GERIATRICS At Your FINGERTIPS®

2014, 16th EDITION

GERIATRICS *At Your* FINGERTIPS®

2014, 16th EDITION

AUTHORS

David B. Reuben, MD

Keela A. Herr, PhD, RN

James T. Pacala, MD, MS

Bruce G. Pollock, MD, PhD

Jane F. Potter, MD

Todd P. Semla, MS, PharmD

Geriatrics At Your Fingertips® is published by the American Geriatrics Society as a service to health care providers involved in the care of older adults.

Although *Geriatrics At Your Fingertips®* is distributed by various companies in the health care field, it is independently prepared and published. All decisions regarding its content are solely the responsibility of the authors. Their decisions are not subject to any form of approval by other interests or organizations.

Some recommendations in this publication suggest the use of agents for purposes or in dosages other than those recommended in product labeling. Such recommendations are based on reports in peer-reviewed publications and are not based on or influenced by any material or advice from pharmaceutical or health care product manufacturers.

No responsibility is assumed by the authors or the American Geriatrics Society for any injury or damage to persons or property, as a matter of product liability, negligence, warranty, or otherwise, arising out of the use or application of any methods, products, instructions, or ideas contained herein. No guarantee, endorsement, or warranty of any kind, express or implied (including specifically no warrant of merchantability or of fitness for a particular purpose) is given by the Society in connection with any information contained herein. Independent verification of any diagnosis, treatment, or drug use or dosage should be obtained. No test or procedure should be performed unless, in the judgment of an independent, qualified physician, it is justified in the light of the risk involved.

Citation: Reuben DB, Herr KA, Pacala JT, *et al. Geriatrics At Your Fingertips: 2014, 16th Edition.* New York: The American Geriatrics Society; 2014.

ISSN 1553-152X
ISBN 978-1-886775-31-2

TABLE OF CONTENTS

Abbreviations and Symbols iii
  Drug Prescribing and Elimination vii
Introduction viii
Formulas and Reference Information 1
Assessment and Approach 4
Appropriate Prescribing, Drug Interactions, and Adverse Events 16
Antithrombotic Therapy and Thromboembolic Disease 24
Anxiety 34
Cardiovascular Diseases 38
Delirium 67
Dementia 71
Depression 78
Dermatologic Conditions 84
Endocrine Disorders 92
Eye Disorders 104
Fall Prevention 112
Gastrointestinal Diseases 118
Hearing Impairment 134
Hematologic Disorders 138
Incontinence—Urinary and Fecal 147
Infectious Diseases 157
Kidney Disorders 176
Malnutrition 185
Musculoskeletal Disorders 191
Neurologic Disorders 211
Osteoporosis 222
Pain 227
Palliative Care and Hospice 241
Preoperative and Perioperative Care 250
Prevention 257
Prostate Disorders 262
Psychotic Disorders 268
Respiratory Diseases 272
Sexual Dysfunction 288
Skin Ulcers 293
Sleep Disorders 304
Substance Use Disorders 310
Women's Health 316
Appendixes
  Assessment Instruments 322
    Mini-Cog Screen for Dementia 322
    Physical Self-Maintenance Scale (Activities of Daily Living, or ADLs) 323
    Instrumental Activities of Daily Living Scale (IADLs) 324
    PHQ-9 and PHQ-2 Quick Depression Assessment 325
    Rapid Estimate of Adult Literacy in Medicine—Short Form (REALM-SF) 327
    Karnofsky Scale 328
    Palliative Performance Scale (PPS) 329
    Reisberg Functional Assessment Staging (FAST) Scale 330
    AUA Symptom Index for BPH 331
    Opioid Risk Tool 332
Coding in Geriatrics 333
Important Telephone Numbers and Web Sites 335
Index 337

AUTHORS

David B. Reuben, MD
Director, Multicampus Program in Geriatric Medicine and Gerontology
Chief, Division of Geriatrics
Archstone Foundation Chair
Professor of Medicine
David Geffen School of Medicine at UCLA, Los Angeles, CA

Keela A. Herr, PhD, RN
Professor and Associate Dean for Faculty
Co-Director, Iowa John A. Hartford Center of Geriatric Nursing Excellence
College of Nursing
The University of Iowa, Iowa City, IA

James T. Pacala, MD, MS
Associate Professor and Associate Head
Distinguished University Teaching Professor
Department of Family Medicine and Community Health
University of Minnesota Medical School, Minneapolis, MN

Bruce G. Pollock, MD, PhD, FRCPC
Vice President, Research
Director, Campbell Family Mental Health Research Institute
Centre for Addiction and Mental Health
Professor of Psychiatry and Pharmacology
Director, Division of Geriatric Psychiatry
University of Toronto, Toronto, Ontario, Canada

Jane F. Potter, MD
Chief, Division of Geriatrics and Gerontology
Director, Home Instead Center for Successful Aging
Harris Professor of Geriatric Medicine
University of Nebraska Medical Center, Omaha, NE

Todd P. Semla, MS, PharmD
National PBM Clinical Pharmacy Program Manager
Department of Veterans Affairs
Pharmacy Benefits Management Services
Associate Professor, Clinical
Departments of Medicine and Psychiatry & Behavioral Sciences
The Feinberg School of Medicine
Northwestern University, Chicago, IL

AAA	abdominal aortic aneurysm
ABG	arterial blood gas
ABI	ankle-brachial index
ACC	American College of Cardiology
ACEI	angiotensin-converting enzyme inhibitor
ACIP	Advisory Committee on Immunization Practices
ACOG	American College of Obstetrics and Gynecology
ACTH	adrenocorticotropic hormone
AD	Alzheimer disease
ADA	American Diabetes Association
ADLs	activities of daily living
ADT	androgen deprivation therapy
AE	adverse event
AF	atrial fibrillation
AFB	acid-fast bacillus
AGS	American Geriatrics Society
AHA	American Heart Association
AIDS	acquired immune deficiency syndrome
AIMS	Abnormal Involuntary Movement Scale
ALT	alanine aminotransferase
AMD	age-related macular degeneration
APAP	acetaminophen
ARB	angiotensin receptor blocker
AS	aortic stenosis
ASA	acetylsalicylic acid or aspirin
ASA Class	American Society of Anesthesiologists grading scale for surgical patients
AST	aspartate aminotransferase
ATA	American Thyroid Association
ATS	American Thoracic Society
AUA	American Urological Association
BC	Beers Criteria
BMD	bone mineral density
BMI	body mass index
BP	blood pressure
BPH	benign prostatic hyperplasia
bpm	beats per minute
BUN	blood urea nitrogen
C&S	culture and sensitivity
CABG	coronary artery bypass graft
CAD	coronary artery disease
CBC	complete blood cell count
CBT	cognitive behavioral therapy
CCB	calcium-channel blocker
cfu	colony-forming unit
$CHADS_2$	Congestive heart failure, Hypertension, Age $\geq$75, Diabetes, Stroke (doubled) (score)

CHA$_2$DS$_2$-VASc	Congestive heart failure, Hypertension, Age ≥75 (doubled), Diabetes, Stroke (doubled), Vascular disease, Age 65–74, and Sex (female) (score)
CHD	coronary heart disease
CKD	chronic kidney disease
CMS	Centers for Medicare and Medicaid Services
CNS	central nervous system
COPD	chronic obstructive pulmonary disease
CPAP	continuous positive airway pressure
Cr	creatinine
CT	computed tomography
CrCl	creatinine clearance
cw	Choosing Wisely recommendation
CXR	chest x-ray
CYP	cytochrome P-450
D&C	dilation and curettage
D5W	dextrose 5% in water
DBP	diastolic blood pressure
D/C	discontinue
DHIC	detrusor hyperactivity with impaired contractility
DM	diabetes mellitus
DMARD	disease-modifying antirheumatoid drug
DSM-5	*Diagnostic and Statistical Manual of Mental Disorders*, 5th ed. (Arlington, VA: American Psychiatric Association; 2013)
DVT	deep-vein thrombosis
ECF	extracellular fluid
ECG	electrocardiogram, electrocardiography
EEG	electroencephalogram
EF	ejection fraction
eGFR	estimated glomerular filtration rate
EPS	extrapyramidal symptoms
ESR	erythrocyte sedimentation rate
FDA	Food and Drug Administration
FEV$_1$	forced expiratory volume in 1 sec
FI	fecal incontinence
FOBT	fecal occult blood test
FRAX	WHO Fracture Risk Assessment Tool
FTD	frontotemporal dementia
FVC	forced vital capacity
GAD	generalized anxiety disorder
GDS	Geriatric Depression Scale
GERD	gastroesophageal reflux disease
GFR	glomerular filtration rate
GI	gastrointestinal
GnRH	gonadotropin-releasing hormone
GU	genitourinary
Hb	hemoglobin
HbA$_{1c}$	glycosylated hemoglobin
HCTZ	hydrochlorothiazide
HDL	high-density lipoprotein

HF	heart failure
HR	heart rate
HT	hormone therapy
HTN	hypertension
hx	history
IADLs	instrumental activities of daily living
IBS	irritable bowel syndrome
IBW	ideal body weight
ICD	implantable cardiac defibrillator
INH	isoniazid
INR	international normalized ratio
IOP	intraocular pressure
iPTH	intact parathyroid hormone
JNC 7	Seventh Joint National Committee on Prevention, Detection, Evaluation, and Treatment of High Blood Pressure
JNC 8	Eighth Joint National Committee on Prevention, Detection, Evaluation, and Treatment of High Blood Pressure
K^+	potassium ion
LBD	Lewy body dementia
LDL	low-density lipoprotein
L-dopa	levodopa
LFT	liver function test
LMWH	low-molecular-weight heparin
LVEF	left ventricular ejection fraction
LVH	left ventricular hypertrophy
MAOI	monoamine oxidase inhibitor
MCV	mean corpuscular volume
MDI	metered-dose inhaler
MDRD	Modification of Diet in Renal Disease
MDS	myelodysplastic syndromes
MI	myocardial infarction
MMA	methylmalonic acid
MMSE	Mini-Mental State Examination (Folstein's)
MoCA	Montreal Cognitive Assessment
MRA	magnetic resonance angiography
MRI	magnetic resonance imaging
MRSA	methicillin-resistant *Staphylococcus aureus*
MSE	mental status examination
NNRTI	non-nucleoside reverse transcriptase inhibitor
NRTI	nucleoside reverse transcriptase inhibitor
NSAID	nonsteroidal anti-inflammatory drug
NPH	neutral protamine Hagedorn (insulin)
OCD	obsessive-compulsive disorder
OGTT	oral glucose tolerance test
OT	occupational therapy
PAD	peripheral arterial disease
PAH	pulmonary arterial hypertension
PCA	patient-controlled analgesia
PDE5	phosphodiesterase type 5
PE	pulmonary embolism

PEF	peak expiratory flow
PNS	peripheral nervous system
POLST	Physician Orders for Life-Sustaining Treatment
POMA	Performance-Oriented Mobility Assessment
PONV	postoperative nausea and vomiting
PPD	purified protein derivative (of tuberculin)
PPI	proton-pump inhibitor
PSA	prostate-specific antigen
PT	prothrombin time *or* physical therapy
PTH	parathyroid hormone
PTT	partial thromboplastin time
PUVA	psoralen plus ultraviolet light of A wavelength
QT_c	QT (cardiac output) corrected for heart rate
RA	rheumatoid arthritis
RBC	red blood cells *or* ranitidine bismuth citrate
RF	rheumatoid factor
RLS	restless legs syndrome
sats	saturations
SBP	systolic blood pressure
SD	standard deviation
SIADH	syndrome of inappropriate secretion of antidiuretic hormone
SNRI	serotonin norepinephrine-reuptake inhibitor
SPEP	serum protein electrophoresis
SSRI	selective serotonin-reuptake inhibitor
sTfR	soluble transferrin receptor
TCA	tricyclic antidepressant
TD	tardive dyskinesia
TDD	telephone device for the deaf
TG	triglycerides
TIA	transient ischemic attack
TIBC	total iron-binding capacity
TSH	thyroid-stimulating hormone
tx	treatment(s), therapy (-ies)
U	unit(s)
UA	urinalysis
UFH	unfractionated heparin
UI	urinary incontinence
UTI	urinary tract infection
UV	ultraviolet
VF	ventricular fibrillation
VIN	vulvar intraepithelial neoplasia
VT	ventricular tachycardia
VTE	venous thromboembolism
WBC	white blood cell(s)
WHO	World Health Organization

Drug Prescribing and Elimination

Drugs are listed by generic names; trade names are in *italics*. An asterisk (*) indicates that the drug is available OTC. Check marks (✔) indicate drugs preferred for treating older adults. A triangle (▲) following the drug name indicates that the drug is available as a generic formulation. A triangle following a combination medication indicates that the combination is available as a generic, not the individual drugs. Note that even though individual drugs in a combination medication are available as generics, the combination may not be. Formulations in text are bracketed and expressed in milligrams (mg) unless otherwise specified. Abbreviations for dosing, formulations, and route of elimination are defined below.

ac	before meals	OU	both eyes
C	capsule, caplet	pc	after meals
ChT	chewable tablet	pch	patch
conc	concentrate	pk	pack, packet
CR	controlled release	po	by mouth
crm	cream	pr	per rectum
d	day(s)	prn	as needed
ER	extended release	pwd	powder
F	fecal elimination	qam	every morning
fl	fluid	qhs	each bedtime
g	gram(s)	S	liquid (includes concentrate, elixir,
gran	granules		solution, suspension, syrup,
gtt	drop(s)		tincture)
h	hour(s)	SC	subcutaneous(ly)
hs	at bedtime	sec	second(s)
IM	intramuscular(ly)	shp	shampoo
inj	injectable(s)	sl	sublingual
IT	intrathecal(ly)	sol	solution
IV	intravenous(ly)	Sp	suppository
K	renal elimination	spr	spray(s)
L	hepatic elimination	SR	sustained release
lot	lotion	sus	suspension
max	maximum	syr	syrup
mcg	microgram(s)	T	tablet
MDI	metered-dose inhaler	tab(s)	tablet(s)
min	minute(s)	tbsp	tablespoon(s)
mo	month(s)	tinc	tincture
npo	nothing by mouth	TR	timed release
NS	normal saline	tsp	teaspoon(s)
ODT	oral disintegrating tablet	wk	week(s)
oint	ointment	XR	extended release
OTC	over-the-counter	yr	year(s)

INTRODUCTION

Providing high-quality health care for older adults requires special knowledge and skills. *Geriatrics At Your Fingertips*® *(GAYF)* is an annually updated, pocket-sized reference that provides quick, easy access to the specific information clinicians need to make decisions about the care of older adults. Since its initial publication in 1998, *GAYF's* up-to-date content and portable format quickly made it the American Geriatrics Society's (AGS) best-selling publication.

In response to the increased use of electronic media in clinical settings, the AGS has also developed *GAYF* for the Web and for mobile devices. Schools can acquire licenses to provide mobile device access for all their faculty and trainees. More information on these formats can be found at www.geriatricscareonline.org.

In this updated 16th edition, we have included major updates of cholesterol treatment based on American College of Cardiology/American Heart Association guidelines, hypertension based on the JNC 8, and arthritis based on new American College of Rheumatology guidelines. We have added new sections on completing a death certificate, multimorbidity (based on the 2012 AGS Expert Panel), methicillin-resistant Staphylococcus aureus (MRSA), edema, and restrictive lung disease. The text and tables contain newly recommended diagnostic tests and management strategies. Among the many updates included in this edition are recommendations about tests and procedures that follow the American Board of Internal Medicine Foundations Choosing Wisely® Campaign (indicated by ^{CW}). Medication tables were updated shortly before publication and include specific caveats and cautions to facilitate appropriate prescribing in older adults. Medications available as generic formulations are indicated, because these are often less expensive.

Given its portable size, *GAYF* does not explain in detail the rationale underlying the strategies presented. Many of these strategies have been derived from guidelines published by the Agency for Healthcare Research and Quality and various medical societies (see the National Guideline Clearinghouse at www.guidelines.gov). When no such guidelines exist, the strategies recommended represent the best opinions of the authors and reviewers, based on clinical experience and the most recent medical literature. References are provided sparingly, but many others are available from the organizations listed below, as well as from the current edition of the AGS *Geriatrics Review Syllabus*.

The authors welcome comments about *GAYF*, which should be addressed to the AGS at info.amger@americangeriatrics.org or 40 Fulton Street, 18th Floor, New York, NY 10038.

The authors are particularly grateful to the following organizations and individuals: the John A. Hartford Foundation, for generously supporting the initial development and distribution of *GAYF* and its PDA version; AGS staff, Nancy Lundebjerg, Carol Goodwin, and Elvy Ickowicz, who have served a vital role in *GAYF's* development and its continued distribution and expansion; and the following experts who reviewed portions of this edition:

Daniel Blumberger, MD
Catherine E. DuBeau, MD
Karen Feldt, PhD, ARNP, GNP
Perry Fine, MD
Gail Greendale, MD
Gerald C. Groggel, MD
Jason M. Johanning, MD

Jerry C. Johnson, MD
James Judge, MD
Joy Laramie, MSN, NP
Andrew Lee, MD
Patrick E. McBride, MD, MPH
Arash Naeim, MD, PhD
Larissa Rodriguez, MD

Guidelines of the following organizations are the basis of parts of specific chapters:

Advisory Committee on Immunization Practices
Agency for Healthcare Research and Quality
Alzheimer's Association
American Academy of Neurology
American Academy of Orthopaedic Surgeons
American Association for Geriatric Psychiatry
American College of Cardiology
American College of Chest Physicians
American College of Gastroenterology
American College of Obstetrics and Gynecology
American College of Rheumatology
American Diabetes Association
American Geriatrics Society
American Heart Association
American Lung Association
American Pain Society
American Psychiatric Association
American Society of Anesthesiologists
American Thyroid Association
American Urological Association
The Endocrine Society
Ethnogeriatrics Committee, American Geriatrics Society
National Cholesterol Education Program
National Heart, Lung and Blood Institute
National Osteoporosis Foundation
U.S. Preventive Services Task Force
World Health Organization

Editorial Staff
Hope J. Lafferty, AM, ELS, Medical Editor
Joseph Douglas, Managing Editor
Pilar Wyman, Medical Indexer

Technical development and production of print and electronic versions:
Fry Communications, Inc.
Melissa Durborow, Group Manager
Rhonda Liddick, Composition Manager
Denise DeNicholas, Composition
Jason Hughes, Technical Services Manager
Julie Stevens, Project Manager

Atmosphere Apps
Eric Poirier, Chief Operations Officer

FORMULAS AND REFERENCE INFORMATION

Table 1. Conversions		
Temperature	**Liquid**	**Weight**
F = (1.8)C + 32	1 fl oz = 30 mL	1 lb = 0.453 kg
C = (F − 32) / (1.8)	1 tsp = 5 mL	1 kg = 2.2 lb
	1 tbsp = 15 mL	1 oz = 30 g

Alveolar-Arterial Oxygen Gradient

$A - a = 148 - 1.2(PaCO_2) - PaO_2$ [normal = 10–20 mmHg, breathing room air at sea level]

Calculated Osmolality

Osm = 2Na + glucose / 18 + BUN / 2.8   [normal = 280–295]

Golden Rules of Arterial Blood Gases

- $PaCO_2$ change of 10 corresponds to a pH change of 0.08.
- pH change of 0.15 corresponds to base excess change of 10 mEq/L.

Creatinine Clearance

See Appropriate Prescribing, p 16.

For renally eliminated drugs, dosage adjustments may be necessary if CrCl <60 mL/min. Cockcroft-Gault formula:

$$\frac{IBW(140 - age)\ (0.85\ if\ female)}{(72)\ (stable\ serum\ Cr)}$$

Many laboratories are reporting MDRD as an estimate of GFR (eGFR). This measure is used for staging CKD. The MDRD has not been validated in adults >70 yr old.

GFR should not be equated to CrCl. The use of the MDRD eGFR to adjust drug dosages overestimates renal function in many older adults. The use of Cockcroft-Gault is more accurate to adjust drug dosages. FDA package insert dosing recommendations are almost entirely based on the Cockcroft-Gault estimate of CrCl.

Erythrocyte Sedimentation Rate

Westergren: women = (age + 10) / 2
       men = age / 2

Ideal Body Weight

- Men = 50 kg + (2.3 kg) (each inch of height >5 feet)
- Women = 45.5 kg + (2.3 kg) (each inch of height >5 feet)

Lean Body Weight

IBW + 0.4 (actual body weight − IBW)

Body Mass Index

$$\frac{\text{weight in kg}}{(\text{height in meters})^2} \quad or \quad \frac{\text{weight in lb}}{(\text{height in inches})^2} \times 704.5$$

Partial Pressure of Oxygen, Arterial (PaO$_2$) While Breathing Room Air

100 − (age/3) estimates decline

Table 2. Motor Function by Nerve Roots			
Level	Motor Function	Level	Motor Function
C4	Spontaneous breathing	L1–L2	Hip flexion
C5	Shoulder shrug	L3	Hip adduction
C6	Elbow flexion	L4	Hip abduction
C7	Elbow extension	L5	Great toe dorsiflexion
C8/T1	Finger flexion	S1–S2	Foot plantar flexion
T1–T12	Intercostal abdominal muscles	S2–S4	Rectal tone

Table 3. Lumbosacral Nerve Root Compression			
Root	Motor	Sensory	Reflex
L4	Quadriceps	Medial foot	Knee jerk
	Dorsiflexors	Dorsum of foot	Medial hamstring
L5	Great toe dorsiflexors	Dorsum of foot	Medial hamstring
S1	Plantar flexors	Lateral foot	Ankle jerk

Figure 1. Dermatomes

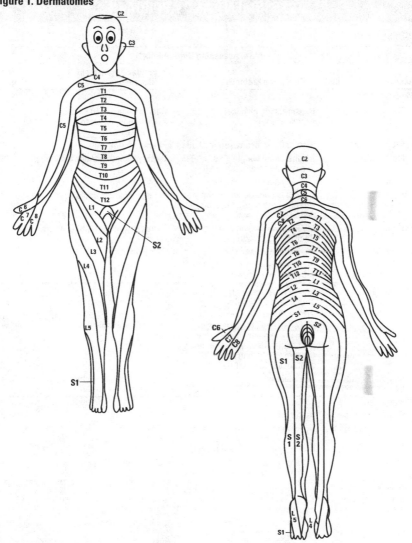

Source: Hamilton, RJ, ed. *The Tarascon Pocket Pharmacopoeia*, 2014 classic shirt-pocket edition. Jones and Bartlett Learning, 2014:143. Sudbury, MA. www.jblearning.com. Reprinted with permission.

ASSESSMENT

Table 4. Assessing Older Adults*

Assessment Domain	Screening Methods	Further Assessment (if screen is positive)	See Page(s)
Medical			
Medical illnesses[a,b]	Hx, screening physical examination	Additional targeted physical examination, laboratory and imaging tests	—
Medications[a,b]	Medications review/reconciliation	Pharmacy referral	16
Nutrition[a,b]	Inquire about weight loss (>10 lb in past 6 mo), calculate BMI	Dietary hx, malnutrition evaluation	185
Dentition	Oral examination	Dentistry referral	—
Hearing[a]	Handheld audioscope, Brief Hearing Loss Screener, whisper test	Ear examination, audiology referral	134
Vision[a]	Inquire about vision changes, Snellen chart testing	Eye examination, ophthalmology referral	104
Pain	Inquire about pain	Pain inventory	227
Urinary incontinence	Inquire if patient has lost urine >5 times in past year	UI evaluation	147
Mental			
Cognitive status[a,b]	3-item recall, Mini-Cog	MSE, dementia evaluation	322
Emotional status[a]	PHQ-2: "Over the past month, have you often had little interest or pleasure in doing things? Over the past month, have you often been bothered by feeling down, depressed, or hopeless?"	PHQ-9 or other depression screen, in-depth interview	325
Spiritual status	Spiritual hx	In-depth interview, chaplain or spiritual advisor referral	—
Physical			
Functional status[a]	ADLs, IADLs	PT/OT referral	323–324
Balance and gait[a]	Observe patient getting up and walking, orthostatic BP and HR, Romberg test, semitandem stand	POMA scale	
Falls	Inquire about falls in past year and difficulty with walking or balance	Falls evaluation	112
Environmental			
Social, financial status[a]	Social hx, assess risk factors for mistreatment	In-depth interview, social work referral	10–12
Environmental hazards[a]	Inquire about living situation, home safety checklist	Home evaluation	116

(cont.)

Table 4. Assessing Older Adults* (cont.)			
Assessment Domain	**Screening Methods**	**Further Assessment** (if screen is positive)	**See Page(s)**
Care Preferences			
Life-sustaining tx[a,b]	Inquire about preferences; complete POLST form		10

*See also Assessment Instruments, p 322.
[a]Required elements of the Medicare Initial Annual Wellness Visit
[b]Required elements of Medicare Subsequent Annual Wellness Visits

Medicare Annual Wellness Visit (AWV)

• Can be performed by a physician, physician assistant, nurse practitioner, clinical nurse specialist, or a health professional (eg, health educator, dietitian) under the direct supervision of a physician.
• Initial and subsequent AWVs must include documentation of elements indicated in **Table 4**, plus the following items that are to be established at the initial AWV and updated at subsequent AWVs:
  ○ A family hx
  ○ A list of current providers caring for the patient
  ○ A written 5- to 10-yr schedule of screening activities based on USPSTF/CDC recommendations (see Prevention, p 236)
  ○ A list of risk factors and conditions for which primary, secondary, and tertiary preventive interventions are being applied

INTERPROFESSIONAL GERIATRIC TEAM CARE

• Most effective for care of frail older adults with multiple comorbidities
• Also appropriate for management of complex geriatric syndromes (eg, falls, confusion, dementia, depression, incontinence, weight loss, persistent pain, immobility)
• Common features of team care include:
  ○ Proactive assessment of multiple domains (see **Table 4**)
  ○ Care coordination, usually performed by an advanced practice nurse or social worker
  ○ Care planning performed by team members (see **Table 5**)

Table 5. Interprofessional Team Members[a]

Profession	Degree/Certification	Training	Team Role/Expertise
Advance practice nurse	APRN	2–4 yr PB	Disease management, care coordination, patient education, primary care, skin and pain assessment
Nurse	RN/LPN (LVN)	2–4 yr B/1–2 yr B	Care coordination, patient education, skin and pain assessment, ADL/IADL screening
Occupational therapist	OTR	2–4 yr PB	ADL/IADL assessment and improvement (including driving and home safety assessments)
Pharmacist	PharmD	4 yr PB ± 1–2 yr PG	Medication review/reconciliation, patient education, drug monitoring
Physical therapist	PT	2–3 yr PB	Mobility, strength, upper extremity assessment and improvement
Physician	MD, DO	4 yr PB + 3 or more yr PG	Diagnosis and management of medical problems, primary care
Social worker	MSW, DSW	2–4 yr PB	Complete psychosocial assessment and improvement, individual and family counseling

Note: B = baccalaureate (post-high school), PB = post-baccalaureate, PG = post-graduate (ie, residency training)

[a]This is not an exhaustive list. Other common team members include audiologists, dentists, dietitians, physician assistants, speech therapists, and spiritual care professionals.

Table 6. Sites of Care[a]		
Site	**Patient Needs and Services**	**Principal Funding Source**
Home	ADL or IADL assistance	PP for caregiving services
	Skilled nursing and/or rehabilitation services when patient can only occasionally leave the home at great effort	Medicare Part A for nonphysician homecare services (eg, nursing, OT, PT); Part B for outpatient PT/ST/OT services independent of a home care agency;[b] PP for caregiving services
Senior citizen housing	Housing	PP[c]
Assisted living, residential care, board-and-care facilities	IADL assistance, primarily with meals, housekeeping, and medication management	PP, Medicaid for some facilities
Hospital		
Acute care	Acute hospital care	Medicare Part A
Chronic care	Chronic skilled care (eg, chronic ventilator)	Medicare Part A, PP, Medicaid
Inpatient rehabilitation	Intensive multidisciplinary team rehabilitation	Medicare Part A[d]
Skilled nursing facility		
Transitional care unit	Skilled nursing care and/or intensive multidisciplinary team rehabilitation	Medicare Part A[d]
Short stay/ Rehabilitation	Skilled nursing care and/or straight-forward rehabilitation	Medicare Part A[d]
Long-term care	ADL assistance and/or skilled nursing care	PP, Medicaid
Continuing care retirement communities	Variety of living arrangements ranging from independent to skilled	PP
Hospice (home or facility-based)	Palliative/comfort care for life expectancy <6 mo	Medicare Part A

Note: PP = private pay (may include long-term care insurance)

[a] For useful information about sites of care for patients and families, see www.payingforseniorcare.com.

[b] A yearly cap of $1900 for these services can be exceeded if the therapist documents a "medically reasonable and necessary" exception.

[c] May be subsidized for older adults spending over one-third of income for rent. Some facilities may have access to a social worker or caregiving services for hire.

[d] Medicare Part A pays for 20 d after a hospital stay of ≥3 d, patient or co-insurance pays $152/d (in 2014) for days 21–100 with Part A covering the rest; patient or co-insurance pays 100% after day 100.

HOSPITAL CARE

Common Problems to Monitor
- Delirium (see p 67)
- Intra- and postoperative coronary events: postoperative ECG to check
- Malnutrition (see p 185)
- Pain (see p 227)
- Polypharmacy: review medications daily
- Pulmonary complications: minimized by incentive spirometry, coughing, early ambulation after surgery
- Rehabilitation: encourage early mobility
- Skin breakdown (see p 293)

Discharge Planning
- Ideally, all team members should participate in discharge planning, beginning early in the hospitalization.
- For a safe and effective transfer from the hospital to the nursing home, the following should be completed by the time the patient arrives at the nursing home:
  - Interfacility transfer form (the medication administration record is inadequate) that includes a discharge medication list noting new and discontinued medications, discontinuation dates for short-term medications, and any dosage changes in all medications
  - Discharge summary (performed by physician) that includes the patient's baseline functional status, "red flags" for rare but potentially serious complications of conditions or tx, orders including medications, important tests for which results are pending, and needed next steps
  - Verbal physician-to-physician sign-out
- Tools are available (see www.caretransitions.org) for patients and caregivers to assert care preferences, clarify discharge instructions, resolve medication discrepancies, and facilitate communication across care sites after discharge.
- Site of care after discharge should be warranted by patient's needs (see **Table 6**).

SCHEDULED NURSING-HOME VISIT CHECKLIST
1. Evaluate patient for interval functional change
2. Check vital signs, weight, laboratory tests, consultant reports since last visit
3. Review medications (correlate to active diagnoses)
4. Sign orders
5. Address nursing staff concerns
6. Write a SOAP note (subjective data, objective data, assessment, plan)
7. Revise problem list as needed
8. Update advance directives at least yearly
9. Update resident; update family member(s) as needed

GOAL-ORIENTED CARE, LIFE EXPECTANCY, AND MEDICAL DECISION MAKING
- Goals of care should be established for individual patients
- Goals of care should be based on:
  - Disease-specific care processes and outcomes (eg, HbA_{1c} and retinopathy for patients with DM)—useful for healthier patients with isolated conditions.

- ◦ Goal-oriented outcomes (an individual's goals potentially encompassing a variety of dimensions, including symptoms, functional status, social engagement, etc)—useful for patients with multiple conditions or who are frail.
- Many medical decisions are predicated on estimated life expectancy of the patient. **Table 7** shows life expectancy by age and sex.
- Life expectancy is associated with a number of factors in addition to age and sex, including health behaviors, presence of disease, nutritional status, race/ethnicity, and educational and financial status.
- Conditions commonly leading to death are frailty, cancer, organ failure (heart, lung, kidney, liver), and advanced dementia.
- Active life expectancy reflects the remaining years of disability-free existence. At age 65, active life expectancy is about 90% of total life expectancy; this percentage decreases with further aging.
- Estimated life expectancy can aid individualized medical decision making, particularly when considering preventive tests. A clinician can judge the patient's health status as being above (75th percentile), at (50th percentile), or below average (25th percentile) for age and sex, and then roughly determine life expectancy using **Table 7**. Then, the period of time needed for the tx to result in a positive clinical outcome is estimated and compared with the life expectancy of the patient.
  - ◦ If estimated life expectancy is longer than the time needed to achieve a positive outcome, the tx is encouraged.
  - ◦ If estimated life expectancy is shorter than the time needed to achieve a positive outcome, the tx is discouraged.
  - ◦ If estimated life expectancy is about the same as the time needed to achieve a positive outcome, the potential risks and benefits of the tx should be discussed neutrally with the patient.

For example, the benefit of many cancer screening tests is not realized for ~10 yr after detection of asymptomatic malignancies. If a patient's life expectancy is significantly less than 10 yr based only on age and sex, and the patient has poor overall health status compared with age-matched peers, cancer screening would be discouraged because the likelihood of benefit from having the test is low.

	Table 7. Life Expectancy (yr) by Age (United States)*					
	25th percentile		50th percentile		75th percentile	
Age	Men	Women	Men	Women	Men	Women
65	11	13	17	20	24	26
70	8	10	13	16	19	22
75	5	7	10	12	15	17
80	4	5	7	9	11	13
85	2	3	5	6	8	10
90	2	2	3	4	6	7
95	1	1	2	2	4	5

*Figures indicate the number of years in which a percentage of the corresponding age and sex cohort will die. For example, in a cohort of 65-yr-old men, 25% will be dead in 11 yr (by age 76), 50% will be dead in 17 yr, and 75% will be dead in 24 yr.

Source: Data from Arias E, Rostron BL, Tejada-Vera B. United States Life Tables, 2007. National Vital Statistics Reports, vol 59, no 9, Sept 28, 2011.

INFORMED DECISION MAKING AND PATIENT PREFERENCES FOR LIFE-SUSTAINING CARE

Physicians have no ethical obligation to offer care that is judged to be futile.

Three elements are needed for a patient's choices to be legally and ethically valid:

- A capable decision maker: Capacity is for the decision being made; patient may be capable of making some but not all decisions. If a person is sufficiently impaired, a surrogate decision maker must be involved. (See also **Figure 2**.)
- Patient's voluntary participation in the decision-making process.
- Sufficient information: Patient must be sufficiently informed; items to disclose in informed consent include:
  - Diagnosis
  - Nature, risks, costs, and benefits of possible interventions
  - Alternative tx; relative benefits, risks, and costs
  - Likely results of no tx
  - Likelihood of success
  - Advice or recommendation of the clinician

Ideally, patient preferences for life-sustaining care should be established before the patient is critically ill.

- Preferences should be established for use of the following interventions and the conditions under which they would be used: cardiopulmonary resuscitation, hospitalization, IV hydration, antibiotics, artificially administered nutrition, other life-extending medical tx, and palliative/comfort care (see Palliative Care, p 241).
- Patients should be encouraged to complete a living will and/or to establish a durable power of attorney for health-care decision making.
- Use of a POLST form can be very useful in formalizing patient preferences (see www.polst.org).

MISTREATMENT OF OLDER ADULTS

Risk Factors for Inadequate or Abusive Caregiving

- Cognitive impairment in patient, caregiver, or both
- Dependency (financial, psychological, etc) of caregiver on elderly patient, or vice versa
- Family conflict
- Family hx of abusive behavior, alcohol or drug problems, mental illness, or mental retardation
- Financial stress
- Isolation of patient or caregiver, or both
- Depression or malnutrition in the patient
- Living arrangements inadequate for needs of the patient
- Stressful events in the family, such as death of a loved one or loss of employment

Assessment and Management

- Interview patient and caregiver separately.
- Ask patient some general screening questions, such as, "Are there any problems with family or household members that you would like to tell me about?" Follow up a positive response with more direct questions such as those suggested in **Table 8**.
- On physical examination, look for any unusual marks, signs of injury, or conditions listed in **Table 8**.

Figure 2. Informed Decision Making

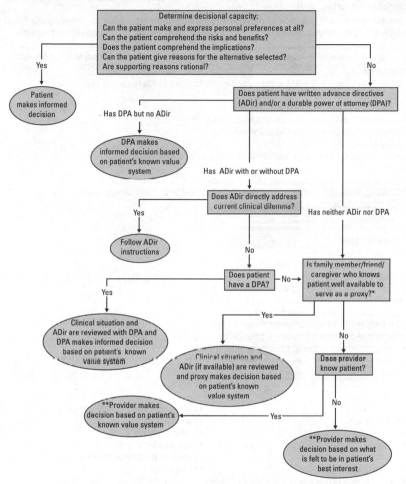

* Most states have laws specifying who should serve as proxy when no ADir or DPA exists. For most of these states, the specified hierarchy of decision makers is (in order): legal guardian, spouse or domestic partner, adult children, parents, adult siblings, closest living relative, close friend.
** Or court-appointed decision maker; laws vary by state.

- If mistreatment is suspected, report case to Adult Protective Services (most states have mandatory reporting laws).
- If patient is in immediate danger of harm, create and implement plan to remove patient from danger (hospital admission, court protective order, placement in safe environment, etc).

Table 8. Determining Suspicion and Clinical Signs of Possible Mistreatment of Older Adults

Abandonment

Question to Ask Patient: Is there anyone you can call to come and take care of you?
Clinical Signs:
- Evidence that patient is left alone unsafely
- Evidence of sudden withdrawal of care by caregiver
- Statements by patient about abandonment

Physical Abuse

Question to Ask Patient: Has anyone at home ever hit you or hurt you?
Clinical Signs:
- Anxiety, nervousness, especially toward caregiver
- Bruising, in various healing stages, especially bilateral or on inner arms or thighs
- Fractures, especially in various healing stages
- Lacerations
- Repeated emergency department visits
- Repeated falls
- Signs of sexual abuse
- Statements by patient about physical abuse

Exploitation

Question to Ask Patient: Has anyone taken your things?
Clinical Signs:
- Evidence of misuse of patient's assets
- Inability of patient to account for money and property or to pay for essential care
- Reports of demands for money or goods in exchange for caregiving or services
- Unexplained loss of Social Security or pension checks
- Statements by patient about exploitation

Neglect

Question to Ask Patient: Are you receiving enough care at home?
Clinical Signs:
- Contractures
- Dehydration
- Depression
- Diarrhea
- Fecal impaction
- Malnutrition
- Inappropriate use of medications
- Poor hygiene
- Pressure ulcers
- Repeated falls
- Repeated hospital admissions
- Urine burns
- Failure to respond to warning of obvious disease
- Statements by patient about neglect

Psychological Abuse

Questions to Ask Patient: Has anyone ever scolded or threatened you? Has anyone made fun of you?
Clinical Signs:
- Observed impatience, irritability, or demeaning behavior toward patient by caregiver
- Anxiety, fearfulness, ambivalence, or anger shown by patient about caregiver
- Statements by patient about psychological abuse

CROSS-CULTURAL GERIATRICS

Clinicians should remember that:

- Individuals within every ethnic group can differ widely.
- Familiarity with a patient's background is useful only if his or her preferences are linked to the cultural heritage.
- Ethnic groups differ widely in
  - approach to decision making (eg, involvement of family and friends)
  - disclosure of medical information (eg, cancer diagnosis)
  - end-of-life care (eg, advance directives and resuscitation preferences)

In caring for older adults of any ethnicity:

- Use the patient's preferred terminology for his or her cultural identity in conversation and in health records.
- Determine whether interpretation services are needed; if possible, use professional interpreter rather than family member. When interpreters are not available, online translation services (eg, www.babelfish.com or http://translate.google.com) can be useful.
- Recognize that the patient may not conceive of illness in Western terms.
- Determine whether the patient is a refugee or survivor of violence or genocide.
- Explore early on the patient's preferences for disclosure of serious clinical findings, and reconfirm at intervals.
- Ask if the patient prefers to involve or defer to others in the decision-making process.
- Follow the patient's preferences regarding gender roles.

For further information, see *Doorway Thoughts: Cross Cultural Health Care for Older Adults Series* (www.americangeriatrics.org/publications/shop_publications/).

COMPLETING A DEATH CERTIFICATE

- The **Cause of Death** statement in Section 32 of a Death Certificate indicates the provider's opinion, with reasonable probability, of the immediate, intermediate, and underlying causes of death and other significant contributing conditions. See below for details on completing this section.
- The **Manner of Death** statement in Section 37 indicates the provider's opinion of whether the death was natural or unnatural. Unnatural deaths will be reviewed by the coroner or medical examiner; the specific criteria for triggering a review vary by county and state.
- If a patient is on hospice care, the hospice provider will usually complete the death certificate.

Immediate Cause of Death Statement (Section 32.Part I.a)

- Indicates the final disease, injury, or complication causing death (eg, aspiration pneumonia, pulmonary embolism, aortic rupture)
- The approximate interval between the onset of the immediate cause and death is estimated (eg, 4 weeks, minutes, 1 hour for the above examples)
- If the cause of death is not apparent, one may indicate "Undetermined natural causes"
- Mechanistic terminal events such as asystole, electromechanical dissociation, cardiac arrest, and respiratory arrest should not be listed in this or any other cause-of-death section

Intermediate/Underlying Causes of Death "Due to/Consequence of" Statement (Section 32.Part I.b–d)

- Indicates conditions and their sequence leading to the immediate cause of death, listed in reverse chronologic order.
- The last of these conditions listed is the underlying cause—the disease or injury that initiated the events leading to the patient's death.
- Examples:
  - A patient with osteoporosis fractures her hip, develops a DVT in the hospital, and dies of a pulmonary embolus. Pulmonary embolus would be cited as the immediate cause in Section 32.I.a., DVT would be cited as an intermediate ("due to/consequence of") cause in Section 32.I.b., hip fracture would be cited as another intermediate cause in Section 32.I.c., and osteoporosis would be entered in Section 32.I.d. as the underlying cause.
  - A patient with late-state Alzheimer disease (AD) dies from apparent aspiration pneumonia. Aspiration pneumonia would be listed as the immediate cause in Section 32.I.a, and AD would be entered as the intermediate/underlying cause in Section 32.I.b.
- The approximate intervals between the onset of the intermediate/underlying causes and death is estimated.

Other Significant Conditions Leading to Death Statement (Section 32.Part II)

- Indicates conditions that likely contributed to death but did not result in underlying causes.
- Risk factors for underlying causes are often listed in this section, eg, hypertension for cerebrovascular disease (the underlying condition) leading to a massive hemorrhagic stroke (the immediate cause of death).

MULTIMORBIDITY

- More than 50% of older adults have ≥3 chronic conditions.
- Management of patients with multimorbidity involves balancing issues of patient preferences and treatment goals, prognosis, the evidence of outcomes for treatment strategies of individual conditions, interactions among conditions and treatments, and feasibility of treatments (see **Figure 3**).

Figure 3. Approach to the Evaluation and Management of the Older Adult with Multimorbidity

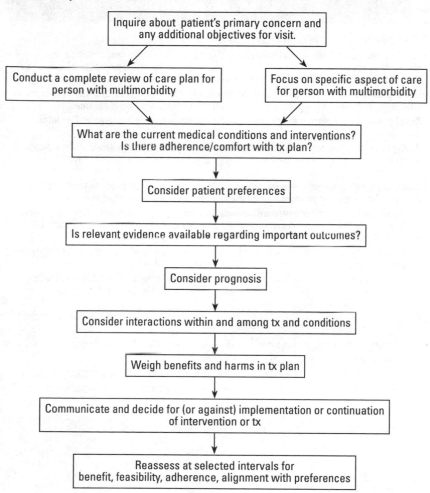

Source: AGS Expert Panel on the Care of Older Adults with Multimorbidity. *J Am Geratr Soc* 2012;60(10):1957–1968.

APPROPRIATE PRESCRIBING, DRUG INTERACTIONS, AND ADVERSE EVENTS

HOW TO PRESCRIBE APPROPRIATELY

- **Obtain a complete medication history.** Ask about previous tx and responses as well as about other prescribers. Ask about allergies, drugs, nutritional supplements, alternative medications, alcohol, tobacco, caffeine, and recreational drugs.

- **Use e-prescribing to reduce risk of transcription and medication errors, check insurance coverage, and avoid a 2% payment penalty on their Medicare Part B services.**

- **Avoid prescribing before a diagnosis is made except in severe acute pain.** Consider nondrug tx.

- **Review medications regularly and before prescribing a new medication.** D/C medications that have not had the intended response, are no longer needed, or do not have a corresponding diagnosis.

- **Know the actions, adverse events, and toxicity profiles of prescribed medications.** Consider how new prescriptions might interact or complement current medications.

- **Consider the following for new medications:** Is the dosing regimen practical? Is the new medication the least expensive alternative if efficacy and safety are comparable to others in the drug class?

- **Start long-term medications at a low dose and titrate dose on the basis of tolerability and response.** Use drug concentration monitoring when available.

- **Attempt to reach a therapeutic dose before switching to or adding another medication.** Use combinations cautiously: titrate each medication to a therapeutic dose before switching to a combination product.

- **Educate patient and/or caregiver about each medication.** Include the regimen, therapeutic goal, cost, and potential AEs or drug interactions. Provide written instructions.

- **Avoid using one medication to treat the adverse events caused by another.**

- **Attempt to use one medication to treat two or more conditions.**

- **Communicate with other prescribers.** Don't assume patients do—they assume you do!

- **Avoid using drugs from the same class or with similar actions** (eg, alprazolam and zolpidem).

Medications listed as Avoid or Use with Caution in the 2012 AGS Beers Criteria are indicated in GAYF by [BC]. An interdisciplinary panel updated the 2003 Beers Criteria and for the first time, graded the evidence. The intent of the update is to improve drug selection and reduce patient exposure to potentially inappropriate medications. Some recommendations state to AVOID the drug without exceptions and others apply only to patients with a specific disease or syndrome, or for a specific duration of use or a specific dose. A detailed description of the 2012 AGS Beers Criteria including evidence tables, useful clinical tools, and patient education materials are available at the AGS website: http://americangeriatrics.org.

WAYS TO REDUCE MEDICATION ERRORS

- Be knowledgeable about the medication's dose, AEs, interactions, and monitoring.
- Write legibly to avoid misreading of the drug name (eg, *Lamictal* vs *Lamisil*).
- Write out the directions:

  (1) strength, route, quantity, and number of refills.

  (2) avoid using abbreviations, especially easily confused ones (qd and qid).

- Always precede a decimal expression of <1 with a zero (0); never use a zero after a decimal.
- Assess patient's or caregiver's ability to correctly and safely administer each medication including health literacy using the Rapid Estimate of Adult Literacy in Medicine – Short Form (REALM-SF) tool. See appendix or http://www.ahrq.gov/populations/sahlsatool.htm
- Avoid confusion: Brand name products can contain different ingredients depending on their indication, eg, *Mylanta Classic*, maximum and regular strength liquid contains aluminum and magnesium hydroxide plus simethicone, while *Mylanta Gel Caps* contain calcium carbonate and magnesium hydroxide; *Lotrimin Ultra* crm contains butenafine, while *Lotrimin AF* and *Gyne-Lotrimin* crm contain clotrimazole, and *Lotrimin AF* aerosol topical contains miconazole.
- Do not use ambiguous directions, eg, as directed (ud) or as needed (prn).
- Include the medication's purpose in the directions (eg, for high BP).
- Write dosages for thyroid replacement tx in mcg, not mg.
- Always re-read what you've written.
- Create a pill card for patients or encourage them to create their own. See AHRQ's software program online at http://www.ahrq.gov/qual/pillcard/pillcard.htm. For more information, see www.fda.gov/Drugs/DrugSafety/MedicationErrors/default.htm or www.ismp.org/tools/abbreviations/

CRITERIA FOR MEDICATIONS OF CHOICE FOR OLDER ADULTS

- Established efficacy
- Compatible safety and adverse-event profile
- Low risk of drug or nutrient interactions
- Half-life <24 h with no active metabolites
- Elimination does not change with age, or there are known dosage adjustments for renal or hepatic function
- Convenient dosing—once or twice daily
- Strength and dosage forms match recommended dosages for older adults
- Affordable for the patient
- See also Medicare Part D Prescription Drug Plan, www.medicare.gov/part-d/index.html or call Medicare at 1-800-633-4227.

DE-PRESCRIBING: WHEN AND HOW TO DISCONTINUE MEDICATIONS

- Recognize opportunities to stop a medication:
  - Care transitions
  - Annual/semiannual medication review
  - Review existing medications before starting a new medication
  - Presentation or identification of a new problem or complaint

- D/C medication if:
  - Harms outweigh benefits
  - Minimal or no effectiveness
  - No indication
  - Not being taken, and adherence is not critical
- Plan, communicate, and coordinate:
  - Include patient, caregiver, and other healthcare providers
  - What to expect/intent
  - Instructions, eg, how to taper (if indicated)
- Monitor and follow-up:
  - Withdrawal reactions
  - Exacerbation of underlying conditions

Examples of medications eligible for de-prescribing: bisphosphonates, antiallergy (seasonal), PPIs and H_2 antagonists, cholinesterase inhibitors, and memantine, iron, antipsychotics, and antidepressants.

Source: Adapted from Bain KT, et al. *JAGS* 2008;56:1946–1952.

CMS GUIDANCE ON UNNECESSARY DRUGS IN THE NURSING HOME

See the complete guidance at www.cms.hhs.gov/transmittals/downloads/R22SOMA.pdf or Appendix PP of the CMS State Operations Manual. Updated survey guidelines for antipsychotic drugs in dementia are at www.cms.gov/Medicare/Provider-Enrollment-and-Certification/SurveyCertificationGenInfo/Downloads/Survey-and-Cert-Letter-13-35.pdf.

PHARMACOLOGIC THERAPY AND AGE-ASSOCIATED CHANGES

Table 9. Age-associated Changes in Pharmacokinetics and Pharmacodynamics

Parameter	Age Effect	Disease, Factor Effect	Prescribing Implications
Absorption	Rate and extent are usually unaffected	Achlorhydria, concurrent medications, tube feedings	Drug-drug and drug-food interactions are more likely to alter absorption
Distribution	Increase in fat:water ratio; decreased plasma protein, particularly albumin	HF, ascites, and other conditions increase body water	Fat-soluble drugs have a larger volume of distribution; highly protein-bound drugs have a greater (active) free concentration
Metabolism	Decreases in liver mass and liver blood flow decrease drug clearance; may be age-related changes in CYP2C19, while CYP3A4 and -2D6 are not affected	Smoking, genotype, concurrent drug tx, alcohol and caffeine intake may have more effect than aging	Lower dosages may be therapeutic
Elimination	Primarily renal; age-related decrease in GFR	Kidney impairment with acute and chronic diseases; decreased muscle mass results in less Cr production	Serum Cr not a reliable measure of kidney function; best to estimate CrCl using formula (see p 1)
Pharmaco-dynamics	Less predictable and often altered drug response at usual or lower concentrations	Drug-drug and drug-disease interactions may alter responses	Prolonged pain relief with opioids at lower dosages; increased sedation and postural instability to benzodiazepines; altered sensitivity to β-blockers

COMPLICATING FACTORS

Drug-Food or -Nutrient Interactions

Physical Interactions: Mg^{++}, Ca^{++}, Fe^{++}, Al^{++}, or zinc can lower oral absorption of levothyroxine and some quinolone antibiotics. Tube feedings decrease absorption of oral phenytoin and levothyroxine.

Decreased Drug Effect: Warfarin and vitamin K-containing foods (eg, green leafy vegetables, broccoli, brussels sprouts, greens, cabbage).

Decreased Oral Intake or Appetite: Medications can alter the taste of food (dysgeusia) or decrease saliva production (xerostomia), making mastication and swallowing difficult. Medications associated with dysgeusia include captopril and clarithromycin. Medications that can cause xerostomia include antihistamines, antidepressants, antipsychotics, clonidine, and diuretics.

Drug-Drug Interactions

A drug's effect can be increased or decreased by another drug because of impaired absorption (eg, sucralfate and ciprofloxacin), displacement from protein-binding sites (eg, warfarin and sulfonamides), inhibition or induction of metabolic enzymes, or because two or more drugs have a similar pharmacologic effect (eg, potassium-sparing diuretics, potassium supplements, and ACEIs). For more information, consult a drug-drug interaction text, software, or Internet resource (eg, http://medicine.iupui.edu/clinpharm/DDIs/).

Drug-induced Changes in Cardiac Conduction

- Intrinsic changes associated with aging in cardiac pacemaker cells and conduction system
- Altered pharmacokinetics
- Increased sensitivity to drug-induced conduction disorders, eg, bradycardia and tachyarrhythmias
- QT_c prolongation exacerbated by drug interactions and medications (see **Table 10**)
- A comprehensive list of drugs that prolong QT_c, increase the risk of Torsades de Pointes, or should be avoided by patients with congenital long QT syndrome is available at crediblemeds.org.

Table 10. Medications That May Prolong the QT$_c$ Interval Alone or in Combination with Other Medications That Affect the QT$_c$ Interval or as a Result of Pharmacokinetic Changes*†

Analgesics	Anti-infectives (cont'd)	Antiretrovirals (cont'd)
Buprenorphine	Ketoconazole	Ritonavir
Methadone	Levofloxacin	Rilpivirine
Oxycodone	Moxifloxacin	Saquinavir
Antidepressants	Telithromycin	Tipranavir
Amitriptyline	Voriconazole	**Cardiovascular**
Citalopram	**Antimigraines**	Amiodarone
Desipramine	Sumatriptan	Disopyramide
Doxepin	Zolmitriptan	Dofetilide
Imipramine	**Antipsychotics**	Dronedarone
Mirtazepine	Clozapine	Ibutilide
Nortriptyline	Fluphenazine	Procainamide
Sertraline	Haloperidol	Quinidine
Trazodone	Loxapine	Sotalol
Venlafaxine	Molindone	**Chemotherapy**
Antiemetics	Olanzapine	Degarelix
Dolasetron	Paliperidone	Dosatinib
Droperidol	Perphenazine	Nilotinib
Granisetron	Pimozide	**Gastrointestinal**
Ondansetron	Quetiapine	Cisapride
Palonosetron	Risperidone	Rantidine
Anti-infectives	Thioridazine	**Urinary**
Azithromycin	Ziprasidone	Alfuzosin
Ciprofloxacin	**Antiretrovirals**	Solfenacin
Clarithromycin	Atazanavir	Tolterodine
Erythromycin	Darunavir	Vardenafil
Gatifloxacin	Fosamprenavir	**Other**
Itraconazole	Indinavir	Tetrabenazine

*Level of risk depends on dosage, baseline QT$_c$ (mild risk if <450 millisec), other patient characteristics, and comorbidity.

† For a comprehensive list, see www.crediblemeds.org.

COMMONLY USED HERBAL AND ALTERNATIVE MEDICATIONS

Note: Herbal and dietary supplements are not subject to the same regulatory process by the FDA as prescription and OTC medications. Product and lot-to-lot variations can occur in composition and concentration of active ingredient(s), or be tainted with heavy metals or prescription medications (eg, sildenafil). Consumers are advised to purchase products by reputable manufacturers who follow good manufacturing procedures.

Chondroitin/Glucosamine

Common Uses: Osteoarthritis, RA

Adverse Events: Chondroitin: Nausea, dyspepsia, changes in IOP; Glucosamine: anorexia, insomnia, painful and itchy skin, peripheral edema, tachycardia.

Comments: Knee pain did not respond better to chondroitin alone or in combination with glucosamine compared with placebo in >1500 patients with osteoarthritis. If patients choose a trial of chondroitin plus glucosamine, it should be glucosamine sulfate.

Coenzyme Q$_{10}$

Common Uses: Cardiovascular diseases (angina, HF, HTN), musculoskeletal disorders, periodontal diseases, DM, obesity, AD; may lessen toxic effects of doxorubicin and daunorubicin

Adverse Events: Abdominal discomfort, headache, nausea, vomiting

Comments: May increase risk of bleeding; use with caution in patients with hepatic impairment, may decrease response to warfarin; may further decrease BP if taking antihypertensives or other medications that decrease BP; ubiquinol is a reduced form of coenzyme Q$_{10}$

Echinacea

Common Uses: Immune stimulant

Adverse Events: Hepatotoxicity, allergic reactions

Drug Interactions: Immunosuppressants; inhibits CYP1A2, –3A4; induces CYP3A4

Comments: D/C ≥2 wk before surgery; cross-sensitivity with chrysanthemum, ragweed, daisy, and aster allergies; kidney disease; immunosuppression; mixed results regarding effectiveness to shorten duration, reduce severity, or prevent colds; should not be taken for >10 d because of concern about immunosuppression

Feverfew

Common Uses: Anti-inflammatory, migraine prophylaxis

Adverse Events: Platelet inhibition, bleeding, GI upset

Drug Interactions: NSAIDs, antiplatelet agents, anticoagulants

Comments: D/C 7 d before surgery, active bleeding; cross-sensitivity with chrysanthemum and daisy; evidence lacking for either indication; minimum of 1-mo trial for migraine prophylaxis suggested

Fish oil (omega-3 fatty acids, *Lovaza*)

Common Uses: Decrease risk of CAD and CHD, hypertriglyceridemia, symptomatic tx of RA, inflammatory bowel disease, asthma, bipolar disorder, schizophrenia and in cases of immunosuppression

Adverse Events: GI upset, dyspepsia, diarrhea, nausea, bleeding, increased ALT and LDL-C

Drug Interactions: Anticoagulants, antiplatelet agents

Comments: Use with caution if allergic to seafood; monitor LFTS, TG, and LDL-C at baseline, then periodically; a 2-mo trial is adequate for hypertriglyceridemia

Flaxseed oil

Common Uses: RA, asthma, constipation, DM, hyperlipidemia, menopausal symptoms, prevention of stroke and CHD, BPH, laxative

Adverse Events: Bleeding, hypoglycemia, hypotension

Drug Interactions: NSAIDs, antiplatelet agents, anticoagulants, insulin and hypoglycemic agents, lithium (mania)

Garlic

Common Uses: HTN, hypercholesterolemia, platelet inhibitor
Adverse Events: Bleeding, GI upset, hypoglycemia
Drug Interactions: NSAIDs, antiplatelet agents, anticoagulants, INH, NNRTIs, protease inhibitors
Comments: D/C 7 d before surgery; effect on lipid lowering modest and of questionable clinical value

Ginger

Common Uses: Antiemetic, anti-inflammatory, dyspepsia
Adverse Events: GI upset, heartburn, diarrhea, irritation of the mouth and throat
Drug Interactions: NSAIDs, antiplatelet agents, anticoagulants
Comments: D/C 7 d before surgery

Ginkgo biloba

Common Uses: AD, memory, intermittent claudication, macular degeneration, diabetic retinopathy, glaucoma
Adverse Events: Bleeding, nausea, headache, GI upset, diarrhea, anxiety
Drug Interactions: MAOIs (increased effect and toxicity), antiplatelet agents, anticoagulants, NSAIDs
Comments: D/C 36 h before surgery; mixed results in dementia trials; recent trials tend to have negative results

Ginseng

Common Uses: Physical and mental performance enhancer, digestive, diuretic
Adverse Events: HTN, tachycardia, insomnia
Drug Interactions: Antiplatelet agents, anticoagulants, NSAIDs
Comments: D/C 7 d before surgery, kidney failure

Glucosamine (see Chondroitin)

Kava kava

Common Uses: Anxiety, sedative
Adverse Events: Sedation, hepatotoxicity, GI upset, headache, dizziness, EPS
Drug Interactions: Anticonvulsants (increased effect), benzodiazepines, CNS depressants
Comments: D/C 24 h before surgery; compared with placebo, kava kava has demonstrated antianxiety efficacy, but effect small and not robust

Melatonin

Common Uses: Sleep disorders, insomnia, jet lag
Adverse Events: Daytime drowsiness, headache, dizziness
Drug Interactions: Warfarin, ASA, clopidogrel, ticlopidine, dipyridamole (loss of hemostasis), antidiabetic agents (decreased glucose tolerance and insulin sensitivity), CNS depressants

Methyl sulfonyl methane (MSM)
Common Uses: Anti-inflammatory, analgesia, osteoarthritis, chronic pain
Adverse Events: Nausea, diarrhea, fatigue, bloating, insomnia
Comments: A derivative of dimethyl sulfoxide (DMSO) that produces less odor

Red yeast rice (*Monascus purpureus*, Xue Zhi Kang)
Common Uses: CHD, DM, hypercholesterolemia
Adverse Events: Nausea, vomiting, GI upset, hepatic disorders, myopathy, rhabdomyolysis
Drug Interactions (theoretical): Cyclosporine, CYP3A4 substrates, digoxin, statins, niacin
Comments: Use with caution in patients taking other lipid-lowering agents

SAMe (S-adenosyl-methionine)
Common Uses: Depression, fibromyalgia, insomnia, osteoarthritis, RA
Adverse Events: GI distress, insomnia, dizziness, dry mouth, headache, restlessness
Drug Interactions: Antidepressants, St. John's wort, NSAIDs, antiplatelet agents, anticoagulants
Comments: Not effective for bipolar depression, hyperhomocysteinemia (theoretical), D/C $\geq$14 d before surgery

Saw palmetto
Common Uses: BPH
Adverse Events: Headache, nausea, GI distress, erectile dysfunction, dizziness
Drug Interactions: Finasteride, a_1-adrenergic agonist properties in vitro may decrease efficacy; may prolong bleeding time so use with caution with antiplatelet agents, anticoagulants, NSAIDs
Comments: Efficacy in BPH did not differ from placebo in an adequately powered, randomized clinical trial

St. John's wort (*Hyporicum perforatum*)
Common Uses: Depression, anxiety
Adverse Events: Photosensitivity, hypomania, insomnia, GI upset
Drug Interactions: Potent CYP3A4 inducer, finasteride (decreased finasteride concentration and possible effectiveness)
Comments: Wear sunscreen with UVA and UVB coverage; avoid in fair-skinned patients; D/C 5 d before surgery; not effective in severe depression; effects reported to vary from those of conventional antidepressants, yet no more effective than placebo; evaluation of effectiveness may be complicated by product, extraction process, and composition

Valerian
Common Uses: Anxiety, insomnia
Adverse Events: Sedation, benzodiazepine-like withdrawal, headache, GI upset, insomnia
Drug Interactions: Benzodiazepines, CNS depressants
Comments: Taper dose several weeks before surgery

NON-VTE INDICATIONS FOR ANTITHROMBOTIC MEDICATIONS

Table 11. Antithrombotic Medications for Selected Conditions

| Indication | Antiplatelet (see Table 16) | Anticoagulant (see Table 17) | | | | | |
		VK Antagonist	Heparin	LMWH	Factor Xa Inhibitor	Direct Thrombin Inhibitor	Glycoprotein IIb/IIIa Inhibitor
Atrial fibrillation	ASA	**Warfarin**	---	---	**Apixaban Rivaroxaban**	Dabigatran	---
Valvular disease	ASA	**Warfarin**	---	---	---	---	---
Acute coronary syndrome	**ASA Clopidogrel** Prasugrel **Ticagrelor**	---	UFH	**Enoxaparin** Dalteparin	Fondaparinux	**Bivalirudin**	**Abciximab Eptifibatide Tirofiban**
Cardiovascular disease prevention	**ASA**	---	---	---	---	---	---
Prior TIA/Stroke	**ASA** Clopidogrel Dipiridamole/ ASA	---	---	---	---	---	---
Peripheral arterial disease	**ASA Clopidogrel**	---	---	---	---	---	---
Heparin-induced thrombocytopenia	---	---	---	---	---	**Argatroban Lepirudin**	---

Notes: **First choice in bold text**; Secondary or alternate choice in regular text; LMWH = low-molecular-weight heparin; UFH = unfractionated heparin; VK = vitamin K

VTE PROPHYLAXIS, DIAGNOSIS, AND MANAGEMENT

Prophylaxis

• Prophylaxis of medical and surgical inpatients is based on patient risk factors and type of surgery.
• See **Tables 12** and **13** for choice of antithrombotic strategy.
• See **Tables 16** and **17** for dosages of antithrombotic medications.

Table 12. DVT/PE Prophylaxis Strategies in Older Medical and Surgical Inpatients

DVT/PE Risk	Surgery Type or Medical Condition	Thromboprophylactic Options
Low	Healthy and mobile patients undergoing minor surgery Brief (<45 min) laparoscopic procedures Transurethral or other low-risk urologic procedures Joint arthroscopy Spine surgery	Aggressive early ambulation after procedure +/– intermittent pneumatic compression
Medium	Immobile (>72 h) patients Inpatients at bed rest with active malignancy, prior VTE, or sepsis Most general surgeries Open abdominopelvic surgeries Thoracic surgery Vascular surgery	Antithrombotic (see **Table 13** and **Table 17**) +/– intermittent pneumatic compression
High	Acute stroke Hip or knee arthroplasty Hip, pelvic, or leg fracture Acute spinal cord injury	See **Table 13**

Table 13. Antithrombotic Medications for VTE Prophylaxis

		Anticoagulant (see Table 17)					
Indication	Antiplatelet (see Table 16)	VK Antagonist	Heparin	LMWH	Heparinoid	Factor Xa Inhibitor	Direct Thrombin Inhibitor
Medical inpatients at moderate-high risk for VTE; patients with acute stroke or spinal cord injury	---	---	UFH	**Enoxaparin Dalteparin**	---	**Fondaparinux**	---
Knee or hip replacement	ASA	Warfarin	UFH	**Enoxaparin Dalteparin**	Danaproid	Fondaparinux Rivaroxaban	Dabigatran Desirudin
Hip fracture surgery	ASA	Warfarin	UFH	**Enoxaparin Dalteparin**	Danaproid	Fondaparinux	---
Nonorthopedic surgery patients at moderate-high risk of VTE	ASA	**Warfarin**	**UFH**	**Enoxaparin Dalteparin**	---	Fondaparinux Rivaroxaban	---

Notes: **First choice(s) in bold text**; Secondary or alternate choice(s) in regular text; LMWH = low-molecular-weight heparin; UFH = unfractionated heparin; VK = vitamin K; VTE = venous thromboembolism (DVT/PE)

DVT Diagnosis

DVT diagnosis is directed by risk score, **D**-dimer testing, and duplex ultrasound imaging.

- Determine risk score
  - 1 point for each of the following:
    - active cancer
    - paralysis, paresis, or plaster immobilization of lower limb
    - bedridden for 3 d or major surgery in past 12 wk
    - localized tenderness along distribution of deep venous system
    - entire leg swelling
    - calf swelling ≥3 cm over diameter of contralateral calf
    - pitting edema confined to symptomatic leg
    - collateral superficial veins
    - prior DVT
  - −2 points for alternative diagnosis as likely as DVT
- Interpret risk score and further testing
  - ≤0 points = low risk: Obtain moderately or highly sensitive D-dimer test. If negative, DVT is excluded. If positive, obtain ultrasound of proximal veins for diagnosis. Don't obtain imaging studies as the initial diagnostic test in patients with low pretest probability (low risk) of VTE.**CW**
  - 1–2 points = moderate risk: Obtain highly sensitive D-dimer. If negative, DVT is excluded. If positive, obtain ultrasound of either proximal veins or whole leg for diagnosis.
  - ≥3 points = high risk: Obtain ultrasound of either proximal veins or whole leg. If proximal leg ultrasound is negative, repeat proximal ultrasound in 1 wk, obtain immediate highly sensitive D-dimer test, or obtain whole leg ultrasound; negative results of any of these rules out DVT.

PE Diagnosis

- Consider PE with any of the following (classic triad of dyspnea, chest pain, and hemoptysis seen in only ≤20% of cases):
  - Chest pain
  - Hemoptysis
  - Hypotension
  - Hypoxia
  - Shortness of breath
  - Syncope
  - Tachycardia
- Calculate clinical probability of PE using clinical decision rule (see **Table 14**), then follow evaluation of PE algorithm (see **Figure 4**). Clinical probability of PE unlikely: total ≤4 points; clinical probability of PE likely: total >4 points.

Table 14. Clinical Decision Rule for PE Probability

Variable	Points
Clinical signs and symptoms of DVT (minimal leg swelling and pain with palpation of the 3 deep veins)	
Alternative diagnosis less likely than PE	3
Heart rate >100/min	1.5
Immobilization (>3 d) or surgery in the previous 4 wk	1.5
Previous PE or DVT	1.5
Hemoptysis	1
Malignancy (receiving tx, treated in last 6 mo, or palliative)	1
Total	

Source: Wells PS, et al. *Thromb Haemost* 2000;83(3):416–420. Reprinted with permission.

Figure 4. Evaluation of Suspected Pulmonary Embolism

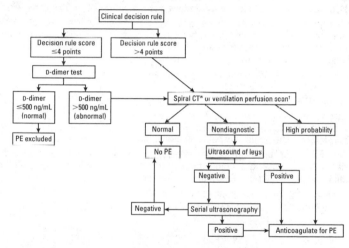

* Multidetector-row CT more sensitive than single-detector CT. Patient must be able to hold breath for 10 sec.
† When unable to use contrast (eg, renal dysfunction), need to avoid ionizing radiation.

Table 15. Antithrombotic Medications for VTE Management

		Anticoagulant (see Table 17)					
Indication	Antiplatelet (see Table 16)	VK Antagonist	Heparin	LMWH	Heparinoid	Factor Xa Inhibitor	Direct Thrombin Inhibitor
Acute VTE tx	—	—	UFH	**Enoxaparin** Dalteparin Tinzaparin	—	**Fondaparinux**	—
Long-term VTE tx	—	**Warfarin**	—	Enoxaparin Dalteparin Tinzaparin	—	Rivaroxaban	Dabigatran

Notes: **First choice(s) in bold text**; Secondary or alternate choice(s) in regular text; LMWH = low-molecular-weight heparin; UFH = unfractionated heparin; VK = vitamin K; VTE = venous thromboembolism (DVT/PE)

- For acute VTE, LMWH or fondaparinux is preferred to UFH in most patients because of lower risk of hemorrhage and mortality. Reduce dosage when CrCl <30 mL/min.

- If warfarin is part of a long-term anticoagulation plan, it may be started the same day as acute anticoagulant. Specific conditions may require a period of overlap when both agents should be used (eg, for DVT or PE, heparin or similar products should be used a minimum of 5 d, including 1–3 d of overlap with therapeutic INR).

- Consider low-dose ASA (100 mg/d) after completion of long-term VTE tx (at least 3 mo of warfarin or other anticoagulant)

- Don't reimage DVT in the absence of a clinical change during DVT tx.[CW]

- Acute massive PE (filling defects in ≥2 lobar arteries or the equivalent by angiogram; about 5% of PE cases) associated with hypotension, severe hypoxia, or high pulmonary pressures on echocardiogram should usually be treated with thrombolytic tx within 48 h of onset.

- Submassive PE (about 20–25% of PE cases) is defined as PE with normotension and right ventricular failure; if present, thrombolytic tx should be considered. Submassive PE can be diagnosed by detection of right ventricular failure through:
  - Physical exam (eg, increased jugular venous pressure)
  - ECG (eg, right bundle branch block [RBBB] or t-wave inversions in leads V_1–V_4)
  - Elevated cardiac troponins
  - Echocardiography (eg, right ventricular hypokinesis and dilatation)
  - Chest CT showing right ventricular enlargement

- Don't perform workup for clotting disorder (order hypercoagulable testing) for patients who develop a first episode of DVT in the setting of a known cause.[CW]

ANTITHROMBOTIC MEDICATIONS
Antiplatelet Agents

Table 16. Antiplatelet Agents			
Agent	**Dose**	**Formulations**	**Comments**
Aspirin (*ASA*)▲	AF, KR, HR, HFS, SP: 75–325 mg/d Valvular disease: 50–100 mg/d ACS: 162–325 mg initially, followed by 75–160 mg/d CVDP, PAD: 75–100 mg/d	T: 81, 162, 325, 500, 650, 975	Risk of GI bleeding is dose-dependent. Use with caution in adults ≥80 yr old for primary prevention of cardiovascular disease.[BC] (L,K)
Dipyridamole/ASA (*Aggrenox*)	SP: 1 tablet q12h	T: 200/25	Headache a common side effect. May decrease effectiveness of cholinesterase inhibitors. (L)
Thienopyridines			Class effect: increased bleeding risk when given with ASA
Clopidogrel (*Plavix*)▲	ACS: 300–600 mg initially, followed by 75 mg/d SP, PAD: 75 mg/d	T: 75, 300	Some patients may be poor metabolizers due to low activity of the CYP2C19 liver enzyme; unclear if testing for this enzyme activity is effective for guiding dosage; unclear if PPIs inhibit activity (L,K)
Prasugrel (*Effient*)	ACS: 60 mg initially, followed by 10 mg/d	T: 5, 10	Use with caution in adults ≥75 yr old.[BC] Consider maintenance dose of 5 mg/d in patients <60 kg (L,K)
Ticagrelor (*Brilinta*)	ACS: 180 mg initially, followed by 90 mg twice daily	T: 90	Should be used with ASA dosage of 75–100 mg/d (K)

Notes: ACS = acute coronary syndrome; CVDP = cardiovascular disease prevention; HFS = hip fracture surgery; HR = hip replacement; KR = knee replacement; SP = secondary stroke prevention after TIA/stroke

		Oral	
Class, Agent	**Dose**	**Formulation**	**Comments**

Table 17. Anticoagulant Agents

Class, Agent	Dose	Oral Formulation	Comments
Heparin			
Unfractionated heparin (*Hep-Lock*)	VTE prophylaxis: 5000 U SC 2 h preop and q12h postop; Acute VTE tx: 5000 U/kg IV bolus followed by 15 mg/kg/h IV; ACS: 60–70 U/kg (max 5000 U) IV bolus, followed by 12–15 U/kg/h IV	NA	Bleeding, anemia, thrombocytopenia, hypertransaminasemia, urticaria (L,K)
LMWH			
Enoxaparin (*Lovenox*)	MP, HR, HFS, NOS: 30 mg SC q12h or 40 mg SC once daily; KR: 30 mg SC q12h; MHS: 40 mg SC once daily; Outpatient tx of DVT: 1 mg/kg SC q12h or 1.5 mg/kg SC once daily; ACS: 30 mg IV bolus, followed by 1 mg/kg SC q12h	NA	Bleeding, anemia, hyperkalemia, hypertransaminasemia, thrombocytopenia, thrombocytosis, urticaria, angioedema (K)
Dalteparin (*Fragmin*)	HR: 2500-5000 U SC preop, 5000 U SC once daily postop; MP, NOS: 2500-5000 U SC preop and postop; LT VTE tx in cancer patients: 200 U/kg SC q24h × 30 d, followed by 150 U/kg SC q24g for the next 5 mo; ACS: 120 IU/kg SC q12h	NA	Same as above (K)
Tinzaparin (*Innohep*)	Acute VTE tx: 175 anti-Xa IU/kg SC once daily	NA	Same as above; contraindicated in older patients with CrCl <30 mL/min (K)
Heparinoid			
Danaparoid (*Orgaran*)	HR, HFS: 750 anti-Xa U SC twice daily	NA	Same as above; also used for heparin-induced thrombocytopenia (K)
Factor Xa Inhibitor			
Apixaban (*Eliquis*)	AF: 5 mg po q12h	T: 2.5, 5	Lower dose to 2.5 mg po q12h if patient has two of the following: age $\geq$ 80, weight $\leq$ 60 kg, Cr $\geq$ 1.5 mg/dL; not recommended in patients with mechanical heart valves
Fondaparinux (*Arixtra*)	MP, KR, HR, NOS: 2.5 mg SC once daily beginning 6–8h postop; Acute VTE tx: weight <50 kg: 5 mg SC once daily, weight 50–100 kg: 7.5 mg SC once daily, weight >100 kg: 10 mg SC once daily	NA	Lower dosage in renal impairment; contraindicated if CrCl <30 mL/min (K)

(cont.)

Table 17. Anticoagulant Agents (cont.)

Class, Agent	Dose	Oral Formulation	Comments
Rivaroxaban (*Xarelto*)	KR, HR, NOS: 10 mg/d po, begin 6–10 h after surgery; AF: 20 mg/d po with evening meal	T: 10, 15, 20	Lower dosage to 15 mg/d in AF patients with CrCl 15–50 mL/min: contraindicated if CrCl <15 mL/min; not recommended in patients with mechanical heart valves; in 1 trial of healthy young subjects, prothrombin complex concentrate reversed the anticoagulant effect of rivaroxaban (L,K)
Direct Thrombin Inhibitors			
Argatroban	HIT + VTE prophylaxis or tx: 2 mcg/kg/min IV infusion	NA	Lower dosage if hepatic impairment (L)
Bivalirudin (*Angiomax*)	ACS: 0.75 mg/kg bolus, followed by 1.75 mg/kg/h IV	NA	(L,K)
Dabigatran (*Pradaxa*)	AF: 150 mg po q12h	T. 75, 150	Reduce dosage to 75 mg po q12h if CrCl = 15–30 mL/min; no known antidote. Contraindicated in patients with mechanical heart valves. Use with caution in adults aged >75 yr old or if CrCl <30 mL/min.[BC] (K)
Desirudin (*Iprivask*)	HR: 15 mg SC q12h starting 5–15 min before surgery	NA	If CrCl = 31–60 mL/min, starting dose is 5 mg; if CrCl <31 mL/min, starting dose is 1.7 mg
Lepirudin (*Refludan*)	HIT + VTE prophylaxis or tx: 4 mcg/kg bolus, then 0.15 mg/kg/h	NA	Lower bolus to 0.2 mg/kg if CrCl <60 mL/min
Glycoprotein IIb/IIIa Inhibitors			
Abciximab (*ReoPro*)	ACS: 0.25 mg/kg IV bolus, followed by 0.125 mcg/kg/min (max 10 mcg/min)	NA	
Eptifibatide (*Integrilin*)	ACS: 180 mcg/kg IV bolus, followed by 2 mcg/kg/min IV	NA	
Tirofiban (*Aggrastat*)	ACS: 0.4 mcg/kg/min IV over 30 min, followed by 0.1 mcg/kg/min	NA	

Notes: ACS = acute coronary syndrome; HFS = hip fracture surgery; HIT = heparin-induced thrombocytopenia; HR = hip replacement; KR = knee replacement; LT = long-term; MP = medical inpatients at moderate-high risk for VTE; NA = not available; NOS = nonorthopedic surgery at moderate-high risk of VTE; VTE = venous thromboembolism (DVT/PE)

Warfarin Therapy

- For anticoagulation in nonacute conditions, initiate tx by giving warfarin▲ *(Coumadin)* 2–5 mg/d as fixed dose [T: 1, 2, 2.5, 3, 4, 5, 6, 7.5, 10]; reduce dose if INR >2.5 on day 3.
- Half-life is 31–51 h; steady state is achieved on day 5–7 of fixed dose.
- Genetic tests for VKORC1 (modulates sensitivity to warfarin) and CYP2C9 (modulates metabolism of warfarin) are available to help guide dosing for initiation of warfarin tx; it is unknown if their routine use significantly improves outcomes. Medicare does not cover genetic testing.
- Home INR testing results in similar outcomes (rates of stroke, death, or severe bleeding episodes) compared with monthly testing in an anticoagulation clinic.
- Warfarin tx is implicated in **many** adverse drug-drug interactions.
- Some drugs that **increase** INR in conjunction with warfarin (type in *italics* = major interaction):

  - alcohol (with concurrent liver disease)
  - amiodarone
  - many antibiotics*
  - APAP (>1.3 g/d for >1 wk)
  - celecoxib
  - *cilostazol*
  - *clofibrate*
  - *duloxetine*
  - flu vaccine
  - INH
  - *ketoprofen*
  - *naproxen*
  - sulindac
  - *tamoxifen*

  *especially fluconazole, itraconazole, ketoconazole, miconazole, ciprofloxacin, erythromycin, *moxifloxacin*, metronidazole, *sulfamethoxazole*, *trimethoprim*

- Some drugs that **decrease** INR in conjunction with warfarin:

  - carbamazepine
  - cholestyramine
  - dicloxacillin
  - nafcillin
  - rifampin
  - vitamin K

Table 18. Indications for Warfarin Anticoagulation in the Absence of Active Bleeding or Severe Bleeding Risk

Condition	Target INR	Duration of Therapy
Hip fracture or replacement surgery, major knee surgery	2–3	10–35 d
VTE secondary to reversible risk factor	2–3	3 mo
Idiopathic VTE	2–3	At least 3 mo
Recurrent VTE	2–3	Indefinitely
AF with CHADS$_2$ or CHA$_2$DS$_2$–VASc score ≥2[a]	2–3	Indefinitely
Rheumatic mitral valvular disease with hx of systemic embolization, left atrial thrombus, or left atrial diameter >5.5 cm	2–3	Indefinitely
Mitral valve prolapse with documented systemic embolism or recurrent TIAs despite ASA tx	2–3	Indefinitely
Mechanical aortic valve	2–3	Indefinitely
Mechanical mitral valve	2.5–3.5	Indefinitely
Mechanical heart valve with AF, anterior-apical STEMI, left atrial enlargement, hypercoagulable state, or low EF	2.5–3.5	Indefinitely
Bioprosthetic mitral valve	2–3	3 mo
Peripheral arterial embolectomy	2–3	Indefinitely

(cont.)

Table 18. Indications for Warfarin Anticoagulation in the Absence of Active Bleeding or Severe Bleeding Risk (cont.)

Condition	Target INR	Duration of Therapy
Cerebral venous sinus thrombosis	2–3	12 mo
MI with large anterior involvement, significant HF, intracardiac thrombosis, or hx of thromboembolic event	2–3	At least 3 mo

[a] See the Atrial Fibrillation section (Table 31, p 60) in the chapter on Cardiovascular Diseases for CHADS$_2$ and CHA$_2$DS$_2$–VASc scoring. Apixaban, dabigatran, and rivaroxaban are alternate options to warfarin. Patients with CHADS$_2$ or CHA$_2$DS$_2$–VASc score=1 or in whom anticoagulation is contraindicated or not tolerated can be treated with ASA 75–325 mg/d; patients with CHADS$_2$ or CHA$_2$DS$_2$–VASc score = 0 should be treated with ASA 75–325 mg/d or receive no tx.

Table 19. Treatment of Warfarin Overdose

INR	Clinical Situation	Action
3.6–10	No bleeding	Omit next 1–2 doses and recheck INR
>10	No bleeding	Omit next 1–2 doses and give Vitamin K 2.5 mg po, recheck INR
Any	Major bleeding	D/C warfarin; give vitamin K 5–10 mg by slow IV infusion plus 4-factor prothrombin complex concentrate

DIAGNOSIS

Anxiety disorders as a whole are the most common mental disorders in older adults. Some anxiety disorders (panic disorder, social phobia) appear to be less prevalent in older than in younger adults. Generalized anxiety disorder (GAD) and new-onset anxiety in older adults are often secondary to physical illness, poorer health-related quality of life, depression, or adverse events of or withdrawal from medications.

DSM-5 recognizes several anxiety disorders:
(Italicized type indicates the most common anxiety disorders in older adults.)
- Agoraphobia
- *GAD*
- *Anxiety disorder due to a general medical condition*
- OCD
- Panic attack
- Social anxiety disorder (social phobia)
- Substance-induced anxiety disorder

DSM-5 Criteria for GAD

- Excessive anxiety and worry on more days than not for ≥6 mo, about a number of events or activities
- Difficulty controlling the worry
- The anxiety and worry are associated with 3 or more of the following symptoms:
  - restlessness or feeling keyed up or on the edge
  - muscle tension
  - being easily fatigued
  - difficulty concentrating
  - irritability
  - sleep disturbance
- Focus of anxiety and worry not confined to features of another primary psychiatric disorder; often, about routine life circumstances; may shift from one concern to another
- Anxiety, worry, or physical symptoms cause clinically significant distress or impairment in social, occupational, or other important areas of functioning
- Disturbance not due to the direct physiologic effects of a drug of abuse, a medication, or to a medical condition; does not occur exclusively during a mood disorder, psychotic disorder, or a pervasive development disorder

DSM-5 Criteria for Panic Attack

An abrupt surge of intense fear or discomfort with ≥4 of the following (also, must peak within minutes):

- Palpitations, pounding heart, or accelerated HR
- Sweating
- Trembling or shaking
- Sensations of shortness of breath or smothering
- Feelings of choking
- Chest pain or discomfort
- Nausea or abdominal distress
- Feeling dizzy, unsteady, lightheaded, or faint
- Chills or heat sensations
- Paresthesias (numbness or tingling sensations)
- Derealization (feelings of unreality) or depersonalization (being detached from oneself)
- Fear of losing your mind or going crazy
- Fear of dying

Differential Diagnosis

- Panic disorder: recurrent, unexpected panic attacks
- Physical conditions producing anxiety
  - Cardiovascular: arrhythmias, angina, MI, HF
  - Endocrine: hyperthyroidism, hypoglycemia, pheochromocytoma
  - Neurologic: movement disorders, temporal lobe epilepsy, AD, stroke
  - Respiratory: COPD, asthma, PE
- Medications producing anxiety
  - Caffeine
  - Corticosteroids
  - Nicotine
  - Psychotropics: antidepressants, antipsychotics, stimulants
  - Sympathomimetics: pseudoephedrine, β-agonists
  - Thyroid hormones: overreplacement

- Withdrawal states: alcohol, sedatives, hypnotics, benzodiazepines, SSRIs
- Depression

EVALUATION

- Past psychiatric hx
- Drug review: prescribed, OTC, alcohol, caffeine
- MSE
- Physical examination: Focus on signs and symptoms of anxiety (eg, tachycardia, tachypnea, sweating, tremor).
- Laboratory tests: Consider CBC, blood glucose, TSH, B_{12}, ECG, oxygen saturation, drug and alcohol screening.

MANAGEMENT
Nonpharmacologic
- CBT may be useful for GAD and panic disorder; efficacy in both individual and group formats.
- Graded desensitization used in panic and phobia relies on gradual exposure with learning to manage resultant anxiety.
- May be effective alone but mostly used in conjunction with pharmacotherapy.
- Requires a cognitively intact, motivated patient.

Pharmacologic (See **Table 41** for dosing of antidepressants and indication of generic status.)
- Panic: sertraline, paroxetine; secondary choices include β-blockers and second-generation antipsychotics
- Social phobia: paroxetine, sertraline, venlafaxine XR
- Generalized anxiety: duloxetine, escitalopram, paroxetine, sertraline, venlafaxine XR
- Post-traumatic stress disorder: paroxetine, sertraline
  - Avoid benzodiazepines.
  - For nightmares, prazosin may be helpful (initiate at 1 mg qhs and titrate slowly to avoid orthostatic syncope).

Buspirone▲ *(BuSpar):*
- Serotonin 1A partial agonist effective in GAD and anxiety symptoms accompanying general medical illness (although geriatric evidence is limited)
- Not effective for acute anxiety or panic disorder
- May take 2–4 wk for therapeutic response
- Recommended starting dosage: 7.5–10 mg q12h [T: 5, 10, 15, 30], up to max 60 mg/d
- No dependence, tolerance, withdrawal, or CNS depression
- Risk of serotonin syndrome with SSRIs, MAOIs, TCAs, 5-hydroxytryptamine 1 receptor agonists, ergot alkaloids, lithium, St. John's wort, opioids, dextromethorphan

Benzodiazepines: (Avoid if hx of falls or fractures.[BC])
- Most often used for acute anxiety, GAD, panic (see **Table 20**)
- Preferred: intermediate–half-life drugs inactivated by direct conjugation in liver and therefore less affected by aging (see **Table 20**)
- Avoid long-acting benzodiazepines (eg, flurazepam, diazepam, chlordiazepoxide)
- Linked to cognitive impairment, falls, sedation, psychomotor impairment, delirium
- Problems: dependence, misuse (p 310), tolerance, withdrawal, more so with short-acting benzodiazepines; seizure risk with alprazolam withdrawal
- Potentially fatal if combined with alcohol or other CNS depressants
- Only short-term (60–90 d) use recommended
- Not covered by Medicare Part D (www.medicare.gov/part-d/index.html or call Medicare at 1-800-633-4227)

Table 20. Benzodiazepines for Anxiety Recommended for Older Adults		
Drug	**Dosage**	**Formulations**
Lorazepam▲ *(Ativan)*	0.5–2 mg in 2–3 divided doses	T: 0.5, 1, 2; S: 2 mg/mL; inj: 2 mg/mL
Oxazepam▲ *(Serax)*	10–15 mg q8–12h	T: 10, 15, 30

Nonbenzodiazepine Hypnotics:
Zolpidem *(Ambien),* zaleplon *(Sonata),* eszopiclone *(Lunesta),* and ramelteon *(Rozerem)* should not be used for tx of anxiety disorders. See Sleep Disorders, **Table 131**.

CARDIOVASCULAR DISEASES

CORONARY ARTERY DISEASE
Calculating Risk in Persons Without Hx of CVD (2013 ACC/AHA Guidelines)

- Quantify CVD risk: every 4–6 yrs in persons up to age 79 without hx of CVD by assessing traditional risk factors
  - Traditional risk factors for quantifying risk are: increasing age, male sex, African American race, total cholesterol >170, HDL-cholesterol <50, SBP >110, tx for high blood pressure, DM, and current smoking
  - 10-yr risk of CVD can be calculated using a downloadable spreadsheet available at http://my.americanheart.org/cvriskcalculator or http://www.cardiosource.org/science-and-quality/practice-guidelines-and-quality-standards/2013-prevention-guideline-tools.aspx
  - If 10-yr risk of CVD is elevated (>7.5%), patient should be considered for intensive lipid management (see **Table 26**, p 47), lifestyle alteration, and assessment and tx for obesity
- If tx decision based on 10-yr CVD risk is uncertain, the presence of one or more of the following other risk factors would suggest further increased risk: first degree relative with hx of premature CVD (male <55, female <65), high-sensitivity C-reactive protein >2 mg/L, coronary artery calcium >30 Agatson units or >75th percentile, ABI <0.9.
- Don't order coronary artery calcium scoring for screening purposes on low-risk asymptomatic individuals except those with a family hx of premature CAD.[CW]
- Don't use coronary artery calcium scoring for patients with known CAD (including stents and bypass grafts).[CW]
- Don't routinely order coronary CT angiography for screening asymptomatic individuals.[CW]

Diagnostic Cardiac Tests

- Cardiac catheterization is the gold standard; cardiac CT angiography is a less invasive, but less accurate, alternative.
- Stress testing: The heart is stressed either through exercise (treadmill, stationary bicycle) or, if the patient cannot exercise or the ECG is markedly abnormal, with pharmacologic agents (dipyridamole, adenosine, dobutamine). Exercise stress tests can be performed with or without cardiac imaging, while pharmacologic stress tests always include imaging. Imaging can be accomplished by echocardiography or single-photon-emission computed tomography (SPECT).
- Don't perform stress cardiac imaging or advanced noninvasive imaging in the initial evaluation of patients without cardiac symptoms unless high-risk markers are present.[CW]
- Don't obtain screening exercise ECG testing in individuals who are asymptomatic and at low risk for coronary heart disease.[CW]

Acute Coronary Syndrome (ACS)

- ACS encompasses diagnoses of ST segment MI (STEMI), non-ST segment MI (NSTEMI), and unstable angina.
- Suspect ACS with anginal chest pain or anginal equivalent: arm, jaw, or abdominal pain (with or without nausea); acute functional decline.

- Diagnosis is based on symptoms along with cardiac serum markers and ECG findings:
  - STEMI: elevated serum markers, elevated ST segments
  - NSTEMI: elevated serum markers, depressed ST segments or inverted T-waves
  - Unstable angina: nonelevated serum markers, normal or depressed ST segments, normal or inverted T-waves
- Measuring cardiac serum markers:
  - Most protocols call for checking troponins T and I and creatine kinase MB isoenzymes (CK-MB) at presentation and 3, 6, 12, and 24 h later.
  - A single negative enzyme measurement, particularly within 6 h of symptom onset, does not exclude MI.
  - Sensitivity of troponins is improved with use of sensitive or ultrasensitive assays.
  - Elevated troponin in the face of normal CK-MB can indicate increased risk of MI in the ensuing 6 mo.
  - Troponins are not useful for detecting reinfarction within first wk of an MI. CK-MB is the preferred marker for early reinfarction.
  - Both CK-MB and cardiac troponins can have false-positive results due to subclinical ischemic myocardial injury or nonischemic myocardial injury.
- Troponin levels can be transiently or persistently minimally elevated by many non-ACS causes, including severe HTN, tachyarrhythmias, coronary spasm, HF, viral myocarditis, endocarditis, myocarditis, pericarditis, malignancy, cancer chemotherapy, trauma, PE, sepsis, renal failure, and stroke. Evaluation (hx, physical examination, assessment of renal function, ECG, echocardiography) should focus on finding and treating the underlying cause.

Initial Management of ACS

- ASA 162–325 mg initially, followed by 75–162 mg/d
- Bed rest with continuous ECG monitoring
- Oxygen to maintain saturation >90%
- D/C NSAIDs
- If ischemia is ongoing (based on symptoms or ECG changes), give nitroglycerin▲ 0.4 mg sl q5min for a total of 3 doses
- Nitroglycerin IV is indicated for persistent ischemia, HTN, large anterior infarction, or HF. Begin at 5–10 mcg/min IV and titrate to pain relief, SBP >90 mmHg, or resolution of ECG abnormalities.
- If chest pain persists on nitroglycerin tx, give morphine sulfate 2–4 mg IV with increments of 2–8 mg IV repeated q5–15 min prn.
- Administer antiplatelet agents, anticoagulants, and glycoprotein IIb/IIIa inhibitors according to reperfusion strategy (see **Tables 11, 16**, and **17**):
  - Thrombolytic tx: ASA, clopidogrel or ticagrelor, and an anticoagulant
  - Early invasive tx with planned percutaneous cardiac intervention: ASA, clopidogrel or prasugrel or ticagrelor, an anticoagulant, and a glycoprotein IIb/IIIa inhibitor
  - Medical management: ASA, clopidogrel or ticagrelor, and an anticoagulant; consider adding a glycoprotein IIb/IIIa inhibitor
  - CABG: ASA and UFH

Ongoing Hospital Management of ACS

- An oral β-blocker should be started within 24 h of symptom onset and continued long term unless there is acute HF, evidence of a low-output state, pronounced bradycardia, or cardiogenic shock.
- An oral ACEI should be started within 24 h of symptom onset for all patients with clinical HF or EF <40% and a systolic BP ≥100 (see **Table 23**). If patient cannot tolerate ACEIs, give oral ARB.
- A statin should be started (if there are no contraindications).
- Lipid-lowering tx, preferably including the use of a high-intensity statin, should be instituted (see Dyslipidemia Management, p 47).
- Anticoagulation with warfarin▲ (see p 32), apixaban (see **Table 17**), rivaroxaban (see **Table 17**), or dabigatran (see **Table 17**) is indicated in post-MI patients with AF. Warfarin is indicated in post-MI patients with left ventricular thrombosis or large anterior infarction (see **Table 18**).
- Patients with a hematocrit ≤30 and who are not in HF should receive a transfusion to increase hematocrit to >33.
- At time of discharge, prescribe rapid-acting nitrates prn: sl nitroglycerin▲ or nitroglycerin spr q5min for max of 3 doses in 15 min. See **Table 21**.
- Longer-acting nitrates should be prescribed if symptomatic angina and tx will be medical rather than surgical or angioplasty. May be combined with β-blockers or calcium channel blockers, or both. See **Table 21**.
- Calcium channel blockers should be used cautiously for management of angina only in non-Q-wave infarctions without systolic dysfunction and a contraindication to β-blockers.

Table 21. Nitrate Dosages and Formulations

Medication	Dosage	Formulations
Oral		
Isosorbide dinitrate▲ *(Isordil, Sorbitrate)*	10–40 mg 3 ×/d (6 h apart)	T: 5, 10, 20, 30, 40; ChT: 5, 10
Isosorbide dinitrate SR *(Dilatrate SR)*	40–80 mg q8–12h	T: 40
Isosorbide mononitrate▲ *(ISMO, Monoket)*	20 mg q12h (8 am and 3 pm)	T: 10, 20
Isosorbide mononitrate SR▲ *(Imdur)*	start 30–60 mg/d; max 240 mg/d	T: 30, 60, 120
Nitroglycerin▲ *(Nitro-Bid)*	2.5–9 mg q8–12h	T: 2.5, 6.5, 9
Sublingual		
Isosorbide dinitrate▲ *(Isordil, Sorbitrate)*	1 tab prn	T: 2.5, 5, 10
Nitroglycerin *(Nitrostat)*	0.4 mg prn	T: 0.15, 0.3, 0.4, 0.6
Oral spray		
Nitroglycerin *(Nitrolingual, NitroMist)*	1–2 spr prn; max 3/15 min	0.4 mg/spr
Ointment		
Nitroglycerin 2%▲ *(Nitro-Bid, Nitrol)*	start 0.5–4 inches q4–8h	2%

Table 21. Nitrate Dosages and Formulations (cont.)		
Medication	**Dosage**	**Formulations**
Transdermal		
Nitroglycerin▲	1 pch 12–14 h/d	(all in mg/h)
(Deponit)		0.2, 0.4
(Minitran)		0.1, 0.2, 0.4, 0.6
(Nitrek)		0.2, 0.4, 0.6
(Nitro-Dur)		0.1, 0.2, 0.3, 0.4, 0.6, 0.8
(Nitrodisc)		0.2, 0.3, 0.4
(Transderm-Nitro)		0.1, 0.2, 0.4, 0.6, 0.8

POST-MI AND CHRONIC STABLE ANGINA CARE

- Unless contraindicated, all post-MI patients should be on ASA, a β-blocker, and an ACEI.
- Give clopidogrel for at least 12 mo in patients receiving drug-eluting stents, and at least 28 d and up to 12 mo in patients who receive a bare metal stent or no stent. Prasugrel or ticagrelor (see **Table 16**) can be given as an alternative to clopidogrel. Prasugrel should be considered only in patients <75 yr old without hx of TIA or stroke. When using ticagrelor, concomitant ASA dosage should not exceed 100 mg/d.
- If β-blockers are contraindicated, use long-acting nitrates or long-acting calcium channel blockers for chronic angina.
- For refractory chronic angina despite tx with β-blocker, calcium channel blocker, or nitrates, consider addition of ranolazine (Ranexa) 500–1,000 mg po q12h [T:500]; contraindicated in patients with QT prolongation or on QT-prolonging drugs, with hepatic impairment, or on CYP3A inhibitors, including diltiazem (see p 54).
- Use sl or spr nitroglycerin for acute angina.
- Treat HTN (see p 49)
- Treat dyslipidemia with high-intensity statin dose (see p 47).
- Treat DM; see p 94 for target goals.
- Weight reduction in obese individuals; goal BMI <25 kg/m^2.
- Aerobic exercise 30–60 min/d, at least intermediate intensity (eg, brisk walking).
- Smoking cessation.
- Increase consumption of oily fish (eg, white canned or fresh tuna, salmon, mackerel, herring) and foods rich in α-linolenic acid (eg, flax-seed, canola, and soybean oils; flax seeds; walnuts). Consider supplementation with fish oil capsules to achieve omega-3 fatty acid intake of 1 g/d; higher dosages are advised in patients with hypertriglyceridemia.
- Strongly consider placement of ICD (see p 66) in patients with LVEF ≤30% at least 40 d after MI or 3 mo after CABG.
- Don't perform routine annual stress testing after coronary artery revascularization.**CW**
- Avoid NSAIDs, especially selective COX-2 inhibitors (see **Table 82**).

HEART FAILURE (HF)
Evaluation and Assessment
- All patients initially presenting with HF should have an echocardiogram to evaluate left ventricular function. An EF of ≤40% indicates systolic dysfunction and a diagnosis of HF with reduced EF (HFrEF). An EF ≥50% indicates diastolic dysfunction and a diagnosis of HF with preserved EF (HFpEF). An EF of 41–49% is a borderline classification but patients usually resemble those with HFpEF.
  - Echocardiography can also evaluate cardiac dyssynchrony (see **Table 22**) in patients with a wide QRS complex on ECG.
  - Echocardiography with tissue doppler imaging may be helpful in diagnosing diastolic dysfunction.
- Other routine initial assessment: orthostatic BPs, height, weight, BMI calculation, ECG, CXR, CBC, UA, electrolytes, calcium, magnesium, Cr, BUN, lipid profile, fasting glucose, LFTs, TSH, UA, functional status.
- Measurement of plasma brain natriuretic peptide (BNP) or N-terminal prohormone brain natriuretic peptide (NT-proBNP) can aid in diagnosis of HF in patients presenting with acute dyspnea.
  - BNP and NT-proBNP levels increase with age.
  - In dyspneic patients >70 yr old:
    - HF very unlikely (likelihood ratio negative = 0.1) if BNP <100 pg/mL (22 mmol/L) or if NT-proBNP <300 pg/mL (35 mmol/L)
    - HF very likely (likelihood ratio positive = 6) if BNP >500 pg/mL (110 mmol/L) or if NT-proBNP >1,200 pg/mL (140 mmol/L)
  - Other conditions causing increased BNP or NT-proBNP levels include impaired renal function, pulmonary disease, HTN, hyperthyroidism, hepatic cirrhosis with ascites, paraneoplastic syndrome, glucocorticoid use, and sepsis.
- Optional: Radionuclide ventriculography, which measures EF more precisely, provides a better evaluation of right ventricular function, and is more expensive than echocardiography.
- If HF is accompanied by angina or signs of ischemia, coronary angiography should be strongly considered.
- Consider coronary angiography if HF presents with atypical chest pain or in patients who have known or suspected CAD.
- Consider stress testing if HF presents in patients at high risk (ie, numerous risk factors) for CAD.

Table 22. Heart Failure Staging and Management

Clinical Profile	ACC/AHA Staging	New York Heart Association Staging	Management[a]
Asymptomatic but at high risk of developing HF (eg, HTN, DM, CAD present)	Stage A	—	RFR, E
Asymptomatic with structural disease: LVH, low EF, prior MI, or valvular disease	Stage B	Class I	RFR, E, ACEI (or ARB if unable to tolerate ACEI), BB
Normal EF; current or prior symptoms (HFpEF)	Stage C	Class I-IV	RFR, drug tx for symptomatic HF, control of ventricular rate
Low EF[b]; currently asymptomatic but with hx of symptoms	Stage C	Class I	RFR, E, DW, SR, ACEI (or ARB if unable to tolerate ACEI), BB
Low EF[b]; patient comfortable at rest but symptomatic on normal physical activity	Stage C	Class II	Class II-IV: RFR, E, DW, SR, drug tx for symptomatic HF (below), consider biventricular pacing if cardiac dyssynchrony is present, consider placement of ICD if LVEF ≤35% (see p 66)
Low EF[b]; patient comfortable at rest but symptomatic on slight physical activity	Stage C	Class III	
Low EF[b]; patient symptomatic at rest	Stage C	Class IV	
Refractory symptoms at rest in hospitalized patient requiring specialized interventions (eg, transplant) or hospice care	Stage D	Class IV	Decide on care preference; above measures or hospice as appropriate

[a] RFR = cardiac risk factor reduction, E = exercise (regular walking or cycling), BB = β-blocker, DW = measurement of daily weight, SR = salt restriction (≤3 g/d if severe HF)
[b] Low EF = EF ≤40%

Drug Therapy for Symptomatic HF (AHA Stage C and D, NYHA Class II–IV)

For information on drug dosages and AEs not listed below, see **Table 28**. Efficacy of different medications may vary significantly across racial and ethnic groups; eg, blacks may require higher doses of ACEIs and β-blockers and may benefit from isosorbide dinitrate combined with hydralazine tx.

• HFrEF:
  ○ Diuretics if volume overload
  ○ ACEIs to target doses (see **Table 23**)
  ○ An angiotensin II receptor blocker is indicated in patients who cannot take ACEIs (see **Table 23**).
  ○ β-blockers to target doses (see **Table 23**) once volume status is stabilized
  ○ Adding an aldosterone antagonist can reduce mortality in patients with NYHA Class II–IV failure. Use either spironolactone[A] (*Aldactone*) 25 mg/d (Avoid doses >25 mg/d[BC] po [T: 25] or eplerenone (*Inspra*) 25–50 mg/d po [T: 25, 50, 100]. Monitor serum potassium carefully and avoid these medications if Cr >2.5 mg/dL in men or >2 mg/dL in women, or serum K+ ≥5.0 mEq/L.

○ Add low-dose digoxin▲ *(Lanoxin)* [T: 0.125, 0.25; S: 0.05 mg/mL]; *(Lanoxicaps)* [T: 0.05, 0.1, 0.2], 0.0625–0.125 mg/d (target serum levels 0.5–0.8 mg/dL) if HF is not controlled on diuretics and ACEIs, with or without an aldosterone antagonist. Avoid doses >0.125 mg/d.[BC] Digoxin may be less effective and even harmful in women.

- Digoxin concentration must be monitored with concomitant administration of many other medications.
  □ The following **increase** digoxin concentration or effect, or both:

amiodarone	esmolol	tetracycline
diltiazem	ibuprofen	verapamil
erythromycin	spironolactone	

  □ The following **decrease** digoxin concentration or effect, or both:

aminosalicylic acid	colestipol	sulfasalazine
antacids	kaolin pectin	St. John's wort
antineoplastics	metoclopramide	
cholestyramine	psyllium	

○ Adding a combination of isosorbide dinitrate and hydralazine (see **Table 21** and **Table 28**; also available as a single preparation: *BiDil* 1–2 tabs po q8h [T: 20/37.5]) can be helpful for patients, particularly African Americans, with persistent symptoms. Use vasodilators with caution in patients with hx of syncope.[BC]

○ Omega-3 polyunsaturated fatty acid supplements can be added as adjunctive tx for symptomatic patients.

○ Correct iron deficiency using IV iron (see **Table 65**) with or without anemia.

○ Calcium channel blockers and Class I antiarrhythmics are not indicated.

• HFpEF:

○ For acute HFpEF with volume overload, loop diuretics and vasodilation with nitroglycerin are indicated. Parenteral nitroglycerin can cause hypotension in HFpEF patients without elevated BP, so use it cautiously if BP is normal or low.

○ For HFpEF without volume overload, pharmacologic management focuses on control of HTN; rate control, especially in patients with AF; and avoidance of digoxin.

• Avoid thiazolidinediones (see **Table 47**) in patients with HF and DM.[BC]

Source: Yancy CW, et al. *Circulation* 2013;128:e240–e327.

Table 23. Target Dosages of ACEIs, Angiotensin II Receptor Blockers, and β-Blockers in Patients with HF and Low EF

Agent	Starting Dosage	Target Dosage
ACEIs		
Benazepril▲	2.5 mg/d	40 mg/d
Captopril▲	6.25 mg q8h	50 mg q8h
Enalapril▲	2.5 mg q12h	10 mg q12h
Fosinopril▲	5 mg/d	40 mg/d
Lisinopril▲	2.5 mg/d	20 mg/d
Perindopril	2 mg/d	8 mg/d
Quinapril▲	5 mg q12h	20 mg q12h
Ramipril▲	1.25 mg/d	10 mg/d
Trandolapril▲	1 mg/d	4 mg/d
Angiotensin II Receptor Blockers		
Candesartan	4 mg/d	32 mg/d
Losartan▲	12.5 mg/d	50 mg q12h
Valsartan	20 mg q12h	160 mg q12h
β-Blockers		
Bisoprolol▲	1.25 mg/d	10 mg/d
Carvedilol▲	3.125 mg q12h	25 mg q12h
Carvedilol ER	10 mg/d	80 mg/d
Metoprolol XR▲	12.5–25 mg/d	200 mg/d
Nebivolol	1.25 mg/d	10 mg/d

LEG EDEMA

Differential

- Acute (<72 h) unilateral: DVT (by far most common and must be ruled out), ruptured Baker's cyst, ruptured medial head of the gastrocnemius
- Acute bilateral: acute worsening of HF, renal disease
- Chronic unilateral: venous insufficiency, secondary lymphedema (from tumor, radiation tx, surgery), cellulitis, reflex sympathetic dystrophy
- Chronic bilateral: venous insufficiency (most common of all causes), HF, pulmonary HTN, drugs (see below), idiopathic edema, obesity, renal disease, liver disease, primary lymphedema, secondary lymphedema (from tumor, radiation tx, surgery)
- Drugs commonly causing edema include:
  - Antihypertensives: calcium channel blockers, β-blockers, clonidine, hydralazine
  - Hormones: corticosteroids, sex hormones
  - NSAIDs

Evaluation

- History: duration and location of edema; overnight improvement (less likely in lymphedema), presence of pain (more likely in DVT, reflex sympathetic dystrophy); medication review; hx of heart, kidney, or liver disease; hx of cancer and/or radiation tx; sleep apnea (increases likelihood of pulmonary HTN)

- Physical exam: BMI; location of edema; tenderness (more likely in DVT); skin changes; signs of heart, kidney, or liver disease; pelvic exam if suspect pelvic tumor
- Diagnostic studies: CBC, UA, electrolytes, Cr, BUN, glucose, TSH, albumin. See p 26 for workup of possible DVT. Other tests obtained according to hx and physical exam findings.

Treatment
- Venous insufficiency: leg elevation, skin care (daily mild soap and moisturizers), and compression stockings worn during the day (see **Table 24**).
  - Below-the-knee stockings are usually sufficient. Above-the-knee stockings are appropriate for more extensive edema and for patients with orthostatic hypotension.
  - ABI measurement should precede use of compression stockings.
  - Compression stockings are not covered under traditional Medicare Part B unless an ulcer is present. Other insurance plans may cover them and require a doctor's prescription for coverage.
  - Anti-embolism stockings (eg, T.E.D.™) are not designed for managing venous insufficiency.
  - Intermittent pneumatic compression pumps can be tried for recalcitrant edema.
  - Compression wraps can be used in patients who have difficulty donning compression stockings.
  - Diuretics should be used only for short-term tx of severe cases; chronic use can lead to intravascular dehydration and electrolyte imbalances.

Table 24. Prescribing Compression Stockings			
Stocking Class (Compression Grade)	Pressure Delivered (mmHg)	Indications	Appropriate ABI Range
1 (light)	20–30	Mild edema Varicose veins	>0.5[a]
2 (medium)	30–40	Mild-moderate edema Pigmentation	>0.8
3 (high)	40–50	Severe edema Lymphedema	>0.8

[a] Use with great caution in patients with ABI of 0.5–0.8.

- Complex decompression physiotherapy is an intensive multiweek intervention that is covered by Medicare for lymphedema.
- See **Table 15** and p 28 for DVT tx.
- Other tx should be directed at the underlying cause.

DYSLIPIDEMIA MANAGEMENT
Nonpharmacologic
A cholesterol-lowering diet should be considered initial tx for dyslipidemia and should be used as follows:

- The patient should be at low risk of malnutrition.
- The diet should be nutritionally adequate, with sufficient total calories, protein, calcium, iron, and vitamins, and low in saturated fats (<7% of total calories), trans-fatty acids, and cholesterol.

- The diet should be easily understood and affordable (a dietitian can be very helpful).
- Plant stanol/sterols (2 g/d), found in many fruits, vegetables, vegetable oils, nuts, seeds, cereals, and legumes, can lower LDL.
- Cholesterol-lowering margarines can lower LDL cholesterol by 10% to 15% *(Take Control* 1–2 tbsp/d, 45 calories/tbsp; *Benecol* 3 servings of 1.5 tsp each/d, 70 calories/tbsp).

Pharmacologic
- Target drug tx according to type of dyslipidemia and cardiovascular risk (**Table 25** and **Table 26**).
- See **Table 27** for dosages of lipid-lowering drugs.
- Statins are dosed according to intensity of lipid lowering: high-intensity (usually lowers LDL ≥50%), moderate-intensity (usually lowers LDL 30–49%), and low-intensity (usually lowers LDL <30%). The LDL-lowering target should be the percentage of lowering rather than an absolute LDL target value.

Table 25. Treatment Choices for Dyslipidemia				
	Type of Dyslipidemia			
Agent	↑LDL	↑TG	↑LDL + ↑TG	↑LDL + ↓HDL + ↑TG
Statin	1	2	1	1
Fibrate		1	2	2
Ezetimibe	2		2,3	2,3
Niacin	2	2		
Bile Acid Sequestrant	2		2,3	2,3
Omega-3 Fatty Acid		2		

1 = First tx choice
2 = Alternate tx choice
3 = Appropriate for combined tx with another agent

Table 26. 2013 ACC/AHA Indications For Statin Therapy						
Risk Categories					**Statin Indication**	
Age	**CVD?**	**LDL ≥190?**	**DM?**	**10-yr risk ≥7.5%?[a]**	**High-Intensity[b]**	**Moderate-Intensity[c]**
40–75	Y	Y/N	Y/N	Y/N	•	
	N	Y	Y/N	Y/N	•	
	N	N	Y	Y	•	
	N	N	Y	N		•
	N	N	N	Y	•	•
>75	Y	Y/N	Y/N	Y/N		•
	N	Y/N	Y/N	Y/N	ND	ND

CVD = CAD (prior MI, angina, ACS, coronary revascularization), stroke, TIA, or PAD; Y = yes; N = no; Y/N = yes or no; • = indication for statin tx; ND = no data, consider potential risk/benefit of primary prevention based on individual CVD risk, co-morbidities, and goals of care.
[a]Calculated 10 yr risk of CVD; the risk calculator can be accessed at
http://my.americanheart.org/cvriskcalculator
[b]High-intensity statin doses usually lower LDL by > 50%. See **Table 27** for dosages.
[c]Moderate-intensity statin doses usually lower LDL by 30–49%. See **Table 27** for dosages.
Source: Stone NJ, et al. *J Am Coll Cardiol* 2013; pii: S0735–1097(13)06028–2.

Table 27. Medications for Dyslipidemia			
Class	**Medication**	**Dosage**[a]	**Formulations**
Statin (HMG-CoA reductase inhibitor)[b]	Atorvastatin▲ (Lipitor)	H: 40–80 mg/d; M: 10–20 mg/d	T: 10, 20, 40, 80
	Fluvastatin▲ (Lescol, Lescol XL)	M: 40 mg q12h or 80 mg XL/d; L: 20–40 mg/d	C: 20, 40; T: ER 80
	Lovastatin▲c (Mevacor, Altoprev)	M: 40 mg/d; L: 10–20 mg/d	T: 10, 20, 40; T: ER 10, 20, 40, 60
	Pitavastatin (Livalo)	M: 2–4 mg/d; L: 1 mg/d	T: 1, 2, 4
	Pravastatin▲ (Pravachol)	M: 40–80 mg/d; M: 10–20 mg/d	T: 10, 20, 40, 80
	ASA/pravastatin (Pravigard PAC)	1 tab/d	T: 81/20, 81/40, 81/80, 325/20, 325/40, 325/80
	Rosuvastatin (Crestor)	H: 20–40 mg/d; M: 5–10 mg/d	T: 5, 10, 20, 40
	Simvastatin▲ (Zocor)	M: 20–40 mg/d; L: 10 mg/d	T: 5, 10, 20, 40, 80
Fibrate (fibric acid derivative)	Fenofibrate▲ (Tricor, Lofibra, Antara)	48–200 mg/d	T: 48, 54, 145, 160 C: 43, 67, 130, 134, 200
	Fenofibrate delayed release (Trilipix)	45–135 mg/d	C: 45, 135
	Gemfibrozil▲ (Lopid)	300–600 mg po q12h	T: 600
Cholesterol absorption inhibitor	Ezetimibe (Zetia)[d]	10 mg/d	T: 10
Nicotinic acid	Niacin▲e	100 mg q8h to start; increase to 500–1000 mg q8h; ER 150 mg qhs to start, increase to 2000 mg qhs prn	T: 25, 50, 100, 250, 500; ER 150, 250, 500, 750, 1000 C: TR 125, 250, 400, 500
	Niacin ER▲ (Niaspan)	500–2000 mg/d	T: 500, 750, 1000
Bile acid sequestrant	Colesevelam (Welchol)	Monotherapy: 1850 mg po q12h; combination tx: 2500–3750 mg/d in single or divided doses	T: 625
	Colestipol▲ (Colestid, Colestid Tablets)	5–30 g mixed with liquid in 1 or more divided doses	Pks or scoops: 5 g, 7.5 g T: 1 g
Fatty acid	Omega-3-acid ethyl esters (Omacor, Lovaza)	4 g/d in single or divided doses	C: 1 g

(cont.)

Table 27. Medications for Dyslipidemia (cont.)

Class	Medication	Dosage[a]	Formulations
Combination preparations	Lovastatin/ niacin combination[b,c,e] (*Advicor*)	20 mg/500 mg ghs to start; max dose 40 mg/2000 mg	T: 20/500, 20/750, 20/1000, 40/1000
	Simvastatin/ niacin ombination[b,e] (*Simcor*)	20 mg/500 mg ghs to start; max dose 40 mg/2000 mg	T: 20/500, 20/750, 20/1000

H = high-intensity statin dose, M = moderate-intensity statin dose, L = low-intensity statin dose

[a] Dosage ranges for statins are listed as high-intensity (usually lowers LDL $\geq$50%), moderate-intensity (usually lowers LDL 30–49%), and low-intensity (usually lowers LDL <30%)

[b] Check fasting lipids and ALT before initiating tx. If ALT is normal, there is no need to recheck LFTs unless hyperbilirubinemia, jaundice, or clinically apparent hepatic disease occurs. There are reports of rare reversible cognitive impairment with statin tx. Statin tx has been uncommonly associated with increases in HbA$_{1c}$ and fasting glucose. Statins should be taken in the evening.

[c] Numerous drug interactions warranting contraindication or dose adjustment of lovastatin; see package insert for details.

[d] Use as monotherapy only in patients unable to tolerate statins, niacin, or a bile acid sequestrant (colesevelam, colestipol) and who have not reached LDL lowering goal.

[e] Monitor for flushing, pruritus, nausea, gastritis, ulcer. Dosage increases should be spaced 1 mo apart. ASA 325 mg po 30 min before first niacin dose of the day is effective in preventing AEs.

HYPERTENSION (HTN)

Goal BP

JNC 8 recommends a goal BP of:

- SBP <150 mmHg or DBP <90 mmHg persons aged 60 and over without DM or CKD.
- SBP <140 mmHg or DBP <90 mmHg in adults of all ages with DM.
- SBP <140 mmHg or DBP <90 mmHg in adults of all ages with CKD and GFR $\geq$60 mL/min/1.73m^2.

In persons aged 70 and over with CKD and GFR <60 mL/min/1.73m^2, there are little data to guide a goal recommendation; tx goals should be individualized according to health status, comorbidities, albuminuria (would suggest lower BP goal), and patient preferences.

Evaluation and Assessment

- Measure both standing and sitting BP after 5 min of rest.
- Base diagnosis on 2 or more readings at each of 2 or more visits. Once diagnosis is made, evaluation includes:
  - Assessment of cardiac risk factors: smoking, dyslipidemia, obesity, and DM are important in older adults.
  - Assessment of end-organ damage: LVH, angina, prior MI, prior coronary revascularization, HF, stroke or TIA, nephropathy, PAD, retinopathy.
  - Routine laboratory tests: CBC, UA, electrolytes, Cr, fasting glucose, total cholesterol, HDL cholesterol, and ECG.
  - Consider renal artery stenosis (RAS) if new onset of diastolic HTN, sudden rise in BP in previously well controlled HTN, HTN despite tx with maximal dosages of 3 antihypertensive agents, or azotemia induced by ACEI/ARB tx.
    - RAS diagnostic test options include renal artery duplex ultrasonography, CT angiography, or MRA.

- Don't screen for RAS in patients without resistant HTN and with normal renal function, even if known atherosclerosis present.[CW]
- Medical tx for RAS includes aggressive management of vascular risk factors and antihypertensive regimens that include an ACEI or ARB (monitor Cr closely).
- Consider renovascular angioplasty in cases of uncontrolled HTN despite aggressive medical tx, sudden or recurrent HF, unstable angina, or progressive decline in renal function.

Aggravating Factors
- Emotional stress
- Excessive alcohol intake
- Excessive salt intake
- Lack of aerobic exercise
- Low potassium intake
- Low calcium intake
- Nicotine
- Obesity

Management
- Initiate pharmacologic tx if goal BP (see above) has not been attained using nonpharmacologic methods.
- Lowering BP below 120/80 mmHg is not recommended. Particularly in patients with "white coat" HTN, home monitoring of BP with a properly calibrated machine can produce more reliable readings than office-based measurements.

Nonpharmacologic:
- Adequate calcium and magnesium intake as well as a low-fat diet for optimizing general health.
- Adequate dietary potassium intake; fruits and vegetables are the best sources.
- Aerobic exercise: 30–45 min most days of the week.
- Moderation of alcohol intake: limit to 1 oz of ethanol/d.
- Moderation of dietary sodium: watch for volume depletion with diuretic use.
  Goal: $\leq$2.4 g Na$^+$/d, optimal $\leq$1.5 g Na$^+$/d.
- Smoking cessation
- Weight reduction if obese: even a 10-lb weight loss can significantly lower BP.
  Goal: BMI <25 kg/m^2.

Pharmacologic: **Table 28** lists commonly used antihypertensives.
- Use antihypertensives carefully in patients with orthostatic BP drop.
- Base tx decisions on standing BP.
- First-line drugs: a thiazide diuretic, an ACEI, an ARB, or a calcium channel blocker.
- Follow-up BP measurements monthly until target BP is attained.
  - If BP is not at target, clinician has the option of increasing the dose of the intial drug or adding a second drug from the first-line list above.
  - Many patients require 2 or more drugs to achieve goal BP.
- Visits may be q3–6mo if BP is stable at target goal.
- If coexisting conditions, tx can be individualized (see **Table 29**).
- Combination drugs for HTN are listed in **Table 30**.
- Available dose formulations of oral potassium supplements▲: [T: (mEq) 6, 7, 8, 10, 20; S: (mEq/15 mL) 20, 40; pwd (mEq/pk) 15, 20, 25]

Hypertensive Emergencies and Urgencies:
- Elevated BP alone without symptoms or target end-organ damage does not require emergent BP lowering.

- Conditions requiring emergent BP lowering include hypertensive encephalopathy, intracranial hemorrhage, unstable angina, acute MI, acute left ventricular failure with pulmonary edema, dissecting aortic aneurysm.
- Most common initial tx for emergent BP lowering is sodium nitroprusside▲ *(Nipride)* 0.25–10 mg/kg/min as IV infusion.
- Nonemergent (ie, urgent) BP lowering is indicated only in cases in which BP needs to be lowered for procedural evaluation or tx (such as β blockade before surgery, see p 250) or in asymptomatic people with SBP >210 mmHg or DBP >120 mmHg.
  - Administer standard dose of a recommended antihypertensive orally (see **Table 28**) or an extra dose of patient's usual antihypertensive.
  - If the patient is npo, give **low** dose antihypertensive IV, titrating upward **slowly**. Options include β-blocker (eg, labetalol 20 mg), ACEI (eg, enalapril at 0.625 mg over 5 min), or diuretic (eg, furosemide 10 mg).

Table 28. Oral Antihypertensive Agents

Class, Medication	Geriatric Dosage Range, Total mg/d (times/d)	Formulations	Comments (Metabolism, Excretion)
Diuretics			↓ potassium, Na, magnesium levels; ↑ uric acid, calcium, cholesterol (mild), and glucose (mild) levels
Thiazides			
✔ Chlorothiazide▲ *(Diuril)*	125–500 (1)	T: 250, 500	
✔ Chlorthalidone▲ *(Hygroton)*	12.5–25 (1)	T: 15, 25, 50, 100	↑ AEs at >25 mg/d (L)
✔ HCTZ▲ *(Esidrix, HydroDIURIL, Microzide, Oretic)*	12.5–25 (1)	T: 25, 50, 100; S: 50 mg/mL; C: 12.5	↑ AEs at >25 mg/d (L)
✔ Indapamide▲ *(Lozol)*	0.625–2.5 (1)	T: 1.25, 2.5	Less or no hypercholesterolemia (L)
✔ Metolazone *(Mykrox)*	0.25–0.5 (1)	T rapid: 0.5	Monitor electrolytes carefully (L)
✔ Metolazone▲ *(Zaroxolyn)*	2.5–5 (1)	T: 2.5, 5, 10	Monitor electrolytes carefully (L)
✔ Polythiazide *(Renese)*	1–4 (1)	T: 1, 2, 4	
Loop diuretics			
♥ Bumetanide▲ *(Bumex)*	0.5–4 (1–3)	T: 0.5, 1, 2	Short duration of action, no hypercalcemia (K)
♥ Furosemide▲ *(Lasix)*	20–160 (1–2)	T: 20, 40, 80; S: 10, 40 mg/5 mL	Short duration of action, no hypercalcemia (K)
♥ Torsemide▲ *(Demadex)*	2.5–50 (1–2)	T: 5, 10, 20, 100	Short duration of action, no hypercalcemia (K)

(cont.)

✔ = preferred for treating older adults; ♥ = useful in treating HF with low EF

* See **Table 23** for target dosages in treating HF.

Note: Listing of AEs is not exhaustive, and AEs are for the drug class except when noted for individual drugs.

Class, Medication	Geriatric Dosage Range, Total mg/d (times/d)	Formulations	Comments (Metabolism, Excretion)
Table 28. Oral Antihypertensive Agents (cont.)			
Potassium-sparing drugs			
Amiloride▲ *(Midamor)*	2.5–10 (1)	T: 5	(L, K)
Triamterene▲ *(Dyrenium)*	25–100 (1–2)	T: 50, 100	Avoid in patients with CKD Stage 4 or 5.[BC] (L, K)
Aldosterone receptor-blockers			
♥ Eplerenone *(Inspra)*	25–100 (1)	T: 25, 50, 100	(L, K)
♥ Spironolactone▲ *(Aldactone)*	12.5–50 (1–2)	T: 25, 50, 100	Gynecomastia; Avoid doses >25 mg/d and avoid if CrCl <30 mL/min.[BC] (L, K)
Adrenergic Inhibitors			
α₁-Blockers[BC]			Avoid as antihypertensive unless patient has BPH;[BC] avoid in patients with syncope;[BC] avoid in patients with HF.[BC]
Doxazosin▲ *(Cardura)*	1–16 (1)	T: 1, 2, 4, 8	(L)
Prazosin▲ *(Minipress)*	1–20 (2–3)	T: 1, 2, 5	(L)
Terazosin▲ *(Hytrin)*	1–20 (1–2)	T: 1, 2, 5, 10; C: 1, 2, 5, 10	(L, K)
Central α₂-agonists and other centrally acting drugs			Sedation, dry mouth, bradycardia, withdrawal HTN
Clonidine▲ *(Catapres, Catapres-TTS)*	0.1–1.2 (2–3) **or** 1 pch/wk	T: 0.1, 0.2, 0.3▲; pch: 0.1, 0.2, 0.3 mg/d	Avoid as first-line antihypertensive.[BC] Continue oral for 1–2 d when converting to patch (L, K)
Guanfacine▲ *(Tenex)*	0.5–2 (1)	T: 1, 2	Avoid.[BC] (K)
Methyldopa▲ *(Aldomet)*	250–2500 (2)	T: 125, 250, 500; S: 250 mg/5 mL	Avoid.[BC] (L, K)
Reserpine▲ *(Serpasil)*	0.05–0.25 (1)	T: 0.1, 0.25	Avoid.[BC] Depression, nasal congestion, activation of peptic ulcer (L, K)
β-Blockers*			Bronchospasm, bradycardia, acute HF, may mask insulin-induced hypoglycemia; less effective for reducing HTN related endpoints in older vs younger patients; lipid solubility is a risk factor for delirium

(cont.)

✔ = preferred for treating older adults; ♥ = useful in treating HF with low EF
* See **Table 23** for target dosages in treating HF.
Note: Listing of AEs is not exhaustive, and AEs are for the drug class except when noted for individual drugs.

Table 28. Oral Antihypertensive Agents (cont.)

Class, Medication	Geriatric Dosage Range, Total mg/d (times/d)	Formulations	Comments (Metabolism, Excretion)
✔ Acebutolol▲ (Sectral)	200–800 (1)	C: 200, 400	β_1, low lipid solubility, intrinsic sympathomimetic activity (L, K)
✔ Atenolol▲ (Tenormin)	12.5–100 (1)	T: 25, 50, 100	β_1, low lipid solubility (K)
✔ Betaxolol▲ (Kerlone)	5–20 (1)	T: 10, 20	β_1, low lipid solubility (L, K)
✔ ♥ Bisoprolol▲ (Zebeta)	2.5–10 (1)	T: 5, 10	β_1, low lipid solubility (L, K)
✔ Carteolol (Cartrol)	1.25–10 (1)	T: 2.5, 5	β_1, low lipid solubility, intrinsic sympathomimetic activity (K)
✔ Metoprolol▲ (Lopressor)	25–400 (2)	T: 25, 50, 100	β_1, moderate lipid solubility (L)
✔ ♥ Long-acting▲ (Toprol XL)	50–400 (1)	T: 25, 50, 100, 200	(L)
Nadolol▲ (Corgard)	20–160 (1)	T: 20, 40, 80, 120, 160	β_1, β_2, low lipid solubility (K)
✔ ♥ Nebivolol (Bystolic)	2.5–40 (1)	T: 2.5, 5, 10	β_1, low lipid solubility (L, K)
Penbutolol (Levatol)	10–40 (1)	T: 20	β_1, β_2, high lipid solubility, intrinsic sympathomimetic activity (L, K)
Pindolol▲ (Visken)	5–40 (2)	T: 5, 10	β_1, β_2, moderate lipid solubility, intrinsic sympathomimetic activity (K)
Propranolol▲ (Inderal)	20–160 (2)	T: 10, 20, 40, 60, 80, 90; S: 4 mg/mL, 8 mg/mL, 80 mq/mL	β_1, β_2, high lipid solubility (L)
Long-acting▲ (Inderal LA, InnoPran XL)	60–180 (1)	C: 60, 80, 120, 160	β_1, β_2, high lipid solubility (L)
Timolol▲ (Blocadren)	10–40 (2)	T: 5, 10, 20	β_1, β_2, low to moderate lipid solubility (L, K)
Combined α- and β-blockers*			Postural hypotension, bronchospasm
✔ ♥ Carvedilol▲ (Coreg)	3.125–25 (2)	T: 3.125, 6.25, 12.5, 25	β_1, β_2, high lipid solubility (L)
✔ ♥ Extended-release (Coreg CR)	10–80 (1)	C: 10, 20, 40, 80	Multiply regular daily dose of carvedilol by 1.6 to convert to CR dose; do not take within 2 h of alcohol ingestion
✔ Labetalol▲ (Normodyne, Trandate)	100–600 (2)	T: 100, 200, 300	β_1, β_2, moderate lipid solubility (L, K)

(cont.)

✔ = preferred for treating older adults; ♥ = useful in treating HF with low EF

* See **Table 23** for target dosages in treating HF.

Note: Listing of AEs is not exhaustive, and AEs are for the drug class except when noted for individual drugs.

Table 28. Oral Antihypertensive Agents (cont.)

Class, Medication	Geriatric Dosage Range, Total mg/d (times/d)	Formulations	Comments (Metabolism, Excretion)
Direct Vasodilators			Headaches, fluid retention, tachycardia
♥ Hydralazine▲ *(Apresoline)*	25–100 (2–4)	T: 10, 25, 50, 100	Lupus syndrome; used in combination with isosorbide dinitrate for HF in blacks (L, K)
Minoxidil▲ *(Loniten)*	2.5–50 (1)	T: 2.5, 10	Hirsutism (K)
Calcium Antagonists			
Nondihydropyridines			Conduction defects, worsening of systolic dysfunction, gingival hyperplasia
✔ Diltiazem SR▲ *(Cardizem CD, Cardizem SR, Dilacor XR, Tiazac)*	120–360 (1–2), max 480	C: 1/d: 120, 180, 240, 300, 360, 420; 2/d: 60, 90, 120; T: 30, 60, 90, 120, ER: 120, 180, 240	Nausea, headache (L)
✔ Verapamil SR▲ *(Calan SR, Covera-HS, Isoptin SR, Verelan PM)*	120–360 (1–2)	T: SR 120, 180, 240; C: SR 100, 120, 180, 200, 240, 300, 360; T: 40, 80, 120	Constipation, bradycardia (L)
Dihydropyridines			Ankle edema, flushing, headache, gingival hypertrophy
✔ Amlodipine▲ *(Norvasc)*	2.5–10 (1)	T: 2.5, 5, 10	(L)
✔ Felodipine▲ *(Plendil)*	2.5–20 (1)	T: 2.5, 5, 10	(L)
✔ Isradipine SR *(DynaCirc CR)*	2.5–10 (1)	T: 5, 10	(L)
✔ Nicardipine▲ *(Cardene)*	60–120 (3)	C: 20, 30	(L)
✔ Sustained release *(Cardene SR)*	60–120 (2)	T: 30, 45, 60	(L)
✔ Nifedipine SR▲ *(Adalat CC, Procardia XL)*	30–60 (1)	T: 30, 60, 90	(L)
✔ Nisoldipine▲ *(Sular)*	10–40 (1)	T: ER 10, 20, 30, 40	(L)
ACEIs*			Cough (common), angioedema (rare), hyperkalemia, rash, loss of taste, leukopenia
✔♥ Benazepril▲ *(Lotensin)*	2.5–40 (1–2)	T: 5, 10, 20, 40	(L, K)

(cont.)

✔ = preferred for treating older adults; ♥ = useful in treating HF with low EF

* See **Table 23** for target dosages in treating HF.

Note: Listing of AEs is not exhaustive, and AEs are for the drug class except when noted for individual drugs.

Table 28. Oral Antihypertensive Agents

Class, Medication	Geriatric Dosage Range, Total mg/d (times/d)	Formulations	Comments (Metabolism, Excretion)
✔ ♥ Captopril▲ *(Capoten)*	12.5–150 (2–3)	T: 12.5, 25, 50, 100	(L, K)
✔ ♥ Enalapril▲ *(Vasotec)*	2.5–40 (1–2)	T: 2.5, 5, 10, 20	(L, K)
✔ ♥ Fosinopril▲ *(Monopril)*	5–40 (1–2)	T: 10, 20, 40	(L, K)
✔ ♥ Lisinopril▲ *(Prinivil, Zestril)*	2.5–40 (1)	T: 2.5, 5, 10, 20, 30, 40	(K)
✔ Moexipril▲ *(Univasc)*	3.75–30 (1)	T: 7.5, 15	(L, K)
✔ ♥ Perindopril▲ *(Aceon)*	4–8 (1–2)	T: 2, 4, 8	(L, K)
✔ ♥ Quinapril▲ *(Accupril)*	5–40 (1)	T: 5, 10, 20, 40	(L, K)
✔ ♥ Ramipril▲ *(Altace)*	1.25–20 (1)	T: 1.25, 2.5, 5, 10	(L, K)
✔ ♥ Trandolapril▲ *(Mavik)*	1–4 (1)	T: 1, 2, 4	(L, K)
Angiotensin II Receptor Blockers (ARBs)*			Angioedema (very rare), hyperkalemia
✔ Azilsartan *(Edarbi)*	20–80 (1)	T: 40, 80	(L, K)
✔ ♥ Candesartan *(Atacand)*	4–32 (1)	T: 4, 8, 16, 32	(K)
✔ Eprosartan *(Teveten)*	400–800 (1–2)	T: 400, 600	(biliary, K)
✔ Irbesartan *(Avapro)*	75–300 (1)	T: 75, 150, 300	(L)
✔ ♥ Losartan▲ *(Cozaar)*	12.5–100 (1–2)	T: 25, 50, 100	(L, K)
✔ Olmesartan *(Benicar)*	20–40 (1)	T: 5, 20, 40	Severe GI symptoms (rare) (L, K)
✔ Telmisartan *(Micardis)*	20–80 (1)	T: 20, 40, 80	(L)
✔ ♥ Valsartan *(Diovan)*	40–320 (1)	T: 40, 80, 160, 320; C: 80, 160	(L, K)
Renin Inhibitor			
Aliskiren *(Tekturna)*	150–300 (1)	T: 150, 300	Monitor electrolytes in patients with renal disease; contraindicated in patients with DM who are also taking an ACEI or ARB

✔ = preferred for treating older adults; ♥ = useful in treating HF with low EF
* See **Table 23** for target dosages in treating HF.
Note: Listing of AEs is not exhaustive, and AEs are for the drug class except when noted for individual drugs.
Source: Data in part from The seventh report of the Joint National Committee on Prevention, Detection, Evaluation, and Treatment of High Blood Pressure: The JNC 7 report. *JAMA* 2003;289:2560–2572.

Table 29. Choosing Antihypertensive Therapy on the Basis of Coexisting Conditions

Condition	Appropriate for Use	Avoid or Contraindicated
Angina	β, D, non-D	
Atrial tachycardia and fibrillation	β, non-D	
Bronchospasm		β, αβ
CKD	AA, ACEI[a]	
DM	ACEI, ARB, β, T[b]	T[b]
Dyslipidemia		β, T[c]
Essential tremor	β	
HF	AA, ACEI, ARB, β, αβ, L	D, non-D[d]
Hyperthyroidism	β	
MI	β, AA, ACEI, ARB	non-D
Osteoporosis	T	
Prostatism (BPH)	α	
Urge UI	D, non-D	L, T

Note: AA = aldosterone antagonist; α = α-blocker; β = β-blocker; αβ = combined α- and β-blocker; D = dihydropyridine calcium antagonist; non-D = nondihydropyridine calcium antagonist; L = loop diuretic; T = thiazide diuretic

[a] Use with great caution in renovascular disease.
[b] Low-dose diuretics probably beneficial in type 2 DM; high-dose diuretics relatively contraindicated in types 1 and 2.
[c] Low-dose diuretics have a minimal effect on lipids.
[d] May be beneficial in HF caused by diastolic dysfunction.

Table 30. Combination Medications Containing an Antihypertensive Agent

Combination Type	Fixed-dose Combination (mg)*	Trade Name
ACEI and calcium channel blocker	Amlodipine/benazepril▲ (2.5/10, 5/10, 5/20, 10/20)	*Lotrel*
	Enalapril/felodipine (5/2.5, 5/5)	*Lexxel*
	Trandolapril/verapamil (2/180, 1/240, 2/240, 4/240)	*Tarka*
ACEI and diuretic	Benazepril/HCTZ▲ (5/6.25, 10/12.5, 20/12.5, 20/25)	*Lotensin HCT*
	Captopril/HCTZ▲ (25/15, 25/25, 50/15, 50/25)	*Capozide*
	Enalapril/HCTZ▲ (5/12.5, 10/25)	*Vaseretic*
	Lisinopril/HCTZ▲ (10/12.5, 20/12.5, 20/25)	*Prinzide, Zestoretic*
	Moexipril/HCTZ▲ (7.5/12.5, 15/12.5, 15/25)	*Uniretic*
	Quinapril/HCTZ▲ (10/12.5, 20/12.5, 20/25)	*Accuretic*
ARB and calcium channel blocker	Amlodipine/valsartan (5/160, 10/160, 5/320, 10/320)	*Exforge*
	Amlodipine/olmesartan (5/20, 5/40, 10/20,10/40)	*Azor*
	Amlodipine/telmisartan (5/40, 5/80, 10/40, 10/80)	*Twynsta*
ARB, calcium channel blocker, and diuretic	Amlodipine/valsartan/HCTZ (5/160/12.5, 10/160/12.5, 5/160/25, 10/160/25, 10/320/25)	*Exforge HCT*

(cont.)

Table 30. Combination Medications Containing an Antihypertensive Agent (cont.)

Combination Type	Fixed-dose Combination (mg)*	Trade Name
ARB and diuretic	Azilsartan/chlorthalidone (40/12.5, 40/25)	*Edarbyclor*
	Candesartan/HCTZ (16/12.5, 32/12.5)	*Atacand HCT*
	Eprosartan/HCTZ (600/12.5, 600/25)	*Teveten HCT*
	Irbesartan/HCTZ (150/12.5, 300/12.5, 300/25)	*Avalide*
	Losartan/HCTZ (50/12.5, 100/12.5, 100/25)	*Hyzaar*
	Olmesartan/HCTZ (20/12.5, 40/12.5, 40/25)	*Benicar HCT*
	Telmisartan/HCTZ (40/12.5, 80/12.5, 80/25)	*Micardis HCT*
	Valsartan/HCTZ (80/12.5, 160/12.5, 160/25, 320/12.5, 320/25)	*Diovan HCT*
β-Blocker and diuretic	Atenolol/chlorthalidone▲ (50/25, 100/25)	*Tenoretic*
	Bisoprolol/HCTZ▲ (2.5/6.25, 5/6.25, 10/6.25)	*Ziac*
	Propranolol LA/HCTZ▲ (40/25, 80/25)	*Inderide*
	Metoprolol succinate/HCTZ (25/12.5, 50/12.5, 100/12.5)	*Dutoprol*
	Metoprolol tartrate/HCTZ▲ (50/25, 100/25, 100/50)	*Lopressor HCT*
	Nadolol/bendroflumethiazide▲ (40/5, 80/5)	*Corzide*
Calcium channel blocker and statin	Amlodipine/atorvastatin (2.5/10, 2.5/20, 2.5/40, 5/10, 5/20, 5/40, 5/80, 10/10, 10/20, 10/40, 10/80)	*Caduet*
Centrally acting drug[a] and diuretic	Methyldopa/HCTZ▲ (250/15, 250/25, 500/30, 500/50)	*Aldoril*
	Reserpine/chlorothiazide▲ (0.125/250, 0.25/500)	*Diupres*
	Reserpine/HCTZ▲ (0.125/25, 0.125/50)	*Hydropres*
Direct vasodilator and nitrate	Isosorbide dinitrate/hydralazine (20/37.5)	*BiDil*
Diuretic and diuretic	Amiloride hydrochloride/HCTZ▲ (5/50)	*Moduretic*
	Spironolactone[b]/HCTZ▲ (25/25, 50/50)	*Aldactazide*
	Triamterene/HCTZ▲ (37.5/25, 50/25, 75/50)	*Dyazide, Maxzide*
Direct renin inhibitor and ARB	Aliskiren/valsartan (150/160, 300/320)	*Valturna*
Direct renin inhibitor and calcium channel blocker	Aliskiren/amlodipine (150/5, 150/10, 300/5, 300/10)	*Tekamlo*
Direct renin inhibitor and diuretic	Aliskiren/HCTZ (150/12.5, 150/25, 300/12.5, 300/25)	*Tekturna HCT*
Direct renin inhibitor, calcium channel blocker, and diuretic	Aliskiren/amlodipine/HCTZ▲ (150/5/12.5, 300/5/12.5, 300/5/25, 300/10/12.5, 300/10/25)	*Amturnide*

*Some drug combinations are available in multiple fixed doses. Each drug dose is reported in mg.
[a]Avoid.**BC**
[b]Avoid doses >25 mg/d or if CrCl <30 mL/min.**BC**

PULMONARY ARTERIAL HYPERTENSION (PAH)

Evaluation and Assessment

- PAH can be primary (unexplained) or secondary to underlying conditions.
- Almost all cases in older adults are secondary, most commonly associated with chronic pulmonary and/or cardiac disease, including COPD, interstitial lung disease, obstructive sleep apnea, pulmonary emboli, HF, and mitral valvular disease.
- Early symptoms are often nonspecific and include dyspnea on exertion, fatigue, and vague chest discomfort.
- Late symptoms include severe dyspnea on exertion, cyanosis, syncope, chest pain, HF, arrhythmias.
- Physical examination findings relate to manifestations of the associated conditions mentioned above.
- Diagnostic tests:
  - ECG may show right-axis deviation, right atrial and ventricular hypertrophy, T-wave changes
  - CXR may show large right ventricle, dilated pulmonary arteries
  - Echocardiography estimates pulmonary arterial pressure and evaluates possible valvular disease
  - Right heart catheterization is gold standard, with PAH defined as mean pulmonary arterial pressure >25 mmHg at rest or >30 mmHg during exercise.
- Additional tests (eg, pulmonary function tests, sleep study) may clarify severity of coexisting conditions.

Management

- Correct/optimize underlying conditions.
- Supplemental oxygen for chronic hypoxemia
- Diuretics for volume overload from HF
- Avoid calcium channel blockers unless they have been shown to be of benefit from a right heart catheterization vasodilator challenge study.
- Other agents have been studied mainly in primary PAH and are of uncertain effectiveness and safety in secondary PAH:
  - Warfarin (see p 24)
  - Prostacyclins: epoprostenol *(Flolan)* by continuous IV infusion, treprostinil *(Remodulin)* by continuous SC infusion, treprostinil or iloprost *(Ventavis)* by inhalation
  - Endothelial receptor antagonists: bosentan *(Tracleer)* 62.5 mg q12h × 4 wk, then 125 mg q12h; ambrisentan *(Letairis)* 5–10 mg/d
  - Sildenafil *(Revatio, Viagra)* po 20–25 mg q8h

ATRIAL FIBRILLATION (AF)

Evaluation and Assessment

Causes:

- Cardiac disease: cardiac surgery, cardiomyopathy, HF, hypertensive heart disease, ischemic disease, pericarditis, valvular disease
- Noncardiac disease: alcoholism, chronic pulmonary disease, infections, pulmonary emboli, thyrotoxicosis

Standard testing: ECG, CBC, electrolytes, Cr, BUN, TSH, echocardiogram

Management
- Correct precipitating cause.
- Patients presenting with AF and hypotension, severe angina, or advanced HF should be strongly considered for acute direct-current cardioversion.
- For acute management of AF with rapid ventricular response in patients who do not receive or respond to cardioversion, ventricular rate should be acutely lowered with one or more of the following medications:
  - β-Blockers, eg, metoprolol▲ 2.5–5 mg IV bolus over 2 min; may repeat twice
  - Diltiazem▲, 0.25 mg/kg IV over 2 min
  - Verapamil▲, 0.075–0.15 mg/kg IV over 2 min
- For patients with minimal symptoms or in whom sinus rhythm cannot be easily achieved, rate control plus antithrombotic tx is the preferred tx strategy. Avoid antiarrhythmic drugs as first-line tx of AF.[BC]
  - Rate control (target <110 bpm) can be achieved with oral metoprolol or other β-blocker, diltiazem, or verapamil.
  - Digoxin▲ can be used as a third-line agent for rate control.
  - For symptomatic patients in whom ventricular rate does not respond to pharmacologic tx, AV node ablation with pacemaker placement can effectively control rate.
  - Antithrombotic tx (**Tables 31** and **32**) should be individualized to balance reduced stroke risk vs increased bleeding risk. Two risk scoring instruments are commonly used for assessing stroke risk while bleeding risk can be assessed using the HAS-BLED score (see **Table 31**). The CHA_2DS_2-VASc classifies many more older adults as warranting anticoagulant tx than the $CHADS_2$.

Table 31. Risk Instruments to Guide Antithrombotic Treatment in AF

Instrument	What is Assessed	Score Calculation	Antithrombotic Tx by Score		
			0	1	≥2
CHADS$_2$	Stroke risk	1 point each for HF, HTN, age ≥75 yr, DM; 2 points for hx of stroke	ASA	ASA or Anticoagulant[a]	Anticoagulant[a]
CHA$_2$DS$_2$–VASc	Stroke risk	1 point each for HF, HTN, DM, vascular disease, age ≥65 yr, female sex; 2 points each for age ≥75 yr, hx of stroke	ASA or no tx	ASA or Anticoagulant[a]	Anticoagulant[a]
HAS–BLED	Bleeding risk of anticoagulant tx	1 point each for HTN, abnormal renal function, abnormal liver function, prior stroke, prior major bleeding, labile INRs, age ≥65 yr, alcohol use, drug use	If CHADS$_2$ or CHA$_2$DS$_2$–VASc score is 1, the risk of bleeding with anticoagulant tx may outweigh the risk of stroke if the HAS-BLED score is >2. If CHADS$_2$ or CHA$_2$DS$_2$–VASc score is ≥2, the risk of bleeding from anticoagulant tx may outweigh the risk of stroke if the HAS-BLED score exceeds the CHADS$_2$ or CHA$_2$DS$_2$–VASc score.		

[a]Apixaban, dabigatran, rivaroxaban, or warfarin; see **Tables 17** and **18** for dosing, **Table 32** for selection of anticoagulant.

Table 32. Effects of Newer Anticoagulants vs Warfarin in AF Treatment

Outcome	Effect of Anticoagulant Compared to Warfarin		
	Apixaban	Dabigatran	Rivaroxaban
All-cause mortality	Lower	Trend lower[a]	Trend lower[a]
Hemorrhagic stroke	Lower	Lower	Lower
Ischemic stroke	Same	Lower	Same
Major bleeding	Lower	Higher[b]	Same
GI bleeding	Same	Higher	Higher

[a] Trend lower means that data are at borderline statistical significance.
[b] Higher major bleeding seen in subjects >75 yr old; rates are the same in younger subjects.

- If anticoagulation is contraindicated or not tolerated in patients with $CHADS_2$ or CHA_2DS_2–VASc scores ≥ 1, use ASA 81–325 mg/d. Addition of clopidogrel 75 mg/d to ASA lowers stroke risk but also increases risk of major hemorrhage. Both ASA and clopidogrel are less effective for stroke prevention in patients ≥ 75 yr of age.
- For patients with unpleasant symptoms or decreased exercise tolerance on rate control tx, rhythm control via direct-current or pharmacologic cardioversion is the preferred tx strategy.
  - For direct-current cardioversion, 3 methods may be used:
    - Early cardioversion (<48 h from onset): proceed with cardioversion; use adjunctive anticoagulation based on risk of thromboembolism (eg, $CHADS_2$ score).
    - Delayed cardioversion (≥ 48 h from onset) with transesophageal echocardiography (TEE): perform TEE to exclude intracardiac thrombus; if no thrombus, begin anticoagulation and cardiovert.
    - Delayed cardioversion (≥ 48 h from onset) without TEE: anticoagulate for at least 3 wk with INR ≥ 2 before cardioversion; continue anticoagulation after cardioversion.
  - For pharmacologic cardioversion and rhythm maintenance (recommended only if AF produces symptoms significantly impairing quality of life), rhythm control drugs may be tried (see **Table 33**).
  - Unless contraindicated, anticoagulation should be continued indefinitely after cardioversion due to the high risk for recurrent AF.
  - In selected patients with symptomatic AF refractory to antiarrhythmic drugs, catheter or surgical AF ablation may be considered.

Table 33. Selected Medications for Rhythm Control in AF

Medication	Dosage	Formulations	Comments (Metabolism)
Amiodarone▲ *(Cordarone, Pacerone)*	100–400 mg/d	T: 200, 400	Most effective antifibrillatory agent but numerous AEs, including pulmonary and hepatic toxic effects, neurologic and dermatologic AEs, hypothyroidism, hyperthyroidism, corneal deposits, warfarin▲ interaction (L)
Propafenone▲ *(Rythmol)*	150–300 mg q8h	T: 150, 225, 300	Contraindicated in patients with ischemic and structural heart disease; AEs include VT and HF (L)
Sotalol▲ *(Betapace, Betapace AF, Sorine)*	80–160 mg q12h	T: 80, 120, 160, 240	Prolongs QT interval; AEs include torsades de pointes, HF, exacerbation of COPD/bronchospasm (K)

AORTIC STENOSIS (AS)

Evaluation and Assessment

- Presence of symptoms—angina, syncope, HF (frequently diastolic dysfunction)—indicates severe disease and a life expectancy without surgery of <2 yr.
- Echocardiography is essential to measure aortic valve gradient (AVG) and aortic valve area (AVA).
  - Moderate AS is indicated by an AVG of 25–50 mmHg and by an AVA of 1–1.5 cm^2.
  - Severe AS is indicated by an AVG of 50–80 mmHg and by an AVA <1 cm^2.
  - Critical AS is indicated by an AVG >80 mmHg and by an AVA <0.5 cm^2.
- For asymptomatic cases, echocardiography should be repeated annually for moderate AS and q6–12 mo for severe AS.
- Don't perform echocardiography as routine follow-up for mild, asymptomatic native valve disease in adult patients with no change in signs or symptoms.[CW]
- ECG and CXR should be obtained initially to look for conduction defects, LVH, and pulmonary congestion.

Treatment

- Aortic valve replacement (AVR)
  - Alleviates symptoms and improves ventricular functioning.
  - In most cases, perform AVR promptly *after* symptoms have appeared.
  - Surgical AVR vs transcatheter AVR (TAVR; a percutaneous procedure in the catheterization lab in which an artificial valve is implanted via a catheter):
    - In low-risk patients (young, no other heart problems or significant comorbidities), AVR surgery is superior to TAVR.
    - In high-risk surgical patients (older, cardiac and/or other significant comorbidities), surgical AVR results in higher 30-d mortality, major bleeding episodes, and new-onset AF, but lower stroke rate than TAVR. Death rates after 1 and 2 yr are the same for both procedures.
    - Relative TAVR contraindications: life expectancy <1 yr, severe mitral regurgitation, subaortic stenosis, low EF, recent MI
- Avoid vasodilators if possible.

ABDOMINAL AORTIC ANEURYSM (AAA)

- Ultrasound should be performed if aortic diameter is felt to be >3 cm on physical examination.
- Ultrasonographic screening for AAA is recommended once for men between age 65 and 75 if former or current smoker.
- Management is based on diameter of AAA
  - <4.5 cm: ultrasound q12mo
  - 4.5–5.4 cm: ultrasound q3–6mo
  - >5.4 cm: surgical referral
- Endovascular repair is associated with significantly less perioperative morbidity and mortality up to 3 yr.

PERIPHERAL ARTERIAL DISEASE (PAD)

Evaluation

Hx should include inquiry regarding the following:

- Lower extremity exertional fatigue or pain, or pain at rest
- Poorly healing or nonhealing wounds
- Cardiac risk factors

Physical examination should include the following:

- Palpation of pulses (brachial, radial, ulnar, femoral, popliteal, posterior tibial, and dorsalis pedis)
- Auscultation for abdominal, flank, and femoral bruits
- Inspection of feet
- Skin inspection for distal hair loss, trophic skin changes, and/or hypertrophic nails

Diagnosis established by ABI <0.9 or other test (see **Table 34**).

Table 34. Management of PAD		
Signs and Symptoms	**Useful Tests**	**Treatment** (see below)
Asymptomatic; diminished or absent peripheral pulses	ABI[a]	Risk factor reduction[b]
Atypical leg pain	ABI, EABI	Risk factor reduction, antiplatelet tx[b]
Claudication: exertional fatigue, discomfort, pain relieved by rest	ABI, EABI, Doppler ultrasound, pulse volume recording, segmental pressure measurement	Risk factor reduction, antiplatelet tx, claudication tx; consider endovascular or surgical revascularization if symptoms persist[b]
Rest pain, nonhealing wound (see also p 293), gangrene	ABI, Doppler ultrasound, angiography (MRI, CT, or contrast)	Risk factor reduction, antiplatelet tx, claudication tx, endovascular or surgical revascularization[b]

Note: EABI = exercise treadmill test with ABI measurement.

[a] Abnormal is <0.9; <0.4 is critical.

[b] Refrain from percutaneous or surgical revascularization of peripheral artery stenosis in patients without claudication or critical limb ischemia.[CW]

Treatment

Risk Factor Reduction

- Smoking cessation
- Lipid-lowering tx (see Dyslipidemia Management, p 46)
- BP control (goal <140/90 mmHg)
- DM tx (see Endocrine chapter p 92)

Antiplatelet Therapy

- ASA[▲] 75–325 mg/d
- Clopidogrel *(Plavix)* 75 mg/d (T: 75) if no response or intolerant of ASA

Claudication Therapy

- Walking program (goal: 50 min of intermittent walking 3–5 ×/wk)

- Cilostazol▲ *(Pletal)* 100 mg q12h, 1 h before or 2 h pc (contraindicated in patients with HF); second-line alternative tx is pentoxifylline▲ *(Trental)* 400 mg q8h [T: 400]
- If ACEI not contraindicated, routine use is recommended to prevent adverse cardiovascular events in patients with claudication.

SYNCOPE

Table 35. Classification of Syncope

Cause	Frequency (%)	Features	Increased Risk of Death
Vasovagal	21	Preceded by lightheadedness, nausea, diaphoresis; recovery gradual, frequently with fatigue	No
Cardiac	10	Little or no warning before blackout, rapid and complete recovery	Yes
Orthostatic	9	Lightheaded prodrome after standing, recovery gradual	No
Medication-induced	7	Lightheaded prodrome, recovery gradual	No
Seizure	5	No warning, may have neurologic deficits, slow recovery	Yes
Stroke, TIA	4	Little or no warning, neurologic deficits	Yes
Other causes	8	Preceded by cough, micturition, or specific situation	No
Unknown	37	Any of the above	Yes

Source: Adapted from Soteriades ES, et al. *N Engl J Med* 2002;347:878–885.

Evaluation
- Focus hx on events before, during, and after loss of consciousness; hx of cardiac disease (significantly worsens prognosis of syncope of all causes); careful medication review.
- Focus on cardiovascular and neurologic systems in physical examination.
- ECG and orthostatic BP or pulse check for all patients.
- The following characteristics are associated with serious outcomes and likely require urgent/emergent further testing and monitoring: age >90 yr, male sex, abnormal ECG, hx of arrhythmia (VT, symptomatic supraventricular tachycardia, third-degree or Mobitz II AV block, sinus pause >3 sec, symptomatic bradycardia), hx of HF, dyspnea, abnormal troponin I, SBP <90 mmHg or >160 mmHg.
- Additional testing as suggested by initial evaluation:
  ○ Ambulatory ECG monitoring for further evaluation of arrhythmia
  ○ Stress testing to investigate ischemic heart disease
  ○ Echocardiography to investigate structural heart disease
  ○ Electrophysiologic studies in patients with prior MI or structural heart disease
  ○ Tilt-table testing for suspected vasovagal cause
  ○ Head imaging, EEG for suspected neurologic cause
  ○ Don't perform imaging of the carotid arteries for simple syncope without other neurologic symptoms.**CW**
  ○ In the evaluation of simple syncope and a normal neurological examination, don't obtain brain imaging studies (CT or MRI).**CW**

- If suspected orthostatic cause, evaluation for Parkinson disease, autonomic neuropathy, DM, hypovolemia

Management

- Patients with cardiac syncope require immediate hospitalization on telemetry; exclude MI and PE.
- Strongly consider hospital admission for patients with syncope due to neurologic or unknown causes, particularly if concurrent heart disease.
- Patients with syncope due to vasovagal, orthostatic, medication-induced, or other causes can usually be managed as outpatients, particularly if there is no hx of heart disease.
- Tx is correction of underlying cause.

ORTHOSTATIC (POSTURAL) HYPOTENSION
See also **Table 54**.

Evaluation and Assessment

- Associated with following symptoms usually after standing: lightheadedness, dizziness, syncope, blurred vision, diaphoresis, head or neck pain, decreased hearing
- Diagnosis: ≥20 mmHg drop in SBP or ≥10 mmHg in DBP within 3 min of rising from lying to standing
- Causes
  - Medications, including antihypertensives, phenothiazines, TCAs, MAOIs, anti-Parkinsonian drugs, PDE5 inhibitors (for erectile dysfunction)
  - Autonomic dysregulation (suggested by lack of compensatory rise in HR with postural hypotension): age-related decreased baroreceptor sensitivity, Parkinson disease and related disorders, peripheral neuropathy, prolonged bed rest
  - Hypovolemia
  - Anemia

Management

- Correct underlying disorder, particularly by discontinuing medications that could exacerbate hypotension
- Alter movement behavior: educate patients to rise slowly, flex calf and forearm muscles when standing, stand with one foot in front of other, avoid straining, and elevate head of bed
- Dietary changes: avoid alcohol, maintain adequate fluid intake, increase salt and caffeine intake
- Above-the-knee compression stockings (at least medium compression strength, eg, Jobst)
- Pharmacologic interventions:
  - First-line: fludrocortisone▲: 0.1–0.2 mg q8–24h [T: 0.1]; use with caution in patients with HF, cardiac disease, HTN, renal disease, esophagitis, peptic ulcer disease, or ulcerative colitis
  - Midodrine▲ *(ProAmatine):* 2.5–10 mg q8–24h [T: 2.5, 5]; use with caution in patients with HTN, DM, urinary retention, renal disease, hepatic disease, glaucoma, BPH
  - Pyridostigmine▲ *(Mestinon):* 60 mg q24h [T: 60]; can be used in combination with midodrine 2.5–5 mg/d.

- ○ Caffeine: 1 cup of caffeinated coffee q8–12h; alternatively, caffeine tabs 100–200 mg q8–12h; useful for postprandial hypotension when taken with meals. Avoid in patients with insomnia.[BC]
- ○ Erythropoietin (see **Table 67**) can be useful for hypotension secondary to anemia if Hb <10 mg/dL

IMPLANTABLE CARDIAC DEFIBRILLATOR (ICD) PLACEMENT

Indications (consider life expectancy and comorbidities)

- Established:
  - ○ Cardiac arrest due to VF or VT
  - ○ Spontaneous sustained VT with structural heart disease
  - ○ Spontaneous sustained VT without structural heart disease not alleviated by other tx
  - ○ Unexplained syncope with hemodynamically significant VF or VT inducible by electrophysiologic study when drug tx is ineffective, not tolerated, or not preferred
  - ○ Nonsustained VT, CAD, and inducible VF by electrophysiologic study that is not suppressed by Class I antiarrhythmic
  - ○ LVEF ≤30%, NYHA Class II or III HF, and CAD >40 d after MI
  - ○ ICD + biventricular pacing for advanced HF (NYHA Class III or IV), LVEF ≤35%, and QRS interval ≥120 millisec or mild HF (NYHA Class I or II), LVEF <30%, and QRS interval ≥130 millisec
- Less established: Nonischemic cardiomyopathy with LVEF <35% and either premature ventricular complexes or nonsustained VT

Contraindications

- Terminal illness with life expectancy <6 mo
- Unexplained syncope without inducible VT or VF and without structural heart disease
- VT or VF due to transient or easily reversible disorder
- End-stage HF (ACC/AHA Stage D) not awaiting cardiac transplant

Complications

- Surgical: infection (1–2%), hematoma, pneumothorax
- Device-related: lead dislodgement or malfunction, connection problems, inadequate defibrillation threshold
- Tx-related: frequent shocks (appropriate or inappropriate), acceleration of VT, anxiety and other psychological stress
- End-of-life planning: discuss and document the circumstances in which the patient would desire the ICD to be turned off. ICDs can be turned off by the cardiologist or the device manufacturer's representative. Don't leave an ICD activated when it is inconsistent with the patient/family goals of care.[CW]

DIAGNOSIS

Diagnostic Criteria—Adapted from *DSM-5*

- Core symptom: disturbed consciousness (ie, decreased attention, environmental awareness)
- Cognitive change (eg, memory deficit, disorientation, language disturbance) or perceptual disturbance (eg, visual illusions, hallucinations)
- Three motoric subtypes: hyperactive, hypoactive, and normal/mild
- Rapid onset (hours to days) and fluctuating daily course
- Evidence of a causal physical condition
- Confusion Assessment Method (CAM): **Both** acute onset and fluctuating course **and** inattention **and either** disorganized thinking **or** altered level of consciousness (Inouye SK. *N Engl J Med* 2006;354[11]:1157–1165). For nonverbal patients, use CAM-ICU to assess attention and level of consciousness (Ely EW. *JAMA* 2001;286[21]:2703–2710).

Risk Factors

- Dementia greatly increases risk of delirium.
- Advanced age, comorbid physical problems (especially sleep deprivation, immobility, dehydration, pain, sensory impairment).
- Hospitalization and/or surgery (see Postoperative Delirium, p 255)

Evaluation

- Assume reversibility unless proven otherwise.
- Thoroughly review prescription and OTC medications, and alcohol usage.
- Exclude infection and other medical causes.
- Laboratory studies may include CBC, electrolytes, LFTs, ammonia, thyroid function tests, renal function tests, serum albumin, B_{12}, serum calcium, serum glucose, UA, oxygen saturation, ABG levels, CXR, and ECG.
- Brain imaging and EEG typically not helpful unless there is evidence of cerebral trauma, possible stroke, focal neurologic signs, or seizure activity.

CAUSES

(Italicized type indicates the most common causes in older adults.)

Medications (see **Table 36** and **Table 37**)

- *Anticholinergics* (Avoid[BC])
- Anti-inflammatory agents, including prednisone
- Benzodiazepines or alcohol—acute toxicity or withdrawal
- Cardiovascular (eg, digoxin, antihypertensives, diuretics)
- Lithium
- Opioid analgesics (especially meperidine) (Avoid[BC])

Table 36. Potentially Differentiating Features of Medication-induced Delirium

Medication type	Early	Late
Anticholinergic	Visual impairment, dry mouth, constipation, urinary retention	↑ HR, mydriasis, ↓ bowel sounds
Serotonin syndrome	Tremor, diarrhea	Hyperreflexia, clonus, myoclonic jerks, ↑ bowel sounds, diaphoresis
Neuroleptic malignant syndrome	↑ EPS	Marked rigidity, bradyreflexia, hyperthermia

* The use of urinary catecholamines and/or metabolics as diagnostic aids require further evaluation.

Table 37. Drugs with Strong Anticholinergic Properties

Antidepressants

Amitriptyline	Doxepin	Paroxetine
Amoxapine	Imipramine	Protriptyline
Clomipramine	Nortriptyline	Trimipramine
Desipramine		

Antihistamines

Brompheniramine	Clemastine	Diphenhydramine
Carbinoxamine	Cyproheptadine	Hydroxyzine
Chlorpheniramine	Dimenhydrinate	Loratadine

Antimuscarinics (urinary incontinence)

Darifenacin	Oxybutynin	Tolterodine
Fesoterodine	Solifenacin	Trospium
Flavoxate		

Antiparkinson agents

Benztropine	Trihexyphenidyl

Antipsychotics

Chlorpromazine	Olanzapine	Promethazine
Clozapine	Perphenazine	Thioridazine
Fluphenazine	Pimozide	Thiothixene
Loxapine	Prochlorperazine	Trifluoperazine

Antispasmodics

Atropine products	Homatropine	Propantheline
Belladonna alkaloids	Hyoscyamine products	Scopolamine
Dicyclomine		

Skeletal Muscle Relaxants

Carisoprodol	Orphenadrine	Tizanidine
Cyclobenzaprine		

* American Geriatrics Society updated Beers Criteria for potentially inappropriate medication use in older adults.
American Geriatrics Society 2012 Beers Criteria Update Expert Panel. *J Am Geriatr Soc.* 2012;60(4):616–631.

Infections
Respiratory, skin, urinary tract, others

Metabolic Disorders
Acute blood loss, *dehydration, electrolyte imbalance,* end-organ failure (hepatic, renal), hyperglycemia, *hypoglycemia, hypoxia*

Cardiovascular
Arrhythmia, *HF, MI,* shock

Neurologic
CNS infections, head trauma, seizures, stroke, subdural hematoma, TIAs, tumors

Miscellaneous
Fecal impaction, *postoperative state,* sleep deprivation, urinary retention

PREVENTIVE MEASURES

Table 38. Preventive Measures for Delirium[a]

Target for Prevention	Intervention
Cognitive impairment	Orientation protocol: board with names, daily schedule, and reorienting communication Therapeutic activities: stimulating activities 3 times/d
Sleep deprivation	Nonpharmacologic: warm milk/herbal tea, music, massage Noise reduction: schedule adjustments and unit-wide noise reduction 0.5 mg melatonin may be protective in acute care
Immobility	Early mobilization: ambulation or range of motion 3 times/d, minimal immobilizing equipment
Visual impairment	Visual aids and adaptive equipment
Hearing impairment	Amplification, cerumen disimpaction, special communication techniques
Dehydration	Early recognition and volume repletion
Infection, HF, hypoxia, pain	Identify and treat medical conditions

[a] May also be valuable for management

MANAGEMENT
Nonpharmacologic
- Ensure safety.
- Use families or sitters as first line.
- Use physical restraints only as last resort to maintain patient safety (eg, to prevent patient from pulling out tubes or catheters).

Pharmacologic
For acute agitation or aggression that impairs care or safety (other than delirium due to alcohol or benzodiazepine withdrawal), choose from one of the following:

- Haloperidol (the most often recommended and studied agent; controls symptoms and may reduce duration and severity of delirium)
  - Because of risk of QT_c prolongation, the IV route is not recommended. *Caution:* If the patient is taking other medications that prolong QT_c (see **Table 10**), D/C all if possible. Even oral or IM dosing may prolong QT_c. Obtain an ECG before the first dose (if possible) or as soon as the patient is calm enough to tolerate the procedure. If QT_c exceeds 500 ms, ***do not*** administer any antipsychotic; all may prolong QT_c. If QT_c >460 ms, correct any deficiency of Mg^{++} and K^+ and recheck.

- Haloperidol *(Haldol)* 0.5–1 mg po [T: 0.5, 1, 2, 5, 10, 20; S: 2 mg/mL]; evaluate effect in 1–2 h.
  - If patient is not able to take medications po, haloperidol 0.5–1 mg IM [5 mg/mL] (twice as potent as po, peak effect 20–40 min). Reevaluate q30–60min for continued troublesome agitation.
  - Double the dosage if initial dose is ineffective. Administer additional doses (IM dose q30min or oral dose q60min) until agitation is controlled. Rarely, additional doubling of the dosage is necessary. Most older patients respond to 1–2 mg total dose.
  - Calculate the total dose administered to achieve control of symptoms, and give half the equivalent oral dose the next day, divided for q12h administration. Hold a dose if sedation occurs.
  - Maintain effective dose for 2–3 d.
  - Slowly taper and D/C haloperidol over 3–5 d while monitoring for recurrence of symptoms. If necessary, continue the minimal dose necessary to control symptoms.
  - EPS will develop with prolonged use. If use exceeds 1 wk, switch to a second-generation antipsychotic agent.
- Quetiapine is the drug of choice for patients with LBD, Parkinson disease, AIDS-related dementia, or EPS. Initial dosage 12.5–25 mg po daily or q12h, increase q2d prn to a max of 100 mg/d (50 mg/d in frail older adults). Once symptoms are controlled, administer half the dose needed to control symptoms for 2–3 d; then taper as described above.
- Quetiapine 50 mg q12h with prn IV haloperidol may result in faster resolution of delirium and less agitation. Quetiapine may be increased by 50 mg q24h.

When delirium is due to alcohol or benzodiazepine withdrawal, use a benzodiazepine, eg, lorazepam in dosages of 0.5–2 mg IV q30–q60min or po q1–2h and titrated to effect. Validated scales are used to guide dosing of benzodiazepines in alcohol withdrawal (www.chce.research.va.gov/apps/PAWS/content/1.htm). Because these agents themselves may cause delirium, gradual withdrawal and discontinuation are desirable. If delirium is secondary to alcohol, also use thiamine at 100 mg/d (po, IM, or IV).

DEMENTIA SYNDROME (*DSM–5:* MAJOR NEUROCOGNITIVE DISORDER)

Definition

Chronic acquired decline in one or more cognitive domains (learning and memory, complex attention, language, visual-spatial, executive) sufficient to affect daily life.

Estimated Frequencies of Causes of Dementia

- AD: 60–70%
- Other progressive disorders: 15–30% (eg, vascular, Lewy body [LBD], frontotemporal [FTD])
- Completely reversible dementia (eg, drug toxicity, metabolic changes, thyroid disease, subdural hematoma, normal-pressure hydrocephalus): 2–5%

Screening

- Dementia is largely unrecognized and underdiagnosed. Clinicians should have a low threshold for triggering an investigation for possible cognitive impairment.
- The value of dementia screening in older adults is controversial. Some professional organizations strongly endorse screening while others do not recommend it, citing lack of evidence of benefit.
- Screening for cognitive impairment is a required element of the initial and subsequent Medicare Annual Wellness Visit.
- Suitable screening tests in primary care include the Mini-Cog (p 322) the Memory Impairment Screen (MIS), General Practitioner Assessment of Cognition and the Informant (GPCOG), and the Informant Questionnaire on Cognitive Decline in the Elderly (IQCODE).

EVALUATION

Although completely reversible dementia (eg, drug toxicity) is rare, identifying and treating secondary physical conditions may improve function.

- Hx: Obtain from family or other caregiver
- Physical and neurologic examination
- Assess functional status (p 323–324)
- Exclude depression (PHQ-9 [p 325], GDS)
- Evaluate mental status for attention, immediate and delayed recall, remote memory, and executive function. If Mini-Cog is positive, use MoCA (www.mocatest.org) to evaluate attention, immediate and delayed recall, remote memory, and executive function, and use MMSE for staging.

Clinical Features Distinguishing AD and Other Types of Dementia

- AD: Memory, language, visual-spatial disturbances, indifference, delusions, agitation
- FTD: Personality change, executive dysfunction, hyperorality, relative preservation of visual-spatial skills
- LBD: visual hallucinations, delusions, EPS, fluctuating mental status, sensitivity to antipsychotic medications
- Vascular dementia: abrupt onset, stepwise deterioration, prominent aphasia, motor signs

Laboratory Testing

CBC, TSH, B_{12}, folate, serum calcium, liver and kidney function tests, electrolytes; HIV, and serologic test for syphilis (selectively); genetic testing and commercial "Alzheimer blood tests" are not currently recommended for clinical use.

Neuroimaging

The likelihood of detecting structural lesions is increased with:

- Onset age <60 yr
- Focal (unexplained) neurologic signs or symptoms
- Abrupt onset or rapid decline (weeks to months)
- Predisposing conditions (eg, metastatic cancer or anticoagulants)

Neuroimaging may detect the 5% of cases with clinically significant structural lesions that would otherwise be missed.

FDG-PET scans approved by Medicare for atypical presentation or course of AD in which FTD is suspected. See www.petscaninfo.com/portals/pat/medicare_guidelines_alzheimers. Florbetapir F18 (*Amyvid*) has been approved by the FDA for the detection of amyloid plaques. A positive scan does not establish diagnosis. Medicare will not cover.

DIAGNOSIS OF AD

- Dementia syndrome
- Gradual onset and continuing decline
- Not due to another physical, neurologic, or psychiatric condition or to medications
- Deficits not seen exclusively during delirium
- No validated biomarkers

PROGRESSION OF AD

- 2011 National Institute on Aging/Alzheimer's Association research criteria identify preclinical stages using PET and CSF biomarkers of $A\beta$ or neuronal injury.
- Mild cognitive impairment (MCI) requires "modest" cognitive decline that does not interfere with "capacity for independence in everyday activities" (eg, paying bills or taking medications correctly).
- Cognitive decline meets the "major" criteria (ie, dementia syndrome) when "significant" impairment is evident or reported and when it does interfere with a patient's independence to the point that assistance is required.

Mild Cognitive Impairment (preclinical)   *MMSE 26–30; CDR 0.5; FAST 3; MoCA <26 (more sensitive)

- Report by patient or caregiver of memory loss
- Objective signs of memory impairment
- No functional impairment
- Mild construction, language, or executive dysfunction

- 6–15% annual conversion rate to dementia syndrome
- Some cases of mild cognitive impairment may not progress to AD
- Treating vascular risk factors (HTN, DM, high cholesterol) may reduce risk of progression to AD

Early, Mild Impairment (yr 1–3 from onset of symptoms)   *MMSE 21–25; CDR 1; FAST 4

- Disoriented to date
- Naming difficulties (anomia)
- Recent recall problems
- Mild difficulty copying figures
- Decreased insight
- Social withdrawal
- Irritability, mood change
- Problems managing finances

Middle, Moderate Impairment (yr 2–8)   *MMSE 11–20; CDR 2; FAST 5–6

- Disoriented to date, place
- Comprehension difficulties (aphasia)
- Impaired new learning
- Getting lost in familiar areas
- Impaired calculating skills
- Delusions, agitation, aggression
- Not cooking, shopping, banking
- Restless, anxious, depressed
- Problems with dressing, grooming

Late, Severe Impairment (yr 6–12)   *MMSE 0–10; CDR 3; FAST 7

- Nearly unintelligible verbal output
- Remote memory gone
- Unable to copy or write
- No longer grooming or dressing
- Incontinent
- Motor or verbal agitation

* MMSE = Mini-Mental State Examination; CDR = Clinical Dementia Rating Scale; FAST = Reisberg Functional Assessment Staging Scale (p 330); MoCA = Montreal Cognitive Assessment

Prognosis

- Among nursing-home residents with advanced dementia, 71% die within 6 mo of admission.
- Distressing conditions common in advanced dementia include pressure ulcers, constipation, pain, and shortness of breath.

NONCOGNITIVE SYMPTOMS

Psychotic Symptoms (eg, delusions, hallucinations)

- Seen in about 20% of AD patients
- Delusions may be paranoid (eg, people stealing things, spouse unfaithful)
- Hallucinations (~11% of patients) are more commonly visual

Depressive Symptoms

- Seen in up to 40% of AD patients; may precede onset of AD
- May cause acceleration of decline if untreated
- Suspect if patient stops eating or withdraws

Apathy

- High prevalence and persistence throughout course of AD
- Causes more impairment in ADL than expected for cognitive status
- High overlap with depressive symptoms but lacks depressive mood, guilt, and hopelessness

Agitation or Aggression

- Seen in up to 80% of patients with AD
- A leading cause of nursing-home admission
- Consider superimposed delirium or pain as a trigger (see Pain chapter)

RISK AND PROTECTIVE FACTORS FOR DEMENTIA

Definite Risks

Age
APOE-E4 (whites)
Atrial fibrillation
Depression
Down syndrome
Family hx

Possible Risks

Delirium
Head trauma
Heavy smoking
Hypercholesterolemia
HTN
Lower educational level
Other genes
Postmenopausal HT

Possible Protections

Antioxidants (eg, vitamin E,
  beta carotene)
Mediterranean diet
Physical activity

TREATMENT

Primary goals of tx are to improve quality of life and maximize functional performance by enhancing cognition, mood, and behavior.

General Treatment Principles

- Identify and treat comorbid physical illnesses (eg, HTN, DM)
- Promote brain health by exercise, balanced diet, stress reduction
- Supervised exercise, whether individual or group, slows disability and prevent falls
- Avoid anticholinergic medications, eg, benztropine, diphenhydramine, hydroxyzine, oxybutynin, TCAs, clozapine, thioridazine
- Set realistic goals
- Limit prn psychotropic medication use
- Specify and quantify target behaviors
- Maximize and maintain functioning
- Establish and maintain alliance with patient and family
- Assess and monitor psychiatric status
- Intervene to decrease hazards of wandering
- Advise patient and family concerning driving
- Advise family about sources of care and support, financial and legal issues
- Consider referral to hospice (FAST = 7 [p 330])
- Identify and examine context of behavior (is it harmful to patient or others) and environmental triggers (eg, overstimulation, unfamiliar surroundings, frustrating interactions); exclude underlying physical discomfort (eg, illnesses or medication); consider nonpharmacologic strategies.

Nonpharmacologic Approaches for Problem Behaviors

To improve function:

- Behavior modification, scheduled toileting, and prompted toileting (see p 147) for UI
- Graded assistance (as little help as possible to perform ADLs), practice, and positive reinforcement to increase independence

For problem behaviors:
- Music during meals, bathing
- Walking or light exercise
- Simulate family presence with video or audio tapes
- Pet tx
- Speak at patient's comprehension level
- Bright light, "white" noise (ie, low-level, background noise)

Pharmacologic Treatment of Cognitive Dysfunction
- Patients with a diagnosis of mild or moderate AD should receive a trial of a cholinesterase inhibitor; donepezil also approved for severe AD (see **Table 39**).
  - Only 10–25% of patients taking cholinesterase inhibitors show modest global improvement, but many more have less rapid cognitive decline.
  - Initial studies show benefits of cholinesterase inhibitors for patients with dementia associated with LBD, Parkinson disease and vascular dementia. May worsen behavioral variant FTD.
  - Cholinesterase inhibitors may attenuate noncognitive symptoms and delay nursing-home placement.
  - AEs increase with higher dosing. Possible AEs include nausea, vomiting, diarrhea, dyspepsia, anorexia, weight loss, leg cramps, bradycardia, syncope, insomnia, and agitation.
  - Vitamin E at 2000 IU/d adjunctive to cholinesterase inhibitors found to delay functional decline in mild to moderate AD (caution: meta-analysis found doses ≥400 IU may increase mortality).
- Patients with moderate to severe AD may benefit from trial of Memantine *(Namenda)*
  - Side effects minimal (confusion, dizziness, constipation, headache)
  - Recent controlled trial did not demonstrate significant advantage to the combination of memantine and donepezil compared with donepezil alone in patients with severe dementia.
  - To evaluate response:
    - Elicit caregiver observations of patient's behavior (alertness, initiative) and follow functional status (ADLs [p 323] and IADLs [p 324]).
    - Follow cognitive status (eg, improved or stabilized) by caregiver's report or serial ratings of cognition (eg, Mini-Cog [p 322]; MMSE).
- D/C cognitive enhancers when FAST = 7 (see p 330).

Table 39. Cognitive Enhancers

Medication	Formulations	Dosing (Metabolism)
Cholinesterase Inhibitors		
Donepezil *(Aricept)* [a,b]	T: 5▲, 10▲, 23; ODT: 5, 10; S: 5 mg/mL	Start at 5 mg/d, increase to 10 mg/d after 1 mo (CYP2D6, -3A4); must be on 10 mg/d ≥3 mo to consider increasing to 23 mg/d in moderate to severe AD. Avoid if hx of syncope.[BC] (L)
Galantamine▲ *(Razadyne)* [a,c]	T: 4, 8, 12; S: 4 mg/mL	Start at 4 mg q12h, increase to 8 mg q12h after 4 wk; recommended dosage 8 or 12 mg q12h (CYP2D6, -3A4). Avoid if hx of syncope.[BC] (L)
(Razadyne ER)	C: 8, 16, 24	Start at 1 capsule daily, preferably with food; titrate as above
Rivastigmine▲ *(Exelon)* [a]	C: 1.5, 3, 4.5, 6; S: 2 mg/mL; pch: 4.6, 9.5	Start at 1.5 mg q12h and gradually titrate up to minimally effective dosage of 3 mg q12h; continue up to 6 mg q12h as tolerated; for pch, start at 4.6 mg/d, may be increased after ≥ 4 wk to 9.5 mg/d (recommended effective dosage): retitrate if drug is stopped. Avoid if hx of syncope.[BC] (K)
Memantine *(Namenda* [NMDA antagonist])[b,d]	T: 5, 10; S: 2 mg/mL	Start at 5 mg/d, increase by 5 mg at weekly intervals to max of 10 mg q12h; if CrCl <30 mL/min, max of 5 mg q12h (K)
(Namenda XR)	C: 7, 14, 21, 28	Start at 7 mg/d, increase by 7 mg at weekly intervals to max of 18 mg; if severe renal impairment, max of 14 mg daily (L)

[a] Cholinesterase inhibitors. Continue if improvement or stabilization occurs; stopping medications can lead to rapid decline.

[b] Approved by FDA for moderate to severe AD.

[c] Increased mortality found in controlled studies of mild cognitive impairment.

[d] Tablets will be discontinued in Aug 2014.

- Ginkgo biloba is not generally recommended (see p 220).
- *Axona* (medium-chain TG) has insufficient evidence to support its value in preventing or treating AD, and long-term effects are uncertain.

Treatment of Agitation

- Consider nonpharmacologic approaches first before pharmacologic tx (see **Table 40**).
- Steps to reduce nonverbalized pain (see p 227).
- Cognitive enhancers may slow deterioration, and agitation may worsen if discontinued. Low doses of antipsychotic medications have limited role but may be necessary. Note this use is off-label and increases risk of death compared with placebo in patients with AD. CATIE-AD trial (*NEJM* 2006;355:1525–1538) showed modest tx benefit compared with placebo for olanzapine and risperidone that was mitigated by greater EPS, sedation, and confusion. In this trial, quetiapine did not appear to be efficacious compared with placebo but caused greater sedation. See also **Table 108** and **Table 109**.
- CATIE-AD reported second-generation antipsychotics cause weight gain, particularly in women treated with olanzapine or quetiapine; olanzapine tx was also associated with decreased HDL cholesterol.
- Behavioral variant FTD: consider Memantine or SSRI.

Treatment of Apathy

- Assess and treat underlying depression.
- Cholinesterase inhibitors help.
- Methylphenidate (5–20 mg/d), very limited data, may cause agitation and psychosis.

Table 40. Pharmacologic Treatment of Agitation

Symptom	Medication	Dosage	Formulations
Agitation in context of psychosis	Aripiprazole[a,b] *(Abilify)*	2.5–12.5 mg/d	T: 5, 10, 15, 20, 30
	Olanzapine[a,b] *(Zyprexa) (Zydis)*	2.5–10 mg/d	T: 2.5, 5, 7.5, 10, 15, 20 ODT: 5, 10, 15, 20
	Quetiapine[a,b] *(Seroquel)*	12.5–100 mg/d	T: 25, 100, 200, 300
	Risperidone[▲a,b] *(Risperdal)*	0.25–3 mg/d	T: 0.25, 0.5, 1, 2, 3, 4; S: 1 mg/mL
Agitation in context of depression	SSRI, eg, citalopram[▲] *(Celexa)*	10–20 mg/d	T: 20, 40; S: 2 mg/mL
Anxiety, mild to moderate irritability	Buspirone[▲] *(BuSpar)*	15–60 mg/d[c]	T: 5, 7.5, 10, 15, 30
	Trazodone[▲] *(Desyrel)*	50–100 mg/d[d]	T: 50, 100, 150, 300
Agitation or aggression unresponsive to first-line tx	Carbamazepine[▲] *(Tegretol)*	300–600 mg/d[e]	T: 200; ChT: 100; S: sus 100/5 mL
	Divalproex sodium[▲] *(Depakote, Epival)*	500–1500 mg/d[f]	T: 125, 250, 500; S: syr 250 mg/mL; sprinkle capsule: 125
	Olanzapine[b,g] *(Zyprexa IntraMuscular)*	2.5–5 mg IM	Inj
Sexual aggression, impulse control symptoms in men	Second-generation antipsychotic or divalproex[▲]	See dosages above	
	If no response, estrogen[▲] *(Premarin)*	0.625–1.25 mg/d	T: 0.3, 0.625, 0.9, 1.25, 2.5
	or medroxyprogesterone[▲] *(Depo-Provera)*	100 mg IM/wk	Inj

[a] Avoid.[BC]

[b] Increased risk of mortality and cerebrovascular events compared with placebo; use with particular caution in patients with cerebrovascular disease or hypovolemia.

[c] Can be given q12h; allow 2–4 wk for adequate trial.

[d] Small divided daytime dosage and larger bedtime dosage; watch for sedation and orthostasis.

[e] Monitor serum levels; periodic CBCs, platelet counts secondary to agranulocytosis risk. Beware of drug-drug interactions.

[f] Can monitor serum levels; usually well tolerated; check CBC, platelets for agranulocytosis, thrombocytopenia risk in older adults.

[g] For acute use only; initial dose 2.5–5 mg, second dose (2.5–5 mg) can be given after 2 h, max of 3 injections in 24 h (max daily dose 20 mg); should not be administered for >3 consecutive d.

CAREGIVER ISSUES

- Over 50% develop depression.
- Physical illness, isolation, anxiety, and burnout are common.
- Intensive education and support of caregivers may delay institutionalization.
- Adult day care for patients and respite services may help.
- Alzheimer's Association offers support, education services (eg, Safe Return); chapters are located in major cities throughout US (see p 335 for telephone, Web site).
- Family Caregiver Alliance offers support, education, information for caregivers (see p 335 for telephone, Web site).

DEPRESSION

EVALUATION AND ASSESSMENT

Recognizing and diagnosing late-life depression can be difficult. Older adults may complain of lack of energy or other somatic symptoms, attribute symptoms to old age or other physical conditions, or neglect to mention them to a health care professional.

Consider screening with Patient Health Questionnaire 2 (PHQ-2):

• Over the past 2 wk, have you often had little interest or pleasure in doing things?

• Over the past 2 wk, have you often been bothered by feeling down, depressed, or hopeless?

Score each item: 0 = not at all, 1 = several days, 2 = more than half the days, 3 = nearly every day; a score ≥3 indicates high probability of depressive disorder.

Follow-up and/or assess tx with structured self-assessment scale such as the GDS or the PHQ-9 (see p 325).

Medical Evaluation

TSH, B_{12}, calcium, liver and kidney function tests, electrolytes, UA, CBC

DSM-5 Criteria for Major Depressive Disorder (Abbreviated)

Five or more of the following criteria have been present during the same 2-wk period and represent a change from previous functioning; at least one of the symptoms is either depressed mood *or* loss of interest or pleasure. Do not include symptoms that are clearly due to a medical condition.

• Depressed mood
• Loss of interest or pleasure in activities
• Significant weight loss or gain (not intentional), or decrease or increase in appetite
• Insomnia or hypersomnia
• Psychomotor agitation or retardation

• Fatigue or loss of energy
• Feelings of worthlessness or excessive or inappropriate guilt
• Diminished ability to think or concentrate, or indecisiveness
• Recurrent thoughts of death; suicidal ideation, attempt, or plan

The *DSM-5* criteria are not specific for older adults; cognitive symptoms may be more prominent.

Subsyndromal Depression

Subsyndromal depression does not meet full criteria for major depressive disorder and may include adjustment disorders and milder depression with anxiety symptoms but can be serious and associated with functional impairment. In older adults, subsyndromal depression may actually reflect major depression not diagnosed by current diagnostic criteria and may require pharmacologic and nonpharmacologic intervention.

MANAGEMENT

Tx should be individualized on the basis of hx, past response, and severity of illness as well as concurrent illnesses.

Nonpharmacologic

For mild to moderate depression or in combination with pharmacotherapy: CBT, interpersonal tx, problem-solving tx, or repetitive transcranial magnetic stimulation (rTMS) (see p 82), bright light tx in morning for seasonal depression.

For severe or psychotic depression, consider electroconvulsive tx (ECT) (see p 81).

Pharmacologic

For mild, moderate, or severe depression: the duration of tx should be at least 6–12 mo after remission for patients experiencing their first depressive episode. Most older adults with major depression require maintenance antidepressant tx. Ensure adequate initial trial of 4–6 wk after titrating up to therapeutic dosage; if inadequate response, consider switching to a different first-line agent or second-line tx or psychiatric referral/consult. Combining antidepressants can lead to significant adverse effects. SSRIs may increase hemorrhagic stroke risk; low initial dosages and monitoring are recommended, especially in patients at risk of stroke. Check sodium before starting SSRI and after a few weeks of tx; high index of suspicion for hyponatremia. SSRIs are also associated with increased risk of GI and postsurgical bleeding.

Choosing an Antidepressant (see **Table 41** and list on p 81)

First-line Therapy: SSRI; consider sertraline.

Second-line Therapy: Consider venlafaxine▲, duloxetine, mirtazapine▲, or bupropion▲.

Third-line Therapy: Consider augmentation of first- or second-line antidepressants with aripiprazole or quetiapine, or SSRI with buspirone▲ or bupropion▲.

Table 41. Antidepressants Used for Older Adults

Class, Medication	Initial Dosage	Usual Dosage	Formulations	Comments (Metabolism, Excretion)
SSRIs				*Class AEs:* EPS, hyponatremia, increased risk of upper GI bleeding, suicide (early in tx), lower BMD and fragility fractures, risk of toxicity if methylene blue or linezolid co-administered. Avoid if hx of falls or fracture; caution if hx of SIADH.[BC] (L, K [10%])
Citalopram▲ *(Celexa)*	10–20 mg qam	20 mg/d	T: 20, 40, 00; S: 5 mg/10 mL	20 mg/d is max dosage in adults >60 yr old
Escitalopram *(Lexapro)*	10 mg/d	10 mg/d	T: 10, 20	10 mg/d is max dosage in adults >60 yr old
Fluoxetine▲ *(Prozac)*	5 mg qam	5–60 mg/d	T: 10; C: 10, 20, 40; S: 20 mg/5 mL; C: SR 90 (weekly dose)	Long half-lives of parent and active metabolite may allow for less frequent dosing; may cause more insomnia than other SSRIs; CYP2D6, -2C9, -3A4 inhibitor (L)
Fluvoxamine▲ *(Luvox)*	25 mg qhs	100–300 mg/d	T: 25, 50, 100	Not approved as an antidepressant in US; greater likelihood of GI AEs; CYP1A2, -3A4 inhibitor (L)

(cont.)

Table 41. Antidepressants Used for Older Adults (cont.)

Class, Medication	Initial Dosage	Usual Dosage	Formulations	Comments (Metabolism, Excretion)
Paroxetine▲ (Paxil)	5 mg	10–40 mg/d	T: 10, 20, 30, 40	Increased risk of withdrawal symptoms (dizziness); anticholinergic AEs; CYP2D6 inhibitor (L)
(Paxil CR)	12.5 mg/d	12.5–37.5 mg/d	T: ER 12.5, 25, 37.5; S: 10 mg/5 mL	Increase by 12.5 mg/d no faster than once/wk (L)
Sertraline▲ (Zoloft)	25 mg qam	50–200 mg/d	T: 25, 50, 100; S: 20 mg/mL	Greater likelihood of GI AEs (L)
Additional Medications				
Bupropion▲ (Wellbutrin)	37.5–50 mg q12h	75–150 mg q12h	T: 75, 100	Consider for SSRI, TCA nonresponders; safe in HF; may be stimulating; can lower seizure threshold. Avoid.[BC] (L)
(Wellbutrin SR▲, Zyban▲)	100 mg q12h or q24h	100–150 mg q12h	T: 100, 150, 200	
(Wellbutrin XL)	150 mg/d	300 mg/d	T: 150, 300	
Methylphenidate▲[BC] (Ritalin)	2.5–5 mg at 7 AM and noon	5–10 mg at 7 AM and noon	T: 5, 10, 20	Short-term tx of depression or apathy in physically ill older adults; used as an adjunct; avoid if insomnia.[BC] (L)
Mirtazapine▲ (Remeron)	15 mg qhs	15–45 mg/d	T: 15, 30, 45	May increase appetite; sedating; ODT (SolTab) available (L)
Vilazodone (Viibryd)	10 mg/d for 7 d, then 20 mg/d	40 mg/d	T: 10, 20, 40	Metabolized by CYP3A4; limited geriatric data; AEs: diarrhea and nausea
TCAs				Avoid.[BC]
◆Desipramine▲ (Norpramin)	10–25 mg qhs	50–150 mg/d	T: 10, 25, 50, 75, 100, 150	Therapeutic serum level >115 ng/mL (L)
◆Nortriptyline▲ (Aventyl, Pamelor)	10–25 mg qhs	75–150 mg/d	C: 10, 25, 50, 75; S: 10 mg/5 mL	Therapeutic window (50–150 ng/mL) (L)
SNRIs				Caution if hx of SIADH.[BC]
◆Duloxetine (Cymbalta)	20 mg/d, then 20 mg q12h	40–60 mg q24h or 30 mg q12h	C: 20, 30, 60	Most common AEs: nausea, dry mouth, constipation, diarrhea, urinary hesitancy; reduce dosage if CrCl 30–60 mL/min; contraindicated if CrCl <30 mL/min (L)

(cont.)

Table 41. Antidepressants Used for Older Adults (cont.)

Class, Medication	Initial Dosage	Usual Dosage	Formulations	Comments (Metabolism, Excretion)
Venlafaxine▲ (Effexor)	25–50 mg q12h	75–225 mg/d in divided doses	T: 25, 37.5, 50, 75, 100	Low anticholinergic activity; minimal sedation and hypotension; may increase BP and QT$_C$; may be useful when somatic pain present; EPS, withdrawal symptoms, hyponatremia (L)
(Effexor XR)	75 mg qam	75–225 mg/d	C: 37.5, 75, 150	Same as above
Desvenlafaxine (Pristiq)	50 mg/d	50 mg; max 400 mg	SR tab: 50, 100	Active metabolite of venlafaxine; adjust dosage when CrCl <30 mL/min (L, K 45%)

◆ = Also has primary indication for neuropathic pain.

Antidepressants to Avoid in Older Adults

- Amitriptyline▲ (eg, *Elavil*): anticholinergic, sedating, hypotensive
- Amoxapine▲ *(Asendin)*: anticholinergic, sedating, hypotensive; also associated with EPS, TD, and neuroleptic malignant syndrome
- Doxepin▲ (eg, *Sinequan*): anticholinergic, sedating, hypotensive
- Imipramine▲ *(Tofranil)*: anticholinergic, sedating, hypotensive
- Maprotiline▲ *(Ludiomil)*: seizures, rashes
- Protriptyline▲ *(Vivactil)*: very anticholinergic; can be stimulating
- St. John's wort: drug interactions, photosensitivity, hypomania
- Trimipramine *(Surmontil)*: anticholinergic, sedating, hypotensive

Electroconvulsive Therapy (ECT)

Generally safe and very effective. Potential complications include temporary confusion, anterograde and retrograde amnesia, arrhythmias, aspiration, falls.

Indications: Severe depression when a rapid onset of response is necessary; when depression is resistant to drug tx; for patients who are unable to tolerate antidepressants, have previous response to ECT, have psychotic depression, severe catatonia, or depression with Parkinson disease.

Evaluation: Before ECT, perform CXR, ECG, serum electrolytes, and cardiac examination. Additional tests (eg, stress test, neuroimaging, EEG) are used selectively.

Contraindications:

- Increased intracranial pressure
- Intracranial tumor
- MI within 3 mo (relative)
- Stroke within 1 mo (relative)

Consider Maintenance ECT:

- Hx of ECT-responsive illness
- Resistance or intolerance to medications alone
- Serious medical comorbidity
- More effective than pharmacotherapy after successful ECT

Repetitive Transcranial Magnetic Stimulation (rTMS)

- Series of magnetic pulses directed to brain at frequency of 1–20 stimulations per sec. Each tx session lasts ~30 min, and a full course of tx may be as long as 30 sessions.
- Placebo-controlled studies have demonstrated moderate effect sizes for tx-resistant depression in younger adults and appears safe with minimal adverse effects.
- Limited experience with rTMS in tx-resistant late-life depression; rTMS tx parameters may need to be optimized to address age-related changes such as prefrontal cortical atrophy.

Depression and Parkinson Disease

Patients with Parkinson disease and depression may benefit more from nortriptyline than SSRIs. Pramipexole may also reduce depressive symptoms independent of effect on motor symptoms. See also p 215.

Psychotic Depression

- Psychosis accompanying major depression; increased disability and mortality
- ECT is the tx of choice
- Olanzapine 15–20 mg/d added to sertraline 150–200 mg/d significantly improves remission rate vs placebo.

BIPOLAR DISORDER

See **Table 42**.

- 5–19% of mood disorders in older adults.
- Usually begins in early adulthood, family hx.
- 10% may develop after age 50.
- Distinct period of abnormally and persistently elevated, expansive, or irritable mood for longer than 1 wk.
- Symptoms may include racing thoughts, pressured speech, decreased need for sleep, distractibility, grandiose delusions.
- A single manic episode is sufficient for a diagnosis if secondary causes are excluded.
- Late-onset mania may be secondary to head trauma, stroke, delirium, other neurologic disorders, alcohol abuse, or medications (eg, corticosteroids, L-dopa, thyroxine).
- Use aripiprazole, olanzapine, quetiapine, risperidone▲, or ziprasidone for acute mania (see **Table 108**) and D/C antidepressants if taking.
- If depression emerges in bipolar disorder, lamotrigine▲ may be helpful.
- Initiate long-term tx (see **Table 43**) as soon as patient is able to comply with oral tx.

Table 42. Medications for Management of Bipolar Disorders

Medication	Mania		Depression	
	Acute	**Maintenance**	**Acute**	**Maintenance**
Second-generation antipsychotics	All +	Aripiprazole + Olanzapine +/−	Quetiapine + Olanzapine +/−	Olanzapine +/−
Mood stabilizers				
Lithium▲	+	+	+	+
Valproate▲	+	+/−	−	+/−
Lamotrigine▲	−	+/−	+	+
Carbamazepine▲	+	+/−	?	+/−
Antidepressants				
SSRIs	Avoid	Avoid	+	+
TCAs	Avoid	Avoid	−	−

Note: + = evidence to support use; +/− = some evidence to support use; − = evidence does not support use; ? = has not been studied

Table 43. Long-term Treatment of Bipolar Disorders*

Medication	Initial Dosage	Usual Dosage	Formulation	Comments
Lithium▲ *(Eskalith, Eskalith CR, Lithobid)*	150 mg/d	300–900 mg/d Levels 0.4–0.8 mEq/L	T: 300; T: ER 300; T: CR 450; C: 150, 300, 600; syr 300 mg/mL	Risk of CNS toxicity; cognitive impairment; hypothyroidism; interactions with diuretics, ACEIs, calcium channel blockers, NSAIDs
Carbamazepine▲ *(Tegretol, Tegretol XR)*	100 mg q12h	800–1200 mg/d Levels 4–12 mcg/L	T: 100, 200, 400	Many drug interactions; may cause SIADH; risk of leukopenia, neutropenia, agranulocytosis, thrombocytopenia; monitor CBC; drowsiness, dizziness
Valproic acid▲ *(Depacon, Depakene, Depakote)*	125 mg q12h	750 mg/d in divided doses Levels 50–125 mcg/L	T: 125, 250, 500	Can cause weight gain, tremor, several drug interactions; risk of hepatotoxicity, pancreatitis, neutropenia, thrombocytopenia; monitor LFTs and platelets
Lamotrigine▲ *(Lamictal)*	25 mg/d	100–200 mg/d	T: 25, 100, 150, 200	D/C if rash; interaction with valproate (when used together, begin at 25 mg q48h, titrate to 25–100 mg q12h); prolongs PR interval; somnolence, headache common

*Limited evidence base in older adults. See www.healthquality.va.gov. (See also **Table 91**.)

DERMATOLOGIC CONDITIONS COMMON IN OLDER ADULTS

For numerous dermatologic images, see http://hardinmd.lib.uiowa.edu/dermpictures.html.

Actinic Keratosis

Erythematous, flat, rough, scaly papules 2–6 mm; may be easier felt than seen; precancerous (can develop into squamous or basal cell carcinoma); cutaneous horn may develop; affects sun-exposed areas, including lips (actinic cheilitis)

Risk Factors: UV light exposure (amount and intensity), increased age, fair coloring, immunosuppression

Prevention: Limit UV light exposure, use sunscreen with UVA and UVB coverage, wear protective clothing

Treatment

- Topical 5-fluorouracil *(Carac* crm 0.5% daily × 4 wk, *Efudex* crm 5% q12h × 2–4 wk, *Fluoroplex* crm 1% to face, 5% elsewhere, q12h × 2–6 wk) to entire area affected
- Imiquimod 3.75% pk *(Zyclara)*. Apply 1 or 2 pk to face or scalp (not both) qhs × 14 d, wash off with soap and water after 8 h. Rest 14 d, then repeat another 14 d. Max. 56 pk/2 cycles
- Imiquimod 5% pk *(Aldara)*. Apply 1 or 2 pk to face or scalp (not both) qhs × 16 d, wash off with soap and water after 8 h. Rest 14 d, then repeat another 14 d. Max. 56 pk/2 cycles
- Cryosurgery
- Aminolevulinic acid *(Levulan Kerastick* 20%) applied to lesions with blue light illumination after 14–18 h, repeat in 8 wk
- Ingenol mebutate 0.015% gel *(Picato)*. Face and scalp: apply q24h × 3 d; trunk and extremities: apply q24h × 2 d. Allow gel to dry × 15 min, do not wash or touch for 6 h
- Curettage with or without electrosurgery
- Chemical peels, dermabrasion, laser tx

Basal Cell Carcinoma

Can affect any body surface exposed to the sun, most often head and neck

Types

- Nodular: pearly papule or nodule over telangiectases with a rolled border; may contain melanin; most common type
- Superficial: scaly erythematous patch or plaque, may contain melanin
- Morpheaform: indurated, whitish, scar-like plaque with indistinct margins

Risk Factors

- Exposure to UV radiation, especially intense intermittent exposure during childhood or adolescence
- Physical factors: fair skin, light eye color, red or blonde hair
- Exposure to ionizing radiation, arsenic, psoralen, UV-A radiation, smoking
- Immunosuppression (eg, after solid-organ transplant)

Prevention: Avoid sun exposure, use sunscreen with UVA and UVB coverage, wear protective clothing

Treatment: (localized control)

- Surgical: Mohs micrographic surgery, cryosurgery, excision, curettage and electrodessication
- Nonsurgical: radiotherapy, imiquimod 5% crm *(Aldara)* applied daily 5 d/wk × 6 wk (not for use on face, hands, or feet); photodynamic tx; 5-fluorouracil 0.5% crm or sol q12h × 3–6 wk or longer

Candidiasis

Erythema, pustules, or cheesy, whitish matter in body folds; satellite lesions

Treatment: See intertrigo; antifungal powders (see **Table 44**)

Cellulitis

Ill-defined erythema, pain, blisters and exudates; most often affects lower dermis and subcutaneous tissue, commonly the legs; group A streptococci and *Staphylococcus aureus* most frequent pathogens

Treatment

- Antistaphylococcal penicillin, amoxicillin-clavulanate▲ × 10 d
- Macrolide (eg, erythromycin▲), 1st-generation cephalosporin (eg, cephalexin▲), or tetracycline▲ if penicillin allergy
- MRSA suspected or known
  - Oral empiric options: clindamycin, TMP/SMX, doxycycline, minocycline, or linezolid
  - Tailor tx to culture and sensitivity results when available

Erysipelas

Bright red, edematous, and tender with unilateral distribution; orange peel appearance; well-demarcated border with vesicles and bullae; affects lower dermis and subcutaneous tissue, face and legs

Treatment: Penicillin; erythromycin, clindamycin, linezolid, or cephalosporin if penicillin allergy

Folliculitis

Multiple small, erythematous papules and pustules surrounding a hair; most often affects areas with coarse, short hair (ie, neck, beard, buttocks, thighs)

Treatment

- Mild localized cases—topical antibiotic: mupirocin 2%▲ *(Bactroban)*, erythromycin, or clindamycin
- Extensive or severe cases—oral antistaphylococcal penicillin, amoxicillin-clavulanate, or erythromycin

Impetigo

Very contagious; nonbullous and bullous variants; honey-colored crusts on face around nose and mouth

Treatment

- Small, localized lesions: topical mupirocin 2%▲ *(Bactroban)* q8h × 7–10 d, topical retapamulin 1% oint *(Altabax)* q12h × 5 d
- Widespread: oral antistaphylococcal penicillin, erythromycin, or a cephalosporin × 10 d

Intertrigo

Moist, erythematous lesions with local superficial skin loss; satellite lesions caused by *Candida*; can affect any place two skin surfaces rest against one another (eg, under breasts, between toes)

Treatment
- Keep area dry.
- Topical antifungals, (see **Table 44**), absorbent pwd, 1–2% hydrocortisone▲ or 0.1% triamcinolone▲ crm q12h × 1–2 d if inflamed

Melanoma

Less common than nonmelanoma lesions; usually asymptomatic
Clinical Features
Asymmetry: a line down the center of the lesions does not create a mirror image
Border: irregular, ragged, fuzzy, or scalloped
Color: nonuniform throughout the lesion
Diameter: >6 mm (considered relatively insensitive as an independent factor)
Types
- Lentigo maligna: most often located on atrophic, sun-damaged skin; irregular-shaped tan or brown macule; slow growing
- Superficial spreading: occur anywhere; irregular-shaped macule, papule, or plaque; coloration varies
- Nodular: a rapidly growing, often black or gray papule or nodule
- Acral lentiginous: located on the palms, soles, or nail beds; dark brown or black patch; more common in Hispanic, black, and Asian individuals
Risk Factors
- Very fair skin type
- Family hx
- Dysplastic or numerous nevi
- Sun exposure; blistering sunburns as a child

Prevention: Avoid sun exposure, use sunscreen with UVA and UVB coverage, wear protective clothing
Treatment: Surgical excision

Neurodermatitis

Generalized or localized itching, redness, scaling; can affect any skin surface
Treatment: Mid- to higher-potency topical corticosteroids (see **Table 45**); exclude other causes (eg, allergies, irritants, xerosis)

Onychomycosis

Thickening and discoloration; affects nails *(Tinea unguium)*
Treatment: Obtain nail specimens for laboratory culture to confirm diagnosis before prescribing itraconazole or terbinafine.
- Itraconazole▲ *(Sporanox* [C: 100; S: 100 mg/mL]), contraindicated in HF (L), mycologic cure rate on pulse tx 63%
  ○ Toenails: 200 mg po q24h × 3 mo—23% complete cure rate (negative mycologic analysis and normal nail) reported with this regimen, or 200 mg po q12h × 1 wk/mo × 3 mo
  ○ Fingernails: 200 mg po q12h × 1 wk/mo × 2 mo ("Pulse Therapy") or 200 mg q24h × 12 wk
- Fluconazole▲ *(Diflucan* [T: 50, 100, 150, 200; S: 10, 40 mg/mL]) (L), mycologic cure rate 48%
  ○ Toenails: 150 or 300 mg po/wk × 6–12 mo
  ○ Fingernails: 150 or 300 mg po/wk × 3–6 mo

- Terbinafine▲ *(Lamisil* [T: 250]), avoid if CrCl <50 mL/min, mycologic cure rate 76%
  - Toenails: 250 mg po q24h × 12 wk—48% complete cure rate reported with this regimen
  - Fingernails: 250 mg po q24h × 6 wk
- Ciclopirox▲ *(Loprox, Penlac):* Toenails and fingernails—apply lacquer q12h to nails and adjacent skin; remove with alcohol q7d—8% complete cure rate reported with this regimen
- Mentholatum (eg, *Vicks VapoRub*) applied 2–3 ×/d for several months has been reported as a tx for fungal infections of the nail but has not been compared with marketed tx or placebo
- OTC lacquers (eg, *Fungi-Nail*) treat the fungus around the nail but do not penetrate the nail
- Laser tx: improves appearance; not covered by insurance

Psoriasis

Well-defined, erythematous plaques covered with silver scales; severity varies; can affect all skin areas, nails (pitting)

Treatment

- Topical corticosteroids, UV light, PUVA, methotrexate, cyclosporine, etretinate, sulfasalazine, tacrolimus, pimecrolimus *(Elidel)*, tazarotene gel 0.05%, 0.1%, anthralin preparations, and tar + 1–4% salicylic acid
- Calcipotriene for nonfacial areas
- Cyclosporine, methotrexate, and biological agents for extensive and recalcitrant disease

Rosacea

Vascular and follicular dilatation; mild to moderate; can accompany seborrhea; can affect face (nose, chin, cheeks, forehead) or eyes (dryness, blepharitis, conjunctivitis)

Prevention: Avoid triggers (stress, prolonged sun exposure and exercise, hot and humid environment, alcohol, hot drinks, spicy foods); may be worsened by vasodilators, niacin, or topical corticosteroids. Wear sunscreen with UVA and UVB coverage (SPF ≥15) or sunblock with titanium and zinc oxide. See www.rosacea.org.

Treatment

- Topical (for mild cases and maintenance)
  - Azelaic acid 15% gel *(Finacea)* q12–24 h or 20% crm *(Azelex, Finevin)* q12h
  - Benzoyl peroxide 2.5, 5, 10% crm, gel, wash, soap q12–24h
  - Metronidazole 0.75% crm▲ *(MetroCream)* q12h or 1% crm or gel *(Noritate, MetroGel)* q24h
  - Sodium sulfacetamide 10% + sulfa 5% (*Rosula* aqueous gel, *Clenia* crm, foaming wash) q12–24h, avoid if sulfa allergy or kidney disease (K)
  - Erythromycin 2% sol▲ q12h
  - Tretinoin▲ 0.025% crm or liq, 0.01% gel qhs
- Oral (for moderate to severe papular-pustular rosacea)
  - Tetracycline▲ 500 mg q8–12h × 6–12 wk
  - Doxycycline▲ 50–100 mg q12–24h × 6–12 wk
  - Minocycline▲ 50–100 mg q12–24h × 6–12 wk
  - Clarithromycin▲ 250–500 mg q12h × 6–12 wk
  - Metronidazole▲ 200 mg q12–24h × 4–6 wk
  - Erythromycin▲ 250–500 mg q12–24h × 6–12 wk
  - Azithromycin▲ 250–500 mg q24h × 6–12 wk

Scabies

Burrows, erythematous papules or rash, dry or scaly skin, pruritus (worse at night); spread by close, skin-to-skin or sexual contact; can affect interdigital webs, flexor aspects of wrists, axillae, umbilicus, nipples, genitalia. Diagnostic confirmation by microscopic exam of skin scrapings in mineral oil.

Treatment

• Infestation can result in epidemics; treat all contacts and treat environment

• Oatmeal baths, topical corticosteroids, or emollient creams for symptom relief

• Apply topical products from head to toe:

  ○ Permethrin 5% crm▲ *(Elimite)*, wash off after 8–14 h, repeat in 7–10 d if symptomatic or if live mites were found.

  ○ Lindane 1% crm▲ *(K-well, Scabene)*, wash off after 8–12 h

  ○ Crotamiton 10% crm *(Eurax)*, less effective, leave on 48 h, repeat in 7–10 d if necessary

  ○ Ivermectin *(Stromectol)* 200 mcg/kg po, may repeat once in 1 or 2 wk [T: 3, 6]

Seborrheic Dermatitis

Greasy, yellow scales with or without erythematous base; common in Parkinson disease and in debilitated patients; can affect nasal labial folds, eyebrows, hairline, sideburns, posterior auriculare and midchest

Treatment

• Hydrocortisone 1% or 2% crm▲ q12h or triamcinolone 0.1% oint q12h × 2 wk

• Scalp: shampoo containing selenium sulfide, zinc, or tar

• Ketoconazole 2% crm▲ for severe conditions if *Pityrosporum orbiculare* infection suspected

Skin Maceration

Erythema; abraded, excoriated skin; blisters; white and silver patches; can affect any area constantly in contact with moisture, covered by occlusive dressing or bandage; skin folds, groin, buttocks

Prevention and Treatment

• Eliminate cause of moisture.

  ○ Toileting program for incontinence (p 147)

  ○ Condom catheter

  ○ Indwelling catheter (reserve for most intractable conditions)

  ○ FI collector

• Protect skin from moisture.

  ○ Clean gently with mild soap after each incontinent episode.

  ○ Apply moisture barrier (eg, *Vaseline, Proshield, Smooth and Cool, Calmoseptine*).

  ○ Use disposable briefs that wick moisture from the skin; use linen incontinence pads when disposable briefs worsen perineal dermatitis.

Urticaria

Hives

• Uniform, red edematous plaques surrounded by white halos, can affect any skin surface

• Treatment

  ○ Identify cause.

  ○ Oral H_1 antihistamines (see **Table 115**) or oral H_2 antihistamines (see **Table 56**)

- Oral glucocorticoids (eg, prednisone 40 mg q24h)
- Doxepin▲ (po or topical *Zonalon* 5%) for refractory cases

Angioedema
- Larger, deeper than hives; can affect lips, eyelids, tongue, larynx, GI tract
- Treatment
  - Oral H_1 antihistamines (see **Table 115**)
  - Oral glucocorticoids
  - For severe reactions, epinephrine 0.3 mL of a 1:1000 dilution *(EpiPen)* SC

Cholinergic
- Round, red papular wheals; can affect any skin surface
- Treatment
  - Hot shower may relieve itching
  - Oral H_1 antihistamines (see **Table 115**) 1 h before exercise

Xerosis
Dull, rough, flaky, cracked; nummular; can affect all skin surfaces

Treatment
- Increase humidity
- Avoid excess bathing, sponges, brushes, and use of bath oils, which can lead to falls from slippery feet
- Tepid water in baths or showers
- Oatmeal baths
- Apply emollient oint (eg, *Aquaphor*) or crm (eg, *Eucerin*) immediately after bathing
- Hydrocortisone 1% oint

DERMATOLOGIC MEDICATIONS

Table 44. Topical Antifungal Medications

Medication	Formulation	Dermatologic Indications	Dosing Frequency
Butenafine *(Lotrimin ultra*, Mentax)*	1% crm	*Tinea pedis, T cruris, T corpis, T versicolor*	q24h × 2–4 wk
Ciclopirox▲ *(Loprox, Penlac)*	0.77% crm, gel, lot, sus; 1% shp; 8% lacquer	*Tinea pedis, T cruris, T corpis, T versicolor;* candidiasis; scalp seborrhea; onychomycosis	2 times/wk × 4 wk; shp 3 ×/wk; lacquer qhs
Clotrimazole▲* *(Cruex, Mycelex, others)*	1% crm, sol	Candidiasis, dermatophytoses; superficial mycoses	q12h
Econazole▲ nitrate *(Spectazole)*	1% crm	Candidiasis; *Tinea cruris, T corpis, T versicolor*	q24h × 2–4 wk
Ketoconazole▲ *(Nizoral, Nizoral A-D*)*	2% crm, 1% shp	Candidiasis; seborrhea; *Tinea cruris, T corpis, T versicolor*	q12–24h; shp 2 ×/wk

(cont.)

Table 44. Topical Antifungal Medications (cont.)

Medication	Formulation	Dermatologic Indications	Dosing Frequency
Miconazole▲* (eg, *Micatin, Monistat-Derm)*	2% crm, lot, pwd, spr, tinc	*Tinea cruris, T corpis, T pedis*	q12h × 2–4 wk
Naftifine *(Naftin)*	1% crm, gel	*Tinea cruris, T corpis, T pedis*	crm; gel q12h
Nystatin▲ *(Mycostatin, Nilstat, Nystex)*	100,000 U/g crm, oint, pwd	Mucocutaneous candidiasis	q8–12h up to 4 wk
Oxiconazole *(Oxistat)*	1% crm, lot	*Tinea corpis, T cruris, T pedis, T versicolor*	q12–24h × 2–4 wk
Sertraconazole *(Ertaczo)*	2% crm	*Tinea pedis*	q12h × 4 wk
Sulconazole *(Exelderm)*	1% crm, sol	*Tinea corpis, T cruris*	q12–24h × 3–4 wk
Terbinafine▲ *(Lamisil, LamisilAT*)*	1% crm▲, sol	*Tinea cruris, T corpis, T pedis, T versicolor*	q12h × 1–4 wk
Tolnaftate▲* *(Absorbine Jr. Antifungal, Tinactin, others)*	1% crm▲, gel, S▲, pwd▲, spr	*Tinea cruris, T corpis, T pedis*	q12h × 2–4 wk
Triacetin *(Myco–Nail*)*	25% sol	*Tinea pedis*	q12h, continue for 7 d after symptoms have resolved
Undecylenic acid *(Fungi–Nail*)*	25% sol	*Tinea pedis*, ringworm (except nails and scalp)	q12h × 4 wk

*OTC

Table 45. Topical Corticosteroids

Medication	Strength and Formulations	Frequency of Application
Lowest Potency		
Hydrocortisone▲a	0.5%, 1%, 2.5% crm, oint, lot, sol	q6–8h
Low Potency		
Alclometasone dipropionate▲a *(Aclovate)*	0.05% crm, oint	q8–12h
Desonide▲ *(DesOwen, Tridesilon)*	0.05% crm, oint, foam, lot, gel	q6–12h
Fluocinolone acetonide▲ *(Synalar)*	0.01% crm, sol	q6–12h
Mid-potency		
Betamethasone dipropionate▲ *(Diprosone)*	0.05% lot	q6–12h
Betamethasone valerate▲ *(Valisone)*	0.1% crm	q6–12h
Clocortolone pivalate▲ *(Cloderm)*	0.1% crm	q6–24h
Desoximetasone▲ *(Topicort)*	0.05% crm	q12h
Fluocinolone acetonide▲ *(Synalar)*	0.025% crm, oint	q6–12h
Flurandrenolide *(Cordran)*	0.05% crm, oint, lot, tape	q12–24h

(cont.)

Table 45. Topical Corticosteroids (cont.)

Medication	Strength and Formulations	Frequency of Application
Fluticasone propionate▲ *(Cutivate)*	0.05% crm, 0.005% oint	q12h
Hydrocortisone butyrate *(Locoid)*	0.1% oint	q12–24h
Hydrocortisone valerate▲ *(Westcort)*	0.2% crm, oint	q6–8h
Mometasone furoate▲ᵃ *(Elocon)*	0.1% crm, lot, oint	q24h
Prednicarbate▲ *(Dermatop)*	0.1% crm, lot	q12h
Triamcinolone acetonide▲ *(Aristocort, Kenalog)*	0.025%, 0.1% crm, oint, lot	q8–12h
Higher Potency		
Amcinonide▲ *(Cyclocort)*	0.1%, crm, oint, lot	q8–12h
Betamethasone dipropionate▲ *(Diprolene AF)*	0.05% augmented crm	q6–12h
Betamethasone dipropionate▲ *(Diprosone)*	0.05%, crm, oint	q6–12h
Betamethasone valerate▲ *(Valisone)*	0.1% oint	q6–12h
Desoximetasone▲ *(Topicort)*	0.25% crm, oint, spr; 0.05% gel	q12h
Diflorasone diacetate▲ *(Florone, Maxiflor)*	0.05%, crm, oint	q6–12h
Fluocinonide▲ *(Lidex)*	0.05% crm, oint, gel	q6–12h
Halcinonide▲ *(Halog)*	0.1% crm, oint	q8–24h
Triamcinolone acetate▲	0.5% crm, spr	q8–12h
Super Potency		
Betamethasone dipropionate▲ *(Diprolene)*	0.05% oint, lot, gel (augmented)	q6–12h
Clobetasol propionate *(Temovate)*	0.05% crm▲, oint▲, lot, gel▲, shp, spr	q12h
Diflorasone diacetate▲ *(Psorcon)*	0.05% optimized oint	q8–24h
Halobetasol propionate▲ *(Ultravate)*	0.05% crm, oint	q12h

ᵃ Hydrocortisone (all forms), alclometasone, and mometasone are nonfluorinated.

HYPOTHYROIDISM

Common Causes
• Autoimmune (primary thyroid failure)
• Following tx for hyperthyroidism
• Pituitary or hypothalmic disorders (secondary thyroid failure)
• Medications, especially amiodarone (rare after first 18 mo of tx) and lithium

Screening for hypothyroidism in asymptomatic older persons is controversial

Evaluation
TSH, and if high, free T_4

Pharmacotherapy
• Tx of subclinical hypothyroidism (TSH 5–10 mIU/L, normal free T_4 concentration, and no overt symptoms) is controversial and should be tailored to the individual patient based on symptoms, atherosclerotic heart disease, heart failure, or risk factors for these diseases.
• Levothyroxine▲ (T_4 *[Eltroxin, Levo-T, Levothroid, Synthroid]* [T: 25, 50, 75, 88, 100, 112, 125, 137, 150, 175, 200, 300 mcg]) given on empty stomach and waiting for 1 h before eating or hs (4 h after last meal), which is more potent. Start at 25–50 mcg and increase by 12- to 25-mcg intervals q4–8wk with repeat TSH testing until TSH is in normal range. Prescribe product from same manufacturer for individual patients for consistent bioavailability.
• Combinations of levothyroxine and L-triiodothyronine (T_3) are not recommended.
• For myxedema coma: Load T_4 400 mcg IV or 100 mcg q6–8h for 1 d, then 100 mcg/d IV (until patient can take orally) and give stress doses of corticosteroids (see p 103); then start usual replacement regimen.
• Thyroid USP is not recommended.(Avoid.**BC**) To convert thyroid USP to thyroxine: 60 mg USP = 50 mcg thyroxine.
• If patients are npo and must receive IV thyroxine, dose should be half usual po dose.
• If tx has been interrupted for <6 weeks and without an intercurrent cardiac event or marked weight loss, previous full replacement dose can be resumed
• Monitor TSH level at least q12mo (ASCE/ATA) in patients on chronic thyroid replacement tx.

HYPERTHYROIDISM

Common Causes
• Graves' disease
• Toxic nodule
• Toxic multinodular goiter
• Medications, especially amiodarone (can occur any time during tx)

Evaluation
TSH, free T_4
• If TSH is low and free T_4 is normal, recheck TSH in 4–6 wk; if TSH is still low, check free T_3.
• If TSH is low and free T_4 or free T_3 is high, check radioactive iodine uptake and, if thyroid nodularity, thyroid scan.

Pharmacotherapy

- β-blockers (see p 52) if symptomatic hyperthyroidism
- Radioactive iodine ablation is usual tx of choice for older persons, but surgery (works faster but more likely to become hypothyroid) or medical tx are options. Pretreat with methimazole and β-blockers before iodine ablation if symptomatic or if free $T_4 > 2-3 \times$ normal. Monitor free T_4 and total T_3 within 1–2 mo after tx. Pretreat with methimazole and β-blockers before surgery. Give potassium iodide in immediate preoperative period. After surgery, measure calcium or intact PTH, stop antithyroid drugs, and taper β-blockers.
- Methimazole▲ (*Tapazole* [T: 5, 10]): First-line drug tx; start 5–20 mg po q8h, then adjust. If used as primary tx, continue for 12–18 m then DC or taper if TSH is normal. Check CBC, LFTs before starting.
- Propylthiouracil (PTU [T: 50]): Use only if allergic to or intolerant of methimazole; can cause serious liver injury; start 100 mg po q8h, then adjust up to 200 mg po q8h prn. Check CBC, LFTs before starting.
- When dose has stabilized, follow TSH per hypothyroid monitoring.
- Adjunctive tx with β-blockers (see **Table 28**) or calcium antagonists (see **Table 28**) may improve symptoms.
- In older adults, treat both symptomatic hyperthyroidism and subclinical hyperthyroidism (low TSH and normal serum free T_4 and T_3 concentrations confirmed by repeat testing in 3–6 m) if TSH <0.1 mIU/L or if TSH 0.1–0.5 mIU/L and underlying cardiovascular disease or low BMD.

EUTHYROID SICK SYNDROME

Definition
Abnormal thyroid function tests in nonthyroidal illness

Evaluation
- Do not assess thyroid function in acutely ill patients unless thyroid dysfunction is strongly suspected.
- Low T_3, high reverse T_3, low T_4, low or high TSH may be seen.
- If TSH is very low (<0.1 mIU/L in high sensitivity assays), then hyperthyroidism is likely.
- If TSH is very high (>20 mIU/L), then hypothyroidism is likely.
- If thyroid disease is not strongly suspected, recheck in 3–6 wk.

SOLITARY THYROID NODULE

Evaluation
- Ultrasound of thyroid
- TSH
  - If TSH is normal or high, perform fine-needle aspirate. Do not perform radioclidescan.[CW]
  - If TSH is low, perform radionuclide scan; if "hot," then rarely cancer and manage as described below; if "cold," perform fine-needle aspirate.

Management
- Benign nodules: follow clinically and with ultrasound q6–12mo initially
- "Hot" nodules: radioactive iodine or surgery
- Malignant nodules, suspicious for malignancy, and follicular neoplasm: surgery

- Inconclusive biopsy of nodules: follow clinically and with ultrasound, and repeat fine-needle aspirate.

DIABETES MELLITUS

Definition and Classification (ADA)

DM is a group of metabolic diseases characterized by hyperglycemia resulting from defects in insulin secretion, insulin action, or both.

Type 1: Caused by an absolute deficiency of insulin secretion.

Type 2: Caused by a combination of resistance to insulin action and an inadequate compensatory insulin secretory response. Type 2 DM is a progressive disorder requiring higher dosages or additional medications over time.

Screening—Screen asymptomatic older adults if BMI >25 kg/m^2 with HbA$_{1c}$, fasting plasma glucose or OGTT if patient is likely to benefit from identification and tx based on current health and prognosis; repeat at 3-yr intervals.

Criteria for Diagnosis—One or more of the following:
- Symptoms of DM (eg, polyuria, polydipsia, unexplained weight loss) plus casual plasma glucose concentration ≥200 mg/dL
- Fasting (no caloric intake for ≥8 h) plasma glucose ≥126 mg/dL
- 2-h plasma glucose ≥200 mg/dL during an OGTT.
- Unless hyperglycemia is unequivocal, diagnosis should be confirmed by repeat testing.
- HbA$_{1c}$ >6.5

Pre-diabetes—Any of the following:
- Impaired fasting glucose: defined as fasting plasma glucose ≥100 and <126 mg/dL
- Impaired glucose tolerance: 2-h plasma glucose 140–199 mg/dL
- HbA$_{1c}$ 5.7–6.4%

Prevention/Delay of Type 2 DM in Patients with Pre-diabetes

- Lifestyle modification (most effective)
  - Weight loss (target 7%) if overweight
  - Reduction in total and saturated dietary fat
  - High dietary fiber (14 g fiber/1000 kcal) and whole grains
  - Exercise (at least 150 min/wk of moderate activity, such as walking)
- Pharmacologic
  - Metformin (850 mg q12h) (less effective than lifestyle modification)
  - Valsartan (beginning 80 mg/d and increased to 160 mg/d after 2 wk as tolerated) slightly reduces risk of developing DM but does not reduce rate of cardiovascular events.
  - Acarbose (100 mg q8h) (less effective than lifestyle modification)

Management of Diabetes

Evaluate for Comorbid Conditions (AGS, ADA): Depression (see p 78), polypharmacy (see p 116), cognitive impairment (see p 322), UI (see p 147), falls (see p 112), pain (see p 227) (AGS), PAD (claudication hx and assessment of pedal pulses) (see p 63) (ADA), stress test screening for CAD is of no benefit in asymptomatic patients (see p 38).

Goals of Treatment (ADA, AGS):

Older adults who are functional, cognitively intact, and have significant life expectancy should receive diabetes care with goals similar to those developed for younger adults (ADA) (see **Table 46**).

Patient Health	A_{1c} goal	FPG or PPG, mg/dL	Bedtime glucose, mg/dL	BP goal, mm/Hg	Lipid Tx
Healthy	7.0–7.5%	90–130	90–150	<140/80	Statin
Complex/intermediate[a]	7.5–8.0%	90–150	100–180	<140/80	Statin
Very complex/poor health[b]	8.5%–9.0%	100–180	110–200	<150/90	Consider statin

Table 46. Goals of Treatment for Older Patients with Diabetes Mellitus

Notes: FPG = fasting plasma glucose; PPG = post-prandial glucose
[a]multiple (3+) coexisting chronic illness or 2+ instrumental ADL impairments or mild-to-moderate cognitive impairment
[b]LTC or end-stage chronic illnesses or moderate-to-severe cognitive impairment or 2+ ADL dependencies

- Inpatient: If critically ill, 140–180 mg/dL; if noncritically ill, there are no clear evidence-based guidelines, but fasting <140 mg/dL and random <180 mg/dL are suggested (might be relaxed if severe comorbidities [ADA]). Scheduled basal and prandial insulin doses with correction doses with rapid-acting analog (aspart, glulisine, or lispro).[BC]
- Long-term care: Do not use sliding-scale insulin in chronic glycemic management.[BC]

Nonpharmacologic Interventions:

- Individualize medical nutrition tx to achieve tx goals (diet plus exercise is more effective than diet alone)
- Lifestyle (eg, regular exercise for ≥150 min/wk, resistance training 3 ×/wk if not contraindicated, alcohol and smoking cessation)
- Weight loss if overweight or obese
- Limit saturated fat to <7% of total calories
- Minimize intake of trans fat
- Low-carbohydrate, low-fat calorie-restricted; or Mediterranean diet
- Limit protein intake to ≤0.8 g/kg/d if any CKD
- For younger and healthier older adults with BMI >35 kg/m² who have type 2 DM that is difficult to control with lifestyle and pharmacotherapy, consider bariatric surgery.
- High-fiber diet (25 g insoluble and 25 g soluble/d)
- Limit alcohol intake to <1 drink/d in women and <2 drinks/d in men
- Patient and family education for self-management (reimbursed by Medicare)
- Psychosocial assessment and care

Pharmacologic Interventions for Type 2:

If diet and exercise have not achieved target HbA_{1c} in 6 mo, begin drug tx.

- Management of glycemia: stepped tx* (ADA), see **Table 47**.

Step 1: Metformin▲ (reduce dose in Stage 3 CKD; avoid in Stage 4 CKD) beginning 500 mg q12h or q24h; can titrate up q5–7d to max of 2000 mg/d if no AEs and blood glucose uncontrolled.

Step 2: Add one of the following:

- Basal insulin (intermediate at bedtime or long-acting at bedtime or morning) 10 U or 0.2 U/kg; can increase by 2–4 U q3d depending on fasting blood glucose. When fasting blood glucose is at goal, recheck HbA_{1c} in 2–3 mo. If hypoglycemia or fasting blood glucose <70 mg/dL, reduce dose by 4 U or 10%, whichever is greater. If above target HbA_{1c}, check pre-lunch, dinner, and bedtime blood glucose concentrations and add rapid- or intermediate-acting insulin (see **Table 48**).
  - Use 4-mm, 32-gauge needle if BMI <40 kg/m^2.
  - Injection sites for human insulin: fastest onset is abdomen and slowest onset is thigh.
  - Timing for prandial insulin: if blood glucose is in 100s, give 10 min before eating; if blood glucose is in 200s, give 20 min before eating; if blood glucose is in 300s, give 30 min before eating.
- Sulfonylurea (glipizide preferred)
- Less well-validated *Step 2* tx
  - Pioglitazone
  - GLP-1 agonists

Step 3: Combine *Step 2* agents. D/C sulfonylureas and meglitinides when insulins are started.

Step 4: Other agents (see **Table 47**) may be appropriate for selected patients.

*Reinforce lifestyle modifications at every visit.

- Management of tx-associated hypoglycemia (most common with insulin, sulfonylurea, α-glucosidase inhibitors, and meglitinides)
  - If conscious, patients should have fast-acting carbohydrate (eg, glucose tabs, hard candy, paste (Instant Glucose), or instant fruit that provides 15–20 g of glucose.
  - Effects may last only 15 min, so need to eat and recheck blood glucose.
  - If hypoglycemia is severe (patient unconscious or cannot ingest carbohydrate), then glucagon 0.5–1 mg SC or IM.
  - In medical settings, 25–50 g of D50 IV restores glucose quicker.
- Tx of comorbid conditions should be individualized based on life expectancy, patient preferences, and tx goals.
- Manage HTN (BP goal <140/80 mmHg; also see HTN, p 49) beginning with ACEI, ARB, CCB, or thiazide diuretic. If patient is black, CCB or thiazide diuretic (JNC 8).
- Treat lipid disorders (see p 46). If no overt cardiovascular disease and ≤75 yr old, use high-intensity statin (AHA-ACC). If >75 yr old, use moderate-intensity statin (see Cardiovascular). If DM, no overt cardiovascular disease, and ≤75 yr old, use moderate-intensity statin or high-intensity statin if estimated 10-yr risk of cardiovascular disease is ≥7.5%.
- ACEI or angiotensin II receptor blocker if albuminuria, HTN, or another cardiovascular risk factor. Check kidney function and serum potassium within 1–2 wk of initiation of tx, with each dosage increase, and at least yearly.

- ASA 75–162 mg/d if hx of heart disease but value in primary prevention is uncertain; consider using if 10-yr risk of CAD >10% (see http://hp2010.nhlbihin.net/atpiii/calculator); if allergic, clopidogrel 75 mg/d
- Pneumococcal vaccination
- Annual influenza vaccination
- Smoking cessation

Table 47. Non-insulin Agents for Treating Diabetes Mellitus

Medication	Dosage	Formulations	Comments (Metabolism)
Oral Agents			
Biguanide			Decrease hepatic glucose production; lower HbA_{1c} by 1.0–2.0%; do not cause hypoglycemia
Metformin▲ *(Glucophage)*	500–2550 mg divided	T: 500, 850, 1000	Avoid in patients with Cr ≥1.5 mg/dL (men) or ≥1.4 mg/dL (women) or eGFR <30 mL/1.73 m², HF, COPD, ↑ LFTs; hold before contrast radiologic studies; may cause weight loss (K)
(Glucophage XR)▲	1500–2000 mg/d	T: ER 500, 750	
2nd-Generation Sulfonylureas			Increase insulin secretion; lower HbA_{1c} by 1.0–2.0%; can cause hypoglycemia and weight gain
Glimepiride▲ *(Amaryl)*	4–8 mg once (begin 1–2 mg)	T: 1, 2, 4	Numerous drug interactions, long-acting (L, K)
Glipizide▲ *(Glucotrol)* *(Glucotrol XL)*	2.5–40 mg once or divided	T: 5, 10	Short-acting (L, K)
	5–20 mg once	T: ER 2.5, 5, 10	Long-acting (L, K)
Glyburide▲ (generic or *Diaβeta, Micronase)*	1.25–20 mg once or divided	T: 1.25, 2.5, 5	Long-acting, ↑ risk of hypoglycemia; not recommended for use in older adults (L, K)
Micronized glyburide *(Glynase)*	1.5–12 mg once	T: 1.5, 3, 4.5, 6	Long-acting, ↑ risk of hypoglycemia; not recommended for use in older adults (L, K)
α-Glucosidase Inhibitors			Delay glucose absorption; lower HbA_{1c} by 0.5–1.0%; can cause hypoglycemia and weight gain
Acarbose▲ *(Precose)*	50–100 mg q8h, just ac; start with 25 mg/d	T: 25, 50, 100	GI AEs common, avoid if Cr >2 mg/dL, monitor LFTs (gut, K)
Miglitol *(Glyset)*	25–100 mg q8h, with 1st bite of meal; start with 25 mg/d	T: 25, 50, 100	Same as acarbose but no need to monitor LFTs (L, K)

(cont.)

Table 47. Non-insulin Agents for Treating Diabetes Mellitus (cont.)

Medication	Dosage	Formulations	Comments (Metabolism)
DPP–4 Enzyme Inhibitors			Protect and enhance endogenous incretin hormones; lower HbA$_{1c}$ by 0.5–1%; do not cause hypoglycemia, weight neutral
Alogliptin *(Nesina)*	25 mg once daily; 1.5 mg/d if CrCl 31–50 mL/min; 6.25 mg/d if CrCl<30 mL/min	T: 25, 12.5, 6.25	K
Linagliptin *(Tradjenta)*	5 mg	T: 5 mg	L
Sitagliptin *(Januvia)*	100 mg once daily as monotherapy or in combination with metformin or a thiazolidinedione; 50 mg/d if CrCl 31–50 mL/min; 25 mg/d if CrCl <30 mL/min	T: 25, 50, 100	
Saxagliptin *(Onglyza)*	5 mg; 2.5 mg if CrCl <50 mL/min	T: 2.5, 5	K
Meglitinides			Increase insulin secretion; lower HbA$_{1c}$ by 1.0–2.0%; can cause hypoglycemia and weight gain
Nateglinide▲ *(Starlix)*	60–120 mg q8h	T: 60, 120	Give 30 min ac
Repaglinide *(Prandin)*	0.5 mg q6–12h if HbA$_{1c}$ <8% or previously untreated; 1–2 mg q6–12h if HbA$_{1c}$ ≥8% or previously treated	T: 0.5, 1, 2	Give 30 min ac, adjust dosage at weekly intervals, potential for drug interactions, caution in hepatic, renal insufficiency (L)
Thiazolidinediones			Insulin resistance reducers; lower HbA$_{1c}$ by 0.5–1.5%; ↑ risk of HF; avoid if NYHA Class III or IV cardiac status; D/C if any decline in cardiac status; weight gain
			Check LFTs at start, q2mo during 1st yr, then periodically; avoid if clinical evidence of liver disease or if serum ALT levels >2.5 times upper limit of normal; may Increase risk of fractures in women (L, K)
Pioglitazone▲ *(Actos)*	15 or 30 mg/d; max 45 mg/d as monotherapy, 30 mg/d in combination tx	T: 15, 30, 45	

(cont.)

Table 47. Non-insulin Agents for Treating Diabetes Mellitus (cont.)

Medication	Dosage	Formulations	Comments (Metabolism)
SGLT2 Inhibitor Canagliflozin *(Invokana)*	100–300 mg/d	T: 100, 300	Decreases glucose reabsorption from kidney; lowers HbA_{1c} by 0.5–1.5%; Initial dose 100 mg and no more than 100 mg if eGFR 45–59/1.73 m^2 (L)
Rosiglitazone *(Avandia)*	4 mg q 12–24h	T: 2, 4, 8	Prescribing and dispensing restrictions were removed in 2014.
Other Bromocriptine *(Cycloset)*	1.6–4.8 once	0.8	Start 0.8 and increase 0.8 weekly; lowers HbA_{1c} by 0.5% (L)
Colesevelam *(Welchol)*	3750 mg once or 1875 mg twice	T: 625, 1875 pwd pk: 3750	Give with meals; lowers HbA_{1c} by 0.5%; not absorbed (GI)
Combinations Glipizide and metformin▲ *(METAGLIP)*	2.5/250 mg once; 20/2000 in 2 divided doses	T: 2.5/250, 2.5/500, 5/500	Avoid in patients >80 yr, Cr >1.5 mg/dL in men, Cr >1.4 mg/dL in women; see individual drugs (L, K)
Glyburide and metformin▲ *(Glucovance)*	1.25/250 mg initially if previously untreated; 2.5/500 mg or 5/500 mg q12h with meals; max 20/2000/d	I: 1.25/250, 2.5/500, 5/500	Starting dose should not exceed total daily dose of either drug; see individual drugs (L, K)
Pioglitazone and metformin *(ACTO plus met)*	15/850 mg q12–24h	T: 15/850	See individual drugs.
Repaglinide and metformin *(PrandiMet)*	1/500 mg to 4/1000 mg twice q12h or q8h ac; max 10/2500 mg/d	T: 1/500, 2/500	See Individual drugs.
Pioglitazone and glimepiride *(Duetact)*	30/2 mg initially; max 45/8 mg	T: 30/2, 30/4	See individual drugs.
Saxagliptin and metformin *(Kombiglyze XR)*	5/1000–2000 mg once	T: ER 5/500, 5/1000, 2.5/1000	See individual drugs.

(cont.)

Table 47. Non-insulin Agents for Treating Diabetes Mellitus (cont.)			
Medication	**Dosage**	**Formulations**	**Comments (Metabolism)**
Sitagliptin and metformin *(Janumet)*	Begin with current doses; max 100/2000 mg in 2 divided doses	T: 50/500, 50/1000	See individual drugs.
(Janumet XR)	Begin with current doses; once a day doses	T: 50/500, 50/1000, 100/1000 mg ER	
Linagliptin and metformin *(Jentadueto)*	Begin with current doses; twice daily with meals	T: 2.5/500, 2.5/800, 2.5/1000	See individual drugs.
Alogliptin and metformin *(Kazano)*	Begin with current doses	T: 12.5/500, 12.5/1000	See individual drugs.
Alogliptin and pioglitazone tablet *(Oseni)*	Begin with current doses	T: 25/15, 25/30 25/45	See individual drugs.
Injectable Agents			Hypoglycemia common if combined with sulfonyl urea or insulin
Exenatide *(Byetta)*	5–10 mcg SC twice daily with meals	1.2-, 2.4-mL prefilled syringes	Incretin mimetic; lowers HbA_{1c} by 0.4–0.9%; nausea and hypoglycemia common; less weight gain than insulin; avoid if CrCl <30 mL/min (K)
Extended release *(Bydureon)*	2 mg SC once/wk	2-mg prefilled syringes	
Liraglutide *(Victoza)*	0.6–1.8 mg SC once daily	0.6, 1.2, 1.8 (6 mg/mL) in prefilled, multidose "pen"	Glucagon-like peptide-1 (GLP-1) receptor agonist; lowers HbA_{1c} by 1%; risks include acute pancreatitis and possibly medullary thyroid cancer (L)
Pramlintide *(Symlin)*	60 mcg SC immediately before meals	0.6 mg/mL in 5-mL vial	Amylin analog; lowers HbA_{1c} by 0.4–0.7%; nausea common; reduce pre-meal dose of short-acting insulin by 50% (K)

Table 48. Insulin Preparations

Preparation	Onset	Peak	Duration	Number of Injections/d
Rapid-acting				
Insulin glulisine (Apidra)	20 min	0.5–1.5 h	3–4 h	3
Insulin lispro (Humalog)	15 min	0.5–1.5 h	3–4 h	3
Insulin aspart (NovoLog)	30 min	1–3 h	3–5 h	3
Regular (eg, Humulin, Novolin) [a]	0.5–1 h	2–3 h	5–8 h	1–3
Intermediate or long-acting				
NPH (eg, Humulin, Novolin) [a]	1–1.5 h	4–12 h	24 h	1–2
Insulin detemir (Levemir)	3–4 h	6–8 h	6–24 h depending on dose	1–2
Insulin glargine (Lantus) [b]	1–2 h	—	24 h	1
Isophane insulin and regular insulin inj, premixed (Novolin 70/30)	30 min	2–12 h	24 h	1–2

[a] Also available as mixtures of NPH and regular in 50:50 proportions.
[b] To convert from NPH dosing, give same number of units once a day. For patients taking NPH q12h, decrease the total daily units by 20%, and titrate on basis of response. Starting dosage in insulin-naive patients is 10 U once daily hs.

Monitoring
Initial
- Screen for PAD by checking pedal pulses and asking about claudication (see p 63)
- Screen for signs and symptoms of cardiovascular autonomic neuropathy
- Comprehensive dilated eye and visual examinations by an ophthalmologist or optometrist who is experienced in management of diabetic retinopathy at time of diagnosis and annually

Ongoing
- Self-monitor blood glucose (SMBG) >3 ×/d if multiple daily injections or using insulin pump
- The value of SMBG in type 2 DM is unclear. For older adults treated with medications that do not cause hypoglycemia, SMBG may be unnecessary and there is no consensus about the frequency of monitoring patients on medications that may cause hypoglycemia.

More frequently than annually
- BP evaluation at each visit
- HbA$_{1c}$ twice/yr in patients with stable glycemic control; quarterly, if poor control

Annually
- Annual comprehensive foot examination, including monofilament testing at 4 plantar sites (great toe and base of first, third, and fifth metatarsals), plus testing any one of: tuning fork, pinprick sensation, ankle reflexes, or vibration perception threshold; assessment of foot pulses; and inspection. Insensate feet should be inspected q3–6mo; well-fitted walking or athletic shoes may be of benefit; refer those with sensory and structural abnormalities to foot care specialists.
- Lipid profiles q1–2yr depending on whether values are in normal range
- Annual test for microalbuminuria by measuring albumin:Cr ratio in a random spot collection
- Annual serum Cr

ADRENAL INSUFFICIENCY

Common Causes

Secondary (more common; mineralocorticoid function is preserved, no hyperkalemia or hyperpigmentation, dehydration is less common)

- Abrupt discontinuation of chronic glucocorticoid administration
- Megestrol acetate
- Brain irradiation
- Traumatic brain injury
- Pituitary tumors

Primary (less common)

- Autoimmune
- Tuberculosis

Evaluation

- Basal (morning) plasma cortisol >18 mcg/dL excludes adrenal insufficiency, and <3 mcg/dL is diagnostic.
- ACTH stimulation test: tetracosactin *(Synacthen Depot)* 250 mcg IV; best administered in the morning; peak value at 30–60 min >18 mcg/dL is normal, <15 mcg/dL is diagnostic.
- If adrenal insufficiency is diagnosed with high ACTH (eg, >100 pg/mL), then insufficiency is primary.

Pharmacotherapy

For corticosteroid dose equivalencies, see **Table 49**. Hydrocortisone preferred for adrenal insufficiency (10–25 mg/m²/d) in 2 or 3 divided doses. If primary adrenal insufficiency, add fludrocortisone▲ to glucocorticoids.

Management

Stress doses of corticosteroids for patients with severe illness, injury, or undergoing surgery: In emergency situations, do not wait for test results. Give hydrocortisone 100 mg IV bolus (or if patient has not been previously diagnosed, dexamethasone 4 mg IV bolus). Also treat with IV fluids (eg, saline). For less severe stress (eg, minor illness), double or triple usual oral replacement dosage for 3 d.

- For chronic adrenal insufficiency, hydrocortisone in 2 or 3 divided doses (total dose of 10 to 12 mg/m²/d). Alternatives are dexamethasone or prednisone.
- For minor surgery (eg, hernia repair), hydrocortisone 25 mg/m²/d on day of surgery and return to usual dosage on following day.
- For moderate surgical stress (eg, cholecystectomy, joint replacement), total 50–75 mg/d on the day of surgery and the first postoperative day, then usual dosage on the second postoperative day.
- For major surgical procedures (eg, cardiac bypass), total 100–150 mg/d given in divided doses for 2–3 d, then return to usual dosage.

Table 49. Corticosteroids					
Medication	Approx Equivalent Dose (mg)	Relative Anti-inflammatory Potency	Relative Mineralo-corticoid Potency	Biologic Half-life (h)	Formulations
Betamethasone▲ (Celestone)	0.6–0.75	20–30	0	36–54	T: 0.6; S: 0.6 mg/5 mL
Cortisone▲ (Cortone)	25	0.8	2	8–12	T: 5; S: 50 mg/mL
Dexamethasone▲ (Decadron, Dexone, Hexadrol)	0.75	20–30	0	36–54	T: 0.25, 0.5, 0.75, 1, 1.5, 2, 4; S: elixir 0.5 mg/5 mL; inj
Fludrocortisone▲ (Florinef)*	NA	10	4	12–36	T: 0.1
Hydrocortisone▲ (Cortef, Hydrocortone)	20	1	2	8–12	T: 5, 10, 20; S: 10 mg/5 mL; inj
Methylprednisolone▲ (eg, Medrol, Solu-Medrol, Depo-Medrol)	4	5	0	18–36	T: 2, 4, 8, 16, 24, 32; inj
Prednisolone▲ (eg, Delta-Cortef, Prelone Syrup, Pediapred)	5	4	1	18–36	S: 5 mg/5 mL; syr 5, 15 mg/5 mL
Prednisone▲ (Deltasone, Liquid Pred, Meticorten, Orasone)	5	4	1	18–36	T: 1, 2.5, 5, 10, 20, 50; S: 5 mg/5 mL
Triamcinolone (eg, Aristocort, Kenacort, Kenalog)	4	5	0	18–36	T: 1, 2, 4, 8; S: syr 4 mg/5 mL

Note: NA = not available

* Usually given for orthostatic hypotension at 0.1 mg q8–24h (max 1 mg/d) and at 0.05–0.2 mg/d for primary adrenal insufficiency.

VISUAL IMPAIRMENT

Definition

Visual acuity 20/40 or worse; severe visual impairment (legal blindness) 20/200 or worse in the better eye.

Evaluation

- Acuity testing
  - Near vision: check each eye independently with glasses using handheld Rosenbaum card at 14" or Lighthouse Near Acuity Test at 16". *Note:* Distance must be accurate.
  - Far vision: Snellen wall chart at 20'
- Visual fields (by confrontation)
- Ophthalmoscopy
- Emergent referral for acute change in vision

Prevention

Biennial full eye examinations for people >65 yr old, annually for people with DM.

SPECIFIC CONDITIONS ASSOCIATED WITH VISUAL IMPAIRMENT

Refractive Error

The most common cause of visual impairment.

Cataracts

Lens opacity on ophthalmoscopic examination. Risk factors: age, sun exposure, smoking, corticosteroids, DM, alcohol, low vitamin intake, quetiapine.

Nonpharmacologic Treatment:

- Reduce UV light exposure.
- Surgery (American, Canadian, and Royal [British] Academies of Ophthalmology):
  - if visual function no longer meets the patient's needs and cataract surgery is likely to improve vision
  - if clinically significant disparity between eyes due to cataract
  - when cataract removal will treat another lens-induced disease (eg, glaucoma)
  - when cataract coexists with retinal disease requiring unrestricted monitoring (eg, diabetic retinopathy)
  - Do not perform preop medical tests for eye surgery without specific indications. Reasonable indications include an ECG in patients with heart disease, serum K^+ in patients on diuretics, and serum glucose in patients with DM.[CW]

Age-related Macular Degeneration (AMD)

Atrophy of cells in the central macular region of retinal pigmented epithelium; on ophthalmoscopic examination, white-yellow patches (drusen) or hemorrhage and scars in advanced stages. Risk factors: age, smoking, sun exposure, family hx, white race. AMD has "wet" and "dry" forms.

- Dry AMD: Accounts for ~90% of cases, is characterized by abnormalities in the retinal pigment with focal drusen, and has a natural hx of slow gradual loss of vision.

- **Wet AMD:** Only 10% of cases are wet or neovascular, which is characterized by often rapid visual loss. Early intervention when the dry form converts to the wet form saves vision.

Nonpharmacologic Treatment:

- Monitor daily for conversion from dry to wet form using Amsler grid.
- Patients with large drusen most at risk of conversion to wet AMD.
- Thermal laser photocoagulation may be appropriate for select patients with extrafoveal choroidal neovascularization.
- Dietary modification reduces risk of progression to neovascular AMD: high intake of beta-carotene, vitamin C, zinc, n-3 long-chain polyunsaturated fatty acids, and fish.

Pharmacologic Treatment of Wet AMD:

- Vascular endothelial growth factor (VEGF) inhibitors reduce neovascularization, eg, bevacizumab *(Avastin)* or ranibizumab *(Lucentis)* intravitreal monthly or aflibercept (*Eylea, Zaltrap*) q 4–8 wks for up to 2 yr; maintains vision in the majority and improves it in a significant minority. As-needed drug administration (ie, only when signs of exudation are present) is as effective as monthly injections. Complications of the intraocular injections include retinal detachment or endophthalmitis and visual loss in 1–2% of patients.
- Radiation tx can be used to augment the effect of VEGF inhibitors reducing the number and frequency of injections needed.

Pharmacologic Treatment of Dry AMD:
In intermediate or more advanced stages, zinc oxide 80 mg, cupric oxide 2 mg, beta-carotene 15 mg, vitamin C 500 mg, and vitamin E 400 IU taken in divided doses q12h reduces risk of progression (eg, *Ocuvite PreserVision* 2 tabs po q12h). Not recommended for smokers (beta-carotene) or for people with CAD (vitamin E).

Diabetic Retinopathy

Microaneurysms, dot and blot hemorrhages on ophthalmoscopy with proliferative retinopathy ischemia and vitreous hemorrhage. Risk factors: chronic hyperglycemia, smoking.

Treatment:

- Laser tx of proliferative retinopathy or macular edema; panretinal photocoagulation for severe disease
- Moderate evidence that VEGF inhibitors work as well or better than laser for macular edema, with the number needed to treat of 5–7 for one to have significantly better visual outcomes. Requires 7–10 injections in year 1 and 2 in year 2.

Diabetic Management

Glycemic control to HbA$_{1c}$ of 7 vs 9 improves visual outcomes at 7–10 yr (see Diabetes, p 94). BP control to a mean of 144/80 mmHg improves visual outcomes compared with higher BPs. Control of lipids and use of antiplatelet agents do not affect visual outcomes.

Glaucoma

Characteristic optic cupping and nerve damage, and loss of peripheral visual fields. Risk factors: black race, age, family hx, increased ocular pressures. Most common cause of blindness in black Americans. Primary open-angle glaucoma is most common, a chronic disease of older adults. Angle-closure glaucoma is an acute disease requiring emergent management.

Glaucoma Surgery:

- Open angle—laser trabeculoplasty, surgical trabeculectomy (most effective but higher complication rates), canuloplasty, aqueous shunt
- Angle closure—laser iridotomy with or without iridoplasty

- Used primarily when pressures or optic nerve damage are poorly controlled by topicals.
- Outcomes with surgery similar to pharmacotherapy.

Pharmacologic Treatment:
Treat when there is optic nerve damage or visual field loss (see **Table 50**). Prostaglandin analogs are first-line tx.

Tx reduces IOP. Instill 1 gtt under lower lid, close eye for at least 1 min to reduce systemic absorption; repeat if a second drop is needed. Systemic absorption is further reduced by teaching the patient to compress the lacrimal sac for 15–30 sec after instilling a drop. Always wait 5 min before instilling a second type of drop.

Table 50. Medications for Treating Glaucoma			
Medication	**Strength**	**Dosage**	**Comments (Metabolism)**
α₂-Agonists (bottles with purple caps)			*Class AEs:* low BP, fatigue, drowsiness, dry mouth, dry nose, ocular AEs, hyperemia, burning, foreign-body sensation (unknown)
Brimonidine▲ *(Alphagan)*	0.2%	1 gtt q8–12h	
(Alphagan P)	0.1%, 0.15%	1 gtt q8–12h	
α-β Agonist			
Dipivefrin▲ *(AKPro, Propine)*	0.1%	1 gtt q12h	HTN, headache, tachycardia, arrhythmia (eye, L)
β-Blockers (bottles with yellow caps)			*Class AEs:*
✔Betaxolol *(Betoptic▲, Betoptic-S)*	0.25%, 0.5%	1–2 gtt q12h	hypotension, bradycardia, HF, bronchospasm, anxiety, depression, confusion, hallucination, diarrhea, nausea, cramps, lethargy, weakness, masking of hypoglycemia, sexual dysfunction. Avoid in patients with asthma, bradycardia, COPD (L)
✔Carteolol▲ *(Ocupress)*	1%	1 gtt q12h	
✔Levobunolol▲ *(AKBeta, Betagan)*	0.25%, 0.5%	1 gtt q12h	
✔Metipranolol▲ *(OptiPranolol)*	0.3%	1 gtt q12h	
✔Timolol drops▲ *(Betimol, Timoptic)*	0.25%, 0.5%	1 gtt q12h	Not all formulations available as generic
Cholinergic Agonists (bottles with green caps)			*Class AEs:* brow ache, corneal toxicity, red eye, retinal detachment
Pilocarpine gel *(Pilopine HS)*	4%	1/2″ qhs	Systemic cholinergic effects are rare (tissues, K)
(Ocusert)	20, 40 mcg/h	weekly	

(cont.)

Table 50. Medications for Treating Glaucoma (cont.)			
Medication	**Strength**	**Dosage**	**Comments (Metabolism)**
Pilocarpine▲ *(Adsorbocarpine, Akarpine, Isopto Carpine, Pilagan, Pilocar, Piloptic, Pilostat)*	0.25–10%	1 gtt q6h	
Miotic, Cholinesterase Inhibitor (bottles with green cap)			*Class AEs:* cholinomimetic effects (sweating, tremor, headache, salivation), confusion, high or low BP, bradycardia, broncho-constriction, urinary frequency, cramps, diarrhea, nausea
Echothiophate *(Phospholine)*	0.03–0.25%	1 gtt q12h	
Carbonic Anhydrase Inhibitors (bottles with orange caps)			
Topical			Caution in kidney failure and after corneal transplant (K)
✔Brinzolamide *(Azopt)*	1%	1 gtt q8h	
✔Dorzolamide▲ *(Trusopt)*	2%	1 gtt q8h	
Oral			
Acetazolamide▲ (eg, *Diamox*)	125–500 mg, SR 500 mg	250–500 mg q6–12h, SR 500 mg q12h	*Class AEs:* fatigue, weight loss, bitter taste, paresthesias, depression, COPD exacerbation, cramps, nausea, diarrhea, kidney failure, blood dyscrasias, hypokalemia, myopia, renal calculi acidosis; not recommended in kidney failure (K)
Methazolamide▲ (eg, *Neptazane*)	25–50 mg	50–100 mg q8–12h	(L, K)
Prostaglandin Analogs (bottles with turquoise caps)			First-line tx *Class AEs:* change in eye color and periorbital tissues, hyperemia, itching
✔Bimatoprost *(Lumigan)*	0.03%	1 gtt qhs	(L, K, F)
✔Latanoprost▲ *(Xalatan)*	0.005%	1 gtt qhs	(L)
Tafluprost* *(Zioptan)*	0.0015%	1 gtt qhs	(L)
✔Travoprost *(Travatan)*	0.004%	1 gtt qhs	(L)
Combinations			
Dorzolamide/timolol *(Cosopt)*	0.05%/0.2%	1 gtt q12h	See individual agents (K, L)
Brimonidine/timolol *(Combigan)*	0.2%/0.5%	1 gtt q12h	See individual agents (K, L)
Brinzolamide/brimonidine *(Simbrinza)*	1%/0.2%	1 gtt 2×/d	See individual agents (unknown, L)

✔ = preferred for treating older adults, * = preservative-free
Note: Patients may not know names of drugs but instead refer to them by the color of the bottle cap. The usual colors are listed above.

ADDITIONAL CONSIDERATIONS IN MANAGEMENT OF EYE DISORDERS

Topical Steroid Treatment

Patients on topical steroids for ocular inflammatory disease require periodic monitoring by an ophthalmologist. Serious and potentially vision-threatening adverse effects can occur from chronic topical corticosteroid use, including glaucoma and cataract or superinfection. Patients on chronic topical steroids should be followed by an ophthalmologist and there should be a legitimate indication for continued tx.

Low-vision Services

• Address the full range of functional visual impairment from blindness to partial sight. Refer patients with uncompensated visual loss that reduces function.

• Recommend optical aids:
  ○ Electronic video magnifiers
  ○ Spectacle-mounted telescopes for distance vision
  ○ Closed-circuit television to enlarge text
  ○ A variety of high-technology devices are available (see www.lighthouse.org).
  ○ Optical aids (like the above) may improve mood unlike traditional aids such as talking books, Braille watches, etc, which do not.

• Environmental modifications that improve function include color contrast, floor lamps to reduce glare, motion sensors to turn on lights, talking clocks, spoken medication reminders.

• Many states have "Services for the Visually Impaired" through the health department.

Dual Sensory Impairment (DSI)

• 9–21% of adults >70 yr old have loss of both vision and hearing.

• Compared with single-sensory impairment, DSI is more often associated with depression, poor self-rated health, reduced social participation, IADL, and cognitive impairment.

• Management currently limited to vibrating devices such as alarm clocks, door bells, smoke alarms, etc.

RED EYE

The "red eye" is an eye with vascular congestion: some conditions that cause this pose a threat to vision and warrant prompt ophthalmologic referral. (See **Table 51**). Acute conjunctivitis and allergic conjunctivitis are common causes of red eye. Diagnosis and tx of those conditions are discussed below (see p 109).

Table 51. Signs and Symptoms of Serious Conditions in Patients with Red Eye	
Red Flag Signs and Symptoms	**Potentially Dangerous Condition(s)**
Lid or lacrimal sac swelling or proptosis	Orbital cellulitis, orbital tumor
Subnormal visual acuity, foreign-body sensation, severe pain, photophobia, or circumcorneal hyperemia (ciliary flush)	Keratitis, anterior uveitis; acute angle closure glaucoma; endophthalmitis, episcleritis and scleritis
Proptosis, chemosis, visual loss, and ophthalmoplegia	Cavernous sinus arteriovenous fistula

Acute Conjunctivitis

Symptoms: Red eye, foreign body sensation, discharge, photophobia

Signs: Conjunctival hyperemia and discharge

Etiology: Viral, bacterial, chlamydial

Viral Versus Bacterial:

Viral—profuse tearing, minimal exudation, preauricular adenopathy common, monocytes in stained scrapings and exudates

Bacterial—moderate tearing, profuse exudation, preauricular adenopathy uncommon, bacteria and polymorphonuclear cells in stained scrapings and exudates

Both—minimal itching, generalized hyperemia, occasional sore throat and fever

Treatment: Majority are viral; do not treat viral infections with antibiotics; if diagnosis is uncertain, patients may be followed closely for resolution.[CW]

Treat viral infections with artificial tears and cool compresses. If purulent discharge, suspect bacterial; start broad-spectrum topical antibiotics (see **Table 52**). If severe, obtain culture and Gram stain, then start tx.

If signs and symptoms do not improve in 24–48 h, refer to ophthalmologist.

Other: Wash hands frequently and use separate towels to avoid spread.

Table 52. Treatment for Acute Bacterial Conjunctivitis[a]

Medication	Formulations[b]	Comments
Besifloxacin *(Besivance)*	0.6% sol	Very broad spectrum, well tolerated, a first choice in severe cases, expensive
Ciprofloxacin *(Ciloxan)*	0.3% sol▲, 0.3% oint	See besifloxacin
Erythromycin ophthalmic▲ *(AK-Mycin, Ilotycin)*	5 mg/g oint	Good if staphylococcal blepharitis is present
Gatifloxacin *(Tequin)*	0.3% sol	See besifloxacin
Moxifloxacin *(Avelox)*	0.5% sol	See besifloxacin
Ofloxacin▲ *(Floxin, Ocuflox)*	0.3% sol, 0.3% oint	See besifloxacin; generic available
Sulfacetamide sodium▲ *(Sodium Sulamyd)*	10%, 30% drops, 10% oint	Well tolerated
Tobramycin *(AKTob, Tobrex)*	3 mg/g oint, 3 mg/mL sol▲	Well tolerated but more corneal toxicity
Trimethoprim and polymyxin▲ *(Polytrim)*	1 mg/mL, 10,000 IU/mL sol	Well tolerated but some gaps in coverage

[a] Do not use steroid or steroid-antibiotic preparations in initial tx.

[b] In mild cases, solution is applied q6h and gel or oint q12h for 5–7 d. In more severe cases, solution is applied q2–3h and oint q6h; as the eye improves, solution is applied q6h and oint q12h.

Allergic Conjunctivitis

Symptoms: Prominent itching, watery discharge accompanied by nasal stuffiness (see allergic rhinitis, p 274)

Signs: Eyelid edema, conjunctival bogginess, and hyperemia (all bilateral)

Etiology: IgE–mediated hypersensitivity to airborne pollen

Treatment: Start a nonsedating oral H_1 antihistamine (see **Table 115**); if symptoms persist, add or substitute a topical H_1 antihistamine or topical mast cell stabilizer/antihistamine (see **Table 53**). If these are ineffective, try topical ketorolac (see **Table 53**). Nasal steroids reduce ocular symptoms to some degree (see **Table 115**). If the above do not relieve symptoms, refer to an ophthalmologist (topical steroids [p 108] may be necessary but should be prescribed only by an ophthalmologist). Oral mast cell stabilizers are not used in the tx of acute ocular allergies. The OTC vasoconstrictor/antihistamines are for short-term use only (see **Table 53**).

DRY EYE SYNDROME
Symptoms: Itchy or sandy eyes (foreign body sensation)

Etiology: Altered tear film composition, reduced tear production, poor lid function, environment, drug-induced causes (eg, anticholinergics, estrogens, SSRIs), or diseases such as Sjögren's syndrome; refer to ophthalmology for diagnostic assistance.

Therapy:
- Artificial tear formulations (eg, *HypoTears*) administer q1–6h prn. Preservatives may cause eye irritation. Preservative-free preparations, available in single-dose vials, are expensive. Ointment preparations can be used at night or also during the day in severe cases.
- *Lacrisert* is an insert that gradually releases hydroxypropyl cellulose after placement in the inferior conjunctival sac.
- Environmental strategies: room humidifiers, frequent blinking, and swim goggles or moisture chambers fit to eye glasses are all helpful.
- Cyclosporine ophthalmic emulsion 0.05% *(Restasis)* 1 gtt OU q12h. Indicated when tear production is suppressed by inflammation. May take 4–6 wk to achieve results. Does not increase tears in people using topical anti-inflammatories or punctal plugs. AEs: burning, hyperemia, discharge, pain, blurring. Patients should have a complete ophthalmologic examination before receiving a prescription.
- Temporary or permanent punctal plugs; do not place punctal plugs for mild dry eye before trying other medical tx.[CW]

Table 53. Topical Therapy for Allergic Conjunctivitis

Category/Medication	Formulation and Dosing	Adverse Events[a]
H₁ Antihistamines		
Alcaftadine *(Lastacaft)*	0.25%, 1 gtt OU q24h	Itching, erythema
Azelastine▲ *(Optivar)*	0.05%, 1 gtt OU q6h	Headache, rhinitis
Bepotastine *(Bepreve)*	1.5%, 1 gtt OU q12h	Dysgeusia
Emedastine *(Emadine)*	0.05%, 1 gtt OU q12h	
Epinastine *(Elestat)*	0.5%, 1 gtt OU q12h	
Ketotifen▲ *(Zaditor, Alaway)*	0.025%, 1 gtt OU q8–12h	
Olopatadine *(Patanol)*	0.1%, 1 gtt OU q12h	
Olopatadine *(Pataday)*	0.2%, 1 gtt OU q24h	Cold syndrome, dysgeusia, headache, keratitis
NSAID		
Ketorolac▲ *(Acular)*	0.5%, 1 gtt OU q6h	Ocular irritation, burning
Mast cell stabilizers[b]		
Lodoxamide *(Alomide)*	0.1%, 1–2 gtt OU q6h	Ocular irritation, burning
Nedocromil *(Alocril)*	2%, 1–2 gtt OU q12h	Headache, ocular irritation, burning
Pemirolast *(Alamast)*	0.1%, 1–2 gtt OU q6h	Headache, rhinitis, flu-like symptoms, ocular irritation, burning

(cont.)

Table 53. Topical Therapy for Allergic Conjunctivitis (cont.)		
Category/Medication	**Formulation and Dosing**	**Adverse Events[a]**
Vasoconstrictor/Antihistamine combinations		
Naphazoline▲ (0.1%, 0.12%) (Naphcon)	OTC; 1–2 gtt q3–4h as needed	*Class effects*: Caution in heart disease, HTN, BPH, narrow angle glaucoma; chronic use can cause follicular reactions or contact dermatitis
Pheniramine maleate 0.315%/ naphazoline hydrochloride 0.02675% (Opcon-A)	OTC; 1–2 gtt up to q6h for no more than a few days	
Pheniramine maleate 0.3%/ naphazoline hydrochloride 0.025% (Naphcon-A)	1–2 gtt up to q6h for no more than a few days	

[a] Any may cause stinging, which can by reduced by refrigerating drops.
[b] Not used in acute allergy; use when allergen exposure can be predicted, and use well in advance of exposure.

SYSTEMIC MEDICATIONS WITH OCULAR ADVERSE EVENTS (SYMPTOMS, SIGNS)
- Amiodarone: halos, blurred vision, corneal changes, optic neuropathy
- Anticholinergics: blurry near vision, angle-closure glaucoma (rare)
- Bisphosphonates: scleritis (and perhaps uveitis), ocular pain, red eye, blurred vision
- Carbamazepine and phenytoin: at toxic levels, blurred vision, diplopia, nystagmus
- Cisplatin: optic neuritis, papilledema, retrobulbar neuritis, cortical blindness
- Corticosteroids: cataracts, glaucoma
- Digoxin: yellowish orange vision; snowy, flickering vision
- Ethambutol or INH: loss of color vision, visual acuity, visual field
- Floxacins: diplopia, retinal detachment
- Hydroxychloroquine or chloroquine: loss of color vision, visual acuity, visual field
- Minocycline: increased intracranial pressure, papilledema, blurred vision, visual loss
- Niacin: decreased visual field, maculopathy
- Sildenafil: color tinge in vision, increased sensitivity to light, blurred vision. Nonarteritic ischemic optic neuropathy has been reported in association with PDE5 inhibitors.
- Tamoxifen: retinopathy with cumulative dose of 100 g or as little as 7 g (blurred vision, macular edema)
- Topiramate: acute angle-closure glaucoma (ocular pain, blurred vision, red eye)
- Vincristine: sixth cranial nerve palsy (ptosis, diplopia, abduction deficits)

FALL PREVENTION

DEFINITION

An event whereby an individual unexpectedly comes to rest on the ground or another lower level without known loss of consciousness (AGS/BGS Clinical Practice Guideline: Prevention of Falls in Older Persons, 2010). Excludes falls from major intrinsic event (eg, seizure, stroke, syncope) or overwhelming environmental hazard.

ETIOLOGY

Typically multifactorial. Composed of intrinsic (eg, poor balance, weakness, chronic illness, visual or cognitive impairment), extrinsic (eg, polypharmacy), and environmental (eg, poor lighting, no safety equipment, loose carpets) factors. Commonly a nonspecific sign for one of many acute illnesses in older adults.

RISK FACTORS

Focus on most common risk factors, which include:

- hx of falls
- fear of falling
- gait deficit
- balance deficit

Other risk factors include:

- muscle weakness
- use of assistive devices
- visual deficit, particularly unilateral visual loss
- arthritis
- impaired ADLs
- depression
- cognitive impairment
- >80 yr old
- ≥2 pain locations
- higher pain severity
- pain interference with activities

MEDICATIONS ASSOCIATED WITH FALLS

- Antisychotics (Avoid[BC])
- Sedatives (Avoid[BC]), hypnotics (including benzodiazepines)
- MAOIs, SSRIs, TCAs (Avoid[BC])
- Antiarrhythmics (Class 1A)
- Anticonvulsants (Avoid unless safer alternatives are not available; avoid except if seizure disorder.[BC])
- Anxiolytics (including benzodiazepines) (Avoid[BC])
- Antihypertensives
- Diuretics
- Systemic glucocorticoids
- Skeletal muscle relaxants (Avoid[BC])

EVALUATION

Exclude acute illness or underlying systemic or metabolic process (eg, infection, electrolyte imbalance as indicated by hx, examination, and laboratory studies). Determine if fall is syncopal or nonsyncopal (see Syncope, p 64).

See **Figure 5** for recommended assessment and prevention strategies. USPSTF does not recommend multifactorial assessment, although small benefit (11% reduction in fall risk; 11% in those with risk factors).

History

- Circumstances of fall (eg, activity and footwear at time of fall, location, time, lighting)
- Associated symptoms (eg, lightheadedness, vertigo, syncope, weakness, confusion, palpitations, joint pain, joint stability, feelings of pitching [common in Parkinsons], foot pain, ankle instability)
- Relevant comorbid conditions (eg, prior stroke, parkinsonism, cardiac disease, DM, seizure disorder, depression, anxiety, hyperplastic anemia, sensory deficit, osteoarthritis, osteoporosis, hyperthyroidism, glucocorticoid excess, GI or chronic renal disease, myeloma)
- Medication review, including OTC medications and alcohol use; note recent changes in medications (see p 16)

Physical Examination

Look for:

- Vital signs: postural pulse and BP lying and 3 min after standing, temperature
- Head and neck: visual impairment (especially poor acuity, reduced contrast sensitivity, decreased visual fields, cataracts), motion-induced nystagmus (Dix-Hallpike test), bruit, nystagmus
- Musculoskeletal: arthritic changes, motion or joint limitations (especially lower extremity joint function), postural instability, skeletal deformities, podiatric problems, muscle strength
- Neurologic: slower reflexes, altered proprioception, altered mental status, focal deficits, peripheral neuropathy, gait or balance disorders, hip flexor weakness, instability, tremor, rigidity
- Cardiovascular: heart arrhythmias, cardiac valve dysfunction (peripheral vascular changes, pedal pulses)

Diagnostic Tests

- Laboratory tests for people at risk: CBC, serum electrolytes, BUN, Cr, glucose, B_{12}, thyroid function, 25-hydroxy vitamin D
- Bone densitometry in all women >65 yr old
- Cardiac workup if symptoms of syncope or pre-syncope (see Syncope Evaluation, p 64)
- Imaging: neuroimaging if head injury or new, focal neurologic findings on examination or if a CNS process is suspected; spinal imaging to exclude cervical spondylosis or lumbar stenosis in patients with abnormal gait, neurologic examination, or lower extremity spasticity or hyperreflexia
- Drug concentrations for anticonvulsants, antiarrhythmics, TCAs, and high-dose ASA

Gait, Balance, and Mobility Assessment

- Functional gait: observe patient rising from chair, walking (stride, length, velocity, symmetry), turning, sitting (Get Up and Go test, POMA)
- Balance: semi-tandem, and full tandem stance; Functional Reach test; POMA; Berg Balance Scale (especially retrieve object from floor)

Figure 5. Assessment and Prevention of Falls

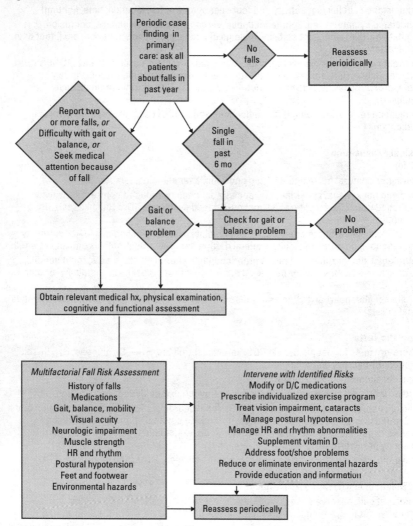

Sources: American Geriatrics Society and British Geriatrics Society. *Clinical Practice Guideline for the Prevention of Falls in Older Persons.* New York: American Geriatrics Society; 2010; www.medcats.com/FALLS/frameset.htm; and Pighills AC, et al. *J Am Geriatr Soc* 2011; 59:26–33.

- Mobility: observe patient's use and fit of assistive device (eg, cane, walker) or personal assistance, extent of ambulation, restraint use, footwear evaluation
  - Cane fitting: top of the cane should be at the top of the greater trochanter or at the break of the wrist; when the patient holds the cane, there is approximately a 15-degree bend at the elbow. Canes are most often used to improve balance but can also be used to reduce weight-bearing on the opposite leg.
  - Walker fitting: walkers are prescribed when a cane does not offer sufficient stability. Front-wheeled walkers allow a more natural gait and are easier for cognitively impaired patients to use. Four-wheeled rolling walkers (rollators) have the advantage for a smoother faster gait, but require more coordination because of the brakes; however, they are good for outside walking because the larger wheels move more easily over sidewalks.
- ADLs: complete ADL skill evaluation, including use of adaptive equipment and mobility aids as appropriate

PREVENTION

Goal is to minimize risk of falling without compromising mobility and functional independence. Recommendations are primarily based on studies of community-dwelling older adults with limited evidence from randomized controlled trials regarding single or multifactorial interventions in the long-term-care setting and in cognitively impaired. USPSTF recommends 3 factors to identify increased risk for falls in older adults: hx of falls, hx of mobility problems, and poor performance on the timed Get Up and Go test.

Also consider balance of benefits and harms, based on prior falls circumstances, medical comorbid conditions, and patient values, in providing comprehensive multifactorial assessment and intervention.

Other assessment considerations include:

- Assess risk of falling as part of routine primary health care visit (at least annually). Risk of falling significantly increases as number of risk factors increases. Falling is more frequent in ambulatory residents in long-term care and in acute care settings (Hendrich II Fall Risk Model), see http://consultgerirn.org/uploads/File/trythis/try_this_8.pdf.
  - Screen for fall risk in nursing home (Morse Fall Scale, see www.primaris.org/node/816).
- Assess for risk factors using a multidisciplinary approach, including PT and OT if problems with gait, balance, or lower extremity strength identified.
- Complete environmental assessment, including home safety, and mitigate identified hazards.
- Diagnose and treat underlying cause.
- Begin fall prevention program targeting interventions for risk factors (see **Table 54**).
- Preventive home visits (n = 3) that included risk assessment, home counseling, and booster showed a 37% reduction in the rate of falls in RCT with functionally impaired patients aged 80 and older, although cost-effectiveness is a concern. (Source: Luck T et al. *Clin Interv Aging* 2013;8:697–702.)

Table 54. Preventing Falls: Selected Risk Factors and Suggested Interventions

Factors	Suggested Interventions (Outcome Reduction*)
General Risk	Offer: exercise program to include combination of aerobic, resistance (strength) training, gait, and balance training • medical assessment before starting • tailor to individual capabilities • initiate with caution in those with limited mobility not accustomed to physical activity • prescribed by qualified healthcare provider • regular review and progression
	($\downarrow$ risk 13% [USPSTF];
	$\downarrow$ risk 15%; $\downarrow$ rate 29% [Cochrane];
	Tai Chi: $\downarrow$ risk 29%, $\downarrow$ rate 22% [Cochrane]
	Education and information, CBT intervention to decrease fear of falling and activity avoidance (limited evidence [Cochrane])
	Recommend daily supplementation of vitamin D (at least 800 IU) to achieve 25-hydroxy level >30 (see Osteoporosis, p 222).
	($\downarrow$ risk 17% [Cochrane])
Medication-related Factors	
Use of benzodiazepines, sedative-hypnotics, antidepressants, or antipsychotics	Consider agents with less risk of falls
	Avoid if hx of falls or fracture.[BC]
	Taper and D/C medications, as possible
	Address sleep problems with nonpharmacologic interventions (see p 307)
	Educate regarding appropriate use of medications and monitoring for AEs
Recent change in dosage or number of prescription medications *or* use of ≥4 prescription medications *or* use of other medications associated with fall risk	Review medication profile and reduce number and dosage of all medications, as possible
	(Withdrawal of antipsychotics; no $\downarrow$ risk; $\downarrow$ rate 66% [Cochrane])
	Monitor response to medications and to dosage changes
Mobility-related Factors	
Environmental hazards (eg, improper bed height, cluttered walking surfaces, lack of railings, poor lighting)	Improve lighting, especially at night
	Remove floor barriers (eg, loose carpeting)
	Replace existing furniture with safer furniture (eg, correct height, more stable)
	Install support structures, especially in bathroom (eg, railings, grab bars, elevated toilet seats)
	Use nonslip bathmats
	($\downarrow$ risk 12%; $\downarrow$ rate 19%; more effective delivered by OT [Cochrane])

(cont.)

Table 54. Preventing Falls: Selected Risk Factors and Suggested Interventions (cont.)	
Factors	**Suggested Interventions (Outcome Reduction*)**
Impaired gait, balance, or transfer skills	Refer to PT for comprehensive evaluation and rehabilitation
	Refer to PT or OT for gait training, transfer skills, use of assistive devices, balancing, strengthening and resistance training, and evaluation for appropriate footwear
Impaired leg or arm strength or range of motion, or proprioception	Refer to PT or OT
Medical Factors	
Parkinson disease, osteoarthritis, depressive symptoms, impaired cognition, carotid sinus hypersensitivity, other conditions associated with increased falls	Optimize medical tx
	Monitor for disease progression and impact on mobility and impairments
	Determine need for assistive devices
	Use bedside commode if frequent nighttime urination
	Cardiac pacing in patients with carotid sinus hypersensitivity who experience falls due to syncope
	($\downarrow$ rate 27%, but not risk [Cochrane])
Postural hypotension: drop in SBP $\geq$20 mmHg (or $\geq$20%) with or without symptoms, within 3 min of rising from lying to standing	See orthostatic postural hypotension, p 65
Visual (see Eye Disorders, p 104)	Cataract extraction (first eye cataract removal, rate $\downarrow$ 34%, but not second eye)
	Avoid wearing multifocal lenses while walking, particularly up stairs

*risk of falls = # people falling; rate of falling = # falls per person
Sources: Available evidence on rate of falling and risk for falling from Gillespie LD, et al. *Cochrane Database Syst Rev.* 2012 Sep 12;9:CD007146; Moyer VA, USPSTF. *Ann Intern Med.* 2012;157(3):197–204.

GASTROINTESTINAL DISEASES

DYSPHAGIA
See also p 247.

Types/Presentation/Patient Complaints

Table 55. Dysphagia Complaints

Classification	Presentation and Signs	Common Causes
Oral	Inability to move food or medication from mouth to pharynx. Food deposits in cheeks	Dementia
Pharyngeal	Impaired involuntary food transport pharynx to esphogus with airway protection. Coughing, choking, or nasal regurgitation	Stroke, Parkinson disease, CNS tumor, ALS, local strictures
Esophageal	Sensation that food is stuck in the throat	Impaired esophageal motility, obstruction, medication

Evaluation
- Physical examination
  - Oral cavity, head, neck, and supraclavicular region
  - All cranial nerves with emphasis on nerves V, VII, IX, X, XI, XII
- Review medications for those that can decrease saliva production (eg, anticholinergics)
- Referral to speech-language pathologists
- Diagnostic tests (as indicated)
  - Modified barium swallow or videofluoroscopy to assess swallowing mechanism; may document aspiration
  - Upper endoscopy
  - Fiberoptic nasopharyngeal laryngoscopy provides detailed evaluation of lesions in oropharynx, hypopharynx, larynx, and proximal esophagus; also visualizes pooled secretions or food
  - Esophageal manometry often used in combination with barium radiography; more useful for assessment of esophageal dysphagia

Treatment
- Identify and treat underlying cause (eg, endoscopic dilation, cricopharyngeal myotomy, botulinum toxin injection in cricopharyngeal muscle)
- Dietary modifications based on recommendation of speech pathologist or dietitian
- Swallowing rehabilitation, eg, multiple swallows, tilt head back and place bolus on strong side, or chin tuck
- Avoid rushed or forced feeding
- Sit upright at 90 degrees
- Elevate head of the bed at least 30 degrees
- Review medications and administration for unsafe practices, eg, crushing enteric-coated or ER formulations

• Symptomatic presbyesophagus responds to esophageal dilatation

Food Consistencies
• Pureed: thick, homogenous textures; pudding-like
• Ground/minced: easily chewed without coarse texture; excludes most raw foods except mashed bananas
• Soft or easy to chew: soft foods prepared without a blender; tender meats cut to ≤1-cm pieces; excludes nuts, tough skins, and raw, crispy, or stringy foods
• Modified general: soft textures that do not require grinding or chopping

Fluid Consistencies and Thickening Agents
• Thin: regular fluids
• Nectar-like: thin enough to be sipped through a straw or from a cup, but still spillable (eg, eggnog, buttermilk); 2–3 tsp of thickening powder to ½ cup (4 fl oz) of liquid
• Honey-like: thick enough to be eaten with a spoon, too thick for a straw, not able to independently hold its shape (eg, yogurt, tomato sauce, honey); 3–5 tsp of thickening powder to ½ cup (4 fl oz) of liquid
• Spoon-thick: pudding-like, must be eaten with a spoon (eg, thick milk pudding, thickened applesauce); 5–6 tsp of thickening powder to ½ cup (4 fl oz) of liquid
• Thickening agents are starch- or gum-based. Liquids thickened with modified starch continue to thicken or over-thicken over time. The thicker the product, the less consumed and the greater risk for dehydration.

GASTROESOPHAGEAL REFLUX DISEASE (GERD)

Evaluation and Assessment
Empiric tx is appropriate when hx is typical for uncomplicated GERD.
• Endoscopy (if symptoms are chronic or persist despite initial management, atypical presentation)
• Ambulatory pH testing

Risk Factors
• Obesity
• Hiatal hernia
• Use of estrogen, nitroglycerin, tobacco

Symptoms Suggesting Complicated GERD and Need for Evaluation
• Dysphagia
• Bleeding
• Weight loss
• Anemia
• Choking, cough, shortness of breath, hoarseness
• Chest pain
• Pain with swallowing
• Vomiting

Management

- Acid suppression with a PPI or H$_2$ antagonist (see **Table 56**)
- Antacids
- Avoid alcohol and fatty foods
- Avoid lying down for 3 h after eating
- Avoid tight-fitting clothes
- Change diet (avoid pepper, spearmint, chocolate, spicy or acidic foods, carbonated beverages)
- Drink 6–8 oz water with all medications

- Chew gum or use oral lozenges to stimulate salivation, which neutralizes gastric acid
- Elevate head of the bed (6–8 in)
- Lose weight (if overweight)
- Stop drugs that may promote reflux or can induce esophagitis
- Stop smoking
- Consider surgery (not recommended for PPI nonresponders)

Treatment with PPIs

- Initial tx: 8 wk with once-a-day PPI with morning meal

- Maintenance tx if symptoms remain after stopping or if complicated by erosive esophagitis or Barrett esophagus

Table 56. Pharmacologic Management of GERD[aCW]

Medication	Initial Oral Dosage	Formulations (Metabolism, Excretion)
PPIs[b]		
Dexlansoprazole *(Dexilant)*	30 mg/d × 4 wk	C: ER 30, 60 (L)
✔ Esomeprazole *(Nexium)*	20 mg/d × 4 wk	C: ER 20, 40 (L)
✔ Lansoprazole▲* *(Prevacid)*	15 mg/d × 8 wk	C: ER 15, 30; gran for susp: 15, 30/pk (L)
✔ Omeprazole▲* *(Prilosec)*	20 mg/d × 4–8 wk	C: ER 10, 20,[c] 40; T: enteric-coated 20 (L)
✔ Pantoprazole *(Protonix)*	40 mg/d × 8 wk	T: enteric-coated 20, 40; inj (L)
✔ Rabeprazole *(AcipHex)*	20 mg/d × 4–8 wk; 20 mg/d maintenance, if needed	T: ER enteric-coated 20 (L)
H$_2$ Antagonists (for less severe GERD) (Avoid.[BC])		
Cimetidine▲*d *(Tagamet HB 200)*	400 or 800 mg q12h	S: 200 mg/20 mL, 300 mg/5 mL with alcohol 2.8%; T: 100, 200,[c] 300, 400, 800; inj (K, L)
✔ Famotidine▲* *(Pepcid)*	20 mg q12h × 6 wk	S: oral sus 40 mg/5 mL; T: film-coated 10,[c] 20, 40; ODT 20, 40; C (gel): 10[c]; ChT: 10[c]; inj (K)
✔ Nizatidine▲ *(Axid)*	150 mg q12h	C: 150, 300; T: 75 (K)
Ranitidine▲* *(Zantac)*	150 mg q12h	Pk: gran, effervescent (EFFERdose) 150 mg; S: syr 15 mg/mL; T: 75,[c] 150, 300; T: effervescent (EFFERdose) 150; inj (K, F)

(cont.)

Table 56. Pharmacologic Management of GERD[a][CW] (cont.)

Medication	Initial Oral Dosage	Formulations (Metabolism, Excretion)
Prokinetic Agents[g]		
✔ Domperidone[e]	10 mg 15–30 min ac and hs	T: 10 mg (L)
Metoclopramide[▲][f] *(Reglan)*	5 mg q6h, ac, and hs	S: syr, sugar-free 5 mg/5 mL, conc 10 mg/mL; T: 5, 10; inj (K, F)

✔ = preferred for treating older adults

* Available OTC

[CW] Use lowest dose needed to achieve symptom control

[a] PPIs more effective than H_2 antagonists for tx and maintenance

[b] Associated with osteopenia/osteoporosis; can inhibit CYP2C19 and -3A4; prolonged exposure may increase risk of fractures, community-acquired pneumonia, *Clostridium difficile* diarrhea, hypomagnesemia; reduce vitamins C and B_{12} concentrations, and gastric atrophy. Monitor magnesium if taken long term or with digoxin.

[c] OTC strength

[d] Inhibits CYP1A2, -2D6, -3A4

[e] Available in the United States only through an Investigational New Drug application for compassionate use in patients refractory to other tx (see www.fda.gov); domperidone is approved in Canada as a tx for upper GI motility disorders associated with gastritis and diabetic gastroparesis, and for prevention of GI symptoms associated with use of dopamine-agonist anti-Parkinson agents.

[f] Risk of EPS high in people >65 yr old.

[g] No role in absence of gastroparesis.

Source: Data from Katz PO, et al. *Am J Gastroenterol.* 2013;108:308–328.

PEPTIC ULCER DISEASE

Causes

Helicobacter pylori is the major cause. NSAIDs are the second most common cause.

Diagnosis of *H pylori*

- Endoscopy with biopsy
- Serology
- Urea breath test
- Fecal antigen test

Initial Treatment Options

- Empiric anti-ulcer tx for 6 wk
- Definitive diagnostic evaluation by endoscopy
- Noninvasive testing for *H pylori* and tx with antibiotics for those that test positive (see **Table 57** for regimens)
- Review patient's chronic medications for drug interactions before selecting regimen; many potential drug interactions and adverse drug events.

Table 57. Pharmacotherapeutic Management of *H pylori* Infection		
Regimen	**Duration**	**Comments**
Triple Therapy		Preferred if no previous macrolide exposure
PPI[a] q12h[b] *plus* Clarithromycin 500 mg q12h *plus* Amoxicillin 1000 mg q12h	10–14 d	Example: *PrevPac* (includes lansoprazole 30 mg)
PPI[a] q12h[b] *plus* Clarithromycin 500 mg q12h *plus* Metronidazole 500 q12h	10–14 d	Preferred if penicillin allergy or unable to tolerate bismuth quadruple tx
Second-line Triple Therapy		
PPI[a] q24h *plus* Amoxicillin 1 g *plus* Metronidazole 500 mg q12h	7–14 d	
Quadruple Therapy		
PPI[a] q12h[b] or H$_2$ antagonist *plus* Bismuth subsalicylate 525 mg q6h *plus* Metronidazole 250 mg q24h *plus* Tetracycline 500 mg q24h *(Helidac)*	10–14 d	
PPI[a] q12h[b] or H$_2$ antagonist *plus* Bismuth subcitrate 425 mg q24h *plus* Metronidazole 250 mg q24h *plus* Tetracycline 500 mg q24h *(Plyera)*	10–12 d	Consider if penicillin allergy or previous macrolide exposure, *or* as second-line if triple tx fails

[a] Associated with osteopenia/osteoporosis; can inhibit CYP2C19 and -3A4; prolonged exposure may increase risk of fractures, community-acquired pneumonia, hospital-acquired *Clostridium difficile* diarrhea; reduce vitamins C and B$_{12}$ concentrations

[b] Esomeprazole is dosed 40 mg q24h.

Source: Adapted from Chey WD, et al. *Am J Gastroenterol.* 2007;102(8):1808–1825.

Medications

Bismuth subsalicylate▲ *(Pepto-Bismol)* [T: 324; ChT: 262; S: sus 262 mg/15 mL, 525 mg/15 mL]

Antibiotics: (for complete information, see **Table 77**)

Amoxicillin▲ *(Amoxil)* [C: 250, 500; ChT: 125, 250; S: oral sus 125 mg/5 mL, 250 mg/5 mL]

Clarithromycin▲ *(Biaxin)* [T: film-coated 250, 500; S: oral sus 125 mg/5 mL, 250 mg/5 mL]

Metronidazole▲ *(Flagyl)* [T: 250, 500, 750; C: 375]

Tetracycline▲ *(Achromycin, Sumycin)* [T: 250, 500; S: oral sus 125 mg/5 mL]

PPIs: See **Table 56**.

STRESS-ULCER PREVENTION IN HOSPITALIZED OLDER ADULTS

Risk Factors (in order of prevalence in older adults)

- Hx of GI ulceration or bleed in past year
- Sepsis
- Multiple organ failure
- Hypotension
- Mechanical ventilation for >48 h
- Kidney failure
- Major trauma, shock, or head injury
- Glasgow Coma Scale <10

- Coagulopathy (platelets <50,000/µL, INR >1.5, or PTT >2 × control)
- Burns over >25% of body surface area
- Hepatic failure/partial hepatectomy
- Intracranial HTN
- Spinal cord injury
- Quadraplegia

Prophylaxis

- H_2 antagonists (see **Table 56**)
- PPIs (see **Table 56**)
- Sucralfate▲ (see **Table 56**)
- Antacids

- Enteral feedings
- D/C H_2 antagonists, PPIs, and other tx for stress-ulcer prevention before transfer or discharge from hospital

Key Points

- Prophylaxis has not been shown to reduce mortality.
- No one regimen has shown superior efficacy.
- Choice of regimen depends on access to and function of GI tract and presence of nasogastric suction.

IRRITABLE BOWEL SYNDROME (IBS)

Signs and Symptoms

Symptoms should be present ≥12 wk.

Consistent with IBS:

- Abdominal pain
- Bloating

- Constipation
- Diarrhea

Not Consistent with IBS:

- Weight loss
- First onset after age 50
- Nocturnal diarrhea
- Family hx of cancer or inflammatory bowel disease
- Rectal bleeding or obstruction
- Laboratory abnormalities
- Presence of fecal parasites

Diagnosis (of exclusion)

Exclude ischemia, diverticulosis, colon cancer, inflammatory bowel disease by physical examination and testing (colonoscopy, CT scan, or small-bowel series). Do not repeat CT unless major changes in clinical findings.[CW]

Treatment

- Reassurance; not life threatening; focus on relief of physical and emotional symptoms
- Dietary modification
  - Avoid foods that trigger symptoms or produce excess gas or bloating
  - Consider a trial of a lactose-free diet
- Behavioral interventions: hypnosis, biofeedback, psychotherapy have been shown to be more effective than placebo. Other interventions: increase physical activity, trials of gluten-free diet.
- Fiber supplements (see **Table 58**)
  - Synthetic: polycarbophil▲ (*FiberCon* [caplet: 625], others), methylcellulose▲ (*Citrucel, Fiber Ease* [C, sus, pwd])
  - Natural: psyllium▲ (*Metamucil* [C, T, wafer, pwd], others)
- Antispasmodics (short-term use only)
  - Dicyclomine (Avoid unless no other alternatives.[BC]) (*Bentyl* [C: 10▲; T: 20▲; syr: 10 mg/5 mL; inj]) 10–20 mg po q6h prn (L)
  - Hyoscyamine▲[BC] (*Anaspaz, Levsin, Levsin/SL,* others [T (sl): 0.125, 0.15; T ER, C: 0.375; inj: 125 sol]) 0.125–0.25 mg po/sl q6–8h prn (L, K)
- Antidiarrheals: may be helpful for diarrhea but not for global IBS symptoms, abdominal pain, or constipation
  - Loperamide▲ (*Imodium A-D* [C, T: 2; sol 1 mg/5 mL]) 4 mg × 1, then 2 mg after each loose bowel movement; max 16 mg/24 h
- Antidepressants
  - TCAs and SSRIs may be beneficial for patients with diarrhea or pain. See Depression, p 78, for dosing.
- Laxative for IBS constipation
  - Linaclotide (*Linzess* [C:145, 290 mcg]): 290 mcg q24h on empty stomach
- Serotonin agent
  - Alosetron (*Lotronex* [T: 0.5, 1 mg]): serotonin 3 antagonist; tx of women with severe diarrhea-predominant IBS who have not responded to conventional tx (restricted distribution in the US); 0.5 mg po q12h × 4 wk, increase to 1 mg q12h × 4 wk, stop if no response (K, L)

CONSTIPATION

Definition

Frequency of bowel movements <2–3 times/wk, straining at defecation, hard feces, or feeling of incomplete evacuation. Clinically, large amount of feces in rectum on digital examination and/or colonic fecal loading on abdominal radiograph.

Medications That Constipate

- Analgesics—opioids
- Antacids with aluminum or calcium
- Anticholinergic drugs
- Antidepressants, lithium
- Antihypertensives
- Antipsychotics
- Barium sulfate
- Bismuth
- Calcium channel blockers
- Diuretics
- Iron

Conditions That Constipate

- Colon tumor or mechanical obstruction
- Dehydration
- Depression
- DM
- Hypercalcemia
- Hypokalemia
- Hypothyroidism
- Immobility
- Low intake of fiber
- Panhypopituitarism
- Parkinson disease
- Spinal cord injury
- Stroke
- Uremia

Management of Chronic Constipation

Step 1: Stop all constipating medications, when possible.

Step 2: Increase dietary fiber to 6–25 g/d, increase fluid intake to ≥1500 mL/d, and increase physical activity; or add bulk laxative (see **Table 58**), provided fluid intake is ≥1500 mL/d. If fiber exacerbates symptoms or is not tolerated, or patient has limited mobility, go to Step 3.

Step 3: Add an osmotic (eg, 70% sorbitol sol, polyethylene glycol *[MiraLAX]*).

Step 4: Add stimulant laxative (eg, senna, bisacodyl), 2–3 times/wk. (Alternative: saline laxative, but avoid if CrCl <30 mL/min.)

Step 5: Use tap water enema or saline enema 2 times/wk.

Step 6: Use oil-retention enema for refractory constipation.

Table 58. Medications That May Relieve Constipation

Medication	Onset of Action	Starting Dosage	Site and Mechanism of Action
Bulk laxatives—not useful in managing opioid-induced constipation			
Methylcellulose▲ *(Citrucel)* *	12–24 h (up to 72 h)	2–4 caplets or 1 heaping tbsp with 8 oz water q8–24h	Small and large intestine; holds water in feces; mechanical distention
Psyllium▲ *(Metamucil)* *ᵃ	12–24 h (up to 72 h)	1–2 capsules, pks, or tsp with 8 oz water or juice q8–24h	Small and large intestine; holds water in feces; mechanical distention
Polycarbophil▲ *(FiberCon, others)*ᵃ	12–24 h (up to 72 h)	1250 mg q6–24h	Small and large intestine; holds water in feces; mechanical distention
Wheat dextrin *(Benefiber)* OTC	24–28 h		Small and large intestine; holds water in feces; mechanical distention
Chloride channel activator			
Lubiprostone *(Amitiza)*	24–28 h	24 mcg q12h with food C: 8, 24 mcg	Enhances chloride-ion intestinal fluid secretion; does not affect serum Na⁺ or K⁺ concentrations. For idiopathic chronic constipation.
Linaclotide *(Linzess)*		145 mcg q24h without food	

(cont.)

Table 58. Medications That May Relieve Constipation (cont.)

Medication	Onset of Action	Starting Dosage	Site and Mechanism of Action
Opioid antagonists			
Alvimopan *(Entereg)*	NA	Initial: 12 mg po 30 min to 5 h before surgery Maintenance: 12 mg po q12h the day after surgery × 7 d max	Hospital use only; for accelerating time to recovery after partial large- or small-bowel resection with primary anastomosis; contraindicated if >7 consecutive d of therapeutic opioids (L, K, F)
Methylnaltrexone *(Relistor)*	30–60 min	Weight-based dosing: <38 kg: 0.15 mg/kg 38 to <62 kg: 8 mg 62–114 kg: 12 mg >114 kg: 0.15 mg/kg (all SC q48hr); if CrCl <30 mL/min, decrease dosage 50%	Peripheral-acting opioid antagonist for the tx of opioid-induced constipation in palliative care patients who have not responded to conventional laxatives (L, K, F)
Osmotic laxatives			
Lactulose▲ *(Chronulac)*	24–48 h	15–30 mL q12–24h	Colon; osmotic effect
Polyethylene glycol▲ *(Miralax)* *	48–96 h	17 g pwd q24h (~1 tbsp) dissolved in 8 oz water	GI tract; osmotic effect
Sorbitol 70%▲*	24–48 h	15–30 mL q12–24h; max 150 mL/d	Colon; delivers osmotically active molecules to colon
Glycerin supp*	15–30 min		Colon; local irritation; hyperosmotic
Sodium, potassium, and magnesium sulfate *(Suprep* bowel prep kit)	24 h		Small and Large intestine; hyperosmotic
Saline laxatives			
Magnesium citrate▲ *(Citroma)* *	30 min–3 h	120–240 mL × 1; 10 oz q24h or 5 oz q12h followed by 8 oz water × ≤5 d	Small and large intestine; attracts, retains water in intestinal lumen; potential hypermagnesemia in patients with renal insufficiency
Magnesium hydroxide▲ *(Milk of Magnesia)* *	30 min–3 h	30 mL q12–24h 311-mg tab (130 mg magnesium); 400, 800 mg/5 mL sus	Osmotic effect and increased peristalsis in colon; potential hypermagnesemia in patients with renal insufficiency
Sodium phosphate/ biphosphate emollient enema▲ *(Fleet)* *	2–15 min	14.5-oz enema × 1, repeat prn	Colon; osmotic effect; potential hypermagnesemia in patients with renal insufficiency
Stimulant laxatives			
Bisacodyl tablet▲ *(Dulcolax)* *	6–10 h	5–15 mg × 1	Colon; increases peristalsis
Bisacodyl suppository▲ *(Dulcolax)* *	15 min–1 h	10 mg × 1	Colon; increases peristalsis
Senna▲ *(Senokot)* *	6–10 h	1–2 tabs or 1 tsp qhs	Colon; direct action on intestine; stimulates myenteric plexus; alters water and electrolyte secretion

(cont.)

Table 58. Medications That May Relieve Constipation (cont.)

Medication	Onset of Action	Starting Dosage	Site and Mechanism of Action
Surfactant laxative (fecal softener)			
Docusate▲ *(Colace)**	24–72 h	100 mg q12–24h	Small and large intestine; detergent activity; facilitates admixture of fat and water to soften feces (effectiveness questionable); does not increase frequency of bowel movements

* Available OTC

a Psyllium caplets and packets contain ≥3 g dietary fiber and 2–3 g soluble fiber each. A teaspoonful contains ~3.8 g dietary fiber and 3 g soluble fiber.

NAUSEA AND VOMITING

Causes

- CNS disorders (eg, motion sickness, intracranial lesions)
- Drugs (eg, chemotherapy, NSAIDs, opioid analgesics, antibiotics, digoxin)
- GI disorders (eg, mechanical obstruction; inflammation of stomach, intestine, or gallbladder; pseudo-obstruction; motility disorders; dyspepsia; gastroparesis)
- Infections (eg, viral or bacterial gastroenteritis, hepatitis, otitis, meningitis)
- Metabolic conditions (eg, uremia, acidosis, hyperparathyroidism, adrenal insufficiency)
- Psychiatric disorders

Evaluation

- If patient is not seriously ill or dehydrated, can probably wait 24–48 h to see if symptoms resolve spontaneously.
- If patient is seriously ill, dehydrated, or has other signs of acute illness, hospitalize for further evaluation.
- If symptoms persist, evaluate on the basis of the most likely causes.

Pharmacologic Management

- If analgesic drug is suspected, decrease dosage, consider adding antiemetic until tolerance develops, or change to a different analgesic drug.
- Drugs that are useful in the management of nausea and vomiting are listed in **Table 59**.

Table 59. Antiemetic Therapy

Class/Site of Action	Dosage (Metabolism)	Formulation
Dopamine antagonists/CTZ[a] vomiting center		
Haloperidol[▲b]	IM, po: 0.5–1 mg q6h (L, K)	See p 264.
Metoclopramide[▲b] *(Reglan)*	PONV: 5–10 mg IM near the end of surgery Chemotherapy (IV): 1–2 mg/kg 30 min before and q2–4h or q4–6h (K)	T: 5, 10 S: 10 mg/mL; syr (sugar-free): 5 mg/mL Inj: 5 mg/mL
Prochlorperazine[▲b] *(Compazine)*	IM, po: 5–10 mg q6–8 h, usual max 40 mg/d IV: 2.5–10 mg, max 10 mg/dose or 40 mg/d; may repeat q3–4h prn (L)	T: 5, 10, 25 mg C: 10, 15, 30 mg Syr: 5 mg/5 mL Inj: 5 mg/mL Sp: 2.5, 10, 25
Serotonin (5-HT$_3$) antagonists/CTZ, gut		
✔Ondansetron[▲] *(Zofran)*	PONV: 16 mg po 1 h before anesthesia IM, IV: 4 mg immediately before anesthesia; repeat if needed (L) Radiation tx: 8 mg po 1–2 h before, then 8 mg po q8h × 1–2 d	T: 4, 8, 24 mg ODT: 4, 8 mg S: 4 mg/5 mL Inj: 2 mg/mL
Granisetron *(Kytril)*	PONV: 1 mg IV before anesthesia or anesthesia reversal Chemotherapy: 2 mg/d po (L, K) Radiation tx: 2 mg po 1 h before	T: 1 mg S: 2 mg/10 mL Inj: 1 mg/mL Pch: 3.1 mg/24 h
Dolasetron *(Anzemet)*	PONV: 100 mg po 2 h before surgery; 12.5 mg IV 15 min before stopping anesthesia (L)	T: 50, 100 mg Inj: 20 mg/mL
Antimuscarinic/H$_1$ antagonist/vestibular apparatus		
Diphenhydrinate[▲cBC] *(Dramamine)* *	IM, IV, po: 50–100 mg q4–6h; max 400 mg/d (L)	T, ChT: 50 mg S: 12.5 mg/4 mL, 16.62 mg/5 mL Inj: 10 mg/mL
Meclizine[▲cBC] *(Antivert)* *	Motion sickness: 12.5–25 mg 1 h before travel, repeat dose q12–24h if needed Vertigo: 25–100 mg/d in divided doses (L)	T: 12.5, 25, 50 mg ChT: 25 mg C: 25, 30 mg
Scopolamine[cBC] *(Transderm Scop)*	Motion sickness: apply 1 pch behind ear ≥4 h before travel/exposure; change q3d (L)	Pch: 1.5 mg

✔ = preferred for treating older adults

Note: PONV = postoperative nausea and vomiting

* Available OTC

[a] Chemoreceptor trigger zone

[b] Avoid.[BC]

[c] Avoid unless no other alternatives.[BC]

Note: All have potential CNS toxicity. Metoclopramide associated with EPS and TD.

DIARRHEA

Causes
- Drugs (eg, antibiotics [see **Table 77** and below], laxatives, colchicine)
- Fecal impaction
- GI disorders (eg, IBS, malabsorption, inflammatory bowel disease)
- Infections (eg, viral, bacterial, parasitic)
- Lactose intolerance

Evaluation
- If patient is not seriously ill or dehydrated and there is no blood in the feces, can probably wait 48 h to see if symptoms resolve spontaneously.
- If patient is seriously ill, dehydrated, or has other signs of acute illness, hospitalize for further evaluation.
- If diarrhea persists, evaluate on the basis of the most likely causes.

Pharmacologic Management
Drugs that are useful in the management of diarrhea are listed in **Table 60**.

Table 60. Antidiarrheals		
Drug	**Dosage (Metabolism)**	**Formulations**
✔ Attapulgite *(Kaopectate)**	1200–1500 mg after each loose bowel movement or q2h; 15–30 mL up to 9 × /d, up to 9000 mg/24 h (not absorbed)	S: oral conc 600, 750 mg/15 mL; T: 750; ChT. 300, 600
✔ Bismuth subsalicylate▲* *(Pepto-Bismol)*	2 tabs or 30 mL q30–60min prn up to 8 doses/24 h (L, K)	S: 262 mg/15 mL, 525 mg/15 mL; T: 324; ChT: 262
Diphenoxylate with atropine▲ *(Lomotil)* [a]	15–20 mg/d of diphenoxylate in 3–4 divided doses; maintenance 5–15 mg/d in 2–3 divided doses (L)	S: oral, diphenoxylate hydrochloride 2.5 mg + atropine sulfate 0.025 mg/5 mL; T: diphenoxylate hydrochloride 2.5 mg + atropine sulfate 0.025 mg
✔ Loperamide▲ *(Imodium A-D)**	Initial: 4 mg followed by 2 mg after each loose bowel movement, up to 16 mg/d (L)	Caplet: 2; C: 2; T: 2; S: oral, 1 mg/5 mL

✔ = preferred for treating older adults
* Available OTC
[a] Anticholinergic, potential CNS toxicity

ANTIBIOTIC-ASSOCIATED DIARRHEA (AAD)
(Antibiotic-associated pseudomembranous colitis [AAPMC])

Definition
A specific form of *Clostridium difficile* pseudomembranous colitis

Risk Factors
- Almost any oral or parenteral antibiotic and several antineoplastic agents, including cyclophosphamide, doxorubicin, fluorouracil, methotrexate
- Advanced age
- Duration of hospitalization
- PPI

Prevention
The use of probiotic products to prevent primary infection remains controversial. Two systematic reviews and meta-analyses found that they significantly reduce the risk of AAD and *C difficile* diarrhea. Since their publication, the largest trial, conducted in elderly inpatients, found the combination lactobacilli and bifidobacteria did not reduce the risk of AAD or *C difficile* diarrhea. Probiotics should be used with caution by immunocompromised patients.

Presentation
- Abdominal pain, cramping
- Dehydration
- Diarrhea (can be bloody)
- Fecal leukocytes
- Fever (100–105°F)
- Hypoalbuminemia
- Hypovolemia
- Leukocytosis

Symptoms appear a few days after starting to 10 wk after discontinuing the offending agent.

Evaluation and Empiric Management
- D/C unnecessary antibiotics, and agents that can slow gastric motility such as opioids and antidiarrheal agents.
- Initiate empiric tx if severe or complicated *C difficile* suspected.
- Perform *C difficile* toxin test on 2 separate bowel movements. If suspicion remains after 2 negative tests, a third toxin test can be performed. Some laboratories perform *C difficile* A and B toxin DNA testing, which is highly sensitive; repeat testing is unnecessary unless symptoms or clinical situation change.
- Place patient in contact isolation and observe infection control procedures. Hand washing is crucial and must be done with soap and water to remove spores. Hand sanitizers do not kill or remove spores.
- Provide adequate fluid and electrolyte replacement.
- Consider empiric metronidazole (see **Table 61** for dosing).

Diagnosis
- Only stools from patients with diarrhea should be tested for *C difficile*
- Isolation of *C difficile* or its toxin from symptomatic patient
- Nucleic acid amplification tests (NAAT) for toxin genes is superior to toxin A + B enzymeimmunoassays
- Negative fecal examinations are needed to exclude diagnosis
- Repeated testing is discouraged
- Testing for a cure should not be performed

Table 61. Treatment of Suspected or Confirmed *Clostridium difficile* Infection

Clinical Definition	Supportive Clinical Data	Treatment
Toxin negative on 2 specimens		D/C contact isolation D/C metronidazole/vancomycin Begin antidiarrheal agent Evaluate other causes
Initial episode, mild or moderate	Leukocytosis (WBC ≤15,000 cells/μL), serum Cr <1.5 times premorbid level	Metronidazole 500 mg po q8h × 10–14 d Fidaxomicin* 200 mg po q12h × 10 d
Initial episode, severe	Leukocytosis (WBC >15,000 cells/μL), which signifies colonic inflammation; serum Cr ≥1.5 times premorbid level, which signifies dehydration	Vancomycin 125 mg po q6h × 10–14 d Oral vancomycin is available as a capsule (125, 250) or by reconstituting the powder for injection for oral administration.
Initial episode, severe, complicated	Hypotension or shock, ileus, megacolon in the absence of abdominal distention	Vancomycin 500 mg po or nasogastric tube q6h plus metronidazole IV 500 mg q8h; if complete ileus or toxic megacolon, add vancomycin 500 mg/500 mL pr is an option.
First recurrence		Same as initial episode, unless severe, then use vancomycin
Second recurrence		Vancomycin in a tapered and/or pulsed regimen

Source: Adapted from Cohen SH, et al. *Infect Control Hosp Epidemiol* 2010;31(5):431–455.
*Fidaxomicin *(Dificid)* [T: 200 mg; 92% F, minimal systemic absorption]. Clinical trials did not include patients with life-threatening or fulminant *C difficile* infection, toxic megacolon, or with >1 *C difficile* infection in the previous 3 mo. Fidaxomicin is not in the SHEA/IDSA guideline. Cure rates between vancomycin and fidaxomicin do not differ. With both tx, age (per decade) is associated with a decreased cure rate, decrease in sustained response, and increased recurrence rate.

• Oral vancomycin is an option for patients allergic to or who cannot tolerate metronidazole.
• Fecal transplant is a promising alternative tx to antibiotics. It is not universally available, nor has its place in tx been determined.

HEMORRHOIDS
Contributing Factors
• Constipation
• Prolonged straining
• Exercise
• Gravity
• Low-fiber diet
• Pregnancy
• Increased intra-abdominal pressure
• Irregular bowel habits
• Age

Classification
• External: distal to the dentate line and painful if thrombotic, itchy

- Internal: proximal to the dentate line without sensitivity to pain, touch, or temperature; mucous discharge; feeling of incomplete evacuation
  - *Grade*
    - First-degree: no prolapse, may bleed after defecation, only seen via anoscope
    - Second-degree: prolapse outside anal canal with defecation and retract spontaneously
    - Third-degree: prolapse and require manual reduction
    - Fourth-degree: prolapsed, nonreducible

Treatment
Diet and Lifestyle Changes
- High-fiber diet (20–35 g/d) or psyllium, methylcellulose, or calcium polycarbophil
- Increased fluid intake
- Avoid prolonged time on commode
Topical Treatments
- Sitz baths (40°C)
- Protectants plus vasoconstrictor, eg, light mineral oil, petrolatum, shark liver oil *plus* phenylephrine *(Preparation H*, Anucort*, Cortifoam*)*, or with hydrocortisone (oint, crm, gel, foam, supp, wipes); apply/insert up to 4 times/d.
Procedures
- Office-based
  - Rubber band ligation: for first-, second-, or third-degree internal hemorrhoids
    - Contraindicated in patients who are anticoagulated
    - D/C antiplatelet drugs (including ASA) for 5–7 d before and after banding
  - Sclerotherapy
  - Bipolar diathermy
  - Infrared photocoagulation
- Surgical
  - Open (Milligan-Morgan) hemorrhoidectomy
  - Closed (Ferguson) hemorrhoidectomy
  - Doppler-guided transanal hemorrhoidal ligation
  - Circular stapled hemorrhoidopexy (for prolapsed hemorrhoids)
- Postoperative complications
  - Bleeding
  - Urinary retention
  - Wound infection

DRUG-INDUCED LIVER DISEASE
Risk Factors
- Advanced age
- Sex (drug-specific)
- Alcohol use
- Genetic predisposition

Diagnosis: Clinical features consistent with acute hepatitis or cholestatic liver disease

Classification

- Intrinsic hepatotoxicity (predictable): dose-related, short-term exposure (eg, APAP overdose)
- Idiosyncratic hepatotoxicity (unpredictable):
  - Allergic (hypersensitivity): clinical features—fever, rash, eosinophilia, recurrence with rechallenge; usual timeframe 1–5 wk
  - Nonallergic (idiosyncratic) clinical features—allergic features absent; usual timeframe weeks to months

Table 62. Presentation and Management of Drug-induced Liver Disease

Condition	Liver Enzymes/Presentation	Management and Prognosis
Acute Hepatitis		
Hepatocellular necrosis (APAP, halothane, labetalol, methyldopa, herbals, hydralazine, INH, NSAIDs)	ALT >2 × upper limit of normal or ALT:alk phos ratio >5 Asymptomatic to jaundice, fatigue, anorexia, nausea, coagulopathy, ascites	Withdrawal of drug, supportive care; N-acetylcysteine for APAP toxicity; mortality rate 10–50% if jaundice present
Cholestatic (amoxicillin ± clavulanate, erythromycin, dicloxacillin, methyldopa, herbals, hydralazine, sulindac, naproxen)	ALT >2 × upper limit of normal or ALT:alk phos ratio <2; increased GGT Jaundice, pruritus, pale feces, dark urine, abdominal pain, fever, chills	Withdrawal of drug, resolves in a few weeks
Mixed hepatocellular-cholestatic (captopril, herbals, sulindac, nabumetone, naproxen, carbamazepine, phenytoin)	Jaundice, resembles biliary obstruction without pain and fever	Withdrawal of drug, resolves in few weeks
Acute hyperbilirubinemia (rifampin, anabolic steroids)	Increased indirect bilirubin, increased direct bilirubin	
Chronic Hepatitis		
(nitrofurantoin, herbals)	Increased ALT, PT; prolonged drug exposure, women more likely to be affected than men; increased serum globulin concentration; autoantibodies (ANA); enlarged liver, splenomegaly, ascites, cirrhosis, fibrosis, jaundice, anorexia, fatigue	Withdrawal of drug, resolves in a few weeks

Note: alk phos = alkaline phosphatase; GGT = gamma glutamyl transferase

DEFINITION

The most common sensory impairment in old age; presbycusis affects 40% of the population older than 75 yrs. To quantify hearing ability, the necessary intensity (decibel = dB) and frequency (Hertz) of the perceived pure-tone signal must be described.

Importance: Hearing impairment is strongly correlated with depression, decreased quality of life, poorer memory and executive function, and incident dementia.

EVALUATION

Screening and Evaluation

- Note problems during conversation.
- Ask the question: Do you feel you have hearing loss? A "yes" response should prompt referral to audiology.
- Test with handheld audioscope or whisper test. Refer patients who screen positive for audiologic evaluation.

- Whisper test: stand behind patient at arm's length from ear, cover untested ear, fully exhale, whisper a combination of 3 numbers and letters (eg, 6-K-2) and ask patient to repeat the set; if patient unable to repeat all 3, whisper a second set. Inability to repeat at least 3 of 6 is positive for impairment.

Audiometry

- Documents the dB loss across frequencies
- Determines the pattern of loss (see Classification, below)

- Determines if loss is unilateral or bilateral and assesses speech discrimination.

CLASSIFICATION

See **Table 63**. Mixed hearing disorders are quite common, particularly involving features of age-related presbycusis and conductive loss. Central auditory processing disorders become clinically important when superimposed on other ear pathology.

Table 63. Classification of Hearing Disorders			
	Sensorineural Hearing Loss	**Conductive Hearing Loss**	**Central Auditory Processing Disorder**
Pathologic process	Cochlear or retrocochlear (cranial nerve VIII) pathology	Impaired transmission to inner ear from external or middle ear pathology	CNS change interfering with ability to discriminate speech, particularly when background noise is present
Weber test findings	Lateralizes away from impaired ear	Lateralizes toward impaired ear	Normal
Rinne test findings	Normal	Abnormal in impaired ear	Normal
Audiogram/ Audiometry findings	Air and bone conduction thresholds equal	Air conduction thresholds greater than bone conduction thresholds	Normal for pure tone audiometry; impaired for speech discrimination

(cont.)

Table 63. Classification of Hearing Disorders (cont.)

	Sensorineural Hearing Loss	Conductive Hearing Loss	Central Auditory Processing Disorder
Common causes	Age-related presbycusis (high frequency loss, problems with speech discrimination) most common	Cerumen impaction	Dementia
		Otosclerosis	Stroke
	Excessive noise exposure	RA	Presbycusis
	Acoustic neuroma	Paget disease	Possibly normal aging
	Ménière disease (both high- and low-frequency loss)		
	Ototoxic drugs		

MANAGEMENT

Remove Ear Wax

Ear wax causes conductive loss and further reduces hearing. Soft wax can be flushed with a syringe, removed with a cerumen scoop, or suctioned. Dry wax should be softened before removal by doing the following:

Fill ear canal with 5–10 gtt water and cover with cotton q12h × ≥4 d. Liquid must stay in contact with ear for ≥15 min. Hearing may worsen as cerumen expands. Water is as effective as commercial preparations (eg, *Debrox, Cerumenex, Colace*). Use of any of the commercial preparations >4 d may cause ear irritation.

Table 64. Rehabilitation of Hearing Loss, by Level of Loss

Level of Loss (dB)	Difficulty Understanding	Need for Hearing Technology
16–25 (slight)	None	None
26–40 (mild)	Normal speech	Hearing aid or MEI in specific situations
41–55 (moderate)	Loud speech	Hearing aid or MEI in many situations
56–69 (moderately severe)	Anything but amplified speech	Hearing aid, MEI, or EAS for all communication
70–90 (severe)	Even amplified speech	EAS or cochlear implant
≥91 (profound)	Even amplified speech	Cochlear implant and/or speech reading, aural rehabilitation, sign language

Note: MEI = middle ear implant; EAS = electric acoustic stimulation

Hearing Technology

Hearing Aids: Digital devices enhance select frequencies for each ear. Amplification in both ears (binaural) provides best speech understanding; unilateral aid may be appropriate if hearing loss is asymmetrical, if hearing-aid care is challenging, or if cost is a factor. Features that enhance sound and speech quality include directional microphones, open-fit hearing aids, ear-to-ear wireless coordination, and in the canal extended-wear aids *(Lyric)*.

Cochlear Implants: Bypass the middle ear, directly innervate auditory nerve. Results after age 65 comparable to those in younger people. Failure rate <1%, but patient selection important. Selection criteria:

- Severe to profound bilateral sensorineural hearing loss
- <40% correct on sentence recognition test in best aided ear

- Benefit from aids less than that expected from implant
- No external or middle ear pathology
- No medical contraindication to general anesthesia
- No contraindication to surgical placement of device
- Family support, motivation, appropriate expectations

Middle Ear Implants: A fully implantable ossicular stimulator; all components (including battery) are implanted under the skin; for adults who cannot wear hearing aids for medical (eg, collapsed ear canal, inability to handle device) or personal (ie, cosmetic) reasons.

Electric Acoustic Stimulation: Use of a cochlear implant and hearing aid in the same ear; for patients who have ≥60 dB hearing loss at frequencies >1000 Hz, even though they may have mild to moderate hearing loss at frequencies ≤1000 Hz. The hearing aid amplifies residual hearing at low frequencies, while the cochlear implant provides electric stimulation to the high frequencies. Users still perform well when using the implant without the hearing aid.

Assistive Devices: Microphone placed close to sound source transmits to headphones or earpiece. Transmission is by wire or wireless (FM or infrared); these systems increase signal-to-noise ratio, which is useful for people with central auditory processing disorder. Personal pocket devices (eg, *Pocket Talker*) are relatively inexpensive; every care setting should have one. Also consider recommending flashing fire alarms, amplified telephones, closed captioning.

Telephone Device for the Deaf (TDD): Receiver is a keyboard that allows the hearing-impaired person to respond.

Tips for Communication with Hearing-impaired People
- Ask the person how best to communicate
- Stand 2–3 ft away
- Have the person's attention
- Have the person seated in front of a wall, which helps reflect sound
- Speak toward the better ear
- Use lower-pitched voice
- Speak slowly and distinctly; don't shout
- Rephrase rather than repeat
- Pause at the end of phrases or ideas
- Ask the person to repeat what was heard

Tips for Approaches to Patients Resistant to Acquiring/Using Hearing Aids
Set appropriate expectations, inform the patient, support and assist the patient during the period of adjustment.
- Hearing aids do not produce normal hearing; they are aids to hearing
- Hearing aids usually need adjustments over months; expect to see the audiologist often
- Report problems: hearing or understanding speech in specific situations (eg, noisy environments); difficulty operating the hearing aid; aid-associated discomfort
- Inquire how the patient feels about hearing aid appearance
- Recommend group audiologic visits of newly fitted patients, if available
- Include caregivers in the process of fitting hearing aids
- Regularly examine ears for cerumen or other pathology

Tips for Treating Hearing Loss in Older Adults with Frailty or Multiple Morbidities
- Include hearing evaluation in team-based geriatric assessment
- Assess, and when possible, improve visual function
- Assess and treat physical, cognitive, and affective disorders
- For patients with hearing aids and problems with manual dexterity, consider easier-to-use hearing aid models (eg, behind-the-ear or in-the-ear types)

- For hearing-impaired patients with advanced cognitive deficits
  - Prevent loss of hearing aid by attaching a metal loop to its body and tying a thin nylon line through the loop, fasten the other end of the line to the patient's clothing
  - Educate caregivers on proper use of hearing aids
  - Consider use of personal amplifier ("pocket-talker") or other assistive listening device if patient is unable to use a hearing aid
- Assess for hearing deficits and correct them in patients presenting with geriatric syndromes

TINNITUS

Definition
The perception of sound in the absence of external acoustic stimulation; may be ringing, crackling, or whistling; may be continuous or intermittent

Objective Tinnitus
Noise heard by both patient and examiner (rare); usually due to abnormal blood flow in or around ear (normal anatomic variants or a pathologic condition)

Subjective Tinnitus
- Cannot be heard externally by others (common)
- Normal tinnitus lasts <5 min, <once/wk
- Pathologic tinnitus lasts >5 min, >weekly (usually in people with hearing loss)

Evaluation
- Auscultate the head and neck near ear orbits, mastoids for objective tinnitus.
  - If pulsatile, obtain CT/MRA for vascular cause.
  - If continuous, obtain MRI looking for patulous Eustachian tube; other causes include palatal myoclonus, stapedial muscle spasm.
  - Refer to otolaryngology.
- Examine ear canals for cerumen, otitis externa or interna; treat and reassess.
- Assess hearing (as above); unilateral hearing loss and tinnitus suggest acoustic neuroma; obtain MRI.
- Audiometry (see p 137)
- Check medication list for drugs associated with tinnitus, eg, NSAIDs, ASA, antibiotics (especially erythromycin), loop diuretics (especially furosemide), chemotherapy, quinine.

Treatment
- Objective tinnitus: refer to otolaryngology.
- Subjective tinnitus without distress:
  - Normal tinnitus: reassure patient.
  - Pathologic tinnitus: educate patient, encourage amplification for those with hearing impairment.
- Subjective tinnitus with distress: warrants referral to otolaryngology.
  - Severe complaints about tinnitus are often a sign of depression; treat if indicated (see p 78).
  - Tx may include tinnitus control instruments and desensitization tx.
- Tinnitus retraining tx (a form of desensitization, combined with counseling) may be the most effective approach (www.tinnitus-pjj.com).

ANEMIA
Evaluation

- Hematopoietic reserve capacity declines with age, eg, slower return of Hb to normal after phlebotomy.
- Evaluate people >65 yr old when Hb <13.
- Evaluate if Hb falls >1 g/dL in 1 yr.
- Physical examination and laboratory tests for kidney or liver disease.
- Evaluate GI and GU source if iron deficient.
- Check WBC and peripheral blood smear; pursue suspected causes as appropriate.
- Combined deficiencies are common in older adults; reasonable to check B_{12}, folate, and iron in all cases. MCV is not reliable in combined deficiency states.
- Check reticulocyte count and reticulocyte index.
  - Reticulocyte count or index high: adequate response, suspect blood loss or RBC destruction
  - Reticulocyte count or index normal or low: evaluate for possible B_{12} or folate deficiency (see **Figure 6**), and possible iron deficiency (see **Figure 7**)

Common Anemias of Later Life: Diagnosis and Treatment
Iron deficiency anemia: (see **Figure 7**)

- Serum iron and iron saturation are both low, transferrin is high, and ferritin ≤15
- Begin tx with oral iron using the steps outlined in **Table 65**.
- If oral iron replacement is inadequate or not tolerated, parenteral replacement is used (see **Table 66**).

Anemia of inflammation (also known as anemia of chronic inflammation or chronic disease):

- Most common causes in older adults:
  - Acute and chronic infection
  - Chronic inflammation
  - Malignancy
  - Protein calorie malnutrition
  - Unidentified chronic disease
- Laboratory tests: usually low iron, low or normal TIBC, ferritin >100 ng/mL
- Type determines treatability:
  - "Rheumatoid arthritis type" responds to erythropoietin at usual dosages (see **Table 67**).
  - "Cancer type" may respond to erythropoietin at high dosages (see **Table 67**).
- Restoring Hb to 10–11 g/dL improves quality of life, function, and possibly survival.

Combined iron deficiency and anemia of inflammation:

- Usual laboratory values (iron, TIBC, ferritin) less reliable in presence of inflammatory conditions (see **Figure 7**).
- Anemia often more severe than in chronic inflammation alone. Iron, transferrin, and saturation reduced. If ferritin ≤45, iron deficiency is confirmed. If 45–99, iron deficiency is possible; either treat presumed iron deficiency and evaluate response by reticulocyte count at 2 wks or check soluble transferrin receptor (sTfR). If sTfR/log ferritin >1.5, iron deficiency is confirmed.

Figure 6. Evaluation of Hypoproliferative Anemia Due to Possible B_{12} or Folate Deficiency

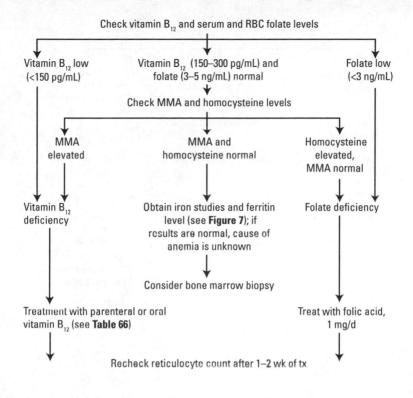

Source: Balducci L. *J Amer Geriatr Soc* 2003; 51(3 Suppl):S2–9. Reprinted with permission.

Figure 7. Evaluation of Hypoproliferative Anemia Due to Possible Iron Deficiency

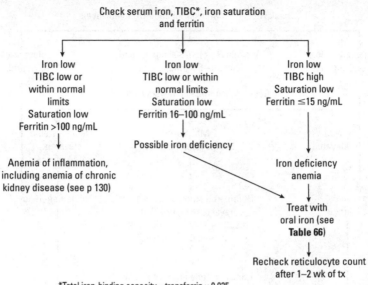

Check serum iron, TIBC*, iron saturation and ferritin

Iron low
TIBC low or within normal limits
Saturation low
Ferritin >100 ng/mL

↓

Anemia of inflammation, including anemia of chronic kidney disease (see p 130)

Iron low
TIBC low or within normal limits
Saturation low
Ferritin 16–100 ng/mL

↓

Possible iron deficiency

Iron low
TIBC high
Saturation low
Ferritin ≤15 ng/mL

↓

Iron deficiency anemia

↓

Treat with oral iron (see **Table 66**)

↓

Recheck reticulocyte count after 1–2 wk of tx

*Total iron-binding capacity = transferrin × 0.025

Table 65. Steps in Oral Iron Replacement

		Hb (g/dL)	Elemental iron total replacement dose (mg)
		>11	5,000
Step 1: Estimate iron replacement		9–11	10,000
dose based on Hb		<9	15,000

	Preparation*	Number of tables to achieve 5000-mg elemental iron replacement
Step 2: Select an oral iron preparation (only 10% of oral iron is absorbed)	Ferrous sulfate (324-mg tab, 65 mg elemental iron)	75
	Elixir 2.7 mg/15 mL Ferrous gluconate (300-mg tab, 36 mg elemental iron)	140
	Ferrous fumarate (100-mg tab, 33 mg elemental iron)	150
	Iron polysaccharide (150-mg tab, 150 mg elemental iron)	33
Step 3: Decide on dosing frequency	Many patients cannot tolerate more than a single tablet daily. Iron may be dosed up to 3 ×/d if tolerated. Iron is best absorbed on an empty stomach. Assess tolerance after 1 wk (phone call); if not tolerating, adjust dose, interval, or preparation.	
Step 4: Recheck Hb and ferritin after each 5000-mg cycles	Give additional 5000-mg cycles prn.	

*Tolerance to GI side effects improves, however cost increases going down the list of preparations.
Note: 1 unit packed RBCs replaces 500 mg iron, or approximately the same as is absorbed from a 5000-mg cycle of oral iron. Reticulocytosis should occur in 7–10 d. Lack of correction with replacement suggests nonadherence, malabsorption, or ongoing blood loss. H_2-blockers, antacids, and PPIs reduce absorption, and some patients will need parenteral replacement (see **Table 66**). Enterically coated preparations are less well absorbed.

Anemia of chronic kidney disease:

- Caused by decreased erythropoietin production; check erythropoietin level, iron studies, B_{12}, and folate.
- Correct all correctable causes of anemia (iron deficiency, inflammation) before using erythropoiesis-stimulating agents (ESAs). Keep transferrin saturation 20–50% and ferritin 100–500 ng/mL. Oral iron absorption is poor in CKD; parenteral replacement often needed.
- Restoring Hb levels with ESAs decreases transfusions and fatigue but doubles stroke risk in people with diabetes, CKD, and anemia.
- Guidelines (www.kdigo.org), recommend individualized tx.
  - Use ESAs with caution (if at all) in patients with malignancy, hx of stroke, or hx of malignancy.
  - For most patients, consider ESA and iron replacement when Hb is 9–10 g/dL with the goal of avoiding Hb <9 and the need for transfusion.
  - Some patients will have improved quality of life with Hb above 11.5 and will accept the risk; do not let Hb exceed 13.
  - Begin erythropoietin based on body weight (see **Table 67**); check Hb q2wk with target increase of 0.5–1 g/dL/wk, not more. Adjust erythropoietin dosage q4wk; increase or

decrease by 25% to reach goal. Reduce dose or frequency of ESA when Hb exceeds target, rather than stopping.

- Some patients will not respond to usual dosages, and it may be that risk of cardiovascular events are a result of high dosages. Failure to respond to ESAs in the first month of usual weight-based dosing is ESA hyporesponsiveness. In these patients do not use more than twice the weight-based dose.
- Evaluate for antibody-mediated pure red cell aplasia in patients using ESAs for >8 wk if Hb declines 0.5–1 g/wk.

Anemia of B_{12} and folate deficiency (see Figure 6):

- Laboratory tests: anemia or pancytopenia, macrocytosis
- Serum B_{12} 65–95% sensitivity for clinical deficiency at concentrations <200 pg/mL (or lower limit of lab normal); deficiency is possible at concentrations of <350 pg/mL; check serum methylmalonic acid level (MMA) before replacement to confirm deficiency.
- Treatment:
  - B_{12} 1000 mcg IM daily × 5 d, then weekly × 4 wk, then 1000 mcg IM every mo.
  - Alternates for maintenance replacement include: 100 mcg/d po or 2500 mcg sl once daily or nasal spr *(Nascobal)* 500 mcg intranasally in one nostril once weekly (nasal spr should be administered ≥1 h before or after ingestion of hot foods or liquids), or folate 1 mg/d po for 1–4 mo or until complete hematologic recovery.

Anemia of unknown cause:

- No evidence of B_{12} or folate deficiency, iron studies all normal, CrCl >30 mL/min; hypocellular bone marrow; erythropoietin levels low for degree of anemia; inflammatory markers not elevated.
- Prevalence: <1/3 of all anemias after age 65
- May be age-related decline in hematopoietic reserve, low erythropoietin, or poor response to endogenous erythropoietin
- At follow-up, about 25% evolve to a myelodysplastic syndrome; for the other 75%, prognostic significance is not known.

Hemolytic anemia:

- Hallmark is high reticulocyte count.
- About 2% of all anemias after age 65.
- Causes if Coombs' test positive: chronic lymphocytic leukemia, medications, lymphoma, collagen vascular disease, idiopathic
- Causes if Coombs' test negative: vascular, intrinsic

Table 66. Parenteral Iron Replacement	
Medication	**Formulation and Dosage**
Iron sucrose *(Venofer)*	200 mg IV, injected undiluted over 2–5 min on 5 different occasions within 14-d period (total cumulative dose of 1000 mg) Other recommended dosing options: • 100 mg, dilute to max of 100 mL in NS and infuse over ≥15 min • 300 mg, dilute to max of 250 mL in NS and infuse over 1.5 h • 400 mg, dilute to max of 250 mL in NS and infuse over 2.5 h
Ferumoxytol *(Feraheme)*:	510 mg IV × 1 dose followed by 510 mg 3–8 d later
Ferric carboxymaltose *(Injectafer)*	750 mg IV followed by 750 mg IV 7 d later; total cumulative dose not to exceed 1500 mg elemental iron; weight less than 50 kg, 15 mg/kg IV followed by 15 mg/kg IV 7 d later
Sodium ferric gluconate complex* *(Ferrlecit, Nulecit)*	10 mL IV (125 mg elemental iron) in 100 mL NS, over 1 h OR slow IV (12.5 mg/min) undiluted; usual minimum cumulative dose 1 g elemental iron over 8 consecutive dialysis sessions

*Hemodialysis: iron deficiency anemia, during epoetin tx.

Table 67. Erythropoiesis-stimulating Agents		
Medication	**Formulation and Dosage**	**Comments**
Epoetin alfa *(Epogen, Procrit)*	50–150 U/kg SC or IV 3×/wk in CKD; 150 U/kgSC 3×/wk U/wk in chemotherapy	*Caution.* Raise Hb only to avoid need for transfusion; higher Hb increases cardiovascular events. *All Agents*: Monitor BP, adjust dosage q4–6 wk based on response. Use in cancer patients not on chemotherapy increases risk of death. Use in patients on chemotherapy reduces need for transfusion but increases risk of thromboembolic events.
Darbepoetin alfa *(Aranesp)*	2.25 mcg/kg/wk in chemotherapy; 0.45 mcg/kg/wk in CKD; dose q2–4 wk when Hb stable.	
Methoxy polyethylene glycol-epoetin beta (*Mircera*)	0.6 mcg/kg IV q 2 wks on CKD	

PANCYTOPENIA

Unless due to B_{12} deficiency or drug-induced (eg, chloramphenicol, NSAIDs, antithyroid drugs, corticosteroids, penicillamine, allopurinol, gold, etc), bone marrow aspirate is indicated; causes include cancer, fibrosis, myelodysplasia, and aplastic anemia.

Aplastic Anemia

• Hematopoietic stem cell failure; in 78%, cause is idiopathic but felt to be immune mediated.

• Diagnosis: hypocellular bone marrow

• Treatment: 75% respond to immunosuppressive tx.

Myelodysplastic Syndromes (MDS)

A group of stem cell disorders with decreased production of blood elements causing risk of symptomatic anemia infection, and bleeding; risk of transformation to acute leukemia varies by syndrome.

Diagnosis

The diagnosis of MDS should be considered in any older patient with unexplained cytopenia(s) or monocytosis. Inspection of the peripheral blood smear and bone marrow aspirate is a next step in diagnosis. Because these alone are not diagnostic of MDS, in vitro bone marrow progenitor cultures, trephine biopsies, flow cytometry, immunohistochemical studies, and chromosome analysis are routinely needed for diagnosis.

Staging and Prognosis

- Four different classification systems are available to help estimate prognosis, but none explain most of the variability in survival.
- Classification systems stratify patients from low- to high-risk groups based on various characteristics that differ by classification system.
- In general, poorer survival occurs with: higher proportion of blast cells, complex (>3 different) karyotypes or abnormal chromosome 7, and greater number of cell lines with cytopenias (Hb <10 g/dL, absolute neutrophils <1800/µL, platelet count <100,000).
- Median survival of high-risk patients is independent of age and is under 6 months. However, among low-risk patients, survival is substantially affected by age with mean survival for those <60 yr old about 11.8 yr, >60 yr old about 4.8 yr, and >70 yr old about 3.9 yr.
- The higher the blast count the more likely the conversion to acute myelogenous leukemia (AML); but the most common causes of death are complications of the cytopenias, not acute leukemia.

Therapy

- Tx of asymptomatic patients does not improve survival, and supportive care remains a mainstay of tx at all stages of the disease.
- Tx is warranted with symptomatic cytopenias, although there is no consensus regarding standard tx and patients should be encouraged to join clinical trials.
- Lower-risk patients are generally treated with low-intensity tx including: growth factors, DNA hypomethylating agents, immunosuppressive tx, and lenalidomide.
- High- and intermediate-risk patients receive high-intensity tx including: combination chemotherapy and stem cell transplant.
- Only stem cell transplant holds a hope for cure, but is not usually an option for patients aged >60–65 yr old.

PRIMARY MYELOPROLIFERATIVE DISORDERS

Polycythemia Vera

- Diagnosis: elevated RBC mass with normal arterial oxygen saturation and splenomegaly
- If no splenomegaly, 2 of the following: leukocytosis, increased leukocyte alkaline phosphatase, or increased B_{12}; or genetic testing showing JAK-2
- Treatment: phlebotomy to achieve iron deficiency and hematocrit ≤45, and ASA 325 mg/d

Essential Thrombocytosis

- Platelet count >600,000/µL on two occasions ≥1 mo apart; Hb <13 mg/dL or normal RBC mass

- Normal iron marrow stores and no splenomegaly; exclude reactive thrombocytosis
- No Philadelphia or *bcr-abl* gene rearrangements or myelofibrosis in marrow
- Treatment: For patients at high risk of thrombohemorrhagic events, use low-dose ASA and hydroxyurea. Anagrelide is less effective at preventing thrombosis.

Chronic Myelogenous Leukemia
- Leukocytosis with early myeloid forms evenly distributed in peripheral blood
- Philadelphia chromosome in >95% of cases
- Leukocyte alkaline phosphatase score low
- Treatment: chronic and acute phases—imatinib *(Gleevec)*; acute-phase tx for select patients is stem cell transplantation.

Myelofibrosis
- Pancytopenia, splenomegaly, and other extramedullary hematopoiesis
- Marrow fibrosis (dry tap) and peripheral blood: leukoerythroblastosis, tear-drop cells
- Acute leukemia develops in 5–20%
- Tx for patients with symptomatic anemia: androgens, steroids, transfusion; erythropoietin probably has limited effectiveness.

MONOCLONAL GAMMOPATHY AND MULTIPLE MYELOMA

Monoclonal Gammopathy of Undetermined Significance (MGUS)
- Definition: monoclonal immunoglobulin concentration in serum ≤3 g/dL; no lytic bone lesions, anemia, hypercalcemia, or renal insufficiency; plasma cells in marrow ≤10%
- Prevalence increases with age: 3.2% at ≥50 yr; 6.6% at ≥80 yr.
- Evaluation: SPEP, serum immunofixation, and serum $\kappa{:}\lambda$ light-chain ratio.
  - If initial monoclonal protein is <1.5 g/dL and no other risk factors (see below), repeat laboratory testing at 6 mo and q2–3 yr thereafter if stable.
  - If initial monoclonal protein is ≥1.5 g/dL or any other of the below risk factors is abnormal, obtain bone marrow biopsy and skeletal survey, and repeat laboratory testing at 6 mo and annually.
  - If monoclonal protein is IgM, obtain abdominal CT to exclude a lymphoproliferative process.
- 0.4–1%/yr progress to multiple myeloma. Risk of progression to myeloma increases with increasing number of these risk factors: monoclonal protein ≥1.5 g/dL, monoclonal immunoglobulin other than IgG, abnormal serum free light chain ratio ($\kappa{:}\lambda$ light chains) of <0.26 or >1.65.
- Increased risk of vertebral fracture; bone turn-over markers are normalized with use of bisphosphonates.

Multiple Myeloma
- Definition: an incurable clonal B-cell malignancy; most have MGUS years before diagnosis
- Median age at diagnosis is 68 yr; incidence in black Americans is double that in whites
- Smoldering myeloma (asymptomatic stage)
  - Initial evaluation: SPEP, 24-h urine with electrophoresis, serum $\kappa{:}\lambda$ ratio, serum calcium, Cr, and CBC. Also obtain bone marrow biopsy and skeletal survey. Repeat serum calcium, CBC at 2–3 mo to check for stability.

- Diagnosis: marrow plasmacytosis >10%, and serum or urine (or both) monoclonal protein ≥3 g/dL; bisphosphonates reduce skeletal events but not disease progression.
- Symptomatic stage: above plus evidence of end-organ damage, hypercalcemia, lytic lesions, renal failure, anemia, or recurrent infection
- Treat symptomatic patients. First, determine eligibility for stem cell transplant:
  - If eligible, induction with thalidomide, dexamethasone, and bortezomib, followed by autologous transplant.
  - If not eligible, melphalan, prednisone, plus bortezomib improves survival and time to progression in patients >75 yr old.
  - Zoledronic acid (not all bisphosphonates) started at the time of diagnosis reduces skeletal events and improves overall survival independent of skeletal events. This effect was seen whether patients received transplant or oral agents.
  - Adverse effects of bisphosphonates include hypocalcemia, fever, and in 1/163 osteonecrosis of the jaw. Risk of osteonecrosis of jaw is reduced with good oral hygiene and prophylactic antibiotics if oral surgery is required.
- Patients at all stages are at risk of venous and possibly also arterial thrombosis related to both the disease and its tx (eg, thalidomide).
- Supportive care for all patients with advanced disease
  - Anemia may require transfusion. Erythropoietin is generally reserved for patients on chemotherapy with Hb <10 g/dL.
  - IV immunoglobulins monthly for recurrent bacterial infections and hypogammaglobulinemia; administer pneumococcal but not varicella vaccine.
  - Radiation to specific symptomatic bone lesions, or vertebroplasty or kyphoplasty.
  - Maintain hydration with at least 2 L/d and avoid NSAIDs and contrast because of renal dysfunction.
  - Provide adequate analgesia.

URINARY INCONTINENCE (UI)

UI is the complaint of involuntary leakage of urine. In older adults, it is most often multifactorial and results from some combination of lower urinary tract abnormalities, changes in neurologic control of voiding, multimorbidity, and functional impairment. Like other geriatric syndromes, effective tx requires addressing more than one factor.

Classification of UI

Transient and Functional Causes of Incontinence: UI is caused or exacerbated by factors outside the lower urinary tract (eg, comorbidities, medications, mobility). However, UI from these sources is transient only if they are recognized and addressed, and these same factors are frequent contributors to UI in patients with urge, stress, and other causes of persistent UI.

Table 68. Types of Persistent Urinary Incontinence: Characteristics and Causes

Type	Characteristic	Causes
Urge	UI with compelling and often sudden need to void	Idiopathic or associated with CNS lesions or bladder irritation from infection, stones, or tumors
Stress	UI with increased intra-abdominal pressure (eg, cough or sneeze)	Due to failure of sphincter mechanisms to remain closed during bladder filling; insufficient pelvic support in women; prostate surgery in men
Mixed	UI with both urgency and increases in intra-abdominal pressure	Some of the above
Overflow	UI is continual, and postvoid residual urine is increased	Impaired detrusor contractility from neuropathy, DM, vitamin B_{12} deficiency, tabes dorsalis, alcoholism, spinal disease, or bladder outlet obstruction in men most often due to BPH, cancer, or stricture; in women due to prior incontinence surgery or a large cystocele

Other (rare): Bladder-sphincter dyssynergia, fistulas, reduced detrusor compliance
Overactive Bladder: Frequency and urgency without UI; tx is the same as for urge UI.

Evaluation
History

- Determine type of UI (see **Table 68**)

- Identify "red flag" symptoms including sudden onset of UI, pelvic pain (constant, worsened, or improved with voiding), and hematuria. These suggest neoplastic or neurologic disease and require prompt referral to a urologist if UTI is excluded.

- Lower urinary tract symptom review: frequency, nocturia, slow stream, hesitancy, interrupted voiding, terminal dribbling

- Medical condition status and medications used to treat them, reviewed in association with onset or worsening of UI

- Ask "How does UI affect your life?" and also ask about the presence of FI.

Physical Examination
- Functional status (eg, mobility, dexterity)
- Mental status (important for planning tx)
- Findings:
  - Bladder distention
  - Cord compression (interosseus muscle wasting, Hoffmann's or Babinski's signs)
  - Rectal mass or impaction
  - Sacral root integrity (anal sphincter tone, anal wink, perineal sensation)
  - Volume overload, edema

Male GU
Prostate consistency; symmetry; if uncircumcised, check phimosis, paraphimosis, balanitis

Female GU
Atrophic vaginitis (see p 291); pelvic support (cystocele, rectocele, prolapse; see p 319)

Testing
- **Bladder Diary:** Record time and volume of incontinent and continent voids, activities and time of sleep; knowing oral intake is sometimes helpful.
- **Postvoid Residual:** If available, bladder ultrasound after voiding is preferred to catheterization. If >100 mL, repeat; still >100 mL suggests detrusor weakness, neuropathy, medications, fecal impaction, outlet obstruction, or DHIC. Even if postvoid residual is not available, begin tx steps as shown in **Figure 8**.
- **Laboratory:** UA to check for hematuria or glycosuria; urine C&S if onset of UI or worsening of UI is acute; serum glucose and calcium if polyuric; renal function tests and B_{12} if urinary retention; urine cytology if hematuria or pain.
- **Urodynamic Testing:** Usually not needed; indicated before corrective surgery, when diagnosis is unclear, when empiric tx is ineffective, or if postvoid residual volume >200–300 mL (possibly lower in men).

Management in a Stepped Approach (see Figure 8)
Contributing Factors
- Environment: ensure adequate access
- Mentation: If the patient is cognitively impaired, recommend prompted toileting (see p 149, Prompted toileting).
- Manual dexterity: compensate for deficits, eg, by adapting clothing
- Medical conditions: optimize tx for HF, COPD, or chronic cough
- Medications: eliminate or minimize those with adverse effects (see **Table 69**)
- Mobility: improve mobility or adapt environment

Lifestyle Factors
- Caffeine and diuretic (including carbonated) beverages produce rapid bladder filling
- Fluid intake: avoid extremes of fluid intake, reduce fluids after supper time to avoid nocturia
- Constipation: produces urethral obstruction or places pressure on bladder
- Weight loss: 60% UI reduction with large weight loss (≥16 kg); 30% decrease in odds for stress UI with 3.5 kg loss
- Smoking: produces chronic cough, encourage patient to quit

Behavioral Therapy

- Efficacy for behavioral tx: >35% reduction in UI; 50% greater patient perception of cure.
- Two components of bladder training for urge UI:
  1) Voiding on schedule during the day (start q2h) to keep bladder volume low. When no incontinence for 2 d, increase voiding interval by 30–60 min until voiding q3–4h.
  2) Urge suppression (see **Figure 9**), which retrains the CNS and pelvic mechanisms to inhibit contractions and leakage.
- Tx for stress UI involves timed toileting (as above) and also pelvic muscle (Kegel) exercises—isolate pelvic muscles (avoid thigh, rectal, buttocks contraction); perform slow velocity contraction, sustained for 6–8 sec in sets of 8–12 contractions, 3–4 d/wk for at least 15–20 wk. Handout alone can reduce leakage by 50% (see www.nlm.nih.gov/medlineplus/ency/patientinstructions/000141.htm). Biofeedback can help with teaching; covered by Medicare if patient unsuccessful after 4 wk of conventional teaching (refer to PT).
- Tx for post-prostatectomy UI
  ○ Pelvic floor electrical stimulation and biofeedback begun soon after catheter removal in post-prostatectomy patients improves early recovery of continence.
  ○ Even for those with UI ≥1 yr after prostatectomy, pelvic floor exercises and urge control (see **Figure 9**) reduces the number of incontinence episodes by more than half. Send patients to an experienced continence specialist for training (nurse practitioner or PT).
- Behavioral tx is at least as effective for overactive bladder symptoms in men on α-blocker tx as antimuscarinic tx. For benefit, patients should not have outlet obstruction (ie, PVR not >150 mL) (also see Prostate, p 262)
- DHIC is first treated with behavioral methods; may add detrusor muscle-relaxing medications but follow postvoid residual; clean intermittent self-catheterization if needed.

Pharmacotherapy

- Eliminate medications causing/exacerbating UI if possible (see **Table 69**).
- Data suggesting benefit of topical postmenopausal estrogen tx in urge and possibly stress UI are limited. See **Table 136** for available preparations.
- See **Table 70** for antimuscarinics for urge and mixed UI. All have shown equal efficacy in randomized controlled clinical trials. No oral agent is clearly superior in terms of cognitive adverse events.
- No oral antimuscarinic is clearly superior in terms of cognitive AEs. Combining antimuscarinics and cholinesterase inhibitors should be avoided.
- Significant benefit (≥50% reduction in UI) from pharmacotherapy occurs in <20% of patients.
- Select among alternative medications based on drug-related AEs (harms) (see **Table 70**).
- >50% of patients stop tx by the end of 1 yr.
- Chronic antimuscarinic use is associated with tooth loss and caries; routine dental care is important.
- Reevaluate use of these agents regularly after they are prescribed for lack of efficacy. D/C medication if not effective. Avoid use of anticholinergic agents.[BC]

Figure 8. Stepwise Evaluation and Treatment of Common UI Conditions

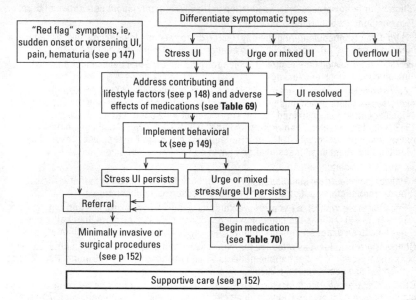

*Referral to differentiate neuropathy from obstruction (also see **Table 68**)

Figure 9. Urge Suppression

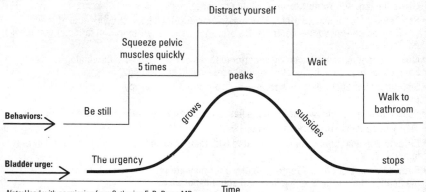

Note: Used with permission from Catherine E. DuBeau, MD

Table 69. Medications Commonly Associated with UI

Medication/Class	Adverse Effects/Comments
Alcohol	Frequency, urgency, sedation, immobility
α-Adrenergic agonists	Outlet obstruction (men)
α-Adrenergic blockers	Stress leakage (women), avoid[BC]
Anticholinergics	Impaired emptying, delirium, fecal impaction
Calcium channel blockers	Impaired detrusor contraction, edema with nocturnal diuresis
Estrogen (oral, transdermal)	Stress and mixed UI (women), avoid systemic estrogens in women with UI[BC]
GABA-ergics (gabapentin, pregabalin)	Edema, nocturnal diuresis
Loop diuretics	Polyuria, frequency, urgency
NSAIDs/thiazolidinediones	Edema, nocturnal diuresis
Sedative hypnotics	Sedation, delirium, immobility
Opioid analgesics	Constipation, sedation, delirium
Tricyclic antidepressants/ antipsychotics	Anticholinergic effects, sedation, immobility; avoid[BC]

Table 70. Pharmacotherapy for Urge or Mixed Urinary Incontinence

Medication	Dosage	Formulations	Adverse Events/Comments (Metabolism)
Antimuscarinics			*Class adverse events:* dry mouth, blurry vision, dry eyes, delirium/confusion, constipation
Oxybutynin *(Ditropan*▲*, Ditropan XL*▲*, Gelnique, Oxytrol for Women)*	2.5–5 mg q8–12h 5–20 mg/d 1 g gel topically q24h 3.9 mg/d (apply pch 2 × /wk)	T: 5; S: 5 mg/5 mL SR: 5, 10, 15 10% gel, unit dose (1.14 mL) Transdermal pch 39 cm^2	Dry mouth and constipation less with XL and pch than immediate release Pch/Gel: rotate sites to reduce skin irritation (L)
Tolterodine *(Detrol, Detrol LA)*	2 mg q12h 4 mg/d	T: 1, 2 C: ER 2, 4	Withdrawl from tx trials for drug-related AEs not different from placebo; P450 interactions (L, CYP3A4 and CYP2D6)
Trospium *(Sanctura, Sanctura XR)*	20 mg q12–24h (on empty stomach) 60 mg/d (XR)	T: 20 C: ER 60	Dyspepsia, headache; caution in liver dysfunction; dose once daily at hs in patients ≥75 yr old or with CrCl <30 mL/min; XR formulation not recommended if CrCl <30 mL/min (L, K)
Darifenacin *(Enablex)*	7.5–15 mg/d	T: 7.5, 15	Gastric retention; not recommended in severe liver impairment. Withdrawal from tx trials for drug-related AEs not different from placebo. (L, CYP3A4 and CYP2D6)

(cont.)

Table 70. Pharmacotherapy for Urge or Mixed Urinary Incontinence (cont.)

Medication	Dosage	Formulations	Adverse Events/Comments (Metabolism)
Solifenacin (VESIcare)	5–10 mg/d	T: 5, 10	Same as darifenacin; max dose 5 mg if CrCl <30 mL/min or moderate liver impairment. Women with urge UI who have taken other antimuscarinics that have failed may benefit from a trial dose of the 5-mg dose (no additional benefit at the 10-mg dose) (L, CYP3A4)
Fesoterodine (TOVIAZ)	4–8 mg/d	T: 4, 8	Max dose 4 mg if CrCl <30 mL/min (L, CYP3A4, CYP2D6)
β-3 agonist			
Mirabegron (Myrbetriq)	25–50 mg/d	T: 25, 50	Hypertension (monitor BP), nausea, headache, dizziness, tachycardia (AF). Max dose 25 mg if CrCl <30 mL/min; not recommended in severe kidney or severe liver impairment; raises digoxin and reduces metoprolol levels. Do not use in combination with antimuscarinics. (L, CYP2D6)

Note: For prostate obstruction UI, see Benign Prostatic Hyperplasia, p 262.

Minimally Invasive Procedures

• Sacral nerve neuromodulation can be effective for refractory urge UI and urinary retention (both idiopathic and neurogenic). Electrode is implanted to stimulate S3; done as a trial before permanent device.

• Pessaries may benefit women with vaginal (see p 319) or uterine prolapse who experience retention and stress or urge UI.

• Botulinum toxin is also effective for refractory urge UI (not FDA approved for this purpose), but patients must be willing to perform self-catheterization because risk of retention is high.

Surgical Therapy

• Consider for the 50% of women whose stress UI does not respond adequately to behavioral tx and exercise.

• Type of surgery depends on type of urethral function impairment, patient-related factors, and coexisting conditions (eg, prolapse).

Supportive Care

• Pads and protective garments should be chosen on the basis of gender and volume of urine loss. Medicaid (some states) covers pads; Medicare does not.

• Because of expense, patients may not change frequently enough.

Nocturnal Frequency in the Absence of HF

- Two voidings per night is probably normal for older adults.

- Exclude sleep difficulties as nocturia is a common symptom of sleep apnea (see Sleep Disorders, p 304); then consider if the condition is due to excessive output or urinary tract dysfunction.

- Bladder diary with measured voided volumes can be very helpful. Voiding more than ⅓ of total 24-h output between bedtime and awakening is excessive nocturnal fluid excretion.

- Patients should restrict fluid (especially alcohol) intake 4 h before bedtime.

- If stasis edema is present, have patient wear pressure-graded stockings during the day.

- If no stasis edema, a potent, short-acting loop diuretic can be used in the afternoon or early evening to induce a diuresis before bedtime, eg, bumetanide 0.5–1.5 mg titrated to achieve a brisk diuresis.

- Evaluate for other factors contributing to volume overload or diuresis (eg, HF, poorly controlled DM).

UI in Nursing-home Residents and People with Cognitive Impairment

- Rather than bladder diaries, observe toileting patterns and UI episodes over several days.

- Trial of prompted toileting in patients who are able to state their name and transfer with assist of no more than one. Continue prompted schedule; ability to toilet at least 75% of the time during a 3-d trial is considered success.

- **Prompted toileting** consists of:
  - Asking if patient needs to void, and taking him or her to toilet starting at 2- to 3-h intervals during day; encourage patients to report continence status; praise patient when continent and responds to toileting.
  - Simply asking the patient if they need to toilet will NOT improve UI.

- Consider use of antimuscarinics in patients with urge UI who succeed with prompted toileting and still have UI episodes.

- Do not neglect evaluation for stress UI and outlet obstruction.

Catheter Care

- Use catheter **only** for chronic urinary retention, to protect pressure ulcers, and when requested by patients or families to promote comfort (eg, at end of life).

- Leakage around catheter can be caused by large Foley balloon, too large catheter diameter, constipation, impaction.

- Bacteriuria is universal; treat only if symptoms (eg, fever, inanition, anorexia, delirium) or if bacteriuria persists after catheter removal.

- Suprapubic catheters reduce meatal and penile trauma but not infection. Condom catheters are less painful and have a somewhat lower complication rate.

- Replace catheter if symptomatic bacteriuria develops, then culture urine from new catheter.

- Nursing-facility patients with catheters should reside in separate rooms.

- For acute retention, catheterize for 7–10 d, then do voiding trial after catheter removal.

Replacing Catheter: Routine replacement not necessary. Changing q4–6wk is reasonable to prevent blockage. Patients with recurrent blockage need increased fluid intake, possibly acidification of urine, or change of catheter q7–10d.

FECAL INCONTINENCE (FI)

Definition
"Involuntary loss of liquid or solid stool that is a social or hygienic problem" (International Continence Society)

Prevalence
After age 65: 6–10% of men and 15% of community-dwelling women, 14% of hospitalized, 45% of nursing-home residents

Risk Factors
Constipation, age >80 yr, female sex, UI, impaired mobility, dementia, neurologic disease

Age-related Factors
Decreased strength of external sphincter and weak anal squeeze; increased rectal compliance, decreased resting tone in internal sphincter, and impaired anal sensation

Causes: FI is commonly multifactorial.
- Overflow: from colonic distention by excessive feces, causing continuous soiling
- Loose feces: caused by medications, neoplasia, colitis, lactose intolerance
- Functional incontinence: associated with poor mobility
- Dementia related: uninhibited rectal contraction, often have UI
- Anorectal incontinence: weak external sphincter (surgery, multiparity, etc)
- Comorbidity: stroke, DM (autonomic neuropathy), sacral cord dysfunction

Evaluation
History
- Ask about "red flag" symptoms/signs that signal serious disease and require prompt referral to a gastroenterologist (ie, hematochezia, anemia, unexplained weight loss, refractory constipation, new onset constipation or diarrhea, and positive family hx of colon cancer or inflammatory bowel disease)
- Description of FI (eg, diarrhea, hard feces, etc), including usual bowel habit, change in habit, usual fecal consistency
- Frequency, urgency, ability to delay, difficulty wiping, post-defecation soiling, ability to distinguish feces and flatus
- Evacuation difficulties: straining, incomplete emptying, rectal prolapse or pain
- Functional: communication of needs, need for assistance, toilet access
- Other: bowel medications, other medications, UI, prior tx (eg, pads)

Examination
- Examine/palpate abdomen for colonic distention, and visually inspect anus for fissures and hemorrhoids.
- Check for rectal prolapse while patient seated on commode; check for rectocele in women.
- Perform rectal examination for sphincter tone, volume and consistency of feces; heme test.
- Observe gait, mobility, dressing, hygiene, mental status.

Laboratory
- TSH, electrolytes, calcium

Bowel investigations
• Abdominal radiograph: may identify colonic distention by excessive feces
• Colonoscopy: only when pathology suspected (unexplained loose feces, bleeding)
• Anorectal physiology tests: not generally needed for tx but may be important in patients who do not respond to usual tx.

Treatment: Multiple interventions may be required.
Main approach is to simulate the patient's usual bowel pattern.
• Use rectal evacuants to stimulate evacuation and to establish a bowel pattern.
• Use evacuants in the following order: glycerine Sp, bisacodyl Sp, microenemas (eg, *Enemeez*, docusate 5 mL), phosphate or tap water enemas; digital stimulation.
• Use antidiarrheals to slow an overactive bowel or to enable planned evacuation with rectal preparations.
Constipation (see p 124): often plays a role; evaluate (if needed) and treat
Modify fecal consistency to achieve soft, formed feces.
• Loose feces: use fiber or loperamide titrated to effect, sometimes as little as q48h.
• Hard feces: modify diet; add MgSO or MgOH at low dosages. In poorly mobile people, bran and fiber may exacerbate constipation.
Patient education
• Respond promptly on urge to defecate, heed the gastrocolic reflex.
• Take loperamide 2–4 mg 45 min before meal or social event to prevent evacuation.
• Use coffee to stimulate the gut.
• Position on toilet with back support, foot stool to achieve squat position.
• Exercise to improve bowel motility.
• Those who are able may be taught rectal sphincter exercises (tighten rectal sphincter for 10 sec 50 times/d) or may use biofeedback.
Rectal evacuation and toilet training
• Following a regimen improves bowel control.
• When no spontaneous bowel action, stimulate with suppositories or enemas (see **Table 58**); those with incompetent sphincters may not retain usual enemas.
• Bed pans should not be used; bedside commodes are not as good as toilets.
Nursing-home residents and very disabled older adults: FI is most often due to colonic loading and overflow. Treat as follows:
• Daily enemas until no more results.
• Add a daily osmotic laxative (see **Table 58**) and follow bowel training (above).
• Fecal transit can be stimulated with abdominal massage in direction of colonic transit.
Other therapies
• Manual evacuation may be appropriate in some patients.
• Skin care: Wet wipes better than dry; commercial preparations better than soap and water; toilet tongs and bottom wipers help those with shoulder disease.
• Surgery:
  ◦ Full-thickness rectal prolapse usually requires surgery using a transanal approach.
  ◦ Denervation of the sphincter can be repaired, but long-term results are often unsatisfactory.

- Division of the external anal sphincter or anal fissure can be repaired, but long-term results are less than satisfactory.
- Selected patients have improved quality of life through creation of a stoma.
- Sacral nerve stimulation for patients with both intact and defective rectal sphinters is FDA-approved for chronic FI in patients who cannot tolerate more conservative tx or in whom such tx has not been effective. Patients must show appropriate response to a trial of stimulation and must be able to operate the device.
- A perianal bulking agent *(Solesta)* is available for patients in whom other tx has failed. The gel is injected into the tissue below the anal lining to promote tissue growth. In turn, the anal opening narrows, and patients may have better control of the muscles in that area. Tx is contraindicated in active inflammatory bowel disease, immunodeficiency disorders, previous pelvic radiation, and significant rectal prolapse.

ANTIMICROBIAL STEWARDSHIP: PRINCIPLES FOR PRESCRIBERS
• Collaborate with local antimicrobial stewardship teams and efforts.
• Be familiar with formulary restrictions and preauthorization requirements.
• Participate in educational offerings on antimicrobials and antimicrobial stewardship.
• Streamline or de-escalate empirical antimicrobial tx based on C&S results.
• Optimize and individualize antimicrobial dose.
• Switch eligible patients from IV to oral antimicrobials.

PNEUMONIA
Presentation
Can range from subtle signs such as lethargy, anorexia, dizziness, falls, and delirium to septic shock or acute respiratory distress syndrome. Pleuritic chest pain, dyspnea, productive cough, fever, chills, or rigors are not consistently present in older adults.

Evaluation and Assessment
• Physical examination: Respiratory rate >20 breaths/min; low BP; chest sounds may be minimal, absent, or consistent with HF; 20% are afebrile.
• CXR: Infiltrate may not be present on initial film if the patient is dehydrated.
• Sputum: Gram's stain and culture (optional per ATS guidelines)
• CBC with differential: Up to 50% of patients have a normal WBC count, but 95% have a left shift.
• BUN, Cr, electrolytes, glucose
• Blood culture × 2
• Oxygenation: ABG or oximetry
• Test for *Mycobacterium tuberculosis* with acid-fast bacilli stain and culture in selected patients.
• Test for *Legionella* spp in patients who are seriously ill without an alternative diagnosis, are immunocompromised, are nonresponsive to β-lactam antibiotics, have clinical features suggesting this diagnosis, or in outbreak setting. Urinary antigen testing is highly specific for serotype 1 but lacks specificity for other serotypes. Value and use vary by geographic region.
• Test for urinary antigen for pneumococcus if ICU admission, antibiotic failure, active alcohol abuse, pleural effusion, leucopenia, or asplenia.
• Thoracentesis (if moderate to large effusion)

Aggravating Factors (* indicates modifiable)
• Age-related changes in pulmonary reserve
• Alcoholism
• Altered mental status
• Aspiration
• Comorbid conditions that alter gag reflexes or ciliary transport

- COPD or other lung disease
- Heart disease
- Heavy sedation* or paralytic agents
- Hyperglycemia*
- Intubation, mechanical ventilation (orotracheal intubation and orogastric tubation preferred)
- Malnutrition
- Medications*: immunosuppressants, sedatives, anticholinergic or other agents that dry secretions, agents that increase gastric pH
- Nasogastric tubes
- Oral care* (manual brushing plus rinse with fluoride/chlorhexidine 0.12% × 30 sec/d)
- Poor compliance with infection control* (eg, hand disinfection)
- Supine positioning* (semi-recumbent, 30–45 degrees preferred)
- Swallowing* (eat/feed upright at 90 degrees over 15–20 min)

Predominant Organisms by Setting

Community-acquired:
- *Streptococcus pneumoniae*
- *Legionella* spp
- Respiratory viruses
- *Haemophilus influenzae*
- Gram-negative bacteria
- *Chlamydia pneumoniae*
- *Moraxella catarrhalis*
- *M tuberculosis*
- Endemic fungi
- Anaerobes

Nursing-home–acquired:
- *Strep pneumoniae*
- Gram-negative bacteria
- *Staphylococcus aureus* (including methicillin-resistant *S aureus*)
- Anaerobes
- *H influenzae*
- Group B streptococci
- *Chlamydia pneumoniae*

Hospital-acquired:
- Gram-negative bacteria
- Anaerobes
- Gram-positive bacteria
- Fungi

Supportive Management
- Chest percussion
- Inhaled β-adrenergic agonists
- Mechanical ventilation (if indicated)
- Oxygen as indicated
- Rehydration

Empiric Antibiotic Therapy (see Table 77)
The antibiotic regimen should be narrowed if the causative organism has been identified.

Table 71. Treatment of Community-acquired Pneumonia for Immunocompetent Patients by Clinical Circumstances or Setting[a]

Clinical Circumstances or Setting	Treatment Options
Outpatient, previously healthy and no antibiotic tx in past 3 mo	Azithromycin, clarithromycin, or erythromycin Alternative: doxycycline
Outpatient, with comorbidities[b] or antibiotic tx in past 3 mo[d]	A fluoroquinolone[c] alone *or* Azithromycin, clarithromycin, or erythromycin *plus* amoxicillin (high dose) or amoxicillin-clavulanate Alternative β-lactams: ceftriaxone, cefpodoxime, or cefuroxime Alternative to a macrolide: doxycycline
Hospitalized patient	A fluoroquinolone[c] alone *or* Azithromycin or clarithromycin *plus* cefotaxime, ceftriaxone, or ampicillin Alternative β-lactam: ertapenem Alternative to a macrolide: doxycycline
Hospitalized patient, intensive care unit	
No concern about *Pseudomonas*	Cefotaxime, ceftriaxone, or ampicillin-sulbactam *plus* azithromycin or fluoroquinolone[c]
No concern about *Pseudomonas* but β-lactam allergy	Fluoroquinolone[c] *plus* aztreonam
Concern about *Pseudomonas*	Piperacillin-tazobactam, imipenem, meropenem, or cefepime *plus* ciprofloxacin or levofloxacin; *or* Piperacillin-tazobactam, imipenem, meropenem, or cefepime *plus* an aminoglycoside *and* azithromycin, ciprofloxacin, or levofloxacin
Concern about *Pseudomonas* and β-lactam allergy	Aztreonam *plus* ciprofloxacin or levofloxacin *plus* an aminoglycoside
Nursing-home patient[e,f]	Fluoroquinolone[d] alone *or* Azithromycin, clarithromycin, or erythromycin *plus* amoxicillin (high dose) or amoxicillin-clavulanate

[a] Because of the geographical variability in antimicrobial resistance patterns, refer to local tx recommendations.
[b] Comorbidities: chronic heart, lung, liver, or kidney disease; DM; alcoholism; malignancies; asplenia; immunosuppressing conditions or drugs
[c] Fluoroquinolones (respiratory): moxifloxacin, levofloxacin, or gemifloxacin
[d] Choice of antibiotic should be from a different class
[e] Patients being treated in the nursing home; for tx of nursing-home patients who are hospitalized, see hospitalized patient or intensive care unit.
[f] Because of the incidence of gram-negative and atypical bacterial pneumonia in nursing-home patients, experts in geriatric infectious disease often recommend expanded gram-negative antibiotic coverage.
Source: Mandell LA, et al. *Clin Infect Dis* 2007;44:S27–72.

Nursing-home or Hospital-acquired Pneumonia Requiring Parenteral Treatment: Alternative Recommendations

Antipseudomonal cephalosporin (cefepime or ceftazidime) *or*
Antipseudomonal carbepenem (imipenem or meropenem) *or*
β-lactam/β-lactamase inhibitor (piperacillin-tazobactam)

plus

Antipseudomonal fluoroquinolone (ciprofloxacin or levofloxacin) *or*
Aminoglycoside (amikacin, gentamicin, or tobramycin)

plus

Linezolid or vancomycin (if risk factors for methicillin-resistant *S aureus* are present or if local incidence is high)

For both sets of empiric tx guidelines, the choice of combination depends on local bacteriologic patterns.

Source: Adapted from: ATS and IDSA Guidelines for the management of adults with hospital-acquired, ventilator-associated, and healthcare-associated pneumonia. *Am J Resp Crit Care Med* 2005;171:388–416.

Duration of Treatment

Inpatient—until clinical indicators have been reached:

- Temperature <100°F (37.8°C)
- HR <100 bpm
- Respiratory rate <25/min
- SBP >90 mmHg
- O_2 saturation >90%
- Ability to maintain oral intake

Switch from parental to oral antibiotics when patient is hemodynamically stable, shows clinical improvement, is afebrile for 16 h, and can tolerate oral medications; total duration of tx 7–14 d depending on clinical response. Tx courses of 7–8 d are recommended for clinically improving hospital-acquired pneumonia not caused by *Pseudomonas spp, Steriotrophous*, or other nonfermenting gram-negative bacilli.

Outpatient and long-term care facility—usually 10–14 d

Note: The empiric use of vancomycin should be reserved for patients with a serious allergy to β-lactam antibiotics or for patients from environments in which methicillin-resistant *S aureus* is known to be a problem pathogen. For all cases, antimicrobial tx should be individualized once Gram's stain or culture results are known.

URINARY TRACT INFECTION OR UROSEPSIS

Definition

Bacteriuria is the presence of a significant number of bacteria in the urine without reference to symptoms.

- **Symptomatic bacteriuria** usually has signs of dysuria and increased frequency of urination; fever, chills, nausea may be present; $>10^5$ cfu/mL of the same organism from a single specimen supports the diagnosis of UTI, counts $\geq 10^3$ cfu/mL are diagnostic for specimens obtained by in and out catheterization. New onset or worsening of UI may be the only symptom.

- **Asymptomatic bacteriuria** is seen when there is an absence of symptoms, including absence of fever (<100.4°F [38°C]) plus:

  ○ the same organism(s) ($\geq 10^5$ cfu/mL) is found on 2 consecutive cultures in women

  ○ one bacterial species ($\geq 10^5$ cfu/mL) in a single clean-catch specimen in men

  ○ one bacterial species ($\geq 10^2$ cfu/mL) in a catheterized specimen in men and women

- **Complicated UTI in women**—affecting the lower or upper urinary tract and associated with underlying condition that increases risk of infection and of tx failure (eg, obstruction, anatomical abnormality, resistant organisms, or urologic dysfunction).

Risk Factors

- Abnormalities in function or anatomy of the urinary tract
- Catheterization or recent instrumentation
- Comorbid conditions (eg, DM, BPH)
- Female gender
- Limited functional status

Assessment and Evaluation

Choice is based on presenting symptoms and severity of illness.

- UA with culture (do not obtain sample from catheter bag)
- Blood culture × 2
- BUN, Cr, electrolytes
- CBC with differential

Expected Organisms

Noncatheterized Patients: Most common: *Escherichia coli, Proteus* spp, *Klebsiella* spp, *Providencia* spp, *Citrobacter* spp, *Enterobacter* spp, coagulase-negative staphylococci, *Gardnerella vaginalis*, group B streptococci, and *Pseudomonas aeruginosa* if recent antibiotic exposure, known colonization, or known institutional flora

Nursing-Home–Catheterized Patients: All of the above plus enterococci, staphylococcus aureus, and fungus (eg, candida)

Empiric Antibiotic Treatment

- Routine tx of asymptomatic bacteriuria is not recommended.[CW]
  - Asymptomatic bacteriuria has not been associated with adverse outcomes
  - Screening and tx is recommended before a urologic procedure anticipated to result in mucosal bleeding
- Empiric regimens should be changed based on C&S results, patient factors, and tx costs.
- Tx duration should be at least 3–7 d for women with uncomplicated UTI; 7–12 d for complicated UTI; and >14 d and up to 6 wk for men if prostatitis present.

Community-Acquired or Nursing-Home–Acquired Cystitis or Uncomplicated UTI (oral route): TMP/SMZ DS, cephalexin, ampicillin, or amoxicillin. Amoxicillin-clavulanate should be reserved for patients with sulfa allergy and for settings with known β-lactam resistance. Fluoroquinolones should be reserved for patients with allergies to sulfa or β-lactams, or for settings with known resistance.

Suspected Urosepsis (IV route): Third-generation cephalosporin plus aminoglycoside, aztreonam, or fluoroquinolone ± aminoglycoside.

Vancomycin should be reserved for patients with a serious allergy to β-lactam antibiotics.

UTI Prophylaxis

- Leads to antibiotic resistance regardless of patient's catheter status or duration of catheterization; generally not recommended. Noncatheterized women with a hx of UTI, especially if caused by *E coli*, may benefit from prophylaxis with cranberry juice (250–300 mL/d). Time to benefit may be ≥ 2 mo.
- Vaginal atrophy due to estrogen depletion may predispose women to recurrent UTIs. Local topical estrogen replacement may be indicated.

METHICILLIN-RESISTANT STAPHYLOCOCCUS AUREUS (MRSA)

Risk Factors

- Long-term care residence
- Hemodialysis or peritoneal dialysis
- IV drug use
- DM
- Recent surgery
- Previous colonization
- Poor functional status
- Wounds
- Invasive devices, (eg, catheters, feeding tube)

Types
Community-acquired
Usually skin and soft tissue infection (SSTI) or severe necrolyzing pneumonia
Usual tx: clindamycin, doxycycline, minocycline or TMP-SMX
Hospital-acquired
Usual tx: vancomycin +/− aminoglycoside and/or rifampin; daptomycin; or linezolid
Alternative tx for complicated SSTI: ceftaroline or telavancin
Duration of Treatment
- SSTI or pneumonia: 7–10 d
- Bacteremia, (−) valve endocarditis: 4 wk after culture negative
- Osteomyelitis or infected prosthetics: >6 wk

Decolonization with mupirocin or other antiseptics should be restricted to MRSA outbreaks and recurrent infections.

HERPES ZOSTER ("SHINGLES")

Definition
Cutaneous vesicular eruptions followed by radicular pain secondary to the recrudescence of varicella zoster virus. Recurrence may occur but rare in immunocompetent older people.

Prevention
Zoster vaccine live (Zostavax) for individuals ≥50 yr who are immunocompetent and without contraindication to the vaccine. Patients who have had shingles in the past can receive the vaccine to prevent future episodes. There is no specific period of time that needs to have elapsed, but the rash should have resolved before administering the vaccine. (See Table 105.)

Clinical Manifestations
- Abrupt onset of pruritus or pain along a specific dermatome (see Figure 1)
- Macular, erythematous rash that becomes vesicular and pustular (Tzanck cell test positive) after ~3 d, crusts over and clears in 10–14 d
- Complications: post-herpetic neuralgia, visual loss or blindness if ophthalmic involvement

Pharmacologic Management
When started within 72 h of the rash's appearance, antiviral tx (see Table 72) decreases the severity and duration of the acute illness and possibly shortens the duration and reduces the risk of post-herpetic neuralgias. Corticosteroids can also decrease the risk and severity of post-herpetic neuralgias. (See p 220 for tx of post-herpetic neuralgia.)

Table 72. Antiviral Treatments for Herpes Zoster

Medication, Route	Dosage	Formulations	Reduce dosage when
Acyclovir▲ *(Zovirax)*			
Oral	800 mg 5 ×/d for 7–10 d	T: 400, 800; C: 200; S: 200 mg/5 mL	CrCl[a] <25 mL/min
IV[b]	10 mg/kg q8h for 7 d	500 mg/10 mL	CrCl[a] <50 mL/min
Famciclovir▲ *(Famvir)*			
Oral	500 mg q8h for 7 d	T: 125, 250, 500	CrCl[a] <60 mL/min
Valacyclovir▲c *(Valtrex)*			
Oral	1000 mg q8h for 7 d	C: 500, 1000	CrCl[a] <50 mL/min

[a] The CrCl listed is the threshold below which the dosage (amount or frequency) should be reduced. See package insert for detailed dosing guidelines.

[b] Use IV for serious illness, ophthalmic infection, or patients who cannot take oral medication.

[c] Preferred to po acyclovir; prodrug of acyclovir with serum concentrations equal to those achieved with IV administration.

INFLUENZA

Vaccine Prevention (ACIP Guidelines)

Yearly vaccination is recommended for all adults ≥65 yr old and all residents and staff of nursing homes, or residential or long-term–care facilities. Nursing-home residents admitted during the winter months after the vaccination program has been completed should be vaccinated at admission if they have not already been vaccinated. The influenza vaccine is contraindicated in people who have an anaphylactic hypersensitivity to eggs or any other component of the vaccine. Dose: 0.5 mL IM once in the fall for those living in the northern hemisphere.

Table 73. Diagnostic Tests for Influenza

Method	Test Time	Acceptable Specimens, Detection and Differentiation
Viral cell culture (conventional)	3–10 d	NP swab, throat swab, NP or bronchial wash, nasal or endotracheal aspirate, sputum
Reverse-transcriptase-polymerase chain reaction (RT-PCR)	1–6 h	Detect and differentiate Types A and B, including subtypes NP swab, throat swab, NP or bronchial wash, nasal or endotracheal aspirate, sputum
		Detect and differentiate Types A and B, including H1N1 and avian H5N1 subtypes
Immunofluorescence, direct (DFA) or indirect (IFA) antibody staining	1–4 h	NP swab or wash, bronchial wash, nasal or endotracheal aspirate
		Detect and differentiate between Types A and B, between A/B, and other respiratory viruses
Rapid influenza diagnostic tests	<30 min	NP swab (throat swab), nasal wash, nasal aspirate
		Antigen (EIA) detects and differentiates between A and B, and detection of Type B varies with EIA.

Note: EIA = enzyme immunoassay; NP = nasopharyngeal

Pharmacologic Prophylaxis and Treatment with Antiviral Agents
Indications:

- Prevention (during an influenza outbreak): people who are not vaccinated, are immunodeficient, or may spread the virus

- Prophylaxis: during 2 wk required to develop antibodies for people vaccinated after an outbreak of influenza A

- Reduction of symptoms, duration of illness when started within the first 48 h of symptoms

- During epidemic outbreaks in nursing homes

- Resistance to antivirals and the emergence of specific strains of influenza (eg, H1N1) have led to frequent updates of recommendations for prophylaxis and tx. Check the CDC Web site for the most current information and guidance (www.cdc.gov/flu/professionals/antivirals/).

Duration: Tx of symptoms: 3–5 d or for 24–48 h after symptoms resolve. Prophylaxis during outbreak: min 2 wk or until ~1 wk after outbreak ends.

Table 74. Antiviral Treatment of Influenza

Agent	Formulation	Dosage
Amantadine▲ *(Symmetrel)* [a]	C: 100 mg S: 50 mg/5 mL	100 mg/d po[b]
✔ Oseltamivir *(Tamiflu)* [c]	C: 75 mg S: 12 mg/mL	Tx: 75 mg po q12h × 5 d (75 mg/d po if CrCl 10–30 mL/min); not recommended if CrCl <10 mL/min Prophylaxis: 75 mg/d po × ≥7 d up to 6 wk if immunocompetent (12 wk if not) (75 mg po q48h if CrCl 10–30 mL/min); not recommended if CrCl <10 mL/min
Rimantadine *(Flumadine)* [a]	T▲: 100 mg	100 mg/d po for adults aged ≥65 yr old including nursing-home residents
Zanamivir *(Relenza)* [c,d]	Inh: 5 mg/blister	Tx: 2 × 5-mg inhalations q12h × 5 d Give doses on first d ≥2 h apart Prophylaxis: 2 × 5-mg inhalations q24h; household setting—start 36 h after onset of signs and symptoms of initial case, duration 10 d; community—begin within 5 d of outbreak, duration 30 d.

✔ = preferred for treating older adults

[a] No longer recommended for prophylaxis.

[b] Dosage adjustments for kidney function, CrCl (mL/min): ≥30 = 100 mg/d; 20–29 = 200 mg 2 ×/wk; 10–19 = 100 mg 3 × /wk; <10 = 200 mg alternating with 100 mg q7d.

[c] Must be started within 2 d of symptom onset or of contact with an infected individual.

[d] Do not use in patients with COPD or asthma.

TUBERCULOSIS (TB)

TB in older adults may be the reactivation of old disease or a new infection due to exposure to an infected individual. Tx recommendations differ; if a new infection is suspected or the patient has risk factors for resistant organisms, then bacterial sensitivities must be determined.

Risk or Reactivating Factors

- Chronic institutionalization
- Corticosteroid use
- DM
- Malignancy
- Malnutrition
- Kidney failure

Risk Factors for Resistant Organisms

- HIV infection
- Homelessness, institutionalization (other than a nursing home)
- IV drug abuse
- Origin from geographic regions with a high prevalence of resistance (New York, Mexico, Southeast Asia)
- Exposure to INH-resistant TB or hx of ineffective chemotherapy
- Previous tx for TB
- AFB-positive sputum smears after 2 mo of tx
- Positive cultures after 4 mo of tx

Diagnosis

- Mantoux tuberculin skin test (TST): 0.1 mL of tuberculin PPD intradermal injection into the inner surface of the forearm
- Read 48–72 h after injection (see **Table 70** for interpretation).
- Repeat ("booster") 1–2 wk after initial skin testing can be useful for nursing-home residents, healthcare workers, and others who are retested periodically to reduce the likelihood of misinterpreting a boosted reaction to subsequent TSTs.

Treatment

Latent Infection: See **Table 75** and **Table 76**.

Table 75. Identification of Patients at High Risk of Developing TB Who Would Benefit from Treatment of Latent Infection

Population	Minimum Induration Considered a Positive Test
Considered positive in any person, including those considered low risk	15 mm
Residents and employees of hospitals, nursing homes, and long-term facilities for older adults, residential facilities for AIDS patients, and homeless shelters	10 mm
Recent immigrants (<5 yr) from countries where TB prevalence is high	10 mm
Injectable-drug users	10 mm
People with silicosis; DM; chronic kidney failure; leukemia; lymphoma; carcinoma of the head, neck, or lung; weight loss of ≥10%; gastrectomy or jejunoileal bypass	10 mm
Recent contact with TB patients	5 mm
Fibrotic changes on CXR consistent with prior TB	5 mm
Immunosuppressed (receiving the equivalent of prednisone at ≥15 mg/d for ≥1 mo), organ transplant recipients, patients receiving TNF-α inhibitors	5 mm
HIV-positive patients	5 mm

Table 76. Treatment of Latent Tuberculosis in HIV(-) Adults

Self-administration	Direct Observation Treatment (DOT)
INH▲ 5 mg/kg (max 300 mg/d) × 6 or 9 mo	INH 900 mg 2/wk × 6 or 9 mo
	Weekly INH 15 mg/kg (rounded to the nearest 50 or 100 mg) plus rifapentine 32.1–49.9 kg = 750 mg or if ≥50.0 kg, 900 mg max

Notes: INH; no dose adjustment in renal impairment; multiple CYP effects; T: 100, 300 mg; Sol: 50 mg/mL; Inj Rifapentine: no dose adjustment in renal impairment; strong inducer of CYP2C8, 2C9, and 3A4; T: 50 mg

Active Infection:
Refer to CDC guidelines at www.cdc.gov/mmwr/preview/mmwrhtml/rr5211a1.htm#tab2.

HUMAN IMMUNODEFICIENCY VIRUS (HIV)

Reasons for increase in HIV infection in adults ≥50 yr old:
- Increased survival of people with HIV
- Age-associated decrease in immune function with resultant increased susceptibility
- Tx for erectile dysfunction leading to more sexual activity
- Difficulty with condom use secondary to erectile dysfunction
- Less condom use by partners of postmenopausal women
- Older women with vaginal dryness and thinning
- Older adults think only the young are at risk

HIV differences young vs old:
- Persons aged ≥65 yr old have a lower CD_4 count at diagnosis
- Viral load suppression greatest in ≥60 yr old after initiating antiretroviral tx
- HIV-1 RNA suppression old > young
- CD_4 response to tx young > old
- Mortality old > young secondary to non-HIV-related causes

Presentation
Many symptoms that may delay diagnosis are common in older adults:
- Anorexia
- Arthralgias
- Earlier, more symptomatic menopause
- Fatigue
- Flu-like symptoms
- Forgetfulness
- Hypogonadism
- Insomnia
- Myalgias
- Pain in hands or feet (neuropathy)
- Recurrent pneumonia
- Sexual disorders
- Weight loss

Comorbidities common in older adults that can occur earlier in people with HIV:
- Cancers (eg, anal, liver, lung)
- Cirrhosis
- Cognitive deficits
- CAD
- DM
- Dyslipidemia
- HTN
- Obstructive lung disease
- Osteoporosis
- Vascular disease

Laboratory Abnormalities
- Anemia
- Leukopenia
- Low cholesterol
- Transaminitis

Screening

Routine screening of adults ≥65 yr old is not recommended.
Screening is recommended regardless of age if:

- Starting tx for TB
- Treating a sexually transmitted disease
- Other HIV risk factors are present: unprotected sex and multiple partners, hazardous alcohol or illicit drug use
- Unexplained anemia
- Peripheral neuropathy
- Oral candidiasis
- Herpes zoster (widespread infection)
- Recurrent bacterial pneumonia
- Unexplained weight loss or pronounced fatigue

Treatment

Antiretroviral tx is recommended in patients aged >50 yr old, regardless of CD_4 count.
For complete guidelines on antiretroviral regimens, see
http://aidsinfo.nih.gov/contentfiles/AA_Tables.pdf.
Tx-naive patients:

- Non-nucleoside reverse transcriptase inhibitor (NNRTI) + 2 nucleoside reverse transcriptase inhibitors (NRTIs) *or*
- Protease inhibitor with ritonavir (preferred) + 2 NRTIs, *or*
- Integrase strand transfer inhibitor + 2 NRTIs

Pre-exposure prophylaxis:

The combination of emtricitabine and tenofovir (*Truvada*; T 200 mg/300 mg; K<60mL/min) in combination with safer sex practices is approved for pre-exposure prophylaxis to reduce the risk of sexually-acquired HIV-1 in adults at high risk.

Complications of Pharmacotherapy

- Increased cholesterol (accelerated atherosclerosis)
- Glucose intolerance
- Drug-drug interactions
- Drug toxicity
- Little data on the effects of age on drug pharmacokinetics in HIV-positive patients
- Increased pill burden

Monitor

- BMD
- Kidney function
- Liver function

ANTIBIOTICS

Table 77. Antibiotics				
Antimicrobial Class, *Subclass*	**Dosage**	**Adjust When CrCl[a] Is: (mL/min)**	**Formulations**	**Route of Elimination (%)**
β-Lactams ***Penicillins***				
Amoxicillin▲ *(Amoxil)*	po: 250 mg–1 g q8h	<50	T: film coated 500, 875 C: 250, 500 ChT: 125, 200, 250, 400 S: 125, 200, 250, 400 mg/5 mL	K (80)
Ampicillin▲	po: 250–500 mg q6h IM/IV: 1–2 g q4–6h	<30	C: 250, 500 S: 125, 250 mg/5 mL Inj	K (90)
Penicillin G▲	IV: 3–5 × 10⁶ U q4–6h IM: 0.6–2.4 × 10⁶ U q6–12h	<30	Inj procaine for IM	K L (30)
Penicillin VK▲	po: 125–500 mg q6h	b	T: 250, 500 S: 125, 250 mg/5 mL	K, L
Antipseudomonal Penicillin				
Piperacillin▲ *(Pipracil)*	IM: 1–2 g q8–12h IV: 2–4 g q6–8h	<40	Inj	K, F (10–20)
Antistaphylococcal Penicillins				
Dicloxacillin▲ *(Dycill, Pathocil)*	po: 125–500 mg q6h	NA	C: 125, 250, 500 S: 62.5 mg/5 mL	K (56–70)
Nafcillin▲	IM: 500 mg q4–6h IV: 500 mg–2 g q4–6h	NA	Inj	L
Oxacillin▲ *(Bactocill)*	po: 500 mg–1 g q4–6h IM, IV: 250 mg–2 g q6–12h	<10	C: 250, 500 S: 250 mg/5 mL Inj	K
Monobactam (antipseudomonal)				
Aztreonam▲ *(Azactam)*	IM: 500 mg–1 g q8–12h IV: 500 mg–2 g q6–12h	<30	Inj	K (70)
Carbapenems				
Doripenem *(Doribax)*	IV: 500 mg q8h	<50	Inj	K (>70)
Ertapenem *(Invanz)*	IM, IV: 1 g q24h × 3–14 d IM × 7 d max IV × 14 d max	<30	Inj	K (80), F (10)
Imipenem-cilastatin▲ *(Primaxin)*	IM: 500 mg–1 g q8–12h IV: 500 mg–2 g q6–12h	<70	Inj	K (70)
Meropenem▲ *(Merrem IV)*	IV: 1 g q8h	≤50	Inj	K (75), L (25)

(cont.)

Table 77. Antibiotics (cont.)

Antimicrobial Class, *Subclass*	Dosage	Adjust When CrCl[a] Is: (mL/min)	Formulations	Route of Elimination (%)
Penicillinase-resistant Penicillins				
Amoxicillin–clavulanate▲ *(Augmentin)*	po: 250 mg q8h, 500 mg q12h, 875 mg q12h	<30	T: 250, 500, 875 ChT: 125, 200, 250, 400 S: 125, 200, 250, 400 mg/5 mL	K (30–40), L
Ampicillin–sulbactam▲ *(Unasyn)*	IM, IV: 1–2 g q6–8h	<30	Inj	K (85)
Penicillinase-resistant and Antipseudomonal Penicillins				
Piperacillin–tazobactam▲ *(Zosyn)*	IV: 3.375 g q6h	<40	Inj	K (70), F (10–20)
Ticarcillin–clavulanate *(Timentin)*	IV: 3 g q4–6h	<60	Inj	K, L
First-generation Cephalosporins				
Cefadroxil▲ *(Duricef)*	po: 500 mg–1 g q12h	<50	C: 500 T: 1 g S: 125, 250, 500 mg/5 mL	K (90)
Cefazolin▲ *(Ancef, Kefzol)*	IM, IV: 500 mg–2 g q12h	<55	Inj	K (80–100)
Cephalexin▲ *(Keflex)*	po: 250 mg–1 g q6h	<40	C: 250, 500 T: 250, 500; 1 g S: 125, 250 mg/5 mL	K (80–100)
Cephalothin▲ *(Keflin)*	IM, IV: 500 mg–2 g q4–6h	<50	Inj	K (50–75)
Cephradine *(Anspor)*	po, IM, IV: 500 mg–2 g q6h	<20	C: 250, 500 T: 1 g S: 125, 250 mg/5 mL Inj	K (80–90)
Second-generation Cephalosporins				
Cefaclor▲ *(Ceclor)*	po: 250–500 mg q8h	<50	C: 250, 500 S: 125, 187, 250, 375 mg/5 mL T: ER 375, 500	K (80)
Cefotetan▲ *(Cefotan)*	IM, IV: 1–3 g q12h or 1–2 g q24h (UTI)	<30	Inj	K (80)
Cefoxitin▲ *(Mefoxin)*	IM, IV: 1–2 g q6–8h	<50	Inj	K (85)
Cefprozil▲ *(Cefzil)*	po: 250–500 mg q12–24h	<30	T: 250, 500 S: 125, 250 mg/5 mL	K (60–70)
Cefuroxime axetil▲ *(Ceftin)*	po: 125–500 mg q12h IM, IV: 750 mg–1.5 g q6h	<20	T: 125, 250, 500▲ S: 125, 150 mg/5 mL Inj▲	K (66–100)

(cont.)

Table 77. Antibiotics (cont.)

Antimicrobial Class, *Subclass*	Dosage	Adjust When CrCl[a] Is: (mL/min)	Formulations	Route of Elimination (%)
Third-generation Cephalosporins				
Cefdinir▲ *(Omnicef)*	po: 300 mg q12h or 600 mg/d × 10 d	<30	C: 300 S: 125 mg/5 mL	K
Cefditoren▲ *(Spectracef)*	po: 400 mg q12h × 10 d (bronchitis) 400 mg q12h × 14 d (pneumonia) 200 mg q12h × 10 d (soft tissue or skin)	<50	T: 200, 400	K
Cefixime *(Suprax)*	po: 400 mg/d	<60	T: 400; CT: 100, 200 S: 100, 200 mg/5 mL	K (50)
Cefotaxime▲ *(Claforan)*	IM, IV: 1–2 g q6–12h	<20	Inj	K, L
Cefpodoxime▲ *(Vantin)*	po: 100–400 mg q12h	<30	T: 100, 200 S: 50, 100 mg/5 mL	K (80)
Ceftazidime▲ *(Ceptaz, Fortaz)*	IM, IV: 500 mg–2 g q8–12h UTI: 250–500 mg q12h	<50	Inj	K (80–90)
Ceftibuten▲ *(Cedax)*	po: 400 mg/d	<50	C: 400 S: 90, 180 mg/5 mL	K (65–70)
Ceftriaxone▲ *(Rocephin)*	IM, IV: 1–2 g q12–24h	NA	Inj	K (33–65)
Fourth-generation Cephalosporins				
Cefepime▲ *(Maxipime)*	IV: 500 mg–2 g q12h	<60	Inj	K (85)
Fifth-generation Cephalosporin				
Ceftaroline fosamil *(Tefloro)*	400–600 mg q12h	≤50	IV: 400, 600 mg	K (88)
Aminoglycosides				
Amikacin▲ *(Amikin)*	IM, IV: 15–20 mg/kg/d divided q12–24h; 15–20 mg/kg q24–48h	<60, TDM	Inj	K (95)
Gentamicin▲ *(Garamycin)*	IM, IV: 2–5 mg/kg/d divided q12–24h; 5–7 mg/kg q24–48h	<60, TDM	Inj ophth sus, oint	K (95)
Streptomycin▲	IM, IV: 10 mg/kg/d not to exceed 750 mg/d	<50	Inj	K (90)
Tobramycin▲ *(Nebcin)*	IM, IV: 2–5 mg/kg/d divided q12–24h; 5–7 mg/kg q24–48h	<60, TDM	Inj ophth sus, oint	K (95)
Macrolides				
Azithromycin▲ *(Zithromax)*	po: 500 mg on day 1, then 250 mg/d IV: 500 mg/d	NA	S: 100, 200 mg/5 mL, 1 g (single-dose pk) T: 250, 500, 600 mg Inj	L

(cont.)

Table 77. Antibiotics (cont.)

Antimicrobial Class, *Subclass*	Dosage	Adjust When CrCl[a] Is: (mL/min)	Formulations	Route of Elimination (%)
Clarithromycin▲ *(Biaxin, Biaxin XL)*	po: 250–500 mg q12h ER: 1000 mg/d	<30	S: 125, 250 mg/5 mL T: 250, 500 ER: 500	L, K (20–30)
Erythromycin▲	po: Base: 333 mg q8h Stearate or base: 250–500 mg q6–12h Ethylsuccinate: 400–800 mg q6–12h IV: 15–20 mg/kg/d divided q6h	NA	Base: C, T: 250, 333, 500 Stearate: T: 250 Ethylsuccinate: S: 100, 200, 400 mg/5 mL T: 400 Inj	L
Fidaxomycin *(Dificid)*	po: 200 mg q12h	NA	T: 200 mg	F (92)
Ketolide				
Telithromycin *(Ketek)*	po: 800 mg/d × 5–10 d	<30	T: 300, 400	L, K
Quinolones				
Ciprofloxacin▲ *(Cipro)* *(Cipro XR)*	po: 250–750 mg q12h ophth: see **Table 52** IV: 200–400 mg q12h	po: <50 IV: <30	T: 100, 250, 500, 750▲ S: 250 mg/5 mL, 500 mg/5 mL Ophth sol:▲ 3.5 mg/5 mL Inj XR▲: 500, 1000	K (30–50), L, F (20–40)
Gemifloxacin *(Factive)*	po: 320 mg/d	≤40	T: 320 mg	K, L, F
Levofloxacin▲ *(Levaquin)*	po, IV: 250–500 mg/d	<50	T: 250, 500 S: 125 mg/5 mL	K
Moxifloxacin *(Avelox)*	po: 400 mg/d	NA	T: 400 Inj	L (~55), F (25), K (20)
Norfloxacin *(Noroxin)*	po: 400 mg q12h	<30	T: 400	K (30), F (30)
Ofloxacin▲ *(Roxin)*	po, IV: 200–400 mg q12–24h ophth: see **Table 52**	<50	T: 200, 300, 400▲ Ophth: 0.3%▲ Inj	K
Tetracyclines				
Doxycycline▲ (eg, *Vibramycin*)	po, IV: 100–200 mg/d given q12–24h	NA	C: 50, 100 T: 50, 75, 100, 150 S: 25, 50 mg/5 mL Inj	K (25), F (30)
Minocycline▲ *(Minocin)*	po, IV: 200 mg once, then 100 mg q12h	NA	C, T: 50, 75, 100 S: 50 mg/5 mL Inj	K
Tetracycline▲	po, IV: 250–500 mg q6–12h	NA	C: 250, 500	K (60)

(cont.)

Table 77. Antibiotics (cont.)

Antimicrobial Class, *Subclass*	Dosage	Adjust When CrCl[a] Is: (mL/min)	Formulations	Route of Elimination (%)
Glycycline				
Tigecycline *(Tygacil)*	IV: 100 mg once, then 50 mg q12h × 5–14 d	NA	Inj	K (33), F (59), L
Other Antibiotics				
Chloramphenicol▲ *(Chloromycetin)*	po, IV: 50 mg/kg/d given q6h; max: 4 g/d	NA	Inj	L (90)
Clindamycin▲ *(Cleocin)*	po: 150–450 mg q6–8h; max: 1.8 g/d IM, IV: 1.2–1.8 g/d given q8–12h; max: 3.6 g/d	NA	C: 75, 150, 300▲ S: 75 mg/5 mL▲ Vaginal crm: 2% Topical gel: 1%▲ Inj▲	L (90)
Co-trimoxazole▲ (TMP/SMZ, *Bactrim*)	Doses based on the trimethoprim component: po: 1 double-strength tab q12h; IV: sepsis: 20 TMP/kg/d given q6h	≤30	T: SMZ 400, TMP 80 double-strength: SMZ 800, TMP 160 S: SMZ 200, TMP 40 mg/5 mL Inj	K, L
Daptomycin *(Cubicin)*	IV: 4 mg/kg/d × 7–14 d	<30	Inj	K (78), L (6)
Fosfomycin *(Monurol)*	Complicated UTI: Women—po: 3 g in 90–120 mL water × 1 dose Men—po: 3 g in 90–120 mL water q2–3d × 3 doses Prostate—po: 3 g in 90–120 mL water q3d × 21 d		pwd: 3 g/packet	K, F
Linezolid *(Zyvox)*	po: 600 mg q12h IV: 600 mg q12h	NA	T: 600 S: 100 mg/5 mL Inj	L (65), K (30)
Metronidazole▲ *(Flagyl, MetroGel)*	po: 250–750 mg q6–8h Topical: apply q12h Vaginal: 1 applicator full (375 mg) qhs or q12h	≤10	T: 250, 500▲ ER: 750 C: 375▲ Topical gel: 0.75%▲ (30 g) Vaginal gel: 0.75%▲ (70 g) Inj▲	L (30–60), K (20–40), F (6–15)
Nitrofurantoin▲BC *(Macrobid, Macrodantin)*	po: 50–100 mg q6h	Do not use if <40	C: 25, 50▲, 100▲ S: 25 mg/5 mL▲	L (60), K (40)
Quinupristin-dalfopristin *(Synercid)*	Vancomycin-resistant *E faecium*: IV: 7.5 mg/kg q8h Complicated skin or skin structure infection: 7.5 mg/kg q12h	NA	Inj	L, B, F (75), K (15–19)

(cont.)

Table 77. Antibiotics (cont.)				
Antimicrobial Class, _Subclass_	**Dosage**	**Adjust When CrCl[a] Is: (mL/min)**	**Formulations**	**Route of Elimination (%)**
Telavancin _(Vibativ)_	IV: 10 mg/kg q24h × 1–2 wk	≤50	Inj	K (76)
Vancomycin▲ _(Vancocin)_	po: _C difficile:_ 125–500 mg q6–8h IV: 500 mg–1 g q8–24h Peak: 20–40 mcg/mL Trough: 5–10 mcg/mL	<60	C: 125, 250 Inj	K (80–90)
Antifungals (see also **Table 44**) _Amphotericin_				
Amphotericin B▲ _(Fungizone)_	IV: test dose: 1 mg infused over 20–30 min; if tolerated, initial therapeutic dosage is 0.25 mg/kg; the daily dosage can be increased by 0.25-mg/kg increments on each subsequent day until the desired daily dosage is reached Maintenance dosage: IV: 0.25–1 mg/kg/d or 1.5 mg/kg q48h; do not exceed 1.5 mg/kg/d	c	Topical: crm, lot, oint: 3% Inj	K
Amphotericin B Lipid Complex _(Abelcet)_	2.5–5 mg/kg/d as a single infusion	c	Inj	K
Amphotericin B Liposomal _(AmBisome)_	3–6 mg/kg/d infused over 1–2 h	c	Inj	K
Amphotericin B Cholestreyl Sulfate Complex _(Amphotec)_	3–4 mg/kg/d infused at 1 mg/kg/h; max dosage 7.5 mg/kg/d	c	Inj	K
Azoles Fluconazole▲ _(Diflucan)_	po, IV: first dose 200–800 mg, then 100–400 mg q24h for 14 d–12 wk, depending on indication Vaginal candidiasis: 150 mg as a single dose	<50	T: 50, 100, 150, 200 S: 10 and 40 mg/mL Inj	K (80)
Itraconazole _(Sporanox)_	po: 200–400 mg/d; dosages >200 mg/d should be divided. Life-threatening infections: loading dose: 200 mg q8h should be given for the first 3 d of tx IV: 200 mg q12h × 4 d, then 200 mg/d	<30	C: 100▲, 200 S: 100 mg/10 mL Inj	L

(cont.)

Table 77. Antibiotics (cont.)

Antimicrobial Class, *Subclass*	Dosage	Adjust When CrCl[a] Is: (mL/min)	Formulations	Route of Elimination (%)
Ketoconazole▲ *(Nizoral)*	po: 200–400 mg/d shp: 2/wk × 4 wk with ≥ 3 d between each shp Topical: apply q12–24h	NA	T: 200 shp: 2% crm: 2%	L, F
Miconazole▲ *(Monistat IV)*	IT: 20 mg q1–2d IV: initial: 200 mg, then 1.2–3.6 g/d divided q8h for up to 2 wk	NA	Inj	L, F
Voriconazole *(VFEND)*	IV: loading dose 6 mg/kg q12h for 2 doses, then 4 mg/kg q12h po: >40 kg: 200 mg q12h; ≤40 kg: 100 mg q12h If on phenytoin, IV: 5 mg/kg q12h, and po: >40 kg: 400 mg q12h; ≤40 kg: 200 mg q12h	<50 (IV only)	Inj T: 50, 200 mg	L
Posaconazole *(Noxafil)*	Candida or aspergillosis, invasive: Prophylaxis: T: 300 mg × 1 d; Maintenance: T: 300 mg q24h; Sus: 200 mg q8h. Duration: recovery from neutropenia or immunosuppression. Oropharyngeal infection: Initial: 100 mg q12h × 1 d; maintenance: 100 mg q24h × 13 d.			
	Refractory oropharyngeal infection: Sus: 400 mg q12h; duration based on underlying disease and clinical response.	NA	T: 200 sus: 40 mg/mL	F

(cont.)

Table 77. **Antibiotics (cont.)**

Antimicrobial Class, *Subclass*	Dosage	Adjust When CrCl[a] Is: (mL/min)	Formulations	Route of Elimination (%)
Echinocandins				
Anidulafungin *(Eraxis)*	Esophageal candidiasis: 100 mg on day 1, then 50 mg/d × ≥13 d and 7 d after symptoms resolve	NA	Inj	L, F (30)
Caspofungin *(Cancidas)*	Initial: 70 mg infused over 1 h; esophageal candidiasis: 50 mg/d; dosage with concurrent enzyme inducers: 70 mg/d	NA	Inj	L (50), F (35)
Micafungin *(Mycamine)*	Esophageal candidiasis: 150 mg/d; prophylaxis in stem cell transplant: 50 mg/d	NA	Inj	L, F (71), K (<15)
Other Antifungals				
Flucytosine▲ *(Ancobon)*	po: 50–150 mg/kg/d divided q6h	<40	C: 250, 500	K (75–90)
Griseofulvin▲ *(Fulvicin P/G, Grifulvin V)*	po: Microsize: 500–1000 mg/d in single or divided doses Ultramicrosize: 330–375 mg/d in single or divided doses Duration based on indication	NA	Microsize: S: 125 mg/5 mL T: 125, 250, 500	L
Terbinafine▲ *(Lamisil)*	po: 250 mg/d × 6–12 wk for superficial mycoses; 250–500 mg/d for up to 16 mo Topical: apply q12–24h for max of 4 wk	<50	T: 250 mg▲ crm: 1%▲ Topical S: 1%	L, K (70–75)

Note: NA = not applicable; TDM = adjust dose on basis of therapeutic drug monitoring principles and institutional protocols

[a] The CrCl listed is the threshold below which the dosage (amount or frequency) should be adjusted. See package insert for detailed dosing guidelines.

[b] Dosage should not exceed 250 mg q6h in kidney impairment.

[c] Adjust dosage if decreased kidney function is due to the medication, or give every other day.

[BC] Avoid.

ACUTE KIDNEY INJURY

Definition

An acute deterioration in kidney function defined by decreased urine output or increased values of kidney function tests, or both

Precipitating and Aggravating Factors (Italicized type indicates most common.)

- *Acute tubular necrosis* due to hypoperfusion or nephrotoxins
- Medications (eg, aminoglycosides, radiocontrast materials, NSAIDs, ACEIs), including those causing allergic interstitial nephritis (eg, NSAIDs, penicillins and cephalosporins, sulfonamides, fluoroquinolones, allopurinol, rifampin, PPIs)
- Multiple myeloma
- Obstruction (eg, BPH)
- Vascular disease (thromboembolic, atheroembolic)
- *Volume depletion* or redistribution of ECF (eg, cirrhosis, burns)

Evaluation

- Review medication list
- Catheterize bladder, determine postvoid residual
- UA (see **Table 78** for likely diagnoses)
- Renal ultrasonography
- Renal biopsy in selected cases

- If patient is not on diuretics, determine fractional excretion of sodium (FENa):

$$FENa = \left[\frac{urine\ Na/plasma\ Na}{urine\ Cr/plasma\ Cr} \right] \times 100$$

FENa <1% indicates prerenal cause; FENa >2% generally indicates acute tubular necrosis; FENa 1–2% is nondiagnostic. Note that some older adults who have prerenal cause may have FENa ≥1% because of age-related changes in sodium excretion.

- If patient is receiving diuretics, determine fractional excretion of urea (FEUrea):

$$FEUrea = \left[\frac{urine\ urea\ nitrogen/BUN}{urine\ Cr/plasma\ Cr} \right] \times 100$$

FEUrea ≤35% indicates prerenal azotemia; FEUrea >50% indicates acute tubular necrosis; FEUrea 36–50% is nondiagnostic.

Table 78. Likely Diagnoses Based on UA Findings

Findings	Diagnoses
Hematuria, RBC casts, heavy proteinuria	Glomerular disease or vasculitis
Granular and epithelial cell casts, free epithelial cells	Acute tubular necrosis
Pyuria, WBC casts, granular or waxy casts, little or no proteinuria	Acute interstitial nephritis, glomerulitis, vasculitis, obstruction, renal infarction
Normal UA	Prerenal disease, obstruction, hypercalcemia, myeloma, acute tubular necrosis

Urinary eosinophils are neither sensitive nor specific for acute interstitial nephritis but may be helpful in some cases.

Prevention of Radiocontrast-induced Acute Kidney Failure in High-risk Patients (Cr >1.5 mg/dL, GFR <60 mL/min/1.73 m² body surface area)

- Hold NSAIDs and diuretics for 24 h and metformin for 48 h before administration
- Use low osmolal or iso-osmolal contrast agents in low doses
- Avoid closely spaced repeat studies (eg, <48 h apart)
- Intravenous hydration
  - 0.9% saline IV 1 mL/kg/h for 24 h beginning 2–12 h before administration and continuing 6–12 h after procedure, *or*
  - Sodium bicarbonate (154 mEq/L) 3 mL/kg/h for 1 h before procedure and 1 mL/kg/h for 6 h after procedure, especially if insufficient time for hydration before procedure
- Oral acetylcysteine *(Mucomyst)* (100, 200/mL) 1200 mg po q12h the day before and the day of procedure (controversial); does not reduce the risk in at-risk patients undergoing coronary and peripheral vascular angiography
- Repeat serum Cr 24–48 h after administration

Treatment

- D/C medications that are possible precipitants; avoid contrast dyes.
- If prerenal pattern, treat HF (see p 42) if present. Otherwise, volume repletion. Begin with fluid challenge 500–1000 mL over 30–60 min. If no response (increased urine output), give furosemide 100–400 mg IV.
- If obstructed, leave urinary catheter in place during evaluation and while specific tx is implemented.
- If acute tubular necrosis, monitor weight daily, record intake and output, and monitor electrolytes frequently. Fluid replacement should be equal to urinary output plus other drainage plus 500 mL/d for insensible losses.
- If acute interstitial nephritis (except if NSAID-induced) and does not resolve with 3–7 d, then glucocorticoids (eg, prednisone 1 mg/kg/d) for a minimum 1–2 wk and gradual taper when Cr has returned near baseline for a total duration of 2–3 mo.
- Dialysis is indicated when severe hyperkalemia, acidosis, or volume overload cannot be managed with other tx or when uremic symptoms (eg, pericarditis, coagulopathy, or encephalopathy) are present.

CHRONIC KIDNEY DISEASE

Definition

Kidney damage as evidenced by urinary albumin excretion of >30 mg/d or eGFR <60 mL/min/1.73 m², irrespective of the cause.

Classification (Kidney Disease Outcomes Quality Initiative)

Stage G1: GFR >90 mL/min/1.73 m² and persistent albuminuria

Stage G2: GFR 60–89 mL/min/1.73 m² and persistent albuminuria

Stage G3: GFR 30–59 mL/min/1.73 m²

Stage G4: GFR 15–29 mL/min/1.73 m²

Stage G5: GFR <15 mL/min/1.73 m² or end-stage renal disease

Albumin

A1: Daily albumin excretion rate <30 mg/dL
A2: Daily albumin excretion rate 30–300 mg/dL
A3: Daily albumin excretion rate >300 mg/dL

• Cause of CKD also has prognostic value for kidney outcomes and other complications.
• Refer to a nephrologist for co-management if stages G4 A3 and all stage G5 are at very high risk of complications and need for dialysis. Stages G4 A1 and A2, and G3 A2 and A3 (if GFR <44) and A3 (if GFR 44–59) are at high risk of complications. If stage G4–G5 or additional indications of urine albumin-to-Cr ratio >300 mg/g, resistant hypertension, unexplained hematuria or cause of CKD, >30% decline in GFR in <4 mo, CKD complications (see below).

Evaluation

• Hx and physical examination: assess for DM, HTN, vascular disease, HF, NSAIDs, contrast dye exposure, angiographic procedures with possible cholesterol embolization, glomerulonephritis, myeloma, BPH or obstructive cancers, current or previous tx with a nephrotoxic drug, hereditary kidney disease (eg, polycystic)
• Blood tests (CBC, comprehensive metabolic profile, phosphorus, cholesterol, ESR, serum protein immunoelectrophoresis)
• Progression to kidney failure can be predicted by age, sex, eGFR, urine albumin:Cr ratio, serum calcium, serum phosphate, serum bicarbonate, and serum albumin using equation: http://www.qxmd.com/calculate-online/nephrology/kidney-failure-risk-equation.
• Estimate CrCl or GFR (see p 1). CrCl is usually about 20% higher than true GFR. eGFR based on the MDRD equation and true GFR are very close when the GFR is <60 mL/min/1.73 m^2, but true GFR exceeds eGFR by a small amount when GFR is >60 mL/min/1.73 m^2. Older people with eGFR 45–59 mL/min/1.73 m^2 may have normal kidney function for their age.
• If GFR 15–59 mL/min/1.73 m^2, then measure iPTH; if iPTH >100 pg/mL, then measure serum 25-hydroxy vitamin D
• UA and quantitative urine protein (protein:Cr ratio or 24-h urine for protein and Cr); urine immunoelectrophoresis, if indicated; at all stages, heavier proteinuria is predictive of mortality, ESRD, and doubling of serum Cr
• Renal ultrasound (large kidneys suggest tumors, infiltrating disease, cystic disease; small kidneys suggest CKD; can also identify cysts, stones, masses, and hydronephrosis)
• Exclude renal artery stenosis with MRI angiography, spiral CT with CT angiography, or duplex Doppler ultrasound if acute rise in Cr shortly after beginning tx with ACEI or ARB
• Renal biopsy in selected cases

Treatment

• Attempt to slow progression of kidney failure
  ○ Control BP *most important* (target <130/80 if proteinuria [>500 mg/d] Kidney Diseases: Improving Global Outcomes [KDIGO]); <140/80 regardless of proteinuria (JNC 8). Begin with ACEI or ARB; in black patients without proteinuria, thiazide diuretic or CCB are acceptable options.
  ○ If DM or proteinuria, begin ACEI or ARB (see **Table 23**) regardless of whether or not patient has HTN.
  ○ DM control (see p 94)
  ○ Treat hyperlipidemia (p 181)
  ○ Moderate dietary protein restriction, 0.8–1 g/kg/d, especially if diabetic nephropathy; if stage G4 or G5 CKD, consider low-protein (0.6 g/kg/d) diet.

- ○ Smoking cessation
- ○ Reduction of proteinuria to <1 g/d, if possible and at least to <60% of baseline
- ○ Avoid triamterene and NSAIDs^{CW} in stages 4 and 5 CKD.^{BC}
- Prevent and treat symptoms and complications
  - ○ Hyperkalemia: if present (p 183); low potassium diet <40–70 mEq/d; avoid NSAIDs.
  - ○ Acidosis: Sodium bicarbonate (daily dosage of 0.5–1 mEq/kg) tx to maintain serum bicarbonate concentration >23 mEq/L.
  - ○ Mineral and bone complications:
    - Normalize serum calcium with calcium carbonate▲ (500 mg elemental calcium q6–24h) or calcium acetate *(PhosLo)* (3 or 4 tabs q8h with meals); if hypocalcemia is refractory, consider calcitriol *(Rocaltrol)* 0.25 mcg/d.
    - Normalize serum phosphate (2.7–4.6 g/dL) if not on dialysis and maintain between 3.5 and 5.5 mg/dL if on dialysis; restrict dairy products and cola to phosphate intake <900 mg/d. When hyperphosphatemia is refractory, begin:
      - □ If serum calcium is low, calcium carbonate▲ (1250–1500 mg q8h with meals) or calcium acetate *(PhosLo)* (3 or 4 tabs q8h with meals).
      - □ If serum calcium is normal or calcium supplementation is ineffective:
        - – Sevelamer hydrochloride *(Renagel)* [T: 400, 800; C: 403] or sevelamer carbonate *(Renvela)* [0.8 g pk, T: 800], which does not lower bicarbonate 800–1600 mg po q8h with each meal.
        - – Lanthanum carbonate *(Fosrenol)* [ChT: 250, 500] at initial dosage of 250–500 mg po q8h with each meal, then titrate in increments of 750 mg/d at intervals of 2–3 wk to max of 3750 mg/d.
  - ○ Total elemental calcium (dietary and phosphate should be <2 g)
  - ○ Avoid aluminum and magnesium phosphate binders
  - ○ Treating vitamin D insufficiency improves biochemical markers but the effect on clinical outcomes is uncertain. Use vitamin D_2 (ergocalciferol) 50,000 U/mo or oral vitamin D with calcitriol 25 mcg/d if 25(OH) vitamin D is <30 ng/mL. Stop if corrected serum calcium is >10.2 mg/dL.
  - ○ Anemia: Monitor Hb yearly if stage G3, q6mo if stages G4 or G5, and q3mo if on dialysis. Treat anemia with iron (if iron-deficient) to maintain transferrin saturation >20% and serum ferritin >100 ng/L and, if necessary, erythropoietin-darbepoetin (see **Table 67**) to maintain a target Hb goal of ≤11 g/dL. Don't administer erythropoiesis-stimulating agents to patients with CKD with Hb ≥10 g/dL without signs or symptoms.^{CW}
  - ○ Cardiovascular:
    - Manage volume overload (see HF, p 42).
    - HTN control: target <140/80; <130/80 if proteinuria >500 mg/d
    - Prevent and treat cardiovascular disease (see p 38) with target LDL goal <100 mg/dL. The value of statins for patients on maintenance dialysis is questionable.
  - ○ Prevention: Immunize with *Pneumovax* and, if stage G4 or G5 CKD, hepatitis B vaccines if hepatitis B surface antigen and antibody are negative.
  - ○ Prepare for dialysis or transplant. Educate patients regarding options of hemodialysis, peritoneal dialysis, and kidney transplantation. If estimated GFR <25 mL/min/1.73 m², recommend referral for arteriovenous fistula access, which takes months before it is ready to be used. If estimated GFR <20 mL/min/1.73 m², patients can be listed for cadaveric kidney transplant.

- Dialysis is indicated when severe hyperkalemia, acidosis, or volume overload cannot be managed with other tx or when uremic symptoms (eg, pericarditis, coagulopathy, or encephalopathy) are present.
- Don't perform routine cancer screening for dialysis patients with limited life expectancies without signs or symptoms.[CW]

VOLUME DEPLETION (DEHYDRATION)

Definition
Losses of sodium and water that may be isotonic (eg, loss of blood) or hypotonic (eg, nasogastric suctioning)

Precipitating Factors
- Blood loss
- Diuretics
- GI losses
- Kidney or adrenal disease (eg, renal sodium wasting)
- Sequestration of fluid (eg, ileus, burns, peritonitis)
- Age-related changes (impaired thirst, sodium wasting due to hyporeninemic hypoaldosteronism, and free water wasting due to renal insensitivity to antidiuretic hormone)

Evaluation
Clinical Symptoms
- Anorexia
- Nausea and vomiting
- Orthostatic lightheadedness
- Delirium
- Weakness

Clinical Signs
- Dry tongue and axillae
- Oliguria
- Orthostatic hypotension
- Elevated HR
- Weight loss

Laboratory Tests
- Serum electrolytes
- Urine sodium (usually <10 mEq/L) and FENa (usually <1% but may be higher because of age-related sodium wasting)
- Serum BUN and Cr (BUN:Cr ratio often >20)

Management
- Weigh daily; monitor fluid losses and serum electrolytes, BUN, Cr.
- If mild, oral rehydration of 2–4 L of water/d and 4–8 g Na diet; if poor oral intake, give IV D5W1/2 NS with potassium as needed.
- If hemodynamically unstable, give IV 0.9% saline 1–2 L as quickly as possible until SBP ≥100 mmHg and no longer orthostatic. Then switch to D5W1/2 NS. Monitor closely in patients with a hx of HF. Avoid hyperoncotic starch solutions, which are associated with acute kidney injury and increased mortality.

HYPERNATREMIA

Causes
- Pure water loss
  - Insensible losses due to sweating and respiration
  - Central (eg, post-traumatic, CNS tumors, meningitis) diabetes insipidus or nephrogenic (eg, hypercalcemia, lithium) diabetes insipidus

- Hypotonic sodium loss
  - Renal causes: osmotic diuresis (eg, due to hyperglycemia), postobstructive diuresis, polyuric phase of acute tubular necrosis
  - GI causes: vomiting and diarrhea, nasogastric drainage, osmotic cathartic agents (eg, lactulose)
- Hypertonic sodium gain (eg, tx with hypertonic saline)
- Impaired thirst (eg, delirious or intubated) or access to water (eg, functionally dependent) may sustain hypernatremia

Evaluation
- Measure intake and output.
- Obtain urine osmolality:
  - >800 mOsm/kg suggests extrarenal (if urine Na <25 mEq/L) or remote renal water loss or administration of hypertonic Na^+ salt solutions (if urine Na >100 mEq/L).
  - <250 mOsm/kg and polyuria suggest diabetes insipidus.

Treatment
- Treat underlying causes.
- Correct slowly over at least 48–72 h using oral (can use pure water), nasogastric (can use pure water), or IV (D5W, 1/2 or 1/4 NS) fluids; correct at rate of no more than 1 mmol/L/h if acute (eg, developing over hours) and at no more than 10 mmol/L/d if of longer duration.
- Correct with NS only in cases of severe volume depletion with hemodynamic compromise; once stable, switch to hypotonic solution.
- When repleting fluids, use the following formula to estimate the effect of 1 L of any infusate on serum Na:

$$\text{Change in serum Na} = \frac{\text{infusate Na} - \text{serum Na}}{\text{total body water} + 1}$$

  - Infusate Na (mmol/L). D5W = 0; 1/4 NS = 34; 1/2 NS = 77; NS = 154
  - Calculate total body water as a fraction of body weight (0.5 kg in older men and 0.45 kg in older women).
- Divide tx goal (usually 10 mmol/L/d) by change in serum Na/L (from formula) to determine amount of solution to be given over 24 h.
- Compensate for any ongoing obligatory fluid losses, which are usually 1–1.5 L/d.
- Divide amount of solution for repletion plus amount for obligatory fluid losses by 24 to determine rate per hour.

HYPONATREMIA
Causes
- With increased plasma osmolality: hyperglycemia (1.6 mEq/L decrement for each 100 mg/dL increase in plasma glucose)
- With normal plasma osmolality (pseudohyponatremia): severe hyperlipidemia, hyperproteinemia (eg, multiple myeloma)
- With decreased plasma osmolality:
  - With ECF excess: kidney failure, HF, hepatic cirrhosis, nephrotic syndrome

- With decreased ECF volume: renal loss from salt-losing nephropathies, diuretics, cerebral salt wasting, osmotic diuresis; extrarenal loss due to vomiting, diarrhea, skin losses, and third-spacing (usually urine Na <20 mEq/L, FENa <1%, and uric acid >4 mg/dL)
  - With normal ECF volume: primary polydipsia (urine osmolarity <100 mOsm/kg), hypothyroidism, adrenal insufficiency, SIADH (urine Na >40 mEq/L and uric acid <4 mg/dL)

Management

Treat underlying cause. Specific tx only if symptomatic (eg, altered mental status, seizures) or severe acute hyponatremia (eg, <120 mEq/L).

- If initial volume estimate is equivocal, give fluid challenge of 0.5–1 L of isotonic (0.9%) saline.
- If volume depletion, give saline IV (corrects ~1 mEq/L for every liter given) or oral salt tablets.
- If edematous states, SIADH, or chronic renal failure, fluid restriction to below the level of urine output is the primary tx.
- Hypovolemic hyponatremia is almost always chronic (except for cerebral salt wasting and after diuretic initiation), and hypertonic saline is seldom indicated.
- Euvolemic hyponatremia if acute (<48 h duration) should be corrected promptly with hypertonic (3%) saline; initial infusion rate: body weight (kg) × desired rate of increase in Na (mEq/h); correct 2–4 mEq/L in first 2–4 h if symptomatic.
- Goal is <10 mEq/L/24 h, <18 mEq/L/48 h, and <20 mEq/L/72 h rise in Na (more rapid correction can result in central pontine myelinolysis).
- Monitor Na closely and taper tx when >120 mEq/L or symptoms resolve.
- Arginine vasopressin receptor antagonists
  - Conivaptan *(Vaprisol)* is effective in euvolemic hyponatremia in hospitalized patients; 20 mg IV over 30 min once, followed by continuous infusion of 20–40 mg over 24 h for 4 d max (L) (CYP3A4 interactions).
  - Tolvaptan *(Samsca)* 15–60 mg/d [T:15, 30]: initiate in hospital and monitor blood sodium concentration closely.

SYNDROME OF INAPPROPRIATE SECRETION OF ANTIDIURETIC HORMONE (SIADH)

Definition

Hypotonic hyponatremia (<280 mOsm/kg) with:

- Less than maximally dilute urine (usually >100 mOsm/kg)
- Elevated urine sodium (usually >40 mEq/L)
- Normal volume status
- Normal kidney, adrenal, and thyroid function

Precipitating Factors, Causes

- Medications (eg, SSRIs, SNRIs, chlorpropamide, carbamazepine, oxcarbazepine, NSAIDs, barbiturates, antipsychotics, mirtazapine. Use with caution.[BC])
- Neuropsychiatric factors (eg, neoplasm, subarachnoid hemorrhage, psychosis, meningitis)
- Postoperative state, especially if pain or nausea
- Pulmonary disease (eg, pneumonia, tuberculosis, acute asthma)
- Tumors (eg, lung, pancreas, thymus)

Evaluation

- BUN, Cr, serum cortisol, TSH
- CXR
- Review of medications
- Neurologic tests as indicated
- Urine sodium and osmolality

Management

Acute Treatment: See euvolemic hyponatremia management, p 182.

Chronic Treatment:

- D/C offending medication or treat precipitating illness.
- Restrict water intake to <800 mL/d with goal of Na ≥130 mEq/L.
- Liberalize salt intake or give salt tablets.
- If urinary osmolality is twice the plasma osmolality, loop diuretics (eg, furosemide 20 mg q12h) may help facilitate excess water excretion.
- Demeclocycline▲ *(Declomycin)* 150–300 mg q12h [T: 150, 300] (may be nephrotoxic in patients with liver disease) only if symptomatic and above steps do not work.
- Tolvaptan *(Samsca)* 15–60 mg/d [T:15, 30]: initiate in hospital and monitor blood sodium concentration closely only if symptomatic and above steps do not work. Risk of hepatotoxicity. Do not use for >30 d and not in patients with chronic liver diseases.

HYPERKALEMIA

Causes

- Kidney failure
- Addison disease
- Hyporeninemic hypoaldosteronism
- Renal tubular acidosis
- Acidosis
- Diabetic hyperglycemia
- Hemolysis, tumor lysis, rhabdomyolysis
- Medications (potassium-sparing diuretics, ACEIs, trimethoprim-sulfamethoxazole, β-blockers, NSAIDs, cyclosporine, tacrolimus, pentamidine, heparin, digoxin toxicity)
- Pseudohyperkalemia from extreme thrombocytosis or leukocytosis
- Transfusions of stored blood
- Constipation

Evaluation

- ECG; peaked T waves typically occur when K^+ exceeds 6.5 mEq/L. ECG changes are more likely with acute increases of K^+ than with chronic increases.

Treatment

Minor elevations

- K^+ <6 mEq/L without ECG changes:
  - Low-potassium diet (restrict orange juice, bananas, potatoes, cantaloupe, honeydew, tomatoes)
  - Oral diuretics (eg, oral torsemide or bumetanide, combined oral loop and thiazide-like diuretics; metolazone is the most K^+ wasting); avoid hypovolemia

- Oral NaHCO$_3$ (650–1300 mg q12h)
- Reduce or D/C medications that increase K$^+$

- K$^+$ 6–6.5 mEq/L without ECG changes: above tx plus sodium polystyrene sulfonate▲ *(SPS, Kayexalate)* 15–30 g po q6–24h, or prn as enema 30–50 g in 100 mL of dextrose; full effect takes 4–24 h and generally requires multiple doses over 1–5 d. Can expect approximately 1 mEg/d reduction. Other laxatives (eg, sorbitol).

- K$^+$ 6.5 mEq/L with peaked T waves but no other ECG changes; hospitalization is decided case-by-case based on acuteness of onset, cause, and other patient factors.

Absolute indications for hospitalization

- K$^+$ >8 mEq/L
- ECG changes other than peaked T waves (eg, prolonged PR, loss of P waves, widened QRS)
- Acute deterioration of kidney function

Inpatient management of hyperkalemia

- Antagonism of cardiac effects of hyperkalemia (most rapid-acting acute tx; use only for severe hyperkalemia with significant ECG changes when too dangerous to wait for redistribution tx to take effect)
  - 10% calcium gluconate IV infused over 2–3 min (20–30 min if on digoxin) with ECG monitoring; effect lasts 30–60 min, may repeat if needed

- Reduction of serum K$^+$ by redistribution into cells (acute tx; can be used in combination with calcium gluconate, and different redistribution tx can be combined depending on severity of hyperkalemia)
  - Insulin (regular) 10 U in 500 mL of 10% dextrose over 30–60 min or bolus insulin (regular) 10 U IV followed by 50 mL of 50% dextrose
  - Albuterol 0.5 mg in 100 mL of 5% dextrose given over 10–15 min or nebulized 10–20 mg in 4 mL of NS over 10 min (should not be used as single agent)
  - Sodium bicarbonate use is controversial.

- Removal of potassium from body (definitive tx; work more slowly)
  - Diuretics (eg, oral torsemide or bumetanide, IV furosemide, combined oral loop and thiazide-like diuretics; metolazone is the most K$^+$ wasting). Avoid hypovolemia.
  - Fludrocortisone▲ 0.1–0.3 mg/d
  - Sodium polystyrene sulfonate▲ *(SPS, Kayexalate)* 15–30 g po q6–24h or prn as enema 30–50 g in 100 mL of dextrose; full effect takes 4–24 h; if packaged in sorbitol *(SPS)*, may cause intestinal necrosis.
  - Dialysis

MALNUTRITION

DEFINITION
There is no uniformly accepted definition of malnutrition in older adults. Some commonly used definitions include the following:

Community-dwelling Older Adults
- ASPEN criteria for adult malnutrition (2 of the following):
  - Insufficient energy intake
  - Loss of muscle mass
  - Fluid accumulation (eg, edema)
  - Weight loss
  - Loss of subcutaneous fat
  - Diminished function by hand-grip strength

- Involuntary weight loss (eg, $\geq$2% over 1 mo, >10 lb over 6 mo, $\geq$4% over 1 yr)
- BMI <22 kg/m^2
- Hypoalbuminemia (eg, $\leq$3.8 g/dL)
- Hypocholesterolemia (eg, <160 mg/dL)
- Overweight (BMI 25–29.9 kg/m^2); not associated with increased mortality if >70 yr old
- Obesity (BMI $\geq$30 kg/m^2)
- Specific vitamin or micronutrient deficiencies (eg, vitamin B$_{12}$)
- Cancer-related anorexia/cachexia syndrome: a hypercatabolic state (increased resting energy expenditure) with high levels of tumor-activated or host-produced immune responses (eg, proinflammatory cytokines) to the tumor
- Sarcopenia age-related loss of muscle mass (eg, 2 SDs below mean for young healthy adults) with loss of strength and performance; contributors include decreased sex hormones, increased insulin resistance, increased inflammatory cytokines, decreased physical activity, inadequate protein intake, and spinal cord changes (decreased motor units)

Hospitalized Patients
- Dietary intake (eg, <50% of estimated needed caloric intake)
- Hypoalbuminemia (eg, <3.5 g/dL)
- Hypocholesterolemia (eg, <160 mg/dL)

Nursing-home Patients (Triggered by the Minimum Data Set)
- Weight loss of $\geq$5% in past 30 d; $\geq$10% in 180 d
- Dietary intake <75% of most meals

EVALUATION

Screening
Proposed screening instruments have not been adequately validated or do not demonstrate sufficient sensitivity and specificity to warrant use in clinical practice.

Multidimensional Assessment
In the absence of valid nutrition screening instruments, clinicians should focus on whether the following issues may be affecting nutritional status:

- Economic barriers to securing food
- Social isolation (eg, eating alone)
- Availability of sufficiently high-quality food
- Dental problems that preclude ingesting food
- Medical illnesses that:
  - interfere with ingestion (eg, dysphagia), digestion, or absorption of food
  - increase nutritional requirements or cause cachexia
  - require dietary restrictions (eg, low-sodium diet or npo)
- Functional disability that interferes with shopping, preparing meals, or feeding
- Food preferences or cultural beliefs that interfere with adequate food intake
- Poor appetite
- Depressive symptoms

Anthropometrics
Weight on each visit and yearly height (see p 1)

Evaluation for Comorbid Medical Conditions
- CBC, ESR, and comprehensive metabolic panel (if none abnormal, then likelihood ratio for cancer is 0.2)
- CXR
- TSH

Biochemical Markers
Serum Proteins: All may drop precipitously because of trauma, sepsis, or major infection.
- Albumin (half-life 18–20 d) has prognostic value in all settings.
- Transferrin (half-life 7 d)
- Prealbumin (half-life 48 h) may be valuable in monitoring nutritional recovery.

Serum Cholesterol (Low or Falling Levels): Has prognostic value in all settings but may not be nutritionally mediated.

MANAGEMENT
Universal Recommendations
Vitamin D and Calcium
All older adults should receive calcium 1000 mg/d and vitamin D 800 IU/d. The appropriate use of 25-hydroxy vitamin D levels to detect and monitor vitamin D tx has not been determined. If low, vitamin D should be replaced to levels of ≥30 ng/mL. See Osteoporosis, p 222.

Multivitamins
- Observational data in post-menopausal women indicate no effect on breast, colorectal, endometrial, lung, or ovarian cancers, MI, stroke, VTE, or mortality.
- In clinical trials in middle-aged men, multivitamins have not been shown to decrease cardiovascular disease or mortality, but there is a small reduction in total cancer risk.
- Clinical trial data show no benefit in reducing infections in outpatient and nursing home settings.

Mediterranean Diet
- Observational data indicate improved health status and reductions in cardiovascular disease, cancer, and overall mortality, as well as lower incidences of Parkinson disease and Alzheimer disease
- Clinical trial data demonstrate reduction in major cardiovascular events with Mediterranean diet supplemented by either extra-virgin olive oil or mixed nuts

Calculating Basic Energy (Caloric) and Fluid Requirements
- WHO energy estimates for adults 60 yr old and older:
  - Women (10.5) (weight in kg) + 596
  - Men (13.5) (weight in kg) + 487
- Harris-Benedict energy requirement equations:
  - Women: 655 + (9.6) (weight in kg) + (1.7) (height in cm) − (4.7) (age in yr)
  - Men: 66 + (13.7) (weight in kg) + (5) (height in cm) − (6.8) (age in yr)
- Fluid requirements for older adults without heart or kidney disease are ~30 mL/kg/d. Depending on activity and physiologic stress levels, these basic requirements may need to be increased (eg, 25% for sedentary or mild, 50% for moderate, and 100% for intense or severe activity or stress).

Obesity and Overweight Management
Nonpharmacologic Treatment
- Overweight probably does not increase mortality risk; however, weight loss in obese older adults may decrease mortality risk.
- In younger overweight and obese patients, no particular combination of protein, carbohydrate, and fat in weight loss diets offers any advantage in losing weight.
- Moderate exercise at 90 min/3 x/wk and a caloric prescription to produce a deficit of 500–750 calories/d can lead to weight loss of 10% and improved functional status in younger (mean age 70) obese older persons.

Pharmacologic Treatment
- Drugs to treat obesity have not been studied extensively in older persons.
- Consider if BMI ≥30 or 27–29 if comorbidities.
- When using pharmacologic management, weight loss of 10–15% is considered a good response and >15% is considered excellent.
- Orlistat *(Xenical, Alli)* 120 mg q8h [C: 60 mg *(Alli)* OTC, 120 mg, has the longest-term data on safety and efficacy. Abdominal discomfort and flatus are the most common adverse effects.
- Lorcaserin 10 mg q12h *(Belviq)* [T:10 mg]. D/C if <5% weight loss in 12 wk.
- Phentermine-topiramate *(Qsymia)* [ER T:3.75 mg/23 mg, 7.5 mg/46 mg, 1.25 mg/69 mg, 5 mg/92 mg]. Begin 3.75 mg/23 mg daily for 14 d, then increase; 3.75 mg/46 mg) may be more effective but should not be used if cardiovascular disease or HTN.
- Other drugs have limited effectiveness or high potential for adverse effects or abuse.

Undernutrition Management
- If possible, remove disease-specific (eg, for hypercholesterolemia) dietary restrictions.
- If needed, help arrange shopping, cooking, and feeding assistance, including home-delivered meals and between-meal snacks.
- Increase caloric density of foods.

- Refeeding syndrome caused by the glucose-induced acute transcellular shift of phosphate typically occurs in malnourished patients who have had poor oral intake and then receive IV glucose-containing fluids, or enteral or parenteral nutrition. Symptoms occur most commonly within 2–4 d of refeeding and include hypophosphatemia, hyperglycemia, and hyperinsulinemia, which may be accompanied by hypokalemia, hypomagnesemia, and fluid retention. Supplementing IV fluids with potassium phosphate or oral phosphate and potassium may help prevent this syndrome.
- Post-hospitalization home visits by a dietitian may be valuable.

Appetite Stimulants

- No medications are FDA approved to promote weight gain in older adults.
- Dronabinol and megestrol acetate (Avoid [BC]) (not covered by Medicare Part D) have been effective in promoting weight gain in younger adults with specific conditions (eg, AIDS, cancer). Small clinical trials of megestrol in select groups (eg, after hospitalization, nursing home) have shown benefit for some nutritional markers (eg, prealbumin, weight) but not for clinical outcomes. Avoid megestrol; may increase risk of thrombosis and death.[BC]
- A minority of patients receiving mirtazapine[▲] report appetite stimulation and weight gain.
- All medications used for appetite have substantial potential AEs.

Nutritional Supplements

- Protein and energy supplements in older adults at risk of malnutrition appear to have beneficial effects on weight gain and mortality, and shorten length of stay in hospitalized patients. Among those who are well nourished at baseline, the benefit is less clear. Supplements should be given between rather than with meals.
- For ICU patients, enteral nutrition is preferred over parenteral nutrition and should be started within the first 24–48 h after admission. Absence of bowel sounds and evidence of bowel function (eg, passing flatus or feces) are not contraindications to beginning tube feeding.
- Many formulas are available (see **Table 79** and **Table 80**). Read the content labels and choose on the basis of calories/mL, protein, fiber, lactose, and fluid load.
  - Oral: Many (eg, *Resource Health Shake*) are milk-based and provide ~1–1.5 calories/mL.
  - Enteral: Commercial preparations have between 0.5 and 2 calories/mL; most contain no milk (lactose) products. For patients who need fluid restriction, the higher concentrated formulas may be valuable, but they may cause diarrhea. Because of reduced kidney function with aging, some recommend that protein should contribute no more than 20% of the formula's total calories. If formula is sole source of nutrition, consider one that contains fiber (25 g/d is optimal).

Table 79. Examples of Lactose-free Oral Products

Product	Kcal/mL	mOsm	Protein (g/L)	Water (mL/L)	Na (mEq/L)	K (mEq/L)	Fiber (g/L)
Routine use formulations							
Boost Drink [a]	1.00	625	41.7	850	27.4	49.7	0
Boost Plus	1.50	670	58.3	780	36.7	38.8	0
Ensure [b]	1.05	640	38.0	840	34.8	42.2	0
Ensure Plus	1.50	680	54.9	740	40.4	43.3	0
Low volume (packaged as 45-mL supplement; nutrients are provided per serving)							
Benecalorie	330	NA	7.0	0	0	0	0
Clear liquid							
Boost Breeze	1.06	750	38.0	830	14.8	0.0	0
Ensure Clear	1.01	700	35.4	840	7.3	3.9	0
Diabetes formulations							
Boost Glucose Control	1.06	400	58.2	850	47.8	28.2	14.8
Glucerna shake [c]	0.93	530	41.8	850	38.4	40.1	10.1

NA = not available

[a] Also has "pudding" product that has 160 Kcal/5 oz and 0 g fiber

[b] Also has "pudding" product that has 170 Kcal/4 oz and 1.0 g fiber/serving

[c] Institutional formulation (also available in 8-oz retail bottle with 200 Kcal, 5 g fiber, 10 g protein/serving)

Table 80. Examples of Lactose-free Enteral Products

Product	Kcal/mL	mOsm	Protein (g/L)	Water (mL/L)	Na (mEq/L)	K (mEq/L)	Fiber (g/L)
Diabetes formulations							
Diabetisource AC	1.20	450	60.0	820	46.0	41.0	15.2
Glucerna 1.0 Cal [a]	1.00	355	41.8	850	40.4	40.3	14.4
Low residue							
Isosource HN [b]	1.20	490	53.6	820	49.0	49.0	0
Osmolite 1 Cal [a]	1.06	300	44.3	840	40.4	40.2	0
Nutren 1.0 [c]	1.00	370	40.0	850	38.0	31.7	0
Low volume							
Nutren 2.0	2.00	745	80.0	700	56.5	49.2	0
TwoCal HN	2.00	725	83.5	700	63.6	62.6	5.0
High fiber							
Jevity 1 Cal [a]	1.06	300	44.3	830	40.4	40.2	14.4
Fibersource HN	1.20	490	54.0	810	52.0	48.7	10.0
Nutren 1.0 FIBER	1.00	410	40.0	840	38.0	31.7	14.0

[a] Also has 1.2 and 1.5 calorie formulations

[b] Also has 1.5 calorie formulation with 8 g fiber/L

[c] Also has 1.5 calorie formulation

Important Drug-enteral Interactions

- Soybean formulas increase fecal elimination of thyroxine; time administration of thyroxine and enteral nutrition as far apart as possible.

- Enteral feedings reduce absorption of phenytoin, levodopa, levofloxacin, and ciprofloxacin; administer these medications at least 2 h after a feeding and delay feeding at least 2 h after medication is administered; monitor levels (if taking phenytoin) and adjust dosages, as necessary.

- Check with pharmacy about suitability and best way to administer SR, enteric-coated, and micro-encapsulated products (eg, omeprazole, lansoprazole, diltiazem, fluoxetine, verapamil).

Gastrostomy/Jejunostomy Tube Feeding

- Chronic artificial nutrition and hydration is not a basic intervention and is associated with uncertain benefit and considerable risks and discomfort.
- Artificial nutrition and hydration should be used only for specific medical indications, not to increase patient comfort.
- Some evidence supports the use of gastrostomy tubes in head and neck cancer.
- For dysphagia and aspiration, the evidence for gastronomy tubes is conflicting without support of randomized trials.

Tips for Successful Tube Feeding

- Gastrostomy tube feeding may be either intermittent or continuous.
- Jejunostomy tube feedings must be continuous.
- Polyurethane tubes have less dysfunction than silicone tubes.
- Continuous tube feeding is associated with less frequent diarrhea but with higher rates of tube clogging.
- To prevent clogging and to provide additional free water, flushing with at least 30–60 mL of water q4–6h is recommended. Do not allow formula bags to run dry, fully crush medications, do not give more than one medication at a time, and flush before and after medication administration. Papain and chymopapain are more effective at clearing clogged tubes than sugar-free carbonated beverages or cranberry juice. Commercial devices (eg, Clog-Zapper) may be effective.
- Diarrhea, which develops in 5–30% of people receiving enteral feeding, may be related to the osmolality of the formula, the rate of delivery, high sorbitol content in liquid medications (eg, APAP, lithium, oxybutynin, furosemide), or other patient-related factors such as antibiotic use or impaired absorption.
- To help prevent aspiration, maintain 30- to 45-degree elevation of the head of the bed during continuous feeding and for at least 2 h after bolus feedings.
- Do not administer bulk-forming laxatives (eg, methylcellulose or psyllium) through feeding tubes.
- Check gastric residual volume before each bolus feeding. Gastric residual volumes in the range of 200–500 mL should raise concern and lead to the implementation of measures to reduce risk of aspiration, but automatic cessation of feeding should not occur for gastric residual volumes <500 mL in the absence of other signs of intolerance. If needed, naloxone *(Narcan)* 8 mg q6h per nasogastric tube, metoclopramide▲ *(Reglan)* 10 mg, or erythromycin 250 mg IV [5 mg/5 mL] q6h may be useful for problems with high gastric residual volume once mechanical obstruction has been excluded.
- Tubes removed inadvertently during the first 4 wk should not be reinserted blindly. Rather, they should be endoscopically, radiologically, or surgically reinserted, which can usually be through the same site.

Parenteral Nutrition

- Indicated in those with digestive dysfunction precluding enteral feeding.
- In ICU settings, if enteral nutrition is not feasible, should wait 8 d to begin parenteral nutrition.
- Delivers protein as amino acids, carbohydrate as dextrose (D5 = 170 kcal/L; D10 = 340 kcal/L), and fat as lipid emulsions (10% = 1100 kcal/L; 20% = 2200 kcal/L).
- Usually administered as total parenteral nutrition through a central catheter, which may be inserted peripherally.

MUSCULOSKELETAL DISORDERS

SHOULDER PAIN: DIFFERENTIAL DIAGNOSIS AND TREATMENT

Rotator Cuff Tendinitis, Subacromial Bursitis, or Rotator Tendon Impingement on Clavicle

Dull ache radiating to upper arm. Painful arc is characteristic. Also can be distinguished by applying resistance against active range of motion while immobilizing the neck with hand. May cause shoulder impingement syndrome (insidious onset of anterolateral acromial pain frequently radiating to lateral mid-humerus). Pain is worse at night, exacerbated by lying on the involved shoulder or sleeping with the arm overhead. Active and passive range of motion are normal. Lidocaine injection will result in normal strength and temporary pain relief. See **Table 81**.

Table 81. Use of Lidocaine Injections to Distinguish Different Shoulder Pain Syndromes[a]

	Response to Lidocaine Injection	
Cause of shoulder pain	*Strength/Range of Motion*	*Pain*
Tendinitis, bursitis	Normal	Temporary relief
Rotator cuff tear	Persistent weakness	Temporary relief
Frozen shoulder	No change in range of motion	

[a] Insert a 1½-inch, 22-gauge needle 1½ inches below the midpoint of the acromion to a depth of 1 to 1½ inches. The angle of entry parallels the acromion. One mL of lidocaine is injected into the deltoid, and 1–2 mL into the subacromial bursa. Dramatic relief of pain and improvement of function by injection into subacromial bursa effectively excludes glenohumeral joint process.

Most accurate bedside tests are (muscle being tested):

- Painful arc test: pain on abduction 60–120 degrees and external rotation suggests impingement or rotator cuff disorder due to compression
- Drop arm test (supraspinatus): inability to maintain the arm in an abducted 90-degree position indicates tear
- External rotation resistance test (infraspinatus): elbows flexed, thumbs up with examiner's hands outside patient's elbows; patient is asked to resist inward pressure; pain or weakness indicates tendonitis or tear
- External rotation lag test (supraspinatus and infraspinatus): elbow at 90-degree flexion and 20-degree abduction, examiner passively rotates patient's arm into full external rotation; linability to maintain this position indicates tear
- Internal rotation lag test (subscapularis): elbow at 90-degree flexion, dorsum of hand on back; hand is lifted off back by examiner; inability to maintain position indicates tear

Treatment: Identify and eliminate provocative, repetitive injury (eg, avoid overhead reaching). A brief period of rest and immobilization with a sling may be helpful. Pain control with APAP or a short course of NSAIDs (see **Table 82**), home exercises or PT (especially assisted range of motion and wall walking), and corticosteroid injections (see p 198) may be useful.

Rotator Cuff Tears

Mild to complete; characterized by diminished shoulder movement. Chronic full thickness tear may not have pain but have loss of range of active or passive motion. After lidocaine injection of shoulder, weakness persists despite pain relief. See **Table 81**. MRI or ultrasound when performed by experienced operators establishes diagnosis.

Treatment: If due to injury, a brief period of rest and immobilization with a sling may be helpful. Pain control with APAP or a short course of NSAIDs (see **Table 82**), home exercises or PT (especially assisted range of motion and wall walking) may be useful. Subacromial glucocorticoid injections may provide short-term pain relief, but multiple injections may be deleterious to healthy tendons. If no improvement after 6–8 wk of conservative measures, consider surgical repair.

Bicipital Tendinitis
Pain felt on anterior lateral aspect of shoulder, tenderness in the groove between greater and lesser tuberosities of the humerus. Pain is elicited on resisted flexion of shoulder, flexion of the elbow, or supination (external rotation) of the hand and wrist with the elbow flexed at the side.

Treatment: Identify and eliminate provocative, repetitive activities (eg, avoid overhead reaching). A period of rest (at least 7 d with no lifting) and corticosteroid injections (see p 198) are major components of tx. After rest period, PT should focus on stretching biceps tendon (eg, putting arm on doorframe and hyperextending shoulder, with some external rotation). Tendon sheath injection with corticosteroids may be helpful.

Frozen Shoulder (Adhesive Capsulitis)
Loss of passive external (lateral) rotation, abduction, and internal rotation of the shoulder to <90 degrees. Usually follows three phases: painful (freezing) phase lasting wks to a few mo; adhesive (stiffening) phase lasting 4–12 mo; resolution phase lasting 6–24 mo. Lidocaine injection does not restore range of motion. See **Table 81**.

Treatment: Avoid rest and begin PT and home exercises for stretching the arm in flexion, horizontal adduction, and internal and external rotation. Corticosteroid injections (see p 198) may reduce pain and permit more aggressive PT. If no response after 6–12 mo, consider surgical manipulation under anesthesia or arthroscopic release.

BACK PAIN: DIFFERENTIAL DIAGNOSIS AND TREATMENT
Axial mechanical back pain is associated with osteoporotic fractures, metastatic bone lesions with or without fractures, internal disc disruption (typically in younger patients), and ligament tears.

Lateral mechanical pain can result from facet arthropathy, sacroiliac joint dysfunction, fascial strain or injury (myofascial pain), or ligament strain. These patients may present with different patterns of radiating pain, but typically the pain does not spread to below the knee. In contrast, pain from lumbar spinal stenosis typically radiates below the knee.

Do not perform imaging for lower back pain within the first 6 wk unless red flags are present (severe or progressive neurologic deficits or when serious underlying conditions are present).^{CW}

Acute Lumbar Strain (Low Back Pain Syndrome)
Acute pain frequently precipitated by heavy lifting or exercise. Pain may be central or more prominent on one side and may radiate to sacroiliac region and buttocks. Pain is aggravated by motion, standing, and prolonged sitting, and relieved by rest. Sciatic pain may be present even when neurologic examination is normal. In sciatica, pain radiating below the knee is more likely to represent true radiculopathy than proximal leg pain.

Treatment: Most can continue normal activities. If a patient obtains symptomatic relief from bed rest, generally 1–2 d lying in a semi-Fowler position or on side with the hips and knees flexed with pillow between legs will suffice. Treat muscle spasm with the application of ice, preferably in a massage over the muscles in spasm. APAP or a short course of NSAIDs (see

Table 82) can be used to control pain. Spinal manipulation is also effective for uncomplicated low back pain. As pain diminishes, encourage patient to begin isometric abdominal and lower-extremity exercises. Symptoms often recur. Education on back posture, lifting precautions, and abdominal muscle strengthening may help prevent recurrences.

Acute Disk Herniation

Over 90% of cases have herniation at L4–L5 or L5–S1 levels, resulting in unilateral impairment of ankle reflex, toe and ankle dorsiflexion, and pain (commonly sciatic) on straight leg raising (can be tested from sitting position by leg extension). Pain is acute in onset and varies considerably with changes in position.

Treatment: Initially same as acute lumbar strain (above). The value of epidural injections and surgery for pain without neurologic signs is controversial. Epidural injection of a combination of a long-acting corticosteroid with an epidural anesthetic may provide modest, transient relief. Consider surgery if recurrence or neurologic signs persist beyond 6–8 wk after conservative tx. The value of epidural injections and surgery for pain without neurologic signs is controversial. Surgery for severe sciatica provides faster pain relief and perceived recovery rates but no difference in perceived recovery and disability at 1 yr compared with conservative management. (See **Table 2** and **Table 3**.)

Osteoarthritis and Chronic Disk Degeneration

Characterized by aching pain aggravated by motion and relieved by rest. Occasionally, hypertrophic spurring in a facet joint may cause unilateral radiculopathy with sciatica.

Treatment: Identify and eliminate provocative activities. Education on back posture, lifting precautions, and abdominal muscle strengthening. APAP or a short course of NSAIDs (see **Table 82**). Corticosteroid injections may be useful. Acupuncture and sham acupuncture may provide benefit. Consider opioids and other pain tx modalities for chronic refractory pain (see p 227).

Unstable Lumbar Spine

Severe, sudden, short-lasting, frequently recurrent pain often brought on by sudden, unguarded movements. Pain is reproduced when moving from the flexed to the erect position. Pain is usually relieved by lying supine or on side. Impingement on nerve roots by spurs from facet joints or herniated disks can cause similar complaints, although symptoms in these conditions usually worsen over time. Symptoms can mimic disk herniation or degeneration, or osteoarthritis. Lumbar flexion radiographs can be diagnostic.

Treatment: Abdominal and paraspinal exercises, lumbrosacral corset. Surgery only in severe cases.

Lumbar Spinal Stenosis

Symptoms increase on spinal extension (eg, with prolonged standing, walking downhill, lying prone) and decrease with spinal flexion (eg, sitting, bending forward while walking, lying in the flexed position). Only symptom may be fatigue or pain in buttocks, thighs, and legs when walking (neurogenic or pseudoclaudication). May have immobility of lumbar spine, pain with straight leg raises, weakness of muscles innervated by L4 through S1 (see **Table 3**). Over 4 yr, 15% improve, 15% deteriorate, and 70% remain stable.

Treatment: APAP or a short course of NSAIDs (see **Table 82**), PT, and exercises to reduce lumbar lordosis (eg, bicycling) are sometimes beneficial. Corticosteroid injections may be useful. Surgical decompression (laminectomy and partial fascectomy) is more effective than conservative tx in relieving moderate or severe symptoms; if spondylolithesis or scoliosis, then fusion may be better than simple decompression. Simple and complex fusion have more complications and higher costs than decompression alone. However, recurrence of pain several years after surgery is common. Depression, comorbidity influencing walking capacity, cardiovascular comorbidity, and scoliosis predict worse surgical outcome. Male gender, younger age, better walking ability and self-rated health, less comorbidity, and more pronounced canal stenosis predict better surgical outcome. Intraspinous spacer insertion (distraction) may be effective if no spondylolithesis and is less invasive.

Vertebral Compression Fracture
Immediate onset of severe pain; worse with sitting or standing; sometimes relieved by lying down. CT scan can help determine instability and MRI can determine acuity of fracture.
Treatment: See Osteoporosis, p 222. Bed rest, analgesia, and mobilization as tolerated. Bracing is unproved except for traumatic vertebral fractures. Calcitonin, teriparatide or pamidronate (30 mg/d IV for 3 consecutive d) may provide symptomatic improvement. May require hospitalization to control symptoms. Percutaneous vertebroplasty and kyphoplasty are not recommended. Avoid muscle relaxants. Pain may persist for a year or longer.

Nonrheumatic Pain (eg, Tumors, Aneurysms)
Gradual onset, steadily expanding, often unrelated to position and not relieved by lying down. Night pain when lying down is characteristic. Upper motor neuron signs may be present. Involvement is usually in thoracic and upper lumbar spine.

HIP PAIN: DIFFERENTIAL DIAGNOSIS AND TREATMENT
Trochanteric Bursitis
Pain in lateral aspect of the hip that usually worsens when patient sits on a hard chair, lies on the affected side, or rises from a chair or bed; pain may improve with walking. Local tenderness over greater trochanter is often present, and pain is often reproduced on resisted abduction of the leg or internal rotation of the hip. However, trochanteric bursitis does not result in limited range of motion, pain on range of motion, pain in the groin, or radicular signs.
Treatment: Identify and eliminate provocative activities. Position pillow posterolaterally behind involved side to avoid lying on bursae while sleeping. Check for leg length discrepancy, prescribe orthotics if appropriate. Injection of a combination of a long-acting corticosteroid with an anesthetic is most effective tx.

Osteoarthritis
"Boring" quality pain in the hip, often in the groin, and sometimes referred to the back or knee with stiffness after rest. Passive motion is restricted in all directions if disease is fairly advanced. In early disease, pain in the groin on internal rotation of the hip is characteristic.
Treatment: See also Osteoarthritis, p 198. Chondroitin sulfate, glucosamine, and capsaicin are not recommended. Participation in cardiovascular, resistance, or aquatic exercises. Weight loss if overweight. Elective total hip replacement is indicated for patients who have radiographic evidence of joint damage and moderate to severe persistent pain or disability, or both, that is not substantially relieved by an extended course of nonsurgical management.

Hip Fracture
Sudden onset, usually after a fall, with inability to walk or bear weight, frequently radiating to groin or knee. If hip radiograph is negative and index of suspicion is high, repeat radiograph with hip at 15–20% internal rotation or obtain MRI. Fractures are 45% femoral neck, 45% intertrochanteric, and 10% subtrochanteric.
Treatment: Tx is surgical with open reduction and internal fixation (ORIF), hemiarthroplasty, or total hip replacement (THR), depending on site of fracture and amount of displacement.

Sliding hip screws may have lower complication rates than intramedullary nails for extracapsular fractures. Displaced femoral neck fractures are generally treated with hemiarthroplasty or THR. Subtrochanteric fractures can be treated with intramedullary nails.

Perioperative Care:
- Timing of surgery: Early surgery (within 48 h) is associated with better outcomes but may be due to more comorbidity in those with delayed surgery.
- Treat comorbid conditions (eg, anemia, volume depletion, metabolic abnormalities, infections, HF, CAD).
- Adequate pre- and postoperative analgesia (eg, 3-in-1 femoral nerve block, intrathecal morphine).
- Regional anesthesia if possible
- Antibiotics: Perioperative antibiotics (cefazolin or vancomycin) should be given beginning within 1 h of surgery.
- Pressure-reducing rather than standard mattress; if high risk of pressure sore, use large cell, alternating pressure air mattress.
- Oximetry for at least 48 h with supplemental oxygen prn.
- Graduated compression stockings as soon as possible after admission.
- Intermittent pneumatic leg compression is recommended for the duration of the hospital stay.
- DVT prophylaxis: Give preoperatively if surgery delay is expected to be >48 h; otherwise begin 12–24 h after surgery. First choices are enoxaparin and dalteparin but other agents can be used (see Antithrombotic Therapy and Thromboembolic Disease, p 24, for regimens). Recommended duration is for up to 35 d but at least 10 d and probably 1 mo if patient is inactive or has comorbidities.
- Preoperative traction has no demonstrated benefit.
- Avoid indwelling urinary catheters.
- Nutritional supplements if undernourished.
- Transfuse only if symptomatic or Hb <8 g/dL.
- Begin assisted ambulation within 48 h.
- Monitor for development of delirium, malnutrition, and pressure sores.
- Weightbearing: Usually as tolerated for hemiarthroplasty or THR; toe-touch if ORIF or intertrochanter fracture.
- Hip precautions: No adduction past midline; no hip flexion beyond 90%; no internal rotation (toes upright in bed).
- Treat osteoporosis: Wait 2 wk before starting bisphosphonates; make sure vitamin D is replete (see Osteoporosis, p 222).
- Fall prevention: See Fall Prevention, p 112.

For patients who were nonambulatory before the fracture, conservative management is an option.

Nonrheumatic Pain
Referred pain from viscera, radicular pain from the lower spine, avascular necrosis, Paget disease, metastasis. Tx based on identified etiology.

KNEE PAIN: DIFFERENTIAL DIAGNOSIS AND TREATMENT

Osteoarthritis
Pain usually related to activity (eg, climbing stairs, arising from chair, walking long distances). Morning stiffness lasts <30 min. Crepitation is common. Examination should attempt to exclude other causes of knee pain such as hip arthritis with referred knee pain

(decreased hip range of motion), chondromalacia patellae (tenderness only over patellofemoral joint), iliotibial band syndrome (tenderness is lateral to the knee at site of insertion in fibular head or where courses over lateral femoral condyle), anserine bursitis (tenderness distal to knee over medial tibia), and determination of malalignment varus (bowlegged) or valgus (knock-kneed).

Treatment: See Osteoarthritis Treatment, p 198. Chondroitin sulfate, glucosamine, and capsaicin are not recommended.

HAND PAIN: DIFFERENTIAL DIAGNOSIS AND TREATMENT
Osteoarthritis
Hand pain (including hand aching or stiffness) plus $\geq$ 3 of the following 4 features (ACR):
(1) hard tissue enlargement of 2 of the following: second and third distal interphalangeal (DIP) joints, the second and third proximal interphalangeal (PIP) joints, and the first carpometacarpal (CMC) of both hands
(2) hard enlargement of 2 or more DIP joints
(3) fewer than 3 swollen metacarpophalangeal (MCP) joints
(4) deformity of at least 1 of the 10 joints above.
X-ray confirmation is not necessary.
Treatment: See Osteoarthritis Treatment, p 198. Avoid opioid analgesics and intraarticular tx.

Carpal Tunnel Syndrome
Painful tingling or hypoesthesia, or both, in one or both hands in distribution innervated by median nerve. Causes include:
- Repetitive activities
- DM
- Thyroid disease
- Amyloidosis
- RA
- Space-occupying lesions (eg, lymphoma)
- Trauma (eg, Colles' fracture)

Physical examination demonstrates decreased sensation in palm, thumb, index finger, middle finger, and thumb side of ring finger, weak handgrip, and tapping over median nerve at wrist causes pain to shoot from wrist to hand (Tinel's sign). An acute flexion of wrist for 60 sec (Phalen's test) should also cause pain.
Laboratory studies should include: fasting glucose, TSH, nerve conduction velocity testing (confirms diagnosis).
Treatment (combined modalities may be effective if single modalities fail)
Nonpharmacologic
Modify work or leisure activities to avoid repetitive movement, carpal tunnel mobilization (moving bones in wrist through PT or OT), and yoga may provide some symptom relief. Splinting in neutral position, especially at night; surgery (more effective than splinting) is indicated for prolonged (usually >6 mo) of moderate to severe symptoms (pain and numbness, diminished hand function, thenar eminence atrophy) after confirmation of median nerve injury by electrodiagnostic testing. Nerve and tendon gliding maneuvers have not been shown to be effective.
Pharmacologic
Injectable corticosteroids, (eg, methylprednisolone 15 mg) are more effective than oral; oral corticosteroids, (eg, prednisone 20 mg/d for 1 wk followed by 10 mg/d for a second wk).

COMMON FOOT DISORDERS

Bunion: prominent and dorsal medial eminence of the first metatarsal; associated with hallux valgus

Calluses and corns: diffuse thickening of the stratum corneum in response to repeated friction or pressure (calluses); corns are similar but have a central, often painful core and are often found at pressure points, especially caused by ill-fitting shoes or gait abnormalities

Equinus: tight Achilles tendon

Hallux valgus (ie, bunion): deviation of the tip of the great toe, or main axis of the toe, toward the outer or lateral side of the foot

Hammertoe (digiti flexus): muscle tendon imbalance causing contraction of the proximal or distal interphalangeal joint, or both

Pes cavus: higher than normal arch that can result in excessive pressure, usually placed on the metatarsal heads, and cause pain and ulceration

Tarsal tunnel syndrome: an entrapment neuropathy of the posterior tibial nerve

Treatment:

- Calluses and corns are treated with salicylic acid plaster 40%, available OTC (eg, Mediplast, Sal-acid plaster) after paring skin with a #15 scalpel blade. Remove dead skin with metal nail file or pumice stone each night before replacing the patch. Do not use in patients with peripheral neuropathy.

- Orthoses can be placed either on the foot or into the shoe to accommodate for a foot deformity or to alter the function of the foot to relieve physical stress on a certain portion of the foot. OTC devices made of lightweight polyethylene foam, soft plastics, or silicone are available for a certain size of foot. Custom-made orthoses are constructed from an impression of a person's foot.

- If conservative methods fail, refer to podiatry or orthopedics for consideration of surgery.

PLANTAR FASCIITIS

Definition

Strain or inflammation in plantar fascia causing foot pain that is worse when beginning to walk; 80% resolve spontaneously within 1 yr.

Causes/Risk Factors

- Jumping
- Running
- Rheumatic diseases
- Obesity
- Flat feet
- Plantar spurs

Evaluation

Examiner should dorsiflex toes and then palpate plantar fascia to elicit pain points; posterior heel pain is uncommon and suggests other diagnosis.

Treatment

Nonpharmacologic

- Rest and icing
- Exercises (calf plantar fascia stretch, foot/ankle circles, toe curls)
- Avoid walking barefoot or in slippers
- Prefabricated silicone heel inserts
- Shoes (running, arch support, crepe sole)
- Short-leg walking cast
- Surgery (rarely needed)

Pharmacologic

- NSAIDs (short duration, 2–3 wk)
- Corticosteroid (eg, methylprednisolone 20–40 mg) and analgesic (eg, 1% lidocaine) injection of fascia; use only if conservative measures fail

OSTEOARTHRITIS

Classification

- Noninflammatory: pain and disability are generally the only complaints; findings include tenderness, bony prominence, and crepitus.
- Inflammatory: may also have morning stiffness lasting >30 min and night pain; findings may include joint effusion on examination or radiograph, warmth, and synovitis on arthroscopy.

Nonpharmacologic Approaches

- Superficial heat: hot packs, heating pads, paraffin, or hot water bottles (moist heat is better)
- Deep heat: microwave, shortwave diathermy, or ultrasound
- Biofeedback and transcutaneous electrical nerve stimulation
- Acupuncture and simulated or sham acupuncture have demonstrated benefit for chronic low back pain compared with usual care.
- Exercise (especially water-based), PT, OT: strengthening, stretching, range of motion, functional activities
- Weight loss: especially for low back, hip, and knee arthritis
- Splinting and orthotics: Avoid splinting for long periods (eg, >6 wk) because periarticular muscle weakness and wasting may occur. For base-of-thumb osteoarthritis, use of a custom-made neoprene splint worn only at night results in decreased pain and disability at 12 mo. Medially wedged insoles if knee lateral compartment osteoarthritis. Laterally wedged subtalar strapped insoles if medial compartment osteoarthritis. Bracing (eg, neoprene sleeves over the knee, valgus brace) to correct malalignment is often helpful.
- Assistive devices: Cane should be used in the hand contralateral to the affected knee or hip. Cane length should be to the level of the wrist crease. Use walker if moderate or severe balance impairment, bilateral weakness, or unilateral weakness requiring support of >15–20% of body weight.
- Acupuncture as an adjunct to NSAIDs or analgesics for knee osteoarthritis or chronic low back pain.
- Surgical intervention (eg, debridement, meniscal repair, prosthetic joint replacement).

Pharmacologic Intervention (see Figure 10)

Topical Analgesics: Liniments containing methylsalicylates (see **Table 101**), capsaicin crm, lidocaine 5% pch *(Lidoderm)*, diclofenac gel or pch (see **Table 82**).

Intra-articular, Bursal, and Trigger-point Injections:

- Corticosteroids (eg, methylprednisolone acetate, triamcinolone acetonide, and triamcinolone hexacetonide [longest acting]) may be particularly effective if monoarticular symptoms. Typical doses for all these drugs:
  - 40 mg for large joints (eg, knee, ankle, shoulder)
  - 30 mg for wrists, ankles, and elbows
  - 10 mg for small joints of hands and feet

Often mixed with lidocaine 1% or its equivalent (some experts recommend giving equal volume with corticosteroids, whereas others give 3–5 times the corticosteroid volume depending on size of joint) for immediate relief. Effect typically lasts 1–2 mo. Usually given no more often than 3 times/yr.

- Hyaluronic acid preparations *(Euflexxa, Hyalgan, Orthovisc, Synvisc, Supartz)* 3–5 injections 1 wk apart for knee osteoarthritis. A formulation *(Synvisc-One)* is available that requires only one injection. Benefit is usually modest but may last ≥6 mo.

Nutriceuticals: Glucosamine sulfate (500 mg q8h) with chondroitin (400 mg q8h) has been effective for some patients. Results of clinical trials have been variable, and a recent meta-analysis has shown no benefit for knee or hip osteoarthritis.

APAP: First choice for mild/moderate pain. Fewer AEs although less effective than NSAIDs.

NSAIDs: Topicals are preferred over oral in persons >75 yr old. Often provide pain relief but have higher rates of AEs than APAP (see **Table 82**). Not recommended for long-term use. Combining with APAP is slightly more effective but may increase risk of bleeding. Misoprostol▲ *(Cytotec)* 100–200 mg q6h with food [T: 100, 200], or a PPI (see **Table 56**) may be valuable prophylaxis against NSAID-induced ulcers in high-risk patients. Selective COX-2 inhibitors have lower likelihood of causing gastroduodenal ulcers than nonselective NSAIDs but increase risk of MI more than nonselective NSAIDs. All may increase INR in patients receiving warfarin. Avoid in individuals with HTN, HF, or CKD of all causes, including DM.[CW]

Oral Opioids: Use requires careful risk-benefit analysis (see **Table 99**).

Other:

- Tramadol for knee or hip arthritis. Begin with 25 mg [T: 50] q4–6h, not to exceed 300 mg/d if age >75.

- Colchicine (0.6 mg q12h) may be of benefit in inflammatory osteoarthritis with recurrent symptoms.

- Duloxetine *(Cymbalta)* [C: 20, 30, 60], beginning at 30 mg/d and increasing to 60 mg/d after 1 wk, may have benefit in chronic low-back pain and osteoarthritis, particularly knee.

Figure 10. Pharmacologic Management of Osteoarthritis*

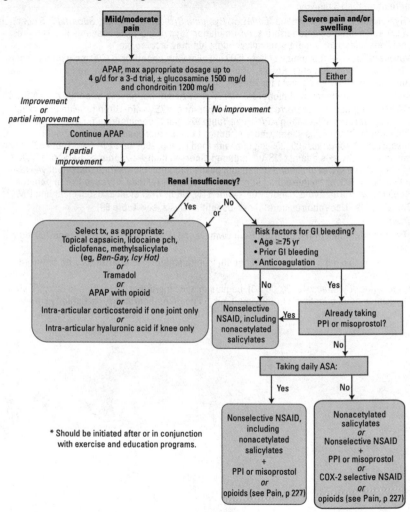

Source: Adapted from original material courtesy of Catherine MacLean, MD, PhD. Reprinted with permission.

Table 82. APAP and NSAIDs

Class, Drug	Usual Dosage for Arthritis	Formulations	Comments (Metabolism, Excretion)
✔APAP▲	650 mg q4–6h (q8h if CrCl <10 mg/mL)	T: 80, 325, 500, 650; C: 160, 325, 500; S: elixir 120/5 mL, 160/5 mL, 167/5 mL, 325/5 mL; S: 160/5 mL, 500/15 mL; Sp: 120, 325, 600	Drug of choice for chronic musculoskeletal conditions; no anti-inflammatory properties and less effective than NSAIDs; hepatotoxic above 4 g/d; at high dosages (≥2 g/d) may increase INR in patients receiving warfarin▲; reduce dosage 50–75% if liver or kidney disease or if harmful or hazardous alcohol intake (L, K)
Extended release	1300 mg q8h	ER: 650	
ASA▲	650 mg q4–6h	T: 81, 325, 500, 650, 975; Sp: 120, 200, 300, 600	(K)
Extended release▲	1300 mg q8h or 1600–3200 mg q12h	CR: 650, 800	
Enteric-coated▲*	1000 mg q6h	T: 81, 162, 325, 500, 650, 975	
Nonacetylated Salicylates			Do not inhibit platelet aggregation; fewer GI and renal AEs; no reaction in ASA-sensitive patients; monitor salicylate concentrations
✔Choline magnesium salicylate▲ *(Tricosal, Trilisate, CMT)*	3 g/d in 1, 2, or 3 doses	T: 500, 750, 1000; S: 500 mg/5 mL	(K)
✔Choline salicylate▲ *(Arthropan)*	4.8–7.2 g/d divided	T: 325, 545, 600, 650 S: 870 mg/5 mL	(L, K)
✔Magnesium salicylate▲* (eg, *Novasal)*	2 tabs q6–8h, max 4800 mg q24h	T: 467, 600, 650	Avoid in kidney failure
✔Salsalate▲	1500 mg to 4 g/d in 2 or 3 doses	T: 500, 750	(K)

(cont.)

✔ = preferred for treating older adults
 * Also OTC in a lower tab strength

Table 82. APAP and NSAIDs (cont.)

Class, Drug	Usual Dosage for Arthritis	Formulations	Comments (Metabolism, Excretion)
Nonselective NSAIDs			Avoid chronic use without GI protection; avoid in HF.[BC]
Diclofenac▲ (Cataflam, Voltaren)	50–150 mg/d in 2 or 3 doses	T: 50, 75; 50, enteric coated	(L)
(Voltaren-XR)	100 mg/d	T: ER 100	(L)
(Zipsor)	25 mg up to q6h	C: 25	(L)
(Zorvolex)	18–25 mg q8h	C: 18, 35	(L)
(Pennsaid)	apply 40 gtt per knee q6h	sol: 1.5%	(L)
✔Enteric coated (Arthrotec 50)	1 tab q8–12h	50 mg with 200 mcg misoprostol	(L)
(Arthrotec 75)	1 tab q12h	75 mg with 200 mcg misoprostol	(L)
✔Gel (Voltaren Gel)	2–4 g q6h	1%	(L)
✔Patch (Flector)	1 q12h	1.3%	(L)
Diflunisal▲ (Dolobid)	500–1000 mg/d in 2 doses	T: 500	(K)
✔Etodolac▲ (Lodine)	200–400 mg q6–8h	T: 400, 500; ER 400, 500, 600	Fewer GI AEs (L)
(Lodine XL)	400–1000 mg/d	C: 200, 300	
Fenoprofen▲ (Nalfon)	200–600 mg q6–8h	C: 200, 300; T: 600	Higher risk of GI AEs (L)
Flurbiprofen▲ (Ansaid)	200–300 mg/d in 2, 3, or 4 doses	T: 50, 100	(L)
✔Ibuprofen▲	1200–3200 mg/d in 3 or 4 doses	T: 100, 200, 300, 400, 600, 800; ChT: 50, 100; S: 100 mg/5 mL	Fewer GI AEs (L)
with famotidine (Duexis)	1 tab q8h	T: 800 with 26.6 mg famotidine	
Injectable (Caldolor)	400–800 mg IV q6h (max 3200 mg/d)	Inj	
✔Ketoprofen▲ (Orudis)	50–75 mg q8h	T: 12.5; C: 50, 75	(L)
Sustained release (Oruvail [Canadian brand])	200 mg/d	C: 200	(L)
Ketorolac▲ (Toradol)	10 mg q4–6h, 15 mg IM or IV q6h	T: 10 Inj	Duration of use should be limited to 5 d (K)
Meclofenamate sodium▲	200–400 mg/d in 3 or 4 doses	C: 50, 100	High incidence of diarrhea (L)
Mefenamic acid▲ (Ponstel)	250 mg q6h	C: 250	(L)
✔Meloxicam▲ (Mobic)	7.5–15 mg/d	T: 7.5, 15 S: 7.5 mg/5mL	Has some COX-2 selectivity; fewer GI AEs (L)

(cont.)

✔ = preferred for treating older adults
 * Also OTC in a lower tab strength

Table 82. APAP and NSAIDs (cont.)

Class, Drug	Usual Dosage for Arthritis	Formulations	Comments (Metabolism, Excretion)
✔Nabumetone▲ (Relafen)	500–1000 mg q12h	T: 500, 750	Fewer GI AEs (L)
✔Naproxen▲ (Naprosyn)	220–500 mg q12h	T: 220, 375, 500, 750 S: 125 mg/5 mL	(L)
Delayed release (EC-Naprosyn)	375–500 mg q12h	T: 375, 500	(L)
Extended release (Naprelan)	750–1000 mg/d	T: 250, 375, 500	(L)
Naproxen sodium▲ (Anaprox)	275 mg or 550 mg q12h	T: 275, 550	(L)
✔Oxaprozin▲ (Daypro)	1200 mg/d	C: 600	(L)
Piroxicam▲ (Feldene)	10 mg/d	C: 10, 20	Can cause delirium (L)
Sulindac▲ (Clinoril)	150–200 mg q12h	T: 150, 200 C: 200	May have higher rate of renal impairment (L)
Tolmetin▲ (Tolectin)	600–1800 mg/d in 3 or 4 doses	T: 200, 600 C: 400	(L)
Trolamine salicylate (Aspercreme and others) OTC	3–4 ×/d	10% sol	
Selective COX-2 Inhibitor			Avoid in HF,[BC]
✔Celecoxib (Celebrex)	100–200 mg q12h	C: 50, 100, 200, 400	Increased risk of MI; less GI ulceration; do not inhibit platelets; may increase INR if taking warfarin▲; avoid if moderate or severe hepatic insufficiency; may induce renal impairment; contra-indicated if allergic to sulfonamides (L)

✔ = preferred for treating older adults
* Also OTC in a lower tab strength

RHEUMATOID ARTHRITIS
Diagnosis

Table 83. 2010 American College of Rheumatology/European League Against Rheumatism (ACR/EULAR) Criteria for Diagnosis of Rheumatoid Arthritis*

A. Joint involvement (any swollen or tender joint excluding first carpometacarpal, metatarsophalangeal, and distal and proximal interphalangeal joints)	
1 large joint (shoulders, elbows, hips, knees, ankles)	0
2 to 10 large joints	1
1 to 3 small joints (with or without involvement of large joints)	2
4 to 10 small joints (with or without involvement of large joints)	3
>10 joints (at least 1 small joint)	5
B. Serology (at least 1 test result is needed for classification)	
Negative RF and negative anticitrullinated protein antibody (ACPA)	0
Low-positive (<3 × upper limit of normal) RF or low-positive ACPA	2
High-positive (>3 × upper limit of normal) RF or high-positive ACPA	3
C. Acute-phase reactants (at least one test result is needed for classification)	
Normal C-reactive protein and normal ESR	0
Abnormal C-reactive protein or abnormal ESR	1
D. Duration of symptoms (by patient self-report)	
<6 wk	0
≥6 wk	1

Scoring: Add score of categories A–D; a score of ≥6/10 is needed for classification of a patient as having definite RA.

* Aimed at classifying newly presenting patients; patients with erosive disease or longstanding disease with a hx of presenting features consistent with these criteria should be classified as having RA.

Note: Adapted from Aletaha D, et al. *Arthritis Rheum* 2010;62(9):2569–2581. This material is reproduced with permission of John Wiley & Sons, Inc.

Staging
- Duration: early <6 mo, intermediate 6–24 mo, late >24 mo
- Activity: low, moderate, high by various criteria; see www.rheumatology.org/practice/clinical/quality/quality.asp
- Poor prognostic factors: functional limitation, extra-articular disease, RF positivity ± anti-CCP antibodies, and/or bony erosions by radiography

Management (co-management with rheumatology)
Nonpharmacologic
- Patient education
- Exercise
- PT and OT
- Atherosclerosis risk factor modification
- Splints and orthotics
- Surgery for severe functional abnormalities due to synovitis or joint destruction
- Bone protection (see Osteoporosis)

Pharmacologic

All patients with established disease should be offered DMARDs as soon as possible; goal is to induce remission and then lower dosages to maintain remission. Tight control of disease activity is associated with better radiographic and functional outcomes.

- Analgesics (see **Table 82** and Pain, p 227)
- NSAIDs (see **Table 82**)
- Glucocorticoids (eg, prednisone ≤15 mg/d or equivalent) with osteoporosis prevention measures (see Osteoporosis, p 222). Avoid in delirium.[BC] Low-dose prednisone (10 mg/d) has benefit as an adjunct to methotrexate.
- Frequent or severe flares should prompt consideration of escalation of dose or modification of regimen.
- Use biologic DMARDs only after failure of nonbiologic DMARDs[CW] (see **Table 84**). Dual and triple nonbiologic DMARD combinations are also used with methotrexate as one component. Triple tx (sulfasalazine, hydroxychloroquine, and methotrexate) is as effective as etanercept plus methotrexate in patients who have active disease despite methotrexate alone. See www.rheumatology.org/practice/clinical/guidelines/Clinical_Practice_Guidelines.

		Table 84. Nonbiologic DMARDs		
Medication	**Starting/ Usual Dosage**	**Formulations**	**Indications**	**Comments***
Hydroxy-chloroquine▲	Begin 200–400 mg/d; dose at <6.5 mg/kg/d to reduce risk of retinal toxicity	T: 200	Monotherapy for durations <24 mo, low disease activity, and without poor prognostic features	Baseline and annual eye examination; contraindicated in G6PD deficiency
Sulfasalazine▲ *(Azulfidine, Azulfidine EN-tabs)*	Begin at 500 mg/d to avoid GI upset; increase dosage by 500 mg every 3–4 d until taking 2–3 g/d split between 2 doses	T: 500	Monotherapy for all disease durations and all degrees of disease activity, and without poor prognostic features	Check CBC, LFTs q8wk
Methotrexate▲ *(Rheumatrex, Trexall)*	10–25 mg/wk, adjust dosage for renal impairment (hold if CrCl <30 mL/min)	T: 2.5 T: 2.5, 5, 7.5, 10, 15	Monotherapy for all disease durations and all degrees of disease activity, irrespective of poor prognostic features	Check for hepatitis B and C; check CBC (hold if WBC <3000/mm^3), LFTs q8wk; give folic acid 1 mg/d; may cause oral ulcers, hepatotoxicity, pulmonary toxicity, cytopenias; avoid if liver disease

(cont.)

Table 84. Nonbiologic DMARDs (cont.)

Medication	Starting/ Usual Dosage	Formulations	Indications	Comments*
Leflunomide▲ *(Arava)*	Begin 100 mg/d × 3 d, then 20 mg/d	T: 10, 20	Monotherapy for all disease durations and all degrees of disease activity, irrespective of poor prognostic features	Check for hepatitis B and C; check CBC (hold if WBC <3000/mm³), LFTs q8wk; may cause hepatotoxicity, cytopenias; avoid if liver disease

* Check baseline CBC, LFTs, Cr for all.

- Biologic DMARDs: Not used in early RA and only low or moderate disease activity; increased risk of serious infections and reactivation of latent infections; check PPD and make sure patient is up-to-date on all vaccinations before starting; check baseline CBC, LFTs, Cr when using any biologic. Hold tx for any infection but can start shortly after bacterial infection is successfully treated; may increase risk of skin cancers. Avoid live vaccinations while on biologics.

  - Anti-TNF-α agents: Used if inadequate response to methotrexate, if moderate disease activity and poor prognostic features, or if high activity regardless of poor prognostic features. May be added to or substituted for methotrexate. Combinations of biologic DMARDs are not recommended.

    □ Adalimumab *(Humira)* 40 mg SC every other wk, or 40 mg SC every wk if not taking methotrexate

    □ Certolizumab *(Cimzia)* 400 mg SC at 0, 2, and 4 wk; then 200 mg q2wk or 400 mg q4wk

    □ Etanercept *(Enbrel)* 50 mg SC once/wk or 25 mg SC twice/wk

    □ Infliximab *(Remicade)* 3 mg/kg IV in conjunction with methotrexate; repeat in 2–6 wk, then q8wk

    □ Golimumab *(Simponi)* 50 mg SC every mo

  - Interleukin-1 receptor antagonist: anakinra *(Kineret)* 100 mg SC daily

- Medications used when response to DMARD has been inadequate:

  - T-cell activation inhibitor: abatacept *(Orencia)* <60 kg: 500 mg; 60–100 kg: 750 mg; >100 kg: 1 g IV at 0, 2, and 4 wk, then q4wk (do not use with anti-TNF-α agents or with anakinra)

  - Anti-CD20 monoclonal antibody: rituximab *(Rituxan)* 1000 mg IV in conjunction with methotrexate; repeat in 2 wk

  - IL-6 inhibitor: tocilizumab *(Actemra)* 4 mg/kg IV over 1h q4wk; if response is not adequate, can increase to 8 mg/kg q4wk

  - Kinase inhibitor: tofacitinib *(Xeljanz)* [T: 5 mg] 5 mg q12h; can use in combination with non-biologics

GOUT
Definition
Urate crystal disease that may be expressed as acute gouty arthritis, usually in a single joint of foot, ankle, knee, or olecranon bursa; or chronic arthritis.

Precipitating Factors

- Alcohol, heavy ingestion
- Allopurinol, stopping or starting
- Binge eating
- Dehydration
- Diuretics
- Fasting
- Infection
- Serum uric acid concentration, any change up or down
- Surgery

Evaluation of Acute Gouty Arthritis

Joint aspiration to remove crystals and microscopic examination to establish diagnosis; serum urate (can be normal during flare).

Management

Treatment of Acute Gouty Flare: Any of the following are appropriate first-line options (ACR):

- Intra-articular injections (see p 198) if only 1 or 2 joints involved
- NSAIDs (see **Table 82**); avoid ASA
- Colchicine 1.2 mg (2 tabs) for the first dose, followed 1 h later by 0.6 mg (total dose 1.8 mg) unless patient has received this regimen within the last 14 d
- Prednisone▲ 5 mg/kg/d for 5–10 d, then stop for 2–5 d at full dose, then taper 7–10 d
- If polyarticular or multiple large joint involvement or severe pain, consider combination tx of methylprednisolone 0.5–2 mg/kg po q12h with taper or ACTH 25–40 IU SC; may repeat daily for 3 d

Pharmacologic anti-inflammatory prophylaxis: Colchicine 0.6 mg/d or twice daily for 2–4 wk before beginning any tx in **Table 85** and continued for up to 6 mo after serum urate has returned to normal.

- Low dose NSAIDs with PPI (if indicated)
- If neither of the above are tolerated, or if either are contraindicated or ineffective, low-dose prednisone or prednisolone (<10 mg/d)

Duration of tx is >6 mo or 3 mo after achieving target urate (if not tophi) or 6 mo after achieving target urate (if tophi)

Treatment of Hyperuricemia

Nonpharmacologic: Lifestyle modification (weight loss if overweight, decrease in saturated fats, substitute low-fat dairy products for red meat or fish, limit alcohol use, avoid organ meats high in purine content [eg, sweetbread, liver, kidney]; avoid high fructose corn syrup—sweetened sodas). D/C nonessential medications that induce hyperuricemia (eg, thiazides and loop diuretics, niacin).

Pharmacologic:

Indications for pharmacologic tx: Established diagnosis of gouty arthritis and:

- Tophus or tophi
- Frequent attacks (≥2/yr)
- CKD stage 2 or worse
- Past urolithiasis

Target is <6 mg/dL and often <5 mg/dL. First-line is either allopurinol or febuxostat. If contraindicated or not tolerated, probenecid. Fenofibrate and losartan are also uricosuric.

Pegloticase is reserved for patients with severe gout disease burden and refractory or intolerance to first-line agents.

Table 85. Medications Useful in Managing Chronic Gout

Medication	Usual Dosage	Formulations	Comments (Metabolism, Excretion)
✔Allopurinol▲ *(Zyloprim, Lopurin)*	100–800 mg/d in divided doses if >300 mg/d	T: 100, 300	Consider if nephrolithiasis, tophi, Cr ≥2 mg/dL, 24-h urinary uric acid >800 mg. Starting dosage should not exceed 100 mg/d and 50 mg/d in ≥stage 4 CKD. Do not initiate during flare; reduce dosage in renal or hepatic impairment; increase dose by 100 mg every 2–5 wk to normalize serum urate level; monitor CBC; rash is common (K)
Colchicine* *(Colcrys)ᵃ*	0.5–0.6 mg/d	T: 0.5, 0.6; Inj	May also be effective in prevention of recurrent pseudogout; monitor CBC (L)
Febuxostat *(Uloric)*	40–80 mg/d	T: 40, 80	Begin 40 mg/d; increase to 80 mg/d if uric acid >6 mg/dL at 2 wk; not recommended if CrCl <30 mL/min (K, L)
Losartan *(Cozaar)*	12.5–100 mg q12–24h	T: 25, 50, 100	Modest uricosuric effect that plateaus at 50 mg/d; may be useful in patients with HTN or HF
Pegloticase *(Krystexxa)*	8 mg IV q2wk	8 mg/1-mL vial	Effective in reducing flares in allopurinol intolerant or refractory patients with high uric acid levels; may cause anaphylaxis, gout flares, and infusion reactions; contraindicated if G6PD deficiency (K)
Probenecid▲* *(Benemid)*	500–1500 mg in 2–3 divided doses	T: 500	Contraindicated as first-line if hx of urolithiasis. Measure urinary uric acid before initiating and if elevated, then contraindicated. Adjust dose to normalize serum urate level or increase urine urate excretion; inhibits platelet function; may not be effective if renal impairment (K, L)

✔ = preferred for treating older adults

*Probenecid (500 mg) and colchicine (0.5 mg) combinations *(ColBenemid, Col-Probenecid, Proben-C)* are available. Available as generic.

ᵃNo longer available as generic.

PSEUDOGOUT

Definition
Crystal-induced arthritis (especially affecting wrists and knees) associated with calcium pyrophosphate. A small proportion have pseudo-RA (chronic crystal inflammatory arthritis) with chronic joint inflammation.

Risk Factors

- Advanced osteoarthritis
- DM
- Gout
- Hemochromatosis
- Hypercalcemia
- Hyperparathyroidism
- Hypomagnesemia
- Hypophosphatemia
- Hypothyroidism
- Neuropathic joints
- Older age

Precipitating Factors

- Acute illness
- Dehydration
- Minor trauma
- Surgery

Evaluation of Acute Arthritis

Joint aspiration and microscopic examination to establish diagnosis; radiograph indicating chondrocalcinosis (best seen in wrists, knees, shoulder, symphysis pubis)

Management of Acute Flare

If single joint, aspiration and intra-articular glucocorticoid may be effective. If multiple joints, see Gout, management (p 207). NSAIDs are often used first, because colchicine is less effective in pseudogout.

Prevention of Recurrence

If >3 attacks/yr, consider colchicine 0.6 mg q12h.

If chronic calcium pyrophosphate crystal inflammatory arthritis (ie, pseudo-RA), then NSAIDs +/− colchicines and, if needed, followed by methotrexate and/or hydroxychloroquine.

POLYMYALGIA RHEUMATICA, GIANT CELL (TEMPORAL) ARTERITIS

Definitions and Evaluation

Polymyalgia Rheumatica: Proximal limb and girdle stiffness usually lasting ≥30 min without tenderness but with constitutional symptoms (eg, fatigue, malaise, weight loss) for ≥1 mo and sedimentation rate elevated to >50 mm/h (7–22% will have normal sedimentation rate), and C-reactive protein; consider ultrasound to demonstrate effusions within shoulder bursae or MRI to demonstrate tenosynovitis or subacromial and subdeltoid bursitis if diagnosis is uncertain.

Giant Cell (Temporal) Arteritis: Medium to large vessel vasculitis that presents with symptoms of polymyalgia rheumatica, headache, unexplained fever or anemia, scalp tenderness, jaw or tongue claudication, visual disturbances, TIA or stroke, and elevated sedimentation rate and C-reactive protein. The presence of synovitis suggests an alternative diagnosis. Giant cell arteritis is confirmed by temporal artery biopsy. The value of other diagnostic tests (Doppler ultrasound, MRI, positron-emission tomography) is still unproved.

Management

Polymyalgia Rheumatica:

- Low-dosage (eg, 10–15 mg/d) prednisone or its equivalent; increase dosage if symptoms are not controlled within 1 wk. If symptoms are not controlled by 20 mg/d, then consider alternative diagnosis (eg, Giant Cell Arteritis, paraneoplastic syndrome)
- Methylprednisolone▲ 120 mg IM q3–4 wk is also effective. After 2–4 wk, begin gradual taper to lowest dose that will control symptoms and C-reactive protein or sedimentation rate. Once-daily dose is 10 mg, taper in 1-mg/mo decrements.
- Some patients with milder symptoms may respond to NSAIDs alone.
- Monitor symptoms and C-reactive protein or sedimentation rate.

- Maintain tx for ≥1 yr to prevent relapse. Relapse occurs in 25–50%, and resuming previous dose that controlled symptoms or increasing steroid dosage if still on steroids is necessary.
- Consider osteoporosis prevention medication (see p 223).

Giant Cell (Temporal) Arteritis:

- Tx should not be delayed while waiting for pathologic diagnosis from temporal artery biopsy. Begin prednisone (40–60 mg/d) or its equivalent while biopsy and pathology are pending.
- Adding methotrexate▲ po 7.5–15 mg/wk and folate 5–7.5 mg/d may reduce the amount of steroid needed and the risk of relapse, but the effect is moderate at best.
- After 2–4 wk, begin taper by 10 mg after 2 wk and another 10 mg prednisone/d at 4 wk, gradual taper (by 10% every 1–2 wk) over 9–12 mo. Once daily dose is 10 mg, taper in 1-mg/mo decrements. Monitor Hb, ESR, C-reactive protein before dose changes, but treat based on symptoms, not lab tests.
- High-dose parenteral steroids (eg, 1000 mg methylprednisolone IV daily for 3 d) for visual loss is controversial.
- For refractory cases, IL–6 receptor inhibitor tocilizumab *(Actemra)* beginning 4 mg/kg every 4 wk with maximum dose 800 mg or cyclophosphamide, mean dose 100 mg/d [T 25, 50] may be helpful.
- Use low-dosage ASA (81–100 mg/d) to reduce risk of visual loss, TIA, or stroke. Combine with PPI or misoprostol.
- Be aware of higher rates of systemic infection during first 6 mo of tx.
- Monitor symptoms and C-reactive protein or sedimentation rate.
- Maintain tx for ≥1 yr to prevent relapse.
- Consider osteoporosis prevention medication (see p 223).
- Monitor for development of thoracic aortic aneurysm with CXR yearly for up to 10 yr.

TREMORS

Table 86. Classification of Tremors

Tremor Type	Hz (cycles/sec)	Associated Conditions	Features	Treatment
Cerebellar	3–5	Cerebellar disease	Present only during movement; ↑ with intention; ↑ amplitude as target is approached	Symptomatic management
Essential	4–12	Familial in 50% of cases	Varying amplitude; common in upper extremities, head, neck; ↑ with antigravity movements, intention, stress, medications	Long-acting propranolol▲ or atonolol▲ (see **Table 28**); or primidone *(Mysoline)* 100 mg qhs start, titrate to 0.5–1 g/d in 3–4 divided doses [T: 50, 250; S: 250 mg/5 mL]; or gabapentin▲ (see **Table 91**)
Parkinson	3–7	Parkinson disease, parkinsonism	"Pill rolling;" present at rest; ↑ with emotional stress or when examiner calls attention to it; commonly asymmetric	See Parkinson disease (p 215)
Physiologic	8–12	Normal	Low amplitude;↑with stress, anxiety, emotional upset, lack of sleep, fatigue, toxins, medications	Tx of exacerbating factor

DIZZINESS

• Medications commonly associated with orthostatic hypotension include:
  ○ Cardiac: α-blockers, β-blockers, ACEIs, diuretics, nitrates, clonidine, hydralazine, methyldopa, reserpine, dipyridamole
  ○ CNS: antipsychotics, opioids, medications for Parkinson Disease, skeletal muscle relaxants, TCAs
  ○ Urologic: antimuscarinic agents for UI, PDE-5 inhibitors
• Caffeine, alcohol, nicotine, and head trauma can also cause or contribute to dizziness.

Table 87. Classification of Dizziness

Primary Symptom	Features	Duration	Diagnosis	Management
Dizziness	Lightheadedness 1–30 min after standing	Seconds to minutes (E)	Orthostatic hypotension	See pp 65–66
	Wobbly/off balance gait; impairment in >1 of the following: vision, vestibular function, spinal proprioception, cerebellum, lower-extremity peripheral nerves	Occurs with ambulation (C)	Multiple sensory impairments including peripheral neuropathy; Parkinson Disease	Correct or maximize sensory deficits; PT for balance and strength training
	Unsteady gait with short steps; ↑ reflexes and/or tone	Occurs with ambulation (C)	Ischemic cerebral disease	ASA▲; modification of vascular risk factors; PT
	Provoked by head or neck movement; reduced neck range of motion	Seconds to minutes (E)	Cervical spondylosis	Behavior modification; reduce cervical spasm and inflammation
Drop attacks	Provoked by head or neck movement, reduced vertebral artery flow seen on Doppler or angiography	Seconds to minutes (E)	Postural impingement of vertebral artery	Behavior modification
Vertigo	Brought on by position change, positive Dix-Hallpike test	Seconds to minutes (E)	Benign paroxysmal positional vertigo	Epley maneuver to reposition crystalline debris (see www.merck.com/mmpe/sec08/ch086/ch086c.html); exercises provoking symptoms may be of help
	Acute onset, nonpositional	Days	Labyrinthitis/vestibular neuronitis	Methylprednisolone▲, 100 mg/d po × 3 d with subsequent gradual taper over 3 wk to improve vestibular function recovery; meclizine▲ (see **Table 59**) for acute symptom relief
	Low-frequency sensorineural hearing loss and tinnitus	Minutes to hours (E)	Ménière disease	Meclizine▲ (see **Table 59**) for acute symptom relief; diuretics and/or salt restriction for prophylaxis
	Vascular disease risk factors, cranial nerve abnormalities	10 min to several hours (E)	TIAs	ASA▲; modification of vascular risk factors

Note: C = chronic; E = episodic

MANAGEMENT OF ACUTE STROKE

Examination

- Cardiac (murmurs, arrhythmias, enlargement)
- Neurologic (serial examinations)
- Optic fundi
- Vascular (carotids and other peripheral pulses)

Tests

- Bloodwork: BUN, CBC with platelet count, Cr, electrolytes, glucose, cardiac troponins, INR, PT, PTT, oxygen saturation
- Emergent brain MRI or noncontrast CT
- ECG
- The National Institutes of Health Stroke Scale (NIHSS; see www.ninds.nih.gov/doctors/NIH_Stroke_Scale.pdf) can quantify stroke severity and prognosis. NIHSS score >15 signifies major or severe stroke with high risk of death or significant permanent neurologic disability; NIHSS score <8 has a good prognosis for neurologic recovery.
- Other tests as indicated by clinical presentation:
  - ABG if hypoxia is suspected
  - Thrombin time and/or ecarin clotting time if patient is taking direct thrombin inhibitor or facter Xa inhibitor
  - Echocardiography (transesophageal preferred over transthoracic) for detection of cardiogenic emboli.
  - Carotid duplex and transcranial Doppler studies for detection of carotid and vertebrobasilar embolic sources, respectively.

Provide Supportive Care

- Maintain O_2 saturation >94%.
- Correct metabolic and hydration imbalances.
- Detect and treat coronary ischemia, HF, arrhythmias.
- In patients with ischemic stroke and restricted mobility, implement DVT/PE prophylaxis with UFH▲, LMWH, or fondaparinux (see **Table 17**).
- Monitor and treat hyperthermia, using antipyretics (eg, acetaminophen) for temperature >100.4°F.
- Monitor for depression.
- Refer to rehabilitation when medically stable.
- Discharge on statin drug (see **Table 25** and **Table 27**).

Antithrombotic Therapy for Ischemic Stroke (AHA/American Stroke Association Guidelines)

- Consider IV thrombolysis if patient presents within 180 min of symptom onset.
  - Data on overall risk/benefit ratio of IV thrombolysis in adults >75 yr old are limited.
  - Absolute contraindications:
    - BP ≥185/110 mmHg
    - subarachnoid hemorrhage or hx of intracranial hemorrhage
    - intracranial neoplasm, arteriovenous malformation, or aneurysm

- head trauma or stroke in past 3 mo
- GI bleed or urinary hemorrhage in past 21 d
- recent intracranial or intraspinal surgery
- active bleeding or acute trauma
- INR >1.7 or PT >15 sec
- heparin use in past 48 h with supranormal PTT
- current use of direct thrombin inhibitor or factor Xa inhibitor with elevated tests for anticoagulation (eg, PTT, INR, thrombin time, ecarin clotting time)
- platelet count <100,000 mm^3
- blood glucose <50 mg/dL
- seizure with postictal neurologic impairment
  - Relative contraindications (carefully consider risk/benefit of thrombolysis if 1 or more are present):
    - minor or rapidly improving stroke symptoms
    - seizure at stroke onset with postictal neurologic impairments
    - major surgery or serious trauma in past 14 d
    - GI or urinary tract hemorrhage in past 21 d
    - acute MI in past 3 mo
  - Use recombinant tissue plasminogen activator (tPA), 0.9 mg/kg IV, max dose 90 mg.
  - Risk of intracranial hemorrhage 3–7%; age >75 yr old and NIHSS >20 are among risk factors for intracranial hemorrhage.
- IV thrombolysis can be considered 3–4.5 h after symptom onset; additional exclusion criteria include age >80 yr old and NIHSS >25.
- Antiplatelet tx: use ASA▲ 162–325 mg/d (initial dose 325 mg), begun within 24–48 h of onset in patients not receiving thrombolytic tx.
- Anticoagulants are not recommended except in DVT/PE prophylactic dosages for medical patients with restricted mobility (see **Table 17**).

Management of Acute Hypertension in Ischemic Stroke
- If patient is otherwise eligible for IV thrombolysis (see contraindications, p 213), attempt to lower BP to ≤185/110 mmHg so that patient may undergo reperfusion tx. Options for lowering BP are:
  - Labetalol▲ *(Normodyne, Trandate)*: 10–20 mg IV over 1–2 min, may repeat once; *or*
  - Nicardipine▲ *(Cardene)*: 5 mg/h IV, increasing by 2.5 mg/h q5–15 min to max of 15 mg/h
- If patient is ineligible or not being considered for thrombolytic tx, do not lower BP if SBP ≤220 mmHg or if DBP ≤120 mmHg; higher BP may be lowered gently, with goal of 15% reduction over first 24 h. Choice of BP-lowering agent should reflect patient's comorbidities (see **Table 28**).

STROKE PREVENTION
Risk Factor Modification
- Stop smoking.
- Reduce BP to at least 140/90 mmHg; <120/80 mmHg is desirable.

- In patients ≥80 yr old with few cardiovascular comorbidities, 150/80 mmHg is a reasonable BP tx goal.
- Treat dyslipidemia (see **Table 25** and **Table 27**).
- Start anticoagulation (see **Table 17**) or antiplatelet (see **Table 16**) tx for AF.
- Low-sodium (≤2–3 g/d), high-potassium (≥4.7 g/d) diet
- Exercise (≥30 min of moderate intensity activity daily)
- Weight reduction (BMI <25 kg/m²)

Antiplatelet Therapy for Patients With Prior TIA or Stroke
- First-line tx is ASA▲ 81–325 mg/d.
- Addition of a combination form of ASA and long-acting dipyridamole *(Aggrenox)* 1 tab q12h [T: 25/200] may provide additional benefit. Watch for AE of headache.
- Clopidogrel▲ *(Plavix)* 75 mg/d [T: 75] if intolerant to ASA or ASA ineffective.
- In the absence of AF, warfarin tx is no more effective and is associated with more bleeding than ASA in preventing strokes.

Table 88. Treatment Options for Carotid Stenosis

Presentation	% Stenosis	Preferred Treatment	Comments
Prior TIA or stroke	≥70	CA or CE	CE superior to medical tx only if patient is reasonable surgical risk and facility has track record of low complication rate for CE (<6%)
Prior TIA or stroke	50–69	CE or MM	Serial carotid Doppler testing may identify rapidly developing plaques
Prior TIA or stroke	<50	MM	CE of no proven benefit in this situation
Asymptomatic	≥80	CA/CE[a] or MM	CA/CE[a] should be considered over MM only for the most healthy
Asymptomatic	<80	MM	CE of no proven benefit in this situation

Note: CA = carotid angioplasty with stent placement in patients with multiple comorbidities and/or at high surgical risk; CE = carotid endarterectomy; MM = medical management
[a]Don't recommend CE for asymptomatic carotid stenosis unless the complication rate is low (<3%).**CW**

PARKINSON DISEASE
Diagnosis Requires:
- Bradykinesia, eg:
  - Slowness of initiation of voluntary movements (eg, glue-footedness when starting to walk)
  - Reduced speed and amplitude of repetitive movements (eg, tapping index finger and thumb together)
  - Difficulty switching from one motor program to another (eg, multiple steps to turn during gait testing)
- **and** one or more of the following:
  - Muscular rigidity (eg, cogwheeling)
  - 3–7 Hz resting tremor
  - Impaired righting reflex (eg, retropulsed during sternal nudge)

- Other clinical features of Parkinson disease:
  - Postural instability and falls
  - Hyposmia
  - Hypophonia
  - Micrographia
  - REM sleep behavior disorder
  - Constipation
  - Masked facies
  - Infrequent blinking
  - Drooling
  - Seborrhea of face and scalp
  - Festinating gait

- Neuropsychiatric conditions are also common usually later in the clinical course: anxiety, depression, dementia, visual hallucinations, dysthymia, psychosis, delirium

Table 89. Distinguishing Early Parkinson Disease From Other Parkinsonian Syndromes

Condition	Tremor	Asymmetric Involvement	Early Falls	Early Dementia	Postural Hypotension
Parkinson disease	+	+	−	−	−
Drug-induced parkinsonism	+/−	−	−	−	−
Vascular parkinsonism	−	+/−	+/−	+/−	−
Dementia with Lewy bodies	+/−	+/−	+/−	+	+/−
Progressive supranuclear palsy	−	−	+	+/−	−
Corticobasilar ganglionic degeneration	−	+	+	−	+
Multiple system atrophy	−	+/−	+/−	−	+

Note: + = usually or always present, +/− = sometimes present, − = absent
Source: Adapted from Christine CW, Aminoff MJ. *Am J Med* 2004;117:412–419.

Nonpharmacologic Management

- Patient education is essential, and support groups are often helpful; see p 335 for telephone numbers, Web sites.
- Monitor for orthostatic hypotension (see p 65).
- Exercise program
- Diet with increased fiber and hydration to minimize constipation; adequate vitamin D and calcium as osteopenia is common

Surgical Treatment—Deep Brain Stimulation (DBS)

- DBS of the globus pallidus or subthalamic nucleus is used for tx of motor complications of Parkinson disease.
- DBS is best suited for patients who have fluctuating motor problems (tremor and other dyskinesias) despite medical tx and who have few comorbidities, especially no dementia.
- Compared with medical tx in selected patients, DBS can significantly increase motor function (several more hours per day of "on" time) and decrease troubling dyskinesias.
- Early (0–3 mo) complications include surgical site infection (~10%), symptomatic intracranial hemorrhage (~2%), death (~1%), cognitive and speech problems (10–15%), and an increased risk of falls.

Pharmacologic Treatment (see Table 90)
- Begin tx when symptoms interfere with function.
- Start at low dose and titrate upward gradually.
- Monitor orthostatic BP during titration of medications.
- Avoid all antipsychotics except quetiapine and clozapine.[BC]
- Avoid metoclopramide, prochlorperazine, and promethazine.[BC]

Table 90. Medications for Parkinson Disease

Class, Medication	Initial Dosage	Formulations	Comments (Metabolism, Excretion)
Dopamine			
✓ Carbidopa-levodopa▲* *(Sinemet, Parcopa)*	1/2 tab of 25/100 q8–12h	T: 10/100, 25/100, 25/250	Mainstay of Parkinson disease tx; increase dose by 1/2–1 tab q1–2wk to achieve minimal target dose of 1 tab q8h, then titrate upward gradually prn; watch for GI AEs, orthostatic hypotension, confusion; long-term tx associated with motor fluctuations and dyskinesias (addition of dopamine agonist may attenuate these effects) (L)
✓ Sustained-release carbidopa-levodopa▲* *(Sinemet CR)*	1 tab/d	T: 25/100, 50/200	Useful at daily dopamine requirement ≥300 mg; slower absorption than carbidopa-levodopa; can improve motor fluctuations (L)
Dopamine Agonists			More CNS AEs than dopamine
Apomorphine *(Apokyn)*	2 mg SC	Inj: 10 mg/mL	Use with extreme caution; can cause severe orthostasis; indicated only for "off" episodes associated with L-dopa tx
Bromocriptine▲ *(Parlodel)*	1.25 mg q12–24h	T: 2.5 C: 5	Increase by 1.25-mg increments q2–5d, titrating to effective dosage (10–30 mg/d) (L)
✓ Pramipexole▲* *(Mirapex)*	0.125 mg/d	T: 0.125, 0.25, 0.5, 1, 1.5	Increase gradually to effective dosage (0.5–1.5 mg q8h) (K)
✓ Ropinirole* *(Requip)*	0.25 mg/d	T▲: 0.25, 0.5, 1, 2, 3, 4, 5 CR: 4, 8	Increase gradually to effective dosage (up to 1–8 mg q8h) (L)
Rotigotine *(Neupro)*	2mg/24 h for early stage disease; 4 mg/24 h for advanced disease	pch: 1, 2, 3, 4, 6, 8 mg/24 h	Increase weekly to effective dosage (max 6 mg/24 h for early stage disease, 8 mg/24 h for advanced disease) (K)
Catechol *O*-Methyl-transferase (COMT) Inhibitors			Adjunctive tx with L-dopa
✓ Tolcapone *(Tasmar)*	100 mg q8h	T: 100, 200	Monitor LFTs q6mo (L, K)
✓ Entacapone *(Comtan)*	200 mg with each L-dopa dose	T: 200	Watch for nausea, orthostatic hypotension (K)
Anticholinergics			
Benztropine▲ᵃ *(Cogentin)*	0.5 mg/d	T: 0.5, 1, 2	Can cause confusion and delirium; helpful for drooling (L, K)

(cont.)

Table 90. Medications for Parkinson Disease (cont.)

Class, Medication	Initial Dosage	Formulations	Comments (Metabolism, Excretion)
Trihexyphenidyl▲ᵃ (Artane, Trihexy)	1 mg/d	T: 2, 5 S: 2 mg/5 mL	Same as above (L, K)
Dopamine Reuptake Inhibitor			
Amantadine▲ (Symmetrel)	100 mg q12–24h	T: 100 C: 100 S: 50 mg/5 mL	Useful in early and late Parkinson disease; watch closely for CNS AEs; do not D/C abruptly (K)
MAO B Inhibitors			
Rasagiline (Azilect)	0.5 mg/d	T: 0.5, 1	Interactions with numerous drugs and tyramine-rich foods; expensive (L, K)
Selegiline▲ (Carbex, Eldepryl, Zelapar)	5 mg qam; 1.25 mg/d for ODT	T: 5 ODT: 1.25	Use as adjunctive tx with dopamine; do not exceed a total dosage of 10 mg/d; metabolized to amphetamine derivatives (L, K)
Combination Medication			
Carbidopa-levodopa + entacapone (Stalevo)	1 tab/d	T: 12.5/50/200, 25/100/200, 37.5/150/200	Should be used only after individual dosages of carbidopa, levodopa, and entacapone have been established (L, K)

✔ = preferred for treating older adults
* = first-line tx
ᵃ Avoid.[BC]

SEIZURES

Classification
- Generalized: All areas of brain affected with alteration in consciousness.
- Partial: Focal brain area affected, not necessarily with alteration in consciousness; can progress to generalized type.

Initial Evaluation, Assessment
- History: neurologic disorders, trauma, drug and alcohol use
- Physical examination: general, with careful neurologic
- Routine tests: BUN, calcium, CBC, Cr, ECG, EEG, electrolytes, glucose, head CT, LFTs, magnesium
- Tests as indicated: head MRI, lumbar puncture, oxygen saturation, urine toxic or drug screen

Common Causes
- Advanced dementia
- CNS infection
- Drug or alcohol withdrawal
- Idiopathic causes
- Metabolic disorders
- Prior stroke (most common)
- Toxins
- Trauma
- Tumor

Management
- Treat underlying causes.
- Institute anticonvulsant tx (see **Table 91**). Virtually all anticonvulsant medications can cause sedation and ataxia.

• Avoid the following drugs, which can lower seizure threshold: bupropion, chlorpromazine, clozapine, maprotiline, olanzapine, thioridazine, thiothixene, and tramadol.[BC]

Table 91. Anticonvulsant Therapy in Older Adults

Medication	Dosage (mg)	Target Blood Concentration (mcg/mL)	Formulations	Comments (Metabolism, Excretion)
◆Carbamazepine▲ (Tegretol, Epitol) (Tegretol XR, Carbatrol, Equetro)	200–600 q12h	4–12	T: 200▲ ChT: 100 S: 100/5 mL▲ T: 100, 200, 400▲ C: ER 100, 200, 300	Many drug interactions; mood stabilizer; may cause SIADH, thrombocytopenia, leukopenia (L, K)
◆Gabapentin▲ (Neurontin)	300–600 q8h	NA	C: 100, 300, 400 T: 600, 800 S: 250/5 mL	Used as adjunct to other agents; adjust dosage on basis of CrCl (K)
Lamotrigine▲ (Lamictal)	100–300 q12h	2–4	T: 25, 100, 150, 200 ChT: 2, 5, 25▲	Prolongs PR interval; risk of severe rash; when used with valproic acid, begin at 25 mg q48h, titrate to 25–100 mg q12h (L, K)
Levetiracetam▲ (Keppra)	500–1500 q12h	NA	T▲: 250, 500, 750 S▲: 100/mL CR: 500, 750	Reduce dosage in renal impairment: CrCl 30–50: 250–750 q12h CrCl 10–29: 250–500 q12h CrCl <10: 500–1000 q24h
Oxcarbazepine (Trileptal)	300–1200 q12h	NA	T▲: 150, 300, 600 ChT: 2, 5, 25 S: 300/5 mL	Can cause hyponatremia, leukopenia (L)
Phenobarbital▲ (Luminal)	30–60 q8–12h	20–40	T: 15, 16, 30, 32, 60, 100 S: 20/5 mL	Many drug interactions; not recommended for use in older adults (L)
Phenytoin▲ (Dilantin)	200–300/d	5–20	C: 30, 100▲ ChT: 50 S: 125/5 mL▲	Many drug interactions; exhibits nonlinear pharmacokinetics (L)
◆Pregabalin (Lyrica)	50–200 q8–12h	NA	C: 25, 50, 75, 100, 150, 200, 225, 300	Indicated as adjunct tx for partial-onset seizures only; not well studied in older adults (K)
Tiagabine (Gabitril Filmtabs)	2–12 q8–12h	NA	T: 2, 4, 12, 16, 20	AE profile in older adults less well described (L)
Topiramate▲ (Topamax)	25–100 q12–24h	NA	T: 25, 100, 200 C, sprinkle: 15, 25	May affect cognitive functioning at high dosages (L, K)
Valproic acid▲ (Depacon, Depakene, Depakote) (Depakote ER)	250–750 q8–12h	50–100	T: 125, 250, 500 C: 125, 250 S: 250/5 mL T: 500	Can cause weight gain, tremor, hair loss; several drug interactions; mood stabilizer; monitor LFTs and platelets (L)
Zonisamide▲ (Zonegran)	100–400/d	NA	C: 25, 100	Anorexia; contraindicated in patients with sulfonamide allergy (K)

Note: NA = not available   ◆ = also has primary indication for neuropathic pain.

Table 92. Aphasias in Which Repetition Is Impaired

Type	Fluency	Auditory Comprehension	Associated Neurologic Deficits	Comments
Broca's	−	+	Right hemiparesis	Patient aware of deficit; high rate of associated depression; message board helpful for communication
Wernicke's	+	−	Often none	Patient frequently unaware of deficit; speech content usually unintelligible; tx often focuses on visually based communication
Conduction	+	+	Occasional right facial weakness	Patient usually aware of deficit; speech content usually intelligible
Global	−	−	Right hemiplegia with right field cut	Most commonly due to left middle cerebral artery thrombosis, which has a poor prognosis for meaningful speech recovery

Note: + = present; − = absent

PERIPHERAL NEUROPATHY

Diagnosis

- Establish pattern of involvement:
  - Focal (entrapment syndromes, compression neuropathies, vasculitis)
  - Multifocal (vasculitis, diabetes)
  - Symmetric
- If symmetric, determine location:
  - Proximal—many causes, including Guillain-Barré syndrome, porphyria, chronic inflammatory demyelinating polyneuropathy, Lyme disease
  - Distal—nerve conduction studies can help distinguish the more common axonal pathologies (diabetes, medication effects, alcohol abuse, kidney failure, malignancy) from demyelinating ones (including Guillain-Barré syndrome and chronic inflammatory demyelinating polyneuropathy)

Treatment

Prevention of Complications:

- Protect distal extremities from trauma—appropriate shoe size, daily foot inspections, good skin care, avoidance of barefoot walking.
- Prevent falls (see pp 115–116)
- Maintain appropriate glycemic control in diabetic neuropathy.

Treatment of Painful Neuropathy: Start at low dosage, increase as needed and tolerated:

- Nortriptyline▲ *(Aventyl, Pamelor)* 10–100 mg qhs [T: 10, 25, 50, 75]; desipramine▲ *(Norpramin)* 10–75 mg qam [T: 10, 25, 50, 75]
- Gabapentin▲ *(Neurontin)* can begin 100–200 mg qhs but may need up to 100–600 mg q8h [C: 100, 300, 400; T: 600, 800; S: 250/5 mL]

- Pregabalin *(Lyrica)* 75–300 mg po q12h [C: 25, 50, 75, 100, 150, 200, 225, 300]: primary indication is for management of post-herpetic neuralgia, diabetic peripheral neuropathy, and fibromyalgia
- Other oral agents that may be effective include:
  - Carbamazepine▲ *(Tegretol)* 200–400 mg q8h [T: 200; ChT: 100; S: 100 mg/5 mL]; *(Tegretol XR)* 200 mg q12h [T: 100, 200, 400; C: CR 200, 300]
  - Duloxetine *(Cymbalta)* 60 mg/d [C: 20, 30, 60]
  - SSRIs have not been shown to be as effective as TCAs (see **Table 41**)
  - Lamotrigine▲ *(Lamictal,* see **Table 91**) 400–600 mg/d
  - Opioids (see **Table 99**); watch for AEs of itching, mood changes, weakness, confusion
  - Tramadol▲ *(Ultram,* see **Table 99**) 200–400 mg/d
- Topical agents that may be effective include:
  - Capsaicin crm▲ (eg, *Zostrix)* 0.075% applied q6–8h [0.025%, 0.075%]
  - Capsaicin cutaneous pch *(Qutenza)* applied by health professional, using a local anesthetic, to the most painful skin areas (max of 4 pchs). Apply for 30 min to feet, 60 min for other locations. Risk of significant rise in BP following placement; monitor patient for at least 1 h [179-mg pch].
  - Transcutaneous electrical nerve stimulation
  - Lidocaine 5% pch *(Lidoderm)* 1–3 patches covering the affected area up to 24 h/d [700-mg pch]

OSTEOPOROSIS

COMMONLY USED DEFINITIONS

- Established osteoporosis: occurrence of a minimal trauma fracture of any bone (WHO).
- Osteoporosis: a skeletal disorder characterized by compromised bone strength (bone density and bone quality) predisposing to an increased risk of fracture (NIH Consensus Development Panel. *JAMA* 2001;285 (6):785–795.)
- Osteoporosis: BMD 2.5 SD or more below that of younger normal individuals (T score) (WHO). Scores between 1 and 2.5 SD below young normals are termed osteopenia. Some experts prefer to use Z score, which compares an individual with a population adjusted for age, sex, and race. For each SD decrement in BMD, hip fracture risk increases about 2-fold; for each SD increment in BMD, hip fracture risk is about halved.

RISK FACTORS FOR OSTEOPOROTIC FRACTURE

- Advanced age*
- Female sex*
- BMI (both low and high)*
- Previous fracture as adult*
- Parent fractured hip*
- Current smoking*
- On glucocorticoids*
- RA*

- Secondary osteoporosis*
- Alcohol (>3 drinks/d)*
- Low BMD*
- Frailty
- Dementia
- Depression
- Impaired vision
- Low physical activity

- Early menopause (<45 yr old)
- Recurrent falls
- Nocturia
- Kidney failure (GFR <45 mL/min/1.73 m^2) body surface area

*indicates included in the WHO Fracture Risk Assessment Tool (FRAX)

TOXINS AND MEDICATIONS THAT CAN CAUSE OR AGGRAVATE OSTEOPOROSIS

- Alcohol (>2 drinks/d)
- ADT
- Anticonvulsants
- Antipsychotics
- Corticosteroids

- Heparin
- Lithium
- Nicotine (ie, smoking)
- Phenytoin
- PPIs (if ≥1 yr)

- SSRIs
- Thyroxine (if overreplaced or in suppressive dosage)

EVALUATION

- BMD at least once in all women after age 65 (and younger if risk is greater than or equal to that of a 65 yr old, using FRAX calculator), insufficient evidence to support screening in men (USPSTF) but National Osteoporosis Foundation (NOF) recommends BMD in all men after age 70, and in men with prior clinical fracture after age 65 (see **Table 105**). Uncertain how often to repeat. Some suggest in 3 yr for patients with osteopenia and in 5 yr for those with normal bone density. Do not routinely repeat more than once every 2 yr.^{CW} Although some professional societies recommend monitoring BMD q2yr, the value of monitoring BMD in patients already receiving tx is unproved. Even patients who continue to lose BMD during tx have benefits in fracture reduction.
- Serum 25-hydroxy vitamin D (treat if <30 ng/mL) expected rise is 1 ng/mL/100 IU vitamin D$_3$; if <20 ng/mL, consider 50,000 U vitamin D$_2$ (ergocalciferol) once/wk.

- Some experts recommend excluding secondary causes (serum PTH, TSH, calcium, phosphorus, albumin, alkaline phosphatase, bioavailable testosterone in men, kidney function tests, LFTs, CBC, UA, electrolytes, protein electrophoresis). Less consensus on 24-h urinary calcium excretion, cortisol, antibodies associated with gluten enteropathy.

MANAGEMENT
Universal Recommendations
- Calcium (elemental) 1200 mg/d for women >50 yr old and men >70 yr old, 1000 mg/d for men <70 yr old. For most patients, calcium carbonate is sufficient and least expensive. For patients on PPIs (see **Table 56**) or who have achlorhydria, calcium citrate should be used. For patients who have difficulty swallowing calcium citrate tabs, smaller tabs of 125 mg *(Freeda Mini Cal-citrate)* and granules, 1 tsp = 760 mg *(Freeda Calcium Citrate Fine Granular)*, are available. Initiating calcium may be associated with a modest increased risk of cardiovascular events (MI or stroke) in women, and the benefits vs risks of supplementation remains to be clarified.
- Vitamin D at least 400 IU (USPSTF) or at least 800 IU (other organizations); D_3 (cholecalciferol) is preferred form
- OTC calcium plus vitamin D preparations vary considerably in amounts of each, so ask patients to read labels (look for elemental calcium) to ensure they are getting adequate amounts.

- Avoid tobacco
- Exercise for muscle strengthening and balance training
- Falls prevention (see **Table 54**)

- No more than moderate alcohol use
- Treat nocturia to lower falls risk

Pharmacologic Prevention and Treatment
- Estimation of 10-yr probability of major osteoporotic or hip fracture based on risk factors with or without BMD can be calculated using FRAX, (www.shef.ac.uk/FRAX/).
- The NOF has recommended initiating pharmacologic management (see **Table 93**) in women with BMD T scores below −2.5 in the absence of risk factors and in women with T scores at any bone site of −1 to −2.5 if 10-yr risk (based on FRAX) of hip fracture is >3% or 10-yr risk of major osteoporotic fracture (cervical spine, forearm, hip, or shoulder) is >20%.
- Some question NOF guidelines because application would result in pharmacotherapy for 72% of white women >65 yr old and 93% of women >75 yr old compared with bone density criteria alone, which would result in pharmacotherapy of 50% of women in both age groups. Also should consider patient's expected survival and whether patient will live long enough to accrue benefit of tx.
- The risk of fracture can be determined from the WHO/FRAX tool (www.shef.ac.uk/FRAX/).
- Bisphosphonates are first-line tx but are contraindicated in renal failure. If CrCl <35 mL/m, denosumab is alternative. However, few data supporting efficacy in Stage 4 and 5 CKD and CKD increases risk of hypocalcemia.
- IV bisphosphonates are generally used in patients with GI contradindications (eg, esophageal disorders, feeding tubes) or are unable to sit up following oral dosing.
- Begin bisphosphonate tx in patients receiving or who will receive chronic glucocorticoids (≥5 mg prednisone or equivalent for ≥3 mo) who have other fracture risk factors or if T score is less than −1.0.

- Bisphosphonate tx of patients with locally advanced or high-risk prostate cancer receiving ADT is cost-effective if osteoporosis on BMD, prior fracture, or age >80.
- Some experts recommend using bisphosphonates that have demonstrated efficacy in reducing hip fractures and shorter-acting agents as preferred initial tx (see **Table 94**).
- PPIs reduce the effectiveness of oral bisphosphonates, and some experts recommend holding the PPI the day before bisphosphonate administration and not administering the PPI until >60 min after the bisphosphonate has been taken.
- Bisphosphonates are more effective in preventing hip fracture when adherence is >80% (compared with adherence <50%). Adherence is better with weekly compared to daily regimens.
- The duration of bisphosphonate tx is uncertain. The risk of subtrochanteric or femoral shaft fractures increases with tx beyond 1 yr. An FDA analysis concluded that there was no clear benefit nor harm for overall osteoporotic fracture risk by continuing bisphosphonates beyond 5 yr. However, continuing tx beyond 5 yr reduces the risk of vertebral fractures. One suggested approach is to measure BMD and those with femoral neck T score below −2.5 (or < −2.0 with a previous spine fracture) should remain on tx. Once bisphosphonates have been discontinued, there are no data on whether or when to resume tx.

Table 93. Pharmacologic Prevention and Treatment of Osteoporosis[a]

Medication	Dosage	Formulations	Comments
Bisphosphonates			*Class effect:* Esophagitis; bone, joint, or muscle pain; osteonecrosis of jaw (estimated 1–28 cases/100,000 patient-yrs with oral tx)[b]; occipital inflammation; possibly atrial fibrillation); association with atypical femoral fractures rare (<6/10,000 patient-yrs). Do not use if CrCl <35 mL/min. Consider discontinuing or suspending after 5 yr
Alendronate▲ *(Fosamax)*	Prevention: 5 mg/d or 35 mg/wk Tx: 10 mg/d or 70 mg/wk	T: 5, 10, 35, 40, 70	Must be taken fasting with water; patient must remain upright and npo for ≥30 min after taking; do not use if CrCl <35 mL/min; relatively contraindicated in GERD
Effervescent *(Binosto)* with cholecalciferol	70 mg/wk 1 tab/wk	T: 70 T: 70/2800U; 70/5600U	
Ibandronate *(Boniva)*	Tx and prevention: po: 150 mg/mo or 2.5 mg/d IV: 3 mg q3mo	T: 2.5, 150 IV: 1 mg/mL (available in 3-mL prefilled syringes)	Must be taken fasting with water; patient must remain upright and npo for ≥60 min after taking; do not use if CrCl <30 mL/min
Risedronate▲ *(Actonel)*	Tx and prevention: 35 mg/wk, 5 mg/d, or 150 mg/mo	T: 5, 30, 35, 150	Must be taken fasting or ≥2 h after evening meal; patient must remain upright and npo for 30 min after taking; do not use if CrCl <30 mL/min

(cont.)

Medication	Dosage	Formulations	Comments
Delayed release (Atelvia)	35 mg/wk	T: 35 DR	
Zoledronic acid (Reclast)	5 mg IV given over >15 min every yr for tx or q2yr for prevention	5 mg/100 mL	May cause acute renal failure in patients using diuretics
Others			
Raloxifene (Evista)	60 mg/d	T: 60	Used more often for prevention because of reduced risk of breast cancer; may cause hot flushes, myalgias, cramps, and limb pain
Calcitonin (Calcimar, Cibacalcin, Miacalcin, Osteocalcin, Salmonine)	Tx and prevention: 100 IU/d SC (human) or 200 IU intranasally (salmon) in alternate nostrils q48h	Inj: human (Cibacalcin) 0.5 mg/vial▲ Intranasal▲: salmon 200 U/mL (Miacalcin)	May also be helpful for analgesic effect in patients with acute vertebral fracture (see also p 194); rhinitis in 10–12%; increased risk of cancer
Estrogen▲	See p 319		For use in select patients; for risks and benefits see p 320
Teriparatide (Forteo)	Tx: 20 mcg/d for up to 24 mo	Inj: 3 mL, 28-dose disposable pen device	Contraindicated in patients with Paget disease or prior skeletal radiation tx; can cause hypercalcemia (L, K); tx for 1 yr followed by 1 yr of bisphosphonates or raloxifene can maintain 1-yr gains in BMD
Denosumab (Prolia)	60 mg SC q6mo	Inj: 60 mg/mL in pre-filled syringe	Skin infections, dermatitis, osteoneorosis of jaw, hypocalcemia especially if CrCl <30 mL/min and uncorrected calcium. Risk of atypical fracture is expected to be similar to bisphosphonates.

[a] Unless specified, medication can be used for prevention or tx.

[b] Risk factors include IV tx (little data on osteoporosis doses); cancer; dental extractions, implants, and poor-fitting dentures; glucocorticoids; smoking; and preexisting dental disease. Some experts recommend that bisphosphonates be stopped for several months before and after elective complex oral procedures (or, if procedures are emergent, that bisphosphonates be held for several months after).

Pharmacologic Treatment Regimens for Those with Prior Osteoporotic Fractures

- BMD measurement is unnecessary. See **Table 93** for tx regimens.
- Combination tx (eg, estrogen plus bisphosphonate or calcitonin) is slightly more effective in improving BMD but has not been proved to affect fracture rates.
- For high-risk patients with multiple fractures who continue to fracture after 1 yr of bisphosphonate tx or who are intolerant of bisphosphonates, consider teriparatide.
- Denosumab is an alternative for those who are intolerant of bisphosphonates.

Osteoporosis in Men

- If symptomatic hypogonadism or a cause for hypogonadism, then testosterone replacement.

- In general, nonpharmacologic tx, indications for pharmacologic tx, and choices of drugs are the same as for women. Bisphosphonate tx has been evaluated less in men. Zoledronic acid reduces the risk morphometric vertebral fractures.

Table 94. Bone Outcomes of Medications for Osteoporosis Based on Randomized Clinical Trials[a]

Medication	Spine BMD and Fracture	Hip BMD	Hip Fracture	All Nonspinal Fractures
Estrogen[▲]	improved	improved	reduced	reduced
Raloxifene	improved	improved	no data	no effect
Alendronate[▲]	improved	improved	reduced	reduced
Ibandronate	improved	improved	no data	no effect
Risedronate	improved	improved	reduced	reduced
Calcitonin (nasal)[b]	improved	no effect	no effect	no effect
Zoledronic acid	improved	improved	reduced	reduced
Teriparatide[c]	improved	improved	no data	reduced
Denosumab	improved	improved	reduced	reduced

[a] The populations studied, sample sizes of individual studies, and duration of follow-up vary considerably; hence, this summary must be interpreted cautiously. Moreover, several randomized clinical trials are currently in progress and new findings may appear.
[b] Based on observational data, calcitonin appears to be less effective in preventing nonspinal fractures.
[c] More effective than bisphosphonates in increasing BMD and reducing spinal fractures in patients receiving systemic glucocorticoid tx for ≥3 mo.

Table 95. Effects on Other Outcomes, Level of Evidence,[a] and Risks of Medications for Osteoporosis

Medication	CHD Risk Factors	CHD Prevention	CHD Treatment	Breast Cancer	Deep-vein Thrombosis
Estrogen[▲b]	improved (R)	↑ risk (R)	no effect (R)	↑ risk (R)	↑ risk (R)
Raloxifene	improved (R)	no effect	↓ risk (R)	↓ risk (R)	↑ risk (R)
Bisphosphonates[c]	no data	no data	no data	↓ risk of invasive ↑ risk of ductal carcinoma in situ (O)	no data
Calcitonin[d] (nasal)	no data	no data	no data	no data	no data

Note: R = randomized clinical trial; O = observational study

[a] The populations studied, sample sizes of individual studies, and duration of follow-up vary considerably; hence, this summary must be interpreted cautiously. Moreover, several randomized clinical trials are currently in progress and new findings may appear.
[b] In the Women's Health Initiative estrogen-alone trial, only stroke and PE risk were increased.
[c] Alendronate[▲], ibandronate, risedronate, zoledronic acid
[d] Risk of any cancer is increased

PAIN

DEFINITION
An unpleasant sensory and emotional experience associated with actual or potential tissue damage (International Association for Study of Pain taxonomy)

Acute Pain
Distinct onset, usually evident pathology, short duration; common causes: trauma, postsurgical pain

Persistent Pain
Pain due to ongoing nociceptive, neuropathic, or mixed pathophysiologic processes, often associated with functional and psychologic impairment; can fluctuate in character and intensity over time (see **Table 96**)

Table 96. Types of Pain, Examples, and Treatment

Type of Pain and Examples	Source of Pain	Typical Description	Effective Drug Classes and Nonpharmacologic Treatments
Nociceptive: somatic			
Arthritis, acute postoperative, fracture, bone metastases	Tissue injury, eg, bones, soft tissue, joints, muscles	Well localized, constant; aching, stabbing, gnawing, throbbing	APAP, opioids, NSAIDs; PT and CBT
Nociceptive: visceral			
Renal colic, constipation	Viscera	Diffuse, poorly localized, referred to other sites, intermittent, paroxysmal; dull, colicky, squeezing, deep, cramping; often accompanied by nausea, vomiting, diaphoresis	Tx of underlying cause, APAP, opioids; PT and CBT
Neuropathic			
Cervical or lumbar radiculopathy, postherpetic neuralgia, trigeminal neuralgia, diabetic neuropathy, post-stroke syndrome, herniated intervertebral disc	PNS or CNS	Prolonged, usually constant, but can have paroxysms; sharp, burning, pricking, tingling, electric-shock–like; associated with other sensory disturbances, eg, paresthesias and dysesthesias; allodynia, hyperalgesia, impaired motor function, atrophy, or abnormal deep tendon reflexes	TCAs, SNRIs, anticonvulsants, opioids, topical anesthetics; PT and CBT
Undetermined			
Myofascial pain syndrome, somatoform pain disorders	Poorly understood	No identifiable pathologic processes or symptoms out of proportion to identifiable organic pathology; widespread musculoskeletal pain, stiffness, and weakness	Antidepressants, antianxiety agents; PT, CBT, and psychological tx

EVALUATION

Key Points, Approach

- Perform comprehensive evaluation for cause of pain, pain characteristics, and impact of physical and psychosocial function.
- Use multidisciplinary assessment and tx (eg, pharmacists, physical therapists, psychologists) when possible, particularly for persistent pain.
- Consider patient's report as the most reliable evidence of pain intensity.
- Assess for pain on each presentation (older adults may be reluctant to report pain).
- Use synonyms for pain (eg, burning, aching, soreness, discomfort).
- Use a standard pain scale (eg, Numeric Rating Scale, Verbal Descriptor Scale, or Faces Pain Scale; see www.geriatricsatyourfingertips.org); adapt for sensory impairments (eg, large print, written vs spoken).
- Use simple pain tools (eg, scale with none, mild, moderate, or severe pain) or questions with yes/no answers to solicit self-report of pain in persons with cognitive impairment.
- Assess pain in persons with severe cognitive impairment or inability to communicate pain using Pain Assessment algorithm (see **Figure 11**), including medical hx and physical examination to identify potential pain etiologies. Ask caregiver about recent changes in function, gait, behavior patterns, mood.
- In those with behavioral disturbances/agitation suspected of an underlying pain etiology for which other causes have been ruled out and behaviors not responding to nondrug intervention, try using a stepwise analgesic trial to evaluate pain as etiology, such as:

  Step 1: Oral APAP, max increase to 3 g/d. Order routinely rather than prn.

  Step 2: Oral morphine sulfate (5 mg q12h to max 10 mg q12h) or topical NSAIDs (second or as add-on tx)

  Step 3: Buprenorphine transdermal pch 5 mcg/h to max 10 mcg/h

  Step 4: Pregabalin 25 mg/d, max 300 mg/d for suspected neuropathic pain

  ○ The first step of an analgesic trial of APAP is often effective in improving behaviors and/or function.

  ○ Carefully monitor response to analgesics at each step of an analgesic trial as agent and dose are titrated to effect or undesirable AEs.
- Reassess regularly for improvement, deterioration, and complications/AEs, and document.

History and Physical Examination

- Focus on a complete examination of pain source and on musculoskeletal, peripheral vascular, and neurologic systems.
- Distinguish new illness from chronic condition.
- Analgesic hx: effectiveness and AEs, current and previous prescription drugs, OTC drugs, "natural" remedies.
- Assess effectiveness of prior nondrug tx.
- Laboratory and diagnostic tests to establish etiologic diagnosis.

Characteristics of Pain Complaint

Provocative (aggravating) and **P**alliative (relieving) factors
Quality (eg, burning, stabbing, dull, throbbing)
Region (eg, pain map)
Severity (eg, scale of 0 for no pain to 10 for worst pain possible)
Timing (eg, when pain occurs, frequency and duration)

Psychosocial Assessment

Depression (see pp 325–326 for screen), anxiety, mental status (see p 322 for screen). Impact on family or significant other. Enabling behaviors by others (eg, oversolicitousness, codependency, reinforcing debility).

Functional Assessment

ADLs, impact on activities (see pp 323–324 for screens), and quality of life

Brief Pain Inventory

Use for comprehensive assessment of pain and its impact (see www.geriatricscareonline.org).

MANAGEMENT

Goal: To find optimal balance in pain relief, functional improvement, and AEs.

Acute Pain and Short-term Management

- Identify cause of pain and treat if possible.
- Use fixed schedule of APAP, NSAIDs (consider nonselective vs celecoxib depending on risk factors and comorbidities, see **Figure 10**), or opioids.
  - IV acetaminophen *(Ofirmev;* 15 mg/kg q6h or 12.5 mg/kg q4h adult dose) option if no other route available; expensive.
- Refer to PT for nonpharmacologic strategies (eg, relaxation, heat or cold, TENS, joint mobilization, stabilizing exercises, assistive devices).
- Patient-controlled analgesia (PCA): Requires patient comprehension of PCA instructions
  - Indications
    - Acute pain (eg, postoperative pain, trauma)
    - Persistent pain in patients who are npo
  - Dosing strategies (see **Table 97**)
    - Titrate up PCA dose 25–50% if pain still not well controlled after 12 h.
    - Unless patient is awakened by pain during sleep, continuous opioid infusion not recommended because of increased risk of opioid accumulation and toxicity.
    - If basal rate used, hourly monitoring of sedation and respiratory status is warranted. If low respiratory rate (≤8) and moderate sedation (difficulty arousing patient from sleep) after expected peak of opioid, withhold further opioid until respiratory rate rises or pain returns. If needed, a small dose of dilute naloxone can be given and repeated.
    - D/C PCA when patient able to take oral analgesics or unable to self-medicate due to altered mental status or physical limitations.

Table 97. Typical Initial Dosing of PCA for Older Adults with Severe Pain		
Medication (usual concentration)	**Usual Dose Range***	**Usual Lockout (min)**
Morphine▲ (1 mg/mL)	0.5–2.5 mg	5–10
Hydromorphone▲ (0.2 mg/mL)	0.05–0.3 mg	5–10

* For opioid-naive patients, consider lower end of dosage range.

Figure 11. Pain Assessment in Older Adults with Severe Cognitive Impairment

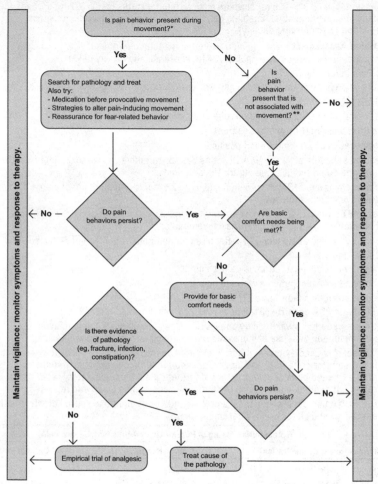

* Examples: grimacing, guarding, combativeness, groaning with movement; resisting care
** Examples: agitation, fidgeting, sleep disturbance, diminished appetite, irritability, reclusiveness, disruptive behavior, rigidity, rapid blinking
† Examples: toileting, thirst, hunger, visual or hearing impairment

Sources: American Geriatrics Society. *J Amer Geriatr Soc* 2002; 50(6, Suppl): S205–S240; and Weiner D, Herr K, Rudy T, eds. Persistent Pain in Older Adults: An Interdisciplinary Guide for Treatment, 2002, Copyright Springer Publishing Company, Inc., New York 10036.

Persistent Pain

- Identify and treat local causes of pain with local tx (eg, manipulation, massage, heat, PT, TENS), minor interventions (eg, steroid joint injection), surgery, or topical anesthetics (eg, lidocaine oint/pch or diclofenac gel/pch/gtt).
- Educate patient for self-management and coping. Include caregiver when possible.
  - Promote healthy behaviors including physical activity, weight control, and sleep.
  - www.healthinaging.org/resources/resource:-2/
  - Explain difference between addiction, physical dependence, and tolerance.
  - www.americanpainsociety.org/resources/content/for-people-in-pain.html
- Emphasize self-administered tx (eg, heat, cold, massage, liniments, and topical agents, distraction, relaxation, music) and self-management approaches (eg, CBT). Prescribe exercise for analgesic effects (see p 260).
- Combine pharmacologic and nonpharmacologic strategies.
  - Add tx taught and/or conducted by professionals (eg, coping skills, biofeedback, imagery, hypnosis) as needed.

Nonpharmacologic Treatment

Table 98. Nondrug Interventions for Persistent Pain in Older Adults

Intervention	Outcomes	Problems Studied
Physical		
Exercise	+	LE OA; chronic pain
Acupuncture	+	Back, knee, shoulder, neck
TENS	+/−	Knee, back
Qigong	+/−	Back, neck
Psychosocial		
Cognitive Behavioral Training	+	Chronic pain
Guided Imagery with Progressive Muscle Relaxation	+	Chronic OA pain
Music	+	Chronic pain
Mindfulness-based Meditation	+/−	Low back pain
Self-Management Education	+/−	Chronic pain, low back

Notes: Short-term efficacy, good tolerance, low risk, low cost; Best format, intensity, duration, content not established; Studies in older adults limited; No clear consensus on best. LE OA = lower extremity osteoarthritis; TENS = transcutaneous electrical nerve stimulation.
Source: Park J et al. *J Am Geriatr Soc*. 2012;60(3):555–568.

- Treat comorbid psychiatric conditions associated with persistent pain including anxiety, depression, and posttraumatic stress disorder.
  - Options include psychotherapy, biofeedback, mindfulness training, counseling (relationship, social, financial, substance abuse)
- When appropriate, obtain:
  - Consult PT and OT for mechanical devices to minimize pain and facilitate activity (eg, splints), transcutaneous electrical nerve stimulation, range-of-motion and ADL programs.
  - Psychiatric pain management consult for somatization or severe mood or personality disorder.
  - Anesthesia pain management consult for possible interventional tx (eg, neuroaxial analgesia, injection tx, neuromodulation) when more conservative approaches are ineffective.
  - Pain or chemical dependency specialist referral for management of at-risk patients and ongoing chemical dependency, "chemical coping," aberrant drug-related behaviors, and drug withdrawal.

Pharmacologic Treatment
Selection of Agent(s)
- Base initial choice of analgesic on the severity and type of pain and impact on function; consider cost, availability, patient preference, comorbidity, and impairments (see **Figure 10**)
- APAP should be considered initial and ongoing pharmacotherapy in treating persistent mild-moderate musculoskeletal pain with maximal dose of 4 g in healthy patients. Advise against alcohol use. (see **Table 82**).
- Consider topical analgesics and NSAIDS with localized neuropathic and/or nonneuropathic persistent pain.
  - Lidocaine pch *(Lidoderm)*, 8% capsaicin pch *(Qutenza)*
  - Diclofenac pch *(Flector)*, topical gel (*Voltaren* 1% Gel) and topical sol (*Pennsaid* 1.5% sol) for local tx of osteoarthritis or musculoskeletal pain
  - Menthol, methyl salicylate, or capsaicin available OTC
- Advise cautious short-term use of carefully selected NSAIDs based on risk/benefit analysis.
- Avoid long-term use of nonselective oral NSAIDs (Avoid NSAIDs without GI protection and in HF[BC]) and COX-2 selective inhibitor (celecoxib; avoid in HF[BC]) for chronic conditions (see **Figure 10**).
  - Nonselective NSAIDs and celecoxib may be considered rarely and with extreme caution in highly selected individuals.
  - If using nonselective NSAID or celecoxib with ASA, use a PPI or misoprostol for GI protection.
  - Do not use ibuprofen when also using ASA for cardioprophylaxis.
  - Consider celecoxib for patients who would benefit from anti-inflammatory medication on a continuous, long-term basis based on risk/benefit assessment (see **Figure 10** and **Table 82**).
  - Routinely assess for GI and renal toxicity, HTN, HF, and drug-drug and drug-disease interactions in patients taking NSAIDs.
  - Vascular risk of high-dose diclofenac and ibuprofen comparable to celecoxib; high-dose naproxen has less vascular risk than other NSAIDs. Data on low doses limited, however ibuprofen and naproxen seem safe at low doses for short-term use.

○ CV risk evident quickly after initiation. GI events confined to current use.
- Patients with moderate to severe pain, pain-related functional impairment, or diminished quality of life due to pain should be considered for opioid tx when other recommended tx aproaches unsuccessful. Careful risk/benefit analysis should be completed when determining appropriate use of opioid tx.
  ○ Ensure no contraindications to opioid tx.
  ○ Select patients who may benefit from low-dose opioid tx in combination with other tx (eg, specific somatic, peripheral, or neuropathic pain).
  ○ Tx not resulting in functional improvement should be tapered or discontinued and other tx options explored.
  ○ Consider fixed-dose combinations (eg, APAP▲ and hydrocodone or tramadol) for moderate pain; do not exceed max dose for APAP (see **Table 99**).
  ○ Consider opioid agonists (see **Table 99**) for severe pain impacting function and quality of life (rating 7–10).
  ○ Fall prevention when initiating opioid tx.
  ○ Avoid using multiple opioids or nonopioids.
  ○ Select least invasive route (usually oral) and fast-onset, short-acting analgesics for episodic or breakthrough pain.
  ○ Use long-acting or SR analgesics for continuous pain after stabilizing dose with short-acting opioid.
    ▪ Medications with long half-life or depot effects (eg, methadone, levorphanol, transdermal fentanyl) should be used and titrated cautiously, with close supervision of effects; duration of effect may exceed usual dose intervals because of reduced metabolism and clearance.
    ▪ Methadone is an option if other long-acting agents are not affordable but should be used with extreme caution and only with expertise and monitoring ability because of highly variable half-life and risk of dose accumulation (for details on methadone prescribing and monitoring, see www.geriatricscareonline.org).
  ○ Assess for ongoing attainment of tx goals, adverse effects and safe and responsible medication use. Long-term safety of opioid use in persistent pain in older adults has not been established.
- Consider adjuvant analgesics (see **Table 101**), including antidepressants and anticonvulsants, for patients with neuropathic pain, fibromyalgia, or refractory persistent pain.
  ○ Effects may be enhanced when used in combination with other pain analgesics and/or nondrug strategies.
  ○ Select agents with lowest AE profiles.
  ○ Begin low and titrate slowly; allow adequate therapeutic trial (may require 2–3 wk for onset of efficacy).

Adjustment of Dosage
- Begin with lowest dose possible, usually 25–50% adult dose, increasing slowly.
- Titrate dose on basis of persistent need for and use of medications for breakthrough pain. If using ≥3 doses/d of breakthrough pain medication, consider increased dosage of SR medication.
- Dose to therapeutic ceiling of nonopioid or NSAID as limited by drug AEs or risk factors.
- Increase opioid dosage until pain relief achieved or AEs unmanageable before changing medications (there is no max dose or analgesic ceiling with opioids).

- Use morphine equivalents as a common denominator for all dose conversions to avoid errors, and titrate to effectiveness. See www.hopweb.org.
- When changing opioids, decrease equivalent analgesic dose by 25–50% because of incomplete cross-tolerance.
- Administer around-the-clock for continuous pain.
- Reassess, reexamine, and readjust tx until pain is relieved.
- Opioid analgesics should not be discontinued abruptly. Gradual tapering is necessary to avoid withdrawal symptoms (eg, nausea, abdominal cramps, irritability, anxiety, diaphoresis, tachycardia, HTN). Decreasing the daily dosage by 10–20% each day for 10 d can wean most patients without adverse responses. Tapering may require conversion to short-acting opioids. For patients at cardiovascular risk, a slower taper with close monitoring for sympathetic hyperactivity is recommended, and low-dose clonidine may be useful in preventing some of the physiologic (and symptomatic) stress related to opioid withdrawal.
- Risk evaluation and mitigation strategy (REMS) requires companies to provide educational materials for patients on safe use of long-acting or extended-release opioids. Prescriber training provided but not required.

Management of Adverse Events
- Anticipate, prevent, and vigorously treat AEs; expect older adults to be more sensitive to AEs.
- Warn patient about risk of sedation with opioids and that gradual resolution occurs within a week.
- Warn about risk of APAP toxicity and importance of including all OTC products with APAP in daily total (not to exceed 4 g/d in healthy older adults).
- Begin prophylactic, osmotic, or stimulant laxative when initiating opioid tx (see **Table 58**); if patient has sufficient fluid intake, cautiously increase fiber or psyllium▲; titrate laxative dose up with opioid dose. Instances of severe opioid-induced constipation may respond to oral naloxone 0.8–2 mg q12h, titrated to a max of 12 mg/d given in water or juice, along with routine bowel regimen; or methylnaltrexone bromide *(Relistor)* SC 8 mg (38–62 kg) to 12 mg (62–114 kg) and 0.15 mg/kg for other weights with one dose q48h. Careful titration and observation are necessary because some patients may experience partial analgesia reversal. (See also p 124.)
- Monitor for dry mouth, constipation, sedation, nausea, delirium, urinary retention, and respiratory depression; tolerance develops to mild sedation, nausea, and impaired cognitive function. Reduce dosage and/or consider adding medication to counter adverse medication events if troublesome until tolerance develops.
- Hyperalgesia, hypogonadism may occur with long-term opioid use.
- Avoid the following medications: carisoprodol, chlorzoxazone, cyclobenzaprine, indomethacin, meperidine, metaxalone, methocarbamol, nalbuphine, pentazocine (see also www.cms.gov/transmittals/downloads/R22SOMA.pdf).

PREVENTION OF OPIOID MISUSE AND WITHDRAWAL
An ongoing tx plan for all patients receiving opioid tx that includes the following is good practice:
- Assess for risk of opioid misuse or abuse (eg, Opioid Risk Tool [ORT] (see Substance Abuse chapter, p 310).
  - Score of 8 or higher is considered high risk. Prescribe opioids only after all other tx modalities exhausted, under close supervision—ideally in consultation with a pain or addiction specialist.

- Perform urine drug testing before initiating opioid tx and at least yearly (be aware that false-negative and -positive results are possible, so cautious interpretation is needed)
- Consider a written opioid agreement (www.aapainmanage.org/literature/Articles/OpioidAgreement.pdf).
- Consult state prescription monitoring program to evaluate multisourcing.
- Avoid opioids in patients with chronic central or visceral pain syndrome, such as fibromyalgia, headaches, or abdominal pain.
- Physical dependence is expected with long-term opioid use (can occur with several weeks of around-the-clock use); it is not the same as substance abuse or addiction.
- Be aware of early symptoms of opioid withdrawal, including agitation, anxiety, muscle aches, increased tearing, insomnia, runny nose, sweating, and yawning.
- Opioid doses exceeding 100 mg of morphine sulfate equivalents may increase risk of overdose and should prompt consideration of tapering and referral to pain specialist.
- Approach to weaning off long-term opioid use can range from a slow 10% dose reduction per wk to a more rapid 25–50% reduction every 2–3 d. Adapt based on comorbidities and withdrawal symptoms when process is begun.

Table 99. Short-acting Opioid Analgesic Drugs

Class, Medication	MS Equiv[a] (Route)	Starting Dosage in Opioid-naïve Patients	Formulations
Mild to Moderate Pain			
Codeine[▲]	200 mg (po)	15 mg q4–6h	T: 15, 30, 60; S: 15/5 mL; Inj
Codeine + APAP[▲][b]	200 mg (po)	1–2 15/325 tabs q4–6h; if 1 tab used, add 325 mg APAP	T: 15/325, 30/325, 60/325, 30/500, 30/650, 7.5/300, 15/300, 30/300, 60/300; S: 12/120/5 mL
Hydrocodone + APAP[▲][b] (eg, *Lorcet, Lortab, Norco, Vicodin*)	30 mg (po)	2.5–5 mg q4–6h	T: 10/325, 5/400, 7.5/400, 10/400, 2.5/500, 5/500, 7.5/500, 10/500, 7.5/650, 7.5/750, 10/650, 10/660; C: 5/500; S: 2.5/167/5 mL (contains 7% alcohol)
Hydrocodone + ibuprofen[▲][c] (eg, *Vicoprofen*)	30 mg	7.5/200	T: 7.5/200
Oxycodone[▲] *(Oxy IR, Oxecta, Roxicodone)*	20 mg (po)	2.5–5 mg q3–4h	T: 5, 15, 30; C: 5; S: 5 mg/mL, 20 mg/mL
Oxycodone + APAP[▲][b] *(Percocet, Tylox)*	20 mg (po)	2.5–5 mg oxycodone q6h	T[▲]: 2.5/325, 5/325, 5/500, 7.5/325, 7.5/500, 10/325, 10/650; C: 5/500; S: 5/325/5 mL
(Magnacet)			T: 2.5/400, 5/400, 7.5/400, 10/400
Oxycodone + ASA[▲] *(Percodan)*	20 mg (po)	2.25–4.5 mg oxycodone q6h	T: 2.25/325, 4.5/325
Moderate to Severe Pain			
Oxycodone + ibuprofen[▲] *(Combunox)*[b,c]	20 mg (po)	1 tab po q6h; do not exceed 4 tabs in 24h	T: 5/400

(cont.)

Table 99. Short-acting Opioid Analgesic Drugs (cont.)

Class, Medication	MS Equiv[a] (Route)	Starting Dosage in Opioid-naive Patients	Formulations
Morphine▲ *(MSIR, Astramorph PF, Duramorph, Infumorph, Roxanol, OMS Concentrate, MS/L, RMS, MS/S)*	30 mg (po), 10 mg (IV, IM, SC)	5 mg po q4h; 1–2 mg IV q3–4h; 2.5–5 mg IM, SC q4h; 5–10 mg Sp q3–4h	C: 15, 30; soluble T: 15, 30; S: 10 mg/5 mL, 20 mg/5 mL, 100 mg/5 mL, 4 mg/mL, 20 mg/mL; Sp: 5, 10, 20, 30; Inj
Hydromorphone▲ *(Dilaudid, Hydrostat)*	7.5 mg (po), 1.5 mg (IV, IM, SC), 6 mg (rectal)	1–2 mg po q3–6h; 0.1–0.3 mg IV q2–3h; 0.4–0.5 mg IM, SC q4–6h; 3 mg Sp q4–8h	T: 2, 4, 8; S: 5 mg/5 mL; Sp: 3; Inj
Oxymorphone *(Opana, Opana injectable)*	10 mg (po), 1 mg (IV, IM, SC)	5 mg po q4–6h; 0.5 mg IM, IV, SC q4–6h	T: 5, 10; Sp: 5; Inj
Tramadol▲BC *(Ultram)* [d,e]	150–300 mg (po)	25 mg q4–6h; not >300 mg for those >75 yr old	T: 50
Tramadol[BC] + APAP▲ *(Ultracet)* [d,e]	37.5/325 mg (po)	2 tabs q4–6h; max 8 tabs/d	T: 37.5/325
Tapentadol *(Nucynta)* [f]	20 mg (po)	50 mg q4–6h	T: 50, 75, 100
Fentanyl *(Actiq)* [g]	NA	Suck on 200 mcg loz over 15 min, effect within 10 min	Loz on a stick: 200, 400, 600, 800, 1200, 1600 mcg
Fentanyl *(Abstral, Fentora)* [g]	NA	100 mcg	sl or buccal: 100, 200, 300, 400, 600, 800 mcg
Fentanyl *(Lazanda)* [g]	NA	100 mcg	Nasal spr: 100, 400mcg/10mcL
Fentanyl *(Subsys)* [g]	NA	100 mcg	sl spr: 100, 200, 400, 600, 800 mcg
Fentanyl *(Onsolis)* [g]	NA	One 200-mcg film, titrate using multiples of the 200-mcg film until patient reaches a dose that provides adequate analgesia with tolerable AEs; do not use >4 of the 200-mcg films simultaneously	Buccal film: 200, 400, 600, 800, 1200 mcg
Fentanyl HCl iontophoretic transdermal system (ITS) [g]	NA	40-mcg dose with 10-min lockout through electrical stimulus	System pch with battery contains 80 doses of 40 mcg each

[BC]Avoid in seizure disorders.

[a] MS Equiv = morphine sulfate (MS) equivalent dose: morphine equivalency = dose of opioid equivalent to 10 mg of parenteral morphine or 30 mg of oral morphine with chronic dosing.

[b] Caution: total APAP dosage should not exceed 4 g/d.

[c] Monitor renal function and use gastric protection.

[d] Tx not to exceed 7 d.

[e] Risk of suicide for patients who are addiction prone, taking tranquilizers or antidepressant drugs, and at risk of overdosage. Additive effects with alcohol and other opioids.

[f] Lowest available dose may be high in opioid-naive patients in unmonitored settings; additional caution is warranted to observe for signs of excessive sedation.

[g] Do not use in opioid-naive; use is for breakthrough pain in those on opioid tx.

Table 100. Long-acting Opioids for Opioid-tolerant [a] Patients with Moderate to Severe Pain

Class, Medication	MS Equiv [b] (Route)	Starting Dose	Formulations
ER Hydromorphone hydrochloride *(Exalgo)*	7.5 mg	*Exalgo:* 8 mg q24h[c]	T: 8, 12, 16, 32
ER Morphine▲ *(MS Contin, Kadian, Oramorph SR, Avinza)*	*MS Contin:* 30 mg (po) *Kadian:* 30 mg (po) *Oramorph SR:* 30 mg (po) *Avinza:* 60 mg (po)	*MS Contin:* 20–30 mg q24h, 15 mg q12h *Kadian:* 20 mg q24h *Oramorph SR:* 15 mg q24h *Avinza:* 30 mg q24h	T: CR 15, 30, 60, 100, 200 C: ER 10, 20, 30, 50, 60, 80, 100, 200 T: SR 15, 30, 60, 100 C: ER 30, 45, 60, 75, 90, 120
ER Morphine/naltrexone hydrochloride *(Embeda)* [d]	30 mg (po)	20 mg/0.8 mg q12–24h	C: ER 20/0.8, 30/1.2, 50/2, 60/2.4, 80/3.2, 100/4
ER Oxycodone▲ *(OxyContin)*	20–30 mg (po)	20 mg q24h, 10 mg q12h	T: CR 10, 20, 40, 80, 160
Oxymorphone ER▲ *(Opana ER)*	10 mg	5 mg q12h; titrate dosage by 5-mg increments q12h	T: 5, 10, 20, 30, 40
Tapentadol ER *(Nucynta ER)*	20 mg (po)	50 mg q12h	T: 50, 100, 150, 200, 250
Tramadol ER[BC] *(Ultram ER, ConZip)*	150–300 mg (po)	100 mg q24h or calculate 24-h total dose for immediate-release tramadol	T: 100, 200, 300 C: 150
Transdermal buprenorphine[e] *(Butrans Transdermal System CIII)*	NA (see package insert)	5 mcg/h if <30 MS equiv for opioid-naive or if taking <30 mg oral morphine equiv; 10 mcg/h if 30–80 oral MS equiv with 1 pch × 7 d.[f]	5, 10, 15, 20 mcg/h
Transdermal fentanyl▲[g] *(Duragesic)*	NA (see package insert)	12 mcg/h or higher q72h (if able to tolerate 60 mg oral morphine equiv/24 h)	12 mcg/h, 25 mcg/h, 50 mcg/h, 75 mcg/h, 100 mcg/h

Note: Conversion from any oral immediate-release opioid should be based on conversion ratios; start by administering 50% of calculated total daily dose of ER opioid, and titrate until adequate pain relief is achieved with tolerable adverse effects.

[BC] Avoid in seizure disorders.

[a] Opioid-tolerant are those taking at least 60 mg/d of oral morphine, 25 mcg/h of transdermal fentanyl, 30 mg/d of oral oxycodone, 8 mg/d of oral hydromorphone, 25 mg/d of oral oxymorphone, or an equianalgesic dosage of another opioid for ≥1 wk.

[b] MS Equiv = morphine sulfate (MS) equivalent dose: morphine equivalency = dose of opioid equivalent to 10 mg of parenteral morphine or 30 mg of oral morphine with chronic dosing.

[c] Starting dose for ER formulation equivalent to total daily dose of oral hydromorphone, taken q24h; titrate every 3–4 d to adequate pain relief. Tablets should be swallowed whole or can lead to rapid release and absorption of potentially fatal dose of hydromorphone.

[d] These products contain an opioid antagonist intended to decrease misuse/abuse. If the product is used as intended and taken whole, analgesia is affected. If the product is altered (eg, chewed, crushed, dissolved), the opioid antagonist is released and can reverse analgesia effects.

(cont.)

Do not exceed one 20 mcg/h Butrans system due to the rise of QT_c prolongation. Avoid exposing Butrans application site and surrounding area to direct external heat sources (eg, heating pads). Temperature-dependent increases in buprenorphine release from the system may result in overdose and death. Caution if switching from pure mu-opioid agonist. Careful patient selection because of abuse potential—monitor for signs of misuse, abuse, and addiction. Indicated for severe, chronic pain requiring around-the-clock analgesia for extended time.

f Initiate dosing regimen on individual basis and consult conversion instructions; do not titrate dose until exposed continuously for 72 h at previous dose.

g *Caution:* Active ingredient accumulates in subcutaneous fat; thus, duration of action may be >17 h. Remove patch before MRI. Do not use in opioid-naive patients. Not recommended for tx of acute pain.

NA = not applicable

Table 101. Adjuvant Medications for Pain Relief in Older Adults

Class, Medication	Formulations and Dosage	Comments
Anticonvulsants (see also **Table 91** and p 226)		If one does not work, try another.
Carbamazepine▲ *(Tegretol)*	T: 200▲ ChT: 100 S: 100/5 mL▲ 200–400 mg q8h	Many drug interactions; mood stabilizer; used for trigeminal or glossopharyngeal neuralgia; may cause SIADH, thrombocytopenia, leukopenia
(Tegretol XR; Carbatrol)	T: 100, 200, 400▲ C: CR 200, 300 200 mg q12h	
Oxcarbazepine *(Trileptal, Oxtellar XR)*	*Trileptal* susp: 300 mg/5 ml *Oxtellar* T: 150, 300, 600 mg 600–2400 mg once	
Gabapentin▲ *(Neurontin)*	C: 100, 300, 400 T: 600, 800 S: 250 mg/5 mL Begin 100–200 mg qhs but may need up to 200–700 mg q12h	If CrCl >15–29 mL/min: dose at 200–700 mg/d; if CrCl >30–59 mL/min, dose at 200–700 q12h; if CrCl ≤15 mL/min, dose at 100–300 mg/d; used for post-herpetic neuralgia and postoperative and chronic pain
Pregabalin *(Lyrica)*	C: 25, 50, 75, 100, 150, 200, 225, 300 75–300 mg q12h	Primary indication is for management of post-herpetic neuralgia, diabetic peripheral neuropathy, and fibromyalgia
Lamotrigine▲ *(Lamictal)*	T: 25, 100, 150, 200 ChT: 2, 5, 25▲ 400–600 mg q24h	Prolongs PR interval; risk of severe rash
Antidepressants (see **Table 41**)		Use low-dose desipramine▲ or nortriptyline▲; data on SSRIs lacking.
Duloxetine *(Cymbalta)*	C: 20, 30, 60 30 mg/d	For management of pain associated with diabetic peripheral neuropathy and tx of chronic musculoskeletal pain, including osteoarthritis and chronic low back pain; most common AEs: nausea, dry mouth, constipation, diarrhea, urinary hesitancy; significant drug-drug interactions.
Venlafaxine▲ *(Effexor)*	T: 25, 37.5, 50, 75, 100 Begin 25–50 mg q12h; 75–225 mg q24h in divided doses	Low anticholinergic activity; minimal sedation and hypotension; may increase BP and QT_c; may be useful when somatic pain present; EPS, withdrawal symptoms, hyponatremia

(cont.)

Table 101. Adjuvant Medications for Pain Relief in Older Adults (cont.)

Class, Medication	Formulations and Dosage	Comments
(Effexor XR)	C: 37.5, 75, 150 Begin 75 mg qam; 75–225 mg q24h	
Milnacipran *(Savella)*	T: 12.5, 25, 50, 100 Begin 12.5 mg q24h; up to 100 mg q24h in divided doses	Dual reuptake inhibitor; used to treat pain of fibromyalgia; contraindicated with MAOI or within 2 wk of MAOI discontinuation
Corticosteroids (see **Table 49**)		Low-dose medical management may be helpful in inflammatory conditions.
Counterirritants		
✔Camphor-menthol- phenol▲ *(Sarna)**	lot: camphor 5%, menthol 5%, phenol 5% prn; max q6h	May be effective for arthritic pain, but effect limited when pain affects multiple joints; can cause skin injury, especially if used with heat or occlusive dressing.
✔Camphor and phenol▲ *(Campho-Phenique)**	S: camphor 5%, phenol 4.7% prn; max q8h	
✔Methyl salicylate and menthol▲		Monitor for salicylate toxicity if used over several areas.
(Ben-Gay oint*, *Icy Hot* crm*)	methyl salicylate 18.3%, menthol 16% q6–8h	Apply to affected area.
(Ben-Gay extra strength crm*)	methyl salicylate 30%, menthol 10% q6–8h	Apply to affected area.
✔Trolamine salicylate▲ *(Aspercreme* rub*)	trolamine salicylate 10% q6h or more frequently	Apply to affected area.
Other		
Baclofen▲ *(Lioresal)*	T: 10, 20; Inj 5 mg up to q8h	Probably increased sensitivity and decreased clearance; monitor for weakness, urinary dysfunction; avoid abrupt discontinuation because of CNS irritability.
Tizanidine▲ *(Zanaflex)*	T: 2, 4 2 mg up to q8h	Monitor for muscle weakness, urinary function, cognitive effects, sedation, orthostasis; potential for many drug-drug interactions.
Clonazepam**BC** *(Klonopin)*	T: 0.5, 1, 2 ODT: 0.125, 0.25, 0.5, 1, 2 0.25–0.5 mg hs	Monitor sedation, memory, CBC.

(cont.)

Table 101. Adjuvant Medications for Pain Relief in Older Adults (cont.)

Class, Medication	Formulations and Dosage	Comments
✔Capsaicin▲ (eg, *Capsin, Capzasin, No Pain-HP, R-Gel, Zostrix, Qutenza*)	crm, lot, gel, roll-on: 0.025%, 0.075%; 179-mg cutaneous pch q6–8h	Renders skin and joints insensitive by depleting and preventing reaccumulation of substance P in peripheral sensory neurons; may cause burning sensation up to 2 wk; instruct patient to wash hands after application to prevent eye contact; do not apply to open or broken skin. Pch should be applied by health professional, using a local anesthetic, to the most painful skin areas (max of 4 pchs). Apply for 30 min to feet, 60 min to other locations. Risk of significant rise in BP after placement; monitor patient for at least 1 h.
✔Lidocaine *(Lidoderm)*	transdermal pch 5% 12 h on, 12 h off; up to 24 h on	Apply over affected area up to 4 patches for 24 h; used for neuropathic pain, may be helpful for low back pain, osteoarthritis.
Onabotulinumtoxin A *(Botox)*	Individualized based on muscle affected, severity of muscle activity, prior experience; not to exceed 360 U q12–16wk	Injected into muscles to treat myofascial pain syndrome resulting from skeletal muscle spasm and migraines when source is neck or facial muscles.

✔ = preferred for treating older adults
* Available OTC
BCAvoid

Note: Various adjuvant classes are useful for tx of neuropathic pain. TCAs are often helpful for migraine or tension headaches and arthritic conditions. Baclofen is particularly useful for muscle-related problems, such as spasms.

DEFINITION

"Palliative care means patient and family-centered care that optimizes quality of life by anticipating, preventing and treating suffering. Palliative care throughout the continuum of illness involves addressing physical, intellectual, emotional, social and spiritual needs to facilitate patient autonomy, access to information and choice." (From National Quality Forum's *National Framework and Preferred Practices for Palliative and Hospice Care*, 2006.)

PRINCIPLES

- Support, educate, and treat both patient and family.
- Address physical, psychologic, social, and spiritual needs.
- Use multidisciplinary team (physicians, nurses, social workers, chaplain, pharmacist, physical and occupational therapists, dietitian, family and caregivers, volunteers).
- Focus on symptom management, comfort, meeting goals, completion of "life business," healing relationships, and bereavement.
- Make care available 24 h/d, 7 d/wk.
- Educate, plan, and document advance directives; health care proxy; family awareness of decisions.
- Coordinate care among various providers. Help integrate potentially curative, disease-modifying, and palliative tx.
- Offer bereavement support.
- Provide therapeutic environment (palliation can be given in any location).
- Advocate comprehensive palliative care for all dying patients.

QUALITY OF LIFE

Ways to help patient and family enhance quality of life with chronic illness and/or at the end of life:

- Communicate, listen
- Teach stress management, coping
- Use all available resources
- Support decision making
- Encourage conflict resolution
- Help complete unfinished business
- Urge focus on nonillness-related affairs
- Urge a focus on one day at a time
- Help anticipate grief, losses
- Help focus on attainable goals
- Encourage spiritual practices
- Promote physical, psychologic comfort
- Refer to PT

DECISIONS ABOUT PALLIATIVE CARE

Follow principles involved in informed decision making (see **Figure 2**).

Communicating Bad News (SPIKES)

S=Setting: Prepare for discussion by ensuring all information/facts/data are available. Deliver in person in private area without interruptions or physical barriers. Determine individuals who patient may want involved.

P=Establish patients' perception of their illness (knowledge and understanding) by asking open-ended questions. Use vocabulary patient uses when breaking bad news.

I=Secure invitation to impart medical information. Determine what/how much patient wants to know.

K=Deliver information in sensitive, straightforward manner; avoid technical language and euphemisms. Check for understanding after small chunks of information and clarify concepts and terms.

E=Use empathetic and exploratory responses; use active listening, encourage expression of emotions, acknowledge patient's feelings.

S=Strategize and summarize and organize an immediate tx plan addressing patient's concerns and agenda. Provide opportunity to raise important issues. Reassess understanding of condition and tx plan and determine need for further education and follow-up with patient and family.

Hospice Referral

- Patients, families, or other health care providers can refer a physician's certification of limited life expectancy (prognosis of ≤6 mo for most hospice programs [see **Table 102**]) is required.

- Encourage nursing home staff to interview residents to determine goals, preferences, and palliative care needs suggestive of appropriateness for hospice. Discuss patient's wishes with primary care provider and evaluate whether patient meets hospice criteria. Fax request for hospice referral to primary care provider effective.

- Referral is appropriate when curative tx is no longer indicated (ie, ineffective, AEs too burdensome) and life is limited to months.

- Course of disability in last year of life does not follow predictable pattern based on the condition leading to death. For advanced dementia, high levels of disability are common. However, for cancer, organ failure, frailty, sudden death, and other conditions, very low levels of disability are seen until only a few months before death. Need for services to assist with ADLs is as great for persons dying from organ failure and frailty as for those with cancer and greater for those with advanced dementia.

- Hospice must be accepted by the patient or family, or both, and can be rescinded at any time.

- Hospice provides palliative medications, durable medical supplies and equipment, team member visits as needed and desired by patient and family (physician, nurses, home health aide, social worker, chaplain), and volunteer services.

- Optimal hospice care requires adequate time in the program; referral when death is imminent does not take full advantage of hospice care.

- Hospice care is usually delivered in patient's home, but it can be delivered in a nursing home or residential care facility (long-term care, assisted living) or in an inpatient setting (hospice-specific or contracted facility) if acuity or social circumstances warrant.

- Coverage of hospice services variable (eg, inpatient availability, amount of home care, sites for care), so determine and discuss with patient/family.

Table 102. Typical Trajectory and Hospice Eligibility for Selected Diseases

Disease	Typical Determinants for Hospice Eligibility*
Cancer	Clinical findings of malignancy with widespread, aggressive, or progressive disease evidenced by increasing symptoms, worsening laboratory values, and/or evidence of metastatic disease Impaired performance status with a Palliative Performance Scale (PPS; see p 329) value of ≤70% Refuses further curative tx or continues to decline in spite of definitive tx
Dementia	FAST Scale Stage 7 (see p 330) **and** • unable to ambulate, dress, bathe without assistance • UI and FI intermittently or constant • no consistently meaningful verbal communication Have had 1 of the following in the past 12 mo: • aspiration pneumonia • decubitus ulcer (multiple, stage 3–4) • inability to maintain sufficient fluid and calorie intake with 10% weight loss during previous 6 mo, or serum albumin < 2.5 g/dL • pyelonephritis or other upper UTI • fever (recurrent after antibiotics)
Failure to thrive	BMI <22 kg/m² and either declining enteral/parenteral nutritional support or not responding to such support, despite adequate caloric intake Karnofsky score ≤40 or PPS value ≤40% (see p 328)
End-stage heart disease	Optimally treated for HD or either not candidates for surgical procedures or who decline those procedures (optimally treated: not on vasodilators have a medical reason for refusing [eg, hypotension or renal disease]) **and** Significant symptoms of recurrent HF at rest and classified as NYHA Class IV (ie, unable to carry on any physical activity without symptoms, symptoms present at rest, symptoms increase if any physical activity is undertaken) Documentation of following will support eligibility but not required: • tx-resistant symptomatic supraventricular or ventricular arrhythmia • hx of cardiac arrest or resuscitation or unexplained syncope • brain embolism of cardiac origin • concomitant HIV disease • documented ejection fraction of ≤20%
End-stage liver disease	Prothrombin time >5 sec longer than control, or INR >1.5 **and** serum albumin <2.5 g/dL At least one of the following: ascites, refractory to tx or patient noncompliant; spontaneous bacterial peritonitis; hepatorenal syndrome (elevated Cr and BUN with oliguria [<400 mL/d]) and urine sodium concentration <10 mEq/L; hepatic encephalopathy, refractory to tx, or patient noncompliant; recurrent variceal bleeding despite intensive tx Documentation of the following will support eligibility, but not required: • progressive malnutrition • muscle wasting with reduced strength and endurance • continued active alcoholism (ethanol intake >80 g/d) • hepatocellular carcinoma; hepatitis B positivity (HBsAg) • hepatitis C refractory to interferon tx Awaiting liver transplant may be certified for Medicare hospice benefit, but if donor organ is procured, patient should be discharged from hospice

(cont.)

Disease	Typical Determinants for Hospice Eligibility*
End-stage pulmonary disease	Disabling dyspnea at rest, poorly or unresponsive to bronchodilators, resulting in decreased functional capacity, eg, bed to chair existence, fatigue, and cough (documentation of FEV_1, after bronchodilator, <30% of predicted is objective evidence for disabling dyspnea, but is not necessary to obtain) **and** Progression of end-stage pulmonary disease, as evidenced by *prior* increased visits to emergency department or *prior* hospitalization for pulmonary infections and/or respiratory failure or increasing physician home visits before initial certification (documentation of serial decrease of FEV_1 >40 mL/yr is objective evidence for disease progression, but is not necessary to obtain) **and** Hypoxemia at rest on room air, as evidenced by pO_2 ≤55 mmHg or O_2 sat ≤88% or hypercapnia, as evidenced by $PaCO_2$ ≥50 mmHg. Values may be obtained from MR within 3 mo. Documentation of the following will support eligibility, but not required: right HF secondary to pulmonary disease (cor pulmonale), unintentional progressive weight loss of >10% of body weight over preceding 6 mo, resting tachycardia >100 bpm
Acute renal failure	Not seeking dialysis or renal transplant or discontinuing dialysis **and** CrCl <10 mL/min (<15 mL/min for DM) **or** Serum Cr >8 mg/dL (>6 mg/dL for DM) Documentation of following will support eligibility, but not required: • mechanical ventilation • malignancy (other organ system) • chronic lung disease • advanced cardiac disease • advanced liver disease • sepsis • immunosuppression/AIDS • albumin <3.5 g/dL • cachexia • platelet count <25,000 • disseminated intravascular coagulopathy • GI bleeding
Chronic renal failure	Not seeking dialysis or renal transplant or discontinuing dialysis **and** CrCl <10 mL/min (<15 mL/min for DM) **or** Serum Cr >8 mg/dL (>6 mg/dL for DM) (<15 mL/min with comorbid CHF; <20 mL/min for diabetics) Documentation following signs and symptoms of renal failure lend support for eligibility: • uremia • oliguria (<400 mL/day) • intractable hyperkalemia (>7) not responsive to tx • uremic pericarditis • intractable fluid overload not responsive to tx • hepatorenal syndrome

* May vary depending on fiscal intermediary; additional supportive indications available for most diagnoses. Source: Adapted from www.montgomeryhospice.org/health-professionals/end-stage-indicators (extracted from CMS documentation LCD for Hospice-Determining Terminal Status [L13653]).

Advance Directives and Living Wills

- Designed to respect patient's autonomy and determine his/her wishes about future life-sustaining medical tx if unable to indicate wishes. (See Assessment regarding Informed Decision-making and Patient Preferences for Life-sustaining Care, p 10.)
- Written by the patient and documented, although not accepted by emergency medical services as legally valid forms; vary from state to state.

Oral Statements

- Conversations with relatives, friends, and clinicians are most common form; should be thoroughly documented in medical record for later reference.
- Properly verified oral statements carry same ethical and legal weight as those recorded in writing.

Instructional Advance Directives (DNR Orders, Living Wills, POLST, MOLST)

- Do-Not-Resuscitate (DNR) orders written by the physician based on the wishes previously expressed by the individual in his or her advanced directive or living will.
- Physician Orders for Life-Sustaining Treatment (POLST) or Medical Orders for Life-Sustaining Treatment (MOLST) include written instructions about the initiation, continuation, withholding, or withdrawal of particular forms of life-sustaining medical tx.
- POLST documents differ from state to state, but are designed to be recognizable (eg, bright pink; posted on refrigerator), used by first responders, and transferred across settings.
- Clinicians who comply with such directives are provided legal immunity for such actions.
- POLST form can be very useful in formalizing patient preferences (www.polst.org). May be revoked or altered at any time by the patient.
- Key elements of POLST Plan of Care address: cardiopulmonary resuscitation; level of medical intervention desired in the event of an emergency (comfort only, limited tx, or full tx); and use of artificial nutrition and hydration. Some states include use of antibiotics, hospitalization and mechanical ventilation.
- To determine whether POLST should be completed, ask "Would I be surprised if this person died in the next year?" If no, the POLST is appropriate.

Durable Power of Attorney for Health Care or Health Care Proxy

A written document that enables a capable person to appoint someone else to make future medical tx choices for him or her in the event of decisional incapacity (see **Figure 2**).

Key Interventions, Treatment Decisions to Include in Advance Directives

- Resuscitation procedures
- Mechanical respiration
- Chemotherapy, radiation tx
- Dialysis
- Simple diagnostic tests
- Pain control
- Blood products, transfusions
- Intentional deep sedation
- ICD and pacemakers

Withholding or Withdrawing Therapy

- There is no ethical or legal difference between withholding an intervention (not starting it) and withdrawing life-sustaining medical tx (stopping it after it has been started).
- Beginning a tx does not preclude stopping it later; a time-limited trial may be appropriate.
- Palliative care should not be limited, even if life-sustaining tx are withdrawn or withheld.
- Decisions on artificial feeding should be based on the same criteria applied to use of ventilators and other medical tx.
- Initiate discussion about pacemaker deactivation only if there is a potential patient benefit; consider the potential negative effects of deactivation before disabling the pacemaker. *Note*: Pacemaker is not a resuscitative device and usually does not keep palliative-care patients alive.
- Reanalyze risk-to-benefit ratio of ICD tx in patients with terminal illness. Life-prolonging tx may no longer be desired.

Euthanasia

- Active euthanasia: direct intervention, such as lethal injection, intended to hasten a patient's death; a criminal act of homicide.
- Passive euthanasia: withdrawal or withholding of unwanted or unduly burdensome life-sustaining tx; appropriate in certain circumstances.

- Assisted suicide: the patient's intentional, willful ending of his or her own life with the assistance of another; a criminal offense in most states.

Death Certificate Completion (see **Assessment and Approach** chapter)

- Certification of death at the end of life is completed by the hospice medical director and provides personal information about the decedent and about circumstances and cause of death
- Information is important for settlement of estate and provides family members closure, peace of mind, and documentation of the cause of death

MANAGEMENT OF COMMON END-OF-LIFE SYMPTOMS
Pain

- Primary goal: to alleviate suffering at end of life. See Pain (p 227) for assessment and interventions.
- The most distressing symptom for patients and caregivers.
- If intent is to relieve suffering, the risk that sufficient medication appropriately titrated will produce an unintended effect (hastening death) is morally acceptable (double effect).
- Alternate routes may be needed, eg, transdermal, transmucosal, rectal, vaginal, topical, epidural, and IT.
- Recommend expert pain management consult if pain not adequately relieved with standard analgesic guidelines and interventions.
- Additional tx may include:
  - radionuclides and bisphosphonates (for metastatic bone pain)
  - radiation tx or chemotherapy directed at source of pain
- Pain crisis: Palliative sedation for intractable pain and suffering is an important option to discuss with patients. Ketamine▲ *(Ketalar)* 0.1 mg/kg IV bolus. Repeat prn q5min. Follow with infusion of 0.015 mg/kg/min IV (if IV access not available, SC at 0.3–0.5 mg/kg). Decrease opioid dosage by 50%. A benzodiazepine may be useful. Observe for problems with increased secretions and treat (see p 248).

Weakness, Fatigue
Nonpharmacologic

- Modify environment to decrease energy expenditure (eg, placement of phone, bedside commode, drinks).
- Adjust room temperature to patient's comfort.
- Teach reordering tasks to conserve energy (eg, eating first, resting, then bathing).
- Modify daily procedures (eg, sitting while showering rather than standing).

Pharmacologic

- Treat remediable causes such as pain, medication toxicity, insomnia, anemia, and depression.
- Consider psychostimulants (eg, dextroamphetamine▲ *[Dexedrine]* [Avoid[BC]] 2.5 mg po qam or q12h, methylphenidate▲ *[Ritalin]* 2.5 mg po qam or q12h to start titrate upward to 3 ×/d or 4 ×/d prn, or modafinil *[Provigil]* 200 mg qam); monitor for signs of psychosis, agitation, or sleep disturbance. Avoid in insomnia.[BC]

Dysphagia (see also p 118)
Nonpharmacologic
- Feed small, frequent amounts of pureed or soft foods.
- Avoid spicy, salty, acidic, sticky, and extremely hot or cold foods.
- Keep head of bed elevated for 30 min after eating. If possible, feed patient sitting upright.
- Instruct patient to wear dentures and to chew thoroughly.
- Use suction machine when necessary.

Pharmacologic
- For painful mucositis: local preparation of "magic mouthwash" (eg, 1:2:8 mixture of diphenhydramine elixir: lidocaine [2–4%]: magnesium-aluminum hydroxide▲ [eg, *Maalox*] as a swish-and-swallow suspension ac).
- For oral candidiasis: clotrimazole 10-mg troches▲, 5 doses/d, *or* fluconazole▲ 150 mg po followed by 100 mg/d po × 5 d.
- For severe halitosis: antimicrobial mouthwash; fastidious oral and dental care; treat putative respiratory tract infection with broad-spectrum antibiotics.

Dyspnea (see p 273)
Nonpharmacologic
- Teach positions to facilitate breathing, elevate head of bed.
- Teach relaxation techniques.
- Eliminate smoke and allergens.
- Ensure brisk air circulation (facial breeze) with a room fan; oxygen is indicated only for symptomatic hypoxemia (ie, SaO_2 <90% by pulse oximetry).

Pharmacologic
- Opioids: oral morphine▲ concentration (20 mg/mL: 1/4 to 1/2 mL sl, po; repeat in 15–30 min prn) *or* morphine tabs 5–10 mg po q2h; if oral route not tolerated, nebulized morphine 2.5 mg in 2–4 mL NS *or* fentanyl 25–50 mcg in 2–4 mL NS; *or* IV morphine 1 mg or equivalent opioid q5–10min.
- Bronchodilators (see **Table 122**).
- Diuretics, if evidence of volume overload (see **Table 28**).
- Anxiolytics (eg, lorazepam▲ po, sl, SC 0.5–2 mg q2–4h or prn); titrate slowly to effect.

Constipation (see p 124)
- Most common cause: adverse effects of opioids, medications with anticholinergic adverse effects. Use stimulant or osmotic laxative (see **Table 58**). Consider enema if no bowel movement for 4 d. Evaluate for bowel obstruction or fecal impaction.
- Opioid-induced constipation not responsive to laxative tx: methylnaltrexone bromide *(Relistor)* SC 8 mg (38–62 kg) to 12 mg (62–114 kg) and 0.15 mg/kg for other weights with 1 dose q48h.

Bowel Obstruction
Indications for Radiographic Evaluation
- To differentiate between constipation and mechanical obstruction
- To confirm the obstruction, determine site and nature if surgery is being considered

Nonpharmacologic Management

- Nasogastric intubation: only if surgery is being considered, for high-level obstructions, and poor response to pharmacotherapy
- Percutaneous venting gastrostomy: for high-level obstructions and profuse vomiting not responsive to antiemetics
- Palliative surgery
- Hydration: IV or hypodermoclysis

Pharmacologic Management (aimed at specific symptoms)

- Nausea and vomiting: haloperidol▲ (Haldol) po, IM 0.5–5 mg (≤10 mg) q4–8h prn; ondansetron▲ (Zofran) IV (over 2–5 min) 4 mg q12h, po 8 mg q12h [inj; T: 4, 8, 24; S: 4 mg/5 mL]; see also **Table 59**.
- Spasm, pain, and vomiting: scopolamine▲ IM, IV, SC 0.3–0.65 mg q4–6h prn; po 0.4–0.8 mg q4–8h prn; transdermal 2.5 cm² pch applied behind the ear q3d [inj; T: 0.4; pch 1.5 mg] **or** hyoscyamine▲ (Levsin/SL) sl [T: 0.125; S: 0.125 mg/mL] 0.125–0.25 q6–8h.
- Diarrhea and excessive secretions: loperamide▲ (Imodium A-D), see **Table 60**; octreotide▲ (Sandostatin) SC 0.15–0.3 mg q12h [inj], very expensive.
- Pain: see **Table 99**.
- Inflammation due to malignant obstruction: dexamethasone▲ (Decadron) po 4 mg q6h × 5–7 d.

Excessive Secretions

Nonpharmacologic: Positioning and suctioning, prn
Pharmacologic: Glycopyrrolate▲ 0.1–0.4 mg IV, SC q4h prn **or** scopolamine▲ 0.3–0.6 mg SC prn **or** transdermal scopolamine pch q72h **or** atropine▲ 0.3–0.5 mg SC, sl, nebulized q4h prn

Cough (see p 272)

Nausea, Vomiting (see p 127)

Determine cause to select appropriate antiemetic based on pathway-mediating symptoms and neurotransmitter involved (see **Table 59**). For refractory nausea and vomiting (ie, not amenable to other tx), a trial of dexamethasone (2 mg q8h) can be tried; risks are dyspepsia, altered mental status

Do not use topical lorazepam (Ativan), diphenhydramine (Benadryl), haloperidol (Haldol) ("ABH") gel for nausea.CW

Anorexia, Cachexia, Dehydration

See also Malnutrition (p 185) and volume depletion (p 180). Universal symptom of patients with serious and life-threatening illness.

Note: Percutaneous feeding tubes are not recommended in patients with dementia; instead offer oral assisted feeding.CW

Reassure patient and caregivers that appetite abates with age and dehydration is not uncomfortable.

Nonpharmacologic

- Educate patient and family on effects of disease progression resulting in lack of appetite and weight loss.
- Promote interest, enjoyment in meals (eg, alcoholic beverage if desired, involve patient in meal planning, small frequent feedings, cold or semi-frozen nutritional drinks).
- Good oral care is important.
- Alleviate dry mouth with ice chips, popsicles, moist compresses, or artificial saliva.

Pharmacologic

- Corticosteroids: dexamethasone▲ 1–2 mg po q8h; methylprednisolone▲ 1–2 mg po q12h; prednisone▲ 5 mg po q8h. Avoid in delirium.[BC]

Note: Avoid prescription appetite stimulants or high-calorie supplements for tx of anorexia or cachexia in older adults; instead, optimize social supports, provide feeding assistance, and clarify patient goals and expectations.[CW]

Altered Mental Status, Delirium (see Delirium, p 67)

Anxiety, Depression

- Provide opportunity to discuss feelings, fears, existential concerns
- Referral to appropriate team members (spiritual, nursing)
- Medicate (see Anxiety, p 34, and Depression, p 78)

Source: Fine P. *The Hospice Companion: Best Practices for Interdisciplinary Assessment and Care of Common Problems During the Last Phase of Life*, 2nd edition. Oxford University Press; 2012.

PREOPERATIVE CARE

Cardiac Risk Assessment

Figure 12. Assessing Cardiac Risk in Noncardiac Surgery

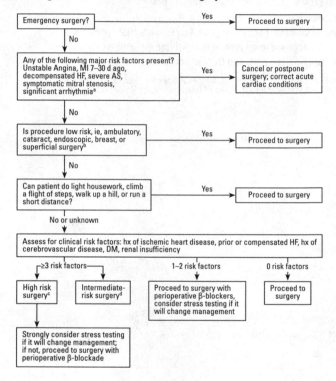

[a] High-grade AV block, Mobitz II AV block, third-degree AV block, symptomatic ventricular arrhythmias, or supraventricular arrhythmias with resting HR >100, newly recognized VT

[b] See next section, "Choosing Wisely Recommendations for Preoperative Cardiac Assessment"

[c] Open aortic or other major vascular surgery, peripheral vascular surgery

[d] Intraperitoneal or intrathoracic surgery, carotid endarterectomy, endovascular AAA repair, head and neck surgery, orthopedic surgery, prostate surgery

Source: Adapted from Fleisher LA, et al. *Circulation* 2007;116:e418-e499.

Choosing Wisely Recommendations for Preoperative Cardiac Assessment

- Don't perform stress cardiac imaging or advanced noninvasive imaging as a preoperative assessment in patients scheduled to undergo low-risk noncardiac surgery.[CW]
- Patients who have no cardiac hx and good functional status do not require preoperative stress testing before noncardiac thoracic surgery.[CW]
- Don't perform preoperative medical tests for eye surgery unless there are specific medical indications.[CW]
- Avoid echocardiograms for preoperative/perioperative assessment of patients with no hx or symptoms of heart disease.[CW]
- Don't order coronary artery calcium scoring for preoperative evaluation for any surgery, irrespective of patient risk.[CW]
- Don't initiate routine evaluation of carotid artery disease before cardiac surgery in the absence of symptoms or other high-risk criteria.[CW]

Pulmonary Risk Assessment

Major risk factors for postoperative pulmonary complications:
- COPD
- ASA Class II – V (I – healthy; II – mild systemic disease; III – moderate/severe systemic disease; IV – life-threatening systemic disease; V – moribund)
- ADL dependence
- HF
- Prolonged (>3 h) surgery; abdominal, thoracic, neurologic, head and neck, or vascular surgery; AAA repair; emergency surgery
- General anesthesia
- Serum albumin <3.5 mg/dL

Minor risk factors:
- Confusion/delirium
- Weight loss >10% in previous 6 mo
- BUN >21 mg/dL or Cr >1.5 mg/dL
- Alcohol use
- Current cigarette use
- Sleep apnea
- Pulmonary hypertension

Reducing risk of postoperative pulmonary complications:
- Smoking cessation 6–8 wk before surgery
- Before cardiac surgery, there is no need for pulmonary function testing in the absence of respiratory symptoms.[CW]
- Preoperative training in incentive spirometry, active-cycle breathing techniques, and forced-expiration techniques
- Postoperative incentive spirometry, chest PT, coughing, postural drainage, percussion and vibration, suctioning and ambulation, intermittent positive-pressure breathing, and/or CPAP
- Nasogastric tube use for patients with postoperative nausea or vomiting, inability to tolerate oral intake, or symptomatic abdominal distention

Other Assessments

Screen for Conditions Associated with Postoperative Complications:

- Cognitive impairment: Mini-Cog (see p 322)
- Depression: PHQ-2 (see p 326)
- Delirium risk factors: see p 67
- Alcohol and substance abuse: CAGE questionnaire (see p 311)
- Functional impairment: ADLs, IADLs
- Malnutrition: BMI <18.5 kg/m^2, >10% unintentional weight loss in past 6 mo, serum albumin <3.0 g/dL
- Frailty syndrome: at least 4 of the following: ≥10 lb unintentional weight loss in past year (shrinkage), decreased grip strength (weakness), self-reported poor energy and endurance (exhaustion), low weekly energy expenditure (low physical activity), slow walking (slowness)

Routine Laboratory Tests

- Recommended: Hb, Cr, BUN, albumin, or basic metabolic panel if it includes these tests and is cheaper
- Not routinely recommended as should be obtained selectively according to the patient's conditions: electrolytes, CBC, platelets, ABG, PT, PTT
- Don't obtain preoperative chest radiography in the absence of clinical suspicion for intrathoracic pathology.[CW]

Cataract Surgery: Routine laboratory testing or cardiopulmonary risk assessment is unneccessary for cataract surgery performed under local anesthesia. If patient is on anticoagulation tx, it should not be interrupted. Use of α_1-blockers for BPH (see p 262) within 14 d of cataract surgery is associated with increased risk of complications (intraoperative floppy iris syndrome), but it is unknown if cessation of α_1-blockers before surgery lowers risk.

Antiplatelet Therapy: If surgery poses high bleeding risk (eg, CABG, intracranial surgery, prostate surgery), D/C antiplatelet tx 7–10 d before procedure.

Patients With Drug-Eluting Stents (DES) on Dual Antiplatelet Therapy:

- If possible, postpone surgery until 12 mo after DES was placed.
- If surgery cannot be delayed until 12 mo after DES placement:
  - For most surgeries, which are at low risk of bleeding, continue dual antiplatelet tx.
  - For surgeries at intermediate risk of bleeding (visceral, cardiovascular, major orthopedic, ENT, and urologic reconstruction surgery), continue dual antiplatelet tx if DES placement was <12 mo previous.
  - For surgeries at intermediate risk of bleeding in patients with DES placement >12 mo previous, D/C clopidogrel or prasugrel 5–7 d before procedure and maintain ASA tx. Because the platelet inhibition of ticagrelor is reversible, it should be stopped 1 d before procedure.
  - For surgeries at high risk of catastrophic bleeding (intracranial, spinal canal, or posterior chamber eye surgery), D/C clopidogrel or prasugrel 5 d before procedure, D/C ticagrelor 1 d before procedure, and consider D/C of ASA 5 d before procedure. Stopping ASA is an individual decision based on patient's risk factors for stent thrombosis and on assessed bleeding risk.

- If both antiplatelet agents need to be stopped, consider bridging tx (requires admitting patient 2–4 d before surgery) with tirofiban or eptifibatide (see **Tables 11 and 17**) in patients felt to be at very high risk of stent thrombosis (consult with cardiology).
- If antiplatelet tx is discontinued, resume it the day of the surgical procedure.

Anticoagulation:

- Cessation of oral anticoagulation tx before surgery:
  - Stop warfarin 5 d before surgery.
  - Bridging tx with LMWH is based on VTE risk (see **Table 103**)
  - DVT tx doses of LMWH (see **Table 17**) should be used for bridging tx. Begin LMWH 3 d before surgery; give last preoperative LMWH dose at one-half of total daily dose 24 h before surgery.
  - Based on surgical bleeding risk, stop dabigatran 1–3 d before surgery (2–4 d if CrCl <50 mL/min) and stop apixaban or rivaroxaban 1–2 d before surgery. Higher-risk procedures include abdominal, thoracic, or orthopedic surgery, spinal puncture, liver or kidney biopsy, TURP, or placement of spinal or epidural catheter/port.
- Resumption of anticoagulation tx after surgery:
  - If bridging, resume LMWH 24 h after surgery, longer (48–72 h) with major surgical procedures or difficulty with hemostasis.
  - Resume warfarin, apixaban, rivaroxaban, or dabigatran 12–24 h after surgery if adequate hemostasis.
- Minor dental procedures: stop warfarin 2–3 d before procedure and recommend administration of prohemostatic agent (eg, tranexamic acid) by dentist.

Table 103. Indications for Perioperative Anticoagulation Bridging Therapy (ACCP Guidelines)

Thromboembolic Risk	Patient Conditions Determining Risk	Recommendations for LMWH Bridging Therapy
Low	• No VTE in past 12 mo • AF without prior TIA/stroke and 0–2 SRF • Bileaflet mechanical aortic valve without AF, prior TIA/stroke, or SRF	Not recommended
Intermediate	• VTE in past 3–12 mo • Recurrent VTE • Active malignancy • AF without prior TIA/stroke and with 3–4 SRF • Bileaflet mechanical aortic valve with AF, prior TIA/stroke, or any SRF	Optional according to individual thrombotic and bleeding risk
High	• VTE within past 3 mo • TIA/stroke within 3 mo • Rheumatic heart disease • AF with prior TIA/stroke and 3–4 SRF • Mechanical mitral valve or ball/cage mechanical aortic valve	Recommended

Note: SRF = stroke risk factors: age ≥75 yr, HTN, DM, HF

Diuretics and Hypoglycemic Agents: Withhold on day of surgery.
SSRIs: SSRIs increase risk of bleeding with surgery, but discontinuing them before surgery is not recommended unless routine medication review indicates no therapeutic need.
Advance Directives: Establish or update.

PERIOPERATIVE MANAGEMENT

Table 104. Perioperative Medical Therapy to Reduce Cardiovascular Complications of Surgery

Agent	Target Conditions to be Prevented	Dosage	Clinical Situation
β-Blocker	MI, cardiac ischemia, death	Long-acting agent begun days to weeks before surgery to achieve resting HR of 60 bpm, and continued throughout postoperative period	Recommended in patients with >1 clinical risk factors and/or demonstrated CAD undergoing vascular (ie, high-risk) or intermediate-risk surgery.[a] Consider in patients with 1 clinical risk factor undergoing intermediate-risk surgery or in patients with no clinical risk factors undergoing vascular surgery.[a] Continue at usual dosage for patients already on a β-blocker.
Statin	MI, cardiac ischemia, death	Uncertain timing, specific drug, and dosage; one randomized trial used atorvastatin 20 mg po q24h begun an average of 30 d before surgery (see **Table 27**)	Consider in all patients undergoing vascular surgery. Consider in patients with >1 clinical risk factor undergoing intermediate-risk surgery.[a] Continue at usual dosage for patients already on a statin.
Antiplatelet	Coronary events, TIA, stroke	ASA[▲] 81–325 mg po q24h; clopidogrel[▲] 75 mg po q24h	Begin ASA <24 h after CABG. For patients already on ASA, consider not withdrawing it before surgery unless patient is undergoing prostate or intracranial surgery. For patients already on clopidogrel, D/C it 5–7 d before CABG and other procedures judged to be high risk for bleeding (see p 253).
Anticoagulant	DVT, PE	See pp 24–33.	For patients >60 yr old, begin after most types of surgery. For patients already on an anticoagulant, see **Table 103** for management guidelines.

(cont.)

Table 104. Perioperative Medical Therapy to Reduce Cardiovascular Complications of Surgery (cont.)

Agent	Target Conditions to be Prevented	Dosage	Clinical Situation
Amoxicillin[▲]	Infective endocarditis	2 g po 30–60 min before procedure[b]	Use in patients with selected cardiac conditions undergoing selected dental, respiratory tract, infected skin, or infected musculoskeletal tissue procedures.[b]
Amiodarone[▲]	AF	5 mg/kg po q12h from 6 d before surgery to 6 d after	Consider in patients undergoing CABG or cardiac valvular surgery.
Hydrocortisone[▲c]	AF	100 mg IV the evening of the operative day, followed by 100 mg IV q8h × 3 d	Consider in patients undergoing CABG or cardiac valvular surgery; concomitant tx with oral metoprolol is advised: 25 mg q12h if HR is 60–70 bpm, 50 mg q12h if HR is 71–80, or 50 mg q8h if HR is >80. Concomitant tx with amiodarone (above) has not been studied.
Insulin	ICU morbidity and mortality	Titrate to maintain blood glucose 140–180 mg/dL (see **Table 48**). Avoid sliding-scale insulin.[BC]	CABG or carotid endarterectomy patients; surgical ICU patients

[a] See **Figure 12** for definitions of clinical risk factors, high-risk surgery, and intermediate-risk surgery.
[b] See Prevention, p 257, for alternative dosing regimens and specific indications.
[c] The efficacy of perioperative steroids in cardiac surgery is not fully established. A trial of intraoperative dexamethasone in patients undergoing cardiac surgery did not result in reduction of major AEs (death, MI, stroke, renal failure, respiratory failure) within 30 d of surgery.

POSTOPERATIVE DELIRIUM (SEE ALSO DELIRIUM, p 67)

Epidemiology and Risk Factors

- Occurs after 15–50% of surgeries depending on type of procedure.
- Most episodes occur in first 2 postoperative days.
- Occurrences after postoperative day 2 are usually due to surgical complications or alcohol/sedative withdrawal.
- Major risk factors:
  ○ age ≥80
  ○ dementia
  ○ recent or unresolved delirium
  ○ major cardiac, open vascular, major abdominal surgery
  ○ emergency surgery
  ○ major surgical complication (eg, cardiogenic shock, prolonged intubation)
  ○ postoperative ICU stay ≥2 d

- Minor risk factors:
  - age 70–79
  - mild cognitive impairment
  - hx of stroke
  - poor functional status
  - significant comorbidity
  - alcohol or sedative use
  - depressive symptoms
  - abdominal, orthopedic, ENT, gynecologic, urologic surgery
  - general anesthesia
  - regional anesthesia with IV sedation
  - minor surgical complication (eg, infection, minor bleeding)
  - poorly controlled pain
  - exposure to opiates or sedatives
  - postoperative ICU stay <2 d

Diagnosis and Management
- The Confusion Assessment Method (CAM; see p 67) is effective for diagnosis.
- Systematic **preoperative** assessment and risk-lowering interventions have been shown to reduce the rate of postoperative delirium. This can be accomplished through proactive geriatrics team consultation/co-management, nurse-run programs to detect and prevent delirium, and the Hospital Elder Life Program (HELP) intervention (see http://www.hospitalelderlifeprogram.org/public/public-main.php).
- See pp 69–70 for delirium management.

PREVENTIVE TESTS AND PROCEDURES

Table 105. Recommended Primary and Secondary Disease Prevention for People Aged 65 and Older

Preventive Strategy	Frequency
USPSTF or CDC[a] Recommendations for Primary Prevention	
BMD (women)	at least once after age 65
BP screening	yearly
DM screening	every 3 yr in people with BP >135/80 mmHg
Exercise, vitamin D supplementation	adults aged ≥65 at increased risk of falls
Herpes zoster immunization	once after age 60 in immunocompetent people[b]
HIV screening	at least once in person ≥65 with risk factors for HIV
Influenza immunization	yearly
Lipid disorder screening	every 5 yr, more often in CAD, DM, PAD, prior stroke
Obesity (height and weight)	yearly
Pneumonia immunization	once at age 65
Smoking cessation	at every office visit
Tetanus immunization	every 10 yr
USPSTF[a] Recommendations for Secondary Prevention	
AAA ultrasonography	once between age 65–75 in men who have ever smoked
Alcohol abuse screening	unspecified but should be done periodically
Depression screening	yearly
FOBT/sigmoidoscopy/colonoscopy	yearly/every 5 yr/every 10 yr from age 50 to age 75[c]
Low-dose CT scanning for lung cancer	yearly in persons aged 55–80 with ≥30 pack-yrs of smoking and currently smoke or have quit in the past 15 yrs
Mammography[d]	every 2 yr in women aged 50–74
Other[e] Recommendations for Primary Prevention	
ASA to prevent MI[f]	daily
BMD (men)	at least once after age 70
Calcium (1200 mg) and vitamin D (≥800 IU) to prevent osteoporosis	daily
Measurement of serum C-reactive protein	at least once in people with one CAD risk factor
Omega-3 fatty acids to prevent MI, stroke	at least 2 ×/wk (see MI care, p 41)
Other[e] Recommendations for Secondary Prevention	
Skin examination	yearly
Cognitive impairment screening	yearly
Glaucoma screening	yearly

(cont.)

Preventive Strategy	Frequency
Hearing impairment screening	yearly
Inquiry about falls	yearly
TSH in women	yearly
Visual impairment screening	yearly

[a] US Preventive Services Task Force (see www.ahrq.gov/clinic/uspstfix.htm); Centers for Disease Control and Prevention (see www.cdc.gov/vaccines/schedules/hcp/adult.html)

[b] May vaccinate patients 1 yr after zoster infection; patients on chronic acyclovir, famciclovir, or valacyclovir tx should D/C the medication 24 h before zoster vaccination and resume the medication 14 d after vaccination.

[c] Do not repeat colorectal cancer screening (by any method) for 10 yr after a high-quality colonoscopy is negative in average-risk individuals.[CW]

[d] Mammograms to age 70 are almost universally recommended; many organizations recommend that mammography should be continued in women over 70 who have a reasonable life expectancy.

[e] Not endorsed by USPSTF/CDC for all older adults, but recommended in selected patients or by other professional organizations.

[f] Use with caution in adults ≥80 yr old.[BC]

For individualized age- and sex-specific USPSTF prevention recommendations, see www.ahrq.gov/clinic/pocketgd.htm.

The USPSTF recommends **against** screening for:

- Asymptomatic bacteriuria with UA
- Bladder cancer with hematuria detection, bladder tumor antigen measurement, NMP22 urinary enzyme immunoassay, or urine cytology
- CAD with ECG, exercise treadmill test, or electron-beam CT in people with few or no CAD risk factors
- Carotid artery stenosis with duplex ultrasonography
- Cervical cancer in women aged ≥65 who have had adequate prior screening or who have had a hysterectomy for benign disease
- Colon cancer with FOBT/sigmoidoscopy/colonoscopy in people ≥85 yr old. Screening may be modestly beneficial in people 76–85 yr old with long life expectancy and no or few comorbidities.
- COPD with spirometry
- Ovarian cancer with transvaginal ultrasonography or CA-125 measurement
- PAD with measurement of ABI
- Pancreatic cancer with ultrasonography or serologic markers
- Prostate cancer with PSA and/or digital rectal examination
- Don't use PET/CT for cancer screening in healthy individuals.[CW]

CANCER SCREENING AND MEDICAL DECISION MAKING
- Many decisions about whether or not to perform preventive activities are based on the estimated life expectancy of the patient. Refer to **Table 7** for life expectancy data by age and sex.

- Most cancer screening tests do not realize a survival benefit for the patient until after 10 yr from the time of the test. Cancer screening should be discouraged or very carefully considered in patients with ≤10 yr of estimated life expectancy.
- Don't recommend screening for breast or colorectal cancer, or prostate cancer (with the PSA test) without considering life expectancy and the risks of testing, overdiagnosis, and overtreatment.[CW]

ENDOCARDITIS PROPHYLAXIS (AHA GUIDELINES)

Antibiotic Regimens Recommended (see **Table 106**)

Cardiac Conditions Requiring Prophylaxis
- Prosthetic cardiac valve
- Previous infective endocarditis
- Cardiac transplant recipients who develop cardiac valvulopathy
- Unrepaired cyanotic congenital heart disease
- Repaired congenital heart disease with residual defects at the site or adjacent to the site of a prosthetic patch or device
- Congenital heart disease completely repaired with prosthetic material or device (prophylaxis needed for only the first 6 mo after repair procedure)

Cardiac Conditions Not Requiring Prophylaxis
All cardiac conditions or procedures not listed above.

Procedures Warranting Prophylaxis (only in patients with cardiac conditions listed above)
- Dental procedures requiring manipulation of gingival tissue, manipulation of the periapical region of teeth, or perforation of the oral mucosa (includes extractions, implants, reimplants, root canals, teeth cleaning during which bleeding is expected)
- Invasive procedures of the respiratory tract involving incision or biopsy of respiratory tract mucosa
- Surgical procedures involving infected skin, skin structures, or musculoskeletal tissue

Procedures Not Warranting Prophylaxis
- All dental procedures not listed above
- All noninvasive respiratory procedures
- All GI and GU procedures

Table 106. Endocarditis Prophylaxis Regimens

Situation	Regimen (Single Dose 30–60 Min Before Procedure)*
Oral	Amoxicillin▲ 2 g po
Unable to take oral medication	Ampicillin▲ 2 g, cefazolin▲ 1 g, or ceftriaxone▲ 1 g IM or IV
Allergic to penicillins or ampicillin	Cephalexin▲ 2 g, clindamycin▲ 600 mg, azithromycin▲ 500 mg, or clarithromycin▲ 500 mg po
Allergic to penicillins or ampicillin and unable to take oral medication	Cefazolin▲ 1 g, ceftriaxone▲ 1 g, or clindamycin▲ 600 mg IM or IV

* For patients undergoing invasive respiratory tract procedures to treat an infection known to be caused by *Staph aureus*, or for patients undergoing surgery for infected skin, skin structures, or musculoskeletal tissue, regimen should include an antistaphylococcal penicillin or cephalosporin.

Source: Wilson W, et al. *Circulation* (online) 2007: http://circ.ahajournals.org/content/116/15/1736.full.pdf.

ANTIBIOTIC PROPHYLAXIS FOR PATIENTS WITH TOTAL JOINT REPLACEMENTS (TJR)

Procedures/Conditions Prompting Consideration of Antibiotic Prophylaxis

- The American Academy of Orthopedic Surgeons in conjunction with the American Dental Association recommend that clinicians consider discontinuing the practice of routine antibiotic prophylaxis in patients with prior TJR who are undergoing dental procedures. (see http://www.aaos.org/Research/guidelines/PUDP/dental_guideline.asp)
  - Bacteremias are produced not just by dental procedures, but also by common daily activities such as tooth brushing.
  - While antibiotic prophylaxis reduces bacteremia after dental procedures, there is no evidence that withholding antibiotics or dental procedures themselves are associated with prosthetic knee or hip infections.
- Antibiotic prophylaxis should be considered for patients with prior TJR, regardless of when joint was replaced, who are undergoing ophthalmic, orthopedic, vascular, GI, head and neck, gynecologic, or GU procedures
- Additional risk factors for considering prophylaxis in patients with prior TJR: immunocompromised state; disease-, radiation-, or drug-induced immunosuppression; inflammatory arthropathies; malnourishment; hemophilia; HIV infection; type 1 DM; malignancy; megaprostheses; comorbidities (eg, DM, obesity, smoking)
- Conditions not requiring prophylaxis: patients with pins, plates, or screws

Suggested Prophylactic Regimens:

- Dental procedures (see those listed on p 259 for endocarditis): amoxicillin▲, cephalexin▲, or cephradine▲ 2 g po 1 h before procedure
- Prophylactic antibiotic recommendations for other types of procedures vary by procedure (see: Antimicrobial Prophylaxis for Surgery. *The Medical Letter, Treatment Guidelines* 2006;4(52):83–88).

Sources: Prevention of Orthopaedic Implant Infection in Patients Undergoing Dental Procedures, the American Academy of Orthopaedic Surgeons & American Dental Association, 2012. (See entire statement at www.aaos.org/research/guidelines/PUDP/PUDP_guideline.pdf) and Antibiotic Prophylaxis for Bacteremia in Patients with Joint Replacements, American Academy of Orthopaedic Surgeons Information Statement, February 2009.

EXERCISE PRESCRIPTION

Before Giving an Exercise Prescription

Screen patient for:

- Musculoskeletal problems: decreased flexibility, muscular rigidity, weakness, pain, ill-fitting shoes
- Cardiac disease: consider stress test if patient is beginning a vigorous exercise program and is sedentary with ≥2 cardiac risk factors (male gender, HTN, smoking, DM, dyslipidemia, obesity, family hx, sedentary lifestyle).

Individualize the Prescription

Specify short- and long-term goals; include the following components (American College of Sports Medicine/AHA recommendations):

Flexibility: Static stretching, at least 2 ×/wk for ≥10 min of flexibility exercises, 10–30 sec per stretch, 3–4 repetitions of major muscle/tendon groups

Endurance: Moderate-intensity activity, ≥30 min ≥5 ×/wk

- Moderate-intensity activities are those that increase HR and would be rated 5–6 on a 10-point intensity scale by the patient (includes activities like brisk walking).

- Using pedometers to record the number of steps in a walking program has been demonstrated to increase physical activity, lower BMI, and lower BP.

Strength: Weight (resistance) training at least 2 ×/wk, 10 exercises on major muscle groups, 10–15 repetitions per exercise

Balance: Balance exercises are recommended for people with mobility problems or who fall frequently.

Patient information: See www.nia.nih.gov/health/publication/exercise-physical-activity-your-everyday-guide-national-institute-aging-1.

See also Assessment and Management of Falls, **Figure 5**.

BENIGN PROSTATIC HYPERPLASIA (BPH)

Lower urinary tract symptoms (increased frequency of urination, nocturia, hesitancy, urgency, and weak urinary stream) may or may not be associated with enlarged prostate gland, bladder outlet obstruction (eg, urinary retention, recurrent infection, renal insufficiency), or histological BPH.

Evaluation

Evaluation of severity of symptoms (see AUA Symptom Index for BPH, p 331): Detailed medical hx focusing on physical examination of the urinary tract, including abdominal examination, digital rectal examination, and a focused neurologic examination; UA and culture if pyuria or hematuria. Postvoid residual (PVR) if neurologic disease or prior procedure that can affect bladder or sphincter function, UI, or reports of incomplete emptying. PVR should be performed before initiating antimuscarinic tx (see below). Measurement of PSA is controversial, but should not be measured if life expectancy is <10 yr. Don't order Cr or upper tract imaging if only lower urinary tract symptoms.[CW]

Management

Mild Symptoms: (eg, AUA/International Prostate Symptom Score [IPSS] <8; see p 331) watchful waiting

Moderate to Severe Symptoms: (eg, AUA score ≥8) watchful waiting, medical or surgical tx

Nonpharmacologic Treatment: Avoid fluids before bedtime, reduce mild diuretics (eg, caffeine, alcohol), double voiding to empty bladder completely.

Pharmacologic Treatment: Combining drugs from different classes may have better long-term effectiveness than single-agent tx. Because of immediate onset of benefit, many recommend beginning with α-adrenergic blockers. If overactive bladder symptoms without evidence of bladder outlet obstruction or high PVR, consider beginning with anti-muscarinics. If large prostate (eg, >30 g), consider beginning with combined tx (α-adrenergic blockers and 5-α reductase inhibitors). No dietary supplements have been demonstrated to be effective.

- α₁-**Blockers** (reduce dynamic component by relaxing prostatic and bladder detrusor smooth muscle). Nonselective and selective agents are equally effective. Do not start in men with planned cataract surgery until after surgery is completed. First-generation drugs appear to have lower rates of intraoperative floppy iris syndrome. Use of PDE5 inhibitors (sildenafil, tadalafil, vardenafil) with α₁-blockers can potentiate hypotensive effect.

  - **First-generation** (can cause orthostatic hypotension and dizziness, which may be potentiated by sildenafil *[Viagra]*, vardenafil *[LEVITRA]*, and perhaps tadalafil *[Cialis]*)

    - Terazosin▲ *(Hytrin)* increase dosage as tolerated: days 1–3, 1 mg/d hs; days 4–7, 2 mg; days 8–14, 5 mg; day 15 and beyond, 10 mg [T: 1, 2, 5, 10]. Avoid use as antihypertensive or in patients with syncope.[BC]

    - Doxazosin▲ *(Cardura)* start 0.5 mg with max of 16 mg/d [T: 1, 2, 4, 8]. Avoid use as antihypertensive or in patients with syncope.[BC]

  - **Second-generation** (less likely to cause hypotension or syncope, also benefits hematuria)

    - Tamsulosin▲ *(Flomax)* 0.4 mg 30 min after the same meal each day and increase to 0.8 mg if no response in 2–4 wk [T: 0.4]; decreases ejaculate volume; increases risk of retinal detachment, lost lens or lens fragment, or endophthalmitis if taken within 14 d before cataract surgery

- Silodosin *(Rapaflo)* 8 mg/d, 4 mg/d in moderate kidney impairment; not recommended in severe kidney or liver impairment [C: 4, 8]; decreases ejaculate volume; retrograde ejaculation in ~30%
  - Alfuzosin ER▲ *(Uroxatral)* 10 mg after the same meal every day [T: 10]
- **5-α Reductase inhibitors** (reduce prostate size and are more effective with large [>30 g] glands; do not use in absence of prostate enlargement; tx for 6–12 mo may be needed before symptoms improve) may help prostate-related bleeding and can decrease libido, ejaculation, and erectile function. Both finasteride and dutasteride reduce the incidence of prostate cancer but may lead to higher incidence of high-grade tumors in later years.
  - Finasteride▲ *(Proscar)* 5 mg/d [T: 5]
  - Dutasteride *(Avodart)* 0.5 mg/d [C: 0.5]
- **Antimuscarinic agents** (bladder relaxants) may have additional benefit beyond α_1-blockers on urinary frequency and urgency (see **Table 70**) but use with caution if PVR >250–300 mL.
- **Phosphodiesterase-5 (PDE-5) inhibitors** may improve symptoms of BPH/lower urinary tract symptoms in men with or without erectile dysfunction but do not improve flow rates. Do not use daily if CrCl <30 mL/m.

Surgical Management: Indicated if recurrent UTI, recurrent or persistent gross hematuria, bladder stones, or renal insufficiency are clearly secondary to BPH or as indicated by severe symptoms (AUA score >16), patient preference, or ineffectiveness of medical tx. For men with moderate symptoms (AUA scores 8–15), surgical tx is more effective than watchful waiting, but the latter is a reasonable alternative.

Surgical options are:

- Transurethral resection of the prostate (TURP); standard tx, best long-term outcome data; 1% risk of UI and no increased risk of sexual dysfunction.
- Transurethral incision of the prostate (TUIP), which is limited to prostates with an estimated resected tissue weight (if done by TURP) of ≤30 g
- Open prostatectomy for large glands (>50 g), usually longer hospital stay and more blood loss
- Transurethral laser enucleation
- Transurethral needle ablation (TUNA) is less effective than TURP but may be an option for men with substantial comorbidity who are poor surgical candidates.
- Transurethral vaporization of the prostate (TUVP) is associated with less hyponatremia (TURP syndrome) but higher rates of postoperative irritative voiding symptoms, dysuria, urinary retention, recatheterization, and re-operation.
- Transuretral microwave thermotherapy (TUMT) is the least operator dependent but has inconsistent results.
- Laparoscopic or robotic prostatectomy may be an option, but few studies have evaluated this and longer operating time.
- Urethral stents may be an option for poor surgical candidates.
- Botulinum toxin may be effective but requires further study before it can be recommended.

PROSTATE CANCER
Screening is not recommended for older men.
Evaluation
Predicting extent of disease:
- PSA (see p 258)

- Biopsy (Gleason primary and secondary grade)
- Digital rectal examination
- CT or MRI abdomen and pelvis (selectively)
- Bone scan (if symptomatic or at increased risk for bone metastases (serum PSA >20 ng/mL, or serum PSA >10 ng/mL with a T2 tumor, or a Gleason 8 lesion, or stage T3 or T4)

Do not perform PET, CT, and radionuclide bone scan in the staging of early prostate cancer at low risk of metastasis.[CW]

Histology

- Gleason score 2–6 has low 15–20 yr morbidity and mortality; watchful waiting usually appropriate.
- Gleason score ≥7, higher PSA and younger age associated with higher morbidity and mortality; best tx strategy (surgery, radiation, androgen suppression, etc) is not known.

Treatment of Early Prostate Cancer

- Based on aggressiveness risk of cancer (National Comprehensive Cancer Network http://www.nccn.org/professionals/physician_gls/pdf/prostate.pdf):
  ○ Very low: T_{1c}, Gleason score <6, <3 positive biopsy cores, <50% cancer in each core, PSA <10 ng/mL, and PSA density 0.15 ng/mL
    If <20 yr expected survival, treat with active surveillance.
  ○ Low: Stage T_1 or T_{2a}, Gleason score 2–6, PSA <10 ng/mL
    Treat with active surveillance (only if >65 yr old), prostatectomy, brachytherapy, or external radiation with adjuvant short-term ADT.
  ○ Intermediate stage: T_{2b} or PSA 10–20 ng/mL, or Gleason score 7
    If <10 yr expected survival, can treat with active surveillance. Otherwise, treat with prostatectomy, brachytherapy, or external radiation tx with short-term ADT. If PSA is still detectable, then evaluate for distant metastasis and if present see below (Therapy for PSA-only Recurrence and Therapy for Metastatic Bone Disease).
  ○ High: T_{3a} or Gleason score 8–10, PSA >20 ng/mL
    Treat with prostatectomy or external radiation tx with adjuvant androgen suppressive tx. At 24 mo, sexual dysfunction rates are similar with prostatectomy, external radiation tx, or brachytherapy.
- Radical prostatectomy (reduced short- and long-term overall and disease-specific mortality, metastasis, and local progression compared with watchful waiting in men <65 yr old with early disease, regardless of histology and PSA, including those who are at low risk. UI is more common but treatable (see tx for post-prostatectomy UI, p 149) and may gradually improve.
- Radiation tx may cause transient PSA increase that does not reflect cancer recurrence. Irritative or obstructive urinary symptoms and bowel frequency and urgency are more common.
  ○ External beam
  ○ Brachytherapy (radioactive seed implantation) has greater effect on prostate than external beam.
- Proton-beam tx is controversial and remains unproved.
- Hormonal tx is reserved for locally advanced or metastatic disease.

Monitoring

After surgery or radiation tx, PSA should be <0.1 ng/mL or undetectable. Monitor PSA every 6–12 mo for 5 y (every 3 mo if high risk), then every year. Digital rectal exam yearly but may be omitted if PSA undetectable. A PSA doubling time of 3–12 mo in the absence of clinical recurrence indicates a higher risk of development of systemic disease and cancer-specific death.

Therapy for Locally Advanced and Metastatic Disease

- For locally advanced (T3) disease (tumor extension beyond prostate capsule or invasion of seminal vesicles), and local disease with unfavorable prognostic factors (eg, Gleason score ≥7, PSA >10 ng/mL), external beam radiation is commonly used with ADT. However, among men with moderate or severe comorbidity, there may be no benefit of ADT beyond radiation tx alone.
- For T3, T4 (invading bladder, levator muscles, and/or pelvic wall), or metastatic disease, use ADT (see **Table 107**).
- Monotherapy can be either bilateral orchiectomy or a GnRH agonist.
- Combined androgen blockade (GnRH agonist plus antiandrogen) is used to avoid "flare" phenomenon (ie, increased symptoms early in tx), but survival benefit is uncertain and side effects are greater than with monotherapy.
- In case of relapse without evidence of metastasis, sequential hormonal manipulations are often used first:
  - Withdrawal of antiandrogen may induce remission.
  - Patients often respond when changed to a second antiandrogen.
  - When antiandrogens no longer control disease, adrenal suppression with aminoglutethimide or ketoconazole and hydrocortisone replacement may be effective.
- If castration-recurrent metastatic disease, maintain castrate levels of testosterone and chemotherapy or autologous cellular immunotherapy.
  (www.nccn.org/professionals/physician_gls/pdf/prostate.pdf)

Therapy for PSA-only Recurrence (no evidence of other disease)

Consider salvage surgery, radiation tx, or cryotherapy if less advanced disease at presentation, long lag between recurrence (>3 yr), or after radical prostatectomy with no nodal involvement. If patient is not a candidate for local tx, then ADT.

Therapy for Metastatic Bone Disease

In men receiving long-term ADT or HT for cancer and in those with bone metastasis, zoledronic acid 5 mg IV annually or denosumab 60 mg SC q6mo reduces the proportion of patients with skeletal-related events or fracture.

Table 107. Common Medications for Prostate Cancer Therapy			
Class, Medication	**Dosage**	**Metabolism**	**Adverse Events/Comments**
GnRH Agonists			*Class AEs:* certain symptoms (urinary obstruction, spinal cord compression, bone pain) may be exacerbated early in tx; risk is less when combined with antiandrogens
Goserelin acetate implant *(Zoladex)*	3.6 mg SC q28d or 10.8 mg q3mo	Rapid urinary and hepatic excretion, no dosage adjustment in renal impairment	Hot flushes (60%), breast swelling, libido change, impotence, nausea

(cont.)

Table 107. **Common Medications for Prostate Cancer Therapy (cont.)**

Class, Medication	Dosage	Metabolism	Adverse Events/Comments
Leuprolide acetate▲ *(Lupron Depot)*	7.5 mg IM qmo or 22.5 mg q3mo or 30 mg q4mo	Unknown; active metabolites for 4–12 wk, dose-dependent	Hot flushes (60%), edema (12%), pain (7%), nausea, vomiting, impotence, dyspnea, asthenia (all 5%), thrombosis, PE, MI (all 1%); headache as high as 32%
Triptorelin *(Trelstar Depot, Trelstar LA)*	Depot: 37.5 mg q28d IM LA: 11.25 mg q84d	Hepatic metabolism and renal excretion (42% as intact peptide)	Hot flushes, ↑ glucose, ↓ Hb, ↓ RBC, ↑ alkaline phosphatase, ↑ ALT or AST, skeletal pain, ↑ BUN
Histrelin acetate *(Vantas)*	50-mg SC implant q12mo	Hepatic metabolism	Hot flushes, fatigue, headaches, nausea, mild renal impairment
Antiandrogens (most often used in combination with GnRH agonists)			*Class AEs:* nausea, hot flushes, breast pain, gynecomastia, hematuria, diarrhea, liver enzyme elevations, galactorrhea
Bicalutamide▲ *(Casodex)*	50 mg/d po [T: 50]	Metabolized in liver, excreted in urine; half-life 10 d at steady state	
Flutamide▲ *(Eulexin)*	250 mg po q8h [C: 125]	Renal excretion; half-life 5–6 h	Greatest GI toxicity in the class; severe liver dysfunction reported
Nilutamide *(Nilandron)*	300 mg/d po for 30 d, then 150 mg/d po [T: 50]	80% protein bound; liver metabolism, renal excretion; half-life 40–60 h	Delayed light adaptation
GnRH Antagonist			
Degarelix *(Firmagon)*	240 mg SC, then 80 mg SC q28d	Liver 70–80%, renal 20–30%	Prolonged QT interval, hot flushes, weight gain, fatigue, ↑ AST and ALT

PROSTATITIS

Definition
Acute or chronic inflammation of the prostate secondary to bacterial (usually Gram-negative organisms) and nonbacterial causes

Symptoms and Diagnosis
Acute: fever; chills; dysuria; obstructive symptoms; tender, tense, or boggy on examination (examination should be minimal to avoid bacteremia); Gram stain and culture of urine.

Chronic: recurrent UTIs, especially with same organism; obstructive or irritative symptoms with voiding, perineal pain (may include chronic pelvic pain syndrome). Examination often indicates hypertrophy, tenderness, edema, or nodularity, but may be normal. Compare first void or midstream urine with prostatic secretion or postmassage urine: bacterial if leukocytosis and bacteria in expressed sample, nonbacterial if sample sterile with leukocytosis

Treatment (see Table 77)

Antibiotic tx should be based on Gram stain and culture. Begin tx for acute prostatitis empirically to cover likely organisms while culture is pending. Do not insert Foley catheter in acute prostatitis. If urinary retention, consult a urologist.

Acute prostatitis (recommend tx for 4–6 wk)

- Co-trimoxazole▲ DS 1 po q12h, *or*
- Ciprofloxacin▲ 500 mg po or 400 mg IV q12h, *or*
- Ofloxacin▲ 400 mg po once, then 300 mg q12h, *or*
- 3rd-generation cephalosporin▲ or aminoglycoside▲ IV
- If patient is toxic, then combine aminoglycoside with fluoroquinolone.

Chronic prostatitis (fluoroquinolones have good penetration of inflamed prostate)

- Co-trimoxazole▲ DS 1 po q12h × 2–4 mo, *or*
- Ciprofloxacin▲ 500 mg po q12h × at least 6 wk, *or*
- Levofloxacin 500 mg po q24h × at least 6 wk, *or*
- Ofloxacin▲ 200 mg q12h × 3 mo

α-blockers may help chronic prostatitis in combination with antibiotics. Less consistent benefits have been demonstrated with anti-inflammatory agents and finasteride.

DIFFERENTIAL DIAGNOSIS
- Bipolar affective disorder
- Delirium
- Dementia
- Medications/drugs: eg, antiparkinsonian agents, anticholinergics, benzodiazepines or alcohol (including withdrawal), stimulants, corticosteroids, cardiac medications (eg, digitalis), opioid analgesics
- Late-life delusional (paranoid) disorder
- Major depression
- Physical disorders: hypo- or hyperglycemia, hypo- or hyperthyroidism, sodium or potassium imbalance, Cushing's syndrome, Parkinson disease, B_{12} deficiency, sleep deprivation, AIDS
- Pain, untreated
- Schizophrenia
- Structural brain lesions: tumor or stroke
- Seizure disorder: eg, temporal lobe

Risk Factors for Psychotic Symptoms in Older Adults: chronic bed rest, cognitive impairment, female gender, sensory impairment, social isolation

MANAGEMENT
- Establish a trusting therapeutic relationship with the patient; focus on empathizing with the distress that symptoms cause rather than reality orientation.
- Encourage patients to maintain significant, supportive relationships.
- Alleviate underlying physical causes.
- Address identifiable psychosocial triggers.
- Before using an antipsychotic to treat behavioral symptoms of dementia, carefully assess for possible psychotic features (ie, delusions and hallucinations) and if psychotic symptoms are severe, frightening, or may affect safety.
- For *DSM–5*, rate presence and severity (most severe in last 7 d) of psychotic symptoms (eg, hallucinations, delusions, disorganized speech) on a 5-point scale ranging from 0 (not present) to 4 (4 present and severe).
- Aripiprazole, olanzapine, quetiapine, risperidone▲ are first choice because of fewer adverse events (TD extremely high in older adults taking first-generation antipsychotics). See **Table 109** and **Table 110** for adverse events of second-generation antipsychotics.
- All antipsychotics are associated with increased mortality in older adults.

Table 108. Representative Medications for Treatment of Psychosis

Class, Medication	Dosage*	Formulations	Comments (Metabolism)
Second-generation Antipsychotics			Avoid for behavioral problems of dementia; avoid if hx of falls or fracture.[BC]
✔Aripiprazole *(Abilify)*	2–5 (1) initially; max 30/d	T: 2, 5, 10, 15, 20, 30 ODT: 10, 15 IM: 9.75 mg/1.3 mL S: 1 mg/mL	Wait 2 wk between dosage changes (CYP2D6, -3A4) (L)
Clozapine▲ *(Clozaril)*	25–150 (1)	T: 25, 100 ODT: 12.5, 25, 100	May be useful for parkinsonism and TD; significant risk of neutropenia and agranulocytosis; weekly CBCs × 6 mo, then biweekly (L)
Lurasidone *(Latuda)*	40 mg	T: 40–80 mg	Very limited geriatric data
✔Olanzapine *(Zyprexa)*	2.5–10 (1)	T: 2.5, 5, 7.5, 10, 15, 20 ODT: 5, 10, 15, 20 IM: 5 mg/mL	Weight gain (L)
Paliperidone *(Invega)*	3–12 (1)	T: ER 3, 6, 9	CrCl 51–80 mL/min, max 6 mg/d; CrCl ≤50 mL/min, max 3 mg/d; very limited geriatric data (K)
✔Quetiapine *(Seroquel)*	25–800 (1–2)	T: 25, 100, 200, 300 T: ER 50, 150, 200, 300, 400	Ophthalmic examination recommended q6mo (L, K)
✔Risperidone▲ *(Risperdal)*	0.25–1 (1–2)	T: 0.25, 0.5, 1, 2, 3, 4 ODT: 0.5, 1, 2, 3, 4 S: 1 mg/mL IM long-acting: 25, 37.5, and 50 mg/2 mL	Dose-related EPS; IM not for acute tx; do not exceed 6 mg (L, K)
Ziprasidone *(Geodon)*	20–80 (1–2)	C: 20, 40, 60, 80 IM: 20 mg/mL	May increase QT$_c$; very limited geriatric data (L)
Low Potency First Generation			
Thioridazine▲ (eg, *Mellaril*)	25–200 (1–3)	T: 10, 15, 25, 50, 100, 150, 200 S: 30 mg/mL	Substantial anticholinergic effects, orthostasis, QT$_c$ prolongation, sedation, TD; for acute use only. Avoid.[BC] (L, K)
Intermediate Potency First Generation			
Perphenazine▲ *(Trilafon)*	2–32 (1–2)	T: 2, 4, 8, 16	Risk of TD with long-term use. Avoid.[BC] (L, K)
High Potency First Generation			Avoid.[BC]
Haloperidol▲ *(Haldol)*	0.5–2 (1–3); depot 25–200 mg IM q4wk	T: 0.5, 1, 2, 5, 10, 20 Conc 2 mg/mL Inj: 5 mg/mL (lactate)	EPS, TD; for acute use only (L, K) Depot form is for chronic use; monitor for TD and D/C if signs appear
Fluphenazine	1–2.5 mg/d (max 5 mg/d) (1)	T: 1, 2.5, 5, 10 S: conc 5 mg/mL IM: 2.5 mg/mL (decanoate)	EPS, TD, akathisia (L, K)

✔= preferred for treating older adults but does not imply low risk; mortality may be increased in patients with dementia.

* Total mg/d (frequency/d)

Table 109. Adverse Events of Preferred Second-generation Antipsychotics

	Aripiprazole	Olanzapine	Quetiapine	Risperidone
Level of Evidence	CR	RCT	RCT	RCT
Cardiovascular				
Hypotension	?	+	+++	+
QT_c prolongation[a]	?	+	+	+
Endocrine/Metabolic				
Weight gain	?	+++	++	++
DM	?	+++	++	++
Hypertriglyceridemia	0	+	0	?
Hyperprolactinemia	?	?	?	+++
Gastrointestinal				
Nausea, vomiting, constipation	0	0	?	?
Neurologic				
EPS	++	+	+	+++
Seizures	?	?	?	ND
Sedation	?	+	+	+
Systemic				
Anticholinergic	0	++	+	0
Neuroleptic malignant syndrome	ND	ND	ND	+

CR = case reports; RCT = randomized clinical trials; ND = no data
? = uncertain effect
0 = no effect
+ = mild effect; ++ = moderate effect; +++ = severe effect
[a]QT_c upper limit of normal = 400 millisec

Table 110. Management of Adverse Events of Antipsychotic Medications

Adverse Event	Treatment	Comment
Drug-induced parkinsonism	Reduce dosage or change drug or drug class	Often dose related; avoid anticholinergic agents
Akathisia (motor restlessness)	Consider adding β-blocker (eg, propranolol▲ *[Inderal]* 20–40 mg/d) or low-dose benzodiazepine (eg, lorazepam▲ 0.5 mg q12h)	Also seen with second-generation antipsychotics; more likely with traditional agents
Hypotension	Slow titration; reduce dosage; change drug class	More common with low-potency agents
Sedation	Reduce dosage; give hs; change drug class	More common with low-potency agents
TD	Stop drug (if possible); consider second-generation antipsychotic (eg, aripiprazole, quetiapine) with lower potential for EPS	Increased risk in older adults; may be irreversible

Note: Periodic (q4mo) reevaluation of antipsychotic dosage and ongoing need is important (see CMS guidance on unnecessary drugs in the nursing home: www.cms.gov/transmittals/downloads/R22SOMA.pdf). Older adults are particularly sensitive to AEs of antipsychotic drugs. They are also at higher risk of developing TD. Periodic use of an AE scale such as the AIMS is highly recommended. (see: www.geriatricscareonline.org)

COUGH

Among the most common symptoms in office practice; consider likely diagnosis based on duration of symptoms and treat the specific disorder (see **Table 111**). **Table 112** lists agents sometimes used in symptomatic management of cough.

Table 111. Diagnosis and Treatment of Cough by Duration of Symptoms

Cause	Preferred Treatment
Acute cough: duration up to 3 wk	
Common cold	Sinus irrigation or nasal ipratropium *(Atrovent NS*, see **Table 115**). Not recommended: sedating antihistamines (dry mouth, urinary retention, confusion); oral pseudoephedrine (HTN, tachycardia, urinary retention)
Allergic rhinitis	See p 274.
Bacterial sinusitis	Oxymetazoline▲ nasal spr (eg, *Afrin)* × 5 d; antibiotic against *Haemophilus influenzae* and streptococcal pneumonia × 2 wk
Pertussis	Macrolide or trimethoprim-sulfa antibiotic × 2 wk
Other: pneumonia, HF, asthma, COPD exacerbation	See pneumonia, p 157; HF, p 42; asthma, p 281; COPD, p 277
Subacute cough: duration 3–8 wk*	
Postinfectious	Inhaled ipratropium *(Atrovent)*; systemic steroids tapered over 2–3 wk; if protracted, dextromethorphan with codeine; use bronchodilators if there is bronchospasm (see **Table 122**)
Subacute bacterial sinusitis	As for acute bacterial sinusitis, but treat for 3 wk
Asthma	See Treatment, p 281
Pertussis	Macrolide or trimethoprim-sulfa antibiotic × 2 wk; may need to treat as above for postinfectious cough
Chronic cough: duration >8 wk*	(25% of patients have more t han 1 cause requiring concurrent tx)
Perennial rhinitis *or postnasal drainage*	See p 274. Tx for 2–4 wk for reduction/resolution
Chronic bacterial sinusitis	Same as for subacute bacterial sinusitis but also cover, mouth anaerobes × 3 wk; may need follow-up course of nasal steroids
Asthma or cough variant asthma	See Treatment, p 281. Tx for 6–8 wk for reduction/resolution
Other: ACEIs, reflux esophagitis	Stop ACEI (cough may persist for 4 wk); treat reflux for 6–8 wk for reduction/resolution using a PPI
Aspiration	See Dysphagia, p 118. Evaluate with modified barium swallow.
Sleep apnea	May present as cough that is also present at night
Nonasthmatic eosinophilic bronchitis	Eosinophils in sputum, but no reversible airway obstruction on spirometry; treat with inhaled glucocorticoids (see p 284) for 3–4 wk.
Smoking	Cessation of smoking for 4 wk
Idiopathic	A proportion of patients do not have identified cause

*Obtain chest radiograph, spirometry, sputums to exclude malignancy, TB; obtain eosinophil count, etc.

Management

- Do not suppress cough in stable COPD.
- For symptomatic relief, see **Table 112**.

Table 112. Antitussives and Expectorants

Medication	Dosage and Formulations	Adverse Events (Metabolism)
Benzonatate[▲a] (Tessalon Perles)	100 mg po q8h (max: 600 mg/d) C: 100, 200	CNS stimulation or depression, headache, dizziness, hallucination, constipation (L)
Dextromethorphan[▲a] (eg, Robitussin DM)	10–30 mL po q4–8h C: 30 S: 10 mg/5 mL	Mild drowsiness, fatigue; interacts with SSRIs and SNRIs; combination may cause serotonin syndrome (L)
Guaifenesin[▲b] (eg, Rohitussin)	5–20 mL po q4h S: 100 mg/5 mL	None at low dosages; high dosages cause nausea, vomiting, diarrhea, drowsiness, abdominal pain (L)
Codeine phosphate/Guaifenesin[▲c]	S: 10 mg/5 mL/100 mg/5 mL; 10 mg/5 mL/300 mg/5 mL T: 10 mg/300 mg	Sedation, constipation (L)
Hydrocodone/Homatropine[▲a] (Hycodan)	5 mL po q4–6h S: 5 mg/5 mL/1.5 mg/mL T: 5 mg/1.5 mg	Sedation, constipation, confusion (L)

[a] Antitussive
[b] Expectorant
[c] Antitussive and expectorant

DYSPNEA

Definition

A subjective experience of breathing discomfort that consists of qualitatively distinct sensations that vary in intensity (ATS)

Characteristics

- >65 yr: occurs in 17% at rest at least occasionally; in 38% when hurrying on level ground or on slight hill
- Hx: consider if level of dyspnea is appropriate to level of exertion (vs suggests pathology)
  - Consider age, peers, usual activities, level of fitness
  - Ask, "What activities have you stopped doing?"
- Associated symptoms: cough, sputum, wheezing, chest pain, orthopnea, paroxysmal nocturnal dyspnea

Evaluation

Hx and physical examination should suggest organ system; then evaluate for cause (see **Table 113**).

Table 113. Diagnosis of Dyspnea

Suspected System	Diagnostic Strategy	Diagnosis
Cardiac	Chest radiograph, ECG, echocardiogram, radionuclide imaging, BNP (p 42)	Ischemic or other form of heart disease
Lung	Spirometry	Asthma, COPD, or restriction
	Diffusing capacity	Emphysema or interstitial lung disease
	Echocardiogram	Pulmonary HTN

(cont.)

Table 113. Diagnosis of Dyspnea (cont.)		
Suspected System	Diagnostic Strategy	Diagnosis
Respiratory muscle dysfunction	Inspiratory and expiratory mouth pressures	Neuromuscular disease
Deconditioning/obesity vs psychological disorders	Cardiopulmonary exercise test	Deconditioning shows decreased maximal oxygen consumption but normal cardiorespiratory exercise responses.

Therapy
Nonpharmacologic
- Exercise reduces dyspnea and improves fitness in almost all older adults regardless of cause; physical conditioning reduces dyspnea during ADLs and exercise, and is primary tx for deconditioning.
  - Use low-impact, indoor activity
  - Base intensity on HR or symptom of dyspnea
  - Recommend 20–30 min on most days
- Indications for pulmonary rehabilitation include the following:
  - Dyspnea during rest or exertion
  - Hypoxemia, hypercapnia
  - Reduced exercise tolerance or a decline in ADLs
  - Worsening dyspnea and a reduced but stable exercise tolerance level
  - Pre- or postoperative lung resection, transplantation, or volume reduction
  - Chronic respiratory failure and the need to initiate mechanical ventilation
  - Ventilator dependence
  - Increasing need for emergency department visits, hospitalization, and unscheduled office visits

Pharmacologic: See specific diseases elsewhere in this chapter.

ALLERGIC RHINITIS
Description
- The most common atopic disorder.
- Symptoms include rhinorrhea; sneezing; and irritated eyes (see Allergic Conjunctivitis, p 109), nose, and mucous membranes.
- May be seasonal, but in older adults is more often perennial.
- Postnasal drip, mainly from chronic rhinitis, is the most common cause of chronic cough.

Therapy
Nonpharmacologic: Avoid allergens, eliminate pets and their dander, dehumidify to reduce molds; saline and sodium bicarbonate nasal irrigation (eg, Sinu*Cleanse*) are helpful as primary or adjunctive tx; reduce outdoor exposures during pollen season; reduce house dust mites by encasing pillows and mattresses. Arachnocides reduce mites.

Pharmacologic: Target tx to symptoms and on whether symptoms are seasonal or perennial; see **Table 114** and **Table 115**.

Stepped tx: For mild or intermittent symptoms, begin with an oral second-generation antihistamine; for moderate or severe symptoms, begin a nasal steroid; if symptoms uncontrolled, add the other agent; if still uncontrolled, add or substitute a leukotriene modifier for one of the other agents.

Ocular symptoms: Oral H_1 antihistamine or topical ophthalmic H_1 antihistamine are drugs of choice (see allergic conjunctivitis, p 109 and **Table 114**).

Table 114. Choosing Medication for Allergic Rhinitis or Conjunctivitis

Medication or Class	Rhinitis	Sneezing	Pruritus	Congestion	Eye Symptoms
Nasal steroids[a]	+++	+++	++	++	++
Ipratropium, nasal[a]	++	0	0	0	0
Antihistamines[b,c]	++	++	++	+	+++
Pseudoephedrine, nasal[d]	0	0	0	++++	0
Cromolyn, nasal[c]	+	+	+	+	0
Leukotriene modifiers	+	+	+	+	++

Note: 0 = drug is not effective; the number of "+'s" grades the drug's effectiveness.

[a] Effective in seasonal, perennial, and vasomotor rhinitis.

[b] Better in seasonal than in perennial rhinitis; nasal, ocular, and oral forms; ocular form effective only for eye symptoms, but nasal form may help ocular symptoms.

[c] Start before allergy season.

[d] Topical tx rapid in onset but results in rebound if used for more than a few days; enhances effectiveness of nasal steroids and improves sleep during severe attacks.

Table 115. Medications for Allergic Rhinitis

Type, Medication	Geriatric Dosage	Formulations	Adverse Events/Comments
H_1-Receptor Antagonists or Antihistamines			*Class AEs:* bitter taste, nasal burning, sneezing (nasal preparations); eye burning, stinging, injection (ocular preparations)
Oral			
✔Cetirizine▲ *(Zyrtec*)*	5 mg/d (max)	T: 5, 10▲; syr 5 mg/5 mL	
✔Desloratadine *(Clarinex)*	5 mg/d	T: 5	
Fexofenadine▲ *(✔Allegra, Allegra-D[a])*	60 mg po q12h; q24h if CrCl <40 mL/min	T▲: 30, 60, 180; C: 60 ODT: 30 S▲: 30/5 mL	Least sedating in the class; fruit juice reduces absorption, so take 4 h before or 1–2 h after ingestion of juice
Levocetirizine *(Xyzal)*	2.5 mg/d po if CrCl 50–80 mL/min; q48h if CrCl 30–50; 2 ×/wk if CrCl 10–30. Not recommended if CrCl <10 mL/min.	T: 5 mg S: 0.5 mg/mL	Somnolence, pharyngitis, fatigue
Loratadine▲* *(✔Claritin, Claritin-D[a])*	5–10 mg/d	T: 10; rapid disintegrating tab 10 mg; syr 1 mg/mL	

(cont.)

Table 115. Medications for Allergic Rhinitis (cont.)			
Type, Medication	**Geriatric Dosage**	**Formulations**	**Adverse Events/Comments**
Chlorpheniramine[▲BC] (eg, *Chlor-Trimeton**)	8–12 mg q12h	T: 4, 8, 12; ChT: 2; CR: 8, 12; S: 2 mg/5 mL	Sedation, dry mouth, confusion, urinary retention; dries lung secretions
Diphenhydramine[▲BC] (eg, *Benadryl**)	25–50 mg q12h	T: 25, 50; S: elixir 12.5 mg/mL	Same as chlorpheniramine
Hydroxyzine[▲BC] (eg, *Atarax*)	25–30 mg q12h	T: 10, 25, 50	Same as chlorpheniramine
Nasal			
✔Azelastine *(Astelin)* *(Astepro)*	2 spr q12h[b]	topical spr 0.1% 0.1%, 0.15%	
✔Olopatadine *(Patanase)*	2 spr q12h	0.6%	Epistaxis
Decongestant			
Pseudoephedrine[▲] (eg, *Sudafed*, combinations*)	60 mg po q4–6h	T: 30, 60; SR: 120; S: elixir 30 mg/5 mL	Arrhythmia, insomnia, anxiety, restlessness, elevated BP, urinary retention in men
Nasal Steroids ✔Beclomethasone (eg, *Beconase, Vancenase*)	1–2 spr q12h[b]	80 spr	*Class AEs:* nasal burning, sneezing, bleeding; septal perforation (rare); fungal overgrowth (rare); no significant systemic effects
✔Budesonide (eg, *Rhinocort*)	1–4 spr/d[b]	200 spr	
✔Ciclesonide *(Omnaris)*	1–2 spr/d[b]	250 spr	
✔Flunisolide[▲] (eg, *Nasalide, Nasarel*)	2 spr/d[b] or 1 spr q8–12h	200 spr	
✔Fluticasone[▲] furoate *(Veramyst)*	2 spr/d[b]	120 spr	
✔Fluticasone propionate[▲] (eg, *Flonase*)	2 spr/d[b]	120 spr	
✔Mometasone *(Nasonex)*	2 spr/d[b]	120 spr	
✔Triamcinolone (eg, *Nasacort*)	2–4 spr/d[b]	100 spr	
Mast Cell Stabilizer Cromolyn[▲] *(NasalCrom)*	1 spr q6–8h[b]; begin 1–2 wk before exposure to allergen	2%, 4%	Nasal irritation, headache, itching of throat

* OTC [BC]Avoid.

(cont.)

Table 115. Medications for Allergic Rhinitis (cont.)

Type, Medication	Geriatric Dosage	Formulations	Adverse Events/Comments
Leukotriene Modifier (see also p 285)			
Montelukast *(Singulair)*	10 mg/d po	T: 10 mg; gran 4 mg/pck	Less effective than nasal steroids
Other			
Ipratropium▲ *(Atrovent NS)*	2 spr q6–12h[b]	0.03, 0.06%[c] sol	Epistaxis, nasal irritation, upper respiratory infection; sore throat, nausea Caution: Do not spray in eyes.

✔ = preferred for treating older adults

[a] *Allegra-D* and *Claritin-D*, also available as *Allegra-D 24 Hour* and *Claritin-D 24 Hour,* are not recommended; all contain pseudoephedrine. Contraindicated in narrow angle glaucoma, urinary retention, MAOI use within 14 d, severe HTN, or CAD. May cause headache, nausea, insomnia.

[b] Spr per nares

[c] Use 0.06% for tx of viral upper respiratory infection.

CHRONIC OBSTRUCTIVE PULMONARY DISEASE

Diagnosis

Consider COPD if any of these factors are present in an individual over 40 yr old. The greater the number of factors, the more likely is the diagnosis.

- **Dyspnea:** that is progressive, worse with exercise, and persistent
- **Chronic cough:** with or without sputum production
- **Hx of exposure to risk factors:** tobacco smoke, smoke from heating fuels, occupational dust, and chemicals
- **Family hx of COPD**

Spirometry is required to establish a diagnosis. Assess airflow limitation based on spirometry measures after bronchodilators. COPD is diagnosed when $FEV_1/FVC <0.70$ or perhaps 0.65 (in patients over age 65) or $FEV_1/FEV_6 <0.70$ in patients over 65 or those with severe disease.

Therapy

- Should be based on 3 factors: symptoms, airflow limitation, and frequency of exacerbations
- Assess symptoms using quantitative scale, eg, The Modified Medical Research Council Dyspnea Scale (MMRC) shown below:

    0 "I only get breathless with strenuous exercise"

    1 "I get short of breath when hurrying on the level or walking up a slight hill"

    2 "I walk slower than people of the same age on the level because of breathlessness or have to stop for breath when walking at my own pace on the level"

    3 "I stopped for breath after walking about 100 yards or after a few minutes on the level"

    4 "I am too breathless to leave the house" or "I am breathless when dressing"

MMRC 0–1, indicates fewer symptoms; MMRC ≥2, indicates more symptoms

- Then determine stage by FEV_1 as follows:

Stage	% predicted
Mild	$FEV_1 \geq 80\%$
Moderate	$50\% \; FEV_1 < 80\%$
Severe	$30\% \; FEV_1 < 50\%$
Very Severe	$FEV_1 < 30\%$

- Classify frequency of exacerbations as follows: low risk ≤ 1 exacerbation/yr, high risk ≥ 2 exacerbations/yr
- Use **Table 116** to classify patients by type and determine tx using **Table 117**.
- The goal of tx is to minimize both symptoms and number of exacerbations. The degree of airflow limitation and risk of exacerbation influences but should not be the sole determinant of tx.

Stepped Approach: Add steps when symptoms inadequately controlled; D/C medication if no improvement. Assess improvement in symptoms, ADLs, exercise capacity, rapidity of symptom relief. See **Table 118** and **Table 122**. Long-term tx with long-acting anticholinergics (eg, tiotropium), long-acting β-agonists, and inhaled steroids slows the loss of FEV_1 and reduces the number of exacerbations and/or hospitalization.

Table 116. Combined Assessment of COPD*

Patient Type	Characteristic	Risk		Symptom Score (eg, mMRC, see p 277)
		Spirometric Classification	Exacerbations per year	
A	low risk, fewer symptoms	mild/moderate	≤ 1	Low 0–1
B	low risk, more symptoms	mild/moderate	≤ 1	High ≥ 2
C	high risk, fewer symptoms	severe/very severe	≥ 2	Low 0–1
D	high risk, more symptoms	severe/very severe	≥ 2	High ≥ 2

* Where assessment of risk is based on the highest risk according to either spirometry or exacerbation hx.
Source: Adapted from www.goldcopd.org.

Table 117. Pharmacotherapy for Stable COPD[a-c]

Patient Group	First Choice	Second Choice	Alternate Choice[d]
A	Short-acting anticholinergic[e] prn **or** Short-acting β_2-agonist prn	Long-acting anticholinergic[e] **or** Long-acting β_2-agonist **or** Short-acting β_2-agonist and short-acting anticholinergic[e]	Theophylline[f]
B	Long-acting anticholinergic[e] **or** Long-acting β_2-agonist	Long-acting anticholinergic[e] and Long-acting β_2-agonist	Short-acting β_2-agonist **and/or** short-acting anticholinergic[e] Theophylline[f]

(cont.)

Table 117. Pharmacotherapy for Stable COPD[a-c] (cont.)

Patient Group	First Choice	Second Choice	Alternate Choice[d]
C	ICS + Long-acting β_2-agonist **or** Long-acting anticholinergic[e]	Long-acting anticholinergic[e] and Long-acting β_2-agonist **or** Long-acting anticholinergic and PDE-4 inhibitor **or** Long-acting β_2-agonist and PDE-4 inhibitor	Short-acting β_2-agonist **and/or** short-acting anticholinergic[e] Theophylline[f]
D	ICS + Long-acting β_2-agonist **and/or** Long-acting anticholinergic[e]	ICS + Long-acting β_2-agonist and Long-acting anticholinergic[e] **or** ICS + Long-acting β_2-agonist and PDE-4 inhibitor **or** Long-acting anticholinergic and Long-acting β_2-agonist **or** Long-acting anticholinergic[e] and PDE-4 inhibitor	Short-acting β_2-agonist **and/or** short-acting anticholinergic Theophylline[f]

ICS, inhaled corticosteroids

[a] Medications in each box are mentioned in alphabetical order and therefore not necessarily in order of preference.

[b] β_2-agonists, anticholinergics, or slow-release theophylline (caution in older adults with other conditions and taking other medications). It is uncertain whether anticholinergics or long-acting β_2-agonists should be used as initial tx.

[c] Consider osteoporosis prophylaxis.

[d] Medications in this column can be used alone or in combination with other options in the First and Second Choice columns.

[e] Avoid inhaled anticholinergics in men with lower urinary tract obstructive sumptoms.[BC]

[f] Avoid in insomia.[BC]

Source: www.goldcopd.org

Other Considerations for Controlling Symptoms

Smoking Cessation: Essential at any age. See p 312.

Anxiety or Major Depression: Seen in up to 40% of patients and should be treated.

Mucolytic Therapy: Not recommended in stable COPD. Consider for patients with chronic productive cough; continue if reduced cough and sputum during a trial. Example tx: guaifenesin▲ long-acting 600 mg po q12h

Rehabilitation: Patients at all stages benefit from exercise training, ie, increased exercise tolerance results in decreased dyspnea and fatigue (p 274).

Long-term Oxygen Therapy: For indications, see **Table 119**. Assess patients with FEV_1 <30%, cyanosis, edema, HF, resting O_2 sats <92%.

Other Considerations in Severe COPD

Patients should be given the opportunity to discuss palliative and end-of-life care. In particular, if the patient should become critically ill, is ICU care consistent with goals of care and are they willing to accept the burdens of such care?

Table 118. COPD Exacerbation: Diagnosis and Therapy

Stage	Treatment
COPD Exacerbation (assess cardinal symptoms: increased dyspnea, sputum volume, and sputum purulence)	
Mild exacerbation (1 cardinal symptom)	Increase dosage and/or frequency of β_2-agonist; no antibiotics; monitor for worsening
Moderate or severe exacerbation (2 or 3 cardinal symptoms)	Add steroid (eg, prednisone 40 mg po every day for 5 d) Add respiratory fluoroquinolone (moxifloxacin, levofloxacin, or gemifloxacin) or amoxicillin-clavulanate; if at risk of *Pseudomonas*, consider ciprofloxacin and obtain sputum culture; if antibiotics in last 3 mo, use alternative class CBC, CXR, ECG, ABG; titrate O_2 to 88–92% sat and recheck ABG If 1 or more of severe dyspnea, signs of respiratory muscle fatigue, or PCO_2 ≥45 or pH <7.35, then noninvasive positive-pressure ventilation reduces risk of ventilator use, mortality and length of hospital stay.

Table 119. Indications for Long-term Oxygen Therapy[a]

PaO_2 Level	SaO_2 Level	Other
≤55 mmHg	≤88%	>15 h/d for benefit[a], greater if 20 h/d[b]
55–59 mmHg	≥89%	Signs of tissue hypoxia (eg, cor pulmonale by ECG, HF, hematocrit >55%); or nocturnal desaturation, sats <90% for >30% of the time
≥60 mmHg	≥90%	Desaturation with exercise Desaturation with sleep apnea not corrected by CPAP

[a] Titrate O_2 saturation to ~90%.
[b] Improves survival, hemodynamics, polycythemia, exercise capacity, lung mechanics, and cognition.
Source: www.goldcopd.org

ASTHMA

Definition

- A chronic inflammatory disorder of airways causing airway hyperresponsiveness and episodic wheezing, breathlessness, chest tightening, and coughing, particularly at night or in the early morning.
- Episodes are usually associated with reversible airflow obstruction.

Diagnosis in Older Adults

- Half of older people with asthma have not been diagnosed.
- Diagnosis is based on symptoms, and after age 65 requires spirometry.
  - Aging reduces FEV_1/FVC and may result in overdiagnosis of COPD. For this reason, some older adults with asthma are misdiagnosed with COPD.
  - If FEV_1/FVC is ≤0.65 and the diffusing capacity of carbon dioxide is reduced, then COPD is likely. The diffusing capacity of carbon dioxide is normal in asthma.
  - If a short-acting β_2-agonist does not reverse airflow obstruction during pulmonary function tests (asthma is not excluded), do one of the following:
    - Perform bronchial provocative testing (induce obstruction), *or*
    - Repeat testing after 2 wk of oral steroids to determine if obstruction seen in the initial test is reversible.
  - Over half of people >65 yr old with airflow obstruction have both COPD and asthma ("overlap" syndrome).

Additional Considerations

- Some adults >65 yr old may have had asthma from a young age, while others develop asthma for the first time in late life. Second peak in incidence after 65 yr; 5–10% after 65 yr are affected and account for two-thirds of asthma deaths.
- Those with long-standing asthma develop fixed obstruction (reduced FEV_1/FVC that is not reversed by bronchodilators) as an effect of both the disease and aging.
- Cough is a common presentation for asthma in those >65 yr old.
- Symptoms may be confused with those of HF, COPD, GERD, chronic aspiration.
- Typical triggers: aeroallergens, irritants (eg, smoke, paint, household aerosols), viral upper respiratory infection, GERD, allergic rhinitis, metabisulfate ingestion (eg, wine, beer, food preservatives), medications (eg, ASA, NSAIDs, β-blockers).
- About 95% of patients with asthma also have perennial rhinitis and tx of both improves asthma outcomes.

Therapy

Nonpharmacologic

Avoid triggers; educate patients on disease management. Peak flow meters are less helpful in monitoring older adults; aging decreases peak flow and increases variability.

Pharmacologic

Good evidence on best tx for older adults with asthma is lacking because most clinical trials exclude people >65 yr old and those with comorbidities or a hx of smoking >10 pack-years. Stepped approach:

- Based on level of symptom control (see **Table 120**).

- Long-acting β-agonists should not be used unless given in combination with an inhaled steroid. Long-acting β-agonists as monotherapy are associated with increased mortality and are contraindicated as monotherapy.
- When symptoms controlled for 3 mo, try stepwise reduction, eg, step down from twice-daily steroid and long-acting β-agonist combination to once daily.
- If control not achieved, step up, but first review medication technique, adherence, and avoidance of triggers (see **Table 120** and **Table 121**).

Use separate AeroChamber for steroids; wash AeroChamber monthly.

Table 120. Levels of Asthma Control

Characteristic	Controlled (all of the following)	Partly Controlled (any measure present in any week)	Uncontrolled
Daytime symptoms	0–2 times/wk	>2 times/wk	
Limitations of activities	None	Any	Three or more
Nighttime symptoms/awakening	None	Any	features of partly
Need for reliever/rescue tx	0–2 times/wk	>2 times/wk	controlled asthma present in any wk
Lung function (PEF or FEV$_1$)	Normal	<80% predicted or personal best (if known)	
Exacerbations	None	≥1/yr[a]	One in any wk[b]

[a] Any exacerbation should prompt review of maintenance tx to ensure that it is adequate.
[b] By definition, an exacerbation in any week makes that an uncontrolled asthma week.
Source: www.ginasthma.org

Table 121. Asthma Therapy for Older Adults

Step*	Treatment Options	Comments
Step 1	Inhaled short-acting β-agonist prn	Anticholinergics are an alternative rescue agent.
Step 2	Low-dose inhaled glucocorticoid (IGC) *or* leukotriene modifier	
Step 3	Low-dose IGC + long-acting β-agonist *or* medium- to high-dose IGC *or* low-dose IGC + leukotriene modifier *or* low-dose IGC + tiotropium or SR-theophylline	The anticholinergic tiotropium is superior to doubling the dose of inhaled steroid and equivalent to adding a long-acting β-agonist in uncontrolled asthma in adults. Leukotriene modifiers are equivalent to long-acting β-agonists in uncontrolled asthma in adults. Many drug interactions with theophylline.
Step 4	**To Step 3 Add**: medium- to high-dose IGC + long-acting β-agonist *or* leukotriene modifier *or* SR-theophylline	Inhaled steroids are associated with bone loss. Never use long-acting β-agonists without an inhaled steroid.
Step 5	**To Step 4 Add**: oral glucocorticoid (lowest dose) and/or anti-IgE tx	Oral steroids are associated with bone loss.

Acute Exacerbation

Mild attacks: reduction in peak flow <20%, nocturnal awakening, and increased use of short-acting β-agonist can usually be managed at home

Moderate attacks may require and severe attacks usually require care in clinic or hospital

(cont.)

Table 121. Asthma Therapy for Older Adults (cont.)

Step*	Treatment Options	Comments

- Begin short-acting β-agonist 2–4 puffs by MDI or neb (possibly with ipratropium) every 20 min × 1 hr, then 2–4 puffs every 3–4 hr (mild) and 6–10 puffs every 2 hr (moderate and severe).
- Oral glucocorticoids (0.5–1.0 mg/kg prednisolone) in moderate/severe attacks
- If hypoxemic, titrate O_2 to 95% saturation
- Combined β-agonist/anticholinergic reduces need for hospitalization
- Do not use theophylline with high doses of β-agonists
- Severe attacks unresponsive to oral steroids and bronchodilators; give 2 g magnesium sulfate IV; Do NOT give: sedatives, mucolytics, chest PT, vigorous hydration, antibiotics, or epinephrine.

* Go to next step if symptoms not controlled.
Source: Adapted from: www.ginasthma.org; and Gibson PG, et al. *Lancet.* 2010;376:803–813.

DELIVERY DEVICES FOR ASTHMA AND COPD

Metered-dose inhalers (MDIs): prescribed as number of puffs. Spacers (require a separate prescription) improve drug delivery and should be used for essentially all older patients. Use separate spacers for steroids. Wash spacer monthly.

Dry powder inhalers (DPIs): prescribed as caps or inhalations; require moderate to high inspiratory flow. DPIs are not used correctly by 40% of people >60 yr old and 60% of those >80 yr old. Instructions should be repeated and reinforced for proper use and effective tx.

Nebulizers: prescribed as milligrams or milliliters of solution. Consider for patients with disabling or distressing breathlessness on maximal tx with inhalers. Often the best choice for patients with cognitive impairment or when patients cannot manage DPIs or MDIs. Caution when patients with glaucoma use nebulized anticholinergics; the mask should fit well, or a T-type delivery device should be used. Ultrasonic and jet nebulizers are available; the latter can be used with supplemental oxygen.

Table 122. Asthma and COPD Medications

Packaging Color (Body/Cap)[a]	Dosage	Adverse Events (Metabolism, Excretion)
Anticholinergics		
✔ Ipratropium *(Atrovent)* (silver/green)	2–6 puffs q6h or 0.5 mg by nebulizer▲ q6h	Dry mouth, urinary retention, possible increase in cardiovascular mortality (lung, poorly absorbed; F)
Tiotropium *(Spiriva)* (gray/green)	1 inhalation cap (18 mcg) daily (inhale twice from cap)	Same as ipratropium except good data on cardiovascular safety (14% K, 86% F)
Short-acting β₂-Agonists (SABA) [b]		*Class AEs:* tremor, nervousness, headache, palpitations, tachycardia, cough, hypokalemia. Caution: use half-doses in patients with known or suspected coronary disease (L)

(cont.)

Table 122. Asthma and COPD Medications (cont.)

Packaging Color (Body/Cap)[a]	Dosage	Adverse Events (Metabolism, Excretion)
✔ Albuterol▲ *(Ventolin)* (yellow/orange) *(Ventolin Rotacaps)* (light blue/dark blue)	2 puffs q4–6h, max 12 puffs/d or 2.5 mg by nebulizer q6h; T: 2, 4 po q6–8h; ER 4–8 mg po q12h 1–2 caps q4–6h; 200 mcg/cap	AEs more common with oral formulation
✔ Bitolterol *(Tornalate)*	1–3 puffs q4–6h	
Levalbuterol *(Xopenex)*	0.31, 0.63, 1.25 mg q6–8h by nebulizer; inhaler 2 puffs q4–6h	Expensive; no advantage over racemic albuterol (intestine, L)
Pirbuterol *(Maxair)* (blue/white)	2–3 puffs q4–6h	Mechanism may be difficult for older adults to trigger (L, K)
Long-acting β-Agonists		*Class AEs:* tremor, nervousness, headache, palpitations, tachycardia, cough, hypokalemia. Caution: use half-doses in patients with known or suspected coronary disease; not for acute exacerbation. These agents should not be used in asthma without an inhaled steroid. (L)
Arformoterol *(Brovana)*	2 mL q12h by nebulizer	
✔ Salmeterol *(Serevent Diskus)* (teal/light teal)	1 cap q12h; 50 mcg/cap	
✔ Formoterol *(Foradil)* (white/light blue)	1 cap q12h; 20 mcg/2 mL q12h per nebulizer	Onset of action 1–3 min (L, K)
Indacaterol *(Arcapta)*	1 cap q-24-hr (75 mcg/cap)	NOT indicated for asthma; greater bronchodilator effect than other long-acting β-agonists, also greater risk of cough after inhalation
Corticosteroids: Inhaled ✔ Beclomethasone *(Beclovent)* (white/brown) *(Vanceril)* (pink/dark pink)	2–4 puffs q6–12h [42, 84 mcg/puff, max 840 mcg/d]	*Class AEs:* nausea, vomiting, diarrhea, abdominal pain; oropharyngeal thrush; dysphonia; dosages >1 mg/d may cause adrenal suppression, reduce calcium absorption and bone density, and cause bruising (L)
✔ Budesonide▲ (eg, *Pulmicort*) (white/brown)	180–800 mcg q 12h [90, 180, 200, 400 mcg/inhalation]	
Budesonide inhalation solution▲ (eg, *Pulmicort Respules*)	0.25, 0.5, 1.0 mg/2 mL q12h	
Ciclesonide *(Alvesco)* (dark orange)	80–320 mcg q12h [80, 160 mcg/inhalation]	
✔ Flunisolide▲ (eg, *AeroBid*) (gray/purple or green)	500 mcg q12h [250 mcg/inhalation]	
✔ Fluticasone▲ (eg, *Flovent*) (orange/light orange)	88–880 mcg q12h [44, 110, 220 mcg/puff]	
Mometasone *(Asmanex)*	1–4 inhalation/d [220 mcg]	
Corticosteroids: Oral		
Prednisone▲ (eg, *Deltasone, Orasone)*	20 mg po q12h [T: 1, 2.5, 5, 10, 20, 50; elixir 5 mg/5 mL]	Leukocytosis, thrombocytosis, sodium retention, euphoria, depression, hallucination, cognitive dysfunction; other effects with long-term use (L)

(cont.)

Table 122. Asthma and COPD Medications (cont)

Packaging Color (Body/Cap)[a]	Dosage	Adverse Events (Metabolism, Excretion)
Methylxanthines Long-acting theophyllines▲		*Class AEs:* atrial arrhythmias, seizures, increased gastric acid secretion, ulcer, reflux, diuresis; clearance ↓ by 30% after 65 yr; initial dosage ≤400 mg/d, titrate using blood levels; 16-fold greater risk of life-threatening events or death after age 75 at comparable blood levels (L)
(eg, *Theo-Dur, Slo-Bid*)	100–200 mg po q12h [T: 100, 200, 300, 450]	
(eg, *Theo-24*)	400 mg/d po [C: 100, 200, 300, T: 400, 600]	
Leukotriene Modifiers		
Montelukast *(Singulair)*	10 mg po in AM [T: 10; ChT: 4, 5]	Headache, drowsiness, fatigue, dyspepsia; minimal data in older adults; leukotriene-receptor antagonist (L)
Zafirlukast *(Accolate)*	20 mg po q12h 1 h ac or 2 h pc [T: 10, 20]	Headache, somnolence, dizziness, nausea, diarrhea, abdominal pain, fever; monitor LFTs; monitor coumarin anticoagulants; leukotriene-receptor antagonist (L, reduced by 50% if >65 yr)
Zileuton *(Zyflo)*	600 mg po q6h [T: 600]	Dizziness, insomnia, nausea, abdominal pain, abnormal LFTs, myalgia; monitor coumarin anticoagulants; other drug interactions; inhibits synthesis of leukotrienes (L)
PDE-4 Inhibitor		
Roflumilast *(Daliresp)*	500 mcg/d po, for use in severe COPD (FEV$_1$ <50%) associated with chronic bronchitis but not emphysema [T: 500 mcg]	Weight loss, nausea, headache, back pain, influenza, insomnia; do not use if acute bronchospasm or moderate or greater liver impairment, caution in patients with depression (suicidality); inhibits CYP3A4 and - 1A2 (eg, erythromycin) (L)
Other Medications		
✔ Albuterol-Ipratropium *(Combivent)* (silver/orange) *(Duoneb)*	0.09/0.018 mg/puff, 2-3 puffs q6h; 3 mg/0.5 mg by nebulizer▲ q6h	Same as individual agents (L, K)
Combivent Respimat	100/20 mcg 1 inhalation q6h (not to exceed 6 inhalations in 24 h)	
✔Budesonide-Formoterol *(Symbicort)* (red/gray)	2 inhalations q12h (80 mcg, 160 mcg/4.5 mcg)	Same as individual agents (L, K)
Cromolyn sodium (eg, *Intal*) (white/blue)	2 mL (10 mg/mL) q6h by nebulizer	Cough, throat irritation (L, K)
✔Formoterol-Mometasone *(Dulera)*	1–2 inhalations (5 mcg/100, 200 mcg per inhalation)	Nasopharyngitis, sinusitis, headache

(cont.)

Table 122. Asthma and COPD Medications (cont.)

Packaging Color (Body/Cap)[a]	Dosage	Adverse Events (Metabolism, Excretion)
Omalizumab *(Xolair)*	150–375 mg SC q2–4wk based on body weight and pre-tx IgE level	Malignancy, rare anaphylaxis; half-life 26 d (L, bile); expensive ($6,000–$25,000/yr)
✔Salmeterol-Fluticasone combination *(Advair Diskus)* (purple/light purple)	1 inhalation q12h (50 mcg/100, 250, or 500 mcg/cap)	
Vilanterol-Fluticasone *(Breo Ellipta)* (light grey/pale blue)	1 inhalation q24h (25 mcg/100 mcg)	

✔ = preferred for treating older adults

[a] Generics may have different color on body and cap.

[b] Older nonselective β_2-agonists such as isoproterenol, metaproterenol, or epinephrine are not recommended and are more toxic.

RESTRICTIVE LUNG DISEASE (RLD)

- Up to 11 of people over age 75 meet criteria for restrictive lung disease (RLD). In old age, RLD is often due to disorders outside of the lung itself. RLD can be disabling and progressive and sometimes treatable.
- RLD is more likely to produce ADL disability (RR = 9.0; 95% CI: 3.1–26.6) than is moderate COPD (RR = 2.3; 95% CI: 0.7–4.5).
- These disorders are characterized by reduced total lung capacity (TLC). However, TLC is not part of routine pulmonary function tests (PFTs). In practice, forced vital capacity (FVC) is used as a surrogate for TLC.

Diagnosis and Staging

- Patients present with exertional dyspnea which often has insidious onset. PFTs show decreased lung volumes (FVC <80% of the lower limit of normal [LLN]), a FEV_1/FVC ratio >85–90%, and flow volume curve shows a complex profile.
- Disease severity is based on the degree of reduction of FVC; FVC 60–80% = mild, 50–60% = moderate, <50% = severe

Differential Diagnosis

The many disorders that cause RLD can be grouped as shown in **Table 123** along with differentiating characteristics and some common causes in the older population.

Table 123. Common Causes of Restrictive Lung Diseases in Older Adults

Category (Mechanism)	Differentiating PFT Findings	Common Causes
Intrinsic lung diseases (inflammation or scarring of the lung tissue)	Abnormal DLCO	Idiopathic pulmonary fibrosis Post-inflammatory lung fibrosis Radiation Drug induced Connective tissue diseases (RA, etc) Chronic heart failure

(cont.)

Category (Mechanism)	Differentiating PFT Findings	Common Causes
Extrinsic disorders (mechanical compression of lungs or limitation of expansion)	Normal DLCO	Kyphosis/Kyphoscoliosis Obesity
Neuromuscular disorders (decreased ability of the respiratory muscles to inflate/deflate lungs)	Normal DLCO Reduced maximal inspiratory and/or expiratory pressures	Amyotrophic lateral sclerosis Thyroid and adrenal disorders Vitamin D deficiency Post-polio syndrome
CNS disorders	Normal DLCO	Parkinson Disease Multisystemic atrophy Progressive supranuclear palsy Multiple sclerosis

Note: DLCO = diffusing capacity of the lung for carbon monoxide

Therapy

Follows the underlying cause. Because many of these disorders are outside of the lung itself, diagnosis and management often falls to geriatric health care providers.

IMPOTENCE (ERECTILE DYSFUNCTION OR ED)

Definition
Inability to achieve sufficient erection for intercourse. Prevalence nearly 70% by age 70.

Causes
Often multifactorial; >50% of cases arterial, venous, or mixed vascular cause (**Table 124**).

Table 124. Causes of Erectile Dysfunction (ED) in Older Men

Causes (in order of frequency)	Associated Findings/Risk Factors	Onset
Vascular	Vascular risk factors; femoral bruits; poor pedal pulses. Venous vascular disease suggested by penile plaques (Peyronie disease).	Gradual
Neuropathic	DM; hx of pelvic trauma, surgery, irradiation; spinal injury or surgery; Parkinson disease, multiple sclerosis; alcoholism; loss of bulbocavernosus reflex or orthostatic BP changes	Gradual
Drug induced (see page 292)	Loss of sleep-associated erections	Sudden
Psychogenic, including bereavement	Sleep-associated erections or erections with masturbation are intact	Sudden
Hypogonadism	Decreased libido >ED; low testosterone, small testes, gynecomastia	Gradual
Thyroid or adrenal disorders or hyperprolactinemia	Rare <5% of cases; other associated symptoms of the underlying problem	Gradual

Diagnosis of Hypogonadism in Middle-aged and Older Men

- Diagnose testosterone deficiency only in men with consistent symptoms and unequivocally low testosterone levels.
- Morning total testosterone level <320 ng/dL (11 nmol/L) that remains <320 ng/dL on repeat testing and a free testosterone level of <640 pg/dL (<220 pmol/L) using a reliable assay suggests deficiency.
- Ask the following questions from the European Male Aging Study Sexual Function Questionnaire. If the answer to **all 3 questions** is the response in **bold**, hypogonadism is likely present.
  - How often did you think about sex? This includes times of just being interested in sex, daydreaming, or fantasizing about sex, as well as times when you wanted to have sex.
    - **2 or 3 times or less in the last month**
    - Once/wk or more often

- It is common for men to experience erectile problems. This may mean that one is not always able to get or keep an erection that is rigid enough for satisfactory activity (including sexual intercourse and masturbation). In the *last month*, are you:
  - Always able to keep an erection that would be good enough for sexual intercourse, or usually able to get and keep an erection that would be good enough for sexual intercourse
  - **Sometimes or never able to get and keep an erection that would be good enough for sexual intercourse**
- How frequently do you awaken with full erection?
  - **Once in the last month or less often**
  - 2 or 3 times or more often in the last month

Therapy

An at-home trial of a PDE5 inhibitor is both diagnostic and therapeutic for the common causes of ED (vascular, neuropathic, mixed).

Table 125. Management of Male Sexual Dysfunction			
Therapy	**Dose**	**Formulation**	**Comments**
PDE5 Inhibitors Avanafil *(Stendra)*	start 50 mg 30 min before sexual activity	50, 100, 200	*All Agents*: Effective in 60–70% of men with ED of various etiologies. Contraindicated with use of nitrates and nonischemic optic neuropathy. PDE5 inhibitors potentiate the hypotensive effects of α-blockers. Potent CYP3A4 inhibitors reduce metabolism of all PDE5 inhibitors and increase risk of toxicity. *Common tx-related AEs*: headache, flushing, rhinitis, dyspepsia *Other tx-related AEs*: priapism, low back pain, bluish discoloration of vision
Sildenafil *(Viagra)*	start 25 mg 1 h before sexual activity	25, 50, 100	*Other AEs*: increased sensitivity to light, blurred vision
Vardenafil *(LEVITRA)*	start 2.5 mg 1 h before sexual activity	2.5, 5, 10, 20	*Other AEs*: Avoid using in congenital or acquired QT prolongation and in patients taking class IA or III antiarrhythmics.
Tadalafil *(Cialis)*	start 5 mg 30–60 min before sexual activity; lasts 24 h	2.5, 5, 10, 20	*Other AEs*: myalgia, pain in limbs; 2.5 mg/d may be as effective as taking higher doses prn.
Androgen (Testosterone) *Injectable* Testosterone enanthate▲	200 mg/mL 50–400 mg IM q2–4 wk	—	Use only when there is clear evidence of deficiency. Not recommended with breast or prostate cancer, prostate nodule or induration or PSA >3 ng/dL, hematocrit >50%, untreated sleep apnea, HF, significant prostate obstructive symptoms. Avoid testosterone/ methyltestosterone unless for moderate to severe hypogonadism.[BC]

(cont.)

Table 125. Management of Male Sexual Dysfunction (cont.)			
Therapy	**Dose**	**Formulation**	**Comments**
Testosterone cypionate▲	100, 200 mg/mL, 50–400 mg IM q2–4wk		Probably effective in the tx of opioid-induced androgen deficiency. Check serum testosterone concentration and adjust dose to achieve concentration in midrange of normal. Monitor AEs and response q3mo. *AEs:* polycythemia, fluid retention, liver dysfunction. Possible increase in cardiovascular events in men with cardiovascular risk factors and poor mobility. Review cautions for individual preparations.
Transdermal			
Androderm, AndroGel	2, 4 mg/24-h pch 12.5 mg/pump starting at 4 pumps/d 20.25 mg/pump starting dose at 2 pumps d	1%, 1.62% by metered-dose pump	
Fortesta	60-g canister (10 mg/spr), 4 spr/d		
Testim	5-g tube (50 mg), 1 tube/d		
Buccal			
Striant	T: 30 mg, 1 tab q12h		
Devices			
Vacuum tumescence devices (*eg, Osbon-Erec Aid, Catalyst Vacuum Device, Pos-T-Vac, Rejoyn*)	N/A	N/A	*Rare:* ecchymosis, reduced ejaculation, coolness of penile tip. Good acceptance in older population; intercourse successful in 70–90% of cases.
Penile prosthesis	N/A	N/A	*Complications:* infection, mechanical failure, penile fibrosis
Prostaglandin E			
Alprostadil	Intracavernosal 5, 40 mcg *or* intraurethral 125–1000 mcg	Intracavernosal: 5, 10, 20, 40 mcg *or* intraurethral: 125, 250, 500, 1000 mcg	*Risks:* hypotension, bruising, bleeding, priapism; erection >4 h requires emergency tx; intraurethral safer and more acceptable. Rarely used since PDE 5 inhibitors became available.

FEMALE SEXUAL DYSFUNCTION

Definition
May involve reduced sex drive, dislike of sexual activity, difficulty with arousal, inability to achieve orgasm, or dyspareunia (pain with intercourse)

Factors Aggravating Dyspareunia
- Anticholinergic medications (produce vaginal dryness)
- Gynecologic tumors
- Interstitial cystitis
- Myalgia from overexertion during Kegel exercises
- Osteoarthritis
- Pelvic fractures
- Retroverted uterus
- Sacral nerve root compression
- Vaginal atrophy from estrogen deprivation
- Vulvar or vaginal infection

Evaluation
- Ask about sexual problems (eg, changes in libido, partner's function, and health issues).
- Screen for depression.
- Perform pelvic examination for vulvovaginitis, vaginal atrophy, conization (decreased distensibility and narrowing of the vaginal canal), scarring, pelvic inflammatory disease, cystocele, and rectocele.

Management
- Identify and treat clinical pathology.
- Educate and counsel patients and/or refer to a certified sex therapist (www.nlm.nih.gov/medlineplus/femalesexualdysfunction.html).
- Water-soluble lubricants (eg, *Replens*) are highly effective as monotherapy for dyspareunia in those who cannot or will not use hormones, or as a supplement to estrogen.
- For vaginismus (vaginal muscle spasm), trial cessation of intercourse and gradual vaginal dilation may help.
- For diminished libido, short-term use of androgens, eg, 300 mcg testosterone pch, provides modest but meaningful improvement (not yet available in the United States).
- Topical estrogens (see **Table 126**) treat symptoms and complications of estrogen deficiency such as dyspareunia and recurrent UTIs with minimal systemic levels when used in dime-size amounts 2–3 ×/wk.
- Dyspareunia (moderate to severe) may also be treated with the selective estrogen-receptor modulator, ospemifene 60 mg orally once daily with food for the shortest duration necessary; in women with a uterus, consider concomitant progestin tx. Contraindications: stroke, MI, DVT, or PE, estrogen-dependent neoplasia, and genital bleeding.
- The OTC botanical massage oil *Zestra* appears to improve desire and arousal in women with mixed desire/interest/arousal/orgasm disorders but can cause vaginal burning.
- Studies of sildenafil have not consistently shown effectiveness.

Table 126. Topical Estrogens Without Systemic Effects

Estrogen	Dosage
Estrogen cream *(Premarin, Ogen, Estrace)*	Use minimum dose (0.5 g for *Premarin*, 2 g for *Ogen* and *Estrace*) daily × 2 wk, then 1–3 ×/wk thereafter
Estradiol vaginal ring *(Estring)*	Insert intravaginally and change q90d
Estradiol vaginal tablets *(Vagifem)*	Insert 25 mcg intravaginally daily ×2 wk, then twice/wk

DRUG-INDUCED SEXUAL DYSFUNCTION

Agents Associated with Sexual Dysfunction in both Men and Women

The following drugs and drug classes are believed to sometimes cause sexual dysfunction. In cases of suspected drug-induced sexual dysfunction, improvement after drug withdrawal provides the best evidence for the adverse effect. Tx with a drug from an alternative class to treat an underlying condition may be necessary.

- Antidepressants: SSRIs (see below) reduce libido and delay orgasm; lithium causes ED, MAOIs may cause ED or anorgasmia
- Antipsychotics: olanzapine produces less loss of libido/ED than risperidone, clozapine, and oral and depot first-generation agents.
- Antihypertensives: any agent may cause ED related to reduced genital blood flow
  - Spironolactone has antiandrogen effect.
  - Centrally acting sympatholytics (eg, clonidine) produce relatively high rates of sexual dysfunction (ED and loss of libido).
  - Peripherally acting sympatholytics, eg, reserpine (ED and loss of libido).
- Digoxin: possibly related to reduced testosterone levels
- Lipid-lowering agents: fibrates (gynecomastia and ED) and many statins (eg, lovastatin, pravastatin, simvastatin, atorvastatin) are the subject of case reports of both ED and gynecomastia. Statins affect the substrate for sex hormones and have been shown to reduce total and sometimes also bioavailable testosterone.
- Acid-suppressing drugs: The histamine$_2$-blockers cimetidine and more rarely ranitidine cause gynecomastia. Famotidine has caused hyperprolactinemia and galactorrhea. The PPI omeprazole has caused gynecomastia.
- Metoclopramide: induces hyperprolactinemia
- Anticonvulsants: phenobarbital, phenytoin, carbamazepine, primidone; all increase metabolism of androgen.
- Anticholinergics and antihistamines produce vaginal dryness.
- Alcohol: high dosages reduce libido.
- Opioids: reduce libido and produce anorgasmia related to reduced testosterone.

Management of SSRI-Induced Sexual Dysfunction

- Wait for tolerance to develop (12 wk of tx may be needed).
- Pharmacologic management:
  - For escitalopram and sertraline (not other SSRIs), reducing dosage or "drug holidays" (skip or reduce weekend dose) may help.
  - In both men and women, sildenafil 50–100 mg po improved sexual function in prospective, parallel-group, randomized, double-blind, placebo-controlled clinical trials.

CHRONIC WOUND ASSESSMENT AND TREATMENT

Wound Assessment

Evaluation of chronic wounds should include the following (see **Table 128** for wound characteristics specific to ulcer type):

- Location
- Wound size and shape: length, width, depth, stage (pressure ulcer), grade (diabetic foot ulcer)
- Wound bed: color, presence of slough, necrotic tissue, granulation tissue, epithelial tissue, undermining or tunneling
- Exudate: purulent vs nonpurulent (serous, serosanguineous)
- Wound edges: distinct, diffuse, rolled under
- Periwound skin and soft tissue: erythema, edema, induration, temperature
- Presence of pain at rest and with wound care procedures
- Signs of wound infection:
  - Increased necrotic tissue
  - Foul odor
  - Purulent exudate
  - Halo of erythema at wound edges
  - Wound breakdown
  - Increasing pain
  - Marked edema
  - Friable granulation tissue
  - Serous exudate with nonspecific inflammation
  - Nonhealing, new tunneling, or enlarged wound
  - Heat
- Swab culture of wound surface exudates is of no value in diagnosing infection due to wound contamination. Educate staff not to collect cultures of wound slough or pus; encourage use of Levine's technique.
  - Levine's technique (cleanse with NS followed by rotating a swab over a 1-cm square area of viable wound tissue (not necrotic) with sufficient pressure to express fluid from the wound tissue beneath the wound surface) produces culture findings most comparable to those of tissue specimens.

Principles of Wound Treatment

- Remove debris from wound surface.
  - Cleanse using NS or Lactated Ringer's with each dressing change. Avoid antiseptics because of cytotoxicity.
  - Irrigate using 4–15 psi to cleanse adherent debris. Use 8 mmHg pressure (19-gauge catheter and 35-mL syringe) when wound is deep, tunneled, or undermined.
- Remove necrotic tissue. Consider combining autolytic or topical enzyme debridement methods with sharp debridement to facilitate more rapid removal of necrotic tissue.
  - Sharp debridement
  - Autolytic methods (eg, moisture-retaining dressings or hydrogels)
  - Mechanical (eg, wet-to-dry dressings)
  - Chemical (eg, topical enzymes such as *Accuzyme, Santyl*)
- Pack dead space (tunnels, undermining) loosely with moistened gauze dressings or strips of calcium alginate.

- Control pain associated with wound care procedures by offering pain medication 30 min before procedure.
  - Gauze-based negative pressure wound tx (TPWT), rather than foam, less painful in older adults, those with bone and tendon exposition wounds
  - For moderate to severe pain not managed by oral medications or with dose-limiting AEs, topical opioids may be used, eg, mixture of 10 mg morphine sulfate injectable combined with 8 g of neutral water-based gel applied 2 ×/d. Can titrate up to 10 mg morphine sulfate injectable with 5 g neutral water-based gel applied 2–3 ×/d.
  - High intensity TENS may help moderate to severe pain during wound care procedures
- Control bacterial burden/infection.
  - Monitor for signs of infection.
  - Debride all necrotic tissue (*except* in lower extremity with arterial insufficiency).
  - If infection is suspected, assess type and quantity of bacteria by validated quantitative swab or tissue biopsy. Suspect infection if epithelialization from margin is not progressing within 2 wk of debridement and initiation of offloading (use of cast, splint, or special shoe to shift pressure from wound to surrounding support structure).
  - For ulcers with ≥1 million CFU/g of tissue or any tissue level of β-hemolytic streptococci, use a topical antimicrobial (eg, *Silvadene* or dressings with bioavailable silver, cadexomer iodine at concentrations up to 0.45%; see **Table 130**). Limit duration of use of topical antimicrobials to avoid cytotoxicity or bacterial resistance.
  - Consider 2-wk trial of topical antibiotic for clean ulcers that are not healing after 2–4 wk optimal care; antibiotic spectrum should include gram-negative, gram-positive, and anaerobic organisms.
  - Use systemic antibiotics if obvious signs of localized infection, cellulitis, osteomyelitis, or systemic inflammatory response (see **Table 127**).
  - Treat cellulitis surrounding ulcer with a systemic gram-positive bactericidal antibiotic (see cellulitis, p 85) unless Gram-negative organisms are suspected and require aggressive IV tx.
  - If osteomyelitis is suspected, evaluate with radiographs, MRI, CT, or radionuclide scan.
  - Referral for surgical evaluation is warranted.

Table 127. Empiric Antibiotic Therapy to Treat Infections in Chronic Wounds

Severity of Infection	Clinical Features	Medication Options	Duration of Treatment
Mild	Superficial, localized signs of inflammation/infection, without signs of a systemic response or osteomyelitis, and ambulatory management planned	Cephalexin Clindamycin Amoxicillin/clavulanate Clindamycin plus ciprofloxacin, moxifloxacin, or linezolid (for MRSA)	2 wk
Moderate	Superficial to deep tissue involvement, a systemic response, no osteomyelitis, and either planned ambulatory or inpatient management	Clindamycin plus ciprofloxacin Clindamycin po plus ceftriaxone IV Vancomycin IV (for MRSA) Linezolid IV (for MRSA)	2–4 wk

(cont.)

Table 127. Empiric Antibiotic Therapy to Treat Infections in Chronic Wounds (cont.)

Severity of Infection	Clinical Features	Medication Options	Duration of Treatment
Severe	Requires inpatient care and involves deep tissue with a systemic response, presence of osteomyelitis, or is life/limb threatening	Clindamycin po plus ceftriaxone IV Piperacillin/tazobactam IV Clindamycin po plus gentamicin IV Imipenem IV Meropenem IV Vancomycin IV (for MRSA) Linezolid IV (for MRSA)	2–12 wk (Bone and joint involvement requires prolonged oral tx after IV tx completed.)

Source: Adapted from Landis, SJ. *Advances in Skin and Wound Care* 2008;21:531–540.

- Provide moist wound environment and control exudates.
  - Dressings (see **Table 129** and **Table 130**)
- Adjunctive tx to support wound healing process
  - Negative-pressure wound tx (ie, vacuum-assisted closure [VAC])
    - Indications: Stage III and IV pressure ulcers, neuropathic ulcers, venous ulcers, dehisced incisions with trapping of third-space fluid around wound
    - Contraindications: Presence of *any* nonviable, necrotic tissue in wound; untreated osteomyelitis; malignancy in or surrounding wound
    - Avoid use in frail elderly patients on anticoagulants (eg, Coumadin, heparin, etc)
    - Guidelines for use:
      - Negative pressure = 75–125 mmHg depending on wound characteristics
      - Dressing change regimen: 48 h after placement, then every other day
      - Cycle: continuous for initial 48 h, then intermittent (5 min negative pressure followed by 2 min of no pressure) for remainder of tx
      - Specialized training in application and monitoring of tx essential for successful outcome
  - Electrical stimulation
    - Indications: Stage III and IV pressure ulcers, arterial ulcers, diabetic foot ulcers, and venous ulcers if no evidence of measurable improvement after ≥30 d of standard wound care
    - Contraindications: presence of cardiac pacemaker, malignancy, osteomyelitis
    - Precautions: avoid placement of electrodes over topical substances containing metal ions, tangential to the heart, or over the carotid sinus
    - Guidelines for use:
      - Refer to PT for stimulation parameters
      - Predominant type of current used is pulsed current (either low- or high-voltage)
      - Electrode placement—two options:
        - One electrode placed directly in contact with saline-moistened gauze on wound surface and second electrode 15–30 cm from wound edge
        - Electrodes placed on skin at wound edges on opposite sides of wound
      - Pulse frequency: 100 pulses/sec with current sufficient to produce tingling sensation
      - Tx administered for 1 h, 5–7 d/wk, continued as long as wound is progressing toward closure

- ◦ Growth factor tx
  - ▪ *Regranex*, a recombinant platelet-derived growth factor, applied topically in thin layer to a clean wound bed for 12 h followed by 12 h of saline-moistened gauze dressing
  - ▪ Indications: Currently for diabetic foot ulcers but may have benefit in other nonhealing wounds.
  - ▪ Contraindications: Not recommended for use in patients with known malignancies.
  - ▪ Guidelines for use:
    - ▫ Must be used in conjunction with offloading of pressure on foot, regular sharp debridement, and maintenance of uninfected status.
    - ▫ If wound closure is not ≥30% in 10 wk or complete in 20 wk, reevaluate tx plan and consider surgical intervention (especially if osteomyelitis is present).
- Prevent further injury
  - ◦ Use pressure-reducing mattresses or chair cushions and heel protectors that float the heels
  - ◦ Reposition q2h and avoid any pressure on the wound
- Support repair process
  - ◦ Protein (1.25–1.5 g/kg/d) and calories (30–35/kg/d) unless contraindicated because of impaired renal function
  - ◦ Correct deficiencies of vitamin C and zinc if suspected
  - ◦ Avoid exposure to cold; vasoconstriction reduces blood flow to wound
  - ◦ Ensure adequate hydration with oral or parenteral fluids
- If ulcer does not show signs of healing over 2-wk period of optimal tx, reevaluate wound management strategies and factors affecting healing.

Table 128. Typical Wound Characteristics by Ulcer Type

	Arterial	Diabetic	Pressure	Venous
Location	Tips of toes or between toes, on pressure points of foot (eg, heel or lateral foot), or in areas of trauma	Plantar surface of foot, especially over metatarsal heads, toes, and heel	Over bony prominences (eg, trochanter, coccyx, ankle)	Gaiter area, particularly medial malleolus
Size and shape	Shallow, well-defined borders	Wound margins with callus	Variable length, width, depth depending on stage (see staging system, p 299)	Edges may be irregular with depth limited to dermis or shallow subcutaneous tissue
Wound bed	Pale or necrotic	Granular tissue unless PAD present	Varies from bright red, shallow crater to deeper crater with slough and necrotic tissue; tunneling and undermining	Ruddy red; yellow slough may be present; undermining or tunneling uncommon
Exudate	Minimal amount due to poor blood flow	Variable amount; serous unless infection present	May be purulent, becoming serous as healing progresses; foul odor with infection	Copious; serous unless infection present

(cont.)

Table 128. Typical Wound Characteristics by Ulcer Type (cont.)

	Arterial	Diabetic	Pressure	Venous
Surrounding skin	Halo of erythema or slight fluctuance indicates infection	Normal; may be calloused	May be distinct, diffuse, rolled under; erythema, edema, induration if infected	May appear macerated, crusted, or scaly; presence of stasis dermatitis, hyperpigmentation
Pain	Cramping or constant deep aching	Variable intensity; none with advanced neuropathy	Painful, unless sensory function impaired or with deep, extensive tissue necrosis	Variable; may be severe, dull, aching, or bursting in character

ARTERIAL ULCERS

Definition

Any lesion caused by severe tissue ischemia secondary to atherosclerosis and progressive arterial occlusion.

Wound Assessment

- See Chronic Wound Assessment (p 293).
- Assess ABI: If ABI <0.5, wound healing unlikely without revascularization.

Management (see also PAD, p 63, and Diabetes, p 94)

Protect from Injury

- Avoid compression of arterial wounds when ABI is <0.8.
- Avoid friction and pressure by using lamb's wool or foam between toes
- Use positioning devices to avoid pressure on feet (eg, heel protectors)

Local Wound Care

Tx dictated by adequacy of perfusion and status of wound bed:

- Avoid debridement of necrotic tissue until perfusion status is determined.
- Assess vascular perfusion and refer for surgical intervention if consistent with overall goals of care.
- If wound is infected, revascularization procedures, surgical removal of necrotic tissue, and systemic antibiotics are tx of choice.
- Topical antibiotics should not be used solely to treat infected ischemic wounds and may cause sensitivity reactions.
- If wound is uninfected and dry eschar is present, maintain dry intact eschar as a barrier to bacteria. Application of an antiseptic may decrease bacterial burden on wound surface although evidence is lacking.
- If wound is uninfected and soft slough and necrotic tissue are present, apply moisture-retaining dressings that allow frequent inspection of wound for signs of infection.

DIABETIC (NEUROPATHIC FOOT) ULCERS

Definition

Any lesion on the plantar surface of the foot caused by neuropathy and repetitive pressure on foot.

Wound Assessment

- See Chronic Wound Assessment (p 293).
- Assess for specific diabetes-related signs of infection:
  - Sudden increase in blood glucose
  - Wound can be probed to the bone—highly sensitive indicator of osteomyelitis
  - Exclude gross arterial disease by assessment for palpable pedal pulses, toe:brachial index >0.7 (or ABI >0.9), a transcutaneous oxygen pressure of >30 mmHg, or normal Doppler-derived wave form.
- Determine grade of ulcer (Wagner Classification)

  Grade 0: Preulcerative lesions; healed ulcers present; bony deformity present

  Grade 1: Superficial ulcer without subcutaneous tissue involvement

  Grade 2: Penetration through subcutaneous tissue

  Grade 3: Osteitis, abscess, or osteomyelitis

  Grade 4: Gangrene of digit

  Grade 5: Gangrene of foot requiring disarticulation

Management (see also Diabetes, p 94)
Local Wound Care

In addition to recommendations under Chronic Wound Treatment (see p 293):

- Debride devitalized tissue and callus: surgical debridement is method of choice for effective, rapid removal of nonviable tissue
- Avoid occlusive dressings to reduce risk of wound infection
- Offload pressure and stress from foot
  - Avoidance of pressure on foot essential to management of diabetic foot ulcer
  - Use orthotic that redistributes weight on plantar surface of foot when ambulating (eg, total contact cast, *DH Pressure Relief Walker)*
- If ulcer does not reduce in size by ≥50% after 4 wk of tx, reassess tx and consider alternative options (eg, negative-pressure wound tx, growth factor tx, skin substitutes, extracellular matrix, hyperbaric oxygen tx).
  - Skin substitutes (*Apligraf, Dermagraft, OrCel, TransCyte*) containing growth factors present in the skin may stimulate healing and decrease time to wound closure. Wound must be granular to be effective.
  - Hyperbaric oxygen tx effective in promoting healing of complicated chronic diabetic foot ulcers is covered by Medicare and some insurance companies. Caution in patients with HF, advanced COPD, and those treated with anticancer drugs. Tx applied in chamber for 1.5–2 h/d for 20–40 d.

PRESSURE ULCERS
Definition

Any lesion caused by unrelieved pressure resulting in damage of underlying tissue; usually develops over bony prominence.

Wound Assessment
- See Chronic Wound Assessment (p 293).
- Determine level of tissue injury by using Pressure Ulcer Staging System:
  - **Stage I:** An observable pressure-related alteration of intact skin that, as compared with an adjacent or opposite area on the body, may include changes in one or more of the following: skin temperature (warmth or coolness), tissue consistency (firm or boggy feel), and/or sensation (pain, itching). The ulcer appears as a defined area of persistent redness in lightly pigmented skin, whereas in darker skin tones, it may appear with persistent red, blue, or purple hues.
  - **Stage II:** Partial-thickness skin loss involving epidermis and/or dermis; presents as abrasion, blister, or shallow crater.
  - **Stage III:** Full-thickness skin loss involving damage or necrosis of subcutaneous tissue that may extend down to, but not through, underlying fascia; presents as deep crater with or without undermining of adjacent tissue.
  - **Stage IV:** Full-thickness skin loss with extensive destruction; tissue necrosis; or damage to muscle, bone, or supporting structures. May have associated undermining of sinus tracts. *Note:* eschar-covered ulcers cannot be staged until eschar is removed.
  - **Suspected Deep Tissue Injury:** Localized area of purple or maroon discoloration of intact skin or blood-filled blister indicating underlying soft-tissue injury due to pressure and/or shear. May be preceded by pain, tissue firmness, mushiness, or bogginess; and cooler or warmer temperature than adjacent tissue.
  - **Unstageable:** Covered with eschar or necrotic tissue.

Management
Local Wound Care

Table 129. Wound and Pressure Ulcer Products, by Drainage and Stage

Product	Drainage			Wound Stage			
	Light	Moderate	Heavy	I	II	III	IV
Transparent film	•			•	•		
Foam island	•	•			•	•	
Hydrocolloids	•	•			•	•	
Collagen	•	•	•			•	•
Calcium alginate		•	•			•	•
Hydrogel	•				•	•	•
Gauze packing (moistened with saline)		•	•			•	•

Table 130. Common Dressings for Pressure Ulcer Treatment

Dressing	Indications/Use	Contraindications
Transparent film (eg, *Bioclusive, 3M Tegaderm, Blisterfilm, ClearSite, Comfeel Film, CarraSmart Film, Dermatell, Polyskin II*)	Stage I, II Protection from friction Superficial scrape Autolytic debridement of slough Apply skin prep to intact skin to protect from adhesive	Draining ulcers Suspicion of skin infection or fungus
Foam (eg, *Allevyn, Lyofoam, COPA, DermaFoam, Flexzan, Mitraflex, 3M Foam, Polyderm, PolyMem, Tielle, VigiFoam*)	Stage II, III Moderate to heavy exudate Leave in place 3–5 d Can apply as window to secure transparent film	Excessive exudate Dry, crusted wound Dry eschar Periwound maceration likely if not changed appropriately
Foam with silver (eg, *PolyMem Silver, Optifoam AG, Contreet Foam*)	Infected Stage II & III ulcer Highly colonized ulcer	Sensitivity to silver Excessive exudate Dry, crusted wound Dry eschar Exudate must be present for silver to be released Inactivates enzymatic debriding agents Periwound maceration likely if not changed appropriately
Hydrocolloids (eg, *DuoDERM, Extra Thin DuoDERM, DuoDERM CGF, DuoDERM Signal, 3M Tegasorb, 3M Tegasorb Thin, Exuderm, RepliCare, RepliCare Thin, Comfeel Plus, Nu-DERM, Cutinova Hydro, Hydrocol II, Restore, Restore CX, Restore Plus, Ultec, Ultec Pro, DermaFilm, Exuderm, Exuderm LP, Sorbex, SignaDRESS, MPM Excel, ProCol, Odor Shield*)	Stage II, III Low to moderate drainage Reduces wound pain Autolytic debridement of slough Preventive for high-risk friction areas Leave in place 3–7 d Can apply as window to secure transparent film or under-taping Can apply over alginate to control drainage Must control maceration Apply skin prep to intact skin to protect from adhesive	Fragile skin Infected ulcers Heavily draining wounds, sinus tracts
Hydrocolloid with silver (eg, *Contreet*)	Infected ulcer Highly colonized ulcer Antimicrobial Leave in place up to 7 d	Sensitivity to silver Ionic silver released only in presence of exudate Inactivates enzymatic debriding agents Fragile skin Heavily draining wounds, sinus tracts

(cont.)

Table 130. Common Dressings for Pressure Ulcer Treatment (cont.)

Dressing	Indications/Use	Contraindications
Hydrogel (amorphous gels) (eg, *Intrasite Gel, AquaSite, Aquasorb, Biolex, CarraDres, Curagel, Restore Gel, SAF-Gel, SoloSite*)	Stage II, III, IV Dermabrasion Skin tears Necrotic ulcers Reduces ulcer pain Rehydrates ulcer bed Softens and loosens slough and necrosis Use in place of saline gauze for packing cavities, tunnels, and undermining Stays moist longer than saline gauze Leave in place 1–3 d depending on type of gel May require secondary dressing	Avoid use with heavily draining wounds May cause periwound maceration
Hydrogel with silver (eg, *SilvaSorb Gel*)	Infected ulcers Highly colonized ulcers Antimicrobial Rehydrates ulcer bed Leave in place maximum of 3 d	Sensitivity to silver Avoid use with topical medications Inactivates enzymatic debriding agents Avoid use with heavily draining wounds May cause periwound maceration Signs of systemic side effects, especially erythema multiforme Fungal proliferation
Hydrogel Sheets (eg, *Vigilon, Restore Impregnated Gauze, 3M Tegagel with Gauze, ClearSite, Aquasorb, Nugel, Curagel, Derma-Gel, FlexiGel*)	Stage II Needs to be held in place with topper dressing	Avoid use in macerated areas Wounds with moderate to heavy exudate
Calcium alginate (eg, *Sorbsan, Kaltostat, Algiderm, NU-DERM Alginate, 3M Tegagen HL & HG Alginate, Curasorb Polymem Alginate, Restore CalciCare, SeaSorb*)	Stage III, IV Excessive drainage Sinus tracts, tunnels, or cavities Apply dressing within wound borders Must use skin prep to protect periwound skin Requires secondary dressing Change q24–48h	Dry or minimally draining wound Dry eschar Superficial wounds with maceration May produce odor during dressing change Can macerate periwound skin

(cont.)

Table 130. Common Dressings for Pressure Ulcer Treatment (cont.)

Dressing	Indications/Use	Contraindications
Calcium alginate with Silver (eg, *Algidex Ag Alginate*)	Infected Stage III & IV ulcers with or without sinus tracts, tunnels, or cavities or excessive drainage Highly colonized ulcer Apply dressing within wound borders Must use skin prep to protect periwound skin Requires secondary dressing Change q24–48h	Sensitivity to silver Exudate must be present for silver to be released Inactivates enzymatic debriding agents Dry or minimally draining wound Dry eschar Superficial wounds with maceration May produce odor with dressing change Can macerate periwound skin
Gauze packing▲ (moistened with saline (eg, square2×2s/4×4s. *Fluffed Kerlix, Curity*)	Stage III, IV Wounds with depth, especially those with tunnels, undermining Must be remoistened at least q4h to maintain moist wound environment	May macerate periwound skin May be painful to remove Can traumatize tissue when removed
Composites (2 or more physically distinct dressing products combined as a single dressing) (eg, *3M Tegaderm, Alldress, CombiDERM, Comfortell, DermaDress, Covaderm Plus, Epigard, Viasorb*)	Stage I, II, III, IV Light, moderate, or heavy exudate Conform to skin surface shape Designed with adhesive border Easy application and removal Dressing change frequency dependent on wound type (follow package insert)	Caution with fragile skin; adhesive may injure skin Some types may be contraindicated with Stage IV ulcers (refer to package insert) May not maintain moist wound environment
Collagen (eg, *CellerateRX Gel/Powder, Fibracol, Kollagen-Medifil* Particles/Gel/Pads, *Promogran Matrix, Stimulen*)	Stage III & selected Stage IV (refer to package insert) Light, moderate, or heavy exudate Chronic, nonhealing ulcers Nonadherent, absorbent, biodegradable gel Accommodates to wound surface May be combined with topical agents Change dressing q1–3d	Sensitivity to collagen or bovine products Avoid use with necrotic ulcers Rehydration may be needed
Collagen with silver (eg, *ColActive AG, Prisma Matrix*)	Infected Stage III & selected Stage IV ulcers Highly colonized ulcers Light, moderate, or heavy exudate Antibacterial Leave in place maximum of 7 d	Sensitivity to collagen, bovine products, or silver Inactivates enzymatic debriding agents

Source: Copyright © 2014 by Rita Frantz. Used with permission.

Surgical Repair
Surgical referral is warranted for Stage IV pressure ulcers and for severely undermined or tunneled wounds.

VENOUS ULCERS
Definition
Any lesion caused by venous insufficiency precipitated by venous HTN

Wound Assessment
- See Chronic Wound Assessment (p 293).
- Assess lower-extremity edema.
- Assess pedal pulses to exclude ischemic ulcers.

Management
Compression Therapy
- Essential component of venous ulcer tx decreases healing time and pain
- Provides externally applied pressure to lower extremity to facilitate normal venous return
- Therapeutic level of compression is 30–40 mmHg at ankle, decreasing toward knee
- Avoid compression tx when ABI ≤0.8
- Types of compression tx:
  - Static compression device
    - Layered compression wraps *(Profore, ProGuide, Dynapress)*
    - Short-stretch wraps *(Comprilan)*
    - Paste-containing bandages *(Unna's boot, Duke boot)*
      - Preferable for actively ambulating patient; support compression of calf muscle "pump"
  - Dynamic compression devices (indicated when static compression not feasible)
    - Pneumatic compression device (intermittent pneumatic pumps)
    - Powered devices that propel venous blood upward when applied to lower leg
  - Compression tx for long-term maintenance
    - Therapeutic compression stockings *(Jobst, Juzo, Sigvaris, Medi-Strumpf, Therapress Duo)*

Local Wound Care
In addition to recommendations under Chronic Wound Treatment (see p 293):
- Use exudate-absorbing dressings (eg, calcium alginate dressings, foam dressings)
- Use skin sealant to protect skin around wound from exudates
- Skin substitutes (eg, *Apligraf, Dermagraft, GammaGraft, OrCel, TransCyte*) containing growth factors present in skin may decrease wound healing time and decrease pain. Wound must be granular to be effective.
- Infected venous ulcers should be treated with systemic antibiotics because of development of resistant organisms with topical antibiotics.

Surgical Intervention
If manifestations of chronic venous insufficiency and ulceration are resistant to more conservative tx or if venous obstruction is present, surgical repair (eg, skin graft) is tx of choice.

SLEEP DISORDERS

CLASSIFICATION
- Circadian rhythm disorders (eg, jet lag)
- **Insomnia** (difficulty initiating or maintaining sleep, or poor quality sleep)
- Parasomnias (disorders of arousal, partial arousal, and sleep stage transition)
- Hypersomnea of central origin (eg, narcolepsy)
- **Sleep-related breathing disorders** (central and obstructive sleep apnea and sleep-related hypoventilation-hypoxia syndromes)
- **Sleep-related movement disorders** (eg, RLS, periodic limb movement disorder)

Bolded disorders are covered here. Others are covered in *JAGS* 2009;57:761–789.

INSOMNIA

Risk Factors and Aggravating Factors
Treatable Associated Medical and Psychiatric Conditions: adjustment disorders, anxiety, bereavement, cough, depression, dyspnea (cardiac or pulmonary), GERD, nocturia, pain, paresthesias, Parkinson disease, stress, stroke

Medications That Cause or Aggravate Sleep Problems: alcohol, antidepressants, β-blockers, bronchodilators, caffeine, clonidine, corticosteroids, diuretics, levodopa, methyldopa, nicotine, phenytoin, progesterone, quinidine, reserpine, sedatives, sympathomimetics including decongestants

Management
- For most patients, behavioral tx should be initial tx.
- Combined behavioral tx and pharmacotherapy is more effective than either alone.
- Sleep improvements are better sustained over time with behavioral tx, including discontinuing pharmacotherapy after acute tx.

Nonpharmacologic
- Stimulus control
  Measures recommended to improve sleep hygiene:
  - During the daytime:
    - Get out of bed at the same time each morning regardless of how much you slept the night before.
    - Exercise daily but not within 2 h of bedtime.
    - Get adequate exposure to bright light during the day.
    - Decrease or eliminate naps, unless necessary part of sleeping schedule.
    - Limit or eliminate alcohol, caffeine, and nicotine, especially before bedtime.
  - At bedtime:
    - If hungry, have a light snack before bed (unless there are symptoms of GERD or it is otherwise medically contraindicated), but avoid heavy meals at bedtime.
    - Don't use bedtime as worry time. Write down worries for next day and then don't think about them.
    - Sleep only in your bedroom.
    - Control nighttime environment, ie, comfortable temperature, quiet, dark.

- □ Wear comfortable bedclothes.
- □ If it helps, use soothing noise (eg, a fan or other appliance or a "white noise" machine).
- □ Remove or cover the clock.
- □ No television watching in the bedroom.
  - ▪ Maintain a regular sleeping time, but don't go to bed unless sleepy.
  - ▪ Develop a sleep ritual (eg, hot bath 90 min before bedtime followed by preparing for bed for 20–30 min, followed by 30–40 min of relaxation, meditation, or reading).
  - ▪ If unable to fall asleep within 15–20 min, get out of bed and perform soothing activity, such as listening to soft music or reading (but avoid exposure to bright light or computer screens).
- CBT combines multiple behavioral approaches (eg, sleep restriction, stimulus control, cognitive tx); preliminary evidence supports this can be delivered by telephone.
- Sleep restriction: reduce time in bed to estimated total sleep time (min 5 h) and increase by 15 min/wk when ratio of time asleep to time in bed is ≥90%.
- Relaxation techniques—physical (progressive muscle relaxation, biofeedback); mental (imagery training, meditation, hypnosis)
- Bright light: 2,500 lux for 2 h/d to 10,000 lux for 30 min/d

Pharmacologic—Principles of Prescribing Medications for Sleep Disorders:
- Combine with behavior tx rather than give medication alone.
- Use lowest effective dose.
- All increase risk of falls.
- Do not use OTC antihistamines to treat insomnia in older adults.
- For patients with anxiety at bedtime, consider SSRIs or buspirone.
- For sleep-onset insomnia, use a shorter-acting agent (eg, zolpidem, zaleplon). For sleep-maintenance insomnia, use a longer-acting agent (eg, eszopiclone, zolpidem ER, doxepin).
- Use intermittent dosing (2–4 times/wk).
- Prescribe medications for short-term use (no more than 3–4 wk).
- D/C medication gradually.
- Be alert for rebound insomnia after discontinuation.

Table 131. Useful Medications for Sleep Disorders in Older Adults

Class, Medication	Usual Dose	Formulations	Half-life	Comments (Metabolism, Excretion)
Antidepressant, sedating				
Trazodone▲ (Desyrel)	25–100 mg	T: 50, 100, 150, 300	12 h	Moderate orthostatic effects; effective for insomnia with or without depression (L)
Doxepin (Silenor)	3–6 mg	T: 3, 6	15.3 h	May cause next-day sedation; many potential drug interactions
Benzodiazepines, intermediate-acting[a]				
Estazolam▲ (ProSom)	0.5–1 mg	T: 1, 2	12–18 h	Rapidly absorbed, effective in initiating sleep; slightly active metabolites that may accumulate (K)

(cont.)

Table 131. Useful Medications for Sleep Disorders in Older Adults (cont.)

Class, Medication	Usual Dose	Formulations	Half-life	Comments (Metabolism, Excretion)
Lorazepam▲ (Ativan)	0.25–2 mg	T: 0.5, 1, 2	8–12 h	Effective in initiating and maintaining sleep; associated with falls, memory loss, rebound insomnia (K)
Temazepam▲ (Restoril)	7.5–15 mg	C: 7.5, 15, 30	8–10 h[b]	Daytime drowsiness may occur with repeated use; effective for sleep maintenance; delayed onset of effect (K)
Nonbenzodiazepines, short-acting[a]				
Eszopiclone (Lunesta)	1–2 mg	T: 1, 2, 3	5–6 h	CYP3A4 interactions; avoid administration with high-fat meal; not for tx of anxiety (L)
Zaleplon▲ (Sonata)	5 mg	C: 5, 10	1 h	Avoid taking with alcohol or food (L)
Zolpidem▲ (Ambien)	5 mg	T: 5, 10	1.5–4.5 h[c]	Confusion and agitation may occur but are rare (L)
(Ambien CR)	6.25 mg	T: 6.25, 12.5	1.6–5.5 h	Do not divide, crush, or chew
(Zolpimist)	5 mg	Spr: 5 mg/spr	2–3 h	Spray over tongue; absorption more rapid
(Intermezzo)	1.75 mg	SL: 1.75, 3.5	2.4 h	SL: For middle-of-the-night insomnia
(Edluar)	5 mg	T: 5, 10 (sl)	2.8 h	
Hormone and Hormone Receptor Agonist				
Melatonin▲	0.3–5 mg	various	1 h	Not regulated by FDA
Ramelteon (Rozerem)	8 mg within 30 min of bedtime	T: 8	Ramelteon: 1–2.6 h; active metabolite: 2–5 h	Do not administer with or immediately after high-fat meal (L, K)

[a] May cause severe allergic reactions and complex sleep-related behavioral disturbances
[b] Can be as long as 30 h in older adults
[c] 3 h in older adults; 10 h in those with hepatic cirrhosis

SLEEP APNEA

Definition
Repeated episodes of apnea (cessation of airflow for ≥10 sec) or hypopnea (transient reduction [≥30% decrease in thoracoabdominal movement or airflow and with ≥4% oxygen desaturation, or an arousal] of airflow for ≥10 sec) during sleep with excessive daytime sleepiness or altered cardiopulmonary function. Predicts future strokes and cognitive impairment. HF (in men), and all-cause mortality (if severe).

Classification
Obstructive (OSA) (90% of cases): Airflow cessation as a result of upper airway closure in spite of adequate respiratory muscle effort
• Mild apnea-hypopnea index (AHI): 5–15
• Moderate: AHI 15–30
• Severe: AHI: >30

Central (CSA): Cessation of respiratory effort
Mixed: Features of both obstructive and central

Associated Risk Factors

Family hx, increased neck circumference, male gender, Asian ethnicity, hx of hypothyroidism (in women), obesity, smoking, upper airway structural abnormalities (eg, soft palate, tonsils), HTN, HF, atrial fibrillation, stroke

Clinical Features

Excessive daytime sleepiness, snoring, choking or gasping on awakening, morning headache, nocturia

Evaluation

- Epworth Sleepiness Scale (www.umm.edu/sleep/epworth_sleep.htm) is useful for documenting and monitoring daytime sleepiness.
- Full night's sleep study (polysomnography) in sleep laboratory is indicated for those who habitually snore and either report daytime sleepiness or have observed apnea.
- Results are reported as AHI, which is the number of episodes of apneas and hypopneas per hour of sleep.
- Medicare reimbursement threshold for CPAP based on a minimum of 2 h sleep by polysomnography is AHI (1) ≥15 or (2) ≥5 and ≤14 with documented symptoms of excessive daytime sleepiness, impaired cognition, mood disorders, or insomnia, or documented HTN, ischemic heart disease, or hx of stroke.

Management

Nonpharmacologic

- Weight loss (eg, using very low-calorie diet) with active lifestyle counseling is effective in mild and probably more severe OSA.
- Exercise (eg, 150 min/wk [4 d/wk] moderate intensity aerobic exercise, even in the absence of weight loss, can improve symptoms.
- Bariatric surgery improves but does not cure moderate or severe OSA.
- CPAP by nasal mask, nasal prongs, or mask that covers the nose and mouth is considered initial tx for clinically important sleep apnea. CPAP may also improve the metabolic syndrome associated with OSA. A short course (14 d) of eszopiclone may facilitate adherence when initiating CPAP.
- Oral appliances that keep the tongue in an anterior position during sleep or keep the mandible forward; less effective than CPAP in reducing AHI but may be better tolerated. Generally used in mild to moderate OSA (AHI <30) for patients who do not want CPAP.
- For moderate sleep apnea (>15 and <30 AHI), oropharyngeal exercises, including tongue, soft palate, and lateral pharyngeal wall, performed daily improves symptoms and reduces AHI.
- Avoidance of alcohol or sedatives.
- Lying in lateral rather than supine position; may be facilitated by soft foam ball in a backpack.
- Weight loss (obese patients) via dieting or bariatric surgery.

Pharmacologic

- Modafinil *(Provigil)* 200 mg qam for excessive daytime sleepiness (CYP3A4 inducer and CYP2C19 inhibitor) [T: 100, 200]; use in addition to (not instead of) CPAP

Surgical

- Palatal implants (for mild to moderate OSA)
- Tracheostomy (indicated for patients with severe apnea who cannot tolerate positive pressure or when other interventions are ineffective)
- Uvulopalatopharyngoplasty (curative in fewer than 50% of cases). Less invasive alternatives include laser-assisted uvulopalatoplasty, radiofrequency ablation, and maxillomandibular advancement. All decrease the AHI but have not been demonstrated to be superior to medical management.
- Maxillofacial surgery (rare cases)

SLEEP-RELATED MOVEMENT DISORDERS

Nocturnal Leg Cramps

No nonpharmacologic approaches have demonstrated effectiveness. Despite evidence of effectiveness, quinine is not recommended for nocturnal leg cramps because of the potential for serious though uncommon AEs. Small studies have supported the use of vitamin B complex and diltiazem. Gabapentin has been used but with little evidence to support its effectiveness. There is no evidence to support the effectiveness of magnesium.

Restless Legs Syndrome (RLS; the majority will also have periodic limb movement disorder)
Diagnostic Criteria

- A compelling urge to move the limbs, usually associated with paresthesias or dysesthesias
- Motor restlessness (eg, floor pacing, tossing and turning in bed, rubbing legs)
- Vague discomfort, usually bilateral, most commonly in calves
- Symptoms occur while awake and are exacerbated by rest, especially at night
- Symptoms relieved by movement—jerking, stretching, or shaking of limbs; pacing

Secondary Causes: Iron deficiency, spinal cord and peripheral nerve lesions, uremia, diabetes, Parkinson disease, venous insufficiency, medications/drugs (eg, TCAs, SSRIs, lithium, dopamine antagonists, caffeine)
Nonpharmacologic Treatment

- Sleep hygiene measures (see p 304).
- Avoid alcohol, caffeine, nicotine.
- Rub limbs.
- Use hot or cold baths, whirlpools.

Pharmacologic Treatment

- Exclude or treat iron deficiency, peripheral neuropathy. Some recommend a trial of iron tx in all patients with RLS, although there is inconsistent evidence to support this.
- If possible, avoid SSRIs, TCAs, lithium, and dopamine antagonists.

Start at low dosage, increase as needed. AASM recommendations:

- Standard medications (best benefit/burden and higher quality of evidence): Dopamine agonists pramipexole (begin at 0.125 mg) or ropinirole (begin at 0.25 mg) 1 h before time of usual onset of symptoms (see **Table 90**).
- Guideline medications (less favorable benefit/burden or lower quality of evidence)
  - Carbidopa-levodopa *(Sinemet)* 25/100 mg, 1–2 h before bedtime. Symptom augmentation may develop earlier in the day (eg, afternoon instead of evening) and may be more severe with carbidopa-levodopa; tx may require reducing dosage or switching to dopamine agonist

- ○ Gabapentin ER formulation, gabapentin enacarbil (*Horizant*) 600 mg [T: 600] daily at 5 PM, has been FDA approved for RLS
- ○ Low-dose opioids
- ○ Cabergoline *(Dostinex)* beginning 0.25 mg twice per wk; [T: 0.5] may also be effective but has potential for causing valvular heart disease.
- Optional medications (lower quality of evidence): carbamazepine, gabapentin, pregabalin (see **Table 91**), clonidine, and for patients with low ferritin levels, iron supplementation.

Periodic Limb Movement Disorder (a minority will also have RLS)
Diagnostic Criteria
- Insomnia or excessive sleepiness
- Repetitive, highly stereotyped limb muscle movements (eg, extension of big toes with partial flexion of ankle, knee, and sometimes hip) that occur during nonREM sleep
- Polysomnographic monitoring showing >15 episodes of muscle contractions per hour and associated arousals or awakenings
- No evidence of a medical, mental, or other sleep disorder that can account for symptoms

Treatment: Indicated for clinically significant sleep disruption or frequent arousals documented on a sleep study.
- Nonpharmacologic: See sleep hygiene measures, p 304.
- Pharmacologic: See RLS, Pharmacologic Treatment, above.

Rapid-Eye Movement (REM) Sleep Behavior Disorder
- Loss of atonia during REM sleep (ranging from simple limb twitches to acting out dreams), exaggeration of features of REM sleep (eg, nightmares), and intrusion of aspects of REM sleep into wakefulness (eg, sleep paralysis)
- High risk of developing neurodegenerative disorder (eg, Parkinson disease, multisystem atrophy, Lewy body dementia)

Pharmacologic Treatment: clonazepam 0.25–1 mg hs, high-dose melatonin 3–6 mg; if associated with Parkinson disease, levodopa, or pramipexole

SLEEP DISORDERS IN LONG-TERM–CARE FACILITIES
Risk Factors
- Medical and medication factors (see insomnia, p 304)
- Environmental factors (eg, little physical activity, infrequent daytime bright light exposure, extended periods in bed, nighttime noise and light interruptions)

Nonpharmacologic Treatment
- Morning bright light tx
- Exercise (eg, stationary bicycle, Tai Chi) and physical activity
- Reduction of nighttime noise and light interruptions
- Multicomponent interventions combining the above and a bedtime routine

Pharmacologic
One small study in a long-term–care facility demonstrated benefit of a supplement (5 mg melatonin, 225 mg magnesium, and 11.25 mg zinc, mixed with 100 g of pear pulp) 1 h before bedtime.

SCOPE OF THE PROBLEM

- Alcohol abuse is the primary substance abuse problem of those ≥50 yr old.
- Baby boomers are likely to maintain higher alcohol consumption than the current cohort of older people.
- 10% of people >65 yr old (12% of men, 8% of women) are current smokers.
- Marijuana use is higher than use of any other illicit drug among baby boomers.
- Although supporting data are sparse, prescription drug misuse is an important problem in the older population.

ALCOHOL USE DISORDERS

Evaluation

Alcohol use disorders are often missed in older adults because of reduced social and occupational functioning; signs more often are poor self-care, malnutrition, and medical illness. Because these disorders occur along a spectrum, it is recommended that all adults are screened for use with validated questionnaires that include the following:

- How many days per week?
- How many drinks on those days?
- Maximal intake on any one day?
- What type (ie, beer, wine, or liquor)?
- What is in "a drink"?

Hazardous or At-Risk Drinking

- Will probably eventually cause harm
- No current alcohol problems
- The National Institute on Alcohol Abuse and Alcoholism (NIAAA) defines at-risk drinking for men as 15 or more drinks/wk or 5 or more on one occasion and for women and anyone >65 yr old as ≥8 drinks/wk or ≥4 drinks on one occasion.
- A standard drink is 12 oz beer, 5 oz of wine, or 1.5 oz of 80-proof liquor.
- Medicare pays for annual screening and up to 4 brief counseling sessions for patients with at-risk drinking who are not yet experiencing adverse effects to their mental or emotional health. No copay or deductible when provided by a primary care provider who accepts assignment.

Harmful Drinking

- Already causing damage to physical or mental health
- Damage may be acute (eg, acute pancreatitis) or chronic (eg, alcohol-related brain damage).
- Do not usually seek tx.

Dependent Drinking (≥3 of the following in the previous year)

- A strong desire or compulsion to drink
- Physiologic withdrawal syndrome (tremors, sweating, anxiety, nausea and vomiting, agitation, insomnia)

- Persistent drinking despite clear evidence of harm
- Difficulty controlling drinking
- Evidence of tolerance
- Neglect of other pursuits because of drinking

Alcohol Misuse Screening: CAGE questionnaire has been validated in the older population.

C Have you ever felt you should **C**ut down?

A Does others' criticism of your drinking **A**nnoy you?

G Have you ever felt **G**uilty about drinking?

E Have you ever had an "**E**ye opener" to steady your nerves or get rid of a hangover?

(Positive response to any suggests problem drinking.)

Aggravating Factors

Alcohol and Aging: Higher blood concentrations per amount consumed due to decreased lean body mass and total body water; concomitant medications may interact with alcohol. Abstain if cognitively impaired, on medications that interact, or comorbidities or disability are present.

Age-related Diseases: Cognitive impairment, HTN.

Medications: Many drug interactions, eg, APAP, anesthetics, antihypertensives, antihistamines, antipsychotics, narcotic analgesics, NSAIDs, sedatives, antidepressants, anticonvulsant medications, nitrates, β-blockers, oral hypoglycemic agents, anticoagulants.

Management of Alcohol Use Disorders

Psychosocial Interventions:

- Hazardous or harmful drinking: Brief intervention; educate patient on effects of current drinking, point out current AEs, specify safe drinking limits (see Medicare Counseling, p 310). Patients who cannot moderate should abstain.
- Dependent drinking: Self-help groups (eg, Alcoholics Anonymous); professional help (eg, psychodynamic, CBT, counseling, social support, family tx, age-specific inpatient or outpatient).
- The NIAAA provides an online resource: Helping Patients Who Drink Too Much: A Clinician's Guide (www.niaaa.nih.gov/guide).

Drug Therapy: Is useful only when used as an adjunct to psychosocial tx.

- Naltrexone▲ *(Depade, REVIA, Trexan)* 25 mg × 2 d po, then 50 mg/d [T: 50]; *(Vivitrol)* 380 mg IM monthly; monitor LFTs, avoid in kidney failure, hepatitis, cirrhosis, and with opioid use; ~10% get nausea, headache (L, K).
- Acamprosate *(Campral)* 666 mg q8h po, reduce dosage to 333 mg q8h if CrCl 30–50 mL/min or weight <132 lb (60 kg) [T: 333]; contraindicated if CrCl <30 mL/min; diarrhea is most common adverse drug event (K). Large US trials have not shown efficacy.
- Topiramate▲ 300 mg/d po is effective at reducing relapse. The magnitude of the effect may be greater than with either acamprosate or naltrexone.

- The duration of drug tx should be at least 3 mo, or up to 12 mo, which is the period when relapse is highest.
- Combining these agents does not improve effectiveness.
- If significant depression persists after 1 wk of abstinence, tx for depression improves outcomes.

Acute Alcohol Withdrawal: See p 70.

SMOKING CESSATION

Nonpharmacologic Therapy
What Health Providers Should Do:
- **Ask** about tobacco use at every visit. **Advise** all users to quit. **Assess** willingness to quit. **Assist** the patient with a quit plan, education, pharmacotherapy.

Making the Decision to Quit:
Patients are more likely to stop smoking if they believe they could get a smoking-related disease and can make an honest attempt at quitting, that the benefits of quitting outweigh the benefits of continued smoking, or if they know someone who has had health problems as a result of smoking.

Setting a Quit Date and Deciding on a Plan:
Pick a specific day within the next month (gives time to develop a plan). Will nicotine replacement tx be used? Will the patient attend a smoking cessation class? On quit day, get rid of all cigarettes and related items.

Managing Symptoms of Withdrawal:
- **Physical:** Pharmacotherapy (see **Table 132**) helps physical symptoms.
  - Nicotine replacement, bupropion, and varenicline are all effective in improving quit rates.
    - Nicotine replacement is contraindicated with recent MI, uncontrolled high BP, arrhythmias, severe angina, gastric ulcer
    - May not be needed if patient smokes fewer than 10 cigarettes/d.
    - The long-term benefits of combining pharmacotherapies remain uncertain.

- **Psychological:**
  - Avoid people and places where tempted to smoke.
  - Alter habits: 1) switch to juices or water instead of alcohol or coffee, (2) take a walk instead of a coffee break, 3) use oral substitutions, eg, sugarless gum or hard candy.
  - Effective interventions include advice from health care provider to quit, self-help materials, proactive telephone counseling, group counseling, individual counseling, intra-tx social support (from a clinician), extra-tx social support (family, friends, coworkers, and smoke-free home).
  - Programs that include counseling in person or by telephone increase quit rates by 10–25% when combined with pharmacotherapy.
  - Medicare pays for up to 8 face-to-face visits/yr focused on counseling for smoking cessation. If there is no smoking-related disease, there is no copay.
  - Allowing the option to quit gradually may be more effective than programs focused on abrupt cessation.

Maintaining Smoking Cessation: Use the same methods that helped during withdrawal.

Source: Adapted from www.goldcopd.org.

Table 132. Pharmacotherapy for Tobacco Abuse

Drug	Dosage	Formulations	Comments (Metabolism, Excretion)
Tobacco Abuse			
Bupropion▲ *(Wellbutrin SR, Zyban)*	150 mg q12h × 7–12 wk	SR: 100, 150	Contraindicated with seizure disorders (L)
Varenicline *(Chantix)* [a]	0.5 mg × 3 d, 0.5 mg q12h × 4 d, then 1 mg q12h × 12–24 wk or longer	0.5, 1	More effective than bupropion in 1 randomized placebo controlled trial for smoking cessation. AEs: nausea, vivid dreams, constipation, depression, suicide, small increased risk of cardiovascular events (L, K); reduce dosage if CrCl <30 mL/min
Nicotine Replacement			
Transdermal patches▲ (eg, *Habitrol, NicoDerm*)	21 mg/d × 4–8 wk[b] 14 mg/d × 2–4 wk 7 mg/d × 2–4 wk	7, 14, 21	Apply to clean, nonhairy skin on upper torso, rotate sites; start 14 mg/d with cardiovascular disease or body weight <100 lb or if smoking <10 cigarettes/d (L)
(Nicotrol)	15 mg/d × 8 wk[b] 10 mg/d × 4–6 wk 5 mg/d × 4–6 wk	5, 10, 15	Gradually released over 16 h (L)
(ProStep)	22 mg/d × 4–8 wk[b] 11 mg/d × 4–8 wk	11, 22	People <100 lb start at lower dosage; reduce or D/C after 4–8 wk (L)
Polacrilex gum▲ *(Nicorette)*	9–12 pieces/d	2, 4	Chew 1 piece when urge to smoke; usual 10–12/d, max 30/d; 4 mg if smoking >21 cigarettes/d (L)
Nasal spray *(Nicotrol NS)* [c]	1 spr each nostril q30–60min	0.5 mg/spr	Do not exceed 5 applications/h or 40 in 24 h (L)
Inhaler *(Nicotrol Inhaler)* [c]	6–16 cartridges/d	4 mg delivered/ cartridge	Max 16 cartridges/d with gradual reduction after 6–12 wk if needed (L)
Lozenge	1 po prn	2, 4	Do not exceed 20/d; do not bite or chew; wean over 12 wk
Lollipop[c]	1 po prn	1, 2, 3, 4	Place in mouth when urge to smoke; remove when craving passes; gradually reduce dose over 4–8 wk; do not exceed 7/d

[a] Partial nicotine agonist that eases withdrawal and blocks effects of nicotine if patients resume smoking.

[b] The next lower dosage is less toxic and probably equally effective.

[c] Available by prescription only.

PRESCRIPTION DRUG MISUSE AND ADDICTION

Definitions

- Misue: Use of a drug that was not prescribed, or using a drug for an experience or feelings it causes rather than for tx of a medical condition
- Addiction: Is characterized by behaviors that include one or more of the 4 Cs: Impaired **Control** over drug use; **Compulsive** use; **Continued** use despite harm; and **Craving**.

Note: Physical dependence to opioids in persons with persistent pain (see page 234) does not meet criteria for misuse or addiction, unless there are maladaptive behaviors (the 4 Cs).

Commonly Abused Prescription Medications

Although many prescription medications can be abused, according to the National Institute of Drug Abuse, the following 3 classes are abused most commonly:

- Opioids—usually prescribed to treat pain
- CNS depressants—used to treat anxiety and sleep disorders
- Stimulants—prescribed to treat attention deficit hyperactivity disorder and narcolepsy

Adverse Events

- Benzodiazepines: falls, mobility and ADL disability, cognitive impairment, motor vehicle accidents, pressure ulcers, UI
- Nonbenzodiazepine sedatives: anxiety, depression, nervousness, hallucinations, dizziness, headache, sleep-related behavioral disturbances
- Opioids: falls and fractures
- If there is a hx or current IV drug abuse, check for hepatitis C infection.

Assessing for Risk of Medication Misuse/Abuse

- Patient education on avoiding misuse is enhanced by a standard patient-prescriber agreement (eg, https://www.tirfremsaccess.com/TirfUI/rems/pdf/ppaf-form.pdf).
- General risk factors include use of a psychoactive drug with abuse potential, use of other substances (alcohol, tobacco, etc), female gender, possibly social isolation, and hx of mental health disorder.
- Addiction to opioids is uncommon in those without hx of substance abuse and in those being treated for pain.
- Screen for risk of opioid misuse/abuse with the Opioid Risk Tool (see p 332); this instrument differentiates low-risk from high-risk patients.

Detection of Medication Misuse/Abuse

- Detection relies on clinical judgment; monitor at-risk patients when prescribing benzodiazepines, stimulants, and opioid analgesics.
- Observe for behavior that may suggest nonadherence to prescribed medication schedule (eg, early fill request, frequent lost prescriptions).
- Record any suspicious drug-seeking or other aberrant behaviors observed or reported by others, along with actions taken.
- Document evaluation process, rationale for long-term tx, and periodic review of patient status.
- Ask about purchases of medication over the Internet. Controlled substances can readily be purchased through illegitimate Internet-based pharmacies.

Treatment for Prescription Drug Abuse/Misuse

- Opioids
  - May need to undergo medically supervised detoxification
  - Gradual tapering of opioids is necessary (see Adjustment of Dosage, p 233).
  - Behavioral tx, usually combined with medications (methadone, buprenorphine), *are* effective.
  - Opioid abuse-deterrent products (eg, *Embeda)* may reduce diversion. These agents do not have street value because they release naltrexone if not used as intended.
- CNS depressants or stimulants
  - Primary provider encouragement to reduce use
  - Short-term substitution of other medications (eg, trazodone) for sleep
  - Gradual slow tapering of the drug
  - CBTs that teach patients skills to cope more effectively with problems; if drug is used for sleep, specific CBT techniques are available (see Sleep Disorders, p 304).

COMMON DISORDERS

Breast Cancer

- Screen with Mammography (see **Table 105**) until age 70–74, perhaps longer in women with life expectancy >10 yrs.

Evaluation of Patients Over Age 65 with Newly Diagnosed Breast Cancer Should Consist of:

- Hx and physical exam
- Diagnostic bilateral mammography and ultrasound if indicated
- CBC, LFTs, serum alkaline phosphatase
- Assessment of:
  - life expectancy (see **Table 7**, p 9)
  - comorbidity (eg, Charlson Index); calculators available online
  - function (ADL and IADL see pp 323, 324 appendix)
- Considering life expectancy, comorbidity, and functional status, discuss goals of care with the patient.
- If the goal of care is cure or life prolongation, the next steps in evaluation are resection of the tumor and possibly sentinel lymph node (SLN) biopsy.
- Older women with clinically negative axillary exams, small (<2-cm tumors), and who will be treated with adjuvant HT may be managed without axillary surgery.
- If a SLN biopsy is positive, axillary lymph node (ALN) dissection is necessary to fully stage disease. Older women are more likely to experience morbidity and lymphedema after ALN dissection.
- Further evaluation depends on the stage of the disease as follows:
  - At Stage I and II no additional evaluation for metastatic disease is needed.
    - Stage I (tumor ≤2 cm), negative nodes (N0), or no more than microscopic (0.2 cm) disease
    - Stage II (tumor >2 and ≤5 cm) with either N0 or N1; or tumor >5 cm and N0. N1 has more than microscopic disease, and mobile nodes (not matted or fixed).
  - At Stage III patients need imaging for bone, liver and pulmonary metastases.
    - Stage III (tumor >5 cm) or tumor of any size with fixed or matted lymph nodes on clinical exam or tumor of any size that extends directly to the chest wall or skin.
  - Stage IV is tumor with metastasis.
- Obtain tumor markers
  - In women over 65 yr old, 85% of tumors are positive for estrogen receptor (ER) and/or progesterone receptor (PR), which predicts response to adjuvant HT.
  - Among women over 85 yr old, ER/PR expression shows a decreased frequency of PR and an increase in androgen receptor positivity.
  - HER2/*neu* overexpression is less common in the tumors of older women, but when present has the same adverse prognosis.

- Patients with limited life expectancy and those who are too ill or frail to undergo surgery for the primary tumor, and whose tumors are ER-positive can be offered tx with tamoxifen or an aromatase inhibitor.

Monitoring Women with a History of Breast Cancer:
- Hx, physical examination q6mo for 5 yr, then annually
- Increase surveillance for second primary in breasts, ovaries, colon, and rectum
- Annual mammography and monthly breast self-examination
- Annual pelvic examination for patients on tamoxifen (higher risk of uterine cancer)

Adjuvant Therapy For Breast Cancer

- *Oral Hormone Adjuvant Therapy:* Postmenopausal women with ER- or PR-positive tumors at high risk of recurrence (tumors >1 cm, or positive nodes) should be treated with oral adjuvant tx. Tx should include an aromatase inhibitor, which may be the initial tx. Options include an aromatase inhibitor for 5 yr, or sequential tx with tamoxifen for 2–3 yr followed by an aromatase inhibitor to complete 5 yr, or tamoxifen for 4.5–6 yr followed by an aromatase inhibitor for 5 yr. See **Table 133**.

- *Adjuvant Chemotherapy:* Is used after resection. Reduces risk of recurrence and improves survival, especially when risk of recurrence is >10% at 10 yr. Recurrence is reduced by 30–50% with greater benefit in ER-poor or -absent breast cancer.

- *Bisphosphonates:* Are commonly used in postmenopausal women on other adjuvant tx for breast cancer. Five yr of zoledronic acid improves invasive disease-free survival in postmenopausal but not premenopausal women.

- *Therapy for Metastatic Bone Disease:* Pamidronate or zoledronic acid reduces morbidity and delays time to onset of bone symptoms.

Vulvar Diseases
Non-neoplastic:
- Lichen sclerosus—Common on vulva of middle-aged and older women; porcelain white appearance in a classic hourglass distribution around the vulva, perineum, and perianal area. May be asymptomatic or cause itching, soreness, or dyspareunia. When clinical diagnosis is straight forward, tx: clobetasol propionate 0.05% q12–24h for 8–12 wk; then taper gradually to zero. Biopsy if diagnosis is in doubt, failure to respond to clobetasol, or if there are any suspicious areas. Lichen sclerosus is a precursor to VIN. Associated with squamous cell cancer in 4–5%. Long-term follow-up advised.
- Squamous hyperplasia—Raised white keratinized lesions difficult to distinguish from VIN; must biopsy to exclude malignancy. Tx: betamethasone dipropionate 0.05% for 6–8 wk, then 1% hydrocortisone if symptoms persist. Long-term follow-up advised.

Neoplastic:
- VIN may be asymptomatic or may cause pruritus; hypo- or hyperpigmented keratinized lesions; often multifocal; inspection ± colposcopy of the entire vulva with biopsy of most worrisome lesions; lesions graded on degree of atypia. Tx: surgical or other ablative tx. Imiquimod 5% topical crm often effective in human papillomavirus-positive patient.
- Vulvar malignancy—Half of cases are in women >70 yr old; 80% are squamous cell, with melanoma, sarcoma, basal cell, and adenocarcinoma <20%; biopsy any suspicious lesion. Tx: vulvectomy, radical local excision, or 3-incision surgical techniques.

Table 133. Oral Agents for Breast Cancer Treatment

Class, Medication	Dosage and Formulations	Monitoring	Adverse Events, Interactions (Metabolism)
Antiestrogen Drugs			
Fulvestrant (Faslodex)	250 mg/mo IM in 1 or 2 injections Inj: 250 mg/5 mL; 125 mg/2.5 mL	Blood chemistry, lipids	Metabolized through CYP3A4; GI reactions, anesthesia, pain (back, pelvic, headache), hot flushes (L)
Tamoxifen▲ᵃ (Nolvadex)	20 mg/d po T: 10, 20	Annual eye examination; endometrial cancer screening	Activated through CYP2D6; avoid fluoxetine, paroxetine, bupropion, duloxetine, and other potent CYPD26 inhibitors that reduce tamoxifen activity; ↑ risk of thrombosis (L)
Toremifene (Fareston)	60 mg/d po T: 60	CBC, Ca, LFTs, BUN, Cr	Drug interactions: CYP3A4–6 inhibitors and inducers; ↑ warfarin effect (L)
Aromatase Inhibitors			
Anastrozole (Arimidex)	1 mg/d po T: 1	Periodic CBC, lipids, serum chemistry profile	Common: arthritis, arthralgia, bone pain, asthenia, cough, dyspnea, pharyngitis, depression, headache, nausea, rash, edema. Less common: anemia, leukopenia, thromboembolism, thrombophlebitis, hypercholesterolemia, fractures, vaginal hemorrhage (L)
Exemestane (Aromasin)	25 mg/d po T: 25	Periodic WBC count with differential, lipids, serum chemistry profile	Common: anxiety, depression, fatigue, insomnia, dyspnea, hot flushes, weight gain, nausea, pain at tumor site. Rare: MI (L)
Letrozole (Femara)	2.5 mg/d po T: 2.5	Periodic CBC, LFTs, TSH	Common: arthralgia, back pain, bone pain, dyspnea, hot flushes, nausea. Less common: fracture, MI or ischemia, pancytopenia, thromboembolism, pleural effusion, PE. Metabolized by CYP3A4, CYP2A6; strongly inhibits CYP2A6 and moderately inhibits CYP2C19 (L)

ᵃ Reduce dosage if CrCl <10 mL/min

Postmenopausal Bleeding

Bleeding after 1 yr of amenorrhea:

- Exclude malignancy, identify source (vagina, cervix, vulva, uterus, bladder, bowel), treat symptoms.
- Examine genitalia, perineum, rectum.
- If endometrial source, use endometrial biopsy or vaginal probe ultrasound to assess endometrial thickness (<5 mm virtually excludes malignancy).
- D&C when endometrium not otherwise adequately assessed.

- Evaluation is needed for:
  - Women on combination continual estrogen and progesterone who bleed after 12 mo.
  - Women on cyclic replacement with bleeding at unexpected times (ie, bleeding other than during the second week of progesterone tx).
  - Women on unopposed estrogen who bleed at any time.

Vaginal Prolapse

- Child-bearing and other causes of increased intra-abdominal pressure weaken connective tissue and muscles supporting the genital organs, leading to prolapse.
- Symptoms include pelvic pressure, back pain, FI or UI, difficulty evacuating the rectum. Symptoms may be present even with mild prolapse.
- The degree of prolapse and organs involved dictate tx; no tx if asymptomatic.
- Estrogen and Kegel exercises (p 149) may help in mild cases.
- Pessary or surgery indicated with increase in symptoms. Surgery needed for fourth-degree symptomatic prolapse.
- Precise anatomic defect(s) dictates the surgical approach. Surgical closure of the vagina is a simple option for frail patients who are not sexually active.
- A common classification (ACOG) for degrees of prolapse:
  - First degree—extension to mid-vagina
  - Second degree—approaching hymenal ring
  - Third degree—at hymenal ring
  - Fourth degree—beyond hymenal ring

HORMONE THERAPY

Symptoms Associated with the Postmenopausal State

- Hot flushes and night sweats
- Sleep disturbances
- Vaginal dryness and dyspareunia
- Depression
- Insufficient evidence exists to link the following commonly reported symptoms to the postmenopausal state: cognitive disturbances, fatigue, sexual dysfunction.

Therapy for Menopausal Symptoms

- Vasomotor and vaginal symptoms respond to estrogen in a dose-response fashion; start at low dosage (eg, oral conjugated or esterified estrogen 0.3 mg/d, which should be combined with medroxyprogesterone in women with an intact uterus), titrate to effect. Dyspareunia and vaginal dryness respond to topical estrogen (see **Table 126** [Sexual Dysfunction chapter]).
- "Bioidentical hormone therapy" refers to the use of naturally occurring (rather than synthetic or animal-derived) forms of progesterone, estradiol, and estriol. These preparations are compounded by pharmacies and readily available over the Internet but are not FDA approved. The FDA and the Endocrine Society believe there is insufficient evidence to evaluate the safety and efficacy of these agents relative to FDA-approved HT.

Risk of Hormone Therapy

- Risks associated with HT use may vary based on the length of time between menopause and initiation of HT. For information on the risks and benefits of HT initiated within the first 5 yr after menopause, see the position statement of the North American Menopause Society (www.menopause.org/docs/default-document-library/psht12.pdf).

- For current understanding of risks for women who start HT ≥10 yr after menopause (generally >63 yr old), see **Table 134**.
- If the woman has a uterus, estrogen combined with progesterone reduces risk of endometrial cancer but increases breast cancer risk and mortality.
- Some women prefer unopposed estrogen and annual endometrial biopsy.
- Older women can get hot flushes if estrogen is discontinued suddenly. Tapering (eg, q48h for 1–2 mo and then q72h for a few months) is better tolerated.
- The fracture-protective effect from HT is lost rapidly after discontinuation; women at risk of fracture should be evaluated and treated with alternative tx (see Osteoporosis, p 222).

Table 134. Risks and Benefits of Systemic Hormone Therapy Initiated After Age 63

Systemic Outcome	Estrogen	Estrogen/Progesterone
MI	none	↑
Thromboembolic disease	↑ DVT	↑ DVT, PE
Stroke	↑	↑
Breast cancer	↓	↑[a]
Hip fracture	↓	↓
Colon cancer	none	uncertain
Kidney stones	↑	↑
Endometrial cancer	↑	no change or ↓
Gallbladder disease	↑	↑
Urogenital disease[b]	↓	↓
Dementia	possibly ↑	↑
Ovarian cancer	↑	↑

Note: ↑ = increased risk; ↓ = decreased risk
[a] Both incidence and breast cancer mortality are increased.
[b] Dyspareunia, UTI, and vaginal dryness; oral HT worsens UI

Contraindications to Hormone Therapy

- Undiagnosed vaginal bleeding
- Thromboembolic disease
- Breast cancer
- Prior stroke or TIA
- Endometrial cancer more advanced than Stage 1
- Possibly gallbladder disease
- CHD

Intolerable Vasomotor Symptoms

- 10% of women continue with vasomotor symptoms 12 yr after menopause.
- HT (estrogen and/or progesterone) is the most effective tx.
- Note contraindications above.
- Assess risk of VTE and cardiovascular disease:
  - VTE risk increased by hx of VTE, malignancy/myeloproliferative disorder, leg immobilization, or both smoking and obesity.
  - Cardiovascular disease risk increased by known CAD, PAD, AAA, carotid artery disease, DM, or risk factors that confer a 10-yr risk of coronary disease >20% (http://hp2010.nhlbihin.net/atpiii/calculator.asp)

- If increased cardiovascular or VTE risk, then oral standard dosage estrogen-progestin should not be used.
- If increased cardiovascular risk (but not VTE risk), attempt to control symptoms with transdermal estrogen.
- If risk of VTE is increased and risk of cardiovascular disease is usual and patient has no uterus, transdermal estrogen may be appropriate; if patient has uterus, adding a progestin raises additional concerns.
- If neither VTE nor cardiovascular disease risk is increased, estrogen (0.3–0.625 mg po daily for women who have had a hysterectomy) or estrogen-progestin (0.45/1.5 mg or 0.625/2.5 mg po daily, for those with an intact uterus) or transdermally at lowest dosage to control symptoms may be appropriate.
- Continue to advocate tapering (see p 320) at 2-yr intervals.
- If estrogen cannot be taken or if risks exceed benefits, try one of these alternatives. Expert opinion based on double-blind randomized trials and demonstrated safety and effectiveness suggests considering agents in the following sequence:
  ○ First, antidepressants: SSRIs: citalopram 10–20 mg/d; paroxetine 7.5–25 mg/d. Avoid SSRIs if patients are receiving tamoxifen; tamoxifen levels will be subtherapeutic. SNRIs: venlafaxine 75 mg/d; desvenlafaxine 50–200 mg/d
  ○ Second, anticonvulsants: gabapentin 900–2700 mg/d; pregabalin 75–300 mg/d
  ○ Third, α_2-Adrenergic agonists: clonidine 0.5–1.5 mg/d (Avoid in HTN[BC]); watch for orthostatic hypotension and rebound increase in BP if used intermittently. Common drug-related AEs: dry mouth, constipation, sedation.

Some assessment instruments commonly used in geriatrics practice are included on the following pages. These instruments, as well as some additional ones, are available on the *Geriatrics At Your Fingertips* Web site (see www.geriatricscareonline.org).

MINI-COG™ SCREEN FOR DEMENTIA

The Mini-Cog™ combines an uncued 3-item recall test with a clock-drawing test (CDT) that serves as the recall distractor. The Mini-Cog™ can be administered in about 3 min, requires no special equipment, and is less influenced by level of education or language differences than many other screens.

Administration

1. Get the patient's attention. Then instruct him or her to listen carefully to, repeat back to you, and remember (now and later) 3 unrelated words. You may present the same words up to 3 times if necessary.

2. Using a blank piece of paper or one with a circle already drawn on it, ask the patient to draw the face of a clock and fill in all the numbers. After he or she adds the numbers, ask him or her to draw the hands to read a specific time (11:10 or 8:20 are most commonly used; other times that use both halves of the clock face may be effective). You can repeat these instructions, but give no additional instructions or hints. If the patient cannot complete the CDT in 3 min or less, move on to the next step.

3. Ask the patient to repeat the 3 previously presented words. Score this step even if the patient was not able to repeat the words in step 1.

Scoring

Give 1 point for each recalled word after the CDT distractor. Score 0–3 for recall.

Give 2 points for a normal CDT, and 0 points for an abnormal CDT. The CDT is considered normal if all numbers are depicted, once each, in the correct sequence and position around the circle, and the hands readably display the requested time. Do not count equal hand length as an error. Add the recall and CDT scores together to get the Mini-Cog score:

- 0–2   positive screen for dementia.
- 3–5   negative screen for dementia.

Sources: Adapted from Borson S et al, *Int J Geriatr Psychiatry*, 2000; 15(11):1021–1027; Borson S et al, *Int J Geriatr Psychiatry*, 2006;21(4):349–355; and Lessig M et al, *Int Psychogeriatr*, 2008; 20(3):459–470.

PHYSICAL SELF-MAINTENANCE SCALE (ACTIVITIES OF DAILY LIVING, OR ADLS)

In each category, circle the item that most closely describes the person's highest level of functioning and record the score assigned to that level (either 1 or 0) in the blank at the beginning of the category.

A. Toilet ____
1. Care for self at toilet completely; no incontinence 1
2. Needs to be reminded, or needs help in cleaning self, or has rare (weekly at most)
   accidents. 0
3. Soiling or wetting while asleep more than once a week 0
4. Soiling or wetting while awake more than once a week 0
5. No control of bowels or bladder 0

B. Feeding ____
1. Eats without assistance. 1
2. Eats with minor assistance at meal times and/or with special preparation of food, or help in
   cleaning up after meals. 0
3. Feeds self with moderate assistance and is untidy. 0
4. Requires extensive assistance for all meals 0
5. Does not feed self at all and resists efforts of others to feed him or her 0

C. Dressing ____
1. Dresses, undresses, and selects clothes from own wardrobe 1
2. Dresses and undresses self with minor assistance 0
3. Needs moderate assistance in dressing and selection of clothes. 0
4. Needs major assistance in dressing but cooperates with efforts of others to help. 0
5. Completely unable to dress self and resists efforts of others to help 0

D. Grooming (neatness, hair, nails, hands, face, clothing) ____
1. Always neatly dressed and well-groomed without assistance 1
2. Grooms self adequately with occasional minor assistance, eg, with shaving. 0
3. Needs moderate and regular assistance or supervision with grooming. 0
4. Needs total grooming care but can remain well-groomed after help from others. 0
5. Actively negates all efforts of others to maintain grooming 0

E. Physical Ambulation ____
1. Goes about grounds or city 1
2. Ambulates within residence on or about one block distant. 0
3. Ambulates with assistance of (check one)
   a ( ) another person, b ( ) railing, c ( ) cane, d ( ) walker, e ( ) wheelchair 0
   1.__Gets in and out without help. 2.__Needs help getting in and out
4. Sits unsupported in chair or wheelchair but cannot propel self without help 0
5. Bedridden more than half the time 0

F. Bathing ____
1. Bathes self (tub, shower, sponge bath) without help. 1
2. Bathes self with help getting in and out of tub. 0
3. Washes face and hands only but cannot bathe rest of body. 0
4. Does not wash self but is cooperative with those who bathe him or her. 0
5. Does not try to wash self and resists efforts to keep him or her clean. 0

For scoring interpretation and source, see note after the next instrument.

INSTRUMENTAL ACTIVITIES OF DAILY LIVING SCALE (IADLS)

In each category, circle the item that most closely describes the person's highest level of functioning and record the score assigned to that level (either 1 or 0) in the blank at the beginning of the category.

A. Ability to Use Telephone   ____
1. Operates telephone on own initiative; looks up and dials numbers. 1
2. Dials a few well-known numbers. 1
3. Answers telephone but does not dial. 1
4. Does not use telephone at all. 0

B. Shopping   ____
1. Takes care of all shopping needs independently. 1
2. Shops independently for small purchases. 0
3. Needs to be accompanied on any shopping trip. 0
4. Completely unable to shop. 0

C. Food Preparation   ____
1. Plans, prepares, and serves adequate meals independently. 1
2. Prepares adequate meals if supplied with ingredients. 0
3. Heats and serves prepared meals or prepares meals but does not maintain adequate diet. 0
4. Needs to have meals prepared and served. 0

D. Housekeeping   ____
1. Maintains house alone or with occasional assistance (eg, domestic help for heavy work). 1
2. Performs light daily tasks such as dishwashing, bedmaking. 1
3. Performs light daily tasks but cannot maintain acceptable level of cleanliness. 1
4. Needs help with all home maintenance tasks. 1
5. Does not participate in any housekeeping tasks. 0

E. Laundry   ____
1. Does personal laundry completely. 1
2. Launders small items; rinses socks, stockings, etc. 1
3. All laundry must be done by others. 0

F. Mode of Transportation   ____
1. Travels independently on public transportation or drives own car. 1
2. Arranges own travel via taxi but does not otherwise use public transportation. 1
3. Travels on public transportation when assisted or accompanied by another. 1
4. Travel limited to taxi or automobile with assistance of another. 0
5. Does not travel at all. 0

G. Responsibility for Own Medications   ____
1. Is responsible for taking medication in correct dosages at correct time. .1
2. Takes responsibility if medication is prepared in advance in separate dosages. 0
3. Is not capable of dispensing own medication. 0

H. Ability to Handle Finances   ____
1. Manages financial matters independently (budgets, writes checks, pays rent and bills, goes to bank); collects and keeps track of income. 1
2. Manages day-to-day purchases but needs help with banking, major purchases, etc. 1
3. Incapable of handling money. 0

Scoring Interpretation: For ADLs, the total score ranges from 0 to 6, and for IADLs, from 0 to 8. In some categories, only the highest level of function receives a 1; in others, two or more levels have scores of 1 because each describes competence at some minimal level of function. These screens are useful for indicating specifically how a person is performing at the present time. When they are also used over time, they serve as documentation of a person's functional improvement or deterioration.

Sources: Lawton MP, Brody EM. *Gerontologist* 1969, 9:179–186. Copyright by the Gerontological Society of America. Reproduced by permission of the Gerontological Society of America.

PHQ-9 AND PHQ-2 QUICK DEPRESSION ASSESSMENT

PHQ-9 Instructions For Use: *for doctor or healthcare professional use only*

For initial diagnosis:

1. Patient completes PHQ-9 Quick Depression Assessment.

2. If there are at least 4 ✔s in the two right columns (including Questions #1 and #2), consider a depressive disorder. Add score to determine severity.

3. *Consider Major Depressive Disorder*
   - if there are at least 5 ✔s in the two right columns (one of which corresponds to Question #1 or #2).

   Consider Other Depressive Disorder
   - if there are 2 to 4 ✔s in the two right columns (one of which corresponds to Question #1 or #2).

Note: Since the questionnaire relies on patient self-report, all responses should be verified by the clinician, and a definitive diagnosis is made on clinical grounds, taking into account how well the patient understood the questionnaire, as well as other relevant information from the patient. Diagnoses of Major Depressive Disorder or Other Depressive Disorder also require impairment of social, occupational, or other important areas of functioning and ruling out normal bereavement, a history of a Manic Episode (Bipolar Disorder), and a physical disorder, medication, or other drug as the biological cause of the depressive symptoms.

To monitor severity over time for newly diagnosed patients or patients in current treatment for depression:

1. Patients may complete questionnaires at baseline and at regular intervals (eg, q2wk) at home and bring them in at their next appointment for scoring, or they may complete the questionnaire during each scheduled appointment.

2. Add up ✔s by column. For every ✔:
   "Several days" = 1   "More than half the days" = 2   "Nearly every day" = 3

3. Add together column scores to get a TOTAL score.

4. Refer to PHQ-9 Scoring to interpret the TOTAL score.

5. Results may be included in patients' files to assist you in setting up a treatment goal, determining degree of response, as well as guiding treatment intervention.

PHQ-9 Scoring For Severity Determination
for healthcare professional use only

Scoring—add up all checked boxes on PHQ-9
For every ✔: Not at all = 0; Several days = 1; More than half the days = 2; Nearly every day = 3

Interpretation of Total Score

Total Score	Depression Severity
0–4	None
5–9	Mild
10–14	Moderate
15–19	Moderately severe
20–27	Severe

PATIENT HEALTH QUESTIONNAIRE-9

Comments

Only the patient (subject) should enter information onto this questionnaire.

Over the *last 2 weeks*, how often have you been bothered by any of the following problems?	Not at all	Several days	More than half the days	Nearly every day
1. Little interest or pleasure in doing things*	0	1	2	3
2. Feeling down, depressed, or hopeless*	0	1	2	3
3. Trouble falling or staying asleep, or sleeping too much	0	1	2	3
4. Feeling tired or having little energy	0	1	2	3
5. Poor appetite or overeating	0	1	2	3
6. Feeling bad about yourself — or that you are a failure or have let yourself or your family down	0	1	2	3
7. Trouble concentrating on things, such as reading the newspaper or watching television	0	1	2	3
8. Moving or speaking so slowly that other people could have noticed? Or the opposite — being so fidgety or restless that you have been moving around a lot more than usual	0	1	2	3
9. Thoughts that you would be better off dead or of hurting yourself in some way	0	1	2	3

If you checked off *any* problems, how *difficult* have these problems made it for you to do your work, take care of things at home, or get along with other people?

Not difficult at all	Somewhat difficult	Very difficult	Extremely difficult
☐	☐	☐	☐

Developed by Drs. Robert L. Spitzer, Janet B.W. Williams, Kurt Kroenke and colleagues, with an educational grant from Pfizer Inc.

* indicates questions of the PHQ-2

I confirm this information is accurate.	Patient's/Subject's initials:	Date:

PHQ-2 Instructions For Use: *for doctor or healthcare professional use only*
The first two questions of the PHQ-9 are often referred to as the PHQ-2. These questions are scored in the same way as the PHQ-9, but are used as an initial screening tool to get a sense of depressed mood and anhedonia over the last 2 wk. The PHQ-2 is not designed to establish a diagnosis of depression, but is used to determine whether the rest of the questions in the PHQ-9 are to be asked. PHQ-2 scores range from 0 to 6, with 3 as the typical score to trigger asking the remaining questions of the PHQ-9.

RAPID ESTIMATE OF ADULT LITERACY IN MEDICINE—SHORT FORM (REALM-SF)

The Rapid Estimate of Adult Literacy in Medicine—Short Form (REALM-SF) is a 7-item word recognition test to provide clinicians with a valid quick assessment of patient health literacy. The REALM-SF has been validated and field tested in diverse research setting, and has excellent agreement with the 66-item REALM instrument in terms of grade-level assignments.

REALM-SF Form

Patient name _____ Date of birth _____ Reading level _____

Date _____ Examiner _____ Grade completed _____

Menopause	☐
Antibiotics	☐
Exercise	☐
Jaundice	☐
Rectal	☐
Anemia	☐
Behavior	☐

Instructions for Administering the REALM-SF

1. Give the patient a laminated copy of the REALM-SF form and score answers on an unlaminated copy that is attached to a clipboard. Hold the clipboard at an angle so that the patient is not distracted by your scoring. Say:

   "I want to hear you read as many words as you can from this list. Begin with the first word and read aloud. When you come to a word you cannot read, do the best you can or say, 'blank' and go onto the next word."

2. If the patient takes more than five seconds on a word, say 'blank' and point to the next word, if necessary, to move the patient along. If the patient begins to miss every word, have him or her pronounce only known words.

Scores and Grade Equivalents for the REALM-SF

Score	Grade range
0	Third grade and below; will not be able to read most low-literacy materials; will need repeated oral instructions, materials composed primarily of illustrations, or audio or video tapes.
1–3	Fourth to sixth grade; will need low-literacy materials, may not be able to read prescription labels.
4–6	Seventh to eighth grade; will struggle with most patient education materials; will not be offended by low-literacy materials.
7	High school; will be able to read most patient education materials.

Health Literacy Measurement Tools. January 2009. Agency for Healthcare Research and Quality, Rockville, MD. http://www.ahrq.gov/populations/sahlsatool.htm

KARNOFSKY SCALE

This 10-point scale is a quick and easy way to indicate how a person is feeling on a given day, without going through several multiple-choice questions or symptom surveys.

Score	Description
100	Able to work; normal, no complaints, no evidence of disease
90	Able to work; able to carry on normal activity, minor symptoms
80	Able to work; normal activity with effort, some symptoms
70	Unable to work or carry on normal activity, cares for self independently
60	Mildly disabled, dependent; requires occasional assistance, cares for most needs
50	Moderately disabled, dependent; requires considerable assistance and frequent care
40	Severely disabled, dependent; requires special care and assistance
30	Severely disabled; hospitalized, death not imminent
20	Very sick; active supportive treatment needed
10	Moribund; fatal processes rapidly progressing

Source: Karnofsky DA, Burchenal JH. The clinical evaluation of chemotherapeutic agents in cancer. In: MacLeon CM, ed. *Evaluation of Chemotherapeutic Agents.* Columbia University Press; 1949:196.

PALLIATIVE PERFORMANCE SCALE, VERSION 2 (PPSv2)

PPS Level (%)	Ambulation	Activity and Evidence of Disease	Self-care	Intake	Conscious Level
100	Full	Normal activity and work, no evidence of disease	Full	Normal	Full
90	Full	Normal activity and work, some evidence of disease	Full	Normal	Full
80	Full	Normal activity with effort, some evidence of disease	Full	Normal or reduced	Full
70	Reduced	Unable to do normal job or work, significant disease	Full	Normal or reduced	Full
60	Reduced	Unable to do hobby or housework, significant disease	Occasional assistance required	Normal or reduced	Full or confusion
50	Mainly sit/lie	Unable to do any work, extensive disease	Considerable assistance required	Normal or reduced	Full or confusion
40	Mainly in bed	Unable to do most activity, extensive disease	Mainly assistance	Normal or reduced	Full or drowsy, ± confusion
30	Totally bed bound	Unable to do any activity, extensive disease	Total care	Normal or reduced	Full or drowsy, ± confusion
20	Totally bed bound	Unable to do any activity, extensive disease	Total care	Minimal to sips	Full or drowsy, ± confusion
10	Totally bed bound	Unable to do any activity, extensive disease	Total care	Mouth care only	Drowsy or coma, ± confusion
0	Death	—	—	—	—

Instructions: PPS level is determined by reading left to right to find a 'best horizontal fit.' Begin at left column reading downwards until current ambulation is determined, then read across to next and downwards until each column is determined. Thus, 'leftward' columns take precedence over 'rightward' columns. Also, see 'definitions of terms' for interpretation of PPSv2 and complete instructions at www.victoriahospice.org. Victoria Hospice Society©

Palliative Performance Scale, Version 2 (PPSv2). *Medical Care of the Dying, 4th ed.* Victoria, BC, Canada: Victoria Hospice Society; 2006:120-121. Reprinted with permission.

REISBERG FUNCTIONAL ASSESSMENT STAGING (FAST) SCALE

This 16-item scale is designed to parallel the progressive activity limitations associated with AD. Stage 7 identifies the threshold of activity limitation that would support a prognosis of ≤6 mo remaining life expectancy.

FAST Scale Item	Activity Limitation Associated with AD
Stage 1	No difficulty, either subjectively or objectively
Stage 2	Complains of forgetting location of objects; subjective work difficulties
Stage 3	Decreased job functioning evident to coworkers; difficulty in traveling to new locations
Stage 4	Decreased ability to perform complex tasks (eg, planning dinner for guests, handling finances)
Stage 5	Requires assistance in choosing proper clothing
Stage 6	Decreased ability to dress, bathe, and toilet independently
Substage 6a	Difficulty putting clothing on properly
Substage 6b	Unable to bathe properly, may develop fear of bathing
Substage 6c	Inability to handle mechanics of toileting (ie, forgets to flush, does not wipe properly)
Substage 6d	Urinary incontinence
Substage 6e	Fecal incontinence
Stage 7	Loss of speech, locomotion, and consciousness
Substage 7a	Ability to speak limited (1–5 words a day)
Substage 7b	All intelligible vocabulary lost
Substage 7c	Nonambulatory
Substage 7d	Unable to smile
Substage 7e	Unable to hold head up

Source: Reisberg, B., *Psychopharmacol Bull* 1988;24(4):653–659.

AUA INTERNATIONAL PROSTATE SYMPTOM SCORE (IPSS) SYMPTOM INDEX FOR BPH

Questions to be answered (circle one number on each line)	Not at all	Less than 1 time in 5	Less than half the time	About half the time	More than half the time	Almost always
1. Over the past month or so, how often have you had a sensation of not emptying your bladder completely after you finished urinating?	0	1	2	3	4	5
2. Over the past month or so, how often have you had to urinate again less than 2 hours after you finished urinating?	0	1	2	3	4	5
3. Over the past month or so, how often have you found you stopped and started again several times when you urinated?	0	1	2	3	4	5
4. Over the past month or so, how often have you found it difficult to postpone urination?	0	1	2	3	4	5
5. Over the past month or so, how often have you had a weak urinary stream?	0	1	2	3	4	5
6. Over the past month or so, how often have you had to push or strain to begin urination?	0	1	2	3	4	5
7. Over the last month, how many times did you most typically get up to urinate from the time you went to bed at night until the time you got up in the morning?	none	1 time	2 times	3 times	4 times	>5 times

AUA Symptom Score = sum of responses to questions 1–7 =_____. For interpretation, see p 262.

Source: Barry MJ, et al. *J Urol* 1992;148(5):1549–1557. Reprinted with permission.

OPIOID RISK TOOL*

Factor	Score**	
	Women	*Men*
Family hx of substance abuse		
Alcohol	1	3
Illegal drugs	2	3
Prescription drugs	4	4
Personal hx of substance abuse		
Alcohol	3	3
Illegal drugs	4	4
Prescription drugs	5	5
Age (if between 16 and 45)	1	1
Hx of preadolescent sexual abuse	3	0
Psychological disease		
Attention-deficit disorder, obsessive-compulsive disorder, bipolar, schizophrenia	2	2
Depression	1	1
TOTAL		

* Main drawback is susceptibility to deception.
** Scoring: 0–3 = low risk, 4–7 = moderate risk, ≥8 = high risk

Note: Adapted from Webster LR, et al. *Pain Med* 2005;6:432–442.

Coding in Geriatrics

Source: Peter Hollmann, MD, AGSF, 9/23/13

Geriatricians focus on Medicare, but private payers including Medicare Advantage plans may use other valid CPT and HCPCS codes. Every procedure code (CPT or HCPCS) must be accompanied with a diagnosis code (ICD-9, to be replaced with ICD-10 October 2014). These codes are particularly relevant for services performed by geriatrics healthcare professionals.

Common Procedure Codes		
Procedure Code	**Description**	**Reference/Notes**
Evaluation and Management		Documentation Guidelines available at: http://www.cms.gov/Outreach-and-Education/Medicare-Learning-Network-MLN/MLNEdWebGuide/EMDOC.html
99201-99215	Office/Outpatient Visits	Also used for Consultations by Medicare
99217-99220 99224-99226 99234-99236	Observation Services	Consultations in Observation are Office/Outpatient codes
99221-99223 99231-99233 99238-99239	Hospital Inpatient Services	Also use for Consultations by Medicare
99241-99245 99251-99255	Consultations	Invalid for Medicare, may be used by other payers
99291-99292	Critical Care	Used in all settings of care, geriatrician relevant
99304-99318	Nursing Facility Services	
99324-99327	Domicilliary Care (eg, ALF)	
99341-99350	Home Services	
99354-99357	Prolonged Services	Time-based codes, track/report time
99387, 99397	Comprehensive Preventive Medicine	Noncovered Medicare (see Medicare Preventive Services), may be used by other payers
99406, 99407	Tobacco Counseling	For Medicare: use is for those with illness, prevention is G code
99495, 99496	Transitional Care Management Services (new 2013)	http://www.cms.gov/Outreach-and-Education/Medicare-Learning-Network-MLN/MLNProducts/Downloads/Transitional-Care-Management-Services-Fact-Sheet-ICN908628.pdf
Medicare Preventive Services		http://www.cms.gov/Outreach-and-Education/Medicare-Learning-Network-MLN/MLNProducts/PreventiveServices.html
G0008, G0009	Flu and Pneumonia Vaccination	Use CPT and Q codes for vaccine supply
G0402	IPPE "Welcome to Medicare" Preventive Exam	http://www.cms.gov/Outreach-and-Education/Medicare-Learning-Network-MLN/MLNProducts/downloads/MPS_QRI_IPPE001a.pdf

(cont.)

Common Procedure Codes

Procedure Code	Description	Reference/Notes
G0438, G0439	Annual Wellness Visits	http://www.cms.gov/Outreach-and-Education/Medicare-Learning-Network-MLN/MLNProducts/Downloads/AWV_Chart_ICN905706.pdf http://www.cms.gov/Outreach-and-Education/Medicare-Learning-Network-MLN/MLNProducts/Downloads/AnnualWellnessVisit-ICN907786.pdf
G0436, G0437	Tobacco Counseling	http://www.cms.gov/Outreach-and-Education/Medicare-Learning-Network-MLN/MLNProducts/downloads/smoking.pdf
G0442, G0443	Alcohol Screening/ Counseling	http://www.cms.gov/Outreach-and-Education/Medicare-Learning-Network-MLN/MLNProducts/Downloads/Reduce-Alcohol-Misuse-ICN907798.pdf
G0444	Depression Screen	http://www.cms.gov/Outreach-and-Education/Medicare-Learning-Network-MLN/MLNProducts/Downloads/Screening-for-Depression-Booklet-ICN907799.pdf
G0445	STI Counseling	Screening lab codes also covered (see Preventive Services publications link)
G0446	Intensive Behavioral Therapy for CVD	https://www.cms.gov/Outreach-and-Education/Medicare-Learning-Network-MLN/MLNProducts/Downloads/Cardiovascular-Disease-Services-Booklet-ICN907784.pdf
G0447	Intensive Behavioral Therapy for Obesity	http://www.cms.gov/Outreach-and-Education/Medicare-Learning-Network-MLN/MLNProducts/Downloads/ICN907800.pdf

Other Important Procedure Codes

G0179, G0180 G0181, G0182	Home Care Certification Home/Hospice Care Plan Oversight	Section 180 of Chapter 12 of 100-4 Medicare Claims Processing manual: http://www.cms.gov/Regulations-and-Guidance/Guidance/Manuals/Downloads/clm104c12.pdf
HCPCS "J" codes	Code range within HCPCS for drugs administered (eg steroid injection)	

Many other codes are relevant to practice (eg ECG), but not listed for brevity. Geriatric Mental Health and Neuropsychological Testing codes not listed; see CPT.
CPT® is a registered Trademark of the American Medical Association. CPT codes, descriptions and other data only are copyright American Medical Association. All Rights Reserved.

General Information on Aging

AARP	www.aarp.org	888-OUR-AARP (888-687-2277)
AGS Foundation for Health in Aging	www.healthinaging.org	800-563-4916
Administration on Aging	www.aoa.gov	202-619-0724
American Geriatrics Society	www.americangeriatrics.org	800-247-4779
American Medical Directors Association	www.amda.com	800-876-2632
American Society of Consultant Pharmacists	www.ascp.com	800-355-2727
Assisted Living Federation of America	www.alfa.org	703-894-1805
CDC National Prevention Information Network	www.cdcnpin.org	800-CDC-INFO (800-232-4636)
Children of Aging Parents	www.caps4caregivers.org	800-227-7294
Family Caregiver Alliance	www.caregiver.org	800-445-8106
Medicare Hotline	www.medicare.gov	800-MEDICARE (800-633-4227) TTY: 877-486-2048
National Adult Day Services Association	www.nadsa.org	877-745-1440
National Council on the Aging	www.ncoa.org	202-479-1200
National Institute on Aging	www.nia.nih.gov	800-222-2225 TTY: 800-222-4225

End-of-Life

National Hospice and Palliative Care Organization	www.nhpco.org	800-658-8898 877-658-8896 (multilingual helpline)

Mistreatment of Older Adults

National Center on Elder Abuse	www.ncea.aoa.gov	855-500-3537 800-677-1116 (help hotline)

Smoking Cessation

CDC National Center for Chronic Disease Prevention and Health Promotion	www.cdc.gov/nccdphp	800-CDC-INFO (800-232-4636) TTY: 888-232-6348
National Cancer Institute	www.smokefree.gov	800-QUITNOW (800-784-8669) TTY: 800-332-8615

Specific Health Problems

Alzheimer's Association	www.alz.org	800-272-3900 TDD: 866-403-3073
Alzheimer's Disease Education and Referral Center	www.nia.nih.gov/alzheimers	800-438-4380
American Academy of Ophthalmology	www.aao.org	877-887-6327
American Association for Geriatric Psychiatry	www.aagponline.org	301-654-7850
American Cancer Society	www.cancer.org	800-ACS-2345 (800-227-2345) TTY: 866-228-4327
American College of Obstetricians and Gynecologists	www.acog.org	800-673-8444

American Diabetes Association	www.diabetes.org	800-DIABETES (800-342-2383)
American Foundation for the Blind	www.afb.org	800-AFB-LINE (800-232-5463)
American Heart Association	www.heart.org	800-AHA-USA1 (800-242-8721)
American Lung Association	www.lung.org	800-LUNG-USA (800-586-4872)
American Pain Society	www.ampainsoc.org	847-375-4715
American Parkinson Disease Association	www.apdaparkinson.org	800-223-2732
American Stroke Association	www.strokeassociation.org	888-4-STROKE (888-478-7653)
American Urological Association	www.auanet.org	866-746-4282
Arthritis Foundation	www.arthritis.org	800-283-7800
Better Hearing Institute	www.betterhearing.org	800-EAR-WELL (800-327-9355)
Endocrine Society and Hormone Foundation (obesity)	www.obesityinamerica.org	301-941-0200
Geriatric Mental Health Foundation	www.gmhfonline.org	301-654-7850
Hearing Loss Association of America	www.hearingloss.org	301-657-2248 (V-TTY)
Lighthouse International	www.lighthouse.org	800-829-0500 TTY: 212-821-9713
Meals On Wheels Association of America	www.mowaa.org	888-998-6525
National Association for Continence	www.nafc.org	800-BLADDER (800-252-3337)
National Diabetes Information Clearinghouse	www.diabetes.niddk.nih.gov	800-860-8747 TTY: 866-569-1162
National Digestive Diseases Information Clearinghouse	www.digestive.niddk.nih.gov	800-891-5389 TTY: 866-569-1162
National Eye Institute	www.nei.nih.gov	301-496-5248
National Heart, Lung, and Blood Institute	www.nhlbi.nih.gov	301-592-8573 TTY: 240-629-3255
National Institute of Arthritis and Musculoskeletal and Skin Diseases	www.niams.nih.gov	877-22-NIAMS (877-226-4267) TTY: 301-565-2966
National Institute of Mental Health	www.nimh.nih.gov	866-615-NIMH (866-615-6464) TTY: 866-415-8051
National Institute of Neurological Disorders and Stroke	www.ninds.nih.gov	800-352-9424 TTY: 301-468-5981
National Institute on Deafness and Other Communication Disorders	www.nidcd.nih.gov	800-241-1044 TTY: 800-241-1055
National Kidney and Urologic Diseases Information Clearinghouse	www.kidney.niddk.nih.gov	800-891-5390 TTY: 866-569-1162
National Osteoporosis Foundation	www.nof.org	800-231-4222
National Parkinson Foundation	www.parkinson.org	800-473-4636 (helpline)
Sexuality Information and Education Council of the US	www.siecus.org	212-819-9770
The Simon Foundation for Continence	www.simonfoundation.org	800-23-SIMON (800-237-4666)

Index

Page references followed by *t* and *f* indicate tables and figures, respectively.

Trade names are in *italics*.

A

AAA (abdominal aortic aneurysm), 62, 257*t*
AAPMC (antibiotic-associated
    pseudomembranous colitis), 129
Abandonment, 12*t*
Abatacept *(Orencia)*, 206
Abbreviations, iii–vii
Abciximab *(ReoPro)*, 24*t*, 31*t*
Abdominal aortic aneurysm (AAA), 62, 257*t*
Abdominal exercises, 193
Abdominal massage, 155
Abdominal radiography, 155
Abdominopelvic surgery, 25*t*
Abelcet (amphotericin B lipid complex), 173*t*
ABI (ankle-brachial index), 63, 63*t*, 297
Abilify, 77*t*, 269*t. See also* Aripiprazole
Absorbine Jr. Antifungal (tolnaftate), 90*t*
Abstral, 236*t. See also* Fentanyl
Abuse
    alcohol, 252, 257*t*, 310–312
    older adults, 10–12, 12*t*, 335
    opioid, 234–235
    prescription drug, 314–315
    substance, 252, 310–315
    tobacco, 313*t*
Acamprosate *(Campral)*, 311
Acarbose *(Precose)*, 94, 97*t*
ACC/AHA heart failure staging, 43*t*
Accolate (zafirlukast), 285*t*
Accupril, 55*t. See also* Quinapril
Accuretic (quinapril hydrochloride with
    HCTZ), 56*t*
Accuzyme, 293
Acebutolol *(Sectral)*, 53*t*
ACEIs (angiotensin-converting enzyme
    inhibitors)
    for ACS, 40
    for chronic angina, 41
    for chronic kidney disease, 178
    and coexisting conditions, 56*t*
    for cough, 272*t*
    for DM type 2, 96
    drug interactions, 19
    for HF, 43, 44
    for HTN, 50, 51, 54*t*–55*t*, 56*t*–57*t*
    and orthostatic hypotension, 211
    for PAD, 64
    for RAS, 50
    target dosages in HF, 45*t*
Aceon, 55*t. See also* Perindopril
Acetaminophen. *See* APAP
Acetazolamide *(Diamox)*, 107*t*
Acetylcysteine *(Mucomyst)*, 177
N-Acetylcysteine, 133*t*
Acetylsalicylic acid. *See* Aspirin (ASA)
Achromycin, 122. *See also* Tetracycline
Acidosis, 179
Acid-suppressing drugs, 292
ACIP (Advisory Committee on Immunization
    Practices) guidelines, 163
AcipHex (rabeprazole), 120*t*
Aclovate, 90*t. See also* Alclometasone
    dipropionate
Acoustic neuroma, 135*t*, 137
Acquired immune deficiency syndrome
    (AIDS), 268
Acral lentiginous melanoma, 86
ACR/EULAR criteria for rheumatoid arthritis,
    204*t*
ACS. *See* Acute coronary syndrome
Actemra (tocilizumab), 206, 210
ACTH (adrenocorticotropic hormone), 207
ACTH stimulation test, 102
Actinic keratosis, 84
Actiq, 236*t. See also* Fentanyl
Activities of daily living (ADLs)
    assessment of, 115
    in COPD therapy, 278
    Instrumental (IADLs), 324
    for pain management, 232
    Physical Self-Maintenance Scale, 323
    preoperative, 252
ACTO plus met (pioglitazone and metformin),
    99*t*
Actonel, 224*t. See also* Risedronate
Actos, 98*t. See also* Pioglitazone

Acuity testing, 104
Acular, 110t. *See also* Ketorolac
Acupuncture, 193, 198, 231t
Acute bacterial conjunctivitis, 109, 109t
Acute care, 7t, 115
Acute coronary syndrome (ACS), 38–40
   anticoagulant agents for, 30t, 31t
   antiplatelet agents for, 29t
   antithrombotic medications for, 24t
Acute hepatitis, 133t
Acute hyperbilirubinemia, 133t
Acute interstitial nephritis, 176t, 177
Acute kidney injury, 176–177, 176t, 244t
Acute tubular necrosis, 176, 176t, 177
Acyclovir *(Zovirax),* 163t
AD. *See* Alzheimer disease
Adalat CC (nifedipine SR), 54t
Adalimumab *(Humira),* 206
Adaptive equipment, 69t
Adenocarcinoma, vulvar, 317
Adenosine stress test, 38
Adhesive capsulitis, 192
ADLs. *See* Activities of daily living
Adrenal disorders, 288t
Adrenal insufficiency, 102, 103t, 182
Adrenergic agonists. *See* α-Adrenergic
   agonists; β-Adrenergic agonists
Adrenergic inhibitors, 52t–53t.
   See also α-Blockers; β-Blockers
Adrenocorticotropic hormone (ACTH), 207
Adrenocorticotropic hormone (ACTH)
   stimulation test, 102
Adsorbocarpine (pilocarpine), 107t
ADT (androgen deprivation therapy), 222,
   264, 265
Adult Protective Services, 12
Advair Diskus (salmeterol-fluticasone), 286t
Advance directives, 244, 245, 254
Advance practice nurses, 6t
Advicor (lovastatin with niacin), 49t
Advisory Committee on Immunization
   Practices (ACIP) guidelines, 163
Aerobic exercise. *See* Exercise
AeroBid, 284t. *See also* Flunisolide
AeroChambers, 282
AF. *See* Atrial fibrillation

Aflibercept *(Eylea, Zaltrap),* 105
Agency for Healthcare Research and Quality
   (AHRQ), 17
Age-related loss of muscle mass, 185
Age-related macular degeneration (AMD),
   104–105
Aggrastat, 31t. *See also* Tirofiban
Aggrenox (ASA and dipyridamole), 29t, 215
Aggression, 69–70, 73, 77t
Agitation
   in delirium, 69–70
   in dementia, 73
   and pain assessment, 228
   treatment of, 76, 77t
AHI (apnea-hypopnea index), 307
AHRQ (Agency for Healthcare Research and
   Quality), 17
AIDS (acquired immune deficiency
   syndrome), 268
AIDS-related dementia, 70
Akarpine (pilocarpine), 107t
Akathisia, 271t
AKBeta (levobunolol), 106t
AK-Mycin (erythromycin ophthalmic), 109t
AKPro (dipivefrin), 106t
AKTob, 109t. *See also* Tobramycin
Alamast (pemirolast), 110t
Alaway (ketotifen), 110t
Albumin, 186
Albuminuria, 96
Albuterol *(Ventolin, Ventolin Rotacaps),* 184,
   284t
Albuterol-ipratropium *(Combivent,
   Combivent Respimat, Duoneb),* 285t
Alcaftadine *(Lastacaft),* 110t
Alclometasone dipropionate *(Aclovate),* 90t,
   91t
Alcohol
   and aging, 311
   delirium secondary to, 70
   and dizziness, 211
   drug interactions, 311
   opioid interactions, 236t
   and osteoporosis, 222
   and sexual dysfunction, 292
   and sleep problems, 304

Alcohol *continued*
  and UI, 151*t*
  warfarin interactions, 32
Alcohol misuse/abuse, 252, 257*t*, 310–312
Alcohol restriction, 95
Alcohol screening/counseling, 334*t*
Alcohol withdrawal, 70
Alcoholism, 243*t*
Aldactazide (spironolactone with HCTZ), 57*t*
Aldactone, 43, 52*t*. *See also* Spironolactone
Aldara, 84, 85. *See also* Imiquimod
Aldomet, 52*t*. *See also* Methyldopa
Aldoril (methyldopa with HCTZ), 57*t*
Aldosterone antagonists
  and coexisting conditions, 56*t*
  for HF, 43, 44
  for HTN, 52*t*
Alendronate *(Fosamax)*, 224*t*, 226*t*
Alendronate effervescent *(Binosto)*, 224*t*
Alfuzosin, 20*t*
Alfuzosin ER *(Uroxatral)*, 263
Algiderm, 301*t*. *See also* Calcium alginate
    dressings
Algidex Ag Alginate, 302*t*
Aliskiren *(Tekturna)*, 55*t*
Aliskiren with amlodipine *(Tekamlo)*, 57*t*
Aliskiren with HCTZ *(Tekturna HCT)*, 57*t*
Aliskiren with HCTZ and amlodipine
    (Amturnide), 57*t*
Aliskiren with valsartan *(Valturna)*, 57*t*
Alldress, 302*t*
Allegra (fexofenadine), 275*t*
Allegra-D (fexofenadine), 275*t*
Allergic conjunctivitis, 109–110, 110*t*–111*t*,
    275*t*
Allergic (hypersensitivity) hepatotoxicity, 133
Allergic rhinitis, 274–275, 275*t*–277*t*
Allevyn, 300*t*. *See also* Foam island
Alli (orlistat), 187
Allopurinol *(Zyloprim, Lopurin)*, 208, 208*t*
ALN (axillary lymph node) dissection, 316
Alocril (nedocromil), 110*t*
Alogliptin *(Nesina)*, 98*t*
Alogliptin with metformin *(Kazano)*, 100*t*
Alogliptin with pioglitazone *(Oseni)*, 100*t*
Alomide (lodoxamide), 110*t*

Alosetron *(Lotronex)*, 124
α-Adrenergic agonists
  combined α- and β-agonists, 106*t*
  for glaucoma, 106*t*
  herbal medicine interactions, 23
  for HTN, 52*t*
  for menopausal symptoms, 321
  and UI, 151*t*
α-Blockers (α-adrenergic inhibitors)
  for BPH, 262–263
  and coexisting conditions, 56*t*
  combined α- and β-blockers, 53*t*, 56*t*
  drug interactions, 289*t*
  for HTN, 52*t*
  and orthostatic hypotension, 211
  for prostatitis, 267
  and UI, 151*t*
Alphagan (brimonidine), 106*t*
Alphagan P (brimonidine), 106*t*
α-Glucosidase inhibitors, 96, 97*t*
Altabax (retapamulin), 85
Altace, 55*t*. *See also* Ramipril
Altered mental status, 67–70
Alternative medications, 20–23
Altoprev, 48*t*. *See also* Lovastatin
Aluminum, 19, 125
Alveolar-arterial oxygen gradient, 1
Alvesco, 284*t*. *See also* Ciclesonide
Alvimopan *(Entereg)*, 126*t*
Alzheimer disease (AD). *See also* Dementia
  clinical features of, 71
  diagnosis of, 72
  pharmacologic treatment of, 75
  progression of, 72–73
  resources for, 335, 336
Alzheimers Association, 77, 335
Amantadine *(Symmetrel)*, 164*t*, 218*t*
Amaryl, 97*t*. *See also* Glimepiride
Ambien, 37, 306*t*. *See also* Zolpidem
Ambien CR, 306*t*. *See also* Zolpidem
AmBisome (amphotericin B liposomal), 173*t*
Ambrisentan *(Letairis)*, 58
Ambulation, 24*t*
Amcinonide *(Cyclocort)*, 91*t*
AMD (age-related macular degeneration),
    104–105

American College of
Rheumatology/European League
Against Rheumatism (ACR/EULAR)
Criteria, 204*t*
American Urological Association (AUA), 331
Amikacin *(Amikin)*, 160, 170*t*
Amikin, 170*t. See also* Amikacin
Amiloride *(Midamor)*, 52*t*
Amiloride hydrochloride with HCTZ
(Moduretic), 57*t*
Aminoglutethimide, 265
Aminoglycosides
for infectious diseases, 170*t*
for MRSA, 162
for pneumonia, 159*t*, 160
for prostatitis, 267
for urosepsis, 161
Aminolevulinic acid *(Levulan Kerastick)*, 84
Aminosalicylic acid, 44
Amiodarone *(Cordarone, Pacerone)*
for AF, 61*t*
drug interactions, 32, 44
ocular adverse events, 111
QTc interval interactions, 20*t*
to reduce cardiovascular complications of
surgery, 255*t*
Amitiza (lubiprostone), 125*t*
Amitriptyline *(Elavil)*, 20*t*, 68*t*, 81
Amlodipine *(Norvasc)*, 54*t*
Amlodipine with aliskiren *(Tekamlo)*, 57*t*
Amlodipine with aliskiren and HCTZ
(Amturnide), 57*t*
Amlodipine with atorvastatin *(Caduet)*, 57*t*
Amlodipine with benazepril hydrochloride
(Lotrel), 56*t*
Amlodipine with olmesartan *(Azor)*, 56*t*
Amlodipine with telmisartan *(Twynsta)*, 56*t*
Amlodipine with valsartan *(Exforge)*, 56*t*
Amlodipine with valsartan and HCTZ
(Exforge HCT), 56*t*
Amoxapine *(Asendin)*, 68*t*, 81
Amoxicillin *(Amoxil)*
for antibiotic prophylaxis, 259*t*, 260
for community-acquired pneumonia, 159*t*
for cystitis or UTI, 161
for *H pylori* infection, 122*t*
for infectious diseases, 168*t*
and liver disease, 133*t*
for peptic ulcer disease, 122
to reduce cardiovascular complications of
surgery, 255*t*
Amoxicillin with clarithromycin and
lansoprazole *(Prevpac)*, 122*t*
Amoxicillin-clavulanate *(Augmentin)*
for cellulitis, 85
for community-acquired pneumonia, 159*t*
for COPD exacerbation, 280*t*
for cystitis or UTI, 161
for folliculitis, 85
for infections in chronic wounds, 294*t*
for infectious diseases, 169*t*
Amoxil, 122, 168*t. See also* Amoxicillin
Amphotec (amphotericin B cholesteryl
sulfate complex), 173*t*
Amphotericin, 173*t*
Amphotericin B *(Fungizone)*, 173*t*
Amphotericin B cholesteryl sulfate complex
(Amphotec), 173*t*
Amphotericin B lipid complex *(Abelcet)*, 173*t*
Amphotericin B liposomal *(AmBisome)*, 173*t*
Ampicillin
for community-acquired pneumonia, 159*t*
for cystitis or UTI, 161
for endocarditis prophylaxis, 259*t*
for infectious diseases, 168*t*
Ampicillin-sulbactam *(Unasyn)*, 159*t*, 169*t*
Amsler grid, 104
Amturnide (aliskiren/amlodipine/HCTZ), 57*t*
Amylin analogs, 101*t*
Amyvid (florbetapin F18), 72
Anagrelide, 145
Anakinra *(Kineret)*, 206
Analgesics. *See also* APAP; Aspirin
abuse/misuse of, 314
for acute vertebral fracture, 225*t*
for arthritis, 201*t*–203*t*
dosage, 233–234
for hip fracture surgery, 195
initial dosing for PCA, 229*t*
management of adverse events, 234
for multiple myeloma, 146
opioids, 235*t*–236*t*, 237*t*–238*t*, 311
for osteoarthritis, 198, 200*f*

Analgesics *continued*
  for pain, 227*t*, 228, 231, 232–233
  patient-controlled, 229, 229*t*
  for plantar fasciitis, 198
  QT_c interval interactions, 20*t*
  for rheumatoid arthritis, 205
  selection of agents, 232–233
  topical, 232
  and UI, 151*t*
Anaprox (naproxen sodium), 203*t*
Anaspaz, 124. *See also* Hyoscyamine
Anastrozole *(Arimidex),* 318*t*
Ancef, 169*t. See also* Cefazolin
Ancobon (flucytosine), 175*t*
Androderm (testosterone), 290*t*
AndroGel (testosterone), 290*t*
Androgen deprivation therapy (ADT), 222, 264, 265
Androgen suppressive therapy, 264
Androgens, 145, 289*t*–290*t*, 291
Anemia, 138–142
  aplastic, 143
  of B_{12} and folate deficiency, 142
  "cancer type," 138
  and chronic kidney disease, 179
  of chronic kidney disease, 141–142
  combined iron deficiency and anemia of inflammation, 138
  hemolytic, 142
  hypoproliferative, 139*f*, 140*f*
  hypotension secondary to, 66
  of inflammation, 138
  "rheumatoid arthritis type," 138
  of unknown cause, 142
Anesthetics, 195, 231, 311
Aneurysm, abdominal aortic (AAA), 62, 257*t*
Angina
  antihypertensive therapy and, 56*t*
  chronic, 41
  unstable, 39, 40
Anginal chest pain or equivalent, 38
Angioedema, 89
Angiography, 38, 42, 63*t*
Angiomax, 31*t. See also* Bivalirudin
Angioplasty, 50, 215*t*
Angiotensin II receptor blockers. *See* ARBs

Angiotensin-converting enzyme inhibitors. *See* ACEIs
Anidulafungin *(Eraxis),* 175*t*
Ankle-brachial index (ABI), 63, 63*t*, 297
Annual Wellness Visit (AWV), 5, 71, 334*t*
Annucort, 132
Anorectal physiology tests, 155
Anorexia, 185, 248–249
Anorgasmia, 292
Ansaid (flurbiprofen), 202*t*
Anserine bursitis, 196
Anspor, 169*t. See also* Cephradine
Antacids
  and constipation, 125
  digoxin interactions, 44
  for GERD, 120
  for stress-ulcer prevention, 123
Antara, 48*t. See also* Fenofibrate
Anthralin, 87
Anthropometrics, 186
Antiandrogens, 265, 266*t*
Antianxiety agents, 227*t*
Antiarrhythmics
  AF refractory to, 61
  drug interactions, 289*t*
  fall risks, 112
  for HF, 44
Antibiotic-associated diarrhea, 129–131
Antibiotic-associated pseudomembranous colitis (AAPMC), 129
Antibiotics
  for acute conjunctivitis, 109
  antimicrobial stewardship, 157
  for arterial ulcer infection, 297
  for community-acquired pneumonia, 159*t*
  drug-food or -nutrient interactions, 19
  for endocarditis prophylaxis, 259*t*
  for folliculitis, 85
  for *H pylori,* 121
  for halitosis at end of life, 247
  for hip fracture surgery, 195
  for infections in chronic wounds, 294*t*–295*t*
  for infectious diseases, 168*t*–176*t*
  for peptic ulcer disease, 122
  for pneumonia, 158
  prophylaxis for patients with TJR, 260

Antibiotics *continued*
  for prostatitis, 267
  for skin ulcer infection, 294
  and tinnitus, 137
  for UTIs, 161
  for venous ulcer infection, 303
  warfarin interactions, 32
Anti-CD20 monoclonal antibody, 206
Anticholinergics
  antidiarrheals, 129*t*
  for asthma, 282*t*, 283*t*
  for COPD, 278, 278*t*–279*t*, 283*t*
  and dementia, 74
  drugs with strong properties, 68*t*
  and dyspareunia, 291
  long-acting, 256*t*, 278
  medication-induced delirium, 68*t*
  ocular adverse events, 111
  for Parkinson disease, 217*t*–218*t*
  and sexual dysfunction, 292
  short-acting, 279*t*
  and UI, 149, 151*t*
Anticoagulation. *See also* Heparin; Warfarin
  for ACS, 39, 40, 41
  for AF, 60*t*, 61
  alcohol interactions, 311
  for antithrombotic therapy, 24*t*
  cessation before surgery, 253
  for dental procedures, 253
  herbal medicine interactions, 21, 22, 23
  indications for, 24*t*
  for ischemic stroke, 214
  newer anticoagulants vs warfarin, 60*t*
  perioperative therapy, 253*t*, 254*t*
  prescribing information, 30*t*–31*t*
  resumption after surgery, 253
  risk instruments to guide, 60*t*
  for stroke prevention, 215
Anticonvulsants
  alcohol interactions, 311
  fall risks, 112
  herbal medicine interactions, 22
  for menopausal symptoms, 321
  and osteoporosis, 222
  for pain, 227*t*, 233, 238*t*
  prescribing information, 219*t*
  for seizures, 218

and sexual dysfunction, 292
Antidepressants. *See also* MAOIs; SSRIs;
    TCAs
  alcohol interactions, 311
  anticholinergic properties, 68*t*
  for bipolar disorders, 83*t*
  choosing, 79
  contraindicated in older adults, 81
  de-prescribing, 18
  for depression, 79, 79*t*–81*t*
  drug interactions, 236*t*
  fall risks, 112
  food interactions, 19
  herbal medicine interactions, 23
  for IBS, 124
  for menopausal symptoms, 321
  for pain, 227*t*, 233, 238*t*–239*t*
  preventing falls with, 116*t*
  QT$_c$ interval interactions, 20*t*
  and sexual dysfunction, 292
  for sleep disorders, 305*t*
  and sleep problems, 304
Antidiabetic agents, 22
Antidiarrheals, 124, 129*t*, 155
Antidiuretic hormone, 180
Anti-embolism stockings, 46
Antiemetics, 20*t*, 127, 128*t*
Antiestrogen drugs, 318*t*
Antifungals
  for candidiasis, 85
  for infectious diseases, 173*t*, 175*t*
  for intertrigo, 86
  prescribing information, 89*t*–90*t*
  topical, 89*t*–90*t*
Antihistamines
  alcohol interactions, 311
  for allergic conjunctivitis, 109, 110, 110*t*,
      111*t*, 275*t*
  for allergic rhinitis, 275, 275*t*–276*t*
  for angioedema, 89
  anticholinergic properties, 68*t*
  for cholinergic reactions, 89
  de-prescribing, 18
  food interactions, 19
  for hives, 88
  and sexual dysfunction, 292

Antihypertensives
    alcohol interactions, 311
    and coexisting conditions, 56*t*
    combination drugs containing, 56*t*–57*t*
    for emergencies and urgencies, 51
    fall risks, 112
    herbal medicine interactions, 21
    for HTN, 50
    oral agents, 51*t*–55*t*
    and sexual dysfunction, 292
    that cause leg edema, 45
Anti-IgE, 282*t*
Anti-infectives, 20*t*
Anti-inflammatory agents, 232, 267. *See also*
        NSAIDs
Antimicrobial stewardship, 157
Antimigraines, 20*t*
Antimuscarinics
    anticholinergic properties, 68*t*
    for BPH, 262, 263
    for nausea and vomiting, 128*t*
    and orthostatic hypotension, 211
    for UI, 149, 151*t*–152*t*, 153
Antineoplastics, 44
Antiparkinson agents, 68*t*
Antiplatelet therapy
    for ACS, 39
    for antithrombotic therapy, 24*t*
    bridging therapy, 253
    cessation before surgery, 252
    dual antiplatelet therapy, 252–253
    herbal medicine interactions, 21, 22, 23
    indications for, 24*t*
    for ischemic stroke, 214
    for PAD, 63, 63*t*
    perioperative use, 254*t*
    prescribing information, 29*t*
    resumption after surgery, 254
    for stroke prevention, 215
    for VTE prophylaxis, 25*t*
Antipseudomonal agents
    for infectious diseases, 168*t*, 169*t*
    for pneumonia, 159, 159*t*, 160
Antipsychotics
    adverse events, 268, 270*t*
    for agitation, 76, 77*t*
    alcohol interactions, 311
    anticholinergic properties, 68*t*
    for delirium, 69
    de-prescribing, 18
    fall risks, 112
    food interactions, 19
    and orthostatic hypotension, 211
    and osteoporosis, 222
    for Parkinson disease, 217
    prescribing information, 269*t*
    preventing falls with, 116*t*
    for psychotic disorders, 268
    QT$_c$ interval interactions, 20*t*
    second-generation, 36, 70, 76, 77*t*, 83*t*,
        269*t*, 270*t*
    and sexual dysfunction, 292
    and UI, 151*t*
Antipyretics, 213
Antiretrovirals, 20*t*, 167
Antiseptics, 297
Antispasmodics, 68*t*, 124
Antistaphylococcal penicillins, 85, 168*t*, 259*t*
Antithrombotic therapy, 24–33
    for AF, 59, 60*t*
    indications for, 24*t*
    for ischemic stroke, 213–214
    risk instruments to guide, 60*t*
    for VTE, 25*t*, 28*t*
Anti-TNF-α agents, 206
Antitussives, 273*t*
Antivert, 128*t*. *See also* Meclizine
Antiviral therapy
    for herpes zoster, 162, 163*t*
    for influenza, 164, 164*t*
Anxiety, 34–37
    agitation treatment guidelines, 77*t*
    at bedtime, 305
    benzodiazepines for, 36, 37*t*
    buspirone management of, 36
    in COPD, 279
    at end of life, 249
    with pain, 232
Anxiolytics, 112, 247
Anzemet, 128*t*. *See also* Dolasetron
Aortic stenosis (AS), 62
Aortic valve replacement (AVR), 32*t*, 62

APAP (acetaminophen)
  for acute lumbar strain, 192–193
  for acute pain, 229
  for acute stroke, 213
  alcohol interactions, 311
  for arthritis, 201*t*
  for back pain, 193
  for chronic disk degeneration, 193
  with codeine, 235*t*
  hepatotoxicity, 133*t*
  for low back pain syndrome, 192–193
  management of adverse events, 234
  for musculoskeletal pain, 232
  with opioids, 200*f*
  for osteoarthritis, 193, 199, 200*f*
  for pain, 227*t*, 228, 229, 232, 235*t*
  for shoulder pain, 191, 192
  warfarin interactions, 32
APAP (acetaminophen) with hydrocodone
      (Lorcet, Lortab, Vicodin), 233, 235*t*
APAP (acetaminophen) with oxycodone
      (Percocet, Tylox, Magnacet), 235*t*
APAP (acetaminophen) with tramadol
      (Ultracet), 233, 236*t*
Apathy, 73, 76
Aphasia, 220*t*
Apidra, 101*t. See also* Insulin glulisine
Apixaban (Eliquis)
  for ACS, 40
  for AF, 60*t*
  for anticoagulation, 30*t*, 33*t*
  for antithrombotic therapy, 24*t*
  cessation before surgery, 253
  resumption after surgery, 253
Aplastic anemia, 143
Apligraf, 298, 303
Apnea-hypopnea index (AHI), 307
Apokyn (apomorphine), 217*t*
Apomorphine (Apokyn), 217*t*
Appetite, decreased, 19. *See also*
      Malnutrition
Appetite stimulants, 188
Apresoline, 54*t. See also* Hydralazine
Aquaphor, 89
AquaSite, 301*t*
Aquasorb, 301*t*
Aqueous shunts, 105

Arachnocides, 274
Aranesp (darbepoetin alfa), 143*t*
Arava (leflunomide), 207*t*
ARBs (angiotensin II receptor blockers)
  for ACS, 40
  for chronic kidney disease, 178
  and coexisting conditions, 56*t*
  for DM type 2, 96
  for HF, 43, 45*t*
  for HTN, 50, 55*t*, 56*t*–57*t*
  for RAS, 50
Arcapta (indacaterol), 284*t*
Arformoterol (Brovana), 284*t*
Argatroban, 24*t*
Arginine vasopressin receptor antagonists,
      182
Aricept, 76*t. See also* Donepezil
Arimidex (anastrozole), 318*t*
Aripiprazole (Abilify)
  for acute mania, 82
  adverse events, 270*t*
  for agitation, 77*t*
  for bipolar disorders, 83*t*
  for depression, 79
  for psychotic disorders, 268, 269*t*
  for tardive dyskinesia, 271*t*
Aristocort, 91*t*, 103*t. See also* Triamcinolone
Arixtra, 30*t. See also* Fondaparinux
Aromasin, 318*t. See also* Exemestane
Aromatase inhibitors, 317, 318*t*
Artane, 218*t. See also* Trihexyphenidyl
Arterial blood gases, 1
Arterial disease, peripheral. *See* Peripheral
      arterial disease (PAD)
Arterial oxygen, 1, 2
Arterial ulcers, 296*t*–297*t*, 297
Arteriovenous fistula access, 179
Arteritis, giant cell (temporal), 209–210
Arthritis. *See also* Osteoarthritis
  acute arthritis, 209
  acute gouty arthritis, 206, 207
  acute gouty flare, 208
  APAP and NSAIDs for, 201*t*–203*t*
  chronic calcium pyrophosphate crystal
      inflammatory arthritis, 209
  chronic crystal inflammatory arthritis, 208
  crystal-induced, 208

Arthritis *continued*
    pain relief, 239t, 240t
    pseudogout, 208–209
    pseudo-rheumatoid arthritis, 208, 209
    recurrent pseudogout, 208t
    resources for, 336
    rheumatoid arthritis, 204–206, 204t
Arthropan (choline salicylate), 201t
Arthrotec (enteric coated diclofenac), 202t
Artificial nutrition, 190, 245
Artificial tears, 109, 110
AS (aortic stenosis), 62
ASA. *See* Aspirin
Asendin, 81. *See also* Amoxapine
Asmanex, 284t. *See also* Mometasone
Aspercreme (trolamine salicylate), 203t, 239t
Aspergillosis, 174t
Aspiration, 190, 272t. *See also* Dysphagia
Aspirin (ASA)
    for ACS, 39
    for AF, 60t, 61
    for antithrombotic therapy, 24t
    for arthritis, 201t
    cessation before surgery, 252
    for chronic angina, 41
    for dizziness, 212t
    for DM type 2, 97
    enteric-coated, 201t
    for essential thrombocytosis, 145
    for giant cell arteritis, 210
    herbal medicine interactions, 22
    for ischemic stroke, 214
    for MI prevention, 257t
    for PAD, 63
    for pain management, 232
    for polycythemia vera, 144
    prescribing information, 29t
    for preventing adverse events, 49t
    to reduce cardiovascular complications of
        surgery, 254t
    for stroke prevention, 215
    and tinnitus, 137
    for vertigo, 212t
    for VTE, 25t, 28
    for warfarin anticoagulation, 33t
Aspirin (ASA) with dipyridamole *(Aggrenox)*,
    29t, 215

Aspirin (ASA) with oxycodone *(Percodan)*,
    235t
Aspirin (ASA) with pravastatin *(Pravigard
    PAC)*, 48t
Assessment, 4–5
    ADLs, 323
    balance, 4t, 113
    cardiac risk, 250, 250f
    care preferences, 5t
    cognitive status, 4t, 71, 75, 322
    depression, 325–326
    dimensions, 4t–5t
    falls prevention, 4t, 114f
    functional, 4t, 113, 229, 323, 324, 330
    gait, 4t, 113
    health literacy, 17, 327
    hearing, 4t
    Instrumental ADLs (IADLs), 324
    instruments, 322–332
    Karnofsky Scale, 328
    medication review, 4t
    mobility, 115
    multidisciplinary, 228
    nutritional, 4t, 185–186
    pain, 4t, 230f
    Palliative Performance Scale, version 2
        (PPSv2), 329
    preoperative, 250–254, 251
    psychosocial, 229
    pulmonary risk, 251
    UI, 4t
    vision testing, 4t, 104
    wound, 293
Assisted feeding, 249
Assisted living, 7t
Assisted suicide, 246
Assistive devices
    functional assessment, 115
    for listening, 136
    optical aids, 108
    for osteoarthritis, 198
    for pain management, 229
    for preventing falls, 117t
Astelin, 276t. *See also* Azelastine
Astepro, 276t. *See also* Azelastine
Asthma, 281–282, 282t, 283t–286t
Astramorph PF, 236t. *See also* Morphine

Atacand, 55t. See also Candesartan
Atacand HCT (candesartan with HCTZ), 57t
Atarax, 276t. See also Hydroxyzine
Atazanavir, 20t
Atelvia (risedronate), 225t
Atenolol (Tenormin), 53t, 212t
Atenolol with chlorthalidone (Tenoretic), 57t
Ativan, 37t, 306t. See also Lorazepam
Atorvastatin (Lipitor), 48t, 254t, 292
Atorvastatin with amlodipine (Caduet), 57t
Atrial fibrillation (AF), 58–60
    anticoagulant agents for, 30t, 31t, 33t
    antihypertensive therapy and, 56t
    antiplatelet agents for, 29t
    antithrombotic medications for, 24t
    perioperative medical therapy to prevent, 255t
    rhythm control drugs for, 61t
    warfarin anticoagulation for, 32t
Atrial tachycardia, 56t
At-risk drinking, 310
Atropine, 68t, 248
Atropine with diphenoxylate (Lomotil), 129t
Atrovent, 283t. See also Ipratropium
Attapulgite (Kaopectate), 129t
AUA IPSS Symptom Index for BPH, 331
Audiometry, 134, 137
Augmentin, 169t. See also Amoxicillin-clavulanate
Autologous cellular immunotherapy, 265
Autolytic debridement, 293
Autonomic dysregulation, 65
Avalide (irbesartan with HCTZ), 57t
Avanafil (Stendra), 289t
Avandia (rosiglitazone), 99t
Avapro, 55t. See also Irbesartan
Avastin (bevacizumab), 105
Avelox, 109t, 171t. See also Moxifloxacin
Aventyl, 80t, 220. See also Nortriptyline
Avinza (morphine), 237t
Avodart (dutasteride), 263
AVR (aortic valve replacement), 32t, 62
AWV. See Annual Wellness Visit
Axid (nizatidine), 120t
Axillary lymph node (ALN) dissection, 316
Axona (medium-chain triglyceride), 76

Azactam, 168t. See also Aztreonam
Azelaic acid (Azelex, Finacea, Finevin), 87
Azelastine (Astelin, Astepro, Optivar), 110t, 276t
Azelex (azelaic acid), 87
Azilect (rasagilene), 218t
Azilsartan (Edarbi), 55t
Azilsartan with chlorthalidone (Edarbyclor), 57t
Azithromycin (Zithromax)
    for community-acquired pneumonia, 159t
    for endocarditis prophylaxis, 259t
    for infectious diseases, 170t
    for rosacea, 87
Azoles, 173t–174t
Azopt (brinzolamide), 107t
Azor (amlodipine with olmesartan), 56t
Aztreonam (Azactam), 159t, 161, 168t
Azulfidine, 206t. See also Sulfasalazine

B
Back pain, 192–194
    low back pain, 192–193, 198, 199, 238t, 240t
    nondrug interventions for, 231t
Baclofen (Lioresal), 239t, 240t
Bacterial conjunctivitis, acute, 109, 109t
Bacterial sinusitis, 272t
Bacteriuria, 153, 160, 258
Bactocill (oxacillin), 168t
Bactrim, 172t. See also Co-trimoxazole
Bactroban, 85. See also Mupirocin
Bad news: communicating, 241–242
Balance assessment, 4t, 113
Balance exercises, 116t, 261
Balance impairment, 117t, 198
Bariatric surgery, 95, 307
Barium swallow, 118
Basal cell carcinoma, 84–85, 317
Basic energy (caloric) requirements, 187
Beclomethasone (Beclovent, Beconase, Vancenase, Vanceril), 276t, 284t
Beclovent, 284t. See also Beclomethasone
Beconase, 276t. See also Beclomethasone
Bedtime glucose, 95t
Beers Criteria, 16
Behavioral disturbances/agitation, 228

Behavioral therapy. *See also* CBT (cognitive-
  behavioral therapy)
  for anxiety, 36
  for dementia, 74
  for DHIC, 149
  for dizziness, 212t
  for drop attacks, 212t
  for IBS, 124
  for opioid abuse/misuse, 315
  for overactive bladder, 149
  for preventing falls, 116t
  procedure codes, 334t
  for sleep disorders, 304, 305
  for smoking cessation, 312
  for UI, 149, 150f
Belladonna alkaloids, 68t
Belviq (lorcaserin), 187
Benadryl, 276t. *See also* Diphenhydramine
Benazepril *(Lotensin)*, 45t, 54t
Benazepril with amlodipine *(Lotrel)*, 56t
Benazepril with HCTZ *(Lotensin HTC)*, 56t
Bendroflumethiazide with nadolol *(Corzide)*,
  57t
Benecalorie, 189t
Benecol, 47
Benefiber (wheat dextrin), 125t
Benemid, 208t. *See also* Probenecid
Ben-Gay (methylsalicylate and menthol),
  200f, 239t
Benicar, 55t. *See also* Olmesartan
Benicar HCT (olmesartan with HCTZ), 57t
Benign paroxysmal positional vertigo, 212t
Benign prostatic hyperplasia (BPH), 56t,
  262–263, 331
Bentyl, 124. *See also* Dicyclomine
Benzodiazepine withdrawal, 70
Benzodiazepines
  abuse/misuse of, 314
  adverse events, 314
  for akathisia, 271t
  for anxiety, 36, 37t
  for delirium, 70
  fall risks, 112
  herbal medicine interactions, 22, 23
  for pain at end of life, 246
  preventing falls with, 116t
  for sleep disorders, 305t–306t

Benzonatate *(Tessalon Perles)*, 273t
Benzoyl peroxide, 87
Benztropine *(Cogentin)*, 68t, 74, 217t
Bepotastine *(Bepreve)*, 110t
Bepreve (bepotastine), 110t
Bereavement, 288t
Berg Balance Scale, 113
Besifloxacin *(Besivance)*, 109t
Besivance (besifloxacin), 109t
β-Adrenergic agonists
  for asthma, 282, 282t, 283t–284t
  combined α- and β-agonists, 106t
  for COPD, 278, 278t–279t, 280t, 283t–284t
  long-acting, 278, 278t–279t, 282, 282t, 284t
  for pneumonia, 158
  short-acting, 278t–279t, 282t, 283t,
    283t–284t
  for UI, 152t
β-Blockers (β-adrenergic inhibitors)
  for ACS, 40
  for AF, 59
  for akathisia, 271t
  alcohol interactions, 311
  for anxiety disorders, 36
  for chronic angina, 41
  and coexisting conditions, 56t
  combined α- and β-blockers, 53t, 56t
  for glaucoma, 106t
  for HF, 43, 45t
  for HTN, 51, 52t–53t, 57t
  for hyperthyroidism, 93
  and leg edema, 45
  and orthostatic hypotension, 211
  perioperative use, 254t
  and sleep problems, 304
β-Carotene, 105
Betagan (levobunolol), 106t
β-Lactams/β-lactamase inhibitors
  for infectious diseases, 168t–170t
  for pneumonia, 159, 159t
Betamethasone *(Celestone)*, 103t
Betamethasone dipropionate *(Diprolene,
    Diprolene AF, Diprosone)*, 90t, 91t, 317
Betamethasone valerate *(Valisone)*, 90t, 91t
Betapace, 61t. *See also* Sotalol

Betapace AF, 61*t. See also* Sotalol
Betaxolol *(Betoptic, Betoptic-S, Kerlone),* 53*t,* 106*t*
Betimol (timolol drops), 106*t*
Betoptic, 106*t. See also* Betaxolol
Betoptic-S, 106*t. See also* Betaxolol
Bevacizumab *(Avastin),* 105
Biaxin, 122, 171*t. See also* Clarithromycin
Biaxin XL, 171*t. See also* Clarithromycin
Bicalutamide *(Casodex),* 266*t*
Bicarbonate, 179
Bicipital tendinitis, 192
BiDil, 44, 57*t. See also* Isosorbide dinitrate and hydralazine
Biguanides, 97*t*
Bile acid sequestrants, 47*t,* 48*t*
Billing codes, 333–334
Bimatoprost *(Lumigan),* 107*t*
Binosto (alendronate), 224*t*
Bioclusive, 300*t. See also* Transparent film
Biofeedback
    for fecal incontinence, 155
    for IBS, 124
    for insomnia, 305
    for osteoarthritis, 198
    for pain, 232
    for UI, 149
Bioidentical hormone therapy, 319
Biolex, 301*t*
Biological agents, 87
Bioprosthetic heart valves, 32*t*
Biopsy, sentinel lymph node (SLN), 316
Bipolar diathermy, 132
Bipolar disorders, 82, 83*t,* 268
Bisacodyl *(Dulcolax),* 125, 126*t,* 155
Bismuth subsalicylate *(Pepto-Bismol),* 122, 122*t,* 129*t*
Bisoprolol *(Zebeta),* 45*t,* 53*t*
Bisoprolol with HCTZ *(Ziac),* 57*t*
Bisphosphonates
    adverse effects of, 146
    for breast cancer, 317
    de-prescribing, 18
    effects on other outcomes, level of evidence, and risks of, 226*t*
    with estrogen, 225

for metastatic bone pain, 246
for multiple myeloma, 145
ocular adverse events, 111
for osteoporosis, 195, 223, 224, 224*t*–225*t,* 225, 226
Bitolterol *(Tornalate),* 284*t*
Bivalirudin *(Angiomax),* 24*t,* 31*t*
Bladder cancer, 258
Bladder diary, 148, 153
Bladder outlet obstruction, 147*t,* 148
Bladder training, 149
Bladder-sphincter dyssynergia, 147
Bleeding, postmenopausal, 318–319
Blepharitis, 109*t*
Blindness. *See* Visual impairment
BlisterFilm, 300*t*
Blocadren, 53*t. See also* Timolol
Blood gases, arterial, 1
Blood glucose monitoring, 101
Blood pressure
    goals of treatment, 95*t*
    high, 49–51, 58
    home monitoring, 50
    low, 103*t,* 117*t,* 212*t,* 270*t,* 271*t*
    management in chronic kidney disease, 178
    management in ischemic stroke, 214
    management in PAD, 63
    management in stroke prevention, 214–215
    screening, 257*t*
Blood urea nitrogen (BUN):creatinine ratio, 180
BMD (bone mineral density), 222, 226*t*
BMI (body mass index), 2, 41, 50
BNP (brain natriuretic peptide), 42
Board-and-care facilities, 7*t*
Body mass index (BMI), 2, 41, 50
Body weight, 1, 2
Bone densitometry (men), 257*t*
Bone densitometry (women), 113, 257*t*
Bone disease, metastatic
    in breast cancer, 317
    pain relief, 246
    in prostate cancer, 264, 265
Bone mineral density (BMD), 222, 226*t*
Boniva, 224*t. See also* Ibandronate

Boost Drink, 189t
Boost Glucose Control, 189t
Boost Plus, 189t
Bortezomib, 146
Bosentan *(Tracleer)*, 58
Botox (onabotulinumtoxin A), 240t
Botulinum toxin, 118, 152, 263
Bowel obstruction, 247–248
Bowel training, 155
BPH (benign prostatic hyperplasia), 56t,
    262–263, 331
Brachytherapy, 264
Bracing, 194, 198
Bradykinesia, 215
Brain natriuretic peptide (BNP), 42
Brain tumor, 268
Breast cancer, 316–317
    medications for osteoporosis and, 226t
    oral agents for, 318t
    recommendations for prevention, 257t
    screening for, 259
Breast self-examination, 317
Breathing disorders, sleep-related, 304
Breo Ellipta (vilanterol-fluticasone), 286t
Brief Pain Inventory, 229
Bright light. *See* Light therapy
Brilinta, 29t. *See also* Ticagrelor
Brimonidine *(Alphagan, Alphagan P)*, 106t
Brimonidine/brinzolamide *(Simbrinza)*, 107t
Brimonidine/timolol *(Combigan)*, 107t
Brinzolamide *(Azopt)*, 107t
Brinzolamide/brimonidine *(Simbrinza)*, 107t
Broca's aphasia, 220t
Bromocriptine *(Cycloset, Parlodel)*, 99t, 217t
Brompheniramine, 68t
Bronchial provocative testing, 281
Bronchitis, 170t, 272t
Bronchodilators, 247, 304
Bronchospasm, 56t
Brovana (arformoterol), 284t
Budesonide *(Pulmicort, Rhinocort, Pulmicort Respules)*, 276t, 284t
Budesonide-formoterol *(Symbicort)*, 285t
Bumetanide *(Bumex)*
    for HTN, 51t
    for hyperkalemia, 183, 184
    for UI, 153

Bumex, 51t. *See also* Bumetanide
BUN:creatinine ratio, 180
Bunion, 197
Buprenorphine, 20t, 315
Buprenorphine, transdermal *(Butrans Transdermal System CIII)*, 228, 237t
Bupropion *(Wellbutrin, Wellbutrin SR, Wellbutrin XL, Zyban)*
    for depression, 79, 80t
    and seizures, 219
    for smoking cessation, 312
    tamoxifen interactions, 318t
    for tobacco abuse, 313t
Bursal injections, 198–199
Bursitis
    anserine, 196
    response to lidocaine injection, 191t
    subacromial, 191, 209
    subdeltoid, 209
    trochanteric, 194
BuSpar, 36, 77t. *See also* Buspirone
Buspirone *(BuSpar)*
    for agitation, 77t
    for anxiety, 36, 305
    for depression, 79
Butenafine *(Lotrimin Ultra, Mentax)*, 17, 89t
Butrans Transdermal System CIII, 237t. *See also* Transdermal buprenorphine
Bydureon (exenatide), 100t
Byetta (exenatide), 100t
Bypass surgery, coronary artery, 39, 254t, 255t
Bystolic, 53t. *See also* Nebivolol

C
Cabergoline *(Dostinex)*, 309
CABG (coronary artery bypass grafting), 39, 254t, 255t
Cachexia, 185, 248–249
CAD. *See* Coronary artery disease
Cadexomer iodine, 294
Caduet (amlodipine with atorvastatin), 57t
Caffeine
    and dizziness, 211
    for fecal incontinence, 155
    for orthostatic (postural) hypotension, 66

Caffeine *continued*
  and sleep problems, 304
  for UI, 148
CAGE questionnaire, 252, 311
Calan SR (verapamil SR), 54*t*
Calcimar, 225*t. See also* Calcitonin
Calcipotriene, 87
Calcitonin *(Calcimar, Cibacalcin, Miacalcin,*
    Osteocalcin, Salmonine)
  bone outcomes, 226*t*
  effects on other outcomes, level of
    evidence, and risks of, 226*t*
  with estrogen, 225
  for osteoporosis, 225, 225*t*
  for vertebral compression fracture, 194
Calcitriol *(Rocaltrol),* 179
Calcium
  antacids with, 125
  drug interactions, 19
  for HTN, 50
  for hypocalcemia, 179
  for malnutrition, 186
  for osteoporosis, 223, 257*t*
  for Parkinson disease, 216
  with vitamin D, 223
Calcium acetate *(PhosLo),* 179
Calcium alginate dressings *(Algiderm,*
    Curasorb Polymem Alginate, Kaltostat,
    NU-DERM Alginate, Restore CalciCare,
    SeaSorb, Sorbsan, 3M Tegagen HL &
    HG Alginate)
  for pressure ulcers, 299*t*, 301*t*, 302*t*
  for skin ulcers, 293
  for venous ulcers, 303
  wound and pressure ulcer products, 299*t*
Calcium alginate with silver *(Algidex Ag*
    Alginate), 302*t*
Calcium antagonists. *See* Calcium-channel
  blockers (CCBs)
Calcium carbonate, 179, 223
Calcium citrate *(Freeda Mini Cal-citrate,*
    Freeda Calcium Citrate Fine Granular),
    223
Calcium gluconate, 184
Calcium polycarbophil, 132
Calcium pyrophosphate, 208
Calcium-channel blockers (CCBs)

for ACS, 40
for chronic angina, 40, 41
for chronic kidney disease, 178
and coexisting conditions, 56*t*
for DM type 2, 96
for HF, 44
for HTN, 50, 54*t*, 56*t*–57*t*
for hyperthyroidism, 93
and leg edema, 45
for PAH, 58
and UI, 151*t*
Caldolor (ibuprofen), 202*t*
Calluses and corns, 197
Calmoseptine, 88
Caloric requirements, 187, 296
CAM (Confusion Assessment Method), 67,
  256
CAM (Confusion Assessment Method)-ICU,
  67
Campho-Phenique (camphor and phenol),
  239*t*
Camphor and phenol *(Campho-Phenique),*
  239*t*
Camphor-menthol-phenol *(Sarna),* 239*t*
Campral (acamprosate), 311
Canagliflozin *(Invokana),* 99*t*
Cancer
  bladder, 258
  breast, 226*t*, 257*t*, 259, 316–317, 318*t*
  cervical, 258
  colon, 258
  colorectal, 259
  decision making, 258–259
  determinants for hospice eligibility, 243*t*
  head and neck, 190
  hospice referral, 242
  lung, 257*t*
  medications for osteoporosis and, 226*t*
  metastatic bone disease, 246, 265, 317
  ovarian, 258
  pancreatic, 258
  prostate, 224, 258, 259, 263–265, 265*t*–266*t*
  resources for, 335, 336
  screening, 257*t*, 258–259
  vulvar, 317
"Cancer type" anemia, 138

Cancer-related anorexia/cachexia syndrome, 185
Cancidas (caspofungin), 175*t*
Candesartan *(Atacand)*, 45*t*, 55*t*
Candesartan with HCTZ *(Atacand HCT)*, 57*t*
Candidiasis, 85
  antibiotics for, 173*t*, 174*t*
  at end of life, 247
  esophageal, 175*t*
  topical antifungals for, 89*t*, 90*t*
  UTI or urosepsis, 161
  vaginal, 173*t*
Cane fitting, 115
Canuloplasty, 105
Capoten, 55*t*. *See also* Captopril
Capozide (captopril with HCTZ), 56*t*
Capsaicin *(Capsin, Capzasin, No Pain-HP, Qutenza, R-Gel, Zostrix)*
  for osteoarthritis, 198, 200*f*
  for pain, 232, 240*t*
  for painful neuropathy, 221
Capsin, 240*t*. *See also* Capsaicin
Capsulitis, adhesive, 192
Captopril *(Capoten)*
  food interactions, 19
  for HF, 45*t*
  for HTN, 55*t*
  and liver disease, 133*t*
Captopril with HCTZ *(Capozide)*, 56*t*
Capzasin, 240*t*. *See also* Capsaicin
Carac, 84. *See also* 5-Fluorouracil
Carbamazepine *(Epitol, Equetro, Carbatrol, Tegretol, Tegretol XR, Carbatrol)*
  for agitation, 77*t*
  for bipolar disorders, 83*t*
  and liver disease, 133*t*
  ocular adverse events, 111
  for pain, 238*t*
  for painful neuropathy, 221
  for restless legs syndrome, 309
  for seizures, 219*t*
  and sexual dysfunction, 292
  warfarin interactions, 32
Carbamide peroxide *(Cerumenex, Debrox)*, 135
Carbapenems, 159, 168*t*–169*t*

Carbatrol, 219*t*, 237*t*. *See also* Carbamazepine
Carbex (selegiline), 218*t*
Carbidopa-levodopa *(Sinemet, Parcopa)*, 217*t*, 308
Carbidopa-levodopa, sustained-release *(Sinemet CR)*, 217*t*
Carbidopa-levodopa + entacapone *(Stalevo)*, 218*t*
Carbinoxamine, 68*t*
Carbohydrates, fast-acting, 96
Carbonic anhydrase inhibitors, 107*t*
Cardene (nicardipine), 54*t*, 214
Cardene SR (nicardipine), 54*t*
Cardiac catheterization, 38
Cardiac conduction, 19, 20*t*
Cardiac CT angiography, 38
Cardiac diagnostic tests, 38
Cardiac enzymes, 39
Cardiac pacing, 117*t*
Cardiac risk assessment, preoperative, 250, 250*f*, 251
Cardiac risk factors, 49, 260
Cardiac syncope, 64–65, 64*t*
Cardiac troponins, 39
Cardiac valvular surgery, 255*t*
Cardiomyopathy, 66
Cardiovascular diseases, 38–66
  behavioral therapy for, 334*t*
  and chronic kidney disease, 179
  determinants for hospice eligibility, 243*t*
  drug-induced changes in cardiac conduction, 19
  drug-QT$_c$ interval interactions, 20*t*
  endocarditis prophylaxis, 259
  exercise prescription, 260
  and intolerable vasomotor symptoms, 320
  prevention of, 24*t*, 29*t*
  resources for, 336
  risks with surgery, 251
Cardioversion, 59, 61
Cardizem CD (diltiazem), 54*t*
Cardizem SR (diltiazem), 54*t*
Cardura (doxazosin), 52*t*, 262
Care preferences assessment, 5*t*
Caregiving, 10, 77, 335. *See also* Mistreatment of older adults

Carisoprodol, 68*t*, 234
Carotid angioplasty, 215*t*
Carotid artery stenosis, 258
Carotid endarterectomy, 215*t*, 255*t*
Carotid sinus hypersensitivity, 117*t*
Carotid stenosis, 215*t*
Carpal tunnel syndrome, 196
CarraDres, 301*t*
CarraSmart Film, 300*t. See also* Transparent
    film
Carteolol *(Cartrol, Ocupress),* 53*t*, 106*t*
Cartrol, 53*t. See also* Carteolol
Carvedilol *(Coreg),* 45*t*, 53*t*
Carvedilol extended-release *(Coreg CR),* 45*t*,
    53*t*
Casodex (bicalutamide), 266*t*
Caspofungin *(Cancidas),* 175*t*
Cataflam, 202*t. See also* Diclofenac
Catalyst Vacuum Device, 290*t*
Catapres, 52*t. See also* Clonidine
Catapres-TTS, 52*t. See also* Clonidine
Cataracts, 104, 117*t*, 252
Catechol *O*-methyltransferase (COMT)
    inhibitors, 217*t*
Catheter ablation, 61
Catheterization, cardiac, 38
Catheters, urinary, 153
CBT (cognitive-behavioral therapy)
    for anxiety, 36
    for dependent drinking, 311
    for depression, 78
    for insomnia, 305
    for pain, 227*t*, 231, 231*t*
    for prescription drug abuse/misuse, 315
    for preventing falls, 116*t*
CCBs. *See* Calcium-channel blockers
Ceclor (cefaclor), 169*t*
Cedax (ceftibuten), 170*t*
Cefaclor *(Ceclor),* 169*t*
Cefadroxil *(Duricef),* 169*t*
Cefazolin *(Ancef, Kefzol),* 169*t*, 195, 259*t*
Cefdinir *(Omnicef),* 170*t*
Cefditoren *(Spectracef),* 170*t*
Cefepime *(Maxipime),* 159, 159*t*, 170*t*
Cefixime *(Suprax),* 170*t*
Cefotan (cefotetan), 169*t*

Cefotaxime *(Claforan),* 159*t*, 170*t*
Cefotetan *(Cefotan),* 169*t*
Cefoxitin *(Mefoxin),* 169*t*
Cefpodoxime *(Vantin),* 159*t*, 170*t*
Cefprozil *(Cefzil),* 169*t*
Ceftaroline fosamil *(Tefloro),* 162, 170*t*
Ceftazidime *(Ceptaz, Fortaz),* 159, 170*t*
Ceftibuten *(Cedax),* 170*t*
Ceftin, 169*t. See also* Cefuroxime axetil
Ceftriaxone *(Rocephin)*
    for community-acquired pneumonia, 159*t*
    for endocarditis prophylaxis, 259*t*
    for infections in chronic wounds, 295*t*
    for infectious diseases, 170*t*
Cefuroxime axetil *(Ceftin),* 159*t*, 169*t*
Cefzil (cefprozil), 169*t*
Celebrex, 203*t. See also* Celecoxib
Celecoxib *(Celebrex),* 32, 203*t*, 232
Celestone (betamethasone), 103*t*
Celexa, 77*t*, 79*t. See also* Citalopram
CellerateRX Gel/Powder, 302*t*
Cellular immunotherapy, autologous, 265
Cellulitis, 85, 108*t*, 294
Central auditory processing disorder,
    134*t*–135*t*, 136
Central sleep apnea (CSA), 307
Cephalexin *(Keflex)*
    for antibiotic prophylaxis, 260
    for cellulitis, 85
    for cystitis or UTI, 161
    for endocarditis prophylaxis, 259*t*
    for infections in chronic wounds, 294*t*
    for infectious diseases, 169*t*
Cephalosporins
    for cellulitis, 85
    endocarditis prophylaxis regimens, 259*t*
    for erysipelas, 85
    for impetigo, 85
    for infectious diseases, 169*t*–170*t*
    for pneumonia, 159
    for prostatitis, 267
    for urosepsis, 161
Cephalothin *(Keflin),* 169*t*
Cephradine *(Anspor),* 169*t*, 260
Ceptaz, 170*t. See also* Ceftazidime
Cerebellar disease, 211*t*
Cerebellar tremor, 211*t*

Cerebral venous sinus thrombosis, 33t
Certolizumab *(Cimzia)*, 206
Cerumen removal, 69t, 135
Cerumenex (carbamide peroxide), 135
Cervical cancer, 258
Cervical spondylosis, 212t
Cetirizine *(Zyrtec)*, 275t
CHADS₂ scoring
    for AF antithrombotic treatment, 60t
    for stroke risk, 59
    for warfarin anticoagulation, 32t, 33t
CHA₂DS₂-VASc scoring, 59, 60t
Chantix, 313t. *See also* Varenicline
Chemical coping, 232
Chemical dependency, 232
Chemical peels, 84
Chemical skin ulcer debridement, 293
Chemotherapy
    antiemetic therapy for, 128t
    for breast cancer, 317
    for myelodysplastic syndromes, 144
    for pain at end of life, 246
    for prostate cancer, 265
    QT_c interval interactions, 20t
    and tinnitus, 137
Chest pain, 38
Chest percussion, 158
Chest radiography, 272t
Chlamydia pneumoniae, 158
Chloramphenicol *(Chloromycetin)*, 172t
Chlordiazepoxide, 36
Chlorhexidine/fluoride, 158
Chloride channel activators, 125t
Chloromycetin (chloramphenicol), 172t
Chloroquine, 111
Chlorothiazide *(Diuril)*, 51t
Chlorothiazide with reserpine *(Diupres)*, 57t
Chlorpheniramine *(Chlor-Trimeton)*, 68t, 276t
Chlorpromazine, 68t, 219
Chlorthalidone *(Hygroton)*, 51t
Chlorthalidone with atenolol *(Tenoretic)*, 57t
Chlorthalidone with azilsartan *(Edarbyclor)*, 57t
Chlor-Trimeton, 276t. *See also* Chlorpheniramine
Chlorzoxazone, 234
Cholecalciferol, 223, 224t

Cholestatic hepatitis, 133t
Cholesterol, serum, 186
Cholesterol absorption inhibitors, 48t
Cholesterol screening. *See* Dyslipidemia
Cholesterol-lowering diet, 46–47
Cholesterol-lowering margarines, 47
Cholestyramine, 32, 44
Choline magnesium salicylate *(Tricosal, Trilisate, CMT)*, 201t
Choline salicylate *(Arthropan)*, 201t
Cholinergic agonists, 106t–107t
Cholinergic urticaria, 89
Cholinesterase inhibitors
    for agitation, 76
    for apathy, 76
    cognitive enhancers, 75, 76t
    de-prescribing, 18
    for glaucoma, 107t
Chondrocalcinosis, 209
Chondroitin, 199
Chondroitin/glucosamine, 20–21
Chondromalacia patellae, 196
Chronic calcium pyrophosphate crystal inflammatory arthritis, 209
Chronic care, 7t
Chronic crystal inflammatory arthritis, 208
Chronic hepatitis, 133t
Chronic kidney disease, 177–180
    anemia of, 141–142
    antihypertensive therapy and, 56t
    determinants for hospice eligibility, 244t
Chronic low back pain, 198, 199
Chronic musculoskeletal pain, 238t
Chronic myelogenous leukemia, 145
Chronic obstructive pulmonary disease (COPD), 277–280
    assessment of, 278t
    with asthma, 281
    exacerbation, 280t
    preoperative risk assessment, 251
    resources for, 335, 336
    screening for, 258
    therapy for, 278t–279t, 280t, 283t–286t
Chronic pain, 231t, 238t
Chronic wounds, 293–296, 294t–295t, 296t–297t
Chronulac (lactulose), 126t

Chymopapain, 190
Cialis (tadalafil), 262, 289*t*
Cibacalcin, 225*t. See also* Calcitonin
Ciclesonide *(Alvesco, Omnaris),* 276*t,* 284*t*
Ciclopirox *(Loprox, Penlac),* 87, 89*t*
Cilastatin-imipenem *(Primaxin),* 168*t*
Cilostazol *(Pletal),* 32, 64
Ciloxan, 109*t. See also* Ciprofloxacin
Cimetidine *(Tagamet HB 200),* 120*t*
Cimzia (certolizumab), 206
Cipro, 171*t. See also* Ciprofloxacin
Cipro XR (ciprofloxacin), 171*t*
Ciprofloxacin *(Ciloxan, Cipro)*
    for acute bacterial conjunctivitis, 109*t*
    for COPD exacerbation, 280*t*
    drug interactions, 19, 32
    enteral nutrition interactions, 189
    for infections in chronic wounds, 294*t*
    for infectious diseases, 171*t*
    for pneumonia, 159*t,* 160
    for prostatitis, 267
    QT$_c$ interval interactions, 20*t*
Ciprofloxacin extended release *(Cipro XR),*
    171*t*
Circadian rhythm disorders, 304
Cirrhosis, hepatic, 181
Cisapride, 20*t*
Cisplatin, 111
Citalopram *(Celexa),* 77*t,* 79*t,* 321
Citrobacter, 161
Citroma (magnesium citrate), 126*t*
Citrucel, 124, 125*t. See also* Methylcellulose
Claforan, 170*t. See also* Cefotaxime
Clarinex (desloratadine), 275*t*
Clarithromycin *(Biaxin, Biaxin XL)*
    for community-acquired pneumonia, 159*t*
    for endocarditis prophylaxis, 259*t*
    food interactions, 19
    for *H pylori* infection, 122*t*
    for infectious disease, 171*t*
    for peptic ulcer disease, 122
    QT$_c$ interval interactions, 20*t*
    for rosacea, 87
Clarithromycin with lansoprazole and
        amoxicillin *(Prevpac),* 122*t*
Claritin, 275*t. See also* Loratadine

Claritin-D, 275*t. See also* Loratadine
Claudication therapy, 63–64, 63*t*
Clavicle: rotator tendon impingement on, 191
Clavulanate, 133*t*
Clavulanate-amoxicillin *(Augmentin)*
    for community-acquired pneumonia, 159*t*
    for COPD exacerbation, 280*t*
    for cystitis or UTI, 161
    for folliculitis, 85
    for infections in chronic wounds, 294*t*
    for infectious diseases, 169*t*
    and liver disease, 133*t*
Clavulanate-ticarcillin *(Timentin),* 169*t*
ClearSite, 300*t,* 301*t. See also* Transparent
        film
Clemastine, 68*t*
Clenia (sodium sulfacetamide), 87
Cleocin, 172*t. See also* Clindamycin
Clindamycin *(Cleocin)*
    for endocarditis prophylaxis, 259*t*
    for erysipelas, 85
    for folliculitis, 85
    for infections in chronic wounds,
        294*t*–295*t*
    for infectious diseases, 172*t*
    for MRSA, 85, 162
Clinoril, 203*t. See also* Sulindac
Clobetasol propionate *(Temovate),* 91*t,* 317
Clocortolone pivalate *(Cloderm),* 90*t*
Cloderm (clocortolone pivalate), 90*t*
Clofibrate, 32
Clog-Zapper, 190
Clomipramine, 68*t*
Clonazepam *(Klonopin),* 239*t,* 309
Clonidine *(Catapres, Catapres-TTS)*
    food interactions, 19
    for HTN, 52*t*
    and leg edema, 45
    for menopausal symptoms, 321
    and orthostatic hypotension, 211
    for restless legs syndrome, 309
    and sexual dysfunction, 292
    and sleep problems, 304
Clopidogrel *(Plavix)*
    for ACS, 39
    for AF, 61
    for antithrombotic therapy, 24*t*

Clopidogrel *continued*
cessation before surgery, 252
for chronic angina, 41
for DM type 2, 97
herbal medicine interactions, 22
for PAD, 63
prescribing information, 29*t*
to reduce cardiovascular complications of
surgery, 254*t*
for stroke prevention, 215
Clostridium difficile
antibiotics for, 173*t*
diagnosis of, 130
evaluation and empiric management of,
130
pseudomembranous colitis, 129
treatment of, 131*t*
Clotrimazole *(Cruex, Lotrimin, Mycelex)*, 89*t*,
247
Clozapine *(Clozaril)*
anticholinergic property, 68*t*
and dementia, 74
for Parkinson disease, 217
for psychosis, 269*t*
QTc interval interactions, 20*t*
and seizures, 219
and sexual dysfunction, 292
Clozaril, 269*t. See also* Clozapine
CMS guidance on unnecessary drugs, 18
CMT (choline magnesium salicylate), 201*t*
CNS depressants
abuse/misuse, 314, 315
herbal medicine interactions, 22, 23
CNS tumors, 118*t*
Cochlear implants, 135–136, 135*t*
Cockcroft-Gault formula, 1
Codeine, 235*t*, 273*t*
Codeine phosphate, 273*t*
Coding, 333–334
Coenzyme Q₁₀, 21
Cogentin, 217*t. See also* Benztropine
Cognitive enhancers, 75, 76, 76*t*
Cognitive impairment
in delirium, 67
and falls, 117*t*
and pain assessment, 228, 230*f*
pharmacologic treatment, 75

preoperative screening for, 252
preventive measures for delirium, 69*t*
progression, 72–73
screening for, 257*t*
UI and, 148, 153
Cognitive status assessment
in cognitive dysfunction, 75
in dementia, 71
Mini-Cog™ screen for dementia, 322
screening assessment, 4*t*
Cognitive-behavioral therapy (CBT). *See* CBT
Colace, 127*t*, 135. *See also* Docusate
ColActive AG, 302*t*
ColBenemid (probenecid with colchicine),
208*t*
Colchicine
for gout, 207, 208*t*
for osteoarthritis, 199
for pseudogout, 209
Colchicine with probenecid *(ColBenemid,
Col-Probenecid, Proben-C)*, 208*t*
Cold therapy, 229, 231
Colesevelam *(WelChol)*, 48*t*, 99*t*
Colestid, 48*t. See also* Colestipol
Colestid Tablets, 48*t. See also* Colestipol
Colestipol *(Colestid, Colestid Tablets)*, 44, 48*t*
Colitis, antibiotic-associated
pseudomembranous, 129
Collagen *(CellerateRX Gel/Powder, Fibracol,
Kollagen-Medifil Particles/Gels/Pads,
Promogran Matrix, Stimulen)*, 299*t*, 302*t*
Collagen with silver *(ColActive AG, Prisma
Matrix)*, 302*t*
Colon cancer, 258
Colonoscopy, 155, 257*t*
Colorectal cancer, 259
Colposcopy, 317
Col-Probenecid (probenecid with
colchicine), 208*t*
Coma, myxedema, 92
CombiDERM, 302*t*
Combigan (brimonidine/timolol), 107*t*
Combivent (albuterol-ipratropium), 285*t*
Combivent Respimat (albuterol-ipratropium),
285*t*
Combunox (oxycodone + ibuprofen), 235*t*
Comfeel Film, 300*t. See also* Transparent film

Comfeel Plus, 300*t*. *See also* Transparent film
Comfortell, 302*t*
Communicating bad news, 241–242
Communication with hearing-impaired people, 136
Community-acquired cystitis, 161
Community-acquired pneumonia, 158, 159*t*
Compazine, 128*t*. *See also* Prochlorperazine
Compression, intermittent pneumatic, 24*t*, 25*t*, 195
Compression devices, 303
Compression fractures, vertebral, 194
Compression stockings
  for hip fracture, 195
  for orthostatic (postural) hypotension, 65
  prescribing information, 46*t*
  for stasis edema, 153
  for UI, 153
  for venous insufficiency, 46
  for venous ulcers, 303
Compression therapy, 65, 303
Compression wraps, 46, 303
Comprilan wrap, 303
Computed tomography (CT), 38, 257*t*
COMT (catechol *O*-methyltransferase) inhibitors, 217*t*
Comtan (entacapone), 217*t*
Conduction aphasia, 220*t*
Conduction disorders, drug-induced, 19
Conductive hearing loss, 134*t*–135*t*
Confusion Assessment Method (CAM), 67, 256
Confusion Assessment Method (CAM)-ICU, 67
Congestion, nasal, 275*t*
Congestive heart failure. *See* Heart failure
Congestive heart failure, Hypertension, Age, Diabetes, Stroke (CHADS). *See* CHADS₂ scoring
Conivaptan *(Vaprisol),* 182
Conjunctival hyperemia, 109
Conjunctivitis, 109
  acute bacterial conjunctivitis, 109*t*
  allergic, 109–110, 110*t*–111*t*, 275*t*
Constipation, 124–125
  drug-induced, 270*t*
  at end of life, 247
  and fecal incontinence, 155
  medications for, 125*t*–127*t*
  opioid-induced, 234
  and UI, 148
Continuing care retirement communities, 7*t*
Continuous positive airway pressure (CPAP), 307
Contreet, 300*t*. *See also* Silver dressings
Contreet Foam, 300*t*
ConZip (tramadol ER), 237*t*
COPA, 300*t*. *See also* Foam island
COPD. *See* Chronic obstructive pulmonary disease
Coping, chemical, 232
Coping skills, 231
Cordarone, 61*t*. *See also* Amiodarone
Cordran (flurandrenolide), 90*t*
Coreg, 53*t*. *See also* Carvedilol
Coreg CR, 53*t*. *See also* Carvedilol extended-release
Corgard, 53*t*. *See also* Nadolol
Corns, 197
Coronary angiography, 42
Coronary artery bypass grafting (CABG), 39, 254*t*, 255*t*
Coronary artery disease (CAD), 38–40
  ICD placement for, 66
  medications for osteoporosis and, 226*t*
  screening for, 258
Coronary risk assessment, preoperative, 250*f*
Cortef, 103*t*. *See also* Hydrocortisone
Corticosteroids. *See also* Glucocorticoids
  for acute bacterial conjunctivitis, 109*t*
  for acute disk herniation, 193
  for adrenal insufficiency, 102, 103*t*
  for allergic conjunctivitis, 109, 275*t*, 276*t*
  for allergic rhinitis, 275, 275*t*, 276*t*
  for anorexia, 249
  for asthma, 282, 282*t*, 284*t*
  for back pain, 193
  for bicipital tendinitis, 192
  for cachexia, 249
  for carpal tunnel syndrome, 196
  for chronic disk degeneration, 193
  for COPD, 278, 279*t*, 280*t*, 284*t*

Corticosteroids *continued*
  for dehydration, 249
  for frozen shoulder (adhesive capsulitis), 192
  for giant cell arteritis, 210
  for herpes zoster, 162
  inhaled, 282*t*
  and leg edema, 45
  and liver disease, 133*t*
  for myelofibrosis, 145
  for myxedema coma, 92
  for neurodermatitis, 86
  ocular adverse events, 111
  for ocular inflammatory disease, 108
  for osteoarthritis, 193, 198–199, 200*f*
  and osteoporosis, 222
  for pain, 231, 239*t*
  for plantar fasciitis, 198
  for scabies, 88
  for shoulder pain, 191, 192
  and sleep problems, 304
  topical, 90*t*–91*t*
  for trochanteric bursitis, 194
Cortifoam, 132
Cortisone *(Cortone),* 103*t*
Cortone (cortisone), 103*t*
Corzide (nadolol with bendroflumethiazide), 57*t*
Cosopt (dorzolamide/timolol), 107*t*
Co-trimoxazole *(Bactrim),* 172*t,* 267
Cough, 272
  antitussives and expectorants, 273*t*
  with asthma, 281
  chronic, 277
  diagnosis and treatment by duration of symptoms, 272*t*
Coumadin, 32. *See also* Warfarin
Counseling
  for dependent drinking, 311
  for female sexual dysfunction, 291
  for pain management, 232
  procedure codes, 333*t,* 334*t*
  for smoking cessation, 312
  telephone counseling, 312
Counterirritants, 239*t*
Covaderm Plus, 302*t*
Covera-HS (verapamil), 54*t*

COX-2 inhibitors
  for arthritis, 199, 200*f,* 203*t*
  for pain, 229, 232
Cozaar, 55*t,* 208*t. See also* Losartan
CPAP (continuous positive airway pressure), 307
Cr (creatinine), 180
Cramps, leg, 308
Cranberry juice, 161
CrCl (creatinine clearance), 1
C-reactive protein (CRP), 38, 257*t*
Creatine kinase MB isoenzymes, 39
Creatinine (Cr), 180
Creatinine clearance (CrCl), 1
Crestor, 48*t. See also* Rosuvastatin
Cricopharyngeal myotomy, 118
Cromolyn *(NasalCrom),* 275*t,* 276*t*
Cromolyn sodium *(Intal),* 285*t*
Cross-cultural geriatrics, 13
Crotamiton *(Eurax),* 88
CRP (C-reactive protein), 38, 257*t*
Cruex, 89*t. See also* Clotrimazole
Cryosurgery, 84, 85
Cryotherapy, 265
Crystal-induced arthritis, 208
CSA (central sleep apnea), 307
CT (computed tomography), 38, 257*t*
Cubicin, 172*t. See also* Daptomycin
Cultural identity, 13
Cupric oxide, 105
Curagel, 301*t*
Curasorb Polymem Alginate, 301*t. See also* Calcium alginate dressings
Curettage, 84, 85, 318
CURITY, 302*t. See also* Gauze packing
Cushing syndrome, 268
Cutaneous capsaicin patches *(Qutenza),* 221, 240*t*
Cutinova Hydro, 300*t. See also* Hydrocolloids
Cutivate, 91*t. See also* Fluticasone propionate
Cyclobenzaprine, 68*t,* 234
Cyclocort (amcinonide), 91*t*
Cyclophosphamide, 210
Cycloset, 99*t. See also* Bromocriptine
Cyclosporine, 23, 87

Cyclosporine ophthalmic emulsion
(Restasis), 110
Cymbalta. See also Duloxetine
for depression, 80t
for osteoarthritis, 199
for pain, 238t
for painful neuropathy, 221
CYP substrates, inducers, and inhibitors, 21,
23, 121t, 289t
Cyproheptadine, 68t
Cystitis, 161
Cytochrome P-450. See CYP substrates,
inducers, and inhibitors
Cytotec, 199. See also Misoprostol

D

Dabigatran (Pradaxa)
for ACS, 40
for AF, 60t
for anticoagulation, 31t, 33t
for antithrombotic therapy, 24t
cessation before surgery, 253
resumption after surgery, 253
for VTE, 25t, 28t
Dalfopristin/quinupristin (Synercid), 172t
Daliresp (roflumilast), 285t
Dalteparin (Fragmin)
for anticoagulation, 30t
for antithrombotic therapy, 24t
for DVT, 195
for VTE, 25t, 28t
Danaparoid (Orgaran), 25t, 30t
Daptomycin (Cubicin), 162, 172t
Darbepoetin alfa (Aranesp), 143t
Darifenacin (Enablex), 68t, 151t
Darunavir, 20t
Daypro (oxaprozin), 203t
DBS (deep brain stimulation), 216
D&C (dilation and curettage), 318
D-dimer test, 26
Deafness. See Hearing impairment
Death certificates, 13–14, 246
Debridement, 293, 298
Debrox (carbamide peroxide), 135
Decadron, 103t, 248. See also
Dexamethasone
Decision making, informed, 10f

cancer screening, 258–259
goal-oriented care, 8–9
life expectancy, 8–9
patient preferences for life-sustaining
care, 10
Declomycin (demeclocycline), 183
Decongestants, 276t, 304
Deep brain stimulation (DBS), 216
Deep tissue injury, 299
Deep-vein thrombosis (DVT)
antithrombotic medications for, 25t
diagnosis of, 26
leg edema, 45
medications for osteoporosis and, 226t
prophylaxis of, 25t, 195, 254t
Degarelix (Firmagon), 20t, 266t
Dehydration, 69t, 180, 248–249. See also
Hydration
Delirium, 67–70
differential diagnosis, 268
medication-induced, 68t
postoperative, 255–256
preventive measures, 69t
Delta-Cortef, 103t. See also Prednisolone
Deltasone, 103t, 284t. See also Prednisone
Delusional (paranoid) disorder, late-life, 268
Delusions, 73
Demadex, 51t. See also Torsemide
Demeclocycline (Declomycin), 183
Dementia, 71–77
AIDS-related dementia, 70
and delirium, 67
dementia syndrome, 71
determinants for hospice eligibility, 243t
differential diagnosis, 268
distinguishing early Parkinson disease
from other parkinsonian syndromes,
216t
gastrointestinal complaints, 118t
Lewy body dementia, 70
management of, 268
Mini-Cog™ screen for dementia, 322
risk and protective factors, 74
Denosumab (Prolia)
bone outcomes, 226t
for metastatic bone disease, 265
for osteoporosis, 223, 225, 225t

Dental care, 149
Dental procedures
    anticoagulation for, 253
    prophylaxis for, 255*t*, 259, 260
Dentition assessment, 4*t*
Depacon, 83*t*, 219*t*. *See also* Valproic acid
Depade (naltrexone), 311
Depakene, 83*t*, 219*t*. *See also* Valproic acid
Depakote (divalproex sodium), 77*t*, 83*t*, 219*t*.
    See also Valproic acid
Depakote ER (divalproex sodium), 219*t*
Depakote extended release (Depakote ER),
    219*t*
Dependency, 232
Dependent drinking, 310–311
Depo-Medrol, 103*t*. *See also*
    Methylprednisolone
Deponit, 41*t*. *See also* Nitroglycerin
Depo-Provera, 77*t*. *See also*
    Medroxyprogesterone
De-prescribing medications, 17–18
Depression, 78–83
    agitation treatment guidelines, 77*t*
    apathy treatment, 76
    in bipolar disorder, 82
    in COPD, 279
    in dementia, 73
    differential diagnosis, 268
    at end of life, 249
    and falls, 117*t*
    medications for management of, 83*t*
    with pain, 232
    and Parkinson disease, 82
    PHQ-2 Quick Depression Assessment, 326
    PHQ-9 Quick Depression Assessment,
        325–326
    postmenopausal, 319
    preoperative screening, 252
    psychotic, 78, 82
    screening for, 257*t*, 334*t*
    subsyndromal, 78
    and tinnitus, 137
Dermabrasion, 84
DermaDress, 302*t*
DermaFilm, 300*t*. *See also* Hydrocolloids
DermaFoam, 300*t*. *See also* Foam island
Derma-gel, 301*t*

Dermagraft, 298, 303
Dermatell, 300*t*. *See also* Transparent film
Dermatitis, seborrheic, 88, 89*t*
Dermatologic conditions, 84–91, 336
Dermatomes, 3*f*
Dermatop (prednicarbate), 91*t*
Dermatophytoses, 89*t*
Desensitization, 36
Desipramine *(Norpramin)*
    anticholinergic property, 68*t*
    for depression, 80*t*
    for pain relief, 238*t*
    for painful neuropathy, 220
    QT$_c$ interval interactions, 20*t*
Desirudin *(Iprivask)*, 25*t*, 31*t*
Desloratadine *(Clarinex)*, 275*t*
Desonide *(DesOwen, Tridesilon)*, 90*t*
DesOwen (desonide), 90*t*
Desoximetasone *(Topicort)*, 90*t*, 91*t*
Desvenlafaxine *(Pristiq)*, 81*t*, 321
Desyrel, 77*t*, 305*t*. *See also* Trazodone
Detrol, 151*t*. *See also* Tolterodine
Detrol LA (tolterodine), 151*t*
Detrusor contractility, impaired, 147
Detrusor hyperactivity with impaired
    contractility (DHIC), 148, 149
Detrusor muscle-relaxing drugs, 149
Dexamethasone *(Decadron, Dexone,
    Hexadrol)*
    for adrenal insufficiency, 102, 103*t*
    for anorexia, cachexia, dehydration, 249
    for inflammation due to malignant
        obstruction, 248
    for multiple myeloma, 146
    for nausea, vomiting, 248
Dexedrine (dextroamphetamine), 246
Dexilant (dexlansoprazole), 120*t*
Dexlansoprazole *(Dexilant)*, 120*t*
Dexone, 103*t*. *See also* Dexamethasone
Dextroamphetamine *(Dexedrine)*, 246
Dextromethorphan *(Robitussin DM)*, 272,
    273*t*
Dextrose solution, 184, 190
DH Pressure Relief Walker, 298
DHIC (detrusor hyperactivity with impaired
    contractility), 148, 149
Diaβeta, 97*t*. *See also* Glyburide

Diabetes control, 41, 178
Diabetes insipidus, 180
Diabetes mellitus (DM), 94–101
   antihypertensive therapy and, 56*t*
   drug-induced, 270*t*
   eye examinations, 104
   goals of treatment, 95*t*
   insulin preparations for, 101*t*
   lactose-free formulations, 189*t*
   non-insulin agents for, 97*t*–100*t*
   and PAD, 63
   post MI, 41
   resources for, 336
   screening for, 257*t*
Diabetic peripheral neuropathy, 221, 238*t*
Diabetic retinopathy, 105
Diabetic ulcers, 296*t*–297*t*, 297–298
Diabetisource AC, 189*t*
Dialysis
   for acute kidney injury, 177
   for chronic kidney disease, 179, 180
   hemodialysis, 179
   for hyperkalemia, 184
   peritoneal dialysis, 179
Diamox (acetazolamide), 107*t*
Diarrhea, 129
   antibiotic-associated, 129–131
   antidiarrheals, 129*t*
   at end of life, 248
   with enteral feedings, 190
   and hyponatremia, 182
Diastolic dysfunction, 42
Diathermy, 198
Diazepam, 36
Diclofenac *(Cataflam, Voltaren, Voltaren-XR, Zipsor, Zorvolex, Pennsaid),* 202*t*, 231, 232
Diclofenac, enteric coated *(Arthrotec),* 202*t*
Diclofenac gel *(Voltaren* Gel*)*
   for arthritis, 198, 202*t*
   for pain, 231, 232
Diclofenac patch *(Flector)*
   for arthritis, 198, 202*t*
   for pain, 231, 232
Dicloxacillin *(Dycill, Pathocil),* 32, 133*t*, 168*t*
Dicyclomine *(Bentyl),* 68*t*, 124
Dietary modification

   for AMD, 105
   for brain health, 74
   cholesterol-lowering diet, 46–47
   for chronic kidney disease, 178
   for constipation, 125
   for diabetes, 94, 95
   for dyslipidemia, 46–47
   for dysphagia, 118
   for fecal incontinence, 155
   for GERD, 120
   gluten-free diet, 124
   for hemorrhoids, 132
   high-fiber diet, 94, 95, 132
   for HTN, 50
   for hyperkalemia, 183
   for hyperuricemia, 207
   for IBS, 124
   lactose-free diet, 124
   low potassium diet, 179
   low-protein diet, 178
   Mediterranean diet, 95, 187
   for orthostatic (postural) hypotension, 65
   for Parkinson disease, 216
   post MI, 41
   for sleep apnea, 307
   for stroke prevention, 215
   weight loss diets, 187
Dietary supplements, 20–21
Dificid (fidaxomicin), 131*t*, 171*t*
Diflorasone diacetate *(Florone, Maxiflor, Psorcon),* 91*t*
Diflucan, 86, 173*t. See also* Fluconazole
Diflunisal *(Dolobid),* 202*t*
Digital rectal examination (DRE), 264–265
Digital stimulation, 155
Digiti flexus (hammertoe), 197
Digoxin *(Lanoxin, Lanoxicaps)*
   for AF, 59
   drug interactions, 44
   herbal medicine interactions, 23
   for HF, 44
   ocular adverse events, 111
   and sexual dysfunction, 292
Dihydropyridines, 54*t*, 56*t*
Dilacor XR (diltiazem), 54*t*
Dilantin, 219*t. See also* Phenytoin
Dilation and curettage (D&C), 318

Dilatrate SR (isosorbide dinitrate SR), 40t
Dilaudid, 236t. See also Hydromorphone
Diltiazem
    for AF, 59
    digoxin interactions, 44
    enteral nutrition interactions, 189
    for nocturnal leg cramps, 308
Diltiazem SR (Cardizem CD, Cardizem SR,
        Dilacor XR, Tiazac), 54t
Dimenhydrinate, 68t
Diovan, 55t. See also Valsartan
Diovan HCT (valsartan with HCTZ), 57t
Diphenhydramine (Benadryl)
    for allergic rhinitis, 276t
    anticholinergic property, 68t
    and dementia, 74
    for painful mucositis, 247
Diphenhydrinate (Dramamine), 128t
Diphenoxylate with atropine (Lomotil), 129t
Dipivefrin (AKPro, Propine), 106t
Diprolene, 91t. See also Betamethasone
        dipropionate
Diprolene AF, 91t. See also Betamethasone
        dipropionate
Diprosone, 90t, 91t. See also Betamethasone
        dipropionate
Dipyridamole
    for antithrombotic therapy, 24t
    herbal medicine interactions, 22
    and orthostatic hypotension, 211
    stress test, 38
    for stroke prevention, 215
Dipyridamole with ASA (Aggrenox), 29t, 215
Direct renin inhibitors, 57t
Direct thrombin inhibitors
    for antithrombotic therapy, 24t
    prescribing information, 31t
    for VTE, 25t, 28t
Discharge planning, 8
Discontinuing medications, 17–18
Disease-modifying antirheumatoid drugs
        (DMARDs), 205–206, 206t–207t
Disk degeneration, chronic, 192–194
Disk herniation, acute, 193
Disopyramide, 20t
Distraction, 231
Ditropan, 151t. See also Oxybutynin

Ditropan XL, 151t. See also Oxybutynin
Diupres (reserpine with chlorothiazide), 57t
Diuretics
    and BPH, 262
    for chronic kidney disease, 178
    and coexisting conditions, 56t
    for DM type 2, 96
    for dyspnea, 247
    fall risks, 112
    food interactions, 19
    for HF, 43, 44
    for HTN, 50, 51, 51t–52t, 56t–57t
    for hyperkalemia, 183, 184
    and hyponatremia, 182
    for nocturnal frequency, 153
    and orthostatic hypotension, 211
    for PAH, 58
    potassium-sparing, 19
    preoperative care, 254
    for SIADH, 183
    and sleep problems, 304
    and tinnitus, 137
    and UI, 148, 151t
    for venous insufficiency, 46
    for vertigo, 212t
Diuril (chlorothiazide), 51t
Divalproex (Depakote, Epival), 77t
Dizziness, 211, 212t
DM. See Diabetes mellitus
DMARDs (disease-modifying antirheumatoid
        drugs), 205–206, 206t–207t
DNA hypomethylating agents, 144
DNR (do-not-resuscitate) Orders, 245
Dobutamine stress test, 38
Docusate (Colace), 127t, 135, 155
Dofetilide, 20t
Dolasetron (Anzemet), 20t, 128t
Dolobid (diflunisal), 202t
Domperidone, 121t
Donepezil (Aricept), 75, 76t
Do-not-resuscitate (DNR) Orders, 245
Dopamine, 217t
Dopamine agonists, 217t, 308
Dopamine antagonists, 128t, 308
Dopamine reuptake inhibitors, 218t
Doppler ultrasound, 42, 63t, 213
Doribax (doripenem), 168t

Doripenem *(Doribax)*, 168*t*
Dorzolamide *(Trusopt)*, 107*t*
Dorzolamide/timolol *(Cosopt)*, 107*t*
Dosatinib, 20*t*
Dostinex (cabergoline), 309
Doxazosin *(Cardura)*, 52*t*, 262
Doxepin *(Silenor, Sinequan, Zonalon)*
    anticholinergic property, 68*t*
    avoid use, 81
    for hives, 89
    QT$_c$ interval interactions, 20*t*
    for sleep disorders, 305, 305*t*
Doxycycline *(Vibramycin)*
    for community-acquired pneumonia, 159*t*
    for infectious diseases, 171*t*
    for MRSA, 85, 162
    for rosacea, 87
DPIs (dry powder inhalers), 283
DPP-4 enzyme inhibitors, 98*t*
Dramamine (diphenhydrinate), 128*t*
DRE (digital rectal examination), 264–265
Dressings
    for arterial ulcers, 297
    for diabetic foot ulcers, 298
    for pressure ulcers, 300*t*–302*t*
    for skin ulcers, 294
    for venous ulcers, 303
    wound and pressure ulcer products, 299*t*
Drinking. *See* Alcohol misuse/abuse
Dronabinol, 188, 239*t*
Drop arm test, 191
Drop attacks, 212*t*
Droperidol, 20*t*
Drug abuse, 234–235, 310, 314–315
Drug interactions
    alcohol interactions, 311
    digoxin interactions, 44
    drug-drug interactions, 19
    drug-food or -nutrient interactions, 19
    drug-induced changes in cardiac
        conduction, 19
    QT$_c$ interval interactions, 20*t*
Drug metabolism, 19
Drug prescribing. *See* Pharmacotherapy
Drug-eluting stents, 253
Drug-induced erectile dysfunction, 288*t*

Dry AMD (age-related macular
    degeneration), 104, 105
Dry eye syndrome, 110
Dry mouth, 248
Dry powder inhalers (DPIs), 283
DSI (dual sensory impairment), 108
DSM-5, 268
Dual antiplatelet therapy, 252–253
Dual sensory impairment (DSI), 108
Duetact (pioglitazone and glimepiride), 99*t*
Duexis (ibuprofen and famotidine), 202*t*
Duke boot, 303
Dulcolax, 126*t*. *See also* Bisacodyl
Dulera (formoterol-mometasone), 285*t*
Duloxetine *(Cymbalta)*
    for anxiety disorders, 36
    for depression, 79, 80*t*
    drug interactions, 32, 318*t*
    for osteoarthritis, 199
    for pain, 238*t*
    for painful neuropathy, 221
DuoDERM, 300*t*. *See also* Hydrocolloids
DuoDERM CGF, 300*t*
DuoDERM Signal, 300*t*
Duoneb (albuterol-ipratropium), 285*t*
Durable power of attorney for health care,
    10, 245
Duragesic, 237*t*. *See also* Fentanyl,
    transdermal
Duramorph, 236*t*. *See also* Morphine
Duricef (cefadroxil), 169*t*
Dutasteride *(Avodart)*, 263
Dutoprol (metoprolol succinate with HCTZ),
    57*t*
DVT. *See* Deep-vein thrombosis
Dyazide (triamterene with HCTZ), 57*t*
Dycill, 168*t*. *See also* Dicloxacillin
DynaCirc CR (isradipine SR), 54*t*
Dynapress wrap, 303. *See also* Compression
    wraps
Dyrenium, 52*t*. *See also* Triamterene
Dysgeusia, 19
Dyslipidemia, 46–47
    antihypertensive therapy and, 56*t*
    in diabetes, 96
    post MI, 41

Dyslipidemia *continued*
  screening for, 257t
  in stroke prevention, 215
  treatment of, 47t, 47t–48t, 48t–49t
Dyspareunia, 291, 319
Dysphagia, 118–119
  at end of life, 247
  gastrostomy tubes for, 190
  types/presentation/patient complaints, 118t
Dyspnea, 273–274
  with COPD, 277, 280t
  diagnosis of, 273t–274t
  at end of life, 247
  exertional, 286
  with HF, 42
  Modified Medical Research Council Dyspnea Scale (MMRC), 277
Dyssynergia, 147

E

E faecium, vancomycin-resistant, 173t
Ear wax removal, 135
EAS (electric acoustic stimulation), 135t, 136
Echinacea, 21
Echinocandins, 175t
Echocardiography
  in acute stroke, 213
  in AF, 61
  in AS, 62
  in CAD, 38
  in HF, 42
  in PAH, 58
Echothiophate *(Phospholine)*, 107t
EC-Naprosyn (naproxen), 203t
Econazole nitrate *(Spectazole)*, 89t
ECT (electroconvulsive therapy), 78, 81, 82
Edarbi, 55t. *See also* Azilsartan
Edarbyclor (azilsartan with chlorthalidone), 57t
Edluar, 306t. *See also* Zolpidem
Effexor, 81t, 238t. *See also* Venlafaxine
Effexor XR, 81t, 239t. *See also* Venlafaxine
Effient, 29t. *See also* Prasugrel
Efudex, 84. *See also* 5-Fluorouracil
Elavil, 81. *See also* Amitriptyline
Eldepryl (selegiline), 218t

Electric acoustic stimulation (EAS), 135t, 136
Electrical stimulation, 149, 295
Electrocardiography, 184
Electroconvulsive therapy (ECT), 78, 81, 82
Electrodessication, 85
Electron-beam computed tomography, 257t
Electrosurgery, 84
Elestat (epinastine), 110t
Elidel (pimecrolimus), 87
Elimite (permethrin), 88
Eliquis, 30t. *See also* Apixaban
Elocon, 91t. *See also* Mometasone furoate
Eltroxin, 92. *See also* Levothyroxine
Emadine (emedastine), 110t
Embeda (ER morphine/naltrexone hydrochloride), 237t, 315
Embolism. *See* Pulmonary embolism (PE)
Emedastine *(Emadine)*, 110t
Emotional status assessment, 4t
Enablex, 151t. *See also* Darifenacin
Enalapril *(Vasotec)*, 45t, 51, 55t
Enalapril maleate with felodipine *(Lexxel)*, 56t
Enalapril maleate with HCTZ *(Vaseretic)*, 56t
Enbrel, 206. *See also* Etanercept
Endocarditis prophylaxis, 255t, 259, 259t
Endocrine disorders, 92–103
End-of-life care, 241–249
  planning, 66
  resources for, 335
  in severe COPD, 280
Endothelial receptor antagonists, 58
Endovascular repair, 62, 63t
Enemas
  for constipation, 125, 126t, 247
  for fecal incontinence, 155
  for hyperkalemia, 184
  for rectal evacuation, 155
Enemeez, 155
Energy requirements, 187
Energy supplements, 188
Enoxaparin *(Lovenox)*
  for anticoagulation, 30t
  for antithrombotic therapy, 24t
  for DVT, 195
  for VTE, 25t, 28t
Ensure, 189t
Ensure Enlive, 189t

Ensure Plus, 189*t*
Entacapone *(Comtan)*, 217*t*
Entacapone + carbidopa-levodopa *(Stalevo)*, 218*t*
Enteral nutrition
    drug interactions, 189
    for ICU patients, 188
    lactose-free products, 189*t*
    for malnutrition, 188
    for stress-ulcer prevention, 123
Entereg (alvimopan), 126*t*
Enterobacter, 161
Enterococci, 161
Enterococcus faecium, vancomycin-resistant, 173*t*
Entricitabine, 167
Environmental hazards assessment, 4*t*
Environmental modification
    for dry eye syndrome, 110
    in end-of-life care, 246
    for insomnia, 304–305
    for preventing falls, 115, 116*t*
    for sleep disorders, 309
    for UI, 148
    for visual impairment, 108
Enzyme immunoassay, 163*t*
Epigard, 302*t*
Epinastine *(Elestat)*, 110*t*
Epinephrine *(EpiPen)*, 89, 286*t*
EpiPen, 89. *See also* Epinephrine
Episcleritis, 108*t*
Epitol, 219*t*. *See also* Carbamazepine
Epival, 77*t*. *See also* Divalproex
Eplerenone *(Inspra)*, 43, 52*t*
Epley maneuver, 212*t*
Epoetin alfa *(Epogen, Procrit)*, 143*t*
Epogen (epoetin alfa), 143*t*
Epoprostenol *(Flolan)*, 58
e-Prescribing, 16
Eprosartan *(Teveten)*, 55*t*
Eprosartan mesylate with HCTZ *(Teveten HCT)*, 57*t*
EPS (extrapyramidal symptoms), 70, 270*t*
Eptifibatide *(Integrilin)*, 24*t*, 31*t*, 253
Epworth Sleepiness Scale, 335
Equetro, 219*t*. *See also* Carbamazepine

Equinus, 197
Eraxis (anidulafungin), 175*t*
Erectile dysfunction, 288–289, 288*t*, 289*t*–290*t*
Ergocalciferol (vitamin D$_2$), 179, 222
Ertaczo (sertraconazole), 90*t*
Ertapenem *(Invanz)*, 159*t*, 168*t*
Erysipelas, 85
Erythrocyte sedimentation rate (ESR), 1
Erythromycin
    for cellulitis, 85
    for community-acquired pneumonia, 159*t*
    drug interactions, 32, 44
    for erysipelas, 85
    for folliculitis, 85
    for high gastric residual volume problems, 190
    for impetigo, 85
    and liver disease, 133*t*
    prescribing information, 171*t*
    QT$_c$ interval interactions, 20*t*
    for rosacea, 87
    and tinnitus, 137
Erythromycin ophthalmic *(AK-Mycin, Ilotycin)*, 109*t*
Erythropoiesis-stimulating agents (ESAs)
    for anemia of CKD, 141, 142
    for CKD, 179
    prescribing information, 143*t*
Erythropoietin
    for anemia of chronic kidney disease, 141–142
    for hypotension secondary to anemia, 66
    for multiple myeloma, 146
    for myelofibrosis, 145
Erythropoietin-darbopoetin, 179
ESAs. *See* Erythropoiesis-stimulating agents
Escherichia coli, 161
Escitalopram *(Lexapro)*, 36, 79*t*, 292
Esidrix, 51*t*. *See also* HCTZ
Eskalith, 83*t*. *See also* Lithium
Eskalith CR, 83*t*. *See also* Lithium
Esmolol, 44
Esomeprazole *(Nexium)*, 120*t*, 122*t*
Esophageal candidiasis, 175*t*
Esophageal dysphagia, 118, 118*t*
Esophageal manometry, 118
Esophagitis, reflux, 272*t*

ESR (erythrocyte sedimentation rate), 1
Essential thrombocytosis, 144–145
Essential tremor, 56t, 211t
Estazolam *(ProSom)*, 305t
Estrace, 291t. *See also* Estradiol
Estradiol *(Estrace)*, 319, 321
Estradiol vaginal ring *(Estring)*, 291t
Estradiol vaginal tablets *(Vagifem)*, 291t
Estring (estradiol vaginal ring), 291t
Estriol, 319
Estrogen
  with bisphosphonate or calcitonin, 225
  with progesterone, 319, 320, 320t
  and UI, 151t
Estrogen therapy
  for agitation, 77t
  bone outcomes, 226t
  for dyspareunia, 291
  effects on other outcomes, level of
    evidence, and risks of, 226t
  for intolerable vasomotor symptoms, 321
  for menopausal symptoms, 319, 320
  for osteoporosis, 225, 225t
  in postmenopausal bleeding, 318
  for recurrent UTIs, 291
  risks, 319–320
  risks and benefits, 320t
  for sexual aggression, impulse-control
    symptoms in men, 77t
  topical, 291, 291t
  transdermal, 321
  for UI, 149
  for UTI prophylaxis, 161
  for vaginal prolapse, 319
Estropipate *(Ogen)*, 291t
Eszopiclone *(Lunesta)*
  for anxiety, 37
  for sleep apnea, 336
  for sleep disorders, 305, 306t
Etanercept *(Enbrel)*, 205, 206
Ethambutol, 111
Ethnic groups, 13
Etodolac *(Lodine)*, 202t
Etodolac extended release *(Lodine XL)*, 202t
Etretinate, 87
Eucerin, 89
Euflexxa, 199. *See also* Hyaluronic acid

Eulexin (flutamide), 266t
Eurax (crotamiton), 88
Euthanasia, 245–246
Euthyroid sick syndrome, 93
Euvolemic hyponatremia, 182
Evista, 225t. *See also* Raloxifene
Exalgo (ER hydromorphone hydrochloride),
  237t
Exelderm (sulconazole), 90t
Exelon (rivastigmine), 76t
Exemestane *(Aromasin)*, 318t
Exenatide *(Byetta)*, 100t
Exenatide extended release *(Bydureon)*, 100t
Exercise treadmill test, 38, 63t
Exercise(s)
  for back pain, 194
  for brain health, 74
  for chronic angina, 41
  for COPD, 280
  for diabetes, 94, 95
  for dyspnea, 274
  for fecal incontinence, 155
  for hip pain, 194
  for HTN, 50
  for low back pain syndrome, 193
  oropharyngeal, 307
  for osteoarthritis, 194, 198
  for osteoporosis, 223
  for PAD, 63
  for pain, 229, 231t
  for Parkinson disease, 216
  pelvic muscle (Kegel), 149, 150f, 319
  for plantar fasciitis, 197
  prescription, 260–261
  for preventing diabetes, 94
  for preventing falls, 74, 116t
  for preventing stroke, 215
  for prevention, 257t
  for problem behaviors, 75
  rectal sphincter, 155
  for rheumatoid arthritis, 204
  for shoulder pain, 191, 192
  for sleep apnea, 307
  for sleep disorders, 309
  for sleep hygiene, 304
  for unstable lumbar spine, 194

Exercise(s) *continued*
  for vaginal prolapse, 319
  for vertigo, 212*t*
  for weight loss, 187
Exforge (amlodipine with valsartan), 56*t*
Exforge HCT (amlodipine/valsartan/HCTZ), 56*t*
Expectorants, 273*t*
Exploitation, 12*t*
External rotation lag test, 191
External rotation resistance test, 191
Extra thin DuoDERM, 300*t*
Extracellular matrix, 298
Extrapyramidal symptoms (EPS), 70, 270*t*
Exuderm, 300*t. See also* Hydrocolloids
Exuderm LP, 300*t*
Eye disorders, 104–111
Eye examinations, 104
Eye symptoms, 275*t*
Eylea (aflibercept), 105
Ezetimibe *(Zetia),* 47*t,* 48*t*

F
Facial weakness, 220*t*
Factive, 171*t. See also* Gemifloxacin
Factor Xa inhibitors
  for antithrombotic therapy, 24*t*
  prescribing information, 30*t*–31*t*
  for VTE, 25*t,* 28*t*
Failure to thrive, 243*t*
Falls prevention, 112–117
  assessment and prevention, 4*t,* 114*f*
  distinguishing early Parkinson disease
    from other parkinsonian syndromes, 216*t*
  general prevention, 74
  for osteoporosis, 223
  in pain management, 233
  recommendations, 258*t*
  risk factors and interventions, 116*t*–117*t*
Famciclovir *(Famvir),* 163*t*
Family Caregiver Alliance, 77
Family education, 95
Family presence, 75
Family therapy, 311
Famotidine *(Pepcid),* 120*t,* 292
Famotidine with ibuprofen *(Duexis),* 202*t*

Famvir (famciclovir), 163*t*
Far vision testing, 104
Fareston (toremifene), 318*t*
Faslodex (fulvestrant), 318*t*
FAST scale, 330
Fasting glucose, impaired, 94
Fasting plasma glucose (FPG), 95*t*
Fatigue, 246
Fatty acid, 48*t*
FDG-PET scans, 72
Febuxostat *(Uloric),* 208, 208*t*
Fecal impaction, 148
Fecal incontinence (FI), 154–156
Fecal occult blood test (FOBT), 257*t*
Fecal softeners, 127*t*
Fecal transplant, 131
Feeding
  assisted, 249
  tube, 19, 190
Feldene (piroxicam), 203*t*
Felodipine *(Plendil),* 54*t*
Felodipine with enalapril maleate *(Lexxel),* 56*t*
Female sexual dysfunction, 291
Femara (letrozole), 318*t*
FENa (fractional excretion of sodium), 176, 180
Fenofibrate *(Tricor, Lofibra, Antara),* 48*t,* 208
Fenofibrate delayed release *(Trilipix),* 48*t*
Fenoprofen *(Nalfon),* 202*t*
Fentanyl *(Abstral, Actiq, Fentora, Lazanda, Onsolis, Subsys),* 236*t,* 247
Fentanyl, transdermal *(Duragesic),* 233, 237*t*
Fentanyl HCl iontophoric transdermal system (ITS), 236*t*
Fentora, 236*t. See also* Fentanyl
Feraheme (ferumoxytol), 143*t*
Ferguson hemorrhoidectomy, 132
Ferric carboxymaltose *(Injectafer),* 143*t*
Ferrlecit (sodium ferric gluconate complex), 143*t*
Ferumoxytol *(Feraheme),* 143*t*
Fesoterodine *(TOVIAZ),* 68*t,* 152*t*
FEUrea (fractional excretion of urea), 176
Feverfew, 21

Fexofenadine *(Allegra, Allegra-D, Allegra-D 24 Hour)*, 275*t*
FI (fecal incontinence), 154–156
Fiber Ease, 124. *See also* Methylcellulose
Fiber supplements, 124
FiberCon, 124, 125*t*. *See also* Polycarbophil
Fiberoptic nasopharyngeal laryngoscopy, 118
Fibersource HN, 189*t*
Fibracol, 302*t*. *See also* Collagen
Fibrates, 47*t*, 48*t*, 292
Fibric acid derivatives, 48*t*
Fibrillation, atrial. *See* Atrial fibrillation (AF)
Fibrillation, ventricular (VF), 66
Fibromyalgia
    pain relief, 233, 238*t*, 239*t*
    treatment of painful neuropathy, 221
Fidaxomicin *(Dificid)*, 131*t*, 171*t*
Finacea (azelaic acid), 87
Financial status assessment, 4*t*
Finasteride *(Proscar)*, 23, 263, 267
Fine-needle aspiration, 94
Finevin (azelaic acid), 87
Firmagon, 266*t*. *See also* Degarelix
Fish oil, 21, 41
5-α Reductase inhibitors, 262, 263
5-Fluorouracil *(Carac, Efudex, Fluoroplex)*, 84, 85
Flagyl, 122, 172*t*. *See also* Metronidazole
Flavoxate, 68*t*
Flaxseed oil, 21
Flector, 202*t*, 232. *See also* Diclofenac patch
Fleet (sodium phosphate/biphosphate emollient enema), 126*t*
FlexiGel, 301*t*
Flexzan, 300*t*. *See also* Foam island
Flolan (epoprostenol), 58
Flomax (tamsulosin), 262
Flonase, 276*t*. *See also* Fluticasone propionate
Florbetapin F18 *(Amyvid)*, 72
Florinef, 103*t*. *See also* Fludrocortisone
Florone, 91*t*. *See also* Diflorasone diacetate
Flovent, 284*t*. *See also* Fluticasone
Floxacins, 111
Floxin, 109*t*. *See also* Ofloxacin

Flu vaccine
    ACIP guidelines, 163
    for DM, 97
    procedure codes, 333*t*
    warfarin interactions, 32
Fluconazole *(Diflucan)*
    for candidiasis, 247
    for infectious diseases, 173*t*
    for onychomycosis, 86
    warfarin interactions, 32
Flucytosine *(Ancobon)*, 175*t*
Fludrocortisone *(Florinef)*
    for adrenal insufficiency, 102, 103*t*
    for hyperkalemia, 184
    for orthostatic (postural) hypotension, 65
Fluffed Kerlix, 302*t*. *See also* Gauze packing
Fluid challenge, 177, 182
Fluid consistencies, 119
Fluid replacement
    in acute kidney injury, 177
    in chronic constipation, 125
    in dehydration, 180
    in hypernatremia, 181
Fluid requirements, 187
Fluid restriction, 182, 183
Flumadine (rimantadine), 164*t*
Flunisolide *(AeroBid, Nasalide, Nasarel)*, 276*t*, 284*t*
Fluocinolone acetonide *(Synalar)*, 90*t*
Fluocinonide *(Lidex)*, 91*t*
Fluoride/chlorhexidine, 158
Fluoroplex, 84. *See also* 5-Fluorouracil
Fluoroquinolones. *See also* Quinolones
    for COPD exacerbation, 280*t*
    for cystitis or UTI, 161
    for pneumonia, 159*t*, 160
    for prostatitis, 267
    for urosepsis, 161
5-Fluorouracil *(Carac, Efudex, Fluoroplex)*, 84, 85
Fluoxetine *(Prozac)*
    for anxiety disorders, 36
    for depression, 79*t*
    drug interactions, 273*t*, 318*t*
    enteral nutrition interactions, 189
Fluphenazine, 20*t*, 68*t*, 269*t*
Flurandrenolide *(Cordran)*, 90*t*

Flurazepam, 36
Flurbiprofen *(Ansaid)*, 202t
Flutamide *(Eulexin)*, 266t
Fluticasone *(Flovent)*, 284t
Fluticasone furoate *(Veramyst)*, 276t
Fluticasone propionate *(Cutivate, Flonase)*,
    91t, 276t
Fluticasone-salmeterol *(Advair Diskus)*, 286t
Fluticasone-vilanterol *(Breo Ellipta)*, 286t
Fluvastatin *(Lescol, Lescol XL)*, 48t
Fluvoxamine *(Luvox)*, 36, 79t
Foam island *(Allevyn, Lyofoam, COPA,
    DermaFoam, Flexzan, Invacore,
    Mitraflx, 3M Foam, Polyderm, PolyMem,
    Tielle, VigiFoam)*, 299t, 300t, 303
Foam with silver *(PolyMem Silver, Optifoam
    AG, Contreet Foam)*, 300t
FOBT (fecal occult blood test), 257t
Folate, 210
Folate deficiency, 139f, 142
Folic acid, 139f
Folliculitis, 85
Fondaparinux *(Arixtra)*
    for anticoagulation, 30t
    for antithrombotic therapy, 24t
    for DVT/PE prophylaxis, 213
    for VTE, 25t, 28t
Food consistencies, 119
Food-drug interactions, 19
Foot disorders, 197
Foot examination, 101
Foot pain, 197
Foot ulcers, diabetic (neuropathic), 297–298
Footwear, 117t, 197
Foradil (formoterol), 284t
Forced vital capacity (FVC), 286
Formoterol *(Foradil)*, 284t
Formoterol-budesonide *(Symbicort)*, 285t
Formoterol-mometasone *(Dulera)*, 285t
Formulas, 1–3, 1t
Fortaz, 170t. *See also* Ceftazidime
Forteo, 225t. *See also* Teriparatide
Fortesta (testosterone), 290t
Fosamax, 224t. *See also* Alendronate
Fosamprenavir, 20t
Fosfomycin *(Monurol)*, 172t

Fosinopril *(Monopril)*, 45t, 55t
Fosrenol (lanthanum carbonate), 179
FPG (fasting plasma glucose), 95t
Fractional excretion of sodium (FENa), 176,
    180
Fractional excretion of urea (FEUrea), 176
Fracture Risk Assessment Tool (FRAX), 222,
    223
Fractures
    hip, 194–195
    medications for osteoporosis and, 226t
    osteoporotic, 222
    prevention of, 224
    risk assessment, 222, 223
    spine, 226t
    vertebral, 194, 225t
Fragmin, 30t. *See also* Dalteparin
Frailty, 136–137, 242, 252
Frailty syndrome, 252
FRAX (Fracture Risk Assessment Tool), 222,
    223
Freeda Calcium Citrate Fine Granular
    (calcium citrate), 223
Freeda Mini Cal-citrate (calcium citrate), 223
Frontotemporal dementia, 71, 76
Frozen shoulder, 191t, 192
Fulvestrant *(Faslodex)*, 318t
Fulvicin P/G (griseofulvin), 175t
Functional assessment
    ADLs, 323
    Instrumental ADLs (IADLs), 324
    in pain, 229
    preoperative, 252
    Reisberg Functional Assessment Staging
        (FAST) scale, 330
    screening assessment, 4t
Functional gait assessment, 113
Fungal infections, 86–87, 158, 161
Fungi-Nail (undecylenic acid), 87, 90t
Fungizone (amphotericin B), 173t
Furosemide *(Lasix)*
    for acute kidney injury, 177
    for HTN, 51, 51t
    for hyperkalemia, 184
    for SIADH, 183
    and tinnitus, 137
FVC (forced vital capacity), 286

G

GABA-ergics, 151*t*
Gabapentin *(Neurontin)*
  for menopausal symptoms, 321
  for nocturnal leg cramps, 308
  for pain, 238*t*
  for painful neuropathy, 220
  for restless legs syndrome, 309
  for seizures, 219*t*
  for tremor, 211*t*
  and UI, 151*t*
Gabapentin enacarbil *(Horizant),* 309
Gabitril Filmtabs (tiagabine), 219*t*
GAD (generalized anxiety disorder), 34, 36
Gait assessment, 4*t*, 113
Gait impairment, 117*t*
Gait training, 116*t*, 117*t*
Galactorrhea, 292
Galantamine *(Razadyne),* 76*t*
Galantamine extended release *(Razadyne ER),* 76*t*
GammaGraft, 303. *See also* Skin substitutes
Garamycin, 170*t*. *See also* Gentamicin
Gardnerella vaginalis, 161
Garlic, 22
Gastritis, 308
Gastroesophageal reflux disease (GERD), 119–120, 120*t*–121*t*
Gastrointestinal (GI) diseases, 20*t*, 118–133, 118*t*
Gastrostomy, percutaneous venting, 248
Gastrostomy tube feeding, 190
Gatifloxacin *(Tequin),* 20*t*, 109*t*
Gauze packing *(CURITY, Fluffed Kerlix)*
  for diabetic foot ulcers, 296
  for pressure ulcers, 302*t*
  for skin ulcers, 293
  wound and pressure ulcer products, 299*t*
Gauze-based negative-pressure wound therapy, 294
Gelnique, 151*t*. *See also* Oxybutynin
Gemfibrozil *(Lopid),* 48*t*
Gemifloxacin *(Factive),* 159*t*, 171*t*, 280*t*
General Practitioner Assessment of Cognition (GPCOG), 71
Generalized anxiety disorder (GAD), 34, 36
Gentamicin *(Garamycin),* 160, 170*t*, 295*t*

Geodon, 269*t*. *See also* Ziprasidone
GERD (gastroesophageal reflux disease), 119–120, 120*t*–121*t*
GI (gastrointestinal) diseases, 20*t*, 118–133, 118*t*
Giant cell (temporal) arteritis, 209–210
Ginger, 22
Ginkgo biloba, 22, 76
Ginseng, 22
Glaucoma, 105–106
  asthma with, 283
  medications for, 106*t*–107*t*
  screening for, 257*t*
  signs and symptoms of, 108*t*
Glaucoma surgery, 105–106
Gleevec (imatinib), 145
Glimepiride *(Amaryl),* 97*t*
Glimepiride with pioglitazone *(Duetact),* 99*t*
Glipizide *(Glucotrol, Glucotrol XL),* 96, 97*t*
Glipizide with metformin *(METAGLIP),* 99*t*
Global aphasia, 220*t*
Glomerular disease or vasculitis, 176*t*
Glomerulitis, 176*t*
GLP-1 (glucagon-like peptide-1) receptor agonists, 96, 101*t*
Glucagon, 97
Glucagon-like peptide-1 (GLP-1) receptor agonists, 96, 101*t*
Glucerna, 189*t*
Glucerna shake, 189*t*
Glucocorticoids. *See also* Corticosteroids
  for acute interstitial nephritis, 177
  for adrenal insufficiency, 102
  for angioedema, 89
  for asthma, 282*t*, 283*t*
  fall risks, 112
  for hives, 89
  medications for osteoporosis and, 226*t*
  for nonasthmatic eosinophilic bronchitis, 272*t*
  for pseudogout, 209
  for rheumatoid arthritis, 205
  for rotator cuff tears, 192
Glucophage, 97*t*. *See also* Metformin
Glucophage XR, 97*t*. *See also* Metformin
Glucosamine, 20–21, 199, 200*f*
Glucose, 94, 95*t*, 101

α-Glucosidase inhibitors, 96, 97*t*
Glucotrol, 97*t. See also* Glipizide
Glucotrol XL, 97*t. See also* Glipizide
Glucovance (glyburide and metformin), 99*t*
Gluten-free diet, 124
Glyburide *(Diaβeta, Micronase),* 97*t*
Glyburide, micronized *(Glynase),* 97*t*
Glyburide with metformin *(Glucovance),* 99*t*
Glycemic control, 63, 95–96, 105
Glycerin suppository, 126*t*, 155
Glycoprotein IIb/IIIa inhibitors, 24*t*, 31*t*, 39
Glycopyrrolate, 248
Glycycline, 172*t*
Glynase (glyburide), 97*t*
Glyset (miglitol), 97*t*
GnRH agonists, 265, 265*t*–266*t*
GnRH antagonists, 266*t*
Goal-oriented care, 8–9
Golimumab *(Simponi),* 206
Gonadotropin-releasing hormone (GnRH)
    agonists, 265, 265*t*–266*t*
Gonadotropin-releasing hormone (GnRH)
    antagonists, 266*t*
Goserelin acetate implant *(Zoladex),* 265*t*
Gout, 206–208, 208–209, 208*t*
GPCOG (General Practitioner Assessment of
    Cognition), 71
Granisetron *(Kytril),* 20*t*, 128*t*
Grifulvin V (griseofulvin), 175*t*
Griseofulvin *(Fulvicin P/G, Grifulvin V),* 175*t*
Group B streptococci, 158, 161
Growth factor therapy, 144, 296, 298
Guaifenesin *(Robitussin),* 273*t*, 280
Guanfacine *(Tenex),* 52*t*
Guided imagery, 231*t*
Gynecomastia, 292
Gyne-lotrimin, 17

H
H$_1$ receptor antagonists
    for allergic conjunctivitis, 109, 110*t*
    for allergic rhinitis, 275, 275*t*–276*t*
    for angioedema, 89
    for cholinergic reactions, 89
    for hives, 88
    for nausea and vomiting, 128*t*

H$_2$ receptor antagonists
    de-prescribing, 18
    for GERD, 120*t*
    for *H pylori* infection, 122*t*
    for hives, 88
    and sexual dysfunction, 292
    for stress-ulcer prevention, 123
Habitrol (transdermal nicotine patch), 313*t*
Haemophilus influenzae, 158
Halcinonide *(Halog),* 91*t*
Haldol, 70, 248, 269*t. See also* Haloperidol
Halitosis, 247
Hallucinations, 73
Hallux valgus, 197
Halobetasol propionate *(Ultravate),* 91*t*
Halog (halcinonide), 91*t*
Haloperidol *(Haldol)*
    for delirium, 69–70
    for nausea and vomiting, 128*t*, 248
    for psychosis, 269*t*
    QT$_c$ interval interactions, 20*t*
Halothane, 133*t*
Hammertoe (digiti flexus), 197
Hand pain, 196
Hand washing, 109, 130
Harmful drinking, 310, 311
Harris-Benedict energy requirement
    equations, 187
HAS-BLED scoring, 59, 60*t*
Hazardous drinking, 310, 311
HCTZ (hydrochlorothiazide) *(Esidrix,
    HydroDIURIL, Microzide, Oretic),* 51*t*,
    56*t*–57*t*
Head and neck cancer, 190
Head trauma, 211
Headache, 240*t*
Health care proxy, 245
Health literacy assessment, 17, 327
Hearing aids (HAs), 135, 135*t*, 136
Hearing assessment, 4*t*
Hearing impairment, 134–137
    classification of, 134*t*–135*t*
    dual sensory impairment (DSI), 108
    effects and rehabilitation, 135*t*
    preventive measures for delirium, 69*t*

Hearing impairment *continued*
  resources for, 336
  screening, 258*t*
Hearing technology, 135–136
Heart disease. *See also* Cardiovascular
    diseases; Heart failure (HF)
  determinants for hospice eligibility, 243*t*
  end-stage, 243*t*
  ICD placement for, 66
  resources for, 336
  valvular, 24*t*, 29*t*, 32*t*, 63
Heart failure (HF), 42–44
  antihypertensive therapy and, 56*t*
  drugs useful in treating, 51*t*–55*t*
  and hyponatremia, 181
  ICD placement for, 66
  management of, 43*t*
  preventive measures for delirium, 69*t*
  staging, 43*t*
  target dosages of ACEIs, ARBs, and β-
    blockers, 45*t*
  warfarin anticoagulation for, 33*t*
Heat therapy, 198, 229, 231
Heel inserts, 197
Heel pain, 197
Heel protectors, 296, 297
Helicobacter pylori infection, 121–122, 122*t*
Helidac, 122*t*. *See also* Tetracycline
HELP (Hospital Elder Life Program), 256
Hematologic disorders, 138–146
Hemiarthroplasty, 194, 195
Hemiparesis, 220*t*
Hemiplegia, 220*t*
Hemodialysis, 179
Hemolytic anemia, 142
Hemorrhoidectomy, 132
Hemorrhoidopexy, 132
Hemorrhoids, 131–132
Heparin. *See also* Anticoagulation
  for anticoagulation, 30*t*
  for antithrombotic therapy, 24*t*
  bridging therapy, 253, 253*t*
  LMWH, 24*t*, 25*t*, 28*t*, 30*t*, 213, 253, 253*t*
  and osteoporosis, 222
  UFH, 24*t*, 25*t*, 28*t*, 30*t*, 39, 213
  for VTE, 25*t*, 28*t*

Heparin-induced thrombocytopenia (HIT),
    24*t*, 30*t*, 31*t*
Heparinoids, 25*t*, 30*t*
Hepatic cirrhosis, 181
Hepatitis, 133*t*
Hepatitis B vaccines, 179
Hepatocellular necrosis, 133*t*
Hepatorenal syndrome, 243*t*
Hepatotoxicity, 133
Herbal medications, 20–23, 69*t*, 133*t*
Herpes zoster ("shingles"), 162
  antiviral treatments, 163*t*
  immunization, 257*t*
  post-herpetic neuralgia, 162, 221
Hexadrol, 103*t*. *See also* Dexamethasone
HF. *See* Heart failure
High-fiber diet, 94, 95, 132
Hip arthroplasty, 25*t*
Hip fracture, 194–195
  medications for osteoporosis and, 226*t*
  prevention of, 224
  risk assessment, 222
Hip fracture surgery, 194–195
  anticoagulant agents for, 30*t*
  antiplatelet agents for, 29*t*
  antithrombotic medications for, 25*t*
  DVT/PE prophylaxis for, 25*t*
  warfarin anticoagulation for, 32*t*
Hip pain, 194–195
Hip replacement
  anticoagulant agents for, 30*t*, 31*t*
  antiplatelet agents for, 29*t*
  antithrombotic medications for, 25*t*
  DVT/PE prophylaxis for, 25*t*
  for hip fracture, 194
  for osteoarthritis, 194
  warfarin anticoagulation for, 32*t*
Histrelin acetate *(Vantas)*, 266*t*
HIT (heparin-induced thrombocytopenia), 24*t*
HIV (human immunodeficiency virus),
    166–167, 257*t*
Hives, 88–89
HMG-CoA reductase inhibitors, 48*t*, 133*t*
Homatropine, 68*t*
Homatropine/hydrocodone *(Hycodan)*, 273*t*
Home BP monitoring, 50

Home care
preventive visits, 115
procedure codes, 333*t*, 334*t*
sites of care, 7*t*
Horizant (gabapentin enacarbil), 309
Hormone receptor agonists, 306*t*
Hormone therapy, 319–321
for anorexia, cachexia, dehydration, 249
bioidentical, 319
for breast cancer, 317
for dyspareunia, 292
estrogen therapy, 225, 225*t*, 226*t*, 319
GnRH agonists, 265, 265*t*–266*t*
for menopausal symptoms, 319
for osteoporosis, 225, 225*t*
for prostate cancer, 264, 265
risks and benefits, 319–320, 320*t*
for sleep disorders, 306*t*
that causes leg edema, 45
for UI, 149
Hospice, 241–249
determinants for eligibility, 243*t*–244*t*
procedure codes, 334*t*
resources for, 335
sites of care, 7*t*
Hospital care, 8
procedure codes, 333*t*
Hospital Elder Life Program (HELP), 256
Hospital sites of care, 7*t*
Hospital-acquired pneumonia, 158, 159–160
Hot flushes, 319
HTN. *See* Hypertension
Humalog, 101*t*. *See also* Insulin lispro
Human immunodeficiency virus (HIV),
166–167, 257*t*
Humira (adalimumab), 206
Humulin, 101*t*. *See also* Insulin
Hyalgan (hyaluronic acid), 199. *See also*
Hyaluronic acid
Hyaluronic acid *(Euflexxa, Hyalgan,
Orthovisc, Synvisc, Supartz)*, 199, 200*f*
Hycodan (hydrocodone/homatropine), 273*t*
Hydralazine *(Apresoline)*
for HTN, 54*t*
and leg edema, 45
and liver disease, 133*t*
and orthostatic hypotension, 211

Hydralazine and isosorbide dinitrate *(BiDil)*,
43, 44, 57*t*
Hydration, 146, 177, 248. *See also*
Dehydration
Hydrochlorothiazide. *See* HCTZ
Hydrocodone with APAP *(Lorcet, Lortab,
Norco, Vicodin)*, 233, 235*t*
Hydrocodone with homatropine *(Hycodan)*,
273*t*
Hydrocodone with ibuprofen *(Vicoprofen)*,
235*t*
Hydrocol II, 300*t*. *See also* Hydrocolloids
Hydrocolloids *(Comfeel Plus, Cutinova
Hydro, DermaFilm, DuoDERM, Exuderm,
Hydrocol II, MediHoney, MPM Excel,
Nu-DERM, Odor Shield, ProCol,
RepliCare, Restore, Sorbex,
SignaDRESS, 3M Tegasorb, Ultec)*, 299*t*,
300*t*
Hydrocortisone *(Cortef, Hydrocortone)*
for adrenal insufficiency, 102, 103*t*
for dermatologic conditions, 90*t*, 91*t*
for hemorrhoids, 132
for intertrigo, 86
for prostate cancer, 265
to reduce cardiovascular complications of
surgery, 255*t*
for seborrheic dermatitis, 88
for squamous hyperplasia, 317
for xerosis, 89
Hydrocortisone butyrate *(Locoid)*, 91*t*
Hydrocortisone valerate *(Westcort)*, 91*t*
Hydrocortone, 103*t*. *See also* Hydrocortisone
HydroDIURIL, 51*t*. *See also* HCTZ
Hydrogel, 293, 299*t*, 301*t*
Hydrogel amorphous gels *(AquaSite,
Aquasorb, Biolex, CarraDres, Curagel,
Intrasite Gel, Restore Gel, SAF-Gel,
SoloSite)*, 301*t*
Hydrogel sheets *(Aquasorb, ClearSite,
Curagel, Derma-Gel, FlexiGel, Nugel,
Restore Impregnated Gauze, 3M
Tegagel with Gauze, Vigilon)*, 301*t*
Hydrogel with silver *(SilvaSorb Gel)*, 301*t*
Hydromorphone *(Dilaudid, Hydrostat)*, 229*t*,
236*t*

Hydromorphone extended release *(Exalgo),* 237*t*
Hydropres (reserpine with HCTZ), 57*t*
Hydrostat, 236*t. See also* Hydromorphone
25-Hydroxy vitamin D, 186
25-Hydroxy vitamin D deficiency, 222
Hydroxychloroquine
  ocular adverse events, 111
  for pseudogout, 209
  for rheumatoid arthritis, 205, 206*t*
Hydroxypropylcellulose *(Lacrisert),* 110
Hydroxyurea, 145
Hydroxyzine *(Atarax),* 68*t,* 74, 276*t*
Hygroton (chlorthalidone), 51*t*
Hyoscyamine *(Anaspaz, Levsin, Levsin/SL),*
  68*t,* 124, 248
Hyperalgesia, 234
Hyperbaric oxygen therapy, 298
Hyperbilirubinemia, acute, 133*t*
Hypercalcemia, 176*t*
Hyperemia, conjunctival, 109
Hyperglycemia, 158, 181, 268
Hypericum perforatum. See St. John's wort
Hyperkalemia, 179, 183–184
Hyperlipidemia, 181. *See also* Dyslipidemia
Hypernatremia, 180–181
Hyperphosphatemia, 179
Hyperprolactinemia, 270*t,* 288*t,* 292
Hyperproteinemia, 181
Hypersensitivity, 117*t,* 133
Hypersomnea, 304
Hypertension (HTN), 49–51
  acute, in ischemic stroke, 214
  in chronic kidney disease, 179
  combination drugs for, 56*t*–57*t*
  in DM type 2, 96
  PAH (pulmonary arterial hypertension), 58
  post MI, 41
Hyperthermia, 213
Hyperthyroidism, 56*t,* 92–93, 268
Hypertonic sodium gain, 181
Hypertriglyceridemia, 41, 270*t*
Hyperuricemia, 207–208
Hypnosis, 124, 231, 305
Hypnotics
  fall risks, 112
  nonbenzodiazepine, 37

  preventing falls with, 116*t*
  and UI, 151*t*
Hypoalbuminemia, 185
Hypoaldosteronism, hyporeninemic, 180
Hypocalcemia, 179
Hypocholesterolemia, 185
Hypodermoclysis, 248
Hypogammaglobulinemia, 146
Hypoglycemia, 96, 268
Hypoglycemics, 22, 254, 311
Hypogonadism, 234, 288–289, 288*t*
Hyponatremia, 181–182
Hypoproliferative anemia, 139*f,* 140*f*
Hyporeninemic hypoaldosteronism, 180
HypoTears, 110
Hypotension
  drug-induced, 270*t,* 271*t*
  orthostatic (postural), 65–66, 103*t,* 117*t,*
    211, 212*t,* 216*t*
  postprandial, 66
  secondary to anemia, 66
Hypothyroidism, 92, 182, 268
Hypotonic hyponatremia, 182
Hypotonic sodium loss, 181
Hypovolemic hyponatremia, 182
Hypoxemia, 58, 247
Hypoxia, 69*t*
Hytrin (terazosin), 52*t,* 262
Hyzaar (losartan with HCTZ), 57*t*

I

IADLs (Instrumental Activities of Daily
  Living) Scale, 252, 324
Ibandronate *(Boniva),* 224*t,* 226*t*
IBS (irritable bowel syndrome), 123–124
Ibuprofen, 44, 202*t,* 232
Ibuprofen, injectable *(Caldolor),* 202*t*
Ibuprofen with famotidine *(Duexis),* 202*t*
Ibuprofen with hydrocodone *(Vicoprofen),*
  235*t*
Ibuprofen with oxycodone *(Combunox),* 235*t*
Ibutilide, 20*t*
ICDs (implantable cardiac defibrillators), 41,
  66, 245
ICU patients, 188, 190
Icy Hot (methylsalicylate and menthol), 200*f,*
  239*t*

Ideal body weight, 1
Iliotibial band syndrome, 196
Iloprost *(Ventavis),* 58
Ilotycin (erythromycin ophthalmic), 109*t*
Imagery, 231, 231*t*, 305
Imdur (isosorbide mononitrate SR), 40*t*
Imipenem, 159, 159*t*, 295*t*
Imipenem-cilastatin *(Primaxin),* 168*t*
Imipramine *(Tofranil),* 20*t*, 68*t*, 81
Imiquimod *(Aldara, Zyclara),* 84, 85, 317
Immobility, 69*t*
Immunization, 163, 257*t*
Immunofluorescence antibody staining, 163*t*
Immunoglobulins, 146
Immunosuppressants, 21, 143, 144
Immunotherapy, autologous cellular, 265
Imodium A-D, 124, 129*t*, 248. *See also*
    Loperamide
Impetigo, 85
Implantable cardiac defibrillators (ICDs), 41,
    66, 245
Impotence, 288–289
    causes of, 288*t*
    drug-induced, 292
    management of, 289*t*–290*t*
Impulse-control symptoms in men, 77*t*
Incontinence, fecal (FI), 154–156
Incontinence, urinary. *See* Urinary
    incontinence (UI)
Incretin mimetics, 101*t*
Indacaterol *(Arcapta),* 284*t*
Indapamide *(Lozol),* 51*t*
Inderal (propranolol), 53*t*, 271*t*
Inderal LA, 53*t*. *See also* Propranolol, long-
    acting
Inderide (propranolol LA with HCTZ), 57*t*
Indinavir, 20*t*
Indomethacin, 234
Infections
    antibiotics for, 168*t*–176*t*
    arterial ulcers, 297
    C difficile, 129, 130, 131*t*, 173*t*
    in chronic wounds, 294*t*–295*t*
    diabetic foot ulcers, 297–298
    empiric antibiotic therapy for, 294*t*–295*t*

fungal, 86–87, 158
H pylori, 121–122, 122*t*
herpes zoster ("shingles"), 162, 163*t*, 221,
    257*t*
influenza, 163–164, 163*t*, 164*t*, 257*t*
MRSA (methicillin-resistant *S aureus*), 85,
    158, 160, 162, 294*t*–295*t*
musculoskeletal tissue procedures, 255*t*
oropharyngeal, 174*t*
pneumonia, 157–160
preventive measures for, 69*t*
prostate, 172*t*
skin and soft tissue, 162, 170*t*, 173*t*
skin procedures, 255*t*
skin ulcers, 294
STI counseling, 334*t*
tuberculosis, 164–166, 165*t*
urinary tract, 160–161, 170*t*, 172*t*, 292
venous ulcers, 303
wound, 293, 297
Infectious diseases, 157–175, 168*t*–176*t*
Infective endocarditis, 255*t*
Inflammation, anemia of, 138
Inflammatory arthritis, 209
Inflammatory disease, ocular, 108
Inflammatory osteoarthritis, 198, 199
Infliximab *(Remicade),* 206
Influenza, 163–164
    antiviral treatment, 164*t*
    diagnostic tests, 163*t*
    immunization, 257*t*
Influenza vaccination, 32, 97, 163
Informant Questionnaire on Cognitive
    Decline in the Elderly (IQCODE), 71
Informed consent, 10
Informed decision making
    algorithm for, 10*f*
    cancer screening, 258–259
    goal-oriented care, 8–9
    life expectancy, 8–9
    patient preferences for life-sustaining
        care, 10
Infrared photocoagulation, 132
Infumorph, 236*t*. *See also* Morphine
Ingenol mebatate *(Picato),* 84
INH. *See* Isoniazid
Inhalers, 283, 313*t*

Injectafer (ferric carboxymaltose), 143*t*
Injection therapy
  for acute gouty flare, 207
  for DM, 100*t*
  for osteoarthritis, 198–199, 200*f*
  for pain, 232
Innohep, 30*t*. *See also* Tinzaparin
InnoPran XL, 53*t*. *See also* Propranolol, long-
    acting
Insomnia, 304–305
Inspra (eplerenone), 43, 52*t*
Instant fruit, 96
Instant Glucose, 96
Instructional advance directives, 245
Instrumental Activities of Daily Living
    (IADLs) Scale, 252, 324
Insulin
  adverse events, 96
  for diabetes, 95, 96
  drug interactions, 98*t*
  herbal medicine interactions, 21
  for hyperkalemia, 184
  preparations, 101*t*
  to reduce cardiovascular complications of
    surgery, 255*t*
Insulin, isophane *(Novolin 70/30)*, 101*t*
Insulin, regular *(Humulin, Novolin)*, 101*t*
Insulin aspart *(NovoLog)*, 95, 101*t*
Insulin detemir *(Levemir)*, 101*t*
Insulin glargine *(Lantus)*, 101*t*
Insulin glulisine *(Apidra)*, 95, 101*t*
Insulin lispro *(Humalog)*, 95, 101*t*
Insulin resistance reducers, 98*t*
Intal (cromolyn sodium), 285*t*
Integrase strand transfer inhibitors, 167
Integrilin, 31*t*. *See also* Eptifibatide
Interleukin-6 inhibitors, 206, 210
Interleukin-1 receptor antagonists, 206
Intermezzo, 306*t*. *See also* Zolpidem
Intermittent pneumatic compression, 25*t*, 46,
    195
Intermittent pneumatic pumps, 303
Internal rotation lag test, 191
International Prostate Symptom Score
    (IPSS) Symptom Index for BPH, 331
Internet-based pharmacies, 314
Interpersonal therapy, 78

Interprofessional geriatric team, 5, 6*t*
Intertrigo, 85–86
Intestinal obstruction, 247–248
Intra-articular injections, 198–199, 200*f*, 207
Intracardiac thrombosis, 33*t*
Intrasite Gel, 301*t*
Intraspinous spacer insertion (distraction),
    194
Intubation, nasogastric, 248
Invacore, 300*t*. *See also* Foam island;
    Transparent film
Invanz, 168*t*. *See also* Ertapenem
Invega (paliperidone), 269*t*
Invokana (Canagliflozin), 99*t*
Iodine, radioactive, 93
Ipratropium *(Atrovent)*, 275*t*, 283*t*
Ipratropium-albuterol *(Combivent,
    Combivent Respimat, Duoneb)*, 285*t*
Iprivask, 31*t*. *See also* Desirudin
IQCODE (Informant Questionnaire on
    Cognitive Decline in the Elderly), 71
Irbesartan *(Avapro)*, 55*t*
Irbesartan with HCTZ *(Avalide)*, 57*t*
Iridoplasty, 105
Iridotomy, laser, 105
Iron deficiency, 44, 138, 140*f*
Iron deficiency anemia, 138, 179
Iron replacement, 141, 141*t*, 143*t*
Iron sucrose *(Venofer)*, 143*t*
Iron supplements, 309
Iron therapy
  for anemia, 138, 140*f*, 141
  de-prescribing, 18
  for restless legs syndrome, 308
Iron-drug interactions, 19
Irritable bowel syndrome (IBS), 123–124
ISMO (isosorbide mononitrate), 40*t*
Isoniazid (INH)
  herbal medicine interactions, 23
  for latent tuberculosis, 165*t*
  and liver disease, 133*t*
  ocular adverse events, 111
  warfarin interactions, 32
Isoproterenol, 286*t*
Isoptin SR (verapamil), 54*t*
Isopto Carpine (pilocarpine), 107*t*
Isordil (isosorbide dinitrate), 40*t*

Isosorbide dinitrate *(Isordil, Sorbitrate)*, 40*t*
Isosorbide dinitrate and hydralazine *(BiDil)*, 43, 44, 57*t*
Isosorbide dinitrate SR *(Dilatrate SR)*, 40*t*
Isosorbide mononitrate *(ISMO, Monoket)*, 40*t*
Isosorbide mononitrate SR *(Imdur)*, 40*t*
Isosource, 189*t*
Isradipine SR *(DynaCirc CR)*, 54*t*
Itraconazole *(Sporanox)*
   for infectious diseases, 173*t*
   for onychomycosis, 86
   QT_c interval interactions, 20*t*
   warfarin interactions, 32
Ivermectin *(Stromectol)*, 88

J

Janumet (sitagliptin and metformin), 100*t*
Janumet XR (sitagliptin and metformin), 100*t*
Januvia (sitagliptin), 98*t*
Jejunostomy tube feeding, 190
Jentadueto (linagliptin with metformin), 100*t*
Jevity 1 Cal, 189*t*
Jobst stockings, 65, 303
Joint arthroscopy, 25*t*
Joint replacement, total (TJR), 194, 260
Juzo stockings, 303

K

Kadian (morphine), 237*t*
Kaltostat, 301*t*. *See also* Calcium alginate
   dressings
Kaolin pectin, 44
Kaopectate (attapulgite), 129*t*
Karnofsky Scale, 328
Kava kava, 22
Kayexalate (sodium polystyrene sulfonate), 184
Kazano (alogliptin with metformin), 100*t*
Keflex, 169*t*. *See also* Cephalexin
Keflin (cephalothin), 169*t*
Kefzol, 169*t*. *See also* Cefazolin
Kegel exercises, 149, 150*f*, 319
Kenacort, 103*t*. *See also* Triamcinolone
Kenalog, 91*t*, 103*t*. *See also* Triamcinolone
Keppra (levetiracetam), 219*t*

Kerlone, 53*t*. *See also* Betaxolol
Ketalar (ketamine), 246
Ketamine *(Ketalar)*, 246
Ketek, 171*t*. *See also* Telithromycin
Ketoconazole *(Nizoral, Nizoral A-D)*
   for dermatologic conditions, 89*t*
   for infectious diseases, 174*t*
   for prostate cancer, 265
   QT_c interval interactions, 20*t*
   for seborrheic dermatitis, 88
   warfarin interactions, 32
Ketolides, 171*t*
Ketoprofen *(Orudis)*, 202*t*
Ketoprofen sustained release *(Oruvail)*, 202*t*
Ketorolac *(Acular, Toradol)*, 109, 110*t*, 202*t*
Ketotifen *(Alaway, Zaditor)*, 110*t*
Kidney disorders, 176–184
   acute kidney injury, 176–177, 176*t*, 177, 244*t*
   chronic kidney disease, 56*t*, 141–142, 177–180, 244*t*
   kidney failure definition, 222
   kidney failure risk equation, 178
   resources for, 336
Kidney transplantation, 179
Kinase inhibitors, 206
Kineret (anakinra), 206
Klebsiella, 161
Klonopin, 239*t*. *See also* Clonazepam
Knee arthroplasty, 25*t*
Knee pain, 195–196, 231*t*
Knee replacement
   anticoagulant agents for, 30*t*, 31*t*
   antiplatelet agents for, 29*t*
   antithrombotic medications for, 25*t*
   DVT/PE prophylaxis for, 25*t*
Knee surgery, 25*t*, 32*t*
Kollagen-Medifil Particles/Gels/Pads, 302*t*.
   See also Collagen
Kombiglyze XR (saxagliptin and metformin), 99*t*
Krystexxa, 208*t*. *See also* Pegloticase
K-well (lindane), 88
Kyphoplasty, 146, 194
Kytril, 128*t*. *See also* Granisetron

L

Labetalol *(Normodyne, Trandate)*
    for HTN, 51, 53*t*, 214
    and liver disease, 133*t*
Laboratory tests, preoperative, 252
Labyrinthitis, 212*t*
Lacrisert (hydroxypropylcellulose), 110
β-Lactam/β-lactamase inhibitors, 159, 159*t*,
    168*t*–170*t*
Lactose-free diet, 124
Lactose-free enteral products, 189*t*
Lactose-free oral products, 189*t*
Lactulose *(Chronulac)*, 126*t*
Lamictal. See also Lamotrigine
    for bipolar disorders, 83*t*
    for pain, 238*t*
    for painful neuropathy, 221
    for seizures, 219*t*
Lamisil (terbinafine), 87, 90*t*, 175*t*
Lamisil AT, 90*t*. *See also* Terbinafine
Lamotrigine *(Lamictal)*
    for bipolar disorders, 83*t*
    for depression, 82
    for pain, 238*t*
    for painful neuropathy, 221
    for seizures, 219*t*
Lanoxicaps, 44. *See also* Digoxin
Lanoxin, 44. *See also* Digoxin
Lansoprazole *(Prevacid)*, 120*t*, 122*t*, 189
Lansoprazole with clarithromycin and
    amoxicillin *(Prevpac)*, 122*t*
Lanthanum carbonate *(Fosrenol)*, 179
Lantus (insulin glargine), 101*t*
Laparoscopic procedures, 25*t*
Laparoscopic prostatectomy, 263
Laser iridotomy, 105
Laser photocoagulation, 105
Laser trabeculoplasty, 105
Laser treatment, 84, 87, 105
Lasix, 51*t*. *See also* Furosemide
Lastacaft (alcaftadine), 110*t*
Latanoprost *(Xalatan)*, 107*t*
Late-life delusional (paranoid) disorder, 268
Latuda (lurasidone), 269*t*
Laxatives
    for constipation, 124, 124*t*, 125, 125*t*, 126*t*,
        234, 247

    for fecal incontinence, 155
    for hyperkalemia, 184
    tube feeding, 190
Lazanda, 236*t*. *See also* Fentanyl
LDL (low-density lipoprotein), 47, 215
Lean body weight, 2
Leflunomide *(Arava)*, 207*t*
Left ventricular thrombosis, 40
Leg compression, pneumatic, 195
Leg cramps, nocturnal, 308
Leg edema, 45–46
Leg fracture surgery, 25*t*
Legal blindness, 104
Legionella, 157, 158
Lenalidomide, 144
Lens correction, 117*t*
Lentigo maligna, 86
Lepirudin *(Refludan)*, 24*t*, 31*t*
Lescol (fluvastatin), 48*t*
Lescol XL (fluvastatin), 48*t*
Letairis (ambrisentan), 58
Letrozole *(Femara)*, 318*t*
Leukemia, chronic myelogenous, 145
Leukotriene modifiers
    for allergic rhinitis, 275, 275*t*, 277*t*
    for asthma, 282*t*, 285*t*
    for conjunctivitis, 275*t*, 277*t*
    for COPD, 285*t*
Leuprolide acetate *(Lupron Depot)*, 266*t*
Levalbuterol *(Xopenex)*, 284*t*
Levaquin, 171*t*. *See also* Levofloxacin
Levatol (penbutolol), 53*t*
Levemir (insulin detemir), 101*t*
Levetiracetam *(Keppra)*, 219*t*
Levine's technique, 293
LEVITRA, 262, 289*t*. *See also* Vardenafil
Levobunolol *(AKBeta, Betagan)*, 106*t*
Levocetirizine *(Xyzal)*, 275*t*
Levodopa, 189, 304, 309
Levodopa-carbidopa *(Sinemet, Parcopa)*,
    217*t*, 308
Levodopa-carbidopa, sustained-release
    (Sinemet CR), 217*t*
Levodopa-carbidopa + entacapone
    (Stalevo), 218*t*

Levofloxacin *(Levaquin)*
  for COPD exacerbation, 280*t*
  enteral nutrition interactions, 189
  for infectious diseases, 171*t*
  for pneumonia, 159*t*, 160
  for prostatitis, 267
Levorphanol, 233
Levo-T, 92. *See also* Levothyroxine
Levothroid, 92. *See also* Levothyroxine
Levothyroxine *(Eltroxin, Levo-T, Levothroid,
  Synthroid),* 19, 92
Levsin, 124. *See also* Hyoscyamine
Levsin/SL, 124, 248. *See also* Hyoscyamine
Levulan Kerastick (aminolevulinic acid), 84
Lewy body dementia. *See also* Dementia
  clinical features of, 71
  distinguishing early Parkinson disease
    from other parkinsonian syndromes,
    216*t*
  pharmacologic management of, 70, 75
Lexapro, 79*t*. *See also* Escitalopram
Lexxel (felodipine with enalapril maleate),
  56*t*
Libido problems, 291, 292
Lichen sclerosus, 317
Lidex (fluocinonide), 91*t*
Lidocaine *(Lidoderm)*
  to distinguish shoulder pain syndromes,
    191*t*
  for frozen shoulder (adhesive capsulitis),
    192
  for osteoarthritis, 198–199, 200*f*
  for pain, 240*t*
  for painful mucositis, 247
  for painful neuropathy, 221
  for persistent pain, 231, 232
  for plantar fasciitis, 198
  for rotator cuff problems, 191
Lidoderm. See also Lidocaine
  for osteoarthritis, 198, 200*f*
  for pain, 232, 240*t*
  for painful neuropathy, 221
Life expectancy, 8–9, 9*t*
Lifestyle modifications
  for DM, 94, 95, 96
  for hemorrhoids, 132
  for hyperuricemia, 207

  for UI, 148, 150*f*
Light therapy
  for problem behaviors, 75
  for seasonal depression, 78
  for sleep disorders, 304, 305, 309
Lighthouse Near Acuity Test, 104
Linaclotide *(Linzess),* 124, 125*t*
Linagliptin (*Tradjent*a), 98*t*
Linagliptin with metformin *(Jentadueto),* 100*t*
Lindane *(K-well, Scabene),* 88
Linezolid *(Zyvox)*
  drug interactions, 79*t*
  for erysipelas, 85
  for infections in chronic wounds,
    294*t*–295*t*
  for infectious diseases, 172*t*
  for MRSA, 85, 162
  for pneumonia, 160
Liniments, 231
α-Linolenic acid, 41
Linzess (linaclotide), 124, 125*t*
Lioresal, 239*t*. *See also* Baclofen
Lipid disorders, 96, 257*t*
Lipidemia. *See* Dyslipidemia
Lipid-lowering therapy
  for ACS, 40
  for dyslipidemia, 47*t*
  for PAD, 63
  and sexual dysfunction, 292
Lipitor, 48*t*. *See also* Atorvastatin
Liquid conversions, 1*t*
Liquid Pred, 103*t*. *See also* Prednisone
Liraglutide *(Victoza),* 100*t*
Lisinopril *(Prinivil, Zestril),* 45*t*, 55*t*
Lisinopril with HCTZ *(Prinzide, Zestoretic),*
  56*t*
Lithium *(Eskalith, Eskalith CR, Lithobid)*
  for bipolar disorders, 83*t*
  herbal medicine interactions, 21
  and osteoporosis, 222
  and restless legs syndrome, 308
  and sexual dysfunction, 292
Lithobid, 83*t*. *See also* Lithium
Livalo (pitavastatin), 48*t*
Liver disease, 133–134, 133*t*, 243*t*
Living wills, 10, 244
LMWH. *See* Low-molecular-weight heparin

Locoid (hydrocortisone butyrate), 91*t*
Lodine (etodolac), 202*t*
Lodine XL (etodolac), 202*t*
Lodoxamide *(Alomide)*, 110*t*
Lofibra, 48*t. See also* Fenofibrate
Lomotil (diphenoxylate with atropine), 129*t*
Long-term care, 7*t*, 115, 309
Loniten (minoxidil), 54*t*
Loop diuretics
  and coexisting conditions, 56*t*
  for HTN, 51*t*
  for hyperkalemia, 183, 184
  for SIADH, 183
  and tinnitus, 137
  and UI, 151*t*, 153
Loperamide *(Imodium A-D)*
  for diarrhea, 129*t*, 248
  for fecal incontinence, 155
  for IBS, 124
Lopid (gemfibrozil), 48*t*
Lopressor, 53*t. See also* Metoprolol
Lopressor HCT (metoprolol tartrate with
  HCTZ), 57*t*
Loprox (ciclopirox), 87, 89*t*
Lopurin, 208*t. See also* Allopurinol
Loratadine *(Claritin, Claritin-D)*, 68*t*, 275*t*
Lorazepam *(Ativan)*
  for akathisia, 271*t*
  for anxiety, 37*t*
  for delirium, 70
  for dyspnea, 247
  for sleep disorders, 306*t*
Lorcaserin *(Belviq)*, 187
Lorcet, 235*t. See also* Hydrocodone with
  APAP
Lortab, 235*t. See also* Hydrocodone with
  APAP
Losartan *(Cozaar)*, 45*t*, 55*t*, 208*t*
Losartan with HCTZ *(Hyzaar)*, 57*t*
Lotensin, 54*t. See also* Benazepril
Lotensin HTC (benazepril with HCTZ), 56*t*
Lotrel (amlodipine with benazepril
  hydrochloride), 56*t*
Lotrimin AF, 17
Lotrimin Ultra (butenafine), 17, 89*t*
Lotronex (alosetron), 124
Lovastatin *(Mevacor, Altoprev)*, 48*t*, 49*t*, 292

Lovastatin with niacin *(Advicor)*, 49*t*
Lovaza, 21, 48*t. See also* Omega-3 fatty acids
Lovenox, 30*t. See also* Enoxaparin
Low back pain
  adjuvant medications for pain relief, 240*t*
  chronic, 198, 199, 238*t*
  nondrug interventions for, 231*t*
Low back pain syndrome, 192–193
Low-density lipoprotein (LDL), 47, 215
Low-molecular-weight heparin (LMWH)
  for antithrombotic therapy, 24*t*
  bridging therapy, 253, 253*t*
  for DVT/PE prophylaxis, 213
  prescribing information, 30*t*
  resumption after surgery, 253
  for VTE, 25*t*, 28*t*
Low-vision services, 108
Loxapine, 20*t*, 68*t*
Lozol (indapamide), 51*t*
Lubiprostone *(Amitiza)*, 125*t*
Lubricants, water-soluble *(Replens)*, 291
Lucentis (ranibizumab), 105
Ludiomil, 81. *See also* Maprotiline
Lumbar spinal stenosis, 193–194
Lumbar spine, unstable, 193
Lumbar strain, acute, 192–193
Lumbosacral corset, 193
Lumbosacral nerve root compression, 2*t*
Lumigan (bimatoprost), 107*t*
Luminal, 219*t. See also* Phenobarbital
Lunesta, 37, 306*t. See also* Eszopiclone
Lung cancer, 257*t*
Lung disease, restrictive, 286–287, 286*t*–287*t*
Lupron Depot (leuprolide acetate), 266*t*
Lurasidone *(Latuda)*, 269*t*
Luvox, 79*t. See also* Fluvoxamine
Lymphedema, 46
Lyofoam, 300*t. See also* Foam island
Lyric hearing aids, 135
Lyrica, 219*t*, 221, 238*t. See also* Pregabalin

M

Maalox (magnesium-aluminum hydroxide),
  247
Macrobid, 172*t. See also* Nitrofurantoin
Macrodantin, 172*t. See also* Nitrofurantoin
Macrolides, 85, 159*t*, 170*t*

Macular degeneration, age-related (AMD), 104–105
Macular edema, 105
Magnacet (oxycodone with APAP), 235*t*
Magnesium, 19, 50, 309
Magnesium citrate *(Citroma)*, 126*t*
Magnesium hydroxide *(Milk of Magnesia)*, 126*t*
Magnesium salicylate *(Novasal)*, 201*t*
Magnesium sulfate, 283*t*
Magnesium sulfate, sodium, and potassium (*Suprep* bowel prep kit), 126*t*
Magnesium-aluminum hydroxide *(Maalox)*, 247
Major neurocognitive disorder, 71
Malalignment valgus, 196
Malalignment varus, 196
Malnutrition, 185–190, 252
Mammography, 257*t*, 316, 317
Mania, 82, 83*t*
MAO B inhibitors, 218*t*
MAOIs (monoamine oxidase inhibitors), 22, 112, 292
Maprotiline *(Ludiomil)*, 81, 219
Marijuana, 310
Massage, 69*t*, 155, 231
Mast cell stabilizers
    for allergic conjunctivitis, 109, 110, 110*t*
    for allergic rhinitis, 276*t*
Mavik, 55*t*. *See also* Trandolapril
Maxair (pirbuterol), 284*t*
Maxiflor, 91*t*. *See also* Diflorasone diacetate
Maxillofacial surgery, 308
Maxipime, 170*t*. *See also* Cefepime
Maxzide (triamterene with HCTZ), 57*t*
MDIs (metered-dose inhalers), 283, 283*t*
Mechanical heart valve, 32*t*
Mechanical skin ulcer debridement, 293
Mechanical ventilation, 158
Meclizine *(Antivert)*, 128*t*, 212*t*
Meclofenamate sodium, 202*t*
Medicaid, 7*t*, 152
Medical decision making, 8–9, 10, 258–259
Medical Orders for Life-Sustaining Treatment (MOLST), 245

Medicare
    alcohol abuse screening and counseling benefits, 310
    Annual Wellness Visit (AWV), 5, 71
    decompression physiotherapy benefits, 46
    education benefits, 95
    hospice benefits, 243*t*
    initial Annual Wellness Visit, 5
    Part A, 7*t*
    Part B, 7*t*, 16, 46
    Part D Prescription Drug Plan, 17
    procedure codes, 333*t*–334*t*
    reimbursement threshold for CPAP, 307
    smoking cessation counseling benefits, 312
Medication history, 16
Medication review, 4*t*
Mediplast, 197
Medi-Strumpf stockings, 303
Meditation, 231*t*, 305
Mediterranean diet, 95, 187
Medrol, 103*t*. *See also* Methylprednisolone
Medroxyprogesterone *(Cycrin, Depo-Provera, Provera)*, 77*t*
Medroxyprogesterone with estrogen *(Prempro, Premphase)*, 319
Mefenamic acid *(Ponstel)*, 202*t*
Mefoxin (cefoxitin), 169*t*
Megestrol acetate, 188
Meglitinides, 96, 98*t*
MEIs (middle ear implants), 135*t*, 136
Melanoma, 86, 317
Melatonin, 22
    for delirium prevention, 69*t*
    for sleep disorders, 306*t*, 309
Mellaril, 269*t*. *See also* Thioridazine
Meloxicam *(Mobic)*, 202*t*
Melphalan, 146
Memantine *(Namenda)*
    for agitation, 76
    for cognitive enhancement, 75, 76*t*
    de-prescribing, 18
Memantine extended release *(Namenda XR)*, 76*t*
Memory. *See* Cognitive impairment; Dementia
Memory Impairment Screen (MIS), 71

Ménière disease, 135*t*, 212*t*
Menopause, 222, 319, 320
Men's health
  benign prostatic hyperplasia (BPH), 56*t*,
    262–263, 331
  bone densitometry, 257*t*
  energy (caloric) and fluid requirements,
    187
  erectile dysfunction, 288–289
  impulse-control symptoms, 77*t*
  osteoporosis, 225–226
  prostate cancer, 263–265, 265*t*–266*t*
  prostate disorders, 262–267
  prostate infection, 172*t*
  prostatitis, 266–267
  sexual dysfunction, 289*t*–290*t*
Mental status, altered, 67–70
Mentax, 89*t. See also* Butenafine
Menthol, 232
Menthol with methylsalicylate (*Ben-Gay, Icy
    Hot*), 239*t*
Mentholatum (Vicks VapoRub), 87
Menthol-camphor-menthol (*Sarna*), 239*t*
Meperidine, 234
Mepore Film, 300*t. See also* Transparent film
Meropenem (*Merrem IV*)
  for infections in chronic wounds, 295*t*
  for infectious diseases, 168*t*
  for pneumonia, 159, 159*t*
Merrem IV, 168*t. See also* Meropenem
Mestinon (pyridostigmine), 65
Metaclopramide, 217, 292
METAGLIP (glipizide and metformin), 99*t*
Metamucil, 124, 125*t. See also* Psyllium
Metastatic bone disease
  in breast cancer, 317
  pain relief, 246
  in prostate cancer, 264, 265
Metaxalone, 234
Metered-dose inhalers (MDIs), 283, 283*t*
Metformin (*Glucophage, Glucophage XR*),
    94, 96, 97*t*
Metformin with alogliptin (*Kazano*), 100*t*
Metformin with glipizide (*METAGLIP*), 99*t*
Metformin with glyburide (*Glucovance*), 99*t*
Metformin with linagliptin (*Jentadueto*), 100*t*

Metformin with pioglitazone (*ACTO plus
    met*), 99*t*
Metformin with repaglinide (*PrandiMet*), 99*t*
Metformin with saxagliptin (*Kombiglyze XR*),
    99*t*
Metformin with sitagliptin (*Janumet*), 100*t*
Methadone, 20*t*, 233, 315
Methazolamide (*Neptazane*), 107*t*
Methicillin-resistant *S aureus. See* MRSA
Methimazole (*Tapazole*), 93
Methocarbamol, 234
Methotrexate (*Rheumatrex, Trexall*)
  for giant cell arteritis, 210
  for pseudogout, 209
  for psoriasis, 87
  for rheumatoid arthritis, 205, 206, 206*t*
Methoxy polyethylene glycol-epoetin beta
    (*Mircera*), 143*t*
Methyl sulfonyl methane (MSM), 23
Methylcellulose (*Citrucel, Fiber Ease*)
  for constipation, 125*t*
  for hemorrhoids, 132
  for IBS, 124
  tube feeding, 190
Methyldopa (*Aldomet*)
  for HTN, 52*t*
  and liver disease, 133*t*
  and orthostatic hypotension, 211
  and sleep problems, 304
Methyldopa with HCTZ (*Aldoril*), 57*t*
Methylnaltrexone bromide (*Relistor*), 126*t*,
    234, 247
Methylphenidate (*Ritalin*), 76, 80*t*, 246
Methylprednisolone (*Medrol, Solu-Medrol,
    Depo-Medrol*)
  for acute gouty flare, 207
  for adrenal insufficiency, 103*t*
  for anorexia, cachexia, dehydration, 249
  for carpal tunnel syndrome, 196
  for giant cell arteritis, 210
  for plantar fasciitis, 198
  for polymyalgia rheumatica, 209
  for vertigo, 212*t*
Methylprednisolone acetate, 198
Methylsalicylate, 198, 232
Methylsalicylate and menthol (*Ben-Gay, Icy
    Hot*), 200*f*, 239*t*

Methylxanthines, 285*t*
Meticorten, 103*t. See also* Prednisone
Metipranolol *(OptiPranolol),* 106*t*
Metoclopramide *(Reglan)*
  digoxin interactions, 44
  for GERD, 121*t*
  for high gastric residual volume problems, 190
  for nausea and vomiting, 128*t*
Metolazone *(Mykrox, Zaroxolyn),* 51*t,* 183, 184
Metoprolol *(Lopressor),* 53*t,* 59, 255*t*
Metoprolol, long-acting *(Toprol XL),* 45*t,* 53*t*
Metoprolol with HCTZ *(Dutoprol),* 57*t*
Metoprolol with HCTZ *(Lopressor HCT),* 57*t*
Metoprolol XR, 45*t*
Metoproterenol, 286*t*
MetroCream, 87. *See also* Metronidazole
MetroGel, 87, 172*t. See also* Metronidazole
Metronidazole *(Flagyl, MetroCream, MetroGel, Noritate)*
  for *C difficile* infection, 130, 131*t*
  for *H pylori* infection, 122*t*
  for infectious diseases, 172*t*
  for peptic ulcer disease, 122
  for rosacea, 87
  warfarin interactions, 32
Mevacor, 48*t. See also* Lovastatin
MGUS (monoclonal gammopathy of undetermined significance), 145
MI. *See* Myocardial infarction
Miacalcin, 225*t. See also* Calcitonin
Micafungin *(Mycamine),* 175*t*
Micardis (telmisartan), 55*t*
Micardis HCT (telmisartan with HCTZ), 57*t*
Micatin, 90*t. See also* Miconazole
Miconazole *(Micatin, Monistat-Derm, Monistat IV),* 32, 90*t,* 174*t*
Microalbuminuria, 101
Micronase, 97*t. See also* Glyburide
Microwave therapy, 198, 263
Microzide, 51*t. See also* HCTZ
Midamor (amiloride), 52*t*
Middle ear implants (MEIs), 135*t,* 136
Midodrine *(ProAmantine),* 65
Miglitol *(Glyset),* 97*t*

Migraine, 240*t*
Milk of Magnesia (magnesium hydroxide), 126*t*
Millgan-Morgan hemorrhoidectomy, 132
Milnacipran *(Savella),* 239*t*
Mindfulness training, 232
Mindfulness-based meditation, 231*t*
Mini-Cog™ screen for dementia assessment instrument, 322
  in cognitive dysfunction, 75
  in dementia, 71
  preoperative, 252
Mini–Mental State Examination (MMSE), 71, 72–73, 75
Minipress, 52*t. See also* Prazosin
Minitran, 41*t. See also* Nitroglycerin
Minocin, 171*t. See also* Minocycline
Minocycline *(Minocin)*
  for infectious diseases, 171*t*
  for MRSA, 85, 162
  ocular adverse events, 111
  for rosacea, 87
Minoxidil *(Loniten),* 54*t*
Miotics, 107*t*
Mirabegran *(Myrbetiq),* 152*t*
MiraLAX (polyethylene glycol), 125, 126*t*
Mirapex, 217*t. See also* Pramipexole
Mircera (methoxy polyethylene glycol-epoetin beta), 143*t*
Mirtazapine *(Remeron),* 79, 80*t,* 188
MIS (Memory Impairment Screen), 71
Misoprostol *(Cytotec)*
  for giant cell arteritis, 210
  for osteoarthritis, 199, 200*f*
  for pain, 232
Misoprostol with diclofenac *(Arthrotec),* 202*t*
Mistreatment of older adults, 10–12, 12*t,* 335
Mitraflx, 300*t*
Mitral valve prolapse, 32*t*
Mitral valve replacement surgery, 32*t*
Mitral valvular disease, rheumatic, 32*t*
MMRC (Modified Medical Research Council Dyspnea Scale), 277
MMSE (Mini–Mental State Examination), 71, 72–73, 75
Mobic (meloxicam), 202*t*

Mobility assessment, 115
MoCA (Montreal Cognitive Assessment), 71
Modafinil *(Provigil)*, 246, 307
Modified Medical Research Council Dyspnea Scale (MMRC), 277
Moduretic (amiloride hydrochloride with HCTZ), 57*t*
Moexipril *(Univasc)*, 55*t*
Moexipril with HCTZ *(Uniretic)*, 56*t*
Mohs micrographic surgery, 85
Moisture-retaining dressings, 293, 297
Molindone, 20*t*
MOLST (Medical Orders for Life-Sustaining Treatment), 245
Mometasone *(Asmanex, Nasonex)*, 276*t*, 284*t*
Mometasone furoate *(Elocon)*, 91*t*
Mometasone-formoterol *(Dulera)*, 285*t*
Monascus purpureus (red yeast rice), 23
Monistat IV, 174*t*. See also Miconazole
Monistat-Derm, 90*t*. See also Miconazole
Monoamine oxidase B inhibitors, 218*t*
Monoamine oxidase inhibitors (MAOIs), 22, 112, 292
Monobactam, 168*t*
Monoclonal gammopathy of undetermined significance (MGUS), 145
Monofilament testing, 101
Monoket (isosorbide mononitrate), 40*t*
Monopril, 55*t*. See also Fosinopril
Montelukast *(Singulair)*, 277*t*, 285*t*
Montreal Cognitive Assessment (MoCA), 71
Monurol (fosfomycin), 172*t*
Mood disorder, 232
Mood stabilizers, 83*t*
Moraxella catarrhalis, 158
Morphine *(Astramorph PF, Duramorph, Infumorph, MSIR, MS/L, MS/S, OMS Concentrate, RMS, Roxanol)*
  for dyspnea, 247
  for hip fracture surgery, 195
  for pain, 229*t*, 236*t*
Morphine extended release *(Avinza, Kadian, MS Contin, Oramorph SR)*, 237*t*
Morphine sulfate, 39, 228, 294
Morphine with naltrexone hydrochloride *(Embeda)*, 237*t*, 315

Motion sickness, 128*t*
Motor function, 2*t*
Motor restlessness (akathisia), 271*t*
Movement behavior, 65
Movement disorders, 304, 308–309
Moxifloxacin *(Avelox)*
  for acute bacterial conjunctivitis, 109*t*
  for community-acquired pneumonia, 159*t*
  for COPD exacerbation, 280*t*
  for infections in chronic wounds, 294*t*
  for infectious diseases, 171*t*
  QT_c interval interactions, 20*t*
  warfarin interactions, 32
MPM Excel, 300*t*. See also Hydrocolloids
MRSA (methicillin-resistant *S aureus*), 162
  in cellulitis, 85
  in chronic wounds, 294*t*–295*t*
  empiric antibiotic therapy against, 160, 294*t*–295*t*
  in pneumonia, 158
MS Contin (morphine), 237*t*
MSIR, 236*t*. See also Morphine
MS/L, 236*t*. See also Morphine
MSM (methyl sulfonyl methane), 23
MS/S, 236*t*. See also Morphine
Mucolytic therapy, 280
Mucomyst (acetylcysteine), 177
Mucositis, painful, 247
Multidisciplinary assessment, 228
Multimorbidity, 14, 15*f*, 136–137
Multiple myeloma, 145–146
Multiple system atrophy, 216*t*
Multivitamins, 186, 257*t*
Mupirocin *(Bactroban)*, 85, 162
Muscle mass, loss of, 185
Musculoskeletal disorders, 191–210, 260, 336
Musculoskeletal pain, 232, 238*t*
Musculoskeletal tissue procedures, 255*t*
Music therapy
  for delirium prevention, 69*t*
  for pain, 231, 231*t*
  for problem behaviors, 75
  for sleep disorders, 305
Mycamine (micafungin), 175*t*
Mycelex, 89*t*. See also Clotrimazole
Mycobacterium tuberculosis, 157, 158
Myco-Nail (triacetin), 90*t*

Mycoses, superficial, 89*t*, 175*t*
Mycostatin (nystatin), 90*t*
Myelodysplastic syndromes, 144
Myelofibrosis, 145
Myeloma, 145–146, 176*t*
Myeloproliferative disorders, primary, 144–145
Mykrox, 51*t. See also* Metolazone
Mylanta Classic, 17
Mylanta Gas Maximum Strength, 17
Myocardial infarction (MI)
   in ACS, 39
   antihypertensive therapy and, 56*t*
   non-ST segment (NSTEMI), 39
   ongoing hospital management of, 40
   prevention of, 254*t*, 257*t*
   ST segment (STEMI), 32*t*, 39
   warfarin anticoagulation for, 33*t*
Myofascial pain syndrome, 240*t*
Myrbetiq (mirabegran), 152*t*
Mysoline, 211*t. See also* Primidone
Myxedema coma, 92

N
Nabumetone *(Relafen),* 133*t*, 203*t*
N-acetylcysteine, 133*t*
Nadolol *(Corgard),* 53*t*
Nadolol with bendroflumethiazide *(Corzide),* 57*t*
Nafcillin, 32, 168*t*
Naftifine *(Naftin),* 90*t*
Naftin (naftifine), 90*t*
Nalbuphine, 234
Nalfon (fenoprofen), 202*t*
Naloxone *(Narcan),* 190, 229, 234
Naltrexone *(Depade,* REVIA, *Trexan, Vivitrol),* 311
Naltrexone with morphine *(Embeda),* 237*t*, 315
Namenda, 75, 76*t. See also* Memantine
Namenda XR, 76*t*
Naphazoline *(Naphcon),* 111*t*
Naphazoline hydrochloride/pheniramine maleate *(Naphcon-A, Opcon-A),* 111*t*
Naphcon (naphazoline), 111*t*

Naphcon-A (pheniramine maleate/naphazoline hydrochloride), 111*t*
Naprelan, 203*t. See also* Naproxen
Naprosyn, 203*t. See also* Naproxen
Naproxen *(Aleve, Naprosyn)*
   for arthritis, 203*t*
   and liver disease, 133*t*
   for pain, 232
   warfarin interactions, 32
Naproxen delayed release *(EC-Naprosyn),* 203*t*
Naproxen extended release *(Naprelan),* 203*t*
Naproxen sodium *(Anaprox),* 203*t*
Narcan, 190. *See also* Naloxone
Narcolepsy, 304
Narcotics. *See* Opioids
Nasacort, 276*t. See also* Triamcinolone
Nasal steroids
   for allergic conjunctivitis, 109, 275*t*, 276*t*
   for allergic rhinitis, 275, 275*t*, 276*t*
NasalCrom, 276*t. See also* Cromolyn
Nasalide, 276*t. See also* Flunisolide
Nasarel, 276*t. See also* Flunisolide
Nasogastric intubation, 248
Nasonex, 276*t. See also* Mometasone
Nateglinide *(Starlix),* 98*t*
National Institutes of Health Stroke Scale (NIHSS), 213
Nausea and vomiting, 127
   antiemetic therapy, 128*t*
   drug-induced, 270*t*
   at end of life, 248
   postoperative, 128*t*
Near vision testing, 104
Nebcin, 170*t. See also* Tobramycin
Nebivolol *(Bystolic),* 45*t*, 53*t*
Nebulizers, 283, 283*t*
Neck pain, 231*t*
Nedocromil *(Alocril),* 110*t*
Needle ablation, transurethral (TUNA), 263
Negative-pressure wound therapy, 294, 295, 298
Neglect, older adults, 10, 12*t*
Nephrotic syndrome, 181
Neptazane (methazolamide), 107*t*

Nerve block, 195
Nerve roots, 2t
Nesina (Alogliptin), 98t
Nesina with metformin *(Kazano)*, 101t
Nesina with pioglitazone *(Oseni)*, 90t
Neupro (rotigotine), 217t
Neuralgia, 162, 221, 238t
Neuroaxial analgesia, 232
Neurocognitive disorder, major, 71
Neurodermatitis, 86
Neuroimaging, 72
Neuroleptic malignant syndrome, 68t, 270t
Neuroleptics. *See* Antipsychotics
Neurologic disorders, 211–221
Neuromodulation, 232
Neurontin, 219t, 220, 238t. *See also*
     Gabapentin
Neuropathic erectile dysfunction, 288t, 289
Neuropathic foot ulcers, 296t–297t, 297–298
Neuropathic pain
   adjuvant drugs for, 238t–240t
   treatment of, 227t, 228, 232, 233
Neuropathy, 148, 220–221, 238t
New York Heart Association (NYHA) heart
     failure staging, 43t
Nexium, 120t. *See also* Esomeprazole
Niacin
   for dyslipidemia, 47t, 48t
   herbal medicine interactions, 23
   ocular adverse events, 111
Niacin extended release *(Niaspan)*, 48t
Niacin with lovastatin *(Advicor)*, 49t
Niacin with simvastatin *(Simcor)*, 49t
Niaspan (niacin ER), 48t
Nicardipine *(Cardene)*, 54t, 214
Nicardipine sustained release *(Cardene SR)*,
     54t
NicoDerm (nicotine patch), 313t
Nicorette (polacrilex gum), 313t
Nicotine, 211, 222, 304
Nicotine lollipops, 313t
Nicotine lozenges, 313t
Nicotine replacement therapy, 312, 313t
Nicotinic acid, 48t
Nicotrol (nicotine patch), 313t

Nicotrol Inhaler, 313t. *See also* Nicotine
     replacement therapy
Nicotrol NS, 313t. *See also* Nicotine
     replacement therapy
Nifedipine SR *(Adalat CC, Procardia XL)*, 54t
Nightmares, 36
NIHSS (National Institutes of Health Stroke
     Scale), 213
Nilandron (nilutamide), 266t
Nilotinib, 20t
Nilstat (nystatin), 90t
Nilutamide *(Nilandron)*, 266t
Nipride (sodium nitroprusside), 51
Nisoldipine *(Sular)*, 54t
Nitrates
   for ACS, 40
   alcohol interactions, 311
   for chronic angina, 40, 41
   dosages and formulations, 40t–41t
   drug interactions, 289t
   for HTN, 57t
   and orthostatic hypotension, 211
Nitrek, 41t. *See also* Nitroglycerin
Nitro-Bid, 40t. *See also* Nitroglycerin
Nitrodisc, 41t. *See also* Nitroglycerin
Nitro-Dur, 41t. *See also* Nitroglycerin
Nitrofurantoin *(Macrobid, Macrodantin)*,
     133t, 172t
Nitroglycerin *(Deponit, Minitran, Nitrek,
     Nitro-Bid, Nitrodisc, Nitro-Dur, Nitrol,
     Nitrolingual, NitroMist, Nitrostat,
     Transderm-Nitro)*
   for ACS, 39, 40
   for acute angina, 41
   dosage and formulations, 40t, 41t
   for HF, 44
Nitrol, 40t. *See also* Nitroglycerin
Nitrolingual, 40t. *See also* Nitroglycerin
NitroMist, 40t. *See also* Nitroglycerin
Nitrostat, 40t. *See also* Nitroglycerin
Nizatidine *(Axid)*, 120t
Nizoral, 89t, 174t. *See also* Ketoconazole
Nizoral A-D, 89t. *See also* Ketoconazole
NMDA antagonists, 76t
NNRTIs (non-nucleoside reverse
     transcriptase inhibitors), 22, 167
No Pain-HP, 240t. *See also* Capsaicin

Nociceptive pain, 227*t*
Nocturnal leg cramps, 308
Nodular melanoma, 86
Nodules, thyroid, 93–94
Noise reduction, 69*t*, 309
Nolvadex, 318*t. See also* Tamoxifen
Non-nucleoside reverse transcriptase
    inhibitors (NNRTIs), 22, 167
Nonsteroidal anti-inflammatory drugs. *See*
    NSAIDs
Norco, 235*t. See also* Hydrocodone with
    APAP
Norfloxacin *(Noroxin),* 171*t*
Noritate, 87. *See also* Metronidazole
Normodyne, 53*t,* 214. *See also* Labetalol
Noroxin (norfloxacin), 171*t*
Norpramin, 80*t,* 220. *See also* Desipramine
Nortriptyline *(Aventyl, Pamelor)*
    anticholinergic property, 68*t*
    for depression, 80*t,* 82
    for pain, 238*t*
    for painful neuropathy, 220
    for Parkinson disease, 82
    QT_c interval interactions, 20*t*
Norvasc, 54*t. See also* Amlodipine
Novasal (magnesium salicylate), 201*t*
Novolin, 101*t. See also* Insulin
Novolin 70/30 (isophane insulin), 101*t*
NovoLog, 101*t. See also* Insulin aspart
Noxafil (posaconazole), 174*t*
NRTIs (nucleos[t]ide reverse transcriptase
    inhibitors), 167
NSAIDs (nonsteroidal anti-inflammatory
    drugs)
    for acute gouty flare, 207
    for acute lumbar strain, 192–193
    for acute pain, 229
    alcohol interactions, 311
    for allergic conjunctivitis, 110*t*
    for anti-inflammatory prophylaxis, 207
    for arthritis, 201*t*–203*t*
    for back pain, 193
    for chronic disk degeneration, 193
    and CKD, 179
    dosage, 233
    herbal medicine interactions, 21, 22, 23
    and leg edema, 45

and liver disease, 133*t*
    for low back pain syndrome, 192–193
    nonselective, 199, 200*f,* 202*t*–203*t*
    for osteoarthritis, 193, 199, 200*f*
    for pain, 227*t,* 228, 229, 232
    for plantar fasciitis, 198
    for polymyalgia rheumatica, 209
    for pseudogout, 209
    for rheumatoid arthritis, 205
    for shoulder pain, 191, 192
    and tinnitus, 137
    and UI, 151*t*
N-terminal prohormone brain natriuretic
    peptide (NT-proBNP), 42
NT-proBNP (N-terminal prohormone brain
    natriuretic peptide), 42
Nucleos(t)ide reverse transcriptase
    inhibitors (NRTIs), 167
Nucynta (tapentadol), 236*t*
Nucynta ER (tapentadol ER), 237*t*
Nu-DERM, 300*t. See also* Hydrocolloids
NU-DERM Alginate, 301*t. See also* Calcium
    alginate dressings
Nugel, 301*t*
Nulecit (sodium ferric gluconate complex),
    143*t*
Nurses, interprofessional team, 6*t*
Nursing-home patients
    advanced dementia in, 73
    catheter care for, 153
    CMS guidance on unnecessary drugs for,
      18
    community-acquired pneumonia in, 159*t*
    fall prevention for, 115
    fecal incontinence treatment for, 155
    influenza treatment for, 164
    influenza vaccination for, 163
    malnutrition in, 185
    procedure codes, 333*t*
    resources for, 335–336
    scheduled visit checklist for, 8
    sites of care, 7*t*
    sleep disorders in, 309
    UI in, 153
Nursing-home–acquired cystitis, 161
Nursing-home–acquired pneumonia, 158,
    159–160

Nutren 1.0, 189*t*
Nutren 2.0, 189*t*
Nutren 1.0 Fiber, 189*t*
Nutriceuticals, 199
Nutrient-drug interactions, 19
Nutrition
  artificial, 190, 245
  enteral, 123, 188, 189, 189*t*
  oral, 188, 189*t*
  parenteral, 190
Nutritional assessment, 4*t*, 185–186
Nutritional supplements, 188, 195
Nutritional support, 188, 189*t*, 296
NYHA (New York Heart Association) heart
    failure staging, 43*t*
Nystatin *(Mycostatin, Nilstat, Nystex),* 90*t*
Nystex (nystatin), 90*t*

O
Oatmeal baths, 88, 89
Obesity, 187
  behavioral therapy for, 334*t*
  definition of, 185
  management of HTN, 50
  post MI, 41
  resources for, 336
  screening for, 257*t*
Obsessive-compulsive disorder (OCD), 36
Obstruction
  bladder outlet, 147*t*, 148
  bowel, 247–248
  renal, 176*t*
Obstructive pulmonary disease, chronic. *See*
    Chronic obstructive pulmonary disease
    (COPD)
Obstructive sleep apnea (OSA), 306–307
Occupational therapy (OT)
  for arthritis, 198, 204
  for carpal tunnel syndrome, 196
  for falls prevention, 115
  interprofessional team, 6*t*
  for pain, 232
  for preventing falls, 117*t*
OCD (obsessive-compulsive disorder), 36
Octreotide *(Sandostatin),* 248
Ocuflox, 109*t. See also* Ofloxacin
Ocular inflammatory disease, 108

Ocular symptoms, 275
Ocupress, 106*t. See also* Carteolol
Ocusert (pilocarpine gel), 106*t*
Ocuvite PreserVision, 105
Odor Shield, 300*t. See also* Hydrocolloids
Ofloxacin *(Floxin, Ocuflox, Roxin),* 109*t,* 171*t,*
    267
Ogen (estropipate), 291*t*
Olanzapine *(Zyprexa, Zydis)*
  for acute mania, 82
  adverse events, 270*t*
  for agitation, 76, 77*t*
  anticholinergic property, 68*t*
  for bipolar disorders, 83*t*
  for psychotic depression, 82
  for psychotic disorders, 268, 269*t*
  QTc interval interactions, 20*t*
  and seizures, 219
  and sexual dysfunction, 292
Olanzapine IM *(Zyprexa IntraMuscular),* 77*t*
Olmesartan *(Benicar),* 55*t*
Olmesartan with amlodipine *(Azor),* 56*t*
Olmesartan with HCTZ *(Benicar HCl),* 57*t*
Olopatadine *(Patanol, Pataday, Patanase),*
    110*t,* 276*t*
Omacor, 48*t. See also* Omega-3 fatty acids
Omalizumab *(Xolair),* 286*t*
Omega-3 fatty acids *(Omacor, Lovaza),* 21
  for chronic angina, 41
  for dyslipidemia, 47*t,* 48*t*
  for HF, 44
  for MI, stroke prevention, 41, 257*t*
Omeprazole *(Prilosec),* 120*t,* 189, 292
Omnaris, 276*t. See also* Ciclesonide
Omnicef (cefdinir), 170*t*
OMS Concentrate, 236*t. See also* Morphine
Onabotulinumtoxin A *(Botox),* 240*t*
Ondansetron *(Zofran),* 20*t,* 128*t,* 248
Onglyza (saxagliptin), 98*t*
Onsolis, 236*t. See also* Fentanyl
Onychomycosis, 86–87, 89*t*
Opana (oxymorphone), 236*t*
Opana ER (oxymorphone ER), 237*t*
Opcon-A (pheniramine maleate/naphazoline
    hydrochloride), 111*t*
Open reduction and internal fixation (ORIF),
    194

Opioid abuse-deterrent products, 315
Opioid antagonists, 126*t*
Opioid Risk Tool, 314, 332
Opioids
  with acetaminophen, 200*f*
  adverse events, 234, 314
  alcohol interactions, 311
  analgesic drugs, 235*t*–236*t*
  dosage, 233, 234
  drug interactions, 236*t*
  for dyspnea, 247
  misuse/abuse of, 234–235, 314, 315
  for opioid-tolerant patients, 237*t*–238*t*
  and orthostatic hypotension, 211
  for osteoarthritis, 199, 200*f*
  for pain, 227*t*, 229, 233, 236*t*–237*t*, 246, 294
  for painful neuropathy, 221
  for restless legs syndrome, 309
  risk evaluation and mitigation strategy
    (REMS), 234
  and sexual dysfunction, 292
  and UI, 151*t*
Op-site, 300*t. See also* Transparent film
Optical aids, 108
Optifoam AG, 300*t*
OptiPranolol (metipranolol), 106*t*
Optivar, 110*t. See also* Azelastine
Oral appliances, 307
Oral care, 158
Oral dysphagia, 118*t*
Oral hypoglycemics, 311
Oral nutrition, 188, 189*t*
Oral procedures, 259, 259*t*, 260
Oral statements, 244
Oramorph SR (morphine), 237*t*
Orasone, 103*t*, 284*t. See also* Prednisone
OrCel, 298, 303
Orchiectomy, 265
Orencia (abatacept), 206
Oretic, 51*t. See also* HCTZ
Organan, 30*t. See also* Danaparoid
Orientation protocols, 69*t*
ORIF (open reduction and internal fixation),
  194
Orlistat *(Xenica, Alli)*, 187
Oropharyngeal exercises, 307
Oropharyngeal infection, 174*t*

Orphenadrine, 68*t*
Orthoses, 197
Orthostatic (postural) hypotension, 65–66
  corticosteroids for, 103*t*
  distinguishing early Parkinson disease
    from other parkinsonian syndromes,
    216*t*
  dizziness in, 212*t*
  medications associated with, 211
  preventing falls with, 117*t*
Orthostatic syncope, 64*t*, 65
Orthotics, 197
  for diabetic foot ulcers, 298
  for osteoarthritis, 198
  for rheumatoid arthritis, 204
  for trochanteric bursitis, 194
Orthovisc, 199. *See also* Hyaluronic acid
Orudis, 202*t. See also* Ketoprofen
Oruvail, 202*t. See also* Ketoprofen
OSA (obstructive sleep apnea), 306–307
Osbon-Erec Aid (vacuum tumescence
  device), 290*t*
Oseltamivir *(Tamiflu)*, 164*t*
Oseni (alogliptin with pioglitazone), 100*t*
Osmolality, 1, 181
Osmolite 1 Cal, 189*t*
Osmotics, 125, 126*t*
Ospemifene, 291
Osteoarthritis, 198–199
  APAP and NSAIDs for, 201*t*–203*t*
  in back, 193
  and falls, 117*t*
  in hand, 196
  in hip, 194
  in knee, 195–196
  pain relief, 231*t*, 232, 238*t*, 240*t*
  pharmacologic management, 200*f*
  resources for, 336
Osteocalcin, 225*t. See also* Calcitonin
Osteomyelitis, 294, 296, 298
Osteopenia, 222
Osteoporosis, 222–226
  antihypertensive therapy and, 56*t*
  bone outcomes of medications for, 226*t*
  effects on other outcomes, level of
    evidence, and risks of medications for,
    226*t*

Osteoporosis *continued*
  prevention and treatment of, 195, 224*t*–225*t*
  resources for, 336
OT. *See* Occupational therapy
Ovarian cancer, 258
Overactive bladder, 147, 149
Overflow incontinence, 147*t*. *See also* Urinary incontinence
Overweight, 185, 187
Oxacillin *(Bactocill)*, 168*t*
Oxaprozin *(Daypro)*, 203*t*
Oxazepam *(Serax)*, 37*t*
Oxcarbazepine *(Trileptal)*, 219*t*, 238*t*
Oxcarbazepine extended release *(Oxtellar XR)*, 238*t*
Oxecta, 235*t*. *See also* Oxycodone
Oxiconazole *(Oxistat)*, 90*t*
Oximetry, 195
Oxistat (oxiconazole), 90*t*
Oxtellar XR (oxcarbazepine), 238*t*
Oxy IR, 235*t*. *See also* Oxycodone
Oxybutynin *(Ditropan, Ditropan XL, Gelnique, Oxytrol)*, 68*t*, 74, 151*t*
Oxycodone *(Oxy IR, Oxecta, Roxicodone)*, 20*t*, 235*t*
Oxycodone extended release *(OxyContin)*, 237*t*
Oxycodone with APAP *(Percocet, Tylox, Magnacet)*, 235*t*
Oxycodone with ASA *(Percodan)*, 235*t*
Oxycodone with ibuprofen *(Combunox)*, 235*t*
OxyContin (oxycodone), 237*t*
Oxygen, 1, 2
Oxygen therapy
  for ACS, 39
  for acute stroke, 213
  for diabetic foot ulcers, 298
  for dyspnea, 247
  for hip fracture, 195
  long-term, 280, 280*t*
  for PAH, 58
  for pneumonia, 158
Oxymorphone *(Opana)*, 236*t*
Oxymorphone extended release (*Opana* ER), 237*t*

Oxytrol for Women, 151*t*. *See also* Oxybutynin

P
Pacemakers, 43*t*, 59, 245
Pacerone, 61*t*. *See also* Amiodarone
PAD. *See* Peripheral arterial disease
Page references followed by *t* and *f* indicate tables and figures, respectively.
PAH (pulmonary arterial hypertension), 58
Pain, 227–240
  acute, 227, 229
  adjuvant drugs for, 238*t*–240*t*
  arthritic, 198–199, 200*f*, 201*t*–203*t*
  assessment of, 4*t*, 230*f*
  back, 192–194
  bowel obstruction, 248
  carpal tunnel syndrome, 196
  chest, 38
  differential diagnosis, 268
  at end of life, 246
  foot, 197
  hand, 196
  heel, 197
  hip, 194–195
  in intercourse, 291
  knee, 195–196
  low back, 198, 199, 238*t*, 240*t*
  metastatic bone, 246
  myofascial pain syndrome, 240*t*
  neuropathic, 227*t*, 228, 232, 233, 238*t*–240*t*
  nociceptive, 227*t*
  nondrug interventions for, 231*t*
  nonrheumatic, 194, 195
  opioids for, 235*t*–236*t*
  persistent, 227, 231–232, 231*t*, 232–233
  preventive measures for delirium, 69*t*
  resources for, 336
  shoulder, 191–192
  stepwise analgesic trial for, 228
  types, examples, and treatment of, 227*t*
Pain crisis, 246
Painful arc test, 191
Painful neuropathy, 227*t*
Palatal implants, 308
Paliperidone *(Invega)*, 269*t*
Palliative care, 241–249, 280, 335

Palliative Performance Scale, version 2 (PPSv2), 329
Palonosetron, 20*t*
Pamelor, 80*t*, 220. *See also* Nortriptyline
Pamidronate, 194, 317
Pancreatic cancer, 258
Pancytopenia, 143–144
Panic attack, 35
Panic disorder, 35, 36
Pantoprazole *(Protonix),* 120*t*
Pao2 (partial pressure of oxygen, arterial), 2
Papain, 190
Paranoid (delusional) disorder, late-life, 268
Parasomnias, 304
Parcopa, 217*t*. *See also* Carbidopa-levodopa
Parenteral iron replacement, 143*t*
Parenteral nutrition, 190
Parkinson disease, 215–217
    classification of, 211*t*
    dementia associated with, 75
    depression and, 82
    differential diagnosis, 268
    distinguishing early Parkinson disease
        from other parkinsonian syndromes,
        216*t*
    and falls, 117*t*
    gastrointestinal complaints, 118*t*
    medications for, 217*t*–218*t*
    pharmacologic management of delirium,
        70
    resources for, 336
Parkinsonism, 211*t*, 216*t*, 271*t*
Parlodel, 217*t*. *See also* Bromocriptine
Paroxetine *(Paxil, Paxil CR)*
    anticholinergic property, 68*t*
    for anxiety disorders, 36
    for depression, 80*t*
    drug interactions, 273*t*, 318*t*
    for menopausal symptoms, 321
Partial pressure of oxygen, arterial (PaO$_2$), 2
Paste-containing bandages, 303
Pataday, 110*t*. *See also* Olopatadine
Patanase, 276*t*. *See also* Olopatadine
Patanol, 110*t*. *See also* Olopatadine
Pathocil, 168*t*. *See also* Dicloxacillin
Patient education, 95, 231, 231*t*

Patient Health Questionnaire-2 (PHQ-2)
    Quick Depression Assessment, 326
Patient Health Questionnaire-9 (PHQ-9)
    Quick Depression Assessment, 325–326
Patient-controlled analgesia (PCA), 229, 229*t*
Paxil, 80*t*. *See also* Paroxetine
Paxil CR, 80*t*. *See also* Paroxetine
PCA (patient-controlled analgesia), 229, 229*t*
PCC (prothrombin complex concentrate), 31*t*
PCI (percutaneous cardiac intervention), 39
PDE-4 (phosphodiesterase-4) inhibitors, 279*t*,
    285*t*
PDE-5 (phosphodiesterase-5) inhibitors
    for BPH, 263
    drug interactions, 262, 289*t*
    for impotence, 289
    for male sexual dysfunction, 289*t*
    and orthostatic hypotension, 211
PE. *See* Pulmonary embolism
Peak flow meters, 281
Pear pulp, 309
Pedal pulse, 298
Pediapred, 103*t*. *See also* Prednisolone
Pedometers, 261
Pegloticase *(Krystexxa),* 208, 208*t*
Pelvic examination, 317
Pelvic floor electrical stimulation, 149
Pelvic fracture surgery, 25*t*
Pelvic muscle (Kegel) exercises, 149, 150*f*,
    319
Pemirolast *(Alamast),* 110*t*
Penbutolol *(Levatol),* 53*t*
Penicillin G, 168*t*
Penicillin VK, 168*t*
Penicillinase-resistant penicillins, 169*t*
Penicillins
    antipseudomonal, 168*t*, 169*t*
    for cellulitis, 85
    endocarditis prophylaxis regimens, 259*t*
    for erysipelas, 85
    for folliculitis, 85
    for impetigo, 85
    for infectious diseases, 168*t*, 169*t*
    penicillinase-resistant, 169*t*
Penile prosthesis, 290*t*
Penlac (ciclopirox), 87, 89*t*

Pennsaid, 202t, 232. See also Diclofenac
Pentazocine, 234
Pentoxifylline (Trental), 64
Pepcid, 120t. See also Famotidine
Peptic ulcer disease, 121–122
Pepto-Bismol (bismuth subsalicylate), 122, 129t
Percocet (oxycodone with APAP), 235t
Percodan (oxycodone with ASA), 235t
Percutaneous cardiac intervention (PCI), 39
Percutaneous venting gastrostomy, 248
Perennial rhinitis, 274, 281
Perianal bulking agents, 156
Perindopril (Aceon), 45t, 55t
Periodic limb movement disorder, 309
Perioperative management, 254
Peripheral arterial disease (PAD), 63–64
    antiplatelet agents for, 24t, 29t
    antithrombotic medications for, 24t
    management of, 63t
    screening for, 101, 258
    warfarin anticoagulation for, 32t
Peripheral neuropathy, 220–221, 238t
Peritoneal dialysis, 179
Permethrin (Elimite), 88
Perphenazine (Trilafon), 20t, 68t, 269t
Personality disorder, 232
Pertussis, 272t
Pes cavus, 197
Pessaries, 152, 319
Pet therapy, 75
Petrolatum, 132
Peyronie's disease, 288t
Phalen's test, 196
Pharmacists, 6t
Pharmacodynamics, 18t
Pharmacokinetics, 18t
Pharmacotherapy, 16–23
    antimicrobial stewardship, 157
    enteral nutrition interactions, 189
    fall risks, 112
    misuse of prescription drugs, 314–315
    for preventing falls, 116t
    prevention of opioid misuse and withdrawal, 234–235
    QTc interval interactions, 20t

systemic medications with ocular adverse events, 111
Pharyngeal dysphagia, 118t
Pheniramine maleate/naphazoline hydrochloride (Naphcon-A, Opcon-A), 111t
Phenobarbital (Luminal), 219t, 292
Phenol and camphor (Campho-Phenique), 239t
Phenol-camphor-menthol (Sarna), 239t
Phentermine-topiramate (Qsmia), 187
Phenylephrine, 132
Phenytoin (Dilantin)
    drug-food or -nutrient interactions, 19
    enteral nutrition interactions, 189
    and liver disease, 133t
    ocular adverse events, 111
    and osteoporosis, 222
    for seizures, 219t
    and sexual dysfunction, 292
    and sleep problems, 304
Phlebotomy, 144
Phobia, 36
PhosLo (calcium acetate), 179
Phosphate, 188
Phosphodiesterase-4 (PDE-4) inhibitors, 279t, 285t
Phosphodiesterase-5 (PDE-5) inhibitors
    for BPH, 263
    drug interactions, 262, 289t
    for impotence, 289
    for male sexual dysfunction, 289t
    and orthostatic hypotension, 211
Phospholine (echothiophate), 107t
Photocoagulation, 105, 132
Photodynamic therapy, 85
PHQ-2 Quick Depression Assessment, 326
PHQ-9 Quick Depression Assessment, 325–326
Physical abuse, 12t
Physical activity
    for chronic constipation, 125
    for IBS, 124
    for pain, 231
    for sleep disorders, 309
Physical restraints, 69
Physical self-maintenance scale, 323

Physical therapy (PT)
  for arthritis, 198, 204
  for balance and strength training, 212*t*
  for bicipital tendinitis, 192
  for carpal tunnel syndrome, 196
  decompression physiotherapy, 46
  for dizziness, 212*t*
  for frozen shoulder (adhesive capsulitis),
    192
  interprofessional team, 6*t*
  for pain, 227*t*, 229, 232
  for preventing falls, 115, 117*t*
  for rotator cuff problems, 191, 192
  for UI, 149
Physician Orders for Life-Sustaining
    Treatment (POLST), 10, 245
Physicians, interprofessional team, 6*t*
Picato (ingenol mebatate), 84
Pilagan (pilocarpine), 107*t*
Pill cards, 17
Pilocar (pilocarpine), 107*t*
Pilocarpine *(Adsorbocarpine, Akarpine,*
    Isopto Carpine, Pilagan, Pilocar,
    Piloptic, Pilostat), 107*t*
Pilocarpine gel *(Ocusert, Pilopine HS),* 106*t*
Pilopine HS (pilocarpine gel), 106*t*
Piloptic (pilocarpine), 107*t*
Pilostat (pilocarpine), 107*t*
Pimeclorimus *(Elidel),* 87
Pimozide, 20*t*, 68*t*
Pindolol *(Visken),* 53*t*
Pioglitazone *(Actos),* 96, 98*t*
Pioglitazone with alogliptin *(Oseni),* 100*t*
Pioglitazone with glimepiride *(Duetact),* 99*t*
Pioglitazone with metformin *(ACTO plus*
    met), 99*t*
Piperacillin *(Pipracil),* 168*t*
Piperacillin-tazobactam *(Zosyn)*
  for infections in chronic wounds, 295*t*
  for infectious diseases, 169*t*
  for pneumonia, 159, 159*t*
Pipracil (piperacillin), 168*t*
Pirbuterol *(Maxair),* 284*t*
Piroxicam *(Feldene),* 203*t*
Pitavastatin *(Livalo),* 48*t*
Pityrosporum orbiculare, 88

Plantar fasciitis, 197–198
Platelet-derived growth factors, 296
Plavix, 29*t*, 63, 215. *See also* Clopidogrel
Plendil, 54*t*. *See also* Felodipine
Pletal, 64. *See also* Cilostazol
Pneumatic compression
  for DVT/PE prophylaxis, 25*t*
  for hip fracture surgery, 195
  for venous insufficiency, 46
  for venous ulcers, 303
Pneumococcal vaccine, 97, 146
Pneumonia, 157–160
  immunization against, 257*t*
  treatment of, 159*t*, 170*t*
  vaccination against, 333*t*
Pneumovax, 179
Pocket Talker, 136
Polacrilex gum *(Nicorette),* 313*t*
POLST (Physician Orders for Life-Sustaining
    Treatment), 10, 245
Polycarbophil *(FiberCon),* 124, 125*t*, 132
Polycythemia vera, 144
Polyderm, 300*t*
Polydipsia, 182
Polyethylene glycol (PEG) *(MiraLAX),* 125,
    126*t*
PolyMem, 300*t*. *See also* Foam island
PolyMem Silver, 300*t*
Polymyalgia rheumatica, 209–210
Polymyxin with trimethoprim *(Polytrim),* 109*t*
Polyskin II, 300*t*. *See also* Transparent film
  for pressure ulcers, 300*t*
Polythiazide *(Renese),* 51*t*
Polytrim (trimethoprim and polymyxin), 109*t*
Polyunsaturated fatty acids, 44, 105
Ponstel (mefenamic acid), 202*t*
Posaconazole *(Noxafil),* 174*t*
Positioning devices, 297
Positive-pressure ventilation, 280*t*
Post-herpetic neuralgia, 162, 221, 238*t*
Postmenopausal bleeding, 318–319
Postmenopausal state, 319
Post-prandial glucose (PPG), 95*t*
Postprandial hypotension, 66
Post-traumatic stress disorder, 36, 232

Postural hypotension. *See* Orthostatic hypotension
Postural impingement of vertebral artery, 212*t*
Pos-T-Vac (vacuum tumescence device), 290*t*
Postvoid residual (PVR), 262
Potassium
  for dehydration, 180
  for HTN, 50
  low potassium diet, 179
  for refeeding syndrome prevention, 188
Potassium, sodium, and magnesium sulfate (*Suprep* bowel prep kit), 126*t*
Potassium imbalance, 268
Potassium iodide, 93
Potassium phosphate, 188
Potassium supplements, 19, 50
Potassium-sparing drugs, 52*t*
Power of attorney for health care, 10, 245
PPG (post-prandial glucose), 95*t*
PPIs. *See* Proton-pump inhibitors
PPSv2 (Palliative Performance Scale, version 2), 329
Pradaxa, 31*t*. *See also* Dabigatran
Pramipexole *(Mirapex)*
  for depression, 82
  for Parkinson disease, 82, 217*t*
  for rapid-eye movement (REM) sleep behavior disorder, 309
  for restless legs syndrome, 308
Pramlintide *(Symlin)*, 100*t*
PrandiMet (repaglinide and metformin), 99*t*
Prandin (repaglinide), 98*t*
Prasugrel *(Effient)*
  for ACS, 39
  for antithrombotic therapy, 24*t*
  cessation before surgery, 252
  for chronic angina, 41
  prescribing information, 29*t*
Pravachol, 48*t*. *See also* Pravastatin
Pravastatin *(Pravachol)*, 48*t*, 292
Pravastatin/ASA *(Pravigard PAC)*, 48*t*
Pravigard PAC (ASA/pravastatin), 48*t*
Prazosin *(Minipress)*, 36, 52*t*
Prealbumin, 186
Precose, 97*t*. *See also* Acarbose

Pre-diabetes, 94
Prednicarbate *(Dermatop)*, 91*t*
Prednisolone *(Delta-Cortef, Prelone Syrup, Pediapred)*, 103*t*, 207, 283*t*
Prednisone *(Deltasone, Liquid Pred, Meticorten, Orasone)*
  for acute gouty flare, 207
  for acute interstitial nephritis, 177
  for adrenal insufficiency, 103*t*
  for anorexia, cachexia, dehydration, 249
  for anti-inflammatory prophylaxis, 207
  for asthma, 284*t*
  for carpal tunnel syndrome, 196
  for chronic adrenal insufficiency, 102
  for COPD, 280*t*, 284*t*
  for giant cell arteritis, 210
  for hives, 89
  for multiple myeloma, 146
  for polymyalgia rheumatica, 209
  for rheumatoid arthritis, 205
Pregabalin *(Lyrica)*
  for menopausal symptoms, 321
  for neuropathic pain, 228
  for pain, 238*t*
  for painful neuropathy, 221
  for restless legs syndrome, 309
  for seizures, 219*t*
  and UI, 151*t*
Prelone Syrup, 103*t*. *See also* Prednisolone
Premarin, 77*t*, 291*t*. *See also* Estrogen therapy
Preoperative care, 250–254, 250*f*
Preparation H, 132
Prerenal disease, 176, 176*t*, 177
Presbycusis, 134, 135*t*
Presbyesophagus, 120
Prescription drug misuse, 310, 314–315
Prescription drugs, 16, 314. *See also* Pharmacotherapy
Pressure stockings, 153, 303. *See also* Compression stockings
Pressure ulcers, 298–303
  dressings for, 300*t*–302*t*
  wound and pressure ulcer products, 299*t*
  wound characteristics, 296*t*–297*t*
Pressure-reducing mattresses, 195, 296
Prevacid, 120*t*. *See also* Lansoprazole

Prevention, 257–261
  of cardiovascular complications of
    surgery, 254t–255t
  of cardiovascular diseases, 24t
  delirium, 69t
  DVT, 25t, 195, 254t
  endocarditis, 259, 259t
  falls, 112–117
  home visits, 115
  influenza, 163, 164
  MI, 254t
  osteoporosis, 224t–225t
  PE, 25t, 254t
  procedure codes, 333t–334t
  recommendations, 257t–258t
  stress ulcer, 123
  stroke, 29t, 214–215, 254t, 257t
  tests, 257t–258t
  TIA, 254t
  visual impairment, 104
  VTE, 22
Prevpac (lansoprazole + clarithromycin +
    amoxicillin), 122t
Prilosec, 120t. See also Omeprazole
Primaxin (imipenem-cilastatin), 168t
Primidone (Mysoline), 211t, 292
Prinivil, 55t. See also Lisinopril
Prinzide (lisinopril with HCTZ), 56t
Prisma Matrix, 302t
Pristiq, 81t. See also Desvenlafaxine
ProAmantine, 65. See also Midodrine
Proben-C (probenecid with colchicine), 208t
Probenecid (Benemid), 208, 208t
Probenecid with colchicine (ColBenemid,
    Col-Probenecid), 208t
Probiotic products, 130
Problem-solving therapy, 78
Procainamide, 20t
Procardia XL (nifedipine SR), 54t
Procedure codes, 333t–334t
Prochlorperazine (Compazine), 68t, 128t, 217
ProCol, 300t. See also Hydrocolloids
Procrit (epoetin alfa), 143t
Profore wrap, 303. See also Compression
    wraps
Progesterone, 304, 319
Progesterone with estrogen, 319, 320, 320t

Progestin, 291, 321
Progestin with estrogen, 321
Progressive muscle relaxation, 231t
Progressive supranuclear palsy, 216t
ProGuide wrap, 303. See also Compression
    wraps
Prokinetic agents, 121t
Prolia, 225t. See also Denosumab
Promethazine, 68t, 217
Promogran Matrix, 302t. See also Collagen
Prompted toileting, 74, 148, 153
Propafenone (Rythmol), 61t
Propantheline, 68t
Propine (dipivefrin), 106t
Propranolol (Inderal), 53t, 271t
Propranolol, long-acting (Inderal LA,
    InnoPran XL), 53t, 211t
Propranolol, long-acting with HCTZ
    (Inderide), 57t
Propylthiouracil (PTU), 93
Proscar, 263. See also Finasteride
Proshield, 88
ProSom (estazolam), 305t
Prostacyclins, 58
Prostaglandin analogs, 106, 107t
Prostate cancer, 263–265
  medications for, 265t–266t
  osteoporosis prevention in, 224
  screening for, 258, 259
Prostate disorders, 262–267
Prostate infection, 172t
Prostatectomy, 149, 263, 264
Prostate-specific antigen (PSA), 264–265
Prostatic hyperplasia, benign (BPH), 56t,
    262–263, 331
Prostatitis, 266–267
ProStep (transdermal nicotine patch), 313t
Prosthesis, penile, 290t
Prosthetic heart valves, 32t
Protease inhibitors, 22, 167
Protein requirements, 296
Protein restriction, 95, 178
Protein supplements, 188
Proteins, serum, 186
Proteinuria, 179
Proteus, 161

Prothrombin complex concentrate (PCC), 31*t*, 33*t*
Proton-beam therapy, 264
Protonix (pantoprazole), 120*t*
Proton-pump inhibitors (PPIs)
  for acute gouty arthritis, 207
  for anti-inflammatory prophylaxis, 207
  de-prescribing, 18
  drug interactions, 224
  for GERD, 120, 120*t*, 121*t*
  for giant cell arteritis, 210
  for *H pylori* infection, 122*t*
  for osteoarthritis, 199, 200*f*
  for pain, 232
  for stress-ulcer prevention, 123
Protriptyline *(Vivactil)*, 68*t*, 81
Providencia, 161
Provigil (modafinil), 246, 307
Prozac, 79*t. See also* Fluoxetine
Pruritus, 275*t*
PSA (prostate-specific antigen), 264–265
Pseudoephedrine *(Sudafed, Sudafed XR),* 275*t*, 276*t*
Pseudogout, 208–209, 208*t*
Pseudohyponatremia, 181
Pseudomembranous colitis, antibiotic-associated, 129
Pseudomonas, 280*t*
Pseudomonas aeruginosa, 159*t*, 161
Pseudo-rheumatoid arthritis, 208, 209
Psoralen plus ultraviolet light (PUVA), 87
Psorcon, 91*t. See also* Diflorasone diacetate
Psoriasis, 87
Psychiatric resources, 336
Psychodynamic therapy, 311
Psychogenic male sexual dysfunction, 288*t*
Psychological abuse, 12*t*
Psychological therapy, 124, 227*t*
Psychosis/psychotic disorders, 268–271
  agitation treatment guidelines, 77*t*
  in dementia, 73
  psychotic depression, 78, 82
  representative medications for treatment, 269*t*
Psychosocial assessment, 95, 229
Psychosocial therapy, 311
Psychostimulants, 246

Psychotherapy, 232
Psychotic depression, 78, 82
Psyllium *(Metamucil)*
  for constipation, 125*t*
  digoxin interactions, 44
  for hemorrhoids, 132
  for IBS, 124
  for opioid-induced constipation, 234
  tube feeding, 190
PT. *See* Physical therapy
PTU (propylthiouracil), 93
Pulmicort, 284*t. See also* Budesonide
Pulmicort Respules, 284*t. See also* Budesonide
Pulmonary arterial hypertension (PAH), 58
Pulmonary disease
  chronic obstructive. *See* Chronic obstructive pulmonary disease (COPD)
  determinants for hospice eligibility, 244*t*
  end-stage, 244*t*
Pulmonary embolism (PE)
  acute massive PE, 28
  clinical decision rule, 27*t*
  diagnosis of, 26
  evaluation algorithm, 27*f*
  medications for osteoporosis and, 226*t*
  prophylaxis of, 25*t*, 254*t*
  submassive PE, 28
Pulmonary rehabilitation, 274
Pulmonary risk assessment, preoperative, 251
Pulse therapy, 86
Punctal plugs, 110
PUVA (psoralen plus ultraviolet light), 87
PVR (postvoid residual), 262
Pylera, 122*t. See also* Tetracycline
Pyridostigmine *(Mestinon),* 65

Q
Qigong, 231*t*
Qsmia (phentermine-topiramate), 187
QT$_c$ interval interactions, 19, 20*t*
Quality of life, 241
Quetiapine *(Seroquel)*
  for acute mania, 82
  adverse events, 270*t*
  for agitation, 76, 77*t*

Quetiapine *continued*
  for bipolar disorders, 83*t*
  for delirium, 70
  for depression, 79
  for Parkinson disease, 217
  for psychosis, 269*t*
  for psychotic disorders, 268
  QT_c interval interactions, 20*t*
  for tardive dyskinesia, 271*t*
Quinapril *(Accupril)*, 45*t*, 55*t*
Quinapril hydrochloride with HCTZ
  (Accuretic), 56*t*
Quinidine, 20*t*, 304
Quinine, 137
Quinolones, 19, 171*t*. *See also*
  Fluoroquinolones
Quinupristin/dalfopristin *(Synercid)*, 172*t*
Qutenza, 221, 232, 240*t*. *See also* Capsaicin

R
Rabeprazole *(AcipHex)*, 120*t*
Radiation therapy
  antiemetic therapy for, 128*t*
  for basal cell carcinoma, 85
  for multiple myeloma, 146
  for pain at end of life, 246
  for prostate cancer, 264, 265
  for wet AMD, 105
Radioactive iodine ablation, 93
Radiocontrast-induced acute kidney failure,
  177
Radiography, abdominal, 155
Radionuclide ventriculography, 42
Radionuclides, 246
Raloxifene *(Evista)*, 225*t*, 226*t*
Ramelteon *(Rozerem)*, 37, 306*t*
Ramipril *(Altace)*, 45*t*, 55*t*
Ranexa (ranolazine), 41
Range-of-motion programs, 232
Ranibizumab *(Lucentis)*, 105
Ranitidine *(Zantac)*, 120*t*, 292
Ranolazine *(Ranexa)*, 41
Rapaflo (silodosin), 263
Rapid Estimate of Adult Literacy in
  Medicine – Short Form (REALM-SF), 17,
  327

Rapid-eye movement (REM) sleep behavior
  disorder, 309
RAS (renal artery stenosis), 49–50
Rasagilene *(Azilect)*, 218*t*
Razadyne (galantamine), 76*t*
Razadyne ER (galantamine extended
  release), 76*t*
REALM-SF (Rapid Estimate of Adult Literacy
  in Medicine – Short Form), 17, 327
Reclast, 225*t*. *See also* Zoledronic acid
Rectal evacuants, 155
Rectal sphincter exercises, 155
Red eye, 108–110, 108*t*
Red yeast rice (*Monascus purpureus*, Xue
  Zhi Kang), 23
Reductase inhibitors
  5-α, 262, 263
  HMG-CoA, 48*t*, 133*t*
Refeeding syndrome, 188
Refludan, 31*t*. *See also* Lepirudin
Reflux, gastroesophageal (GERD), 119–120,
  120*t*–121*t*
Reflux esophagitis, 272*t*
Refractive error, 104
Reglan, 121*t*, 128*t*, 190. *See also*
  Metoclopramide
Regranex, 296
Rehabilitation
  in acute stroke, 213
  for COPD, 280
  of hearing loss, 135*t*
  hospital care, 8
  inpatient, 7*t*
  pulmonary, 274
  short stay, 7*t*
  swallowing, 118
Rehydration, 158, 177, 180
  Reisberg Functional Assessment Staging
  (FAST) scale, 330
Rejoyn (vacuum tumescence device), 290*t*
Relafen, 203*t*. *See also* Nabumetone
Relaxation therapy
  for dyspnea, 247
  for insomnia, 305
  for pain, 229, 231
Relenza (zanamivir), 164*t*

Reliamed, 300*t. See also* Transparent film
Relistor (methylnaltrexone bromide), 126*t,* 234, 247
REM (rapid-eye movement) sleep behavior disorder, 309
Remeron, 80*t. See also* Mirtazapine
Remicade (infliximab), 206
Remodulin (treprostinil), 58
REMS (risk evaluation and mitigation strategy), 234
Renagel (sevelamer hydrochloride), 179
Renal artery stenosis (RAS), 49–50
Renal dialysis, 177
Renal infarction, 176*t*
Renese (polythiazide), 51*t*
Renin inhibitors, 55*t,* 57*t*
Renovascular angioplasty, 50
Renvela (sevelamer carbonate), 179
ReoPro, 31*t. See also* Abciximab
Reordering tasks, 246
Repaglinide *(Prandin),* 98*t*
Repaglinide with metformin *(PrandiMet),* 99*t*
Repetitive transcranial magnetic stimulation (rTMS), 78, 82
Replens (water-soluble lubricant), 291
RepliCare, 300*t. See also* Hydrocolloids
RepliCare Thin, 300*t. See also* Hydrocolloids
Requip, 217*t. See also* Ropinirole
Reserpine *(Serpasil)*
  for HTN, 52*t*
  and orthostatic hypotension, 211
  and sexual dysfunction, 292
  and sleep problems, 304
Reserpine with chlorothiazide *(Diupres),* 57*t*
Reserpine with HCTZ *(Hydropres),* 57*t*
Residential care, 7*t*
Resistance (strength) training, 95, 116*t,* 261
Resource Breeze, 189*t*
Resource Health Shake, 188
Respiratory diseases, 272–287
Respiratory tract procedures, 255*t,* 259
Respiratory viruses, 158
Restasis (cyclosporine ophthalmic emulsion), 110
Restless legs syndrome, 308–309

Restore, 300*t. See also* Hydrocolloids; Silver dressings
Restore CalciCare, 301*t. See also* Calcium alginate dressings
Restore CX, 300*t*
Restore Gel, 301*t*
Restore Impregnated Gauze, 301*t*
Restore Plus, 300*t*
Restoril, 306*t. See also* Temazepam
Restrictive lung disease (RLD), 286–287, 286*t*–287*t*
Retapamulin *(Altabax),* 85
Retinopathy, diabetic, 105
Retirement communities, continuing care, 7*t*
Revascularization, 297
Revatio, 58. *See also* Sildenafil
Reverse-transcriptase polymerase chain reaction (RT-PCR), 163*t*
REVIA (naltrexone), 311
R-Gel, 240*t. See also* Capsaicin
Rheumatic mitral valvular disease, 32*t*
Rheumatoid arthritis, 204–206, 204*t*
"Rheumatoid arthritis type" anemia, 138
Rheumatrex, 206*t. See also* Methotrexate
Rhinitis, 274–275, 275*t*–277*t,* 281
Rhinocort, 276*t. See also* Budesonide
Rhythm control drugs, 61, 61*t*
Rifampin, 32, 133*t,* 162
Rifapentine, 165*t*
Rimantadine *(Flumadine),* 164*t*
Ringworm, 90*t*
Risedronate *(Actonel),* 224*t*–225*t,* 226*t*
Risedronate delayed-release *(Atelvia),* 225*t*
Risk evaluation and mitigation strategy (REMS), 234
Risperdal, 77*t,* 269*t. See also* Risperidone
Risperidone *(Risperdal)*
  for acute mania, 82
  adverse events, 270*t*
  for agitation, 76, 77*t*
  for psychotic disorders, 268, 269*t*
  QT_c interval interactions, 20*t*
  and sexual dysfunction, 292
Ritalin, 80*t,* 246. *See also* Methylphenidate
Ritonavir, 20*t,* 167
Rituxam (rituximab), 206
Rituximab *(Rituxam),* 206

Rivaroxaban *(Xarelto)*
  for ACS, 40
  for AF, 60*t*
  for anticoagulation, 31*t*, 33*t*
  for antithrombotic therapy, 24*t*
  cessation before surgery, 253
  resumption after surgery, 253
  for VTE, 25*t*, 28*t*
Rivastigmine *(Exelon),* 76*t*
RMS, 236*t. See also* Morphine
Robitussin, 273*t. See also* Guaifenesin
Robitussin DM, 273*t. See also*
  Dextromethorphan
Robotic prostatectomy, 263
Rocaltrol, 179. *See also* Calcitriol
Rocephin, 170*t. See also* Ceftriaxone
Roflumilas*t (Daliresp),* 285*t*
Rolling walkers (rollators), 115
Ropinirole *(Requip),* 217*t*, 308
Rosacea, 87
Rosenbaum card testing for near vision, 104
Rosiglitazone *(Avandia),* 99*t*
Rosula (sodium sulfacetamide), 87
Rosuvastatin *(Crestor),* 48*t*
Rotator cuff tears, 191–192, 191*t*
Rotator cuff tendinitis, 191
Rotator tendon impingement on clavicle, 191
Rotigotine *(Neupro),* 217*t*
Roxanol, 236*t. See also* Morphine
Roxicodone, 235*t. See also* Oxycodone
Roxin, 171*t. See also* Ofloxacin
Rozerem (ramelteon), 37, 306*t*
rTMS (repetitive transcranial magnetic
  stimulation), 78, 82
RT-PCR (reverse-transcriptase polymerase
  chain reaction), 163*t*
Rubber band ligation, 132
Rythmol (propafenone), 61*t*

S
Sacral nerve stimulation, 156
Safe sex practices, 167
SAF-Gel, 301*t*
Sal-Acid plaster, 197
Salicylates, nonacetylated, 201*t*
Salicylic acid, 87

Salicylic acid plaster, 197
Saline and sodium bicarbonate
  (Sinu*Cleanse*), 274
Salmeterol *(Serevent Diskus),* 284*t*
Salmeterol-fluticasone *(Advair Diskus),* 286*t*
Salmonine, 225*t. See also* Calcitonin
Salsalate, 201*t*
Salt restriction, 43*t*, 212*t*
Salt tablets, 182, 183
SAMe (S-adenosylmethionine), 23
Samsca (tolvaptan), 182, 183
Sanctura, 151*t. See also* Trospium
Sanctura XR, 151*t. See also* Trospium
Sandostatin (octreotide), 248
Santyl, 293
Saquinavir, 20*t*
Sarcoma, vulvar, 317
Sarcopenia, 185
Sarna (camphor-menthol-phenol), 239*t*
Savella (milnacipran), 239*t*
Saw palmetto, 23
Saxagliptin *(Onglyza),* 98*t*
Saxagliptin with metformin *(Kombiglyze XR),*
  99*t*
Scabene (lindane), 88
Scabies, 88
Scheduled toileting, 74
Schizophrenia, 268
Sciatica, 192, 193
Sclerotherapy, 132
Scopolamine, 68*t*, 128*t*, 248
Seasonal depression, 78
SeaSorb, 301*t. See also* Calcium alginate
  dressings
Seborrheic dermatitis, 88, 89*t*
Secretions, excessive, 248
Sectral (acebutolol), 53*t*
Sedation, 246, 270*t*, 271*t*
Sedatives
  adverse events, 314
  alcohol interactions, 311
  fall risks, 112
  preventing falls with, 116*t*
  for sleep disorders, 305*t*
  and sleep problems, 304
  and UI, 151*t*
Segmental pressure measurement, 63*t*

Seizures, 218–219, 268, 270t
Selective estrogen receptor modulators, 291
Selective serotonin-reuptake inhibitors. *See* SSRIs
Selegiline *(Carbex, Eldepryl, Zelapar),* 218t
Selenium sulfide, 88
Self-help groups, 311
Self-maintenance physical scale (ADLs), 323
Self-management education, 231t
Self-monitor blood glucose (SMBG), 101
Senior citizen housing, 7t
Senna *(Senokot),* 125, 126t
Senokot, 126t. *See also* Senna
Sensorineural hearing loss, 134t–135t
Sensory impairments, 69t, 212t
Sentinel lymph node (SLN) biopsy, 316
Sepsis, 160–161, 172t
Serax (oxazepam), 37t
Serevent Diskus (salmeterol), 284t
Seroquel, 77t, 269t. *See also* Quetiapine
Serotonin 1A partial agonists, 36
Serotonin agents, 124
Serotonin antagonists, 128t
Serotonin norepinephrine-reuptake inhibitors (SNRIs), 80t, 227t, 321
Serotonin syndrome, 36, 68t
Serpasil, 52t. *See also* Resorpine
Sertraconazole *(Ertaczo),* 90t
Sertraline *(Zoloft)*
  for anxiety disorders, 36
  for depression, 79, 80t, 82
  QT_c interval interactions, 20t
  SSRI-induced sexual dysfunction, 292
Sevelamer carbonate *(Renvela),* 179
Sevelamer hydrochloride *(Renagel),* 179
Sex practices, safe, 167
Sex therapy, 291
Sexual aggression, 77t
Sexual dysfunction, 288–292, 289t–290t, 336
$SGLT_2$ Inhibitors, 99t
Shark liver oil, 132
Sharp debridement, 293, 298
Shingles. *See* Herpes zoster
Shoes, 117t, 197
Shoulder impingement syndrome, 191
Shoulder pain, 191–192, 191t, 231t

SIADH (syndrome of inappropriate secretion of antidiuretic hormone), 182–183
Sigmoidoscopy, 257t
SignaDRESS, 300t. *See also* Hydrocolloids
Sig-Varis stockings, 303
Sildenafil *(Revatio, Viagra)*
  α_1-blocker interactions, 262
  ocular adverse events, 111
  for PAH, 58
  for sexual dysfunction, 289t, 292
Silenor, 305t. *See also* Doxepin
Silodosin *(Rapaflo),* 263
Silvadene, 294
SilvaSorb Gel, 301t
Silver dressings, 294
Simbrinza (brinzolamide/brimonidine), 107t
Simcor (simvastatin with niacin), 49t
Simponi (golimumab), 206
Simvastatin *(Zocor),* 48t, 292
Simvastatin with niacin *(Simcor),* 49t
Sinemet (carbidopa-levodopa), 217t, 308
Sinemet CR (carbidopa-levodopa), 217t
Sinequan, 81. *See also* Doxepin
Single-photon emission computed tomography (SPECT), 38
Singulair (montelukast), 277t, 285t
Sinu*Cleanse* (saline and sodium bicarbonate), 274
Sinusitis, bacterial, 272t
Sitagliptin *(Januvia),* 98t
Sitagliptin with metformin *(Janumet, Janumet XR),* 100t
Sites of care, 7t
Sitz baths, 132
Skeletal muscle relaxants, 68t, 112, 211
Skilled nursing facilities, 7t
Skin and soft tissue infection (SSTI), 162, 170t, 173t
Skin care, 46, 155
Skin examination, 257t, 336
Skin graft, 303
Skin losses, 182
Skin maceration, 88
Skin substitutes *(Apligraf, DermaGraft, GammaGraft, OrCel, TransCyte),* 298, 303
Skin ulcers, 293–303, 296t–297t

Sleep, 231
Sleep apnea, 272t, 306–308
Sleep deprivation, 69t, 268
Sleep disorders, 304–309, 305t–306t, 319
Sleep hygiene measures, 304–305, 308, 309
Sleep restriction, 305
Sleep rituals, 305
SLN (sentinel lymph node) biopsy, 316
Slo-Bid, 285t. *See also* Theophylline-SR
SMBG (self-monitor blood glucose), 101
Smoking, 222, 310
Smoking cessation, 312
   for chronic kidney disease, 179
   for COPD, 279
   for cough, 272t
   for DM, 95, 97
   for GERD, 120
   for HTN, 50
   for PAD, 63
   post MI, 41
   preoperative, 251
   for prevention, 257t
   resources for, 335
   for stroke prevention, 214
   for UI, 148
Smoldering myeloma, 145–146
Smooth and Cool, 88
Sneezing, 275t
Snellen wall chart, 104
SNRIs (serotonin norepinephrine-reuptake inhibitors), 80t, 227t, 321
Social phobia, 36
Social status assessment, 4t
Social support, 311, 312
Social workers, 6t
Sodium, fractional excretion of (FENa), 176, 180
Sodium, potassium, and magnesium sulfate (*Suprep* bowel prep kit), 126t
Sodium, urine, 180, 181
Sodium bicarbonate
   for acidosis, 179
   for chronic kidney disease, 179
   for hyperkalemia, 184
   for prevention of radiocontrast-induced acute kidney injury, 177

Sodium bicarbonate and saline (Sinu*Cleanse*), 274
Sodium disorders, 180–181, 181–182
Sodium ferric gluconate complex (*Ferrlecit, Nulecit),* 143t
Sodium imbalance, 268
Sodium nitroprusside (*Nipride),* 51
Sodium phosphate/biphosphate emollient enema (*Fleet),* 126t
Sodium polystyrene sulfonate (SPS, *Kayexalate*), 184
Sodium Sulamyd (sulfacetamide sodium), 109t
Sodium sulfacetamide (*Clenia, Rosula),* 87
Soft tissue or skin infections, 170t
Solesta, 156
Solifenacin (*VESIcare),* 20t, 68t, 152t
SoloSite, 301t
Solu-Medrol, 103t. *See also* Methylprednisolone
Somatic pain, 233, 238t
Somatization, 232
Sonata, 37, 306t. *See also* Zaleplon
Sorbex, 300t. *See also* Hydrocolloids
Sorbitol, 125, 126t, 184
Sorbitrate (isosorbide dinitrate), 40t
Sorbsan, 301t. *See also* Calcium alginate dressings
Sorine, 61t. *See also* Sotalol
Sotalol (*Betapace, Betapace AF, Sorine),* 20t, 61t
Soybean formulas, 189
Spasm, pain, and vomiting, 248
Spasms, muscular, 192, 240t
SPECT (single-photon emission computed tomography), 38
Spectazole (econazole nitrate), 89t
Spectracef (cefditoren), 170t
SPIKES (communicating bad news), 241–242
Spinal cord injury, 25t
Spinal manipulation, 193
Spine fractures, 226t
Spine surgery, 25t
Spiritual status assessment, 4t
Spiriva, 283t. *See also* Tiotropium
Spirometry, 272t

Spironolactone *(Aldactone)*
  digoxin interactions, 44
  for HF, 43
  for HTN, 52*t*
  and sexual dysfunction, 292
Spironolactone with HCTZ *(Aldactazide),* 57*t*
Splinting
  for carpal tunnel syndrome, 196
  for osteoarthritis, 198
  for pain, 232
  for rheumatoid arthritis, 204
Sporanox, 86, 173*t. See also* Itraconazole
Squamous cell carcinoma, vulvar, 317
Squamous hyperplasia, 317
SSRIs (selective serotonin-reuptake
    inhibitors)
  for agitation, 76, 77*t*
  for anxiety at bedtime, 305
  for bipolar disorders, 83*t*
  for depression, 79, 79*t*–80*t*
  fall risks, 112
  for IBS, 124
  for menopausal symptoms, 321
  and osteoporosis, 222
  for pain relief, 238*t*
  for painful neuropathy, 221
  preoperative care, 254
  and restless legs syndrome, 308
  and sexual dysfunction, 292
SSTI (skin and soft tissue infection), 162,
    170*t,* 173*t*
St. John's wort *(Hypericum perforatum),* 23,
    44, 81
Stalevo (carbidopa-levodopa + entacapone),
    218*t*
Staphylococcal blepharitis, 109*t*
Staphylococcus, 161
Staphylococcus aureus
  endocarditis prophylaxis regimens, 259*t*
  methicillin-resistant (MRSA), 85, 158, 160,
    162, 294*t*–295*t*
  in nursing-home–acquired pneumonia,
    158
  in UTI or urosepsis, 161
Starch solutions, 180
Starlix (nateglinide), 98*t*

Statin therapy
  for ACS, 40
  for acute stroke, 213
  adverse events, 49*t*
  and dialysis, 179
  for DM, 95*t,* 96
  for dyslipidemia, 41, 47, 47*t,* 48*t,* 49*t*
  herbal medicine interactions, 23
  for HTN, 57*t*
  indications for, 47*t*
  perioperative use, 254*t*
  and sexual dysfunction, 292
Stem cell transplantation
  antibiotics for, 175*t*
  for chronic myelogenous leukemia, 145
  for multiple myeloma, 146
  for myelodysplastic syndromes, 144
Stendra (avanafil), 289*t*
Stents, 253, 263
Steroids. *See* Corticosteroids;
    Glucocorticoids
STI counseling, 334*t*
Stimulants, 314, 315
Stimulen, 302*t*
Stockings, pressure, 153, 303
Strength training, 116*t,* 212*t,* 261
Streptococcus pneumoniae, 157, 158
Streptomycin, 170*t*
Stress, post-traumatic, 232
Stress incontinence. *See also* Urinary
    incontinence
  characteristics and causes of, 147*t*
  in nursing-home residents, 153
  therapy for, 149, 150*f,* 152
Stress reduction, 74
Stress testing, 38, 42
Stress ulcers, 123
Stretching exercises
  for bicipital tendinitis, 192
  for frozen shoulder (adhesive capsulitis),
    192
  for osteoarthritis, 198
  for plantar fasciitis, 197
  prescription, 260
Striant (testosterone), 290*t*

Stroke
  acute, 25*t*, 213–214
  differential diagnosis, 268
  gastrointestinal complaints, 118*t*
  medications for osteoporosis and, 226*t*
  prevention of, 29*t*, 214–215, 254*t*, 257*t*
  resources for, 336
  risk instruments, 60*t*
Stromectol (ivermectin), 88
Subacromial bursitis, 191, 209
Subdeltoid bursitis, 209
Substance use disorders, 252, 310–315
Subsyndromal depression, 78
Subsys, 236*t. See also* Fentanyl
Sucralfate *(Carafate),* 19, 123
Sudafed, 276*t. See also* Pseudoephedrine
Sular (nisoldipine), 54*t*
Sulbactam-ampicillin *(Unasyn),* 159*t*, 169*t*
Sulconazole *(Exelderm),* 90*t*
Sulfacetamide sodium *(Sodium Sulamyd),*
  109*t*
Sulfamethoxazole, 32
Sulfasalazine *(Azulfidine)*
  digoxin interactions, 44
  for psoriasis, 87
  for rheumatoid arthritis, 205, 206*t*
Sulfonamides, 19
Sulfonylureas, 96, 97*t*
Sulindac *(Clinoril),* 32, 133*t*, 203*t*
Sumatriptan, 20*t*
Sumycin, 122. *See also* Tetracycline
Sunscreens, 84, 86, 87
Supartz, 199. *See also* Hyaluronic acid
Superficial mycoses, 89*t*, 175*t*
Suprax (cefixime), 170*t*
Suprep bowel prep kit (sodium, potassium,
  and magnesium sulfate), 126*t*
Surgery
  abdominopelvic, 25*t*
  for acute disk herniation, 193
  adrenal insufficiency management, 102
  for AF, 61
  anticoagulant agents for, 30*t*, 31*t*
  antithrombotic medications for, 25*t*
  aortic valve replacement (AVR), 32*t*, 62
  for arterial ulcers, 297
  for AS, 63

  for back pain, 193
  bariatric, 95, 307
  for basal cell carcinoma, 85
  for bowel obstruction, 248
  for BPH, 262, 263
  CABG, 39
  cardiac risk assessment for, 250
  cardiac valvular, 255*t*
  for carpal tunnel syndrome, 196
  for cataract, 104, 252
  cessation of anticoagulation before, 253
  cryosurgery, 84, 85
  dental procedures, 253
  for diabetic foot ulcers, 298
  for DM, 95
  DVT/PE prophylaxis in older inpatients, 25*t*
  electrosurgery, 84
  endocarditis prophylaxis, 259, 259*t*
  for fecal incontinence, 155–156
  for foot disorders, 197
  for frozen shoulder (adhesive capsulitis),
    192
  for GERD, 120
  for glaucoma, 105–106
  for hemorrhoids, 132
  for hip fracture, 25*t*, 29*t*, 30*t*, 32*t*, 194–195
  hip replacement, 25*t*, 29*t*, 30*t*, 31*t*, 32*t*
  for hyperthyroidism, 93
  ICD placement, 66
  knee, 25*t*, 29*t*, 30*t*, 31*t*, 32*t*
  for leg fracture, 25*t*
  for lumbar spinal stenosis, 193–194
  maxillofacial, 308
  for melanoma, 86
  mitral valve replacement, 32*t*
  Mohs micrographic surgery, 85
  for osteoarthritis, 198
  for PAD, 63*t*
  for pain management, 231
  for Parkinson disease, 216
  for pelvic fracture, 25*t*
  perioperative management, 254, 254*t*–255*t*
  for plantar fasciitis, 197
  postoperative delirium, 255–256
  postoperative nausea and vomiting, 128*t*
  postoperative pain, 238*t*
  preoperative care, 250–254, 250*f*

Surgery *continued*
  for pressure ulcers, 303
  for prostate cancer recurrence, 265
  pulmonary risk assessment for, 251
  resumption of anticoagulation after, 253
  for rheumatoid arthritis, 204
  for rotator cuff tears, 192
  for sleep apnea, 308
  spine, 25*t*
  thoracic, 25*t*
  for thyroid nodules, 93
  for UI, 150*f*, 152
  for unstable lumbar spine, 193
  urologic procedures, 25*t*
  for vaginal prolapse, 319
  vascular, 25*t*
  for venous ulcers, 303
  for VIN, 317
  for vulvar malignancy, 317
Surmontil, 81. *See also* Trimipramine
Swallowing rehabilitation, 118
Symbicort (budesonide-formoterol), 285*t*
Symlin (pramlintide), 100*t*
Symmetrel (amantadine), 164*t*, 218*t*
Sympathomimetics, 304
Synacthen Depot (tetracosactin), 102
Synalar (fluocinolone acetonide), 90*t*
Syncope, 64–65, 64*t*, 66
Syndrome of inappropriate secretion of
  antidiuretic hormone (SIADH), 182–183
Synercid (quinupristin/dalfopristin), 172*t*
Synthroid, 92. *See also* Levothyroxine
Synvisc, 199. *See also* Hyaluronic acid
Systemic inflammatory response, 294
Systolic dysfunction, 42

T
T_3 (triiodothyronine), 92
T_4 (thyroxine), 92, 189, 222
T scores, 222
Tachycardia, atrial, 56*t*
Tachycardia, ventricular (VT), 66
Tacrolimus, 87
Tadalafil *(Cialis)*, 262, 289*t*
Tafluprost *(Zioptan)*, 107*t*
Tagamet HB 200, 120*t*
Tai Chi, 116*t*, 309

Take Control, 47
Tamiflu (oseltamivir), 164*t*
Tamoxifen *(Nolvadex)*
  for breast cancer, 317, 318*t*
  drug interactions, 32, 321
  ocular adverse events, 111
Tamsulosin *(Flomax)*, 262
Tapazole, 93. *See also* Methimazole
Tapentadol *(Nucynta)*, 236*t*
Tapentadol ER *(Nucynta* ER), 237*t*
Tar, 87, 88
Tardive dyskinesia (TD), 271*t*
Tarka (verapamil with trandolapril), 56*t*
Tarsal tunnel syndrome, 197
Tasmar (tolcapone), 217*t*
Tazarotene gel, 87
Tazobactam-piperacillin *(Zosyn)*
  for infections in chronic wounds, 295*t*
  for infectious diseases, 169*t*
  for pneumonia, 159, 159*t*
TB (tuberculosis), 164–166, 165*t*
TCAs (tricyclic antidepressants)
  for bipolar disorders, 83*t*
  and dementia, 74
  for depression, 80*t*
  fall risks, 112
  for IBS, 124
  and orthostatic hypotension, 211
  for pain, 227*t*, 240*t*
  for painful neuropathy, 221
  and restless legs syndrome, 308
  and UI, 151*t*
T-cell activation inhibitors, 206
TD (tardive dyskinesia), 271*t*
TDD (telephone device for the deaf), 136
TDI (tissue doppler imaging), 42
Team care, 5, 6*t*
T.E.D.™, 46
Tefloro, 170*t*. *See also* Ceftaroline fosamil
Tegretol. *See also* Carbamazepine
  for agitation, 77*t*
  for bipolar disorders, 83*t*
  for pain, 238*t*
  for painful neuropathy, 221
  for seizures, 219*t*

Tegretol XR. See also Carbamazepine
  for bipolar disorders, 83*t*
  for pain, 238*t*
  for painful neuropathy, 221
  for seizures, 219*t*
Tekamlo (aliskiren with amlodipine), 57*t*
Tekturna (aliskiren), 55*t*
Tekturna HCT (aliskiren with HCTZ), 57*t*
Telavancin *(Vibativ),* 162, 173*t*
Telephone counseling, 312
Telephone device for the deaf (TDD), 136
Telithromycin *(Ketek),* 20*t,* 171*t*
Telmisartan *(Micardis),* 55*t*
Telmisartan with amlodipine *(Twynsta),* 56*t*
Telmisartan with HCTZ *(Micardis HCT),* 57*t*
Temazepam *(Restoril),* 306*t*
Temovate, 91*t. See also* Clobetasol
  propionate
Temperature conversions, 1*t*
Temporal (giant cell) arteritis, 209–210
Tendinitis, 191, 191*t,* 192
Tenex (guanfacine), 52*t*
Tenofovir *(Truvada),* 167
Tenoretic (atenolol with chlorthalidone), 57*t*
Tenormin, 53*t. See also* Atenolol
Tenosynovitis, 209
TENS. *See* Transcutaneous electrical nerve
  stimulation
Tequin, 109*t. See also* Gatifloxacin
Terazosin *(Hytrin),* 52*t,* 262
Terbinafine *(Lamisil, Lamisil AT),* 87, 90*t,* 175*t*
Teriparatide *(Forteo)*
  bone outcomes, 226*t*
  for osteoporosis, 225, 225*t*
  for vertebral compression fracture, 194
Tessalon Perles (benzonatate), 273*t*
Testim (testosterone), 290*t*
Testosterone, 289*t–*290*t,* 291
Testosterone, buccal *(Striant),* 290*t*
Testosterone, transdermal *(Androderm,
  AndroGel, Fortesta, Testim),* 290*t*
Testosterone cypionate, 290*t*
Testosterone deficiency, 287
Testosterone enanthate, 289*t*
Testosterone replacement, 225
Tetanus immunization, 257*t*

Tetrabenazine, 20*t*
Tetracosactin *(Synacthen Depot),* 102
Tetracycline *(Achromycin, Helidac, Pylera,
  Sumycin)*
  for cellulitis, 85
  digoxin interactions, 44
  for *H pylori* infection, 122*t*
  for infectious diseases, 171*t*
  for peptic ulcer disease, 122
  for rosacea, 87
Teveten (eprosartan), 55*t*
Teveten HCT (eprosartan mesylate with
  HCTZ), 57*t*
Thalidomide, 146
Theo-24, 285*t. See also* Theophylline-SR
Theo-Dur, 285*t. See also* Theophylline-SR
Theophylline, 278*t–*279*t*
Theophylline-SR *(Slo-Bid, Theo-24, Theo-
  Dur),* 282*t,* 283*t,* 285*t*
Therapress Duo stockings, 303
Thiamine, 70
Thiazide diuretics
  for chronic kidney disease, 178
  and coexisting conditions, 56*t*
  for DM type 2, 96
  for HTN, 50, 51*t*
  for hyperkalemia, 183, 184
Thiazolidinediones, 44, 98*t,* 151*t*
Thickening agents, 119
Thienopyradines, 29*t*
Thioridazine *(Mellaril)*
  anticholinergic property, 68*t*
  and dementia, 74
  for psychosis, 269*t*
  QT_c interval interactions, 20*t*
  and seizures, 219
Thiothixene, 68*t,* 219
Third-spacing, 182
Thirst, impaired, 181
Thoracic surgery, 25*t*
3M Foam, 300*t*
3M Tegaderm, 300*t,* 302*t. See also*
  Transparent film
3M Tegagel with Gauze, 301*t*
3M Tegagen HL & HG Alginate, 301*t. See
  also* Calcium alginate dressings

3M Tegasorb, 300*t*. *See also* Hydrocolloids
3M Tegasorb Thin Exuderm, 300*t*
Thrombocytopenia, heparin-induced (HIT), 24*t*, 30*t*, 31*t*
Thrombocytosis, essential, 144–145
Thromboembolism, 24–33, 25*t*, 28*t*, 30*t*, 31*t*, 32*t*, 321
Thrombolytic therapy, 39, 213–214
Thrombosis
  cerebral venous sinus, 33*t*
  deep-vein (DVT), 25*t*, 26, 45, 195, 226*t*, 254*t*
  intracardiac, 33*t*
  left ventricular thrombosis, 40
Thyroid disorders, 288*t*
Thyroid nodules, 93–94
Thyroid replacement therapy, 17
Thyroid-stimulating hormone (TSH), 258*t*
Thyroxine (T$_4$), 92, 189, 222
TIA (transient ischemic attack), 24*t*, 254*t*
Tiagabine *(Gabitril Filmtabs)*, 219*t*
Tiazac (diltiazem), 54*t*
Ticagrelor *(Brilinta)*
  for ACS, 39
  for antithrombotic therapy, 24*t*
  cessation before surgery, 252
  for chronic angina, 41
  prescribing information, 29*t*
Ticarcillin-clavulanate *(Timentin)*, 169*t*
Ticlopidine, 22
Tielle, 300*t*. *See also* Foam island
Tigecycline *(Tygacil)*, 172*t*
Timentin (ticarcillin-clavulanate), 169*t*
Timolol *(Blocadren)*, 53*t*
Timolol drops *(Betimol, Timoptic)*, 106*t*
Timolol with brimonidine *(Combigan)*, 107*t*
Timolol with dorzolamide *(Cosopt)*, 107*t*
Timoptic (timolol drops), 106*t*
Tinactin (tolnaftate), 90*t*
Tinea corpis, 89*t*–90*t*
Tinea cruris, 89*t*–90*t*
Tinea pedis, 89*t*–90*t*
Tinea unguium, 86
Tinea versicolor, 89*t*–90*t*
Tinel's sign, 196
Tinnitus, 137
Tinnitus retraining therapy, 137
Tinzaparin *(Innohep)*, 28*t*, 30*t*

Tiotropium *(Spiriva)*, 278, 282*t*, 283*t*
Tipranavir, 20*t*
Tirofiban *(Aggrastat)*, 24*t*, 31*t*, 253
Tissue doppler imaging (TDI), 42
Tissue plasminogen activator (tPA), 214
Titanium, 87
Tizanidine *(Zanaflex)*, 68*t*, 239*t*
TJR (total joint replacement), 194, 260
TLC (total lung capacity), 265
TMP/SMZ (trimethoprim/sulfamethoxazole)
  double strength (DS), 161
  for infectious diseases, 172*t*
  for MRSA, 85, 162
TMS (transcranial magnetic stimulation), repetitive, 78, 82
Tobacco abuse, 313*t*. *See also* Smoking
Tobacco counseling, 333*t*, 334*t*
Tobramycin *(AKTob, Nebcin, Tobrex)*, 109*t*, 160, 170*t*
Tobrex, 109*t*. *See also* Tobramycin
Tocilizumab *(Actemra)*, 206, 210
Tofacitinib *(Xelianz)*, 206
Tofranil, 81. *See also* Imipramine
Toilet training, 153
Toileting, prompted, 74, 148, 153
Tolcapone *(Tasmar)*, 217*t*
Tolectin (tolmetin), 203*t*
Tolmetin *(Tolectin)*, 203*t*
Tolnaftate *(Absorbine Jr. Antifungal, Tinactin)*, 90*t*
Tolterodine *(Detrol, Detrol LA)*, 20*t*, 68*t*, 151*t*
Tolvaptan *(Samsca)*, 182, 183
Topamax, 219*t*. *See also* Topiramate
Topicort (desoximetasone), 90*t*, 91*t*
Topiramate *(Topamax)*, 111, 219*t*, 311
Topiramate with phentermine *(Qsmia)*, 187
Toprol XL, 53*t*. *See also* Metoprolol, long-acting
Toradol, 202*t*. *See also* Ketorolac
Toremifene *(Fareston)*, 318*t*
Tornalate (bitolterol), 284*t*
Torsemide *(Demadex)*, 51*t*, 183, 184
Total body water, 181
Total joint replacement (TJR), 194, 260
Total lung capacity (TLC), 265
TOVIAZ, 152*t*. *See also* Fesoterodine

Trabeculectomy, 105
Trabeculoplasty, 105
Tracheostomy, 308
Tracleer (bosentan), 58
Trade names are in *italics.*
Tradjenta (linagliptin), 98*t*
Tramadol *(Ultram)*
  for osteoarthritis, 199, 200*f*
  for pain, 236*t*
  for painful neuropathy, 221
  and seizures, 219
Tramadol extended release *(Ultram* ER,
    ConZip), 237*t*
Tramadol with APAP *(Ultracet),* 233, 236*t*
Trandate, 53*t,* 214. *See also* Labetalol
Trandolapril *(Mavik),* 45*t,* 55*t*
Trandolapril with verapamil *(Tarka),* 56*t*
Tranexamic acid, 253
Transcatheter aortic valve replacement
    (AVR), 62
Transcranial magnetic stimulation, repetitive
    (rTMS), 78, 82
Transcutaneous electrical nerve stimulation
    (TENS)
  for osteoarthritis, 198
  for pain, 229, 231*t,* 232
  for painful neuropathy, 221
TransCyte, 298, 303
Transderm Scop, 128*t. See also* Transdermal
    scopolamine
Transdermal buprenorphine *(Butrans
    Transdermal System CIII),* 228, 237*t*
Transdermal estrogen *(Alora, Climara,
    Divigel, Elestrin, Estraderm, Estrogel,
    Evamist, Fempatch, Vivelle),* 321
Transdermal fentanyl *(Duragesic)*
  iontophoric transdermal system (ITS), 236*t*
  for pain, 233, 237*t*
Transdermal lidocaine patches *(Lidoderm),*
    200*f,* 221, 240*t*
Transdermal nicotine patches *(Habitrol,
    NicoDerm, Nicotrol, ProStep),* 313*t*
Transdermal scopolamine *(Transderm Scop),*
    128*t,* 248
Transdermal testosterone *(Androderm,
    AndroGel, Fortesta, Testim),* 290*t*

Transderm-Nitro, 41*t. See also* Nitroglycerin
Transesophageal echocardiography, 61, 213
Transferrin, 186
Transferrin receptor, soluble (sTFR), 138
Transfusion therapy, 40, 145, 146
Transient ischemic attack (TIA), 24*t,* 254*t*
Transitional care, 7*t,* 333*t*
Transplantation
  fecal, 131
  kidney, 179
  stem cell, 144, 145, 146, 175*t*
Transthoracic echocardiography, 213
Transurethral incision of the prostate (TUIP),
    263
Transurethral laser enucleation, 263
Transurethral microwave thermotherapy
    (TUMT), 263
Transurethral needle ablation (TUNA), 263
Transurethral procedures, 25*t*
Transurethral resection of the prostate
    (TURP), 263
Transurethral vaporization of the prostate
    (TUVP), 263
Travatan (travoprost), 107*t*
Travoprost *(Travatan),* 107*t*
Trazodone *(Desyrel)*
  for agitation, 77*t*
  for prescription drug abuse/misuse, 315
  QT_c interval interactions, 20*t*
  for sleep disorders, 305*t*
Trelstar Depot (triptorelin), 266*t*
Trelstar LA (triptorelin), 266*t*
Tremors, 56*t,* 211*t,* 216*t*
Trental (pentoxifylline), 64
Treprostinil *(Remodulin),* 58
Tretinoin, 87
Trexall, 206*t. See also* Methotrexate
Trexan (naltrexone), 311
Triacetin *(Myco-Nail),* 90*t*
Triamcinolone acetate, 91*t*

Triamcinolone acetonide *(Aristocort, Kenacort, Kenalog, Nasacort)*
for adrenal insufficiency, 103*t*
for allergic rhinitis or conjunctivitis, 276*t*
for dermatologic conditions, 91*t*
for intertrigo, 86
for osteoarthritis, 198
for seborrheic dermatitis, 88
Triamcinolone hexacetonide, 198
Triamterene *(Dyrenium)*, 52*t*, 179
Triamterene with HCTZ *(Dyazide, Maxzide)*, 57*t*
Tricor, 48*t. See also* Fenofibrate
Tricosal (choline magnesium salicylate), 201*t*
Tricyclic antidepressants. *See* TCAs
Tridesilon (desonide), 90*t*
Trifluoperazine, 68*t*
Trigger-point injections, 198–199
Triglycerides, 41
Trihexy, 218*t. See also* Trihexyphenidyl
Trihexyphenidyl *(Artane, Trihexy)*, 68*t*, 218*t*
Triiodothyronine (T_3), 92
Trilafon, 269*t. See also* Perphenazine
Trileptal (oxcarbazepine), 219*t*, 238*t*
Trilipix (fenofibrate delayed release), 48*t*
Trilisate (choline magnesium salicylate), 201*t*
Trimethoprim, 32
Trimethoprim and polymyxin *(Polytrim)*, 109*t*
Trimethoprim/sulfamethoxazole (TMP/SMZ)
double strength (DS), 161
for infectious diseases, 172*t*
for MRSA, 85, 162
Trimipramine *(Surmontil)*, 68*t*, 81
Triptorelin *(Trelstar Depot, Trelstar LA)*, 266*t*
Trochanteric bursitis, 194
Trolamine salicylate *(Aspercreme)*, 203*t*, 239*t*
Troponins, cardiac, 39
Trospium *(Sanctura, Sanctura XR)*, 68*t*, 151*t*
Trusopt (dorzolamide), 107*t*
Truvada (tenofovir), 167
TSH (thyroid-stimulating hormone), 258*t*
TST (tuberculin skin test), 165
Tube feeding, 19, 190
Tuberculin skin test (TST), 165
Tuberculosis (TB), 164–166, 165*t*
Tubular necrosis, acute, 176, 176*t*, 177

TUIP (transurethral incision of the prostate), 263
TUMT (transurethral microwave thermotherapy), 263
TUNA (transurethral needle ablation), 263
TURP (transurethral resection of the prostate), 263
TURP syndrome, 263
TUVP (transurethral vaporization of the prostate), 263
25-Hydroxy vitamin D, 186
25-Hydroxy vitamin D deficiency, 222
TwoCal HN, 189*t*
Twynsta (amlodipine with telmisartan), 56*t*
Tygacil (tigecycline), 172*t*
Tylox (oxycodone with APAP), 235*t*

U
Ubiquinol (coenzyme Q_{10}), 21
UFH. *See* Unfractionated heparin
UI. *See* Urinary incontinence
Ulcers
arterial, 296*t*–297*t*, 297
diabetic, 296*t*–297*t*, 297–298
H pylori-induced, 122*t*
peptic, 121–122
pressure, 296*t*–297*t*, 298–303, 299*t*, 300*t*–302*t*
skin, 293–303, 296*t*–297*t*
stress, 123
venous, 296*t*–297*t*, 303
Uloric, 208*t. See also* Febuxostat
Ultec, 300*t. See also* Hydrocolloids
Ultec Pro, 300*t*
Ultracet, 236*t. See also* Tramadol with APAP
Ultram, 221, 236*t. See also* Tramadol
Ultram ER (tramadol), 237*t*
Ultrasonography
abdominal aortic aneurysm, 62, 257*t*
for osteoarthritis, 198
for thyroid nodules, 93, 94
Ultravate (halobetasol propionate), 91*t*
Unasyn, 169*t. See also* Ampicillin-sulbactam
Undecylenic acid *(Fungi-Nail)*, 87, 90*t*
Undernutrition, 187–188

Unfractionated heparin (UFH)
  for ACS, 39
  for anticoagulation, 30*t*
  for antithrombotic therapy, 24*t*
  for DVT/PE prophylaxis, 213
  for VTE, 25*t*, 28*t*
Uniflex, 300*t*. *See also* Transparent film
Uniretic (moexipril with HCTZ), 56*t*
Univasc, 55*t*. *See also* Moexipril
Unna's boot, 303
Urea, fractional excretion of (FEUrea), 176
Urethral stents, 263
Urge incontinence. *See also* Urinary
    incontinence
  antihypertensive therapy and, 56*t*
  characteristics and causes of, 147*t*
  in nursing-home residents, 153
  therapy for, 149, 150*f*, 151*t*–152*t*, 152
Urge suppression, 150*f*
Urinary incontinence (UI), 147–153
  antihypertensive therapy and, 56*t*
  assessment of, 4*t*
  medications associated with, 151*t*
  mixed, 147*t*, 149, 150*f*, 151*t*–152*t*
  overflow, 147*t*
  resources for, 336
  stepwise evaluation and treatment of, 150*f*
  stress, 147*t*, 149, 150*f*, 152, 153
  types of persistent UI, 147*t*
  urge, 56*t*, 147*t*, 149, 150*f*, 151*t*–152*t*, 152,
    153
Urinary medications, 20*t*
Urinary tract infection (UTI), 160–161
  antibiotics for, 170*t*
  complicated, 160, 172*t*
  recurrent, 291
Urine osmolality, 181
Urine sodium, 180, 181
Urodynamic testing, 148
Urologic procedures, 25*t*
Urosepsis, 160–161
Uroxatral (alfuzosin ER), 263
Urticaria, 88–89
UTI. *See* Urinary tract infection
UV light, 87
Uvulopalatopharyngoplasty, 308

V
VAC (vacuum-assisted closure), 295
Vaccines
  hepatitis B, 179
  influenza, 32, 97, 163, 333*t*
  pneumococcal, 97, 146
  pneumonia, 333*t*
  zoster vaccine live *(Zostavax)*, 162
Vacuum tumescence devices *(Catalyst*
    Vacuum Device, Osbon-Erec Aid, Pos-T-
    Vac, Rejoyn), 290*t*
Vacuum-assisted closure (VAC), 295
Vagifem (estradiol vaginal tablets), 291*t*
Vaginal candidiasis, 173*t*
Vaginal prolapse, 319
Vaginismus, 291
Valacyclovir *(Valtrex)*, 163*t*
Valerian, 23
Valisone (betamethasone valerate), 90*t*, 91*t*
Valproic acid *(Depacon, Depakene,*
    Depakote), 83*t*, 219*t*
Valproic acid extended release *(Depakote*
    ER), 219*t*
Valsartan *(Diovan)*, 45*t*, 55*t*, 94
Valsartan with aliskiren *(Valturna)*, 57*t*
Valsartan with amlodipine *(Exforge)*, 56*t*
Valsartan with amlodipine and HCTZ
    (Exforge HCT), 56*t*
Valsartan with HCTZ *(Diovan HCT)*, 57*t*
Valtrex (valacyclovir), 163*t*
Valturna (aliskiren with valsartan), 57*t*
Valvular heart disease (VD)
  antiplatelet agents for, 24*t*, 29*t*
  antithrombotic medications for, 24*t*
  aortic stenosis, 63
  warfarin anticoagulation for, 32*t*
Valvular surgery, 255*t*
Vancenase, 276*t*. *See also* Beclomethasone
Vanceril, 284*t*. *See also* Beclomethasone
Vancocin, 173*t*. *See also* Vancomycin
Vancomycin *(Vancocin)*
  for *C difficile* infection, 131, 131*t*
  empiric use, 160
  for hip fracture surgery, 195
  for infections in chronic wounds, 295*t*
  for infectious diseases, 173*t*

Vancomycin *continued*
 for MRSA, 162
 for pneumonia, 160
 for UTI or urosepsis, 161
Vancomycin-resistant *E faecium*, 173*t*
Vantas (histrelin acetate), 266*t*
Vantin, 170*t. See also* Cefpodoxime
Vaprisol (conivaptan), 182
Vardenafil *(LEVITRA)*, 20*t*, 262, 289*t*
Varenicline *(Chantix)*, 312, 313*t*
Vascular dementia, 71, 75
Vascular endothelial growth factor (VEGF)
 inhibitors, 105
Vascular erectile dysfunction, 288*t*, 289
Vascular parkinsonism, 216*t*
Vascular surgery, 25*t*
Vasculitis, 176*t*
Vaseline, 88
Vaseretic (enalapril maleate with HCTZ), 56*t*
Vasoconstrictors, 110, 111*t*, 132
Vasodilators
 for aortic stenosis, 62
 for HF, 44
 for HTN, 54*t*, 57*t*
Vasotec, 55*t. See also* Enalapril
Vasovagal syncope, 64, 64*t*, 65
VD. *See* Valvular heart disease
VEGF (vascular endothelial growth factor)
 inhibitors, 105
Venlafaxine *(Effexor, Effexor XR)*
 for anxiety disorders, 36
 for depression, 79, 81*t*
 for menopausal symptoms, 321
 for pain, 238*t*–239*t*
 QT_c interval interactions, 20*t*
Venofer (iron sucrose), 143*t*
Venous insufficiency, 45, 46
Venous thromboembolism (VTE), 24–28
 acute, 28, 28*t*, 30*t*
 and intolerable vasomotor symptoms, 320
 long-term, 28*t*, 30*t*
 management of, 28*t*, 31*t*
 prophylaxis of, 25*t*, 30*t*, 31*t*
 warfarin anticoagulation for, 32*t*
Venous ulcers, 296*t*–297*t*, 303
Ventavis (iloprost), 58
Ventilation, 158, 280*t*

Ventolin, 284*t. See also* Albuterol
Ventolin Rotacaps, 284*t. See also* Albuterol
Ventricular fibrillation (VF), 66
Ventricular tachycardia (VT), 66
Veramyst (fluticasone furoate), 276*t*
Verapamil, 44, 59, 189
Verapamil SR *(Calan SR, Covera-HS, Isoptin
 SR, Verelan PM)*, 54*t*
Verapamil with trandolapril *(Tarka)*, 56*t*
Verelan PM (verapamil), 54*t*
Vertebral artery: postural impingement of,
 212*t*
Vertebral fracture, 194, 225*t*
Vertebroplasty, 146, 194
Vertigo, 128*t*, 212*t*
VESIcare, 152*t. See also* Solifenacin
Vestibular neuronitis, 212*t*
VF (ventricular fibrillation), 66
VFEND, 174*t. See also* Voriconazole
Viagra, 58, 262, 289*t. See also* Sildenafil
Viasorb, 302*t*
Vibativ, 173*t. See also* Telavancin
Vibramycin, 171*t. See also* Doxycycline
Vicks VapoRub (mentholatum), 87
Vicodin, 235*t. See also* Hydrocodone with
 APAP
Vicoprofen (hydrocodone + ibuprofen), 235*t*
Victoza (liraglutide), 100*t*
Videofluoroscopy, 118
VigiFoam, 300*t. See also* Foam island
Vigilon, 301*t*
Viibryd (vilazodone), 80*t*
Vilanterol-fluticasone *(Breo Ellipta)*, 286*t*
Vilazodone *(Viibryd)*, 80*t*
VIN (vulvar intraepithelial neoplasia), 317
Vincristine, 111
Viral conjunctivitis, 109
Vision testing, 4*t*, 104
Visken (pindolol), 53*t*
Visual aids, 69*t*
Visual impairment, 104
 conditions associated with, 104–106
 dual sensory impairment (DSI), 108
 and falls, 117*t*
 preventive measures for delirium, 69*t*

Visual impairment *continued*
  resources for, 336
  screening for, 258*t*
Vitamin B$_{12}$, 121*t*, 139*f*
Vitamin B complex, 308
Vitamin B$_{12}$ deficiency, 139*f*, 142, 268
Vitamin C, 105, 121*t*
Vitamin C deficiency, 296
Vitamin D (ergocalciferol)
  with calcitriol, 179
  calcium plus vitamin D, 223
  for malnutrition, 186
  for osteoporosis, 195, 222, 223, 257*t*
  for Parkinson disease, 216
  for preventing falls, 116*t*
  for vitamin D insufficiency, 179, 222
Vitamin D insufficiency, 179, 222
Vitamin D supplementation, 257*t*
Vitamin E, 75, 105
Vitamin K, 19, 32, 33*t*
Vitamin K antagonists, 24*t*, 25*t*, 28*t*
Vivactil (protriptyline), 81. *See also*
  Protriptyline
Vivitrol (naltrexone), 311
Voltaren, 202*t*. *See also* Diclofenac
Voltaren Gel, 202*t*, 232. *See also* Diclofenac
  gel
Voltaren-XR, 202*t*. *See also* Diclofenac
Volume depletion, 180
Volume overload, 179
Vomiting, 127
  antiemetic therapy, 128*t*
  drug-induced, 270*t*
  at end of life, 248
  and hyponatremia, 182
  postoperative, 128*t*
Voriconazole *(VFEND)*, 20*t*, 174*t*
VT (ventricular tachycardia), 66
VTE. *See* Venous thromboembolism
Vulvar diseases, 317
Vulvar intraepithelial neoplasia (VIN), 317
Vulvectomy, 317

W
Walkers, 115
Walking
  for claudication therapy, 63
  for DM prevention/delay, 94
  exercise prescription, 261
  for PAD claudication therapy, 63
  for problem behaviors, 75
Warfarin *(Coumadin)*, 32. *See also*
  Anticoagulation
  for ACS, 40
  for AF, 60*t*
  cessation before dental procedures, 253
  cessation before surgery, 253
  drug interactions, 19, 32, 61*t*, 203*t*, 318*t*
  food or nutrient interactions, 19
  herbal medicine interactions, 21, 22
  indications for anticoagulation, 32*t*
  indications for antithrombosis, 24*t*
  overdose, 33*t*
  for PAH, 58
  prescribing information, 32
  resumption after surgery, 253
  for stroke prevention, 215
  for VTE, 25*t*, 28, 28*t*
Water loss, pure, 180
Water-soluble lubricants *(Replens)*, 291
Weakness, 198, 220*t*, 246
Weight control, 231
Weight conversions, 1*t*
Weight gain, drug-induced, 270*t*
Weight loss. *See also* Malnutrition
  for diabetes, 94, 95
  for GERD, 120
  for HTN, 50
  for hyperuricemia, 207
  for obesity, 187
  for osteoarthritis, 194, 198
  post MI, 41
  for sleep apnea, 307
  for stroke prevention, 215
  for UI, 148
Weight loss diets, 187
Weight measurement, 43*t*
Weight training, 261
WelChol (colesevelam), 48*t*, 99*t*
Wellbutrin, 80*t*. *See also* Bupropion
Wellbutrin SR, 80*t*, 313*t*. *See also* Bupropion
Wellbutrin XL, 80*t*. *See also* Bupropion
Wellness visits. *See* Annual Wellness Visit
  (AWV)

Wernicke's aphasia, 220*t*
Westcort (hydrocortisone valerate), 91*t*
Westergren sedimentation rate, 1
Wet AMD (age-related macular
  degeneration), 105
Wheat dextrin *(Benefiber),* 125*t*
Whisper test, 134
"White coat" HTN, 50
"White noise," 75, 305
Withholding or withdrawing therapy, 245
Women's health, 316–321
  bone densitometry, 257*t*
  breast cancer, 226*t*, 316–317, 318*t*
  complicated UTI, 160, 172*t*
  dyspareunia, 291
  early menopause, 222
  energy (caloric) and fluid requirements,
    187
  hormone therapy, 319–321
  intolerable vasomotor symptoms, 320–321
  irritable bowel syndrome, 124
  mammography recommendations, 257*t*
  menopausal symptoms, 319
  osteoporosis, 56*t*, 222–226, 226*t*, 336
  postmenopausal bleeding, 318–319
  postmenopausal symptoms, 319
  resources for, 335, 336
  sexual dysfunction, 291
  TSH, 258*t*
  UTI prophylaxis, 161
  vaginal prolapse, 319
  vulvar diseases, 317
World Health Organization Fracture Risk
  Assessment Tool (FRAX), 222, 223
Wound assessment and treatment, 293–296
  arterial ulcers, 297
  diabetic foot ulcers, 297–298
  empiric antibiotic therapy for, 294*t*–295*t*
  pressure ulcers, 298–303
  venous ulcers, 303
  wound and pressure ulcer products, 299*t*

X
Xalatan (latanoprost), 107*t*
Xarelto, 31*t. See also* Rivaroxaban
Xeljanz (tofacitinib), 206
Xenica (orlistat), 187

Xerosis, 89
Xerostomia, 19
Xolair (omalizumab), 286*t*
Xopenex (levalbuterol), 284*t*
Xue Zhi Kang (red yeast rice), 23
Xyzal (levocetirizine), 275*t*

Y
Yoga, 196

Z
Z scores, 222
Zaditor (ketotifen), 110*t*
Zafirlukast *(Accolate),* 285*t*
Zaleplon *(Sonata),* 37, 305, 306*t*
Zaltrap (aflibercept), 105
Zanaflex, 239*t. See also* Tizanidine
Zanamivir *(Relenza),* 164*t*
Zantac, 120*t. See also* Ranitidine
Zaroxolyn, 51*t. See also* Metolazone
Zebeta, 53*t. See also* Bisoprolol
Zelapar (selegiline), 218*t*
Zestoretic (lisinopril with HCTZ), 56*t*
Zestra, 291
Zestril, 55*t. See also* Lisinopril
Zetia, 48*t. See also* Ezetimibe
Ziac (bisoprolol with HCTZ), 57*t*
Zileuton *(Zyflo),* 285*t*
Zinc
  for AMD, 105
  drug interactions, 19
  for seborrheic dermatitis, 88
  for sleep disorders, 309
Zinc deficiency, 296
Zinc oxide, 87, 105
Zioptan (tafluprost), 107*t*
Ziprasidone *(Geodon),* 20*t*, 82, 269*t*
Zipsor, 202*t. See also* Diclofenac
Zithromax, 170*t. See also* Azithromycin
Zocor, 48*t. See also* Simvastatin
Zofran, 128*t*, 248. *See also* Ondansetron
Zoladex (goserelin acetate implant), 265*t*
Zoledronic acid *(Reclast)*
  bone outcomes, 226*t*
  for breast cancer, 317
  effects on other outcomes, level of
    evidence, and risks of, 226*t*

Zoledronic acid *continued*
    for metastatic bone disease, 265, 317
    for multiple myeloma, 146
    for osteoporosis, 225*t*, 226
Zolmitriptan, 20*t*
Zoloft, 80*t. See also* Sertraline
Zolpidem *(Ambien, Ambien CR, Edluar,*
    Intermezzo, Zolpimist), 37, 305, 306*t*
Zolpimist, 306*t. See also* Zolpidem
Zonalon, 89. *See also* Doxepin
Zonegran (zonisamide), 219*t*
Zonisamide *(Zonegran)*, 219*t*
Zorvolex, 202*t. See also* Diclofenac
Zostavax (zoster vaccine live), 162
Zoster ("shingles"). *See* Herpes zoster
Zoster vaccine live *(Zostavax)*, 162
Zostrix, 221, 240*t. See also* Capsaicin
Zosyn, 169*t. See also* Piperacillin-
    tazobactam
Zovirax (acyclovir), 163*t*
Zyban, 80*t*, 313*t. See also* Bupropion
Zyclara, 84. *See also* Imiquimod
Zydis, 77*t. See also* Olanzapine
Zyflo (zileuton), 285*t*
Zyloprim, 208*t. See also* Allopurinol
Zyprexa, 77*t*, 269*t. See also* Olanzapine
Zyprexa IntraMuscular (olanzapine IM), 77*t*
Zyrtec (cetirizine), 275*t*
Zyvox, 172*t. See also* Linezolid